T0211802

Lecture Notes in Computer Science 12484

More information about this subseries at http://www.springer.com/series/7410

Joaquin Garcia-Alfaro · Guillermo Navarro-Arribas ·
Jordi Herrera-Joancomarti (Eds.)

Data Privacy Management, Cryptocurrencies and Blockchain Technology

ESORICS 2020 International Workshops, DPM 2020 and CBT 2020
Guildford, UK, September 17–18, 2020
Revised Selected Papers

Springer

Editors
Joaquin Garcia-Alfaro (iD)
Télécom SudParis
Evry Cedex, France

Jordi Herrera-Joancomarti (iD)
Escola d'Enginyeria
Universitat Autònoma de Barcelona
Cerdanyola del Vallès, Barcelona, Spain

Guillermo Navarro-Arribas (iD)
Departament d'Enginyeria de la Informació i
de les Comunicacions
Universitat Autonoma de Barcelona
Bellaterra, Spain

ISSN 0302-9743   ISSN 1611-3349 (electronic)
Lecture Notes in Computer Science
ISBN 978-3-030-66171-7   ISBN 978-3-030-66172-4 (eBook)
https://doi.org/10.1007/978-3-030-66172-4

LNCS Sublibrary: SL4 – Security and Cryptology

This Springer imprint is published by the registered company Springer Nature Switzerland AG
The registered company address is: Gewerbestrasse 11, 6330 Cham, Switzerland

Foreword from the DPM 2020 Program Chairs

This volume contains the post-proceedings of the 15th Data Privacy Managmeent International Workshop (DPM 2020), which was organized within the 25th European Symposium on Research in Computer Security (ESORICS 2020). The DPM series started in 2005 when the first workshop took place in Tokyo, Japan. Since then, the event has been held in different venues: Atlanta, USA (2006); Istanbul, Turkey (2007); Saint-Malo, France (2009); Athens, Greece (2010); Leuven, Belgium (2011); Pisa, Italy (2012); Egham, UK (2013); Wrocław, Poland (2014); Vienna, Austria (2015); Crete, Greece (2016); Oslo, Norway (2017); Barcelona, Spain (2018); and Luxembourg (2019).

This 2020 edition was intended to be held in the University of Surrey, UK, but was finally held virtually due to the COVID-19 pandemic together with the ESORICS main conference and all its workshops.

We received 38 submissions. The Program Committee performed excellent work and all submissions went through a careful review process. Each paper was evaluated on the basis of significance, novelty, and technical quality. After reviewing the submissions, 12 full papers and 5 short papers were accepted for presentation at the event and further publication in these post-proceedings.

We would like to thank everyone who helped in organizing the event, including all the members of the Organizing Committee of both ESORICS and DPM 2020. Our gratitude goes to Mark Manulis, the workshop chair of ESORICS 2020, and to the ESORICS 2020 general chair, Steve Schneider. During the event, we had the valued assistance and help from Kent Leeding. Thanks also go to Sergi Delgado, CEO of Talaia Labs, Spain, and Marc Juarez, from the University of Southern California, USA, for accepting our invitation to conduct the invited talks. Last, but by no means least, we thank all the DPM 2020 Program Committee members, additional reviewers, all the authors who submitted papers, and all the workshop attendees.

Finally, we want to acknowledge the support received from the sponsors of the workshop: Institut Mines-Telecom and Institut Polytechnique de Paris (Télécom SudParis), France, Universitat Autònoma de Barcelona, Spain, UNESCO Chair in Data Privacy, Cybercat, and projects TIN2017-87211-R and SECURITAS RED2018-102321-T from the Spanish Government.

November 2020

Joaquin Garcia-Alfaro
Guillermo Navarro-Arribas

DPM 2020 Organization

PC Chairs

Joaquin Garcia-Alfaro	Intitut Polytechnique de Paris, France
Guillermo Navarro-Arribas	Universitat Autònoma de Barcelona, Spain

Program Committee

Jordi Casas-Roma	Universitat Oberta de Catalunya, Spain
Jordi Castellà-Roca	Universitat Rovira i Virgili, Spain
Mauro Conti	University of Padua, Italy
Jorge Cuellar	University of Passau, Germany
Sabrina De Capitani di Vimercati	Università degli Studi di Milano, Italy
Jose Maria de Fuentes	Universidad Carlos III de Madrid, Spain
Roberto Di Pietro	Hamad Bin Khalifa University, Qatar
Josep Domingo-Ferrer	Universitat Rovira i Virgili, Spain
Sara Foresti	Università degli Studi di Milano, Italy
Sebastien Gambs	Université du Québec à Montréal, Canada
Javier Herranz	Universitat Politècnica de Catalunya, Spain
Jordi Herrera-Joancomartí	Universitat Autònoma de Barcelona, Spain
Marc Juarez	University of Southern California, USA
Christos Kalloniatis	University of the Aegean, Greece
Florian Kammueller	Middlesex University London, UK, and TU Berlin, Germany
Sokratis Katsikas	Open University of Cyprus, Cyprus
Hiroaki Kikuchi	Meiji University, Japan
Evangelos Kranakis	Carleton University, Canada
Alptekin Küpçü	Koç University, Turkey
Costas Lambrinoudakis	University of Piraeus, Greece
Maryline Laurent	Institut Mines-Télécom, France
Giovanni Livraga	University of Milan, Italy
Brad Malin	Vanderbilt University, USA
Chris Mitchell	Royal Holloway, University of London, UK
Anna Monreale	University of Pisa, Italy
Jordi Nin	ESADE, Universitat Ramon Llull, Spain
Martín Ochoa	AppGate Inc., USA
Melek Önen	EURECOM, France
Gerardo Pelosi	Politecnico di Milano, Italy
Silvio Ranise	Fondazione Bruno Kessler, Italy
Kai Rannenberg	Goethe University Frankfurt, Germany
Ruben Rios	University of Malaga, Spain

Yves Roudier	University of Nice Sophia Antipolis, France
Pierangela Samarati	Università degli Studi di Milano, Italy
David Sanchez	University Rovira i Virgili, Spain
Qiang Tang	Luxembourg Institute of Science and Technology, Luxembourg
Yasuyuki Tsukada	Kanto Gakuin University, Japan
Alexandre Viejo	Universitat Rovira i Virgili, Spain
Isabel Wagner	De Montfort University, UK
Jens Weber	University of Victoria, Canada
Nicola Zannone	Eindhoven University of Technology, The Netherlands

Steering Committee

Joaquin Garcia-Alfaro	Intitut Polytechnique de Paris, France
Guillermo Navarro-Arribas	Universitat Autònoma de Barcelona, Spain
Josep Domingo-Ferrer	Universitat Rovira i Virgili, Spain
Vicenç Torra	Umeå University, Sweden

Additional Reviewers

Tahir Ahmad	Salimeh Dashti
Stefano Berlato	Angeliki Kitsiou
Osman Biçer	Katerina Mavroeidi
Matteo Cardaioli	Luca Pajola
Marco Casagrande	Argyri Pattakou

Foreword from the CBT 2020 Program Chairs

The 4th International Workshop on Cryptocurrencies and Blockchain Technology (CBT 2020) was held in collaboration with the 25th European Symposium on Research in Computer Security (ESORICS 2020) and the 15th International Workshop on Data Privacy Management (DPM 2020). Due to the COVID-19 outbreak, the event was held virtually.

We wish to thank all of the authors who submitted their work. This year, CBT received 24 submissions, out of which, 8 papers were accepted for presentation as full papers, complemented by 4 short papers, 2 invited talks, and a discussion panel. The review process was conducted virtually, involving a rigorous process conducted by the Technical Program Committee (TPC) chairs, all the members of the TPC, and the help of some external reviewers.

The CBT 2020 program was organized in three sessions grouping the contributions into the following topics: Transactions, Mining, Second Layer, Signature Schemes, Formal Methods, Privacy, SNARKs, and Anonymity. The sessions were chaired by members of the TCP, and authors and attendees engaged in exciting discussions on new frontiers in the field of cryptocurrencies and blockchain technology.

We would like to thank all of the people involved in CBT 2020. We are grateful to the TPC members and the external reviewers for their help in providing detailed and timely reviews of the submissions; to Sergi Delgado, CEO of Talaia Labs, Spain, and Marc Juarez, from the University of Southern California, USA, for accepting our invitation to conduct two keynotes, and for their presence during the event and talks; to Shin'ichiro Matsuo (Georgetown University, USA), Pindar Wong (VeriFi Ltd., Hong Kong), Nat Sakimura (OpenID Foundation), Julien Bringer (Convenor of ISO TC307/WG2), Patrick McCorry (PISA Research), and Florian Kammueller (Middlesex University London, UK, and TU Berlin, Germany) for accepting our invitation to conduct a discussion panel on "How cryptocurrency and blockchain technology will become a trust foundation for the New Normal while ensuring data privacy management?" We also thank all the members of the Surrey team, especially to Steve Schneider, Mark Manulis, Kent Leeding, and Mohammed Alsadi, for all their help and support. Thanks also go to Springer for their great support throughout the entire process.

Finally, the organization was made possible through the strong help of our supporters: Institut Mines-Télécom and Institut Polytechnique de Paris, SAMOVAR, France, Universitat Autonoma de Barcelona, Spain, Cybercat, BART (Inria, IRT SYSTEMX, Télécom SudParis, and Télécom Paris, France). A special thank you to all of them. Last, but by no means least, we thank all the authors who submitted papers and talks, and all the workshop attendees.

November 2020

Joaquin Garcia-Alfaro
Jordi Herrera-Joancomartí

CBT 2020 Organization

Program Committee Chairs

Joaquin Garcia-Alfaro   Intitut Polytechnique de Paris, France
Jordi Herrera-Joancomart   Universitat Autònoma de Barcelona, Spain

Program Committee

Daniel Augot   Inria Saclay, France
Alex Biryukov   University of Luxembourg, Luxembourg
Rainer Böhme   Universität Innsbruck, Austria
Joseph Bonneau   New York University, USA
Alexander Chepurnoy   IOHK Research, Russia
Mauro Conti   University of Padua, Italy
Vanesa Daza   Universitat Pompeu Fabra, Spain
Sergi Delgado-Segura   Talaia Labs, Spain
Arthur Gervais   Imperial College London, UK
Hannes Hartenstein   Karlsruhe Institute of Technology, Germany
Ghassan Karame   NEC Research, Germany
Eleftherios Kokoris-Kogias   Novi, Switzerland
Shin'ichiro Matsuo   Georgetown University, USA
Andrew Miller   University of Illinois at Urbana-Champaign, USA
Pedro Moreno-Sanchez   IMDEA, Spain
Guillermo Navarro   Universitat Autònoma de Barcelona, Spain
Cristina Pérez-Solà   Universitat Oberta de Catalunya, Spain
Matteo Signorini   Nokia Bell Labs France, France
Khalifa Toumi   IRT SystemX, France

Steering Committee

Rainer Böhme   Universität Innsbruck, Austria
Joaquin Garcia-Alfaro   Intitut Polytechnique de Paris, France
Hannes Hartenstein   Karlsruher Institut für Technologie, Germany
Jordi Herrera-Joancomart   Universitat Autònoma de Barcelona, Spain

Additional Reviewers

Florian Jacob
Sébastien Andreina
Rahul Saha
Ankit Gangwal
Arantxa Zapico
Oliver Stengele

Federico Franzoni
Daniel Feher
Gulshan Kumar
Alexei Zamyatin
Matthias Grundmann
Abhimanyu Rawat

Contents

**CBT Workshop: Signature Schemes, Formal Methods
and Incentivization**

CBT Workshop: Short Papers

DPM Workshop: Fairness, Differential Privacy and Scalability

Fairness-Aware Privacy-Preserving Record Linkage

Dinusha Vatsalan[1(✉)], Joyce Yu[1], Wilko Henecka[1], and Brian Thorne[2]

[1] CSIRO's DATA61, Eveleigh, NSW 2015, Australia
{dinusha.vatsalan,joyce.yu,wilko.henecka}@data61.csiro.au
[2] Hardbyte, Christchurch, New Zealand
brian@hardbyte.nz

Abstract. Record linkage aims to identify records corresponding to the same real-world entity from different databases, while Privacy-Preserving Record Linkage (PPRL) conducts the linkage in a privacy-preserving context where private and sensitive information about individuals is not compromised. Linking records is considered as a classification task where pairs of records from different databases are classified into matches (i.e. they refer to the same entity) or non-matches (i.e. they refer to different entities). Due to the absence of unique entity identifiers across databases, commonly available quasi-identifiers (QIDs), such as name, gender, address, and date of birth, are used to determine the linkage. The values in such QIDs are often prone to data errors and variations making the linkage task challenging.

Fairness in classification is an emerging concept that determines how much a classifier distorts from producing correct predictions with equal probabilities for individuals across different protected groups based on sensitive features (e.g. gender or race). Developing classifiers that are fair with respect to such sensitive features is an important problem for classification in general and specifically for PPRL to mitigate the bias against sensitive and/or minority groups, for example against female group due to higher likelihood of variations in the QIDs such as last name and address. While there have been increased interest in this field, fairness specifically in PPRL research has not been studied in the literature so far. Fairness for PPRL brings in specific challenges and requirements.

In this paper, we study fairness for PPRL classifiers, analyse appropriate fairness criteria/metric for PPRL, study different forms of fairness-bias for PPRL and investigate the effectiveness of using fairness-aware PPRL. Our experimental results conducted on real and synthetically biased datasets show the efficacy and significance of incorporating fairness constraints in the linkage, leading to higher linkage quality in terms of both correctness and fairness.

Keywords: Entity resolution · Privacy · Correctness · Fairness · Classification

© Springer Nature Switzerland AG 2020
J. Garcia-Alfaro et al. (Eds.): DPM 2020/CBT 2020, LNCS 12484, pp. 3–18, 2020.
https://doi.org/10.1007/978-3-030-66172-4_1

1   Introduction

The demand of record linkage to identify records corresponding to the same real-world entity in different databases has increased significantly in various applications, such as anti-money laundry, clinical data sharing, and fraud prevention [4,17,23]. Due to the absence of unique entity identifiers across databases, personal identifiable information (PII) in commonly available attributes, known as quasi-identifiers (QIDs), such as name, gender, address, occupation, and date of birth, is often used to determine the linkage. Given the sensitivity of the PII used to identify matching records across different organizations and the privacy concerns, privacy-preserving record linkage (PPRL) is required [23]. PPRL (and record linkage) is generally a binary classification problem where pairs of records need to be classified into either 'match' (i.e. the pair of records refer to the same entity) or 'non-match' (i.e. the records in the pair refer to different entities) [7,18,22,23].

Features used in the classification are built by comparing the similarity of encoded QIDs of record pairs and class labels are 'matches' or 'non-matches' of the record pairs. BF encoding of QIDs is a widely used method for PPRL with different variations proposed in the literature [7,18]. Cryptographic Long-term Key is one such BF encoding method that encodes all the QIDs of a record into a single similarity-preserving BF [18]. Similarity of a pair of records encoded into BFs is then calculated using any token-based similarity functions, such as Jacccard, Dice, or Hamming [18].

Different classifiers are used in the record linkage as well as PPRL literature, ranging from simple threshold-based classifiers, rule-based classifiers, to probabilistic linkage and machine learning classifiers [22]. Developing classifiers that are fair with respect to a protected/sensitive feature/attribute [25], such as gender or race, is an important problem for classification in general and specifically for PPRL. Fairness of a classifier with regard to a certain protected feature determines how much the classifier distorts from producing predictions with equal probabilities for individuals across different protected groups/values. There has been increased interest in this field due to the concerns that classifiers may introduce significant bias with respect to a certain protected/sensitive feature, such as race or gender, for example against black people in fraud and crime detection systems [12] or online recommendation systems [20], and against women in job recommendation systems [6], however fairness has not been studied specifically in PPRL literature so far.

As with other classification problems, PPRL can also be biased to certain groups of individuals grouped by one or several protected attributes (e.g. gender or race). This imposes different levels of challenges on classifying record pairs into matches and non-matches for record pairs belonging to different groups. For example, consider a gender attribute that has two values: male and female. Further let's assume that several QIDs exhibit more variance in female records than in their male counterparts. This variance causes record pairs belonging to the female cohort to be more difficult to classify. Another challenge to consider is fairness with regard to record linkage involving minority groups. In supervised machine learning a classifier can learn to ignore poor performance on a small group if it can exploit knowledge about the majority population, potentially leading to unfair outcomes. Without careful treatment a classifier may inadvertently be biased towards the cohort that is easier to classify. These examples show that achieving fair linkage across different groups is a difficult yet important challenge.

In this paper, we study how to improve fairness in PPRL using fairness-aware classifier following the reductions-based approach [1]. Despite PPRL can be considered as a classification problem, there exist several challenges for fairness-aware PPRL classification requiring appropriate fairness definitions and metrics. We define fairness-bias and fairness metrics for binary classification in PPRL. We study different forms of fairness-bias for the PPRL problem. To the best of our knowledge, this is the first work that addresses fairness in PPRL. Our initial experimental results on real and synthetically biased datasets are promising, showing fair and accurate linkage for PPRL.

Outline: We describe the preliminaries in the following section, and discuss fairness metrics for PPRL in Sect. 3. We then describe our approach to reduce fairness-bias in PPRL in Sect. 4. We conduct an experimental study on real and synthetically biased datasets in Sect. 5. Finally, we conclude the paper in Sect. 6 with an outlook to future directions of this work.

2 Preliminaries

In this section, we define the problem and describe the preliminaries required for our study.

We assume p database owners (or parties) $P_1, P_2, \cdots, P_p$ with their respective databases $\mathbf{D}_1, \mathbf{D}_2, \cdots, \mathbf{D}_p$ (containing sensitive or confidential person-specific data) participate in the process. A record in database $\mathbf{D}_i$ is denoted as $r_{i,x}$ with $1 \leq i \leq p$ and $1 \leq x \leq |\mathbf{D}_i|$. We assume a trusted Linkage Unit (LU) is available to conduct the linkage on encoded records sent by the parties, which is a commonly used linkage model in many real applications [17]. We also assume a set of QID attributes A, which will be used for the linkage, is common to all these databases.

PPRL allows the party P_i to determine which of its records $r_{i,x} \in \mathbf{D}_i$ match with records in other database(s) $r_{j,y} \in \mathbf{D}_j$ with $1 \leq i,j \leq p$ and $j \neq i$ based on the similarity/distance between (encoded) QIDs of these records. A binary classifier C is used to classify every pair of records $(r_{i,x}, r_{j,y})$ into 'match' (labeled as 1) where the records $r_{i,x}$ and $r_{j,y}$ refer to the same real-world entity or 'non-match' (labeled as 0) where the records refer to two different entities.

In certain applications, the classifier C classifies record pairs into three classes: match, non-match, and potential match, where the record pairs classified as 'potential match' need to go through a manual clerical review process [4]. However, clerical review is difficult to be conducted in a privacy-preserving setting, and research studies have been done on interactive or semi-supervised methods for clerical review in PPRL [14]. Without loss of generality, we assume a binary classifier with the classes of 'match' and 'non-match' in this paper.

The general PPRL pipeline consists of several steps, starting from pre-processing databases, encoding or encrypting records using the privacy encoding/masking functions [22], then matching records based on their QIDs using similarity functions [4], and finally classifying record pairs into 'matches' and 'non-matches'.

Pre-processing: Each party performs the necessary data pre-processing steps including de-duplication to ensure the quality of their own database. Errors in the data can propagate to other steps in the pipeline, and therefore this step is crucial for quality data linkage. It is a common practice to first internally link (de-duplicate) records within a single database before linking with records from other databases [4,16]. This ensures that there is only one record per entity in a database, and therefore leading to one-to-one linking of records across different databases.

Encoding: QIDs are required to conduct the linkage, however these data often contain PII and therefore cannot be shared or exchanged with or between the LU and/or other database owners. Several encoding or masking functions have been used in the literature [22]. We describe the encoding and matching steps of PPRL using Bloom filter (BF) encoding technique, which is widely used in both research and practical applications of PPRL [3,17,22].

A BF b_i is a bit vector of length l bits where all bits are initially set to 0. k independent hash functions, $h_1, \ldots, h_k$, each with range $1, \ldots l$, are used to map each of the elements s in a set S into the BF by setting the bit positions $h_j(s)$ with $1 \leq j \leq k$ to 1. For PPRL, the set S of q-grams (sub-strings of length q) of QIDs of string values are hash-mapped into BFs [18]. The resulting BFs can be compared in the matching step using a similarity function.

Matching: The encoded record pairs are compared using a similarity function. For example, BF encoding requires token-based similarity functions, such as Jaccard, Dice, and Hamming functions. Dice-coefficient is commonly used for comparing BFs, as it is insensitive to large number of zeros in long BFs. The Dice-coefficient of two BFs (b_1, b_2) is calculated as $\frac{2 \times c}{\sum_{i=1}^{2} x_i}$, where c is the number of common bit positions that are set to 1 in both BFs, and x_i is the number of bit positions set to 1 in b_i, $1 \leq i \leq 2$.

Classification: The calculated similarities are input to a classifier to classify the corresponding record pairs into matches or non-matches. Different classifiers are used in the record linkage as well as privacy-preserving record linkage (PPRL) literature, such as simple threshold-based classifiers, rule-based classifiers, probabilistic linkage and machine learning classifiers [22]. Machine learning classifiers can provide high quality of linkage, however, supervised machine learning classifiers require training data with ground-truth labels of 'matches' and 'non-matches', which are not often available in PPRL context.

Evaluation: The evaluation of the performance of the linkage task consists of three main criteria: computational and communication efficiency, privacy guarantees, and linkage quality. Computation and communication efficiency is measured either theoretically using the big-O notation [5] or empirically using runtime, memory size, number of communication steps, number and size of messages to be communicated, and number of record pair comparisons required [23]. Privacy guarantees are either formally proven or empirically measured using metrics such as Information gain and disclosure risk metrics [22] against privacy attacks.

Linkage quality often refers to the correctness of classification/ prediction and is measured using the standard metrics, such as precision, recall, area under curve (AUC), accuracy, and $f1$-measure [4]. However, linkage quality has another dimension in addition to correctness, which is fairness. Fairness is the accuracy of linkage results with regard to different subgroups of individuals [25], while correctness only considers the overall accuracy of linkage. Different subgroups are based on one or several sensitive/protected features, such as gender or race. Such protected features can either be part of the QIDs or not. Even if the protected feature is not used in the linkage, the linkage can still be biased towards vulnerable sub-groups based on the protected feature, as will be validated in our experimental study in Sect. 5.

3   Fairness Metrics

Fairness of the classifier measures the classification model's behavior towards different individuals grouped by a particular protected or sensitive feature [2]. The protected feature could either be part of the QIDs used to link records or not. Let's assume "gender" is a protected feature dividing a dataset into two groups: male and female. Fairness of a classifier on this dataset would essentially mean whether the model treats both the male and female user groups equally in terms of correct predictions of record pairs belonging to the different groups as 'matches' without giving benefit to one group more than the other. We assume that the protected feature is private and sensitive and therefore not accessible by the classifier used in PPRL.

While PPRL can be considered as a binary classification problem, the main difference is that the input features to the classifier come from pairs of records whereas in general classification problem they are the features of individual records. The features for PPRL classifier are the similarity scores calculated between the encoded QIDs of every record pair. These features can either contain one similarity score of a linkage schema or a list of similarity scores corresponding to different linkage schemas. Without loss of generality, we assume in this work that the features for the classifier contain only one similarity score (resulting from a good or optimal linkage schema).

The classifiers can result in biased predictions for different groups based on the protected feature. For example, with gender as the protected feature, female record pairs might have poor accuracy of linkage compared to male record pairs due to different levels of challenges involved in the linkage. The female group of individuals might have more likelihood of changing their last name or address than the male group due to marriage and/or separation. Additionally, if the classifier is trained on a protected feature-imbalanced dataset, then the predictions could be biased towards the minority group. These challenges impose fairness-bias in PPRL classifiers.

There are many definitions of fairness that have been proposed in the literature for classification tasks, including group fairness, individual fairness, and counterfactual fairness [24]. In this study, we limit our scope to group fairness which states that a classification model is considered fair, if it predicts a particular outcome for individuals (pair of individuals in PPRL) across the protected subgroups with almost equal probability [9,24]. Group fairness has three most commonly used definitions: Demographic Parity, Equal Opportunity, and Equalized Odds. Without loss of generality, we describe these definitions with the assumption that the number of groups based on a protected attribute A is two (a_1 and a_2) and the number of classes is two (1 for matches and 0 for non-matches). Y denotes the true labels and $\hat{Y}$ denotes the predicted labels.

1. Demographic Parity (also known as Independence or Statistical Parity) is one of the most well-known criteria for group fairness. It states that the proportion of each group of a protected attribute (e.g. gender) should receive the positive outcome at equal rates. Positive outcome for the PPRL problem is being classified as a match (1). A classifier C satisfies demographic parity if C is independent of the protected attribute A:

$$P(\hat{Y} = 1|A = a_1) = P(\hat{Y} = 1|A = a_2) \tag{1}$$

The difference between positive outcome rates of different groups should be ideally zero, but this is usually not the case in real applications. Approximate versions of this criteria are:

$$\frac{P(\hat{Y} = 1|A = a_1)}{P(\hat{Y} = 1|A = a_2)} \geq 1 - \epsilon \tag{2}$$

$$|P(\hat{Y} = 1|A = a_1) - P(\hat{Y} = 1|A = a_2)| \leq \epsilon \tag{3}$$

2. Equalized Opportunity (also known as true positive parity) states that each group should get the positive outcome at equal rates, assuming that people in this group qualify for it, i.e. conditioned on the ground truth labels. A classifier C satisfies equalized opportunity criteria if

$$P(\hat{Y} = 1|A = a_1, Y = 1) = P(\hat{Y} = 1|A = a_2, Y = 1) \tag{4}$$

3. Equalized Odds (also known as separation) states that the model should miss-classify positive outcome at equal rates across groups (same False Positive rate across groups), but also miss-classify the negative outcome at equal rates across groups (same False Negative rate). A classifier C satisfies Equalized odds, if it satisfies both

$$P(\hat{Y} = 1|A = a_1, Y = 0) = P(\hat{Y} = 1|A = a_2, Y = 0) \tag{5}$$

and

$$P(\hat{Y} = 0|A = a_1, Y = 1) = P(\hat{Y} = 0|A = a_2, Y = 1) \tag{6}$$

In the PPRL context, predictions of truly matching record pairs as 'matches' are important, i.e. equal true positive and/or false positive rate across different groups. Since Demographic Parity requires equal rate of predictions as 'matches' for both groups regardless of the ground truth, it can result in linkage accuracy loss. Moreover, unlike other classification tasks, PPRL (and record linkage in general) is a class-imbalanced problem with significantly lower number of record pairs truly belonging to 'matches' while the vast majority of record pairs belong to 'non-matches'. This imbalance in ground-truth labels can lead to many false positives with the Demographic Parity fairness criteria.

Equalized Opportunity only takes the true positive rate of the classifier into account, whereas Equalized Odds also considers the errors (false negatives and false positives). In record linkage we are particularly concerned about linkage errors, as linkage is usually only the first step in an analytics task and the errors propagate through the analysis pipeline. Therefore, Equalized Odds is the best fit fairness criteria for PPRL and we therefore use Equalized Odds as the fairness criteria in our study.

We define fairness loss for the Equalized Odds criteria with respect to a binary protected attribute A with two groups (a_1 and a_2) as follows: the average of (a) the absolute difference between (1) the probability of true matching record pairs being classified as non-matches given the protected attribute is a_1 and (2) the probability of true matching record pairs being classified as non-matches given the protected attribute is a_2 and (b) the absolute difference between (1) the probability of true non-matching record pairs being classified as matches given the protected attribute is a_1 and (2) the probability of true non-matching record pairs being classified as matches given the protected attribute is a_2. In other words, it calculates the average of the differences of false positive rates and false negative rates between the two groups.

$$
\begin{aligned}
fairness\_loss = 1/2 \times [abs(Pr(\hat{Y} = 1|A = a_1, Y = 0) \\
- Pr(\hat{Y} = 1|A = a_2, Y = 0)), abs(Pr(\hat{Y} = 0|A = a_1, Y = 1) \\
- Pr(\hat{Y} = 0|A = a_2, Y = 1))],
\end{aligned}
\tag{7}
$$

where Y and $\hat{Y}$ are the true and predicted class labels, respectively, with two values of 1 (for matches) and 0 (for non-matches). Fairness is calculated as:

$$
fairness = 1.0 - fairness\_loss
\tag{8}
$$

4   Reducing Fairness-Bias in PPRL

Fairness-bias in classification models has attracted a large body of research over the past decade. There have been several algorithms and techniques proposed in the literature to improve fairness or mitigate bias in classification problems. These are broadly categorized into: pre-processing, in-processing (i.e. at training time), and post-processing.

1. The aim of pre-processing is to learn a new representation of data such that it removes the information correlated to the sensitive attribute [13,26]. The classifier can thus use the new data representation and produce results that meet the fairness criteria.

   It can only be used for optimizing Demographic Parity or Individual Fairness because it does not have the information of label Y. Further, this category of methods does not perform well compared to the other two categories and inferior to the other two categories in terms of fairness and accuracy (correctness). Moreover, the features in PII are usually correlated. Thus it is pretty much impossible to fully remove the information about the protected feature, for example, the 'female-ness' or 'indigenous-ness' of an entity.

2. In in-processing techniques, the idea is to add a constraint or a regularization term to the existing optimization objective functions of classifiers. Most works in literature fall into this category [1,21,25]. Such methods can be used to optimize for any fairness definition. Moreover, these methods can provide higher flexibility to choose the trade-off between accuracy and fairness measures depending on specific algorithm.

3. Post-processing methods attempt to modify a learned classifier in a way that satisfies fairness constraints. It can be used to optimize most fairness definitions [10,11]. As with pre-processing, any classifier can be supported and no re-training is required. However, it lacks the flexibility of choosing any accuracy–fairness trade-off.

We therefore choose to use in-processing methods to achieve our objective of fair and accurate PPRL. In the following we describe the reductions-based approach using grid search algorithm [1] for fairness-aware PPRL classification.

4.1   Reductions-Based Fairness-Aware Classification Method

Since PPRL is a binary classification problem, we study the applicability of an existing in-processing algorithm for binary classification problem based on reductions approach, as proposed in [1]. The key idea of this method is to reduce fair classification problem to a sequence of cost-sensitive classification problems, whose solutions yield a randomized classifier with the lowest error subject to the desired fairness constraints.

[1] proposes reduction methods to reduce the classification problem to a series of different models. To derive fair classification, the objective function is considered as a saddle point problem from game-theoretic perspective and a Lagrange multiplier λ_k is introduced for each of the constraints in the objective function.

The saddle point can be considered as an equilibrium of a game between two players: the classifier $\mathbf{Q}$ and the Lagrange multipliers λ. The Lagrangian $L(\mathbf{Q}, \lambda)$ specifies how much the $\mathbf{Q}$-player has to pay to the λ-player for each of their choices. At the saddle point, neither player wants to deviate from their choice. [1] proposed a ν-approximate saddle point of the Lagrangian in which neither player can gain more than ν by changing their choice. The algorithm is run iteratively until the ν-approximate saddle point is met.

However, when the number of constraints is very small, as is the case with a binary protected attribute, it is reasonable to consider a grid of values λ_i, and select the best value with the desired trade-off between accuracy and fairness. This algorithm is called grid search algorithm using the reduction approach [1]. In this work, we use the grid search-based reductions algorithm with Equalized Odds constraints to achieve fair and accurate PPRL.

The proposed method tries a series of different models, each parameterized by a Lagrange multiplier λ_i. For each value of λ, the algorithm re-weights and relabels the input data, and trains a new model (note that $\lambda = 0$ corresponds to the unaltered model). The best model found is finally used to predict the binary class labels for PPRL with fairness constraints.

4.2 Efficiency Aspects

The complexity of the fairness-aware classification algorithm depends on the number of candidate record pairs that are input to the classifier. Assuming each of the p databases contains n records ($n \times p$ records in total), the number of similarity/distance comparisons required by the naive linkage techniques (without using any computation reduction methods, such as blocking or filtering [23]) is quadratic in both n and p (i.e. $n^2 \cdot p^2$). The quadratic comparison space can be reduced by using a blocking or computation reduction method [23].

Any machine learning supervised classifier can be used with the reductions-based approach for fairness-aware classification. Different classifiers have different computation complexity. Assuming the number of features is f, number of classes is c, number of training samples (record pairs) is s, and the number of iterations is i, then the complexity of training a logistic regression, for example, is $O((f + 1) \times c \times s \times i)$ (f operations $+1$ for bias). Note that this complexity can change based on things like regularization. The complexity of predictions of s' record pairs using the trained classifier is $O((f + 1) \times c \times s')$.

In order to make the grid search more efficient, we use a two-step approach. In the first step, a set of smaller number of values of λ is used. In the second step, the grid search space is limited to the neighbourhood of values of λ around the λ of the best model found in the first step to improve the model further.

4.3 Privacy Aspects

As with most existing PPRL approaches, we assume the honest-but-curious (semi-honest) adversary model [15]. We also assume the linkage model with a LU to classify the record pairs. There has been a large body of work conducted on the privacy aspect of the blocking and matching steps [18,23]. In this paper, we focus on the classification step of the PPRL pipeline (as described in Sect. 2).

Once the similarities are calculated in the matching step, the classifier uses the similarities of record pairs to classify them into matches and non-matches. Supervised classifiers require training data with ground-truth labels of matches and non-matches. The fairness-aware classifier requires training data with only the similarity scores and the (encoded) protected group values along with the ground truth labels to train the classifier. No information about the QIDs nor encoded QIDs is required.

Similarity scores for different groups would not reveal much information about the PII of individuals in the group, unless the group contains only one or a few individuals, in which case the protected group value can be inferred as well as the individual, especially if it has matching records in the different databases. To improve the privacy guarantees, these scores can be perturbed at the cost of some loss in utility. Furthermore, noise addition mechanisms for similarity scores can be used to meet differential privacy guarantees [8].

5   Experimental Evaluation

In this section, we present the results of our experimental study of our approach for fairness-aware PPRL described in Sect. 4. In our experiments, the similarity scores are calculated based on comparing BF encodings (using the Cryptographic Long-Term Keys method [18]) of record pairs and the protected attribute is assumed to be gender with two groups, which are 'male' and 'female'. The class labels are match/1 and non-match/0.

We conducted experiments on the (encoded) dataset from the Australian Department of Social Science (DSS), Census dataset from the Australian Bureau of Statistic, as well as synthetically biased DSS datasets. 70% of the data are used for training the classifier and 30% as test data. We implemented the prototype for fairness-aware PPRL in Python 3.5.2, and ran all experiments on a server with four 2-core 64-bit Intel Core I7 2.6 GHz CPUs, 8 GBytes of memory and running Ubuntu 16.04. We used logistic regression classifier available in sklearn library for classifying record pairs. We used the grid search algorithm based on reductions approach [1] available in FairLearn library for mitigating fairness-bias in classification. We used 50 iterations for the grid search method.

We evaluate the performance of PPRL in terms of two dimensions, which are correctness and fairness. We use precision, recall, $f1$-measure, and area under curve (AUC) metrics to evaluate the correctness. Precision is the percentage of correctly classified matches against all pairs that are classified as matches and recall is the percentage of correctly classified matches against all true matches. $f1$-measure is the harmonic mean of precision and recall, and is calculated as $f1 = 2 \times \frac{Precision \times Recall}{Precision + Recall}$. AUC measures the 2-dimensional area underneath the curve of false positive rate vs. true positive rate at different points in $[0, 1]$ indicating the trade-off between these two rates. Fairness loss and fairness metrics are calculated using Eqs. 7 and 8, respectively, to evaluate the fairness. The objectives of our experimental study are:

1. Studying the impact of imbalance in the protected feature (gender) on the fairness and correctness of linkage and evaluating how the bias towards the minority group based on the protected feature can be mitigated
2. Evaluating the trade-off between fairness and correctness achieved with fairness-aware model compared to the original (fairness-unaware) model

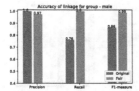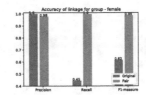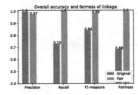

Fig. 1. Comparison of precision, recall, and $f1$-measure of male (left) and female (center) groups, and overall precision, recall, $f1$-measure, and fairness (right) for Original and Fair models on protected feature-imbalanced DSS dataset

3. Studying the impact of bias in QIDs of a certain protected group (e.g. female) using synthetically biased datasets such that female group contains similarity scores that are difficult to be differentiated between matches and non-matches than male group, and evaluating the fairness-bias and the necessity of fairness-aware PPRL
4. Investigating the adverse effect of large bias in QIDs of a certain group to the fair predictions using significantly biased datasets such that the overlap of similarity scores of matches and non-matches is significantly higher for female group than male group, and evaluating the effectiveness of fairness-aware PPRL
5. Investigating if simply removing the protected feature (gender) from encoding, matching, and classification helps overcoming the fairness-bias with respect to the protected feature

In the following, we discuss the results with regard to each of these objectives.

1. Imbalanced protected groups: We first sampled records from the DSS dataset with different numbers for the two groups. In order to evaluate the impact of fairness-bias towards the minority group, we sampled records such that there exist 17760 record pairs belonging to male group and 4000 record pairs belonging to female group. We did not perturb the similarity scores of the record pairs.

We generated predictions from the logistic regression model (labeled as 'Original' in the plots) and fairness-aware logistic regression models with grid search method (labeled as 'Fair'). Figure 1 compares the precision, recall, and $f1$-measure of each group as well as overall precision, recall, $f1$-measure, and fairness of linkage with the original and fair models. As can be seen, the recall of female group with the original model is very low resulting in unfair results for the female (minority) group. Precision of both groups and overall precision, decrease slightly with the fairness-aware model, while recall significantly improves with both groups (especially for the female group) as well as overall. The fairness value improves significantly and reaches to 1.0 with the fair model. As these results show, the overall fairness of the model improves significantly at the cost of some loss in correctness.

2. Trade-off between fairness and correctness: The impact of imposing the fairness constraints in the classification on the correctness of classification

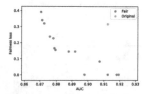 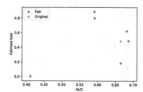 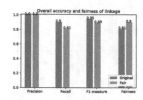

Fig. 2. Comparison of fairness loss vs. AUC on the DSS dataset (left) and DSS-biased dataset (center), and comparison of precision, recall, $f1$-measure, and fairness on the ABS dataset (right) for original and grid/fair models.

depends on the dataset, the fairness definition used, as well as the algorithms used for mitigating unfairness. In general, fairness can have a negative impact on correctness because it diverts the objective from correctness only to both correctness and fairness. However, as is the case with the DSS protected feature-imbalanced dataset, both the overall correctness and fairness could also improve with the fairness-aware linkage.

As shown in Fig. 2 (left), there are several grid models found with the grid search method that achieve both higher AUC and lower fairness loss than the original model (fairness-unaware linkage). However, achieving both higher AUC and lower fairness loss becomes highly challenging with the synthetically biased DSS dataset, as shown in Fig. 2 (center). The trade-off between fairness and correctness results on the ABS dataset is shown in Fig. 2 (right).

3. Bias in QIDs: We next sampled equal number of record pairs from the DSS dataset for male and female groups and then modified the similarity scores of female record pairs in order to make female group of record pairs biased with regard to predictions. We sampled 17760 record pairs for each group (female and male groups) with equal number of matches and non-matches in each group, i.e. 8880 record pairs are matches in each group and 8880 are non-matches. We used this balanced dataset in terms of number of classes and number of protected groups in order to study the sole impact of bias in the QIDs used for linkage on the classification results.

We then modified the similarity scores of record pairs belonging to female group. We have drawn random values from normal distribution in the range of $[0.5, 1.0]$ for matches and $[0.4, 0.8]$ for non-matches and assigned them as similarity scores for female group. The similarity score distributions of matches and non-matches are shown in Figs. 3 (left) and 3 (center), for male and female groups, respectively. As can be seen, there exists a high overlap of similarity scores of matches and non-matches for female group, making the classification task for female group more challenging.

Since the fairness loss of the original model is reasonably low (i.e. fairness-bias is not significant), only one model was identified (with the grid search of 50 iterations) that improves the linkage in terms of both lower fairness loss and higher accuracy values. As shown in Fig. 4, the improvement in fairness is not

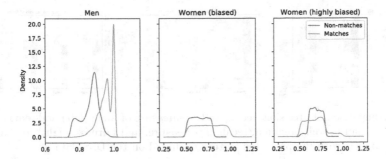

Fig. 3. Similarity score distribution of true matches and true non-matches in different groups in the QID-biased (left and center) and highly QID-biased (left and right) DSS synthetic datasets

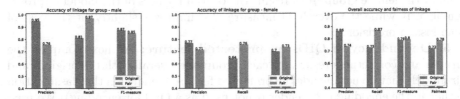

Fig. 4. Comparison of precision, recall, and $f1$-measure of male (left) and female (center) groups, and overall precision, recall, $f1$-measure, and fairness (right) for Original and Fair models on the QID-biased DSS synthetic dataset

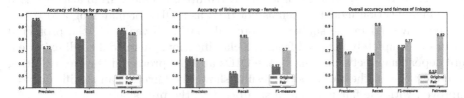

Fig. 5. Comparison of precision, recall, and $f1$-measure of male (left) and female (center) groups, and overall precision, recall, $f1$-measure, and fairness (right) for Original and Fair models on the highly QID-biased DSS synthetic dataset

significant, as similar to the improvement in the recall and $f1$-measure for the female group at the cost of loss in precision in both groups and overall.

4. More biased QIDs: To study the impact of highly biased QIDs on the correctness and fairness of linkage as well as the effectiveness of the fairness-aware model in achieving fair and accurate linkage, we generated a synthetic highly biased dataset from the DSS dataset. The bias is illustrated in Figs. 3 (left) and 3 (right) for male and female groups, respectively, which shows higher bias towards the female group with a large overlap between similarity scores of matches and non-matches making the classification even more challenging. Comparison of fairness and correctness metrics for each group and overall for the original and fair models is shown in Fig. 5. The recall of female group with

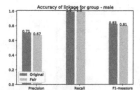 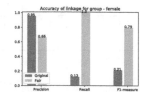 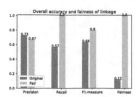

Fig. 6. Comparison of precision, recall, and f1-measure of male (left) and female (center) groups, and overall precision, recall, f1-measure, and fairness (right) for Original and Fair models with the protected feature excluded on the DSS dataset

the original model is significantly low due to the high bias in QIDs, resulting in very low fairness. The fairness-aware model was able to significantly improve the recall of the female group. As a result, the overall fairness of the model improves significantly while the overall f1-measure also improves slightly, at the cost of some loss in precision.

5. Dependency of QIDs on protected feature: We next compare the fairness and correctness results for each group and overall with the original and fair models that do not include the protected feature (gender) in the classification neither in the encoding (i.e. gender is not used as a QID for encoding). We used the highly biased DSS dataset (Figs. 3 (left) and 3 (right)) for this experiment. The results are shown in Fig. 6. As shown in these results, the classification model can still be biased towards a certain vulnerable or minority group based on the protected attribute even if the protected attribute is excluded from features used in the classification model as well as not used as a QID for matching and therefore not involved in the similarity score calculation. Even when the protected feature is completely removed from the classification, there could still exist feature dependency between some of the QIDs and the protected feature, resulting in hidden bias in the data. As the results show, the fairness can significantly be improved with the fair model at a small cost to the precision.

The results of our experimental study explain that fairness-bias exists in various forms for the PPRL problem leading to poor performance of standard classifiers for a certain (vulnerable/minority) group of individuals. Incorporating fairness constraints with Equalized Odds criteria in the classification, a fair and accurate linkage can be achieved for PPRL.

6   Conclusion and Future Work

In this paper, we have studied fairness-bias in privacy-preserving record linkage (PPRL) and investigated appropriate fairness metrics for PPRL and the effectiveness of using fairness-aware classifier based on reductions approach [1] in the context of PPRL binary classification with binary protected attribute. We studied various forms of fairness-bias for the PPRL problem. Experimental evaluation conducted on real datasets from the Australian Department of Social Science (DSS) and Australian Bureau of Statistics (ABS) as well as synthetically biased datasets shows the effectiveness of the method for fairness-aware PPRL.

While the initial results are promising, it opens up several lines of research and experiments in this direction:

1. Evaluating the effectiveness of fairness-aware PPRL algorithm on several real and/or synthetic datasets that are significantly biased
2. Studying fairness constraints with regard to multiple protected attributes (e.g. gender and occupation) as well as with multi-valued (more than two) protected attributes (e.g. race)
3. Investigating fair regression models for continuous similarity values to predict fairly and accurately the similarity scores of record pairs for PPRL
4. Improving efficiency of the grid search method in terms of the number of iterations required, for example, using Bayesian optimization method [19]
5. Studying fairness-aware blocking methods to reduce the computation complexity of PPRL while not affecting the fairness of linkage
6. Finally, conducting extensive set of experiments to understand the fairness-accuracy trade-off with different data, fairness constraints and algorithms

Acknowledgement. This work was funded by the Australian Department of Social Sciences (DSS) as part of the Platforms for Open Data (PfOD) project. We would like to thank Waylon Nielsen and Alex Ware, and Maruti Vadrevu from DSS for their support and feedback on this work.

References

1. Agarwal, A., Beygelzimer, A., Dudík, M., Langford, J., Wallach, H.: A reductions approach to fair classification. arXiv preprint arXiv:1803.02453 (2018)
2. Binns, R.: Fairness in machine learning: lessons from political philosophy. J. Mach. Learn. Res. **81**, 1–11 (2018)
3. Brown, A.P., Randall, S.M., Boyd, J.H., Ferrante, A.M.: Evaluation of approximate comparison methods on bloom filters for probabilistic linkage. Int. J. Popul. Data Sci. **4**(1), 1–16 (2019)
4. Christen, P.: Data Matching - Concepts and Techniques for Record Linkage, Entity Resolution, and Duplicate Detection. Data-Centric Systems and Applications. Springer, Heidelberg (2012). https://doi.org/10.1007/978-3-642-31164-2
5. Dankar, F., El Emam, K.: A method for evaluating marketer re-identification risk. In: EDBT Workshops, No. 28, Lausanne (2010)
6. Datta, A., Tschantz, M.C., Datta, A.: Automated experiments on ad privacy settings. Proc. Priv. Enhanc. Technol. **2015**(1), 92–112 (2015)
7. Durham, E.A.: A framework for accurate, efficient private record linkage. Ph.D. thesis, Vanderbilt University, Nashville, TN (2012)
8. Dwork, C.: Differential privacy. In: Bugliesi, M., Preneel, B., Sassone, V., Wegener, I. (eds.) ICALP 2006. LNCS, vol. 4052, pp. 1–12. Springer, Heidelberg (2006). https://doi.org/10.1007/11787006_1
9. Dwork, C., Hardt, M., Pitassi, T., Reingold, O., Zemel, R.: Fairness through awareness. In: Innovations in Theoretical Computer Science Conference, pp. 214–226. ACM (2012)
10. Dwork, C., Immorlica, N., Kalai, A.T., Leiserson, M.: Decoupled classifiers for group-fair and efficient machine learning. In: Conference on Fairness, Accountability and Transparency, pp. 119–133 (2018)

11. Fish, B., Kun, J., Lelkes, Á.D.: A confidence-based approach for balancing fairness and accuracy. In: SIAM International Conference on Data Mining, pp. 144–152. SIAM (2016)
12. Flores, A.W., Bechtel, K., Lowenkamp, C.T.: False positives, false negatives, and false analyses: a rejoinder to machine bias: there's software used across the country to predict future criminals. And it's biased against blacks. Fed. Probation **80**, 38 (2016)
13. Krasanakis, E., Spyromitros-Xioufis, E., Papadopoulos, S., Kompatsiaris, Y.: Adaptive sensitive reweighting to mitigate bias in fairness-aware classification. In: World Wide Web Conference, pp. 853–862 (2018)
14. Kum, H.C., Krishnamurthy, A., Machanavajjhala, A., Reiter, M.K., Ahalt, S.: Privacy preserving interactive record linkage (PPIRL). JAMIA **21**(2), 212–220 (2014)
15. Lindell, Y., Pinkas, B.: Secure multiparty computation for privacy-preserving data mining. J. Priv. Confidentiality (1) (2009)
16. Naumann, F., Herschel, M.: An introduction to duplicate detection. Synth. Lect. Data Manag. **2**(1), 1–87 (2010)
17. Randall, S.M., Ferrante, A.M., Boyd, J.H., Semmens, J.B.: Privacy-preserving record linkage on large real world datasets. J. Biomed. Inform. **50**(1), 1 (2014)
18. Schnell, R.: Privacy preserving record linkage. In: Harron, K., Goldstein, H., Dibben, C. (eds.) Methodological Developments in Data Linkage, pp. 201–225. Wiley, Chichester (2016)
19. Snoek, J., Larochelle, H., Adams, R.P.: Practical Bayesian optimization of machine learning algorithms. In: Advances in Neural Information Processing Systems, pp. 2951–2959 (2012)
20. Sweeney, L.: Discrimination in online ad delivery. Queue **11**(3), 10–29 (2013)
21. Ustun, B., Liu, Y., Parkes, D.: Fairness without harm: decoupled classifiers with preference guarantees. In: International Conference on Machine Learning, pp. 6373–6382 (2019)
22. Vatsalan, D., Christen, P., Verykios, V.S.: A taxonomy of privacy-preserving record linkage techniques. Inf. Syst. **38**(6), 946–969 (2013)
23. Vatsalan, D., Sehili, Z., Christen, P., Rahm, E.: Privacy-preserving record linkage for big data: current approaches and research challenges. In: Zomaya, A.Y., Sakr, S. (eds.) Handbook of Big Data Technologies, pp. 851–895. Springer, Cham (2017). https://doi.org/10.1007/978-3-319-49340-4_25
24. Verma, S., Rubin, J.: Fairness definitions explained. In: International Workshop on Software Fairness (FairWare), pp. 1–7. IEEE (2018)
25. Zafar, M.B., Valera, I., Rodriguez, M.G., Gummadi, K.P.: Fairness constraints: mechanisms for fair classification. In: International Conference on Artificial Intelligence and Statistics, Florida, USA (2017)
26. Zemel, R., Wu, Y., Swersky, K., Pitassi, T., Dwork, C.: Learning fair representations. In: International Conference on Machine Learning, pp. 325–333 (2013)

Differentially Private Profiling of Anonymized Customer Purchase Records

Hiroaki Kikuchi[(✉)]

Department of Frontier Media Science,
School of Interdisciplinary Mathematical Sciences, Meiji University,
4-21-1 Nakano, Nakano Ku, Tokyo 164-8525, Japan
kikn@meiji.ac.jp

Abstract. In assessing accurately the risk of being compromised, anonymized data must consider the balance between utility and security. In this paper, we propose a new model for profiling customer purchase records. Our model uses a fixed-size vector that indicates the set of all goods that a customer has purchased. Aggregating all records for n customers gives a profile matrix for a customer base. Our interest is in assessing the risk of re-identification by an adversary who has access to the profile matrix as an adversarial knowledge. To evaluate the privacy budget of the differential privacy, we estimate the probability that a dataset has a profile under some reasonable assumptions. This profile probability allows us to estimate not only the privacy of the profile, but also its utility in the form of its mean absolute error.

We have examined the privacy gain expected by performing representative anonymizations, including top/bottom coding, sampling/suppression, and generalization (the fundamental techniques in k-anonymity). These anonymization are modeled by means of simple factors, which allow us to estimate the privacy loss and the mean absolute error under the assumption that the profile's bit errors occur as a sum of independent and identically distributed random variables characterized by the number of records.

1 Introduction

Big data analytics is an increasingly attractive tool for industries, governments and scientists. Businesses acquire data about customers and use their personal data to estimate potential interests and to predict future marketing demands. An efficient marketing technique segments the set of customers into target subsets, such as "valuable" users, and communicates effectively with each of the subsets. This process is referred to as *profiling*. The profiling process extracts features that enable the identification of a target user. Typically, pattern recognition, correlation, and machine learning algorithms are used to extract appropriate features. However, privacy issues have emerged that may have far-reaching consequences.

© Springer Nature Switzerland AG 2020
J. Garcia-Alfaro et al. (Eds.): DPM 2020/CBT 2020, LNCS 12484, pp. 19–34, 2020.
https://doi.org/10.1007/978-3-030-66172-4_2

Mavriki and Karyda [1] identified the privacy threats related to profiling and discussed the implications of profiling for individuals, groups and society.

Anonymization, or de-identification, plays an important role in the safe sharing of data in the age of big data because it enables massive-scale data collection of human activities involving banks, stores, and social networking sites without revealing individual identities. Profiling personally identifiable information (PII) is not only risky, but is also restricted by data protection legislation, such as the EU General Data Protection Regulation [2]. A variety of anonymization techniques have been developed to reduce the re-identification risk. ISO/IEC 20889 [21] classifies the techniques into several categories, namely, statistical tools, cryptographic tools, suppression, pseudonymization, generalization, and randomization. Typically, the risks are evaluated using a range of privacy models in which a privacy condition guarantees an upper bound on the risk of reidentification disclosure by an intruder. Examples of privacy models include k-anonymity [11], ℓ-diversity [12], t-closeness [13], β-likeness [14], ϵ-differential privacy [15], the maximum-knowledge-attacker model [6], general confidentiality metrics [17], and the copula-based model [10].

A new issue in anonymization is *aggregation*. Pyrgelis et al. have pointed out that aggregated location statistics can violate the privacy of individuals [22]. They studied the membership inference threat by an adversary who has access to aggregated location time series. The risks associated with anonymization in aggregated datasets are unclear and are hard to evaluate precisely. Xiao et al. studied privacy in dynamic datasets in [18]. Examples of the features of these datasets include the trajectory of locations [22], the statistics of transactions, the URLs of websites that the target has visited, the titles of movies that the target has seen [20], the items that the customer has rated [7], the medical records of operations that the patient has undergone [5], and the list of goods that the target has purchased [3]. Such features can be used to generate useful profiles for identifying the target individual.

In this paper, we propose a new model for the profile of customer purchase records. Our model uses a fixed-size vector that indicates the set of all goods that a customer has purchased. Aggregating all records for n customers gives the profile matrix a customer base. Our interest is in assessing the risk of re-identification by an adversary who has access the profile matrix as a back-ground knowledge. To evaluate the privacy loss in terms of the differential privacy model [15], we estimate the probability that a dataset represents a profile under some reasonable assumptions. This profile probability allows us to estimate not only the privacy of the profile, but also its utility in the form of its mean absolute error (MAE) of profiles. To reduce the privacy loss from a profile, we consider to perform known anonymization techniques and analyze their expected effects on privacy.

Our contributions of the paper are as follows,

- We propose a new model for profiling cumulative time-series records, e.g., customer purchase records for the year, as an $\ell \times n$ matrix involving the number of goods ℓ and the number of customers n.

- We prove that the profile of customer purchase records meets a differential-privacy criterion involving some parameters and shows an improvement in the privacy budget provided by some representative anonymization techniques.
- We also evaluate the utility loss of an anonymized dataset in terms of the MAE estimated from the probability of inconsistent bits between the original and the anonymized datasets.
- Using the open-access database of the 45,047 customer purchase records in the UCI Machine Learning dataset, we shows a numerical analysis of our proposed model.

The rest of this paper is organized as follows. In Sect. 2, we define the differential-privacy model. In Sect. 3, we give fundamental definitions for profiling, a dataset of purchase records, and an adversary. Section 4 proves the differential privacy of profiling after showing some useful profiling properties and models for typical anonymization techniques. Section 5 evaluates the effects of the various techniques on anonymizations. in terms of the privacy and the utility metrics. After summarizing the trade-off between the privacy and the utility, we conclude our study in Sect. 6.

2   Preliminary

Differential privacy guarantees that a randomized algorithm behaves similarly when applied to similar input databases.

Definition 1 (ϵ-DP). *A randomized algorithm $\mathcal{A}$ is ϵ-differentially private if for any $S \in \text{Range}(\mathcal{A})$ and for any pairs of neighboring datasets D and D',*

$$e^{-\epsilon} \leq \frac{\Pr[\mathcal{A}(D) = S]}{\Pr \mathcal{A}(D') = S]} \leq e^{\epsilon}. \tag{1}$$

Note that we say D and D' are neighboring if a record $t \in D$ does not belong to D'. In practice, ϵ-DP is too strong to be satisfied. It is therefore generalized to allow violation of Eq. (1) with a small failure probability δ as follows.

Definition 2 ((ϵ, δ)-DP). *A randomized algorithm $\mathcal{A}$is (ϵ, δ)-private if for any $S \in \text{Range}(\mathcal{A})$, and for any pairs of neighboring datasets D and D', $\Pr[\mathcal{A}(D) = S] \leq e^{\epsilon} Pr[\mathcal{A}(D') = S] + \delta$.*

This implies that Eq. (1) holds with probability of at least $1 - \delta$.

3   Privacy of Aggregated Purchase Records

3.1   Purchase Records

Anonymization or de-identification is the process that removes the *association* between a set of data attributes and the data principal that they relate to [4]. In our study, we model the association as a linkage, in terms of identity, between the records in an individual master dataset M and the records in a transaction dataset D. We assume that data principals are uniquely identified for the records of table M from certain external knowledge. This assumption is reasonable, given that each data principal is represented by a single record in table M. In contrast, the transaction table D stores multiple records for a data principal, making it relatively difficult to associate records with the correct data principals. Example of purchase record can be found in the Online Retail dataset in the UCI Machine Learning Repository[1]. The master table M describes the customer ID, sex, day of birth, and country for $n = 4$ individuals, expressed as a 4×4 matrix.

3.2   Customer Profiling

Profiling is the process of constructing user profiles aggregated from personal data such as online purchase history, financial records, and credit card transactions. It aims to predict the individual's behavior, interests and decisions. From an industry perspective, profiling is referred to as Customer Relations Management (CRM) or Personalization. We define a simple model of profiling as follows.

A transaction dataset (a matrix) is divided into n subsets according to the n individuals to give $D = D_1 \cup D_2 \cup \cdots \cup D_n$. Let m_i be the number of records in D_i, i.e., $m_i = |D_i|$. Note that the size of each subset depends on the individual concerned. Generally, there is a power-law distribution of m_i, such as Zipf or the Pareto distribution [16].

For simplicity, we suppress redundant columns from a record and regard it as a time series of values in a single column. Let $D_i^{(g)}$ be a projection of dataset D_i to the column regarded as the goods that the i-th customer has purchased during the observation period. Let $G = \{g_1, \ldots, g_\ell\}$ be a set of goods that a shop carries, where the total number of goods is ℓ.

Definition 3 (profile). *Let D_i be a dataset for the i-th user, comprising of m_i records. A profile of i-th user is an ℓ-dimensional vector $\boldsymbol{x} = (x_1, \ldots, x_\ell) \in \{0,1\}^\ell$ where*

$$x_j = \begin{cases} 1 & \text{if } g_j \text{ is in } D_i^{(g)}, \\ 0 & \text{otherwise.} \end{cases}$$

for $j = 1, \ldots, \ell$.

By using $\mathcal{A}(D_i)$, we generate a profile $\boldsymbol{x}$ for the i-th customer. Although this is too simple to model customer profiling in practice, it is significant enough to identify individuals when many records of activities are aggregated over a long period. For example, Narayanan and Shamatikov [20] demonstrated that 500,000 Netflix subscribers can be identified from a very small number of records. After some records are linked to the same customer, an adversary may learn additional private information based on these linked records. This simple model of a profile is therefore critical from the privacy point of view.

---

[1] Available at http://archive.ics.uci.edu/ml/datasets/Online+Retail/.

Table 1. Examples of profiles for $n = 5, m = 13, \ell = 3$

ID i	rank r_i	Profile x_i	# records m_i	Minority
1	1	(1,1,1)	6	0
2	2	(1,0,1)	3	0
3	3	(1,1,0)	2	0
4	4	(0,1,0)	1	1
5	5	(1,0,0)	1	1

Table 2. List of symbols

Symbol	Description	Range
U	Set of customers	$|U| = n$
G	Set of goods	$|G| = \ell$
D	Dataset of purchase records	$|D| = m$
m_i	Number of records that the i-th customer has purchased	$m_{min} \leq m_i \leq m_{max}$
θ	Threshold value used for top/bottom coding	$\theta \in [1, m_{max}]$
β	Random sampling rate	$\beta \in [0, 1]$
c	Generalization factor categorizing c elements together	$1 \geq c$
D_i	Array of m_i records for the i-th customer	$m_i = |D_i|$
$\mathcal{A}(D_i)$	Profile of the i-th customer	$x \in \{0,1\}^\ell$
$\mathcal{A}(\mathcal{D})$	Aggregated customer profiles	$\ell \times n$ matrix

Given an aggregation of n profiles, we define $\mathcal{A}(D)$, as an $\ell \times n$ matrix of binary values, which can be useful to an adversary who wishes to track customers. Table 1 shows an example of profiles for a dataset of $m = 13$ records for $n = 5$ customers. The profile x_i indicates whether the i-th customer has ordered the corresponding goods g_1, g_2, g_3, respectively. For example, suppose the history of orders for the second customer is $D_2 = (g_1, g_3, g_1)$. This customer's history is then profiled as $\mathcal{A}(D_2) = (1, 0, 1)$, where the count of g_1 is ignored. The column labeled as "Minority" relates to differential privacy and will be discussed shortly. In the example, for simplicity, we assign the customer IDs according to their rank r_i in the number of records m_i.

Table 2 gives the list of symbols used in the following definitions and analyses.

3.3 Adversary

Given the aggregated customer profiles $\mathcal{A}(\mathcal{D})$ and an unknown series of records D_i, an adversary may aim to identify the corresponding profile from $\mathcal{A}(D_i)$.

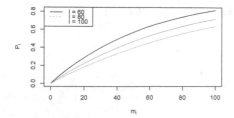

Fig. 1. Probability distribution p_i for parameter m_i (the number of records for the i-th customer)

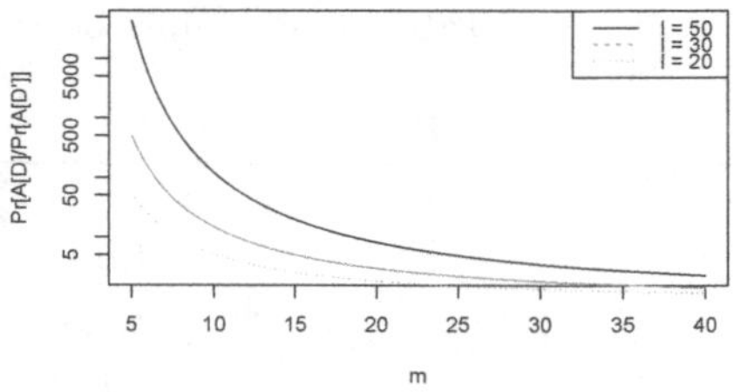

Fig. 2. Distribution of privacy loss with respect to number of records m_i

We are interested in the level of confidence the adversary will have in identifying users based on customer profiles. If we can quantify the risk of being identified from the profile in terms of an accurate probability, we can adaptively control the duration of profile accumulation to maintain an acceptably small risk of privacy breach. Therefore, we evaluate the probabilities related to profiling in the following sections (Fig. 1)

4 Quantifying Privacy

4.1 Profile Probability

Theorem 1 (profile probability). *Let D_i be a sequence of m_i records of purchase for the i-th customer that are independent and identically distributed over G with $1/\ell$ probability. Then, the i-th profile x occurs with $\Pr[\mathcal{A}(D_i) = x] = p_i^z(1 - p_i)^{\ell-z}$, where z is the Hamming weight of x and p_i is the probability that a certain bit of x is 1, computed as*

$$p_i = 1 - (1 - \frac{1}{\ell})^{m_i}. \tag{2}$$

Proof. Under the iid assumption, each g_j of the ℓ elements of G is chosen with probability $1/\ell$. The same good may be purchased many times, but only the first purchase has an effect. Therefore, the probability that g_j is not chosen, even after m_i orders (records), is $(1 - 1/\ell)^{m_i}$, and its complement gives p_i.

All bits of x can be 1 with uniform probability p_i, implying that the probability of x is determined by the number of 1-bits without regards of their locations. Letting z be the number of 1-bits in x, we have the theorem.

Note that the number of 1-bits in x (= Hamming weight z) follows a binomial distribution $B(\ell, p_i)$ whose mean is $E(z) = \ell p_i$.

4.2 Differential Privacy of Profiling

First, we should note a negative aspect of the differential privacy of profiling.

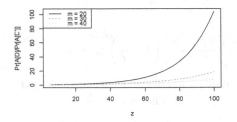

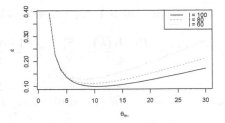

Fig. 3. Distribution of privacy loss with respect to the Hamming weight $z = w_H(\boldsymbol{x})$ ($\ell = 100$)

Fig. 4. Differential privacy for bottom coding θ_{m_-}

Remark 1. The profile $\mathcal{A}(\mathcal{D})$ does not satisfy ϵ-differential privacy.

Suppose two *neighboring* datasets D and D' such that $t \in D$ but $t \notin D'$ for a record t, where t is a record made by the i-th individual, who has m_i records in D and has $m_i - 1$ records in D'. Here, $D_j = D'_j$ for $j \neq i$ and $Pr[\mathcal{A}(D)] = \prod_i Pr[\mathcal{A}(D_i)]$. We are interested in whether

$$\frac{Pr[\mathcal{A}(D) = S]}{Pr[\mathcal{A}(D') = S]} = \frac{\prod_i^n Pr[\mathcal{A}(D_i) = S_i]}{\prod_i^n Pr[\mathcal{A}(D'_i) = S_i]} = \frac{Pr[\mathcal{A}(D_i) = \boldsymbol{x}]}{Pr[\mathcal{A}(D'_i) = \boldsymbol{x}]} \tag{3}$$

$$= \left(\frac{p_i}{p'_i}\right)^z \left(\frac{1 - p_i}{1 - p'_i}\right)^{\ell - z} = \left(\frac{1 - (1 - 1/\ell)^{m_i}}{1 - (1 - 1/\ell)^{m_i - 1}}\right)^z \left(1 - \frac{1}{\ell}\right)^{\ell - z}$$

is bounded within some range for arbitrary $S \in \text{Range}(\mathcal{A})$. Note that the quantity, called *privacy loss*, is monotone increasing with respect to z for $0, \ldots, \ell$, and monotone decreasing with respect to $1 \leq m_i \leq m$. Figure 2 and 3 illustrate the distribution of privacy loss for particular values $\ell = 20, 30, 50$ and $m_i = 20, 30, 40$.

It is clear immediately that $m_i = 1$ maximizes the privacy loss. If the i-th customer has just $m_i = 1$ record in D_i, his profile will be $\boldsymbol{x}_i = (0, \ldots, 1, \ldots, 0)$ (a single bit is 1 and all others are 0) with $1/\ell$ probability. However, he has no record in D'_i, and will never have the same profile as $\boldsymbol{x}_i$, i.e., $Pr[\mathcal{A}(D_i) = \boldsymbol{x}_i] = 0$ and the privacy loss increases to infinity. This implies that any adversary can distinguish D from D' deterministically and ϵ-differential privacy is too strong to guarantee the privacy level of profiling. We therefore need to consider a weaker version of this notion.

Let N_1 be the number of customers who have only one record in D. In many big databases, customers rarely purchase just once and this number may represent only a small fraction. We can then satisfy Eq. (3) with failure probability $\delta_1 = N_1/n$ in terms of the following theorem.

Theorem 2 ((ϵ, δ)-differentially private profile). *A profile $\mathcal{A}(D)$ is (ϵ_2, δ_1)-differentially private with $\epsilon_2 = 2 \ln(2 - 1/\ell) + (\ell - 2) \ln(1 - 1/\ell)$ and $\delta_1 = N_1/n$.*

Proof. For any $m_i > 1$, Eq. (3) will satisfy

$$e^{-\epsilon_-} \leq \frac{Pr[\mathcal{A}(D_i) = S]}{Pr[\mathcal{A}(D_i') = S]} = \left(\frac{1 - (1 - 1/\ell)^{m_i}}{1 - (1 - 1/\ell)^{m_i - 1}}\right)^z \left(1 - \frac{1}{\ell}\right)^{\ell - z} \leq e^{\epsilon_+}$$

for small values of ϵ_- and ϵ_+. If $m_i = 2$, it will be maximized. Because at least one bit must be 1 in the profile of $m_i = 2$, $1 \leq z \leq 2$. Therefore,

$$e^{-\epsilon_-} \leq \left(\frac{1 - (1 - 1/\ell)^1}{1 - (1 - 1/\ell)}\right) \left(1 - \frac{1}{\ell}\right)^{\ell - 1} \leq \left(\frac{1 - (1 - 1/\ell)^2}{1 - (1 - 1/\ell)}\right)^2 \left(1 - \frac{1}{\ell}\right)^{\ell - 2} \leq e^{\epsilon_+}.$$

Taking logarithm gives $\epsilon_- = -\ln(2 - 1/\ell) - (\ell - 1)\ln(1 - 1/\ell)$ and $\epsilon_+ = +2\ln(2 - 1/\ell) + (\ell - 2)\ln(1 - 1/\ell)$. For any $\ell > 2$, $\epsilon_- < \epsilon_+$. Therefore, $\epsilon = \epsilon_+$ and we have the theorem.

4.3   Anonymization Models

Profiling the history of purchased goods allows database user to identify customers in the records of purchase (at least with a certain probability) and to predict future purchase orders that the customer might make. We have estimated the privacy loss when the profile is available to an adversary in the previous section. The risk can be reduced if we modify the dataset slightly before profiling. This process is known as de-identification, or anonymization.

An anonymization technique is designed to reduce the risk of re-identification without decreasing the utility of the anonymized data for intended use cases. Because it is well known that there is a trade-off between utility and privacy (or degree of resilience against an identification threat), much effort has gone into exploring combination of anonymization techniques via parameters such as k-anonymity.

A broad range of algorithms for anonymization have been proposed to date. ISO/IEC 20889 [21] classifies the techniques into several categories: statistical tools, cryptographic tools, suppression, pseudonymization, generalization, and randomization. Here we choose some representative techniques from these categories for evaluation by our profiling model from both the privacy and utility perspectives.

Definition 4 (sampling). *Let β be a sampling rate in $[0, 1]$. Let f_β be random sampling procedure that uses dataset D to output $f_\beta(D)$, which suppress records with a probability of $1 - \beta$.*

After sampling, the number of records for the i-th customer is reduced to $m_i' = \beta m_i$. Note that m_i' can be 0 but we regard the total number of individuals n an unchanged.

Definition 5 (top coding). *Let θ_{m_+} be a threshold for the maximum frequency of records associated with an individual. We use $f_{\theta_{m_+}}(D)$ to denote the suppression of records for all individuals with more than θ_{m_+} records. That is, no one has more than θ_{m_+} records in $f_{\theta_{m_+}}(D)$.*

We do not specify the way to choose the redundant records to suppress in this paper. A reasonable suppression approach is to use random sampling because it preserves the statistical properties within certain bounds.

Definition 6 (bottom coding). *Let θ_{m_-} be a threshold for the minimum frequency of records associated with an individual. We use $f_{\theta_{m_-}}(D)$ to denote the addition of dummy records for all individuals with less than θ_{m_-} records. That is, no one has less than θ_{m_-} records in $f_{\theta_{m_-}}(D)$.*

Similarly to top coding, we do not assume any particular method for generating the dummy records. However, the simple duplication of his/her records is a reasonable approach. Note that, with bottom coding, $\theta_{m_-} > 1$ guarantees that there is no record with $m_i = 1$ in $f_{\theta_{m_-}}(D)$. Therefore, we can avoid the issue of having too few records to satisfy the differential privacy of the anonymized dataset.

Definition 7. *Let c be a generalizing factor in $[1, \ell]$. By f_c, we denote a generalized set of goods G such that $\ell' = \ell/c$, where $\ell = |G|$. Similarly, let $f_c(D)$ be the generalized dataset for which its set of goods is classified into ℓ/c categories.*

A generalizing factor involving real numbers, e.g., $c = 1.2$, is allowed in our model. According to ISO 20889 [21], generalization preserves data truthfulness at the record level. For example, with $c = 2$, we replace values g_1, g_2 by a new category, say, $\{g_1, g_2\}$, and both records with g_1 and g_2 in D preserve the relationship with the new record $\{g_1, g_2\}$ in $f_c(D)$. This is an important interpretation when we evaluate the utility of the generalized dataset.

5   Theoretical Analysis

5.1   Privacy of Anonymizations

We can note that neither top coding nor sampling changes the differential-privacy guarantee.

Remark 2. Given a profile $\mathcal{A}(\mathcal{D})$ that satisfies (ϵ_2, δ_1)-differential privacy, both top coding $f_{\theta_{m_+}}$ and sampling f_β satisfy (ϵ_2, δ_1)-differential privacy.

Sampling reduces the number of records for all individuals with the same probability. The set of individuals having single records in D is therefore reduced to a set of size βN_1. However, the denominator of failure probability will simultaneously decrease with βn. Eventually, the failure probability is the same to δ_1.

Theorem 3. *For any $\theta_{m_-} > 1$, a profiling after bottom coding $\mathcal{A}[f_{\theta_{m_-}}(D)]$ satisfies $(\epsilon_{\theta_{m_-}}, 0)$-differential privacy, where $\epsilon_{\theta_{m_-}} = \theta_{m_-} \ln(1 - (1 - 1/\ell)^{\theta_{m_-}} - \theta_{m_-} \ln(1 - (1 - 1/\ell)^{\theta_{m_-}}).$*

Proof. With a bottom coding of $\theta_{m_-} > 1$, the number of records for any individual m_i is in $1 < \theta_{m_-} \leq m_i \leq m_{\max}$. The privacy loss in Eq. (3) is maximized for $m_i = z = \theta_{m_-}$. Taking logarithms of both sides, we have the privacy budget $\epsilon_{\theta_{m_-}}$.

From the premise of $\theta_{m_-} > 1$, the case of infinite privacy loss will not occur. We therefore have strict differential privacy when $\delta = 0$.

Figure 4 shows the distribution of privacy budget ϵ for a bottom coding threshold of θ_{m_-}. The privacy degree improves as θ_{m_-} increases provided the threshold is below about 10. It slightly increases with θ_{m_-} because ϵ maximizes at the lower bound of $z = \theta_{m_-}$, which increases with θ_{m_-} (i.e., the density of 1-bits increases).

Theorem 4. *For any $c > 1$, a profiling after generalization $\mathcal{A}[f_c(D)]$ satisfies (ϵ_c, δ_1)-differential privacy, where $\epsilon_c = 2\ln(2 - c/\ell) + (\ell - 2)\ln(1 - c/\ell)$.*

Proof. Simply, replacing ℓ in Eq. (3) by $\ell' = \ell/c$ gives ϵ_c. Because N_1 is independent of ℓ', the failure probability δ_1 is unchanged.

The privacy improves as c increases. We will estimate the utility loss incurred by generalization in the next section.

k-anonymity is a privacy model that ensures that every equivalence class contains at least k records. To satisfy k-anonymity, the combination of suppression and generalization is applied with adequate parameters. The above results state that the privacy budget ϵ does not change for any suppression by sampling, but depends on generalization factor c. Hence, we claim that a generalization is a dominant strategy to control the privacy.

5.2   Utility of Anonymizations

Evaluation of MAE. We evaluate the utility loss incurred by anonymization processes in terms of MAE between the original profile matrix $\mathcal{A}(\mathcal{D})$ and the altered profiles $\mathcal{A}(f(D))$ performed by anonymization f.

Definition 8 (MAE). *Given a dataset D involving n individuals and anonymization f, the MAE of $f(D)$ is*

$$w_f(D) = \frac{1}{n}\sum_i^n ||\mathcal{A}(D_i) - \mathcal{A}(f(D_i))|| = \frac{1}{n}\sum_i^n ||\boldsymbol{x}_i - \boldsymbol{x}'_i||,$$

where $||\boldsymbol{x} - \boldsymbol{x}'||$ is the Hamming weight of $\boldsymbol{x}_i \oplus \boldsymbol{x}'_i = (w_1, \ldots, w_\ell)$.

Assuming that $w_1, \ldots, w_\ell$ are independently and identically distributed, we consider a random variable W_j for $j = 1, \ldots, \ell$ for w_j. The random variable W_j is 1 if and only if the bits of two profiles, $\mathcal{A}(D_i)$ and $\mathcal{A}(f(D_i))$, are different, and is 0 otherwise. We can then estimate the conditional probability of $W_j = 1$ given m_i as

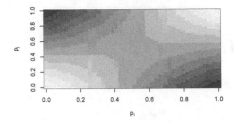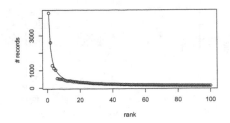

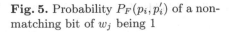

Fig. 5. Probability $P_F(p_i, p'_i)$ of a non-matching bit of w_j being 1

Fig. 6. Number of records in the Online Retail dataset [3] with respect to rank ranging 1 to 100

$$Pr[W_j = 1|m_i] = Pr[x_j = 1, x'_j = 0 \lor x_j = 0, x'_j = 1|m_i]$$
$$= p_i(1 - p'_i) + (1 - p_i)p'_i - p_i(1 - p'_i)p'_i(1 - p'_i),$$

where p_i and p'_i are the probabilities of bits in D_i and $f(D_i)$ being 1, respectively, as defined in Eq. (2). We denote as $P_F(p_i, p'_i)$ the probability that the two profiles characterized by p_i and p'_i take the same value for a certain bit.

Using probability P_F, we estimate MAE as the expected value of W_j, which has a binomial distribution of size ℓ and P_F and is expressed as

$$\hat{w}_f(D) = E[w_f(D)] = E[\sum W_j] = E[B(P_F(p_i, p'_i), \ell)] = \ell \sum_i^n P_F(p_i, p'_i).$$

Figure 5 shows the probability distribution of $P_F(p_i, p_j)$. Note that P_F is not always 0 even if $p_i = p_j$ (the distribution at the orthogonal line in the figure), and it maximizes at $p_i = 0.5$. Therefore, the MAE has $w_f > 0$ even for $f(D_i) = D_i$.

Data. We used the Online Retail dataset ($m = 45,047$ and $\ell = 3,090$) [3] for our analysis. Figure 6 shows the distribution of the number of records m_i with respect to the rank r_i over the range 1 to 100. We can characterize its power-law behavior from the fitted plot of a nonlinear least-squares estimation as $m_i = 4250/r_i^{0.908} + 14.06$.

Top/bottom Coding. Top coding with θ_{m_+} suppresses records whose frequency exceeds the threshold and results in the dataset $f_{\theta_{m_+}}(D)$, where, for $i = 1, \ldots, n$,

$$m'_i = \begin{cases} \theta_{m_+} & \text{if } m_i > \theta_{m_+} \\ m_i & \text{otherwise.} \end{cases}$$

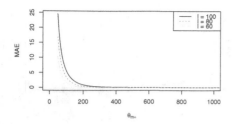 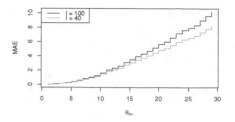

Fig. 7. MAE of top coding   **Fig. 8.** MAE of bottom coding

By letting $r_+ = m_i^{-1}(\theta_{m_+})$ be the lower bound of ranking, for which $m_{r_i} > \theta_{m_+}$ for any $r_i < r_+$, the estimated MAE is

$$\hat{w}_{\theta_{m_+}} = \frac{1}{n}\left(\sum_{r=1}^{r_+} \ell P_F(p_{i_r}, p_{i_{r_+}}) + \sum_{r=r_++1}^{n} ||\boldsymbol{x}_{i_r} - \boldsymbol{x}_{i_r}||\right) \le \frac{r_+}{n}\ell P_F(p_{max}, p_{i_{r_+}}),$$

where $i_1, \ldots, i_n$ are indexes sorted by the number of records. That is, $m_{i_1} \le \cdots \le m_{i_n}$ and $p_{max} = p_{i_{r_1}}$.

The lower bound of rank r_+ increases as the threshold for top coding θ_{m_+} decreases. Accordingly, the MAE increases.

Bottom coding with θ_{m_-} can be made in either by suppressing records whose frequencies are less than θ_{m_-} or by adding dummy records for individuals who otherwise would have too few records. The utility loss of the former may be smaller than the latter, but we should first estimate both worst cases.

Bottom coding is similar to top coding, with the numbers of records being modified to

$$m_i' = \begin{cases} \theta_{m_-} & \text{if } m_i < \theta_{m_-} \\ m_i & \text{otherwise} \end{cases}$$

for $i = 1, \ldots, n$ after the bottom coding. Letting r_- be the upper bound of ranking, for which $m_{i_{r_-}} \le \theta_{m_-}$, the estimated MAE is

$$\hat{w}_{\theta_{m_-}}(D) = \frac{1}{n}\left(\sum_{r=r_-}^{n} \ell Pr(p_{i_r}, p_{i_{r_-}}) + 0\right) \le \frac{n-r_-}{n}\ell P_F(p_{min}, p_{i_{r_-}}),$$

where $p_{min} = p_{i_{r_n}}$. Because p_{min} is very small for most n, and knowing that $P_F(p_i, 0) = p_i$, the estimation can be simplified to $\hat{w}_{\theta_{m_-}} \le (n - r_i)/n\ell p_{i_{r_-}}$.

The threshold in bottom coding θ_{m_-} controls both privacy and utility metrics. If it is high, many records need to be altered and the privacy budget ϵ decreases toward $\epsilon_{\theta_{m_-}}$, resulting in better privacy. However, the utility loss will increase as the threshold increases, in addition to $p_{i_{r_-}}$ increasing, as shown above. Consequently, our analysis confirms that bottom coding involves a trade-off between privacy and utility.

Figure 7 shows that how the estimated MAE decreases as the threshold θ_{m_+} increases. We can observe that the utility loss is limited even if we perform the

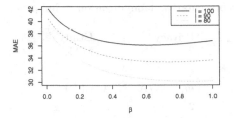

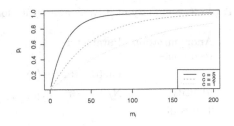

Fig. 9. MAE for sampling

Fig. 10. Probability distributions p_i after generalization with $c = 1, 2, 5$

top coding at $\theta_{m_+} = 200$. This is a consequence of the property of long-tail distribution that a small number of individuals account for most of the records. In contrast, bottom coding has a significant effect on utility, as shown in the distribution of the estimated MAE a range of thresholds in Fig. 8.

Sampling. The sampling process samples the records for every individual in D using a sampling rate β. That is, the number of records for the i-th individual is modified to $m_i' = \beta m_i$. The MAE consequently increases and is expressed as

$$\hat{w}_\beta(D) = \frac{1}{n} \sum_{i=1}^{n} \ell P_F(p_i, \beta p_i) \geq w(D) + \frac{1}{n} \sum_{i=1}^{n} \ell (1 - (1 - \frac{1}{\ell})^{\beta m_i} - (1 - \frac{1}{\ell})^{(1+\beta)m_i}),$$

where $w(D)$ is the MAE without any anonymization. Here, the sampling yields an additional error, given by the second term in the above formula, which is a function of β.

Figure 9 shows the distribution of the estimated MAE with respect to the sampling rate β. The utility is reduced as β approaches 0. The MAE is not exactly zero even if $\beta = 1.0$ (i.e., no sampling is performed) because a type of false positive occurs with $P_F(p_i, 1p_i)$, as discussed in Sect. 5.2.

Generalization uses a generalizing factor $c \in [1, \ell]$ to classify a set of goods (values) into ℓ/c categories $\ell' = \ell/c$, while keeping other parameters such as m_i unchanged. The MAE for generalization is therefore given by

$$\hat{w}_c(D) = \frac{1}{n} \sum_{i=1}^{n} \frac{\ell}{c} P_F(p_i, p_i') = \frac{\ell}{cn} \sum_{i=1}^{n} P_F(1 - (1 - \frac{1}{\ell})^{m_i}, (1 - (1 - \frac{c}{\ell})^{m_i}).$$

It is not useful to evaluate the difference between profiles with different length vectors (ℓ and ℓ/c bits). Instead, we consider the change in the mean probability of non-matching bits of two profiles with respect to the generalizing factor c. Consider two profiles $\mathcal{A}(D_i) = (0, 0, 0, 1)$ and $\mathcal{A}(f_c(D_i)) = (\underline{0}, 1)$ for $c = 2$ and $\ell = 4$, where the first two bits (underlined) are generalized to give the first bit $\underline{0}$ in $\mathcal{A}(f_c(D_i))$. We say the bit is *consistent* if the two bit values (i.e., both are

Table 3. Summary of privacy and utility for representative anonymization techniques

Anonymization techniques f	Parameters			Privacy				Utility MAE
	Factor	Range (m_i)	ℓ'	z	ϵ	δ	
Identity	N/A	$[m_{min}, m_{max}]$	ℓ	m_i	N/A	N/A	$w(D)$
Top coding	θ_{m_+}	$[m_{min}, \theta_{m_+}]$	ℓ	2	ϵ_2	δ_0	$\hat{w}_{\theta_{m_+}}(D)$
Bottom coding	θ_{m_-}	$[\theta_{m_-}, m_{max}]$	ℓ	θ_{m_-}	$\epsilon_{\theta_{m_-}}$	0	$\hat{w}_{\theta_{m_-}}(D)$
Sampling	β	$[\beta m_{min}, \beta m_{max}]$	ℓ	2	ϵ_2	δ_0	$\hat{w}_\beta(D)$
Generalization	c	$[m_{min}, m_{max}]$	ℓ/c	2	ϵ_c	δ_0	$\hat{w}_c(D)$
k-anonymity	c_k	$[m_{min}, m_{max}]$	ℓ/c_k	2	ϵ_{c_k}	δ_0	$\hat{w}_{c_k}(D)$

0 or both are 1). In this example, the profile has one consistent bit and one inconsistent bit.

The bit probability of profile p_i increases as c increases. The mean probability of an inconsistent bit P_F also increases with c. This is unsurprising because generalization involves increasing the MAE. Figure 10 shows the probability distribution p_i for $m_i = 1, \ldots, 200$. The MAE increases as the generalization factor c increases.

We can now address the question: How large is the error associated with k-anonymity? We start by recalling that k-anonymity is ensured by an appropriate combination of generalization and suppression. Suppression can be done via top or bottom coding but either does not contribute the privacy budget ϵ in Sect. 5.1. We, therefore, focus on generalization as an approach to satisfying k-anonymity. We note that k is monotone increasing with respect to generalizing factor c and $k = n$ for the extreme case $c = \ell$. Therefore, there will exist $1 < c_k \leq \ell$ such that all equivalent classes contain at least k records.

Remark 3. k-anonymity generalized with c_k is (ϵ_{c_k}, δ)-differentially private and has an MAE of $\hat{w}_{c_k}$.

5.3   Summary

Table 3 summarizes our analysis from the viewpoints of differential privacy and the utility. We examined several anonymization functions that are modeled as mapping on a dataset D according to the factors θ, β, and c. The anonymized dataset $f(D)$ can have variations in the range of numbers of records per individual m_i (frequency of orders) and in the number of values (categories of goods). From the differential-privacy viewpoint, bottom coding has a significant effect on both ϵ and δ. It ensues that, in the anonymized dataset, no one has purchased on too few occasions, which would aid adversarial identification. It satisfies strict differential privacy with $\delta = 0$. Our analysis gives estimates for privacy and utility with k-anonymity under the assumption that k is achieved via the generalizing factor c_k in the analysis.

6   Conclusions

We have studied the privacy and the utility of profiling cumulative purchase records. We have proposed a model for profiling records that uses a vector of goods that a target customer has purchased at least once during the period of observation. We have analyzed the probability distribution of profiles, given the number of records for each customer, and proved that it does not satisfy a strict differential privacy. This is because some customers may have only one record in the dataset, which can be distinguished easily and implies an infinite privacy loss. Instead, we have developed a weaker differential-privacy measure that has a small probability of failure against an adversary who has a background knowledge of the profiles for all customers.

Some techniques of anonymization are known to reduce the risk of re-identification from an anonymized dataset. We have examined the privacy gain expected by performing representative anonymizations including a top/bottom coding, sampling/suppression, and generalization (the fundamental techniques in k-anonymization). These anonymizations are modeled in terms of simple factors that enable us to estimate the privacy budget and the MAE under the assumption that the profile's bit errors occur as a sum of independent and identically distributed random variables characterized by the number of records.

One of the interesting results from our analysis is that, among the set of anonymization techniques, bottom coding plays the most significant role in characterizing differential privacy. With a threshold on the number of records, bottom coding best suppresses (or hides among dummy records) those risky records that are most likely to be identified by an adversary.

References

1. Mavriki, P., Karyda, M.: Profiling with big data: identifying privacy implications for individuals, groups and society. In: The 12th Mediterranean Conference on Information Systems (MCIS) (2018)
2. General Data Protection Regulation, Regulation (EU) 2016/679 (refereed in 2019). https://gdpr-info.eu
3. Chen, D., Sain, S.L., Guo, K.: Data mining for the online retail industry: a case study of RFM model-based customer segmentation using data mining. J. Database Mark. Cust. Strategy Manag. **19**(3), 197–208 (2012). https://doi.org/10.1057/dbm.2012.17
4. Information Commissioner's Office (ICO): Anonymisation: managing data protection risk code of practice (2012)
5. El Emam, K., Arbuckle, L.: Anonymizing Health Data Case Studies and Methods to Get You Started. O'Reilly, Newton (2013)
6. Domingo-Ferrer, J., Ricci, S., Soria-Comas, J.: Disclosure risk assessment via record linkage by a maximum-knowledge attacker. In: 2015 Thirteenth Annual Conference on Privacy, Security and Trust (PST). IEEE (2015)
7. Linden, G., Smith, B., York, J.: Amazon.com recommendations: item-to-item collaborative filtering. IEEE Internet Comput. **7**(1), 76–80 (2003)

8. Domingo-Ferrer, J., Torra, V.: A quantitative comparison of disclosure control methods for microdata. In: Confidentiality, Disclosure and Data Access: Theory and Practical Applications for Statistical Agencies, pp. 111–133 (2001)

9. Danezis, G., et al.: Privacy and data protection by design - From policy to engineering. ENISA (2014)

10. Rocher, L., Hendrickx, J.M., de Montjoye, Y.-A.: Estimating the success of re-identifications in incomplete datasets using generative models. Nat. Commun. **10**, 1–9 (2019). 3069

11. Samarati, P., Sweeney, L.: Protecting privacy when disclosing information: k-anonymity and its enforcement through generalization and suppression. In: SRI International, Menlo Park, CA, USA, Technical report (1998)

12. Machanavajjhala, A., Gehrke, J., Kiefer, D., Venkatasubramanian, M.: L-diversity: privacy beyond k-anonymity. ACM Trans. Knowl. Discov. Data **1**(1) (2007). Art. no. 3

13. Li, N., Li, T., Venkatasubramanian, S.: t-Closeness: privacy beyond k-anonymity and ℓ-diversity. In: Proceedings of the 23rd IEEE International Conference on Data Engineering (ICDE), pp. 106–115 (2007)

14. Cao, J., Karras, P.: Publishing microdata with a robust privacy guarantee. Proc. VLDB Endow. **5**(11), 1388–1399 (2012)

15. Dwork, C.: Differential privacy. In: Bugliesi, M., Preneel, B., Sassone, V., Wegener, I. (eds.) ICALP 2006. LNCS, vol. 4052, pp. 1–12. Springer, Heidelberg (2006). https://doi.org/10.1007/11787006_1

16. Mitzenmacher, M., Upfal, E.: Probability and Computing: Randomization and Probabilistic Techniques in Algorithms and Data Analysis, 2nd edn., pp. 417–418. Cambridge University Press, Cambridge (2017). Zipf's Law and Other Examples (Sect. 16.2.1)

17. Domingo-Ferrer, J., Muralidhar, K., Bras-Amorós, M.: General confidentiality and utility metrics for privacy-preserving data publishing based on the permutation model. IEEE Trans. Dependable Secure Comput. https://doi.org/10.1109/TDSC.2020.2968027

18. Xiao, X., Tao, Y.: M-invariance: towards privacy preserving re-publication of dynamic datasets. In: Proceedings of the 2007 ACM SIGMOD International Conference on Management of Data, pp. 689–700 (2007)

19. Cummings, R., Krehbiel, S., Lai, K.A., Tantipongpipat, U.: Differential privacy for growing databases. In: Advances in Neural Information Processing Systems, vol. 31, pp. 8864–8873 (2018)

20. Narayanan, A., Shmatikov, V.: Robust de-anonymization of large sparse datasets. In: 2008 IEEE Symposium on Security and Privacy (S&P 2008), pp. 111–125 (2008)

21. ISO/IEC 20889: Privacy enhancing data de-identification terminology and classification of techniques (2018)

22. Pyrgelis, A., Troncoso, C., De Cristofaro, E.: Knock knock, who's there? Membership inference on aggregate location data. In: NDSS 2018 (2018)

P-Signature-Based Blocking to Improve the Scalability of Privacy-Preserving Record Linkage

Dinusha Vatsalan[1]([✉]), Joyce Yu[1], Brian Thorne[2], and Wilko Henecka[1]

[1] CSIRO's DATA61, Eveleigh, NSW 2015, Australia
{dinusha.vatsalan,joyce.yu,wilko.henecka}@data61.csiro.au
[2] Hardbyte, Christchurch, New Zealand
brian@hardbyte.nz

Abstract. Integrating data from multiple sources with the aim to identify records that correspond to the same entity is required in many real-world applications including healthcare, national security, businesses, and government services. However, privacy and confidentiality concerns impede the sharing of personal identifying values to conduct linkage across different organizations. Privacy-preserving record linkage (PPRL) techniques have been developed to tackle this problem by performing clustering based on the similarity between encoded record values, such that each cluster contains (similar) records corresponding to one single entity. When employing PPRL on databases from multiple parties, one major challenge is the prohibitively large number of similarity comparisons required for clustering, especially when the number and size of databases are large. While there have been several private blocking methods proposed to reduce the number of comparisons, they fall short in providing an efficient and effective solution for linking multiple large databases. Further, all private blocking methods are largely dependent on data. In this paper, we propose a novel private blocking method addressing the shortcomings of existing methods for efficiently linking multiple databases by exploiting the data characteristics in the form of probabilistic signatures, and we introduce a local blocking evaluation framework for locally validating blocking methods without knowing the ground-truth data. Experimental results on large datasets show the efficacy of our method in comparison to several state-of-the-art methods.

Keywords: Entity resolution · Privacy · Scalability · Probabilistic signatures · Clustering

1 Introduction

Linking data from multiple sources with the aim to identify matching pairs (from two sources) or matching sets (from more than two sources) of records that correspond to the same real-world entity is a crucial data pre-processing

© Springer Nature Switzerland AG 2020
J. Garcia-Alfaro et al. (Eds.): DPM 2020/CBT 2020, LNCS 12484, pp. 35–51, 2020.
https://doi.org/10.1007/978-3-030-66172-4_3

task for quality data mining and analytics [3]. Various real-world applications require record linkage to improve data quality and enable accurate decision making. Example applications come from healthcare, businesses, the social sciences, government services, and national security.

Record linkage involves several challenges making the process not trivial. Due to the absence of unique entity identifiers across different databases, it is required to use the commonly available quasi-identifiers (QIDs), such as names and addresses, for linking records from those databases. QIDs generally contain personal and often sensitive information about the entities to be linked, which precludes the sharing of such values among different organizations for linkage due to privacy concerns. Known as privacy-preserving record linkage (PPRL) [16,19], this research has attracted increasing interest over the last two decades and has been employed in several real projects [2,6,13].

A prominent challenge of PPRL of multiple large databases is the quadratic complexity of similarity comparisons required between QIDs of records with the number of databases to be linked and their sizes. Blocking techniques are being used in the linkage to reduce the number of comparisons by grouping records according to a certain criteria and limiting the comparison only to the records in the same group [3]. However, existing private blocking methods do not perform well on low latency and high-scale data due to either (1) their dependency on data-sensitive parameters that need to be tuned for different datasets [7,8,10, 11,14,15,20,23], (2) they require external data of similar distribution [8,10,14, 20,23], (3) they require similarity computations for blocking itself which makes them not scalable to linking multiple large databases [1,8,10,14,15], (4) most of them are not developed for linking multiple databases (except [8,11,15]), or (5) they do not support efficient subset matching from any number of databases [8,11,15]. In this paper, we address these shortcomings by developing a novel private blocking method based on probabilistic signatures and proposing a local blocking evaluation framework for tuning data-dependent parameters.

The values in QIDs are often prone to data errors and variations, which impacts the quality of blocking as well as makes the linkage task challenging [3]. Probabilistic signatures (p-signatures) leverage the redundancy in data to reduce the impact of data quality issues on blocking. Subset of information contained in a record that can be used to identify the entity corresponding to that record is called as a signature. For example, 'John Smith' is a frequently occurred name, however, 'John Smith, Redfern' is more unique and more likely to correspond to the real-world entity as similar as 'John Smith, Redfern, NSW 2015'. Probabilistic identification of such signatures for linking records (in the non-PPRL context) has been studied in an existing work [24].

In this paper, we extend the idea of using p-signatures for efficient data-driven blocking for PPRL of multiple databases. Our approach does not depend on external data, and it does not require any similarity computations between records for blocking, as required by most of the existing methods [8,10,14,15]. In addition, our method enables subset matching for multi-party PPRL, which aims to identify matching records from any subset of multiple databases held by different parties, for example, linking patients who have visited at least three out of ten hospitals. Existing blocking methods do not facilitate nor efficiently facilitate blocking for subset matching [8,11,15]. Moreover, existing methods are sensitive to errors and variations in the blocking keys. For example, if a record contains missing values in part of the blocking key, it will be misplaced in a wrong block, while with signatures the part with the missing value will not become a signature and thus will not be placed in a wrong bucket, improving the quality of blocking.

However, as with all existing methods, the blocking quality in terms of effectiveness of reducing the comparison space as well as coverage of true matches depends significantly on the signatures used. We use multi-signature strategy to improve blocking quality. Further, we propose a framework to locally evaluate the blocking quality guarantees individually by the database owners in order to choose an appropriate signature strategy (or parameter settings) depending on the datasets to be blocked. Our proposed local blocking evaluation metrics (which we refer to as **PQR**-guarantees metrics for **P**rivacy, **Q**uality, and **R**eduction guarantees of blocking) can be used to locally evaluate any blocking method for PPRL.

We provide a comparative evaluation of our proposed method with several state-of-the-art blocking methods for PPRL in terms of coverage of true matches, reduction in record comparisons, and privacy guarantees against frequency inference attacks [21] using large datasets. We also evaluate the effectiveness of our blocking method for multi-party PPRL using a black box clustering method [22] and compare the results with no blocking and using an existing multi-party blocking method [11]. Experimental results show that our method outperforms the state-of-the-art methods in terms of all three aspects.

Outline: We describe preliminaries in Sect. 2 and in Sect. 3 we present our protocol. In Sect. 3.1, we introduce a novel method to locally evaluate Privacy, Quality, and Reduction guarantees of any blocking methods. We analyze our protocol in terms of complexity, privacy in Sects. 3.2 and 3.3, respectively, and validate these analyses through an empirical evaluation in Sect. 4. Related work is reviewed in Sect. 5. Finally, we conclude the paper in Sect. 6.

2   Preliminaries

An outline of the general PPRL pipeline is shown in Fig. 1. Assume $P_1, \ldots, P_p$ are the p owners (parties) of the *deduplicated* databases $\mathbf{D}_1, \ldots, \mathbf{D}_p$, respectively. PPRL allows the party P_i to determine which of its records $r_{i,x} \in \mathbf{D}_i$ match with records in other database(s) $r_{j,y} \in \mathbf{D}_j$ with $1 \leq i, j \leq p$ and $j \neq i$ based on the similarity/distance between (masked or encoded) quasi-identifiers (QIDs) of these records. The output of this process is a set $\mathbf{M}$ of match clusters, where a match cluster $m \in \mathbf{M}$ contains a set of matching records of a maximum of one record from each database and $1 < |m| \leq p$. Each $m \in \mathbf{M}$ is identified as a set of

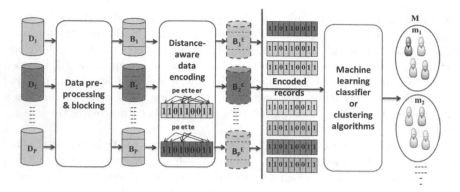

Fig. 1. General pipeline of the PPRL process

matching records representing the same entity. A linkage unit (LU) is generally employed to conduct PPRL using the encoded QID values of records sent by the database owners.

Assuming each of the p databases contains n records ($n \times p$ records in total), the number of similarity comparisons required is quadratic in both n and p (i.e. $n^2 \cdot p^2$). The quadratic comparison space is computationally expensive for clustering techniques with large-scale data. However, majority of the comparisons are between non-matches as record linkage is generally a class-imbalance problem [3]. Blocking aims at reducing the comparison space for linkage by eliminating the comparisons of record pairs that are highly unlikely to be matches. There are numerous blocking strategies [4] developed in the literature for record linkage and PPRL.

Generally, the records are grouped into blocks for each database D_i (denoted as $\mathbf{B}_i$) and the blocks of encoded records of each database (denoted as $\mathbf{B}_i^E$) are sent to a linkage unit (LU) to conduct the linkage of these encoded records from multiple databases using a clustering technique [22]. At the LU, the records are processed block by block (i.e. clustering is applied on each block $B \in \mathbf{B}$, where $\mathbf{B}$ contains the union of blocking keys in $\mathbf{B}_i^E$, with $1 \leq i \leq p$).

The existing blocking methods for PPRL require data dependent parameters to be tuned or external data of similar distribution for blocking. Exploiting the data characteristics, we propose a blocking method based on multiple signatures. Redundancy is one of the common data characteristics in real data as only some information in a record is sufficient to uniquely identify and link records. Such informative part in a record becomes a signature. Each unique signature becomes a blocking key in our blocking method.

Definition 1 (Signature). *Given records R with QIDs A, a signature s is a subset of information in a record $r \in R$, i.e. $s \subset \forall_{a \in A} r.a$, that can uniquely identify the corresponding entity with high probability.*

Example 1: A record r_1 with the values of QIDs $r_1.a_1 = $ 'smith', $r_1.a_2 = $ 'william', $r_1.a_3 = $ 'redfern', $r_1.a_4 = $ '2015', has the signature $s_1 = $ 'smwr316',

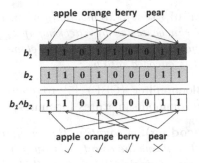

Fig. 2. An example encoding of two sets $S_1 = \{$'apple', 'orange', 'berry', and 'pear'$\}$ and $S_2 = \{$'apple', 'orange', 'berry'$\}$ into BFs b_1 and b_2, respectively, and membership test on the intersected BF ($b_1 \cap b_2$). For example, 'pear' is not a member of $b_1 \cap b_2$.

where the signature is generated based on the concatenation of the first two characters of a_1, first character of a_2, none of the characters of a_4, and phonetic encoding of a_3.

Definition 2 (Signature strategy). *A signature strategy is a function $f(\cdot)$ of generating a signature for each record $r \in R$ from $\forall_{a \in A} r.a$.*

Example 2: $f(a_1[0:2] + a_2.phonetic())$ is a signature strategy, which returns the first two characters and phonetic code of QIDs a_1 and a_2, respectively.

We use multiple such signature strategies to improve the blocking quality (recall of true matches) at the cost of more record pair comparisons. For each of the signature strategies records containing the same signature are grouped into one block, and blocks of records of the same signature across multiple databases are compared and linked using clustering techniques [22].

In order to identify the common blocks (signatures) between two or multiple databases held by different parties without learning the non-common signatures of a party by other parties as well as any signatures by the LU, the parties encode their signatures into a Bloom filter (BF).

Definition 3 (BF encoding). *A BF b_i is a bit vector of length l bits where all bits are initially set to 0. k independent hash functions, $h_1, \ldots, h_k$, each with range $1, \ldots l$, are used to map each of the elements s in a set S into the BF by setting the bit positions $h_j(s)$ with $1 \le j \le k$ to 1.*

Figure 2 illustrates the encoding of two sets $S_1 = \{$'apple', 'orange', 'berry', and 'pear'$\}$ and $S_2 = \{$'apple', 'orange', 'berry'$\}$ into two BFs b_1 and b_2, respectively, of $l = 9$ bits long using $k = 2$ hash functions. Collision of hash-mapping occurs where two different elements are mapped to the same bit position. Collision can result in false positives however providing privacy guarantees through the level of uncertainty about a true mapping at the cost of utility loss.

Definition 4 (Membership test). *Membership of an element s in a set that is encoded into a BF b can be tested by checking if $\forall_{i=1}^{k} b[h_i(s)] == 1$. If at least one of the hash functions returns 0, then the element could not have been a member of the set that is encoded into b.*

We use counting Bloom filter (CBF) [5] to count the number of parties/databases that have common signatures for multi-party PPRL.

Definition 5 (CBF encoding). *A counting Bloom filter (CBF) c is an integer vector of length l bits that contains the counts of values in each position. Multiple BFs can be summarized into a single CBF c, such that $c[\beta] = \sum_{i=1}^{p} b_i[\beta]$, where $\beta, 1 \le \beta \le l$. $c[\beta]$ is the count value in the β bit position of the CBF c. Given p BFs b_i with $1 \le i \le p$, the CBF c can be generated by applying a vector addition operation between the bit vectors such that $c = \sum_i b_i$.*

Secure summation protocols can be used to securely calculate the sum of p values $v_1, \cdots, v_p$ without learning the individual values v_i, but only the sum $\sum_{i=1}^{p} v_i$. v_i can either be a single numeric value or a vector of numeric values.

3   Methodology

In this section we describe the steps of our Privacy Preserving Probabilistic signature (**P3-SIG**) blocking method, which is outlined in Algorithm 1. It consists of three phases:

1. Signature generation: This phase involves identifying and agreeing on signature strategies and generating candidate signatures (lines 1–5 in Algorithm 1). The probability of a candidate signature to appear in records is bounded by the minimum and maximum size of resulting blocks (k_{min} and k_{max}, respectively) for privacy and comparison reduction guarantees, respectively. Signatures that appear in too many records are often redundant (non-informative) and signatures that appear in very few records can be uniquely re-identified against inference attacks.

The resulting candidate signatures are locally evaluated in order to select and agree on a set of good signature strategies to be used by all parties to generate signatures or blocking keys (lines 6–7 in Algorithm 1). We use multi-signature approach where multiple such good signature strategies are used to improve the coverage of true matches. Good signature strategies are determined considering three aspects: (1) comparison reduction, (2) coverage of true matches, and (3) privacy guarantees of the resulting blocks against frequency attack. We will describe the local blocking evaluation in terms of these three aspects in Sect. 3.1.

2. Common signatures identification: Once a set of good signature strategies are agreed upon by all parties, the parties individually generate the signatures for their records using the agreed signature strategies and hash-map the resulting signatures into a Bloom filter (BF) (lines 16–18). If the linkage task is to identify common blocks across all p parties, then the intersected BF of all parties' BFs is sufficient to calculate the common signatures/blocks. The

---

Algorithm 1. P3-SIG blocking (described in Sect. 3)

Input:
- R_i : Party P_i's records, $1 \leq i \leq p$
- S' : A set of signature strategies $f(\cdot)$
- $e(\cdot)$: A function to locally evaluate blocking
- s_m : Minimum subset size, with $2 \leq s_m \leq p$
- $h(\cdot)$: Hash functions for BF encoding
- l : Length of BF
- k : Number of hash functions

Output:
- **C**   : Blocks from all parties

Phase 1 (by each party P_i, with $1 \leq i \leq P$):

1:	**for** $f \in S'$ **do:**	// Iterate strategies
2:	$B_f = \{\}$	// Initialize inverted index
3:	**for** $r \in R_i$ **do:**	// Iterate records
4:	$s = f(r)$	// Signature
5:	$B_f[s].add(r)$	// Store in inverted index
6:	$e(B_f)$	// Evaluate signature strategy
7:	$f' = agree(S', \forall_f e(B_f))$	// Agree on a signature strategy

Phase 2 (by all parties P_i, with $1 \leq i \leq P$):

8:	**for** $1 \leq i \leq P$ **do:**	// Iterate P parties
9:	$B_i = \{\}; bf_i = []$	// Initialization
10:	**for** $r \in R_i$ **do:**	// Iterate records
11:	$s = f'(r)$	// Signature of r
12:	$B_i[s].add(r)$	// Store in inverted index
13:	**for** $s \in B_i$ **do**	// Iterate signatures
14:	**if not** $k_{min} \leq len(B_i(s)) \geq k_{max}$ **do**	// Larger and smaller blocks
15:	$B_i.remove(s)$	// Prune signatures
16:	**for** $s \in B_i$ **do:**	// Iterate signatures
17:	**for** $1 \leq j \leq k$ **do:**	// Hash functions
18:	$bf_i[h_j(s)] = 1$	// Set to 1 in BF
19:	$cbf = sec\_sum(\forall_i bf_i)$	// Generate CBF

Phase 3 (by LU and by each party P_i, with $1 \leq i \leq P$):

20:	$C = \{\}$	// Initialization of **C**
21:	**for** $c \in cbf$	// LU iterates positions in CBF
22:	**if** $c < s_m$ **then**	// Count less than s_m
23:	$c = 0$	// Set to 0
24:	**else**	// Count of at least s_m
25:	$c = 1$	// Set to 1
26:	$\forall_i C.send\_to\_P_i()$	// LU sends Common BF to parties
27:	**for** $1 \leq i \leq P$ **do**	// All parties
28:	**for** $s \in B_i$ **do**	// Iterate signatures
29:	**if not** $\forall_{j=1}^{k} cbf[h_j(s)] == 1$ **then**	// Membership test
30:	$B_i.remove(s)$	// Remove non-matching signatures
31:	$B_i.encode()$	// Encode records and BKVs
32:	$B_i.send\_to\_LU()$	// Send encoded blocks to LU
33:	**for** $1 \leq i \leq P$ **do**	// LU iterates parties
34:	$C = \cup_i B_i$	// Union of blocks from all parties
35:	**return C**	// Output **C**

---

intersected BF contains 1 in positions that have 1 in all parties' BFs and 0 if at least one of the parties does not have 1 in those positions. An example is shown in Fig. 2 for two BFs.

However, for the linkage task of identifying all signatures/blocks that are common in at least s_m of p parties (for subset matching), we propose to use a CBF of p BFs which contains counts of 1-bits from all p BFs. A CBF is generated from all p BFs using a secure summation protocol (line 19). It contains the count values of common signatures (i.e. how many parties have those common signatures), which are in between 0 (if none of the p parties' BFs contain 1 in those bit positions) and p (if all p parties' BFs contain 1).

3. Blocks generation: The LU replaces all the count values in the generated CBF that are below the minimum subset size, s_m, to 0 as these are not common signatures across at least s_m parties, while count values above or equal to s_m are set to 1 (lines 21–25 in Algorithm 1). This implies that blocks need to be common across at least s_m parties for subset matching. The resulting CBF that contains 1s and 0s (which is essentially a BF) is sent to all the parties (line 26). The parties individually perform a membership test (as described in Sect. 2) on the received CBF by checking all their signatures in order to determine if they are common or not (line 27–30 in Algorithm 1).

The encoded records belonging to each of the common signatures/blocks are sent to the LU to perform clustering on records belonging to the same blocks (lines 31–32). The union of blocks from all parties are stored in C and returned by the blocking method (lines 33–35), which will be used as an input to the clustering step.

3.1 Local Blocking Evaluation Framework

The performance of blocking (in terms of comparison space reduction, retaining true matches, and not being susceptible to frequency attacks) depends on the signature strategies (similar to most of the existing blocking methods). For such data-driven blocking techniques, we propose a framework to locally evaluate the blocking performance in order to choose and agree on a signature strategy that performs better in terms of all three aspects. This framework is applicable to any blocking method for local evaluation that provides minimum guarantees of the global blocking results.

Comparison Space Reduction: This refers to the global measure of *reduction ratio* of a blocking method [4]. The reduction ratio measures the percentage of record pair comparisons reduced after blocking from the total number of record pair comparisons. Different signature strategies generate different number and size of blocks and therefore vary by the reduction ratio. Performing blocking with many different strategies across parties and evaluating and comparing their reduction ratio to choose the best strategy is not trivial in a real application due to operational cost and privacy concerns. Therefore, we use a measure to locally evaluate and compare different signature strategies by each party individually on their records.

The statistics of the block sizes for each of the signature strategies can be compared to learn about their impact on the reduction ratio. We consider the average and maximum block sizes as local measures of reduction guarantees. We normalise these values in the range of $[0, 1]$ for comparative evaluation. The Reduction Guarantees metric RG is defined as $RG = 1 - m/n$, where m is the average or maximum block size and n is the total number of records in the dataset. For example, if a blocking strategy results in a maximum block size of $m = 1$ for a dataset of $n = 10000$ records, then $RG_{max} = 1 - 1/10000 = 0.9999$, while a maximum block size of $m = 10000$ results in $RG_{max} = 0.0$.

True Matches Preservation: This refers to the global measure of *pairs completeness* (or *recall*) of a blocking method [4]. Pairs completeness measures the percentage of true matches preserved in the candidate record pairs resulting from blocking in the total number of true matches. Smaller blocks favor the reduction ratio, however, they can have a negative impact on the pairs completeness as they have more likelihood of missing true matches (not grouped into the same block). We use Quality Guarantees (QG) metrics to locally evaluate the likelihood of not missing true matches in the candidate record pairs.

This likelihood is determined by the coverage of records in blocks. We measure the coverage by calculating the statistics of number of blocks per record (average and minimum). The larger the number of blocks where a record appears in, the more likelihood that it will be compared with a potential matching record in one of those blocks. Specifically, a signature strategy that leads records being appear in average m out of b total blocks and at least 1 block (minimum), then the QG metrics are calculated as $QG_{avg} = m/b$ and $QG_{min} = 1/b$.

Privacy Guarantees: While smaller blocks are preferred for reduction guarantees, and overlapping blocks are preferred for quality guarantees, these two have negative impact on the privacy guarantees. Based on the sizes of the blocks, the LU can perform a frequency inference attack by matching the frequency distribution of blocks to a known frequency distribution, as will be detailed in Sect. 3.3). A blocking method that generates blocks with low variance between their sizes is less susceptible to such frequency inference attacks. Moreover, too small blocks are highly vulnerable as they provide information about unique and rare values.

For Privacy Guarantees (PG) metrics, we calculate disclosure risk statistics [21] (average, maximum, and marketer risk) based on the probability of suspicion (P_s) for each record in blocks of a local database **D**. P_s for a record r is calculated as $P_s(r) = 1/n_g$ where n_g is the number of possible matches in the global database $\mathbf{D}_G$ with r. We assume the worst case of $\mathbf{D}_G \equiv \mathbf{D}$, to calculate the minimum local privacy guarantees. Each of the records in a block of k records has the P_s of $1/k$ (i.e. each record matches with k records in the worst case). For example, if $k = 1$, then $P_s = 1.0$, whereas $k = 100$ gives $P_s = 0.01$ for all k records. Based on the P_s values, we calculate the maximum PG as $PG_{max} = max_{r_i \in \mathbf{D}}(P_s(r_i))$, average PG as $PG_{avg} = \sum_i^n P_s(r_i)/n$, and marketer PG as the proportion of records that can be exactly re-identified, i.e. $P_s = 1.0$, $PG_{mar} = |\{r_i \in \mathbf{D} : P_s(r_i) = 1.0\}|/n$ [21].

By locally evaluating and comparing the blocks generated by different blocking strategies using the privacy guarantees (PG), quality guarantees (QG), and reduction guarantees (RG) metrics, the parties can choose and agree on a strategy that can generate good blocking results in terms of the three aspects. We name the family of these metrics for local blocking evaluation as PQR-guarantees metrics, which refer to the Privacy, Quality, and Reduction guarantees of blocking methods.

3.2   Complexity Analysis

Assume p parties participate in the linkage of their respective databases, each containing n records, and b blocks are generated by the blocking function, with each block containing n/b records. Phase 1 has a linear computation complexity for each party as it requires a loop over all records in its database for multiple different signature strategies in a set of strategies, S', and calculating the Privacy, Quality, and Reduction Guarantees (PQR-guarantees) metrics as described in

Sect. 3.1 $(O(n \cdot |S'|))$. Agreeing on a signature strategy across multiple parties based on the PQR-guarantees metrics has a constant communication complexity.

In the second phase, encoding the candidate signatures into a BF of length l bits using k hash functions has a computation complexity of $O(b' \cdot k)$ (assuming b' candidate signatures) for each party, and generating a CBF using secure summation protocol is of $O(l)$ computation and communication complexity. In phase 3, the LU loops through the CBF to generate the intersected BF, which is $O(l)$, and sending to all parties is $O(l \cdot p)$ communication complexity. Each party individually performs membership test of their candidate signatures, which is of $O(b' \cdot k)$. Then the records containing any of the common signatures (assuming b common signatures/blocks) need to be retrieved and sent to the LU, which has a computation and communication complexity of $O(n \cdot b)$. At the LU, the number of candidate record pairs generated is $n^2/b \cdot p^2$. Similar to many existing methods, the reduction in the number of candidate record pairs depends on the number (b) and size of blocks $(n/b$ on average) generated. Therefore, the proposed RG metric based on local block sizes can provide an estimate to locally evaluate the reduction in candidate record pairs.

3.3 Privacy Analysis

As with most existing PPRL methods, we assume that all parties follow the honest-but-curious adversary model [21], where the parties follow the protocol while being curious to find out as much as possible about other parties' data by means of inference attacks on (blocks of) encoded records or by colluding with other parties [21].

In Phase 2, the parties perform secure summation of their BFs, which does not leak any information about the individual BFs. However, secure summation protocols can be susceptible to collusion attacks where two or more parties collude to learn about another party's BF. There have been several extended secure summation protocols developed to reduce their vulnerability to collusion risk. For example, secret sharing-based protocol [17] generates p random shares r_i (one share per party) from the secret input value v_i, such that $\sum_i r_i = v_i$, and therefore even when some of the parties collude, without knowing the shares of other non-colluding parties the input value v_i of a party cannot be learned by the colluding parties.

In Phase 3, since the CBF contains only the summary information (count values), it provides more privacy guarantees than BFs against an inference attack by the LU.

Proposition 1. *The probability of inferring the values of individual signatures s_i of a party P_i (with $1 \leq i \leq p$) given a single CBF c is smaller than the probability of inferring the values of s_i given the corresponding party's BF b_i, $1 \leq i \leq p$.*

Proof. Assume the number of potential matching signatures from an external database that can be matched to a single signature $s \in s_i$ encoded into the BF

b_i through an inference attack is n_g. $n_g = 1$ in the worst case, where a one-to-one mapping exists between the encoded BF b_i and the candidate signatures (based on performing membership test). The probability of inferring the signature value s belonging to a party P_i given its BF b_i in the worst case scenario is therefore $Pr(s \in s_i|b_i) = 1/n_g = 1.0$. However, a CBF represents signatures from p parties and thus $Pr(s \in s_i|c) = 1/p$ in the worst case with $p > 1$. Hence, $\forall_{i=1}^{p} Pr(s \in s_i|c) < Pr(s \in s_i|b_i)$.

Finally, the parties send their blocks of encoded records to the *LU*. If one of the resulting blocks contains only one record, for example, then the likelihood of a successful inference of this record by the *LU* is higher than the inference of a record that belongs to a block of size 100. Similarly, a very large block can be uniquely identified by matching to a frequent value in the global database. Therefore, the variance between block sizes needs to be smaller to reduce the vulnerability of blocking methods to frequency inference attack. Our **P3-SIG** method prunes highly frequent ($> k_{max}$) and rare ($> k_{min}$) blocks to provide privacy guarantees, which can be locally evaluated as discussed in Sect. 3.1.

4   Experimental Evaluation

We conducted our experiments on three different datasets:

(1) **NCVR:** We extracted 4611, 46,116 and 461,116 records from the North Carolina Voter Registration (NCVR) database[1] for two parties with 50% of matching records between the two parties. Ground truth is available based on the voter registration identifiers. We generated another series of datasets where we synthetically corrupted/modified randomly chosen attribute value of records by means of character edit operations and phonetic modifications using the GeCo tool [18].

(2) **NCVR-Subset:** We sampled 10 datasets from the NCVR database each containing 10,000 records such that 50% of records are non-matches and 5% of records are true matches across each different subset size of 1 to 10 (1, 2, 3, $\cdots$, 9, 10), i.e. 45% of records are matching in any 2 datasets while only 5% of records are matching in any 9 out of all 10 datasets. This dataset is used to evaluate our method for multi-party PPRL with different subset sizes.

(3) **ABS Dataset:** This is a synthetic dataset used internally for linkage experiments at the Australian Bureau of Statistics (ABS). It simulates an employment census and two supplementary surveys. There are 120000, 180000 and 360000 records, respectively, with 50000 true matches.

We use six existing private blocking methods as the baseline approaches to compare our proposed approach (**P3-SIG**), which are three-party (two database owners and a *LU*) sorted neighbourhood clustering (SNC)-based blocking (**SNC-3P**) [20], two-party (without *LU*) SNC-based method (**SNC-2P**) [23], hierarchical clustering based approach (**HCLUST**) [14], k-nearest neighbourhood clustering-based method (**k-NN**) [10], Hamming LSH-based blocking

---

[1] Available from ftp://alt.ncsbe.gov/data/.

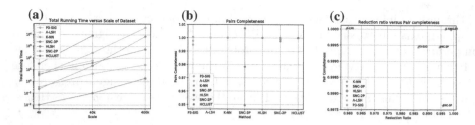

Fig. 3. Comparison of (a) Scalability, (b) Pairs Completeness, and (c) Reduction ratio vs. Pairs Completeness for two-database linking on **NCVR** dataset.

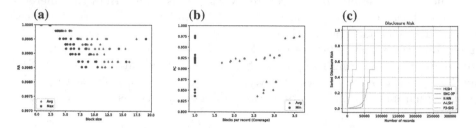

Fig. 4. Correlation between (a) local block sizes and reduction ratio (RR) metric and (b) local coverage and pairs completeness (PC) metric, and comparison of (c) disclosure risk of **P3-SIG** method with baseline methods on **NCVR** dataset.

method (**HLSH**) [7], and λ-fold LSH-based blocking method (λ-**LSH**) [11]. We choose methods for comparison that fall under different categories of shortcomings of existing methods as described in Sect. 1.

We evaluate the complexity (computational efficiency) using *runtime* required for the blocking and *reduction ratio* (RR) of record pair comparisons for the linkage (clustering). RR is calculated as $1.0 - \frac{number\ of\ comparisons\ after\ blocking}{total\ number\ of\ comparisons}$. The quality of the resulting candidate record pairs by a blocking method is measured using the *pairs completeness* (PC) for two-database linking and *set completeness* (SC) for multi-database linking [3,21]. They are calculated as the percentage of true matching pairs/sets that are found in the candidate record pairs/sets in the total number of true matching record pairs/sets, respectively. We evaluate privacy guarantees against frequency attack using block sizes and disclosure risk values [21], as described in Sect. 3.1.

We implemented our **P3-SIG** approach and the competing baseline approaches in Python 3.7.4[2], and ran all experiments on a server with 4-core 64-bit Intel 2.8 GHz CPU, 16 GBytes of memory and running OS X 10.15.1. For the baseline methods, we used the parameter settings as used by the authors in the corresponding methods. For **P3-SIG** method, the default parameter setting is length of BFs $l = 2048$, and number of hash functions $k = 4$. We evaluated multiple different strategies generated from the combinations of first character, first 2 characters, first 3 characters, all characters, phonetic encodings, q-grams,

---

[2] available in http://doi.org/10.5281/zenodo.3653169.

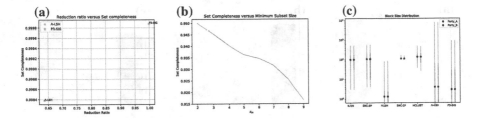

Fig. 5. (a) Reduction ratio vs. Set Completeness for multi-database linking on **ABS** dataset, (b) Set Completeness of **P3-SIG** blocking for subset matching of $p = 10$ databases against s_m on **NCVR**-subset dataset, and (c) comparison of block size distribution of **P3-SIG** method with baseline methods on **NCVR** dataset.

and 'None of the characters' in each of the QID (attribute) values of a record. Based on greedy search parameter tuning method, we used the numerical values in the first four attributes combined with the gender value as the default signature strategy for ABS dataset, and for the NCVR dataset we used the full first and last names, phonetic encoding of the first and last names along with the first one or two characters of first and last names and suburb values.

4.1   Discussion

We compare our method with the baseline methods in terms of runtime, pairs completeness (PC), and reduction ratio (RR) vs. pairs completeness (PC) in Fig. 3 for two-database linkage on the NCVR dataset. In terms of runtime, LSH-based methods and clustering based methods require more time followed by SNC-2P. Our method requires lower runtime than these methods, however SNC-3P is more efficient than our method. Our method however achieves higher RR and PC than the SNC-3P method. LSH-based blocking method generates higher quality blocking results, but they require higher computational cost for blocking. We were unable to conduct experiments for the λ-LSH and HCLUST methods on the largest dataset due to their memory and space requirements.

We next study the effectiveness of our local blocking evaluation framework. The correlation between the local block sizes and global reduction ratio (RR) metric as well the correlation between the local coverage values and global pairs completeness (PC) metric for a set of different signature strategies are shown in Figs. 4(a) and 4(b), respectively. As the results show, there exist a high correlation between them which reveals that local RG and QG metrics can be effectively used for blocking quality evaluation. PC and coverage values have a strong positive correlation, while RR and block sizes are negatively correlated. Figure 4(c) compares the maximum disclosure risk values calculated against a frequency attack in the worst case ($\mathbf{D} \equiv \mathbf{D}^G$) with baseline methods. The privacy guarantees (PG) results show that the disclosure risk values against a frequency inference attack are lower with our method.

We compare our method with the λ-fold LSH multi-party blocking method for multi-party linkage in Fig. 5(a). As can be seen, P3-SIG method outperforms

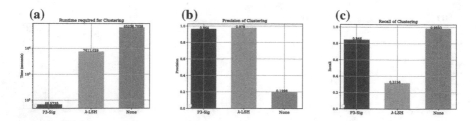

Fig. 6. Comparison of (a) runtime, (b) precision, and (c) recall of clustering for multi-party PPRL [22] with P3-SIG, λ-fold LSH [11], and no blocking on **NCVR** dataset.

λ-fold LSH for multi-party blocking in terms of higher blocking quality. Please note that λ-LSH method works efficiently on small datasets, however on large datasets it requires high runtime and memory space. Figure 5(b) shows the set completeness results for subset matching of $p = 10$ databases from NCVR-Subset dataset against different minimum subset sizes s_m. The larger the value for s_m is, the more difficult it is to find the set of records that match across at least s_m databases/parties. This reflects the challenge of subset matching in multi-party PPRL. These results show that P3-Sig can efficiently be used for multi-party linkage applications. Further, we compare the size of blocks generated by the different blocking methods in Fig. 5(c), which shows that the size of the blocks resulting from our method is similar to that of LSH-based methods, as they both generate overlapping blocks, however our method is more efficient and faster than these methods while achieving similar or superior blocking quality.

Finally, we evaluate our proposed P3-SIG method's performance on a recently developed incremental clustering method for multi-party PPRL [22] and compare with no blocking and λ-fold LSH multi-party blocking method in Fig. 6. The runtime of the PPRL reduces significantly using our method without impacting the linkage quality, which validates the efficacy of our blocking method for efficient clustering required by multi-party PPRL.

5   Related Work

Various blocking techniques have been proposed in the literature tackling the scalability problem of PPRL, as surveyed in [16,19,21]. Most of these methods require external data (reference values) of similar distribution as the original databases to be linked and employ a similarity comparison function to group similar records. For example, in [10] reference values are clustered using the k-nearest neighbor clustering algorithm and then the records are assigned to the nearest cluster. A token-based blocking method is proposed in [1], which requires calculating the TF-IDF distances of the hash signatures of blocking keys.

Similarly, sorted neighbourhood clustering is used in [20] and [23] to group similar reference and record values with and without a LU, respectively. Another method using hierarchical clustering to group similar reference values is proposed in [14] where the records are then assigned to the nearest clusters and differential privacy noise is added to the blocks (clusters) to reduce the vulnerability to inference attacks.

Other set of methods rely on data-specific parameters that are highly sensitive to data. A private blocking method for PPRL of multiple database using Bloom filters and bit-trees is proposed [15]. This method is only applicable to Bloom filter encoded data. The method introduced in [7] uses a set of hash functions (Minhash for Jaccard or Hamming LSH for Hamming distances) to generate keys from records that are encoded into Bloom filters to partition the records, so that similar records are grouped into the same block [12]. [11] proposed a λ-fold LSH blocking approach for linking multiple databases. LSH provides guaranteed accuracy, however, this approach requires data dependent parameters to be tuned effectively and it can be applied only to specific encodings, such as Bloom filters or q-gram vectors.

6 Conclusion

We have presented a scalable private blocking protocol for PPRL that is highly efficient and improves blocking quality compared to existing private blocking approaches. In contrast to most of the existing methods that rely on a clustering technique for blocking records, our method uses signatures in the records to efficiently group records as well as to account for data errors and variations. Further, our blocking method is applicable to linking multiple databases as well as subset matching for multi-party PPRL. We also introduce a local blocking evaluation framework to choose good signature strategies/parameter settings in terms of privacy, blocking quality, and comparison reduction guarantees. Experiments conducted on datasets sampled from two real datasets show the efficacy of our proposed method compared to six state-of-the-art methods.

In future work, we aim to study optimisation techniques, such as Bayesian optimisation, to choose/tune signature strategies for optimal results. We also plan to study parallelisation to improve the scalability of blocking and linkage for multi-party PPRL. Finally, improving privacy guarantees for blocking methods needs to be explored in two different directions: (1) developing methods that provide formal privacy guarantees, such as output-constrained differential privacy [9], without significant utility loss, and (2) developing hybrid methods that combine cryptographic methods with probabilistic encoding methods (such as Bloom filter encoding) without excessive computational overhead.

Acknowledgements. This work was funded by the Australian Department of Social Sciences (DSS) as part of the Platforms for Open Data (PfOD) project. We would like to thank Waylon Nielsen and Alex Ware from DSS for their support on this work.

References

1. Al-Lawati, A., Lee, D., McDaniel, P.: Blocking-aware private record linkage. In: IQIS, pp. 59–68 (2005)

2. Baker, D., et al.: Privacy-preserving linkage of genomic and clinical data sets. Trans. Comput. Biol. Bioinform. **16**, 1342–1348 (2018)
3. Christen, P.: Data Matching. Data-Centric Systems and Applications. Springer, Heidelberg (2012). https://doi.org/10.1007/978-3-642-31164-2
4. Christen, P.: A survey of indexing techniques for scalable record linkage and deduplication. IEEE TKDE **24**(9), 1537–1555 (2012)
5. Cohen, W.W., Ravikumar, P., Fienberg, S.: A comparison of string distance metrics for name-matching tasks. In: IJCAI Workshop on Information Integration on the Web, pp. 73–78 (2003)
6. Condon, J.R., Barnes, T., Cunningham, J., Armstrong, B.K.: Long-term trends in cancer mortality for indigenous Australians in the northern territory. Med. J. Aust. **180**(10), 504 (2004)
7. Durham, E.A.: A framework for accurate, efficient private record linkage. Ph.D. thesis, Vanderbilt University, Nashville, TN (2012)
8. Han, S., Shen, D., Nie, T., Kou, Y., Yu, G.: Private blocking technique for multiparty privacy-preserving record linkage. Data Sci. Eng. **2**(2), 187–196 (2017). https://doi.org/10.1007/s41019-017-0041-5
9. He, X., Machanavajjhala, A., Flynn, C., Srivastava, D.: Composing differential privacy and secure computation: a case study on scaling private record linkage. In: ACM CCS, pp. 1389–1406 (2017)
10. Karakasidis, A., Verykios, V.S.: Reference table based k-anonymous private blocking. In: ACM SAC, Riva del Garda, pp. 859–864 (2012)
11. Karapiperis, D., Verykios, V.S.: A fast and efficient Hamming LSH-based scheme for accurate linkage. Knowl. Inf. Syst. **49**(3), 861–884 (2016). https://doi.org/10.1007/s10115-016-0919-y
12. Kim, H., Lee, D.: HARRA: fast iterative hashed record linkage for large-scale data collections. In: EDBT, Lausanne, Switzerland, pp. 525–536 (2010)
13. Kuehni, C.E., et al. and Swiss Paediatric Oncology Group (SPOG): Cohort profile: the Swiss childhood cancer survivor study. Int. J. Epidemiol. **41**(6), 1553–1564 (2011)
14. Kuzu, M., Kantarcioglu, M., Inan, A., Bertino, E., Durham, E., Malin, B.: Efficient privacy-aware record integration. In: ACM EDBT, Genoa, pp. 167–178 (2013)
15. Ranbaduge, T., Vatsalan, D., Christen, P., Verykios, V.: Hashing-based distributed multi-party blocking for privacy-preserving record linkage. In: Bailey, J., Khan, L., Washio, T., Dobbie, G., Huang, J.Z., Wang, R. (eds.) PAKDD 2016. LNCS (LNAI), vol. 9652, pp. 415–427. Springer, Cham (2016). https://doi.org/10.1007/978-3-319-31750-2_33
16. Schnell, R.: Privacy-preserving record linkage. In: Methodological Developments in Data Linkage, pp. 201–225 (2015)
17. Tassa, T., Cohen, D.J.: Anonymization of centralized and distributed social networks by sequential clustering. IEEE Trans. Knowl. Data Eng. **25**(2), 311–324 (2011)
18. Tran, K.N., Vatsalan, D., Christen, P.: GeCo: an online personal data generator and corruptor. In: ACM Conference in Knowledge Management (CIKM), San Francisco, pp. 2473–2476 (2013)
19. Trepetin, S.: Privacy-preserving string comparisons in record linkage systems: a review. Inf. Secur. J.: Global Perspect. **17**(5), 253–266 (2008)
20. Vatsalan, D., Christen, P.: Sorted nearest neighborhood clustering for efficient private blocking. In: Pei, J., Tseng, V.S., Cao, L., Motoda, H., Xu, G. (eds.) PAKDD 2013. LNCS (LNAI), vol. 7819, pp. 341–352. Springer, Heidelberg (2013). https://doi.org/10.1007/978-3-642-37456-2_29

21. Vatsalan, D., Christen, P., O'Keefe, C.M., Verykios, V.S.: An evaluation framework for privacy-preserving record linkage. JPC **6**(1), 35–75 (2014)
22. Vatsalan, D., Christen, P., Rahm, E.: Incremental clustering techniques for multi-party privacy-preserving record linkage. Data Knowl. Eng. **128**, 101809 (2020)
23. Vatsalan, D., Christen, P., Verykios, V.S.: Efficient two-party private blocking based on sorted nearest neighborhood clustering. In: ACM CIKM, San Francisco, pp. 1949–1958 (2013)
24. Zhang, Y., Ng, K.S., Churchill, T., Christen, P.: Scalable entity resolution using probabilistic signatures on parallel databases. In: ACM CIKM, Turin, Italy, pp. 2213–2221 (2018)

DPM Workshop: Utility, Diversity and Leakage Resistance

Utility Promises of *Self-Organising Maps* in Privacy Preserving Data Mining

Kabiru Mohammed$^{(\boxtimes)}$, Aladdin Ayesh , and Eerke Boiten

Cyber Technology Institute, The Gateway, De Montfort University,
Leicester LE1 9BH, UK
p2432673@my365.dmu.ac.uk, {aayesh,eerke.boiten}@dmu.ac.uk

Abstract. Data mining techniques are highly efficient in sifting through big data to extract hidden knowledge and assist evidence-based decisions. However, it poses severe threats to individuals' privacy because it can be exploited to allow inferences to be made on sensitive data. Researchers have proposed several privacy-preserving data mining techniques to address this challenge. One unique method is by extending anonymisation privacy models in data mining processes to enhance privacy and utility. Several published works in this area have utilised clustering techniques to enforce anonymisation models on private data, which work by grouping the data into clusters using a quality measure and then generalise the data in each group separately to achieve an anonymisation threshold. Although they are highly efficient and practical, however guaranteeing adequate balance between data utility and privacy protection remains a challenge. In addition to this, existing approaches do not work well with high-dimensional data, since it is difficult to develop good groupings without incurring excessive information loss. Our work aims to overcome these challenges by proposing a hybrid approach, combining self organising maps with conventional privacy based clustering algorithms. The main contribution of this paper is to show that, dimensionality reduction techniques can improve the anonymisation process by incurring less information loss, thus producing a more desirable balance between privacy and utility properties.

Keywords: k-anonymity · Clustering · Self Organising Map · Privacy Preserving Data Mining

1 Introduction

Data mining techniques allow the extraction of implicit and useful information from big data. They are programmed to sift through data automatically, seeking patterns that will likely generalise to make evidence-based decisions or accurate predictions that hold in data collections [1]. Although this emerging technology enjoys intense commercial attention, there is a growing concern that data mining results could potentially be exploited to infer sensitive information, therefore potentially breaching individual privacy in a variety of ways [2]. In response to

© Springer Nature Switzerland AG 2020
J. Garcia-Alfaro et al. (Eds.): DPM 2020/CBT 2020, LNCS 12484, pp. 55–72, 2020.
https://doi.org/10.1007/978-3-030-66172-4_4

these privacy concerns, Privacy Preserving Data Mining (PPDM) has been proposed by a number of studies [3–7] as an effective method for accommodating privacy concerns during mining processes to address the risk of re-identification. PPDM aims to provide a trade-off between data utility on one side and data privacy on the other side, by enforcing a certain degree of privacy without relinquishing the purposefulness of the data. It has remained a successful approach, particularly when applied to satisfy anonymisation protection models such as *k-anonymity, l-diversity and t-closeness*. Several published works [8–12] in this area have proposed different clustering techniques to enforce anonymisation models on private data. These techniques work by grouping the data into clusters using a quality measure and then generalising the data in each group separately to achieve an anonymisation threshold [13]. These studies have illustrated that clustering-based methods are able to produce high-quality anonymisation while allowing data mining to take place with less concern about privacy violations. Despite this breakthrough, conventional approaches cannot achieve a good balance between data utility and privacy protection [9,14,15]. They mostly optimise privacy, and as a result cannot guarantee a minimum level of data utility [16]. Our aim is to enhance data utility in PPDM processes, which can further guarantee a greater degree of balance between the two properties.

This paper proposes a hybrid strategy for improving data utility in PPDM techniques. In this approach, conventional clustering algorithms such as *OKA* and *K-member* are applied in combination with a Self-Organising Map (SOM). To illustrate this point, we apply proposed method to the Adult data set [17]. In the first step, the aforementioned clustering algorithms are used to anonymise specific features of the dataset using a selected anonymity threshold. Secondly, a SOM is used to map other data features to a 1-dimensional space of a set of neurons. These data features are otherwise dropped by traditional clustering strategies because they are mostly classified as sensitive attributes, thus they may increase the chances of attribute or membership disclosures. This unsupervised neural network model preserves the topological relationship and increases the correlation between features of the primary data space. Thirdly, the results of the anonymisation methods are fused with the results of the 1-dimensional SOM strategy as a single data domain. Lastly, the newly produced dataset is subjected to several classification techniques that are typically employed on the original Adult data.

The main contribution of this work is to show that the proposed strategy is a more productive approach in scenarios where the need for higher data utility supersedes the need for higher data privacy, particularly if there are no privacy costs associated with the desire for more data utility. Therefore, the results obtained with the application of this strategy justify its use. The remainder of the paper is organised as follows: Sect. 2 presents a brief bibliographical review about privacy preserving data mining algorithms, and Sect. 3 describes the main aspects of the SOM algorithm, detailing its advantages to other unsupervised neural networks. Section 4 describes the Adult data set and its properties, while Sect. 5 presents the strategy for this experiment. In Sect. 6, the methodology for conducting the experiments is expressed, while Sect. 7 presents the outcomes of the proposed strategy, comparing it with results obtained from conventional approaches. Finally, Sect. 8 presents conclusions and the direction of future PPDM research.

2   A Review of PPDM

k-anonymity was first introduced by Samarati and Sweeney [18] in an attempt to prevent possible re-identification of user information from published micro-data. This concept requires that each combination of quasi-identifier values in a released table must be indistinctly matched to at least k respondents [19]. For example, a table $D(S_1, S_2, ..., S_m)$ is said to satisfy k-anonymity if each quasi-identifier QI associated with the values maps to at least k records in a transformed version of the table D^k.[1] More formally, k is the largest number such that the magnitude of each equivalence class in table D is at least k.

The k-anonymity requirement is typically enforced through generalisation, suppression and deletion techniques. Generalisation replaces real values with "less specific but semantically consistent values" [20]. Numerical values are typically specified by a range of values, while categorical values are combined into a set of distinct values based on a hierarchical tree of the data attribute domain. Suppression replaces attribute values with a special symbol, and deletion removes an entire attribute from a dataset. Algorithms based on these techniques are conceptually straightforward; however, there are limitations: the computational complexity of finding an optimal solution for the k-anonymity problem has been shown to be NP-hard [21], possible generalisations are limited by the imposed hierarchical tree [22], also suppression and deletion techniques often compromise data utility by producing results that are unsuitable for further analysis [14]. To overcome these challenges, several PPDM approaches have viewed anonymisation as a clustering problem [6, 8, 10–12]. Clustering-based anonymisation works by partitioning datasets into clusters using a quality measure and generalising the data for each cluster to ensure that they contain at least k records [23]. This method produces high data quality because it reduces data distortion, making the results suitable for further analysis, mining, or publishing purposes. In addition, it is a unified approach, which gives it the benefit of simplicity, unlike the combination of suppression and generalisation techniques in traditional k-anonymity approaches [13]. Several published works in this area have proposed different clustering techniques to enforce anonymisation models on private data.

For instance, Byun et al. in [8] proposed a greedy algorithm for K-member clustering where each cluster must contain at least k records and the sum of all intra-cluster distances is minimised. Although this is shown to be efficient, it is impractical in cases involving categorical attributes which cannot be enumerated in any specific order. Loukides and Shao in [13] improve the greedy clustering algorithm by introducing measures that capture usefulness and protection in

---

[1] D^k denotes a k-anonymised version of the original table D.

k-anonymisation. Thus, they are able to produce better clusters by ensuring a balance between usefulness and protection. However, this approach suffers from the same drawbacks as its predecessor. In [6], Lin et al. propose a new clustering anonymisation method known as *OKA* (One-pass *K*-means Algorithm). Unlike the conventional *K*-means clustering, this only runs for one iteration and proceeds in two phases. In the first phase, all records are sorted by their quasi-identifier. Then *K* records are randomly selected as the seeds (centroids) to build clusters. The nearest records are assigned to a cluster, and the centroid is subsequently updated. In the second phase, formed clusters are adjusted by removing records from clusters with more than *k* records and adding them to ones with less than *k* records. Although this algorithm outperforms the *K*-member algorithm, however the whole process is restricted to one iteration, thus prohibiting the possibility of finding more optimal clustering solutions. The most current modification of the *K*-member clustering is an improved approach proposed in [24], referred to as *K*-member Co-clustering. This approach is adjusted to work in conjunction with maximising the aggregate degree of clustering so that each cluster is composed of records which are mutually related. Despite this, it only performs better than the conventional *K*-member clustering for high anonymity levels ($k > 30$), and has so far been only applied on numerical attributes. Thus, its true performance against other clustering approaches is yet to be fully determined.

So far, clustering approaches have proven to be successful in providing a trade-off between data utility on one side and data privacy on the other side by enforcing a certain degree of privacy without relinquishing the purposefulness of the data. However, there still remain myriad ways of improving the state of the art through hybrid approaches that can sufficiently reduce the risks of inferences while still maintaining maximal data utility with reasonable computational costs.

3   Self-Organising Map

SOM is a variation of the competitive-learning approach in which the goal is to generate a low-dimensional discretized representation of high-dimensional data while preserving its topological and metric relationships [25]. The basic idea in competitive learning is not to map inputs to outputs in order to correct errors or to have output and input layers with the same dimensionality, as in autoencoders. Rather an input layer and output layer are connected to adjacent neurons based on predefined neighbourhood relationships, forming a topographic map [26]. Neurons are tuned to various input patterns until a winning neuron is determined, where the neuron best matches the input vector, more commonly known as the Best Matching Unit (BMU). The BMU (c) for one input pattern (x) can be formally defined by:[2]

$$||x - x_c|| = min||x - x_i|| \tag{1}$$

The closer a node is to the BMU, the more its weights get altered, and the farther away the neighbour is from the BMU, the less it learns. The broad

---

[2] where $|| \cdot ||$ is the measure of distance.

idea of the training occurs in a similar manner to K-means clustering where a winning centroid moves by a small distance towards the training instance once a point is assigned to it at the end of each iteration. SOM allows some variation of this framework, albeit in a different way because it cannot guarantee assigning the same number of instances to each class. Despite this, SOM is an excellent tool that can be used for unsupervised applications like clustering and information compression. A number of frameworks for combining SOM with clustering techniques to improve the solutions of data mining have been proposed in [27–29].

4   Adult Dataset

The Adult dataset[17] is used in a variety of studies on data privacy [8,30–32] and is considered the de facto benchmark for experimenting and evaluating anonymisation techniques and PPDM algorithms. It is an extract of the 1994 U.S. census database and is generally applied to predict whether an individual's annual income exceeds \$50,000 using traditional statistical modeling and machine learning techniques. The data comprises 48,842 entries with 15 different attributes, of which 8 are categorical and 7 numerical.

Table 1 presents all features of the dataset, categorised by their attribute types and their attribute set. 9 features of the dataset have been classified as quasi-identifiers, 5 other features as sensitive attributes, and 1 feature as a non-sensitive attribute. The dataset does not contain any value which can directly identify an individual on its own, thus the lack of an identifier category. This classification of the Adult dataset can be defined as follows:

- **Identifiers:** a data attribute that explicitly declares the identity of an individual e.g. name, social security number, ID number, biometric record.
- **Quasi-Identifiers:** a data attribute that is inadequate to reveal individual identities independently, however, if combined with other publicly available information (quasi-identifiers), they can explicitly reveal the identity of a data subject e.g. date of birth, postcode, gender, address, phone number.
- **Sensitive Attributes:** a data attribute that reveals personal information about an individual that they may be unwilling to share publicly. These attributes can implicitly reveal confidential information about individuals when combined with quasi-identifiers and are likely to cause harm e.g. medical diagnosis, financial records, criminal records.
- **Non-Sensitive Attributes:** a data attribute that may not explicitly or implicitly declare any sensitive information about individuals. These records need to be associated with identifiers, quasi-identifiers or sensitive attributes to determine a respondent's behaviour or action e.g. cookie IDs.

Table 1 also presents the quality of each feature in the Adult dataset using 3 measures, *correlation, id-ness, and stability*.

- Correlation: measures the linear correlation between each feature and the label feature *(Income)*. (A value between 1 and -1)

Table 1. Adult Dataset

TYPE	FEATURES	ATTRIBUTE		CORR.	ID-NESS %	STABILITY %
CATEGORICAL	Workclass	Ⓠ		0.047	0.03	69.70
	Education	Ⓠ		-0.046	0.05	32.5
	Marital-status		Ⓢ	0.003	0.02	45.99
	Occupation	Ⓠ		-0.105	0.05	12.71
	Relationship	Ⓠ		-0.171	0.02	40.52
	Race	Ⓢ		-0.068	0.02	85.43
	Native-country	Ⓠ		0.034	0.13	89.59
	Gender	Ⓢ		-0.216	0.01	66.92
NUMERICAL	Age	Ⓠ		0.234	0.22	2.76
	Fnlwgt		Ⓝ	-0.009	66.48	0.04
	Education-num	Ⓠ		0.335	0.05	32.25
	Capital-gain		Ⓢ	0.266	0.37	91.67
	Capital-loss		Ⓢ	0.139	0.28	95.33
	Hours-per-week		Ⓢ	0.229	0.29	46.73
	Income		Ⓢ	1.000	0.01	75.92

Ⓠ = Quasi-Identifier, Ⓢ = Sensitive, Ⓝ = Non-Sensitive

- ID-ness: measures the fraction of unique values.
- Stability: measures the fraction of constant non-missing values.

All of these measures are essential in identifying patterns in the dataset which can help determine which features to select or deselect when applying a machine learning model for a specific task.

5   Proposed Strategy

This section presents a hybrid strategy for improving data quality and efficiency in PPDM using clustering-based approaches such as OKA and K-member. The proposed strategy works in the following stages:

1. Initially, the dataset is analysed and vertically partitioned based on the attribute set type: categorical or numerical.
2. A traditional k-anonymity clustering algorithm is applied to a local dataset containing the categorical attribute set to produce a k-anonymised result.
3. SOM is applied to compress the local dataset containing the numerical attribute set that are dropped by the clustering-based algorithms and generate a 1-dimensional representation of all input spaces.
4. The partial results are unified in a combined dataset based on their index and reference vectors, ensuring that objects are in the same order as the original dataset.
5. Classification techniques are applied on the combined results for generic data mining tasks.

An overview of the complete architecture is illustrated in Fig. 1.

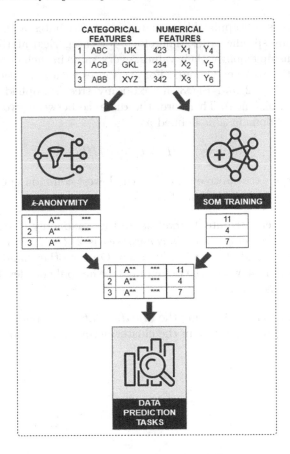

Fig. 1. Architecture of Proposed Strategy

6   Methodology

In order to verify the precision of the proposed strategy, results from this app-roach are compared with those of conventional clustering-based strategies *(OKA and K-member)*. The implementation of these algorithms available from [33] is specifically designed with the purpose of anonymising the Adult dataset, thus making it suitable for this experiment.

In the aforementioned implementation, a distance function is used to measure dissimilarities among data points for both categorical and numerical attributes. For numerical attributes, the difference between two values v_i and v_j of a finite numeric domain D is defined as:

$$\delta_N(v_1, v_2) = |v_1 - v_2|/|D| \tag{2}$$

where the domain size $|D|$ is the difference between the maximum and minimum values in D.

However, this is not applicable to categorical attributes as they cannot be enumerated in any specific order. Therefore, for categorical attributes with no semantic relationship amongst their values, every value in such domain is treated as a different entity to its neighbours. For attributes with semantic relationships as is the case in Fig. 2 and Fig. 3, a taxonomy tree is applied to define the dissimilarity (i.e., distance). Therefore, the distance between two values v_i and v_j of a categorical domain D is defined as:

$$\delta_C(v_1, v_2) = H(\Lambda(v_i, v_j))/H(T_D), \tag{3}$$

where $\Lambda(v_i, v_j)$ is the subtree rooted at the lowest common ancestor of x and y, and $H(T)$ represents the height of tree T.

Example 1. Consider attribute *Workclass* and its taxonomy tree in Fig. 3. The distance between *Federal-gov* and *Never-worked* is $2/2 = 1$, while the distance between *Federal-gov* and *Private* is $1/2 = 0.5$. On the other hand, for attribute *Race* as defined in Fig. 4, where the taxonomy tree has only one level, the distance between all values is always 1.

It is important to note that only the *Marital-status* and *Workclass* attributes have a predefined taxonomy tree in the clustering implementations published in [33].

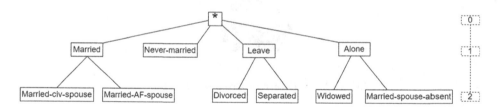

Fig. 2. Taxonomy Tree of *Marital-status*

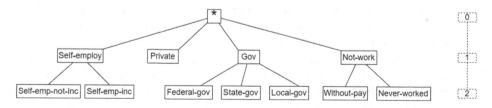

Fig. 3. Taxonomy Tree of *Workclass*

Fig. 4. Taxonomy Tree of *Race*

In our SOM architecture, we use cosine similarity as a distance metric, which ensures the smallest distance between points from the same class and a large margin of separation of points from different classes. This is a particularly useful approach because the Adult dataset has a combination of categorical and numerical data and other more common measures do not translate the distance well between vectors with categorical data. The cosine similarity of two vectors of attributes, a and b, can be formally defined as:

$$C_{(a,b)} = \frac{a * b}{|a| * |b|} \tag{4}$$

Herein, we used a one-dimensional set of 150 neurons. For each sample i, we search for a neuron which is closest to it. The neuron with the smallest distance to the i-th sample is classified as the BMU, and the weight update is executed until all samples are mapped to an output neuron in the set.

We utilise a method known as hyper-parameter optimization for choosing an optimal set of neurons for our SOM based on their correlation with the *Income* attribute. The ultimate goal of the prediction task with the Adult dataset is to identify who earns a certain type of income, thus any set of neurons with the highest correlation with the label feature can enhance this task with the anonymised version of the dataset. With this method, we perform an exhaustive search of all possible neurons within a range of manually set bounds. Following this, the set of neurons with the highest correlation with the label feature (i.e., winning neurons or BMUs) is selected as the optimal neuron set.

Finally, we unify our anonymised features with the SOM feature in a central dataset based on their index and reference vectors. Then, we subject this output to 7 classification models for performing the prediction tasks the Adult dataset is intended for (i.e., income prediction). The seven classification models applied are *Naive Bayes, Generalised Linear Model, Logistic Regression, Deep Learning, Decision Tree, Random Forest* and *Gradient Boosted Trees*.

To validate the experiment, several quality measures were used to evaluate and compare the results of our proposed strategy with the two traditional clustering approaches highlighted earlier *(OKA and K-member)*. The quality measures are as follows:

1. Normalised Certainty Penalty (*NCP*): measures information loss of all formed equivalence classes.

(a) For attributes that are numerical, the NCP score of an equivalence class T is defined as:

$$NCP_{A_{num}}(T) = \frac{max^T_{A_{num}} - min^T_{A_{num}}}{max_{A_{num}} - min_{A_{num}}} \tag{5}$$

Where the numerator and denominator represent attribute ranges of A_{num} for the class T and the whole table, respectively.

(b) For attributes that are categorical, in which no distance function or complete order is present, NCP is described w.r.t the attribute's taxonomy tree:

$$NCP_{A_{cat}}(T) = \begin{cases} 0, & card(u) = 1 \\ card(u)/|A_{cat}|, & otherwise \end{cases} \tag{6}$$

where u represents lowermost common predecessor of all values in A_{cat} that are included in T, $card(u)$ is the number of leaves (i.e., values of attribute) in the subtree of u, and $|A_{cat}|$ represents the total count of discrete values of A_{cat}.

(c) The NCP score of class T over all attributes classified as quasi-identifier is:

$$NCP(T) = \sum_{i=1}^{n} w_i \cdot NCP_{A_i}(T) \tag{7}$$

where n represents number attributes in a quasi-identifier set. A_i can either be a categorical or numerical attribute and has a weight w_i, where $\sum w_i = 1$.

2. Accuracy: measures the percentage of correctly classified instances by the classification model used, which is calculated using the number of *(true positives {TP}, true negatives {TN}, false positives {FP} and false negatives {FN})* [34]. Classification accuracy is defined mathematically as:

$$A = \frac{TP + TN}{TP + TN + FP + FN} \tag{8}$$

3. FMeasure: another classification-based metric used to measure the accuracy of a classifier model. The metric score computes the harmonic mean between precision and recall. Precision p denotes the number of true positives divided by all positive results returned by the classification model, whereas recall r denotes the number of true positives by the number of all samples which should have been returned as positive [34].

$$F_1 = 2 * \left(\frac{p * r}{p + r} \right) \tag{9}$$

4. Time: indicates the length of time it takes to execute an algorithm based on an input data size and a k parameter.

7   Experiments

In this section, we discuss our environment and evaluation methods, which include both information loss and privacy preservation. We have evaluated the accuracy of the proposed approach with conventional classification models on the original and anonymised datasets. The test environment used for our experiment is a Windows platform with an Intel(R) i5-7500T 2.7 GHz 4-core processor and 16 GB of memory. We have also used another platform, a MacBook with a 2.5 GHz dual-core processor and 8 GB memory.

Table 2. *NCP* score and running time of *OKA* and *K-member* algorithms with 3 different k thresholds.

k-VALUE	ALGORITHM	$NCP\%$	TIME (sec)
5-anonymity	*OKA*	9.99	2939.93
	K-member	6.09	6706.59
10-anonymity	*OKA*	16.74	2034.22
	K-member	11.07	7258.76
30-anonymity	*OKA*	32.43	840.12
	K-member	23.90	8518.48

We have evaluated the performance of the proposed approach with respect to privacy, execution time, accuracy, and F-score, where accuracy and F-score are calculated on the original and updated anonymised versions of the Adult dataset.

First, we have evaluated the NCP score of the *K-member* and *OKA* algorithms, considering 3 different k thresholds for anonymity as illustrated in Table 2. We have used the *OKA* and *K-member* algorithms for the purpose of anonymity. It is observed that the NCP score using *OKA* is always higher as compared to *K-member*, and by increasing k threshold for anonymity, the difference in loss also increases. The reason behind this is that *OKA* only uses one iteration for clustering, which leads to higher information loss; however, its one-pass nature makes it more time efficient than *K-member* clustering, thus its execution time is significantly less than that of *K-member* (Fig. 5).

Following this, we have applied SOM clustering on all the numerical features that are dropped by the two algorithms. These features include *(capital-gain, capital-loss, hours-per-week, and fnlwgt)*. Due to categorical features in the Adult dataset, we have used the cosine similarity metric because Euclidean distance-based results are biased. The bias arises because L1 and L2 distances are not applicable for vectors with text. We have used hyper-parameter tuning to identify the correct number of neurons for SOM, setting the stride size equal to 10 and iterating 100–300 times. After this, we determine the co-relation between the results and the actual income group. We have selected the number of neurons with which we got a higher co-relation.

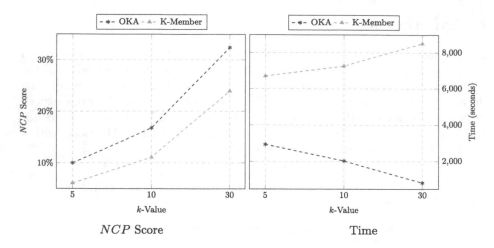

Fig. 5. Information loss & Total time

We have modified the Adult dataset in four versions: one is $OKA+SOM$, in which we have applied OKA and SOM on the original dataset and another version is K-$member+SOM$. The other two versions are obtained by just applying OKA and K-$member$ methods. After this, we have evaluated the performance of the different resulting datasets on the general classification models. We have categorized the performance by different thresholds of k-anonymity: 5, 10, and 30.

In Fig. 6 we have considered 5 members in a cluster. After applying the naive Bayes classification model, we have observed that accuracy of the K-$member+SOM$ version of the Adult dataset provides around 80% accuracy whereas on the original dataset it was around 83%. The $OKA+SOM$ dataset accuracy is bit lower than that of K-$member+SOM$. Even on the original dataset, the lowest accuracy was given by the decision tree method, and the same applies to our versions. The highest accuracy achieved is around 82% using a deep learning classification model, whereas on the original dataset it is around 85%. The same trend is observed for the F-score as well.

In Fig. 7 we have considered the same variations of data with similar models as we used in previous experiment but with a k-anonymity threshold of 10. It is observed that the overall accuracy is lower for all variations of the dataset except for the original one. Still, the dataset generated with K-$member+SOM$ gave higher accuracy than other variations on all of the models. In Fig. 8 we have evaluated our datasets with anonymity threshold of 30, and we have found that the accuracy of our datasets are slightly lower compared to 10-anonymity classification results, but the K-$member+SOM$ dataset still has higher accuracy than other variations of original dataset. The $OKA+SOM$ dataset accuracy has decreased more significantly than the others.

In evaluations, we have observed that, other than the original dataset, accuracy lowered on all other datasets when the cluster size increased from 5 to 10 to 30. K-$member+SOM$ information loss is quite low, which is why its dataset

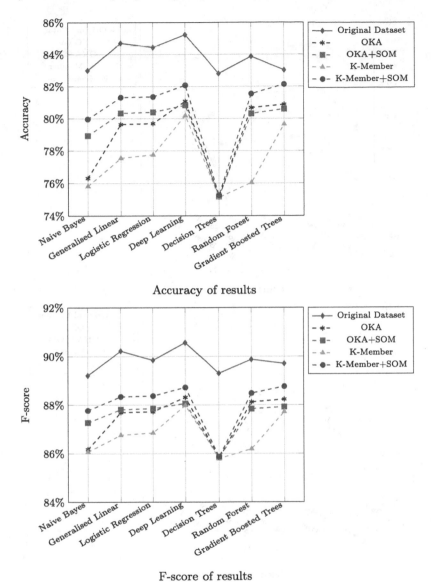

Accuracy of results

F-score of results

Fig. 6. Income prediction task with *5-anonymity* Adult dataset using seven classification models

accuracy improved, however, neither the *K-member* nor *OKA* based dataset performed better. Another aspect to consider is that *OKA+SOM* accuracy is lower than *K-member+SOM* because *OKA* uses only one iteration for clustering, which leads to greater time efficiency but also greater information loss compared to other methods. *K-member+SOM* has a trade-off of data loss with time efficiency. This experiment shows that dimensionality reduction is an effective

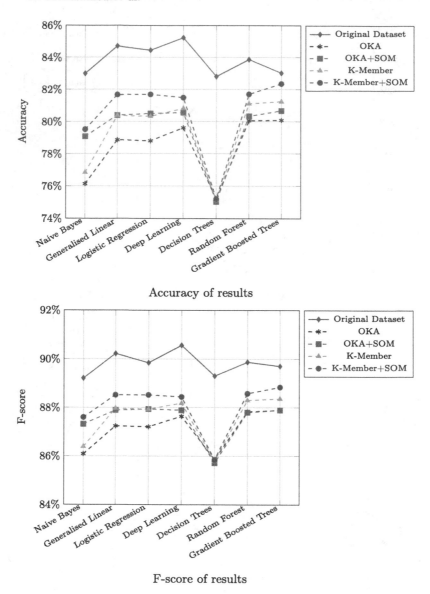

Fig. 7. Income prediction task with *10-anonymity* Adult dataset using seven classification models.

method for preserving the topological and metric relationships of data features, while anonymising its sensitive content. In addition, results obtained from this process improves the utility of data in classification tasks, as shown in Fig. 6, Fig. 7 and Fig. 8.

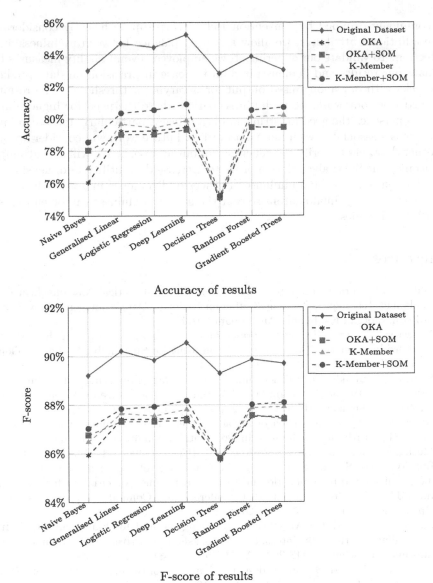

Fig. 8. Income prediction task with *30-anonymity* Adult dataset using seven classification models.

8   Conclusion

In this work, we proposed an effective hybrid strategy for improving data utility in PPDM approaches, which combines self organising maps with conventional privacy based clustering algorithms (OKA & K-Member). To illustrate this approach we apply it to the Adult data set and utilise rarely used attributes that are commonly dropped by conventional clustering approaches. By considering these additional attributes, we allow a revised balance between usefulness and protection. To validate our experiment, we employed several quality measures to evaluate our results and demonstrated an increase in precision on data prediction tasks with our anonymised output for 3 varying k thresholds. The results obtained from our work are useful in scenarios where the need for higher data utility supersedes the need for stringent data privacy, particularly if there are no privacy costs associated with more data utility. Future work will consider applying other data sets to verify the generality of our approach. We will also attempt to optimise our SOM algorithm in order to increase data utility in dimensionality reduction problems and minimise instances of divergence in our results. This will ensure more optimal neurons so that the goal of usefulness can be enhanced in PPDM strategies.

References

1. Witten, I.H., Frank, E., Hall, M.A.: Data Mining: Practical Machine Learning Tools and Techniques. Morgan Kaufmann Series in Data Management Systems, 3rd edn. Morgan Kaufmann, Amsterdam (2011)
2. Narwaria, M., Arya, S.: Privacy preserving data mining – 'a state of the art'. In: 2016 3rd International Conference on Computing for Sustainable Global Development (INDIACom), pp. 2108–2112, March 2016
3. Sharma, S., Shukla, D.: Efficient multi-party privacy preserving data mining for vertically partitioned data. In: 2016 International Conference on Inventive Computation Technologies (ICICT), vol. 2, pp. 1–7, August 2016
4. Kaur, A.: A hybrid approach of privacy preserving data mining using suppression and perturbation techniques. In: 2017 International Conference on Innovative Mechanisms for Industry Applications (ICIMIA), pp. 306–311, February 2017
5. Liu, W., Luo, S., Wang, Y., Jiang, Z.: A protocol of secure multi-party multi-data ranking and its application in privacy preserving sequential pattern mining. In: 2011 Fourth International Joint Conference on Computational Sciences and Optimization, pp. 272–275, April 2011
6. Lin, J.-L., Wei, M.-C.: An efficient clustering method for k-anonymization. In: Proceedings of the 2008 International Workshop on Privacy and Anonymity in Information Society - PAIS 2008. ACM Press (2008)
7. Lin, K.-P., Chen, M.-S.: On the design and analysis of the privacy-preserving SVM classifier. IEEE Trans. Knowl. Data Eng. **23**(11), 1704–1717 (2011)
8. Byun, J.-W., Kamra, A., Bertino, E., Li, N.: Efficient k-anonymization using clustering techniques. In: Advances in Databases: Concepts, Systems and Applications, pp. 188–200 (2007)
9. Oliveira, S., Zaïane, O.: Privacy preserving clustering by data transformation. J. Inf. Data Manage. **1**(1), 05 (2010)
10. Kabir, E., Wang, H., Bertino, E.: Efficient systematic clustering method for k-anonymization. Acta Informatica **48**(1), 51–66 (2011)
11. Xu, X., Numao, M.: An efficient generalized clustering method for achieving k-anonymization. In: 2015 Third International Symposium on Computing and Networking (CANDAR). IEEE, December 2015

12. Zheng, W., Wang, Z., Lv, T., Ma, Y., Jia, C.: K-anonymity algorithm based on improved clustering. In: Algorithms and Architectures for Parallel Processing, pp. 462–476 (2018)
13. Loukides, G., Shao, J.: Clustering-based K-anonymisation algorithms. In: Wagner, R., Revell, N., Pernul, G. (eds.) DEXA 2007. LNCS, vol. 4653, pp. 761–771. Springer, Heidelberg (2007). https://doi.org/10.1007/978-3-540-74469-6_74
14. Ciriani, V., De Capitani, S., di Vimercati, S., Foresti, P.S.: k: anonymous data mining: a survey. In: Aggarwal, C.C., Yu, P.S. (eds.) Privacy-Preserving Data Mining, pp. 105–136. Springer, Boston (2008). https://doi.org/10.1007/978-0-387-70992-5_5
15. Gkoulalas-Divanis, A., Loukides, G.: A survey of anonymization algorithms for electronic health records. In: Gkoulalas-Divanis, A., Loukides, G. (eds.) Medical Data Privacy Handbook, pp. 17–34. Springer, Cham (2015). https://doi.org/10.1007/978-3-319-23633-9_2
16. Pin, L., Wen-bing, Y., Nian-sheng, C. A unified metric method of information loss in privacy preserving data publishing. In: 2010 Second International Conference on Networks Security, Wireless Communications and Trusted Computing, vol. 2, pp. 502–505, April 2010
17. Dua, D., Graff, C.: Adult data set UCI machine learning repository (2017). http://archive.ics.uci.edu/ml
18. Samarati, P.: Protecting respondents identities in microdata release. IEEE Trans. Knowl. Data Eng. **13**(6), 1010–1027 (2001)
19. Ciriani, V., De Capitani Di Vimercati, S., Foresti, S., Samarati, P.: k-anonymity. In: Yu, T., Jajodia, S. (eds.) Secure data management in decentralized systems, pp. 323–353. Springer, Boston (2007). https://doi.org/10.1007/978-0-387-27696-0_10
20. Samarati, P., Sweeney, L.: Generalizing data to provide anonymity when disclosing information (abstract). In: Proceedings of the Seventeenth Symposium on Principles of Database Systems. ACM Press (1998)
21. Meyerson, A., Williams, R.: On the complexity of optimal k-anonymity. In: Proceedings of the Twenty-Third ACM SIGMOD-SIGACT-SIGART Symposium on Principles of Database Systems, PODS 2004, New York, NY, USA, pp. 223–228. Association for Computing Machinery (2004)
22. Tripathy, B.: Database anonymization techniques with focus on uncertainty and multi-sensitive attributes. In: Handbook of Research on Computational Intelligence for Engineering, Science, and Business, pp. 364–383. IGI Global (2013)
23. Friedman, A., Wolff, R., Schuster, A.: Providing k-anonymity in data mining. VLDB J. **17**(4), 789–804 (2008)
24. Kawano, A., Honda, K., Kasugai, H., Notsu, A.: A greedy algorithm for k-member co-clustering and its applicability to collaborative filtering. Procedia Comput. Sci. **22**, 477–484 (2013)
25. Kohonen, T.: Self-Organizing Maps. Springer, Heidelberg (2001). https://doi.org/10.1007/978-3-642-56927-2
26. Aggarwal, C.C.: Neural Networks and Deep Learning. Springer, Cham (2018). https://doi.org/10.1007/978-3-319-94463-0
27. Dogan, Y., Birant, D., Kut, A.: SOM++: integration of self-organizing map and K-Means++ algorithms. In: Perner, P. (ed.) MLDM 2013. LNCS (LNAI), vol. 7988, pp. 246–259. Springer, Heidelberg (2013). https://doi.org/10.1007/978-3-642-39712-7_19
28. Flavius, G., Alfredo, C.J.: PartSOM: a framework for distributed data clustering using SOM and k-means. In: Self-Organizing Maps. IntechOpen, April 2010

29. Tsiafoulis, S., Zorkadis, V.C., Karras, D.A.: A neural-network clustering-based algorithm for privacy preserving data mining. In: Kim, T., Yau, S.S., Gervasi, O., Kang, B.-H., Stoica, A., Ślęzak, D. (eds.) FGIT 2010. CCIS, vol. 121, pp. 269–276. Springer, Heidelberg (2010). https://doi.org/10.1007/978-3-642-17625-8_27

30. Byun, J.-W., Sohn, Y., Bertino, E., Li, N.: Secure anonymization for incremental datasets. In: Jonker, W., Petković, M. (eds.) SDM 2006. LNCS, vol. 4165, pp. 48–63. Springer, Heidelberg (2006). https://doi.org/10.1007/11844662_4

31. Zare-Mirakabad, M.-R., Jantan, A., Bressan, S.: Privacy risk diagnosis: mining *l*-diversity. In: Chen, L., Liu, C., Liu, Q., Deng, K. (eds.) DASFAA 2009. LNCS, vol. 5667, pp. 216–230. Springer, Heidelberg (2009). https://doi.org/10.1007/978-3-642-04205-8_19

32. Wang, K., Fung, B.C.M.: Anonymizing sequential releases. In: Proceedings of the 12th ACM SIGKDD International Conference on Knowledge Discovery and Data Mining, KDD 2006, New York, NY, USA, pp. 414–423. ACM (2006)

33. Gong, Q.: Clustering based k-anonymization. MIT License, January 2016

34. Mishra, A.; Metrics to evaluate your machine learning algorithm (2018). https://towardsdatascience.com/metrics-to-evaluate-your-machine-learning-algorithm-f10ba6e38234

Multi-criteria Optimization Using
l-diversity and t-closeness
for k-anonymization

Clémence Mauger$^{(\boxtimes)}$, Gaël Le Mahec, and Gilles Dequen

Laboratoire MIS, Université de Picardie Jules Verne, UFR des Sciences,
33 rue Saint-Leu, 80000 Amiens, France
{clemence.mauger,gael.le.mahec,gilles.dequen}@u-picardie.fr
https://www.mis.u-picardie.fr

Abstract. k-anonymity is a commonly used anonymization principle. It provides an anonymous table by grouping the individuals of the table in sets of at least k elements. This principle guarantees a good privacy while limiting the data alteration. Within the k-anonymization process, only quasi-identifier attributes are considered. Sensitive attributes are not. As a consequence, in k-anonymous tables, sensitive values might be disclosed. Thus, the concepts of l-diversity and t-closeness have been defined. Considering anonymization principles that take into account the distribution of the sensitive attributes values in the anonymous table, this paper tackles the link between k-anonymity, l-diversity and t-closeness. It then proposes to generate k-anonymous tables which simultaneously optimize data alteration, l-diversity and t-closeness. To do so, this paper describes seven optimization strategies, usable in an anonymization algorithm, that are combinations of minimization of data alteration, maximization of l-diversity and minimization of t-closeness. At the end, this study provides comparative experimental results of these strategies on the *Adult Data Set*, a commonly used data set within the anonymization research field that we extended with randomly generated data following several distributions.

Keywords: k-anonymity · l-diversity · t-closeness · Data anonymization · Optimization

1 Introduction

With the growth of data collected by companies or by public organizations (governments, hospitals), the need to store and protect this large mass of raw data has become a major issue. These data sets, if they are intended for statistical analysis publication, must be anonymized to guarantee to individuals, who have

This research is developed under the Smart Angel project. Smart Angel is sponsored by BPI France as part of Programme d'Investissements d'Avenir (PIA) within the PSPC funding scheme.

© Springer Nature Switzerland AG 2020
J. Garcia-Alfaro et al. (Eds.): DPM 2020/CBT 2020, LNCS 12484, pp. 73–88, 2020.
https://doi.org/10.1007/978-3-030-66172-4_5

voluntarily or not communicated their personal information, the respect of their privacy. Big internet companies are aware of this problem and are already developing tools to protect the privacy of their customers (e.g. Apple's differential privacy deployment or Google's RAPPOR [1]).

In this paper, we focus on *Privacy-Preserving Data Publishing* (PPDP) [2]. It aims to publish data table with respect to the privacy of the individuals of the table. An other research area, mentioned in [2], is the *Privacy-Preserving Data Mining* (PPDM). The authors say that research in PPDM has been motivated by privacy concerns in data mining tools. Dwork *and al.* presented the *differential privacy* in [3] as an anonymization principle to do PPDM. Contrary to PPDP, the data holder in PPDM modifies the data to mask sensitive information while retaining the expected results of the data mining tool. Thus, the data holder must know how the data mining tool works, which is not the case in PPDP.

In this paper, we consider tables composed of records, representing individuals, and columns, representing attributes. The attributes can be separated in three categories. i) The *identifier* attributes are direct links between a record and the identity of an individual (e.g. name, SSN); ii) The *quasi-identifier* (QID) attributes [4] (e.g. age, gender) are a set of attributes that do not reveal information if they are considered separately. However, with the values of the quasi-identifiers and external information (e.g. other public released data sets), an adversary could discover private data about individuals; iii) The *sensitive* attributes contain the information we would like to protect in the table (e.g. a disease, wages). Records could be gathered in *equivalence classes* with respect to their QID attributes' values. We define the *identity disclosure* as the fact to uniquely associate a record with an individual in the anonymous table and the *attribute disclosure* as the fact to learn new information about some individuals after the publication of an anonymous version of the table [5].

2   Related Work

In order to provide PPDP, several anonymization techniques have been enunciated. The simplest one is the *pseudonymization*. It merely consists in removing identifiers or replacing them with unique and random IDs. However, it has been proved in [6] that you can deduce some information about individuals in pseudonymized tables (i.e. *linkage attack*). As a consequence, Samarati presented k-anonymity in [7]. As a definition, we consider that a table is k-anonymous if each record is indistinguishable from at least $k-1$ other records with respect to the set of quasi-identifier attributes. Therefore, within a k-anonymization context, the probability of identity disclosure is at most $\frac{1}{k}$. k-anonymity brings protection against identity disclosure, but it does not protect against attribute disclosure. Indeed, a lack of diversity of the sensitive attributes' values could appear in k-anonymous tables [8]. First stated in [8] in 2006, the principle of l-*diversity* was introduced by Machanavajjhala to face the previous issue. Unlike k-anonymity, this principle takes into account the sensitive attributes' values. l-diversity guarantees that, in each equivalence class, we find at least l sensitive values "well-represented". As a definition, we consider that an equivalence class is "well-represented" by l sensitive values if there exists at least $l \geq 2$ different sensitive values in the equivalence class such that the l most frequent values have roughly the same frequency of appearance. In l-diversity, even if an adversary has information about QID attributes, the diversity of the sensitive values will complicate the discovery of sensitive information. In [9], authors point two drawbacks of l-diversity: the skewness and the similarity attacks. Moreover, they presented a new principle called *t-closeness*. Like l-diversity, t-closeness deals with the distribution of the values of the sensitive attributes in the anonymous table. The distribution of the values of the sensitive attributes in the whole population must be known. An equivalence class is said to have t-closeness if the distance between the distribution of a sensitive attribute in the class and the distribution of the attribute in the whole table is no more than a threshold t. A table is said to have t-closeness if all the equivalence classes have t-closeness. By the work on the sensitive values, attribute disclosure is prevented with t-closeness. Nevertheless, the problem of identity disclosure persists. Authors in [9] advocate to use both t-closeness and k-anonymity to be protected from the two types of disclosure. Like l-diversity, t-closeness manages equivalence classes in order to have a homogeneous distribution of the sensitive attributes values. It could be a weakness for statistical studies.

In [10], the authors conducted a study on the minimization of the data alteration during a k-anonymization process. The quality of a k-anonymous table can be measured thanks to an *information loss metric*. The authors compared the efficiency of seven information loss metrics to maintain data utility during a k-anonymization process. To continue what was undertaken in [10], we study the link between l-diversity, t-closeness and k-anonymity. By influencing the distributions of the sensitive attributes values, it is expected that adding the constraints of l-diversity or t-closeness during the k-anonymization process will enhance the privacy in the anonymous table. We want to measure the impact of these additional constraints on the anonymous table's data utility. We will optimize the anonymous algorithm used in [10] according to strategies mixing information loss metric, l-diversity and t-closeness. We propose seven strategies whose effectiveness is measured by the data alteration and the values of l and t of the k-anonymous tables produced. The rest of the paper is organized as follows. In Sect. 3, we expose the concepts of generalization and information loss metrics, then we justify our choice of metric. In Sect. 4, we present a l-diversity measure and a t-closeness measure for a k-anonymous table. In Sect. 5, we specify the anonymization algorithm used and we present the new optimization strategies. In Sect. 6, we evaluate the optimization strategies on a public table and on simulated data and we present the results obtained. We conclude in Sect. 7.

3 k-anonymity Optimization

The following notations are valid for the rest of the section. Let T be a table with $\mathcal{Q} = \{Q_1, ..., Q_m\}$ its set of quasi-identifier attributes. Let $\mathcal{C}(T)$ be the set of equivalence classes of T.

3.1   The Generalization Technique

To obtain anonymous tables, the generalization technique is a simple and efficient method [7]. For each $Q_i \in \mathcal{Q}$, we build a *generalization hierarchy* denoted by $\mathcal{G}_{Q_i}$. It is a tree in which the leaves correspond to the values without generalization, the internal nodes are generalized values and the root is the most generalized value. The edges are oriented from the leaves to the root. We call *height* of a generalization hierarchy the number of nodes in the longest path of the hierarchy, denoted by h_{Q_i} for each $i \in \{1, ..., m\}$. Figure 1 is an example of a generalization hierarchy.

Fig. 1. A generalization hierarchy

To generalize two equivalence classes, we use the notion of *Lowest Common Ancestor* of two nodes. It is defined in [11] as the ancestor of the two nodes that is located farthest from the root. Let $C_1, C_2 \in \mathcal{C}(T)$ with representatives $c_1 = [x_{Q_1}, ..., x_{Q_m}]$ and $c_2 = [y_{Q_1}, ..., y_{Q_m}]$ respectively. The result of the merging of C_1 and C_2 is $Merge(C_1, C_2) := [LCA(x_{Q_1}, y_{Q_1}), ..., LCA(x_{Q_m}, y_{Q_m})]$, with $LCA(x_{Q_i}, y_{Q_i})$ the lowest common ancestor of x_{Q_i} and y_{Q_i} in $\mathcal{G}_{Q_i}$, $\forall i \in \{1, ..., m\}$.

3.2   Definition of an Information Loss Metric

An *information loss metric* μ is a map that estimates the amount of loss information after an anonymization process using the generalization technique. We use information loss metric to compute the data alteration between a table and an anonymous version of it. We will formally define the expression of the cost of an anonymous table for the metric μ thanks to the modeling presented in [10]. Assume that the table T contains n lines $\{l^1, ..., l^n\}$ and all the values of the table are leaves. Let $\widetilde{T}$ be a version of T in which generalizations have been made and let $\widetilde{T}_{ano}$ be an anonymous version of $\widetilde{T}$ obtained by the generalization technique. We would like to express the cost of $\widetilde{T}_{ano}$ for μ.

Let $Q_i \in \mathcal{Q}$. As explained in [10], each directed edge (x, y) of $\mathcal{G}_{Q_i}$ can be weighted by an *elementary weight* $\omega(x, y)$. We can express the $\omega(x, y)$ for μ (and μ can be characterized by its elementary weights). Then, we build a *matrix of costs* M_{μ, Q_i} from the $\omega(x, y)$. This matrix is indexed by the nodes of the hierarchy $\mathcal{G}_{Q_i}$. An entry (a, b) of M_{μ, Q_i} is defined by $M_{\mu, Q_i}(a, b) = w_{a \to LCA(a,b)}$, with $w_{a \to LCA(a,b)} = \sum_{(x,y) \in E} \omega(x, y)$ for E the set of edges in the path from a to the $LCA(a, b)$.

For each generalization hierarchy $\mathcal{G}_{Q_i}$, let $\mathcal{N}_{Q_i} := \{n_{Q_i}^1, ..., n_{Q_i}^{s_i}\}$ be the set of the nodes of $\mathcal{G}_{Q_i}$. We set $\mathcal{N} := \{[n_{Q_1}^{j_1}, ..., n_{Q_m}^{j_m}] \mid n_{Q_i}^{j_i} \in \mathcal{N}_{Q_i}$ and $j_i \in \{1, ..., s_i\}$ for $i \in \{1, .., m\}\}$. Thanks to the costs matrices M_{μ, Q_i}, we can define the cost of generalization of two m-tuples of $\mathcal{N}$ by:

$$\mu(t^1, t^2) = \sum_{i=1}^{m} M_{\mu, Q_i}(t_{Q_i}^1, t_{Q_i}^2) + M_{\mu, Q_i}(t_{Q_i}^2, t_{Q_i}^1), \tag{1}$$

with $t^1 = [t_{Q_1}^1, ..., t_{Q_m}^1]$ and $t^2 = [t_{Q_1}^2, ..., t_{Q_m}^2]$. By extension, for $C_1, C_2 \in \mathcal{C}(T)$ whose representatives are $c_1 = [x_{Q_1}^1, ..., x_{Q_m}^1]$ and $c_2 = [x_{Q_1}^2, ..., x_{Q_m}^2]$ respectively, we can define:

$$\mu(C_1, C_2) = \sum_{i=1}^{m} M_{\mu, Q_i}(x_{Q_i}^1, x_{Q_i}^2) \times |C_1| + M_{\mu, Q_i}(x_{Q_i}^2, x_{Q_i}^1) \times |C_2|. \tag{2}$$

Formula 2 represents the cost for μ to merge the two equivalence classes.

We can now define the cost of an equivalence class $\widetilde{C}_{ano}$ of $\widetilde{T}_{ano}$ for μ. Let C be the subset of T such that $\widetilde{C}_{ano}$ exactly contains the lines of C generalized. Similarly, let $\widetilde{C}$ be the subset of $\widetilde{T}$ such that $\widetilde{C}_{ano}$ exactly contains the lines of $\widetilde{C}$ generalized. By convention, we set $\mu(\widetilde{C}_{ano}) := \mu(\widetilde{C}_{ano}, C)$ and $\widetilde{\mu}(\widetilde{C}_{ano}) := \mu(\widetilde{C}_{ano}, \widetilde{C})$. Thus, we can define the cost of the anonymous table $\widetilde{T}_{ano}$ for μ as:

$$\mu(\widetilde{T}_{ano}) = \sum_{\widetilde{C}_{ano} \in \mathcal{C}(\widetilde{T}_{ano})} \mu(\widetilde{C}_{ano}). \tag{3}$$

Similarly, we have $\widetilde{\mu}(\widetilde{T}_{ano}) = \sum_{\widetilde{C}_{ano} \in \mathcal{C}(\widetilde{T}_{ano})} \widetilde{\mu}(\widetilde{C}_{ano})$.[1]

3.3   Comparison of Information Loss Metrics

The authors of [10] present seven information loss metrics. Three come from previous papers: *Distortion* defined by Li in [12], *NCP* defined by Xu in [13] and *Total* defined by Byun in [14]. The four other metrics are defined in their paper: *Lost Leaves Metrics (LLM)*, *Normalized LLM (NLLM)*, *Wid LLM (WLLM)* and *Wid Normalized LLM (WNLLM)*. Let *Metric* = {*Distortion, NCP, Total, LLM, NLLM, WLLM, WNLLM*}. For each metric μ of *Metric*, they give the expressions of the elementary weights $\omega(x, y)$ to put in the edges of the hierarchies of the quasi-identifier attributes. Thanks to Sect. 3.2, we can deduce the cost of an anonymous table for each metric in *Metric*.

Then, the authors of [10] introduce an anonymization algorithm. This algorithm, inspired by the work of Li in [12], provides a k-anonymous version of the table T by optimizing the performed mergings thanks to a metric μ. Its formalization is shown in Algorithm 1. Let $\mathcal{C}_k(T) \subseteq \mathcal{C}(T)$ be the set of equivalence

---

[1] $\widetilde{\mu}$ computes the amount of loss information between the table given to be anonymized ($\widetilde{T}$) and its anonymous version ($\widetilde{T}_{ano}$) while μ computes the amount of loss information between the table exclusively composed of leaves (T) and the anonymous table ($\widetilde{T}_{ano}$).

classes of size strictly less than k. While the table T is not k-anonymous, we choose $C_{small} \in \mathcal{C}_k(T)$ among the smallest equivalence classes. We compute the merging cost of C_{small} with the other classes of $\mathcal{C}_k(T)$ according to μ. Finally, we perform in T the merging $Merge(C_{small}, C)$ which has the smallest cost for μ. Thus, we can replace the metric μ in Algorithm 1 by each metric of $Metric$ and obtain k-anonymous tables for each metric. For $k \geq 2$ and $\mu \in Metric$, we denote by $T_{\mu,k}$ the k-anonymous table obtained by using μ as the optimization metric in Algorithm 1.

Algorithm 1. Greedy k-Anonymization Algorithm

1: **procedure** K-ANONYMIZATION(T, k, μ)
2:     **while** $\mathcal{C}_k(T)$ is not empty **do**
3:         Choose arbitrarily a class C_{small} in $\mathcal{C}_k(T)$
4:         Find a class C in $\mathcal{C}_k(T) \backslash C_{small}$ such that $\mu(C_{small}, C)$ is minimal
5:         $\mathcal{C}(T) \leftarrow \mathcal{C}(T) \backslash \{C_{small}, C\} \cup Merge(C_{small}, C)$
6:     **end while**
7: **end procedure**

To compare the quality of the tables obtained previously, the authors introduce the notion of *average percentage of alteration* of a table. First of all, they define the *alteration* for a metric $\nu \in Metric$ of a table $T_{\mu,k}$, for $k \geq 2$ and $\mu \in Metric$, as:

$$A_\nu(T_{\mu,k}) = \frac{\nu(T_{\mu,k})}{\nu(T^*)} \times 100, \qquad (4)$$

with T^* the generalization of T in which all the values are at the root for each $Q_i \in \mathcal{Q}$. Then, they obtain a global measure to compare the anonymous tables given by Algorithm 1: the *average percentage of alteration*. It is defined as $\mathcal{A}(T_{\mu,k}) = \frac{1}{|Metric|} \sum_{\nu \in Metric} A_\nu(T_{\mu,k})$, with $k \geq 2$ and $\mu \in Metric$.

Finally, they confront the experimental protocol on the *Adult Data Set* [15], a table of 30162 lines and 9 quasi-identifier attributes. We denote by *Adult* the *Adult Data Set*. They run Algorithm 1 for 21 values of k between 2 and 15000 for each metric in $Metric$. They compare the quality of the tables $Adult_{\mu,k}$ produced thanks to three criteria: the average percentage of alteration, the number of *modified values* and the number of *deleted values*.

The results show that $NLLM$ is the metric that permits to generate k-anonymous tables with less information loss regards to the three criteria. Thus, we choose $NLLM$ as metric in our experiments on mixing data alteration, l-diversity and t-closeness for k-anonymization. We explicit the expression of the elementary weights and the expression of the cost of an equivalence class for $NLLM$ in Sect. 3.4.

3.4   Expression of $NLLM$

To begin with, we take some notations from the paper [10]. We set $h_{max} = max\{h_{Q_i}, i = 1, ..., m\}$ as the maximum of the heights of the generalization hierarchies of the quasi-identifier attributes. Let $Q_i \in Q$ and $\mathcal{G}_{Q_i}$ be its generalization hierarchy. Let (x, y) be an edge of $\mathcal{G}_{Q_i}$. The *number of leaves* of x, denoted by $nl(x)$, is the number of leaves in the sub-tree of $\mathcal{G}_{Q_i}$ whose root is x.

The elementary weights of $NLLM$ are defined as $\omega(x, y) = \frac{nl(y) - nl(x)}{nl(\mathcal{G}_{Q_i})} \times \frac{h_{max}}{h_{Q_i}}$.

We can compute the cost of an equivalence class for $NLLM$ (and so deduce the cost of an anonymous table for $NLLM$). As in Sect. 3.2, we take an equivalence class $\widetilde{C}_{ano}$ of $\widetilde{T}_{ano}$. We denote by $c = [x_{Q_1}, ..., x_{Q_m}]$ a representative of $\widetilde{C}_{ano}$. The cost of $\widetilde{C}_{ano}$ for $NLLM$ is $NLLM(\widetilde{C}_{ano}) = \sum_{i=1}^{m} \frac{nl(x_{Q_i})}{nl(\mathcal{G}_{Q_i})} \times \frac{h_{max}}{h_{Q_i}}$.

4 *l*-diversity and *t*-closeness as Privacy Quality Measurement

During a k-anonymization process, we work on the QID attributes of the table but the values of the sensitive attributes are not considered at all. Thus, there is no control over the distribution of the sensitive values in the equivalence classes of the k-anonymous table. For a sake of clarity, we will consider that the table has only one sensitive attribute.

For a given table, there potentially exists a lot of k-anonymous versions of it[2] Among those, some better respect l-diversity and t-closeness (i.e. they could have a huge diversity in the sensitive values in each equivalence class or a distribution of the sensitive values very close to the distribution in the whole population). However, it could be synonymous with a large data alteration. Ideally, we would like to be able to compute a k-anonymous table which would be interesting for l-diversity and/or t-closeness and which would preserve a good data utility (by minimizing the data alteration). We will consider the values l of l-diversity and t of t-closeness as quality measures of a k-anonymous table. In the following, we will respectively denote these values l_{div} and t_{close}. Let T be a table with a set Q of QID attributes and a single sensitive attribute S. Let $T_{ano,k}$ be a k-anonymous version of T with $\mathcal{C}(T_{ano,k})$ its set of equivalence classes.

In [8], the authors present several formalizations of l-diversity. In this paper, we use the *entropy l-diversity* definition. We compute l_{div} of $T_{ano,k}$ as $l_{div}(T_{ano,k}) = \min_{C \in \mathcal{C}(T_{ano,k})} l_{div}(C)$ with $l_{div}(C) = \exp(-\sum_{s \in S} (p_{(C,s)} log(p_{(C,s)})))$ and $p_{(C,s)}$ the proportion of the sensitive value s in the equivalence class C.

Similarly, the t_{close} value of $T_{ano,k}$ is $t_{close}(T_{ano,k}) = \max_{C \in \mathcal{C}(T_{ano,k})} t_{close}(C)$ with $t_{close}(C) = \frac{1}{2} \sum_{s \in S} |p_{(C,s)} - p_{(T,s)}|$ and $p_{(T,s)}$ the proportion of the sensitive value s in the whole table T. It is the *Equal Distance* from the *Earth Mover's Distance* used in [9].

Thanks to these formulas, we are able to measure l-diversity and t-closeness on a table. We can now detail the anonymization algorithm used to generate

---

[2] i.e. the number of possible partitions of N elements in subsets of size of at least k is more than $\sum_{i=k}^{N} \binom{N}{i}$ and is of the order of 2^N.

a k-anonymous version of a table and the new optimization strategies that we propose to improve the quality of anonymous tables.

5 Optimization of k-anonymity, l-diversity and t-closeness

Finding an optimal partition of a table that respects an anonymization principle is a difficult issue. Results of NP-hardness for k-anonymity, l-diversity and t-closeness are respectively enunciated within [16,17] and [18].

To provide anonymous tables, researchers develop anonymization frameworks: [14,19] for k-anonymity; [17] for l-diversity; [20] for t-closeness.

As a consequence of the NP-hardness of the underlying problems, to conduct our experiments on the three anonymization principles, we use a classical greedy algorithm providing an anonymous version of a table. It is an extension of Algorithm 1 in Sect. 3.3. More specifically, at each step of our process, we locally choose the optimal merging of two equivalence classes with respect to one or more criteria, and not only according to an information loss metric. Let T be a table to anonymize and let $\mathcal{C}(T)$ be the set of its equivalence classes. Let $\mathcal{P}$ be an anonymization principle (e.g. k-anonymity, l-diversity, t-closeness). Let $Crit$ be a set of criteria that permit the selection of a merging of two classes to perform in T (e.g. the data alteration of the merging is minimal). While T does not respect the $\mathcal{P}$ principle, we choose one of the smallest equivalence class, C_{small}, in $\mathcal{C}(T)$ that does not respect yet the $\mathcal{P}$ principle. Then, we look for a class such that the merging of this class with C_{small} optimizes the criteria of $Crit$. We do the optimal merging in the table. To sum up, we would like to obtain a $\mathcal{P}$ version of T by optimizing the criteria in $Crit$ during the step of classes merging. Algorithm 2 is a formalization of the anonymization process.

Algorithm 2. Greedy Anonymization Algorithm

1: **procedure** ANONYMIZATION(T, $\mathcal{P}$, $Crit$)
2:     **while** T does not respect $\mathcal{P}$ **do**
3:         Choose one of the smallest class C_{small} in $\mathcal{C}(T)$ that does not respect $\mathcal{P}$
4:         Find a class C in $\mathcal{C}(T) \backslash C_{small}$ such that $Merge(C_{small}, C)$ optimizes the criteria in $Crit$
5:         $\mathcal{C}(T) \leftarrow \mathcal{C}(T) \backslash \{C_{small}, C\} \cup Merge(C_{small}, C)$
6:     **end while**
7: **end procedure**

Considering several criteria for optimization, we can combine them in different manners. We can choose a priority criterion on which we select classes to merge, then order the classes by the second criterion (e.g. l-diversity first, then metric ; metric, then t-closeness, ...). Another way to combine these objectives is to define a cost function of the merging of two classes that takes into account the table alteration and the second criterion: $Cost_{crit} : (\mathcal{C} \times \mathcal{C}) \rightarrow \mathbb{R}$ with $\mathcal{C}$

a set of equivalence classes. To co-optimize the data alteration (minimization) and *l*-diversity (maximization), we can define $Cost_{crit}$ as $NLLM_{ldiv}(C_1, C_2) = \frac{NLLM(C_1,C_2)}{l_{div}}$ with l_{div} the *l*-diversity value of $Merge(C_1, C_2)$ and $C_1, C_2 \in C$. To co-optimize the data alteration (minimization) and *t*-closeness (minimization), we define $NLLM_{tclose}(C_1, C_2) = NLLM(C_1, C_2) \times t_{close}$ with t_{close} the *t*-closeness value of $Merge(C_1, C_2)$. Let the following sets:

- $A(C_s, C) = \{C \in C \mid NLLM(Merge(C_s, C)) = \min_{c \in C}(NLLM(C_s, c))\}$

  (i.e. the set of classes $\in C$ that minimize $NLLM$ when merged with C_s)
- $LDIV(C_s, C) = \{C \in C \mid l_{div}(Merge(C_s, C)) = \max_{c \in C}(l_{div}(c))\}$

  (i.e. the set of classes $\in C$ that maximize l_{div} when merged with C_s)
- $TCLOSE(C_s, C) = \{C \in C \mid t_{close}(Merge(C_s, C)) = \min_{c \in C}(t_{close}(c))\}$

  (i.e. the set of classes $\in C$ that minimize t_{close} when merged with C_s)
- $A_{ldiv}(C_s, C) = \{C \in C \mid NLLM_{ldiv}(C_s, C) = \min_{c \in C}(NLLM_{ldiv}(C_s, c))\}$

  (i.e. the set of classes $\in C$ that minimize $NLLM_{ldiv}$ when merged with C_s)
- $A_{tclose}(C_s, C) = \{C \in C \mid NLLM_{tclose}(C_s, C) = \min_{c \in C}(NLLM_{tclose}(C_s, c))\}$

  (i.e. the set of classes $\in C$ that minimize $NLLM_{tclose}$ when merge with C_s)

We propose seven strategies to optimize *l*-diversity and *t*-closeness within the *k*-anonymous tables:

1. A class among those that minimize the merging cost - $Crit : C \in A(C_{small}, C)$
2. A class among those that maximize l_{div} among those that minimize the merging cost - $Crit : C \in LDIV(C_{small}, A(C_{small}, C))$
3. A class among those that minimize the merging cost among those that maximize l_{div} - $Crit : C \in A(C_{small}, LDIV(C_{small}, C))$
4. A class among those that minimize the merging cost divided by l_{div} - $Crit : C \in A_{ldiv}(C_{small}, C)$
5. A class among those that minimize the merging cost among those that minimize t_{close} - $Crit : C \in A(C_{small}, TCLOSE(C_{small}, C))$
6. A class among those that minimize t_{close} among those that minimize the merging cost - $Crit : C \in TCLOSE(C_{small}, A(C_{small}, C))$
7. A class among those that minimize the merging cost multiplied by t_{close} - $Crit : C \in A_{tclose}(C_{small}, C)$

By maximizing the value l_{div} and minimizing the value t_{close}, we seek to preserve the privacy of the individuals in the table by protecting the sensitive values. By minimizing the data alteration, we seek to conserve data utility by keeping information in the quasi-identifier attributes.

6   Experiments

To conduct our experiments, we choose the *Adult Data Set* [15] as experimental table. We conserve 9 columns: *Age, Gender, Race, Marital status, Education, Native country, Work class, Occupation* and *Salary*. We obtain a table of 30162 lines. To evaluate the different strategies, we perform two kind of experiments: using existing attributes of the *Adult data set* as sensitive values, then using simulated attributes of different numbers of possible values and following different distributions.

6.1   Evaluation of the Strategies Using *real* data

At a first step, we evaluate Algorithm 2 for $\mathcal{P}$ is k-anonymity using l-diversity and t-closeness as unique optimization criteria. Figure 2 present the results of such optimizations. For this experiment, we use the *Age* attribute as sensitive value. As expected, Algorithm 2 quickly optimizes the criterion (l-diversity or t-closeness) even for low values of k. Unfortunately, since the selection of the classes to merge does not depend on the QID, in regard to the alteration of the table, this process is equivalent to a random selection. We can see that the table alteration increases very quickly, reducing the data utility, even for very small values of k. It is then necessary to co-optimize the alteration with l-diversity and t-closeness.

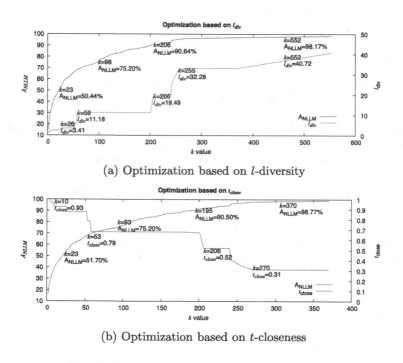

(a) Optimization based on l-diversity

(b) Optimization based on t-closeness

Fig. 2. Optimizing thanks to sensitive attribute

For each strategy, for every possible values of k from 2 to 15000, we measure the alteration and the l_{div} and t_{close} values of the k-anonymous tables obtained when running Algorithm 2. Of course, the largest values of k of these experiments are rarely useful (if they are) in a real application. These largest values are tested to analyse the behavior of Algorithm 2. We evaluate our strategies using two different attributes as sensitive value: the *Age* attribute: 74 different values, maximum $l_{div} = 50$ (Fig. 3) and the *Marital status* attribute: 7 different values, maximum $l_{div} = 3.53$ (Fig. 4).

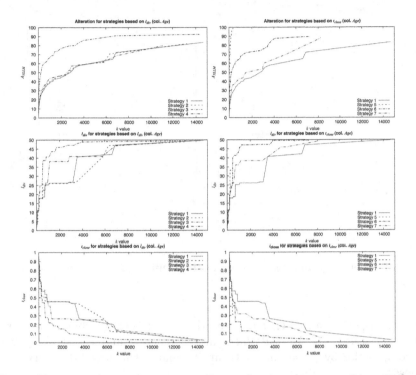

Fig. 3. Alteration, l_{div} and t_{close} according to k using *Age* as sensitive attribute

In Fig. 3 and Fig. 4, we can see that the strategies that prioritize the optimization of *l*-diversity or *t*-closeness (Strategies 3 and 6) give the best results regarding to this criterion but are the worst strategies considering the data alteration. Strategy 5 reaches 100% of data alteration for a very low value of k because it quickly leads to only one equivalence class table (all the lines of the table are generalized in only one class ⇒ $t_{close} = 0$). Strategy 5 is not suitable to preserve data utility. Strategies 1, 2 and 4 are equivalent considering the data alteration, but Strategy 4 outscores Strategies 1 and 2 and is equivalent to Strategy 7 for the *l*-diversity maximization. Strategy 7 alters more the table than Strategy 4 but gives better results considering *t*-closeness when $k > 4000$ when using *Age* as sensitive attribute.

As a whole, when sensitive values are sufficiently numerous (the *Age* attribute for example), Strategy 4 gives good results considering all the criteria and alters less the data than Strategy 7 that is better only for the *t*-closeness criterion

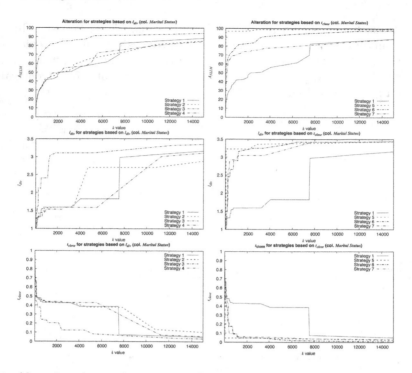

Fig. 4. Alteration, l_{div} and t_{close} according to k using *Marital status* as sensitive attribute

when k is large with a higher data alteration. With few possible values for the sensitive attribute (the *Marital status* attribute for example), Strategy 2 is a good compromise by preserving data utility and optimizing l-diversity and t-closeness.

To summarize, Strategy 4, which consists in taking into account l-diversity when minimizing the data alteration of a k-anonymous table, is efficient and can largely improve l-diversity and t-closeness while preserving data from alteration.

A first conclusion is that the choice of an optimization strategy depends on the primary optimization objective and on the data of the table.

6.2   Evaluation of the Strategies Using *simulated* data

To explore more deeply how our algorithm behaves with any kind of data, we randomly generate data sets to be used as the sensitive values on which we optimize the k-anonymization process. We add these sets as new sensitive columns of the *Adult Data Set*, all the original attributes being *QID*. To cover many possibilities of data distribution, we create sensitive attributes using 5, 10, 20, 50, 100, 200 and 500 possible values. For each new sensitive attribute, we generate sets of values of size 30162 following *Equivalent, Normal* (of parameters $\mu = 0$ and $\sigma = 0.5$) and *Geometric* distributions. Figure 5 presents the distributions of data in the generated sets for three new sensitive attributes. Each figure presents the number of occurrences of each possible value in the generated sets.

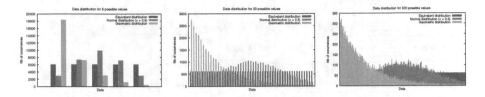

Fig. 5. Sensitive values distributions

In order to analyse the global behavior of the optimization algorithm, we conduct experiments for a large set of k values: k is between 2 and 5000. For each number of possible values among 5, 10, 20, 50, 100, 200 and 500, for each distribution among *Equivalent*, *Geometric* and *Normal* distributions, we evaluate the seven strategies by computing the alteration and the l_{div} and t_{close} values of the obtained k-anonymous tables (147 experiments) for k from 2 to 5000. We then compute the area under the curves (AUC) of alteration, l-diversity and t-closeness to rank the strategies considering these three values. Figure 6a summarizes the results we obtain, ranking the strategies considering data alteration, l-diversity and t-closeness from 1 (best) to 7 (worst). For more details, Fig. 6b shows the deviation from the mean as a color gradient (red is far less good than the mean, green is far better than the mean). At first look, it is clear that Strategy 5 gives the worst results for a large majority of sensitive data distribution and for almost all the criteria. Strategy 1, considering only the data alteration as optimization criterion, preserves data utility better than the other strategies but for most of the sensitive data distribution, it gives less good results for l-diversity and t-closeness. Strategy 2, considering data alteration first, then l-diversity, is among the better for minimizing data alteration but gives few improvements considering l-diversity and t-closeness. Strategy 3, considering l-diversity first, then data alteration is the best strategy to improve l-diversity and t-closeness among all the strategies. But, except Strategy 5, it is also the worst considering the data alteration. Strategy 6 alters the data almost as much as Strategy 3 with overall lower performance considering l-diversity and t-closeness. Strategy 4 that we identified as a good trade-off preserves data utility as well as Strategy 2 but improves l-diversity and t-closeness. Strategy 7 gives similar results to Strategy 4 with better l-diversity and t-closeness results for small data sets (5 or 10 possible values), but it alters more the data than Strategy 4. To conclude, Strategy 4 (we optimize with l-diversity and data alteration in the same time) is a good trade-off to maintain an acceptable data utility in the table while conserving a good diversity of the sensitive values, and so the privacy. Our results are consistent with the ones obtained on real data in Sect. 6.1.

		Equivalent distribution							Geometric distribution							Normal distribution						
		5	10	20	50	100	200	500	5	10	20	50	100	200	500	5	10	20	50	100	200	500
Strategy 1	Alteration	1	1	1	1	1	1	1	1	1	2	1	1	1	2	1	1	1	1	1	1	1
	l-diversity	6	7	5	6	6	6	5	5	6	3	5	2	4	5	6	4	5	6	5	6	4
	t-closeness	5	7	5	5	6	5	4	4	6	6	4	5	5	6	6	6	6	5	4	5	5
Strategy 2	Alteration	3	3	3	3	3	3	3	2	2	3	3	4	2	1	3	3	3	2	3	3	2
	l-diversity	7	6	6	5	4	5	3	4	6	3	5	3	3	4	4	6	4	4	4	2	5
	t-closeness	7	5	6	4	4	5	5	5	5	4	6	3	4	3	5	4	5	4	5	4	3
Strategy 3	Alteration	5	5	5	5	5	5	5	6	6	6	6	6	6	6	6	5	6	6	6	6	4
	l-diversity	4	2	1	2	2	2	1	2	2	1	1	1	1	1	2	1	1	2	1	1	1
	t-closeness	3	2	1	1	2	2	1	2	2	1	1	2	1	1	2	2	2	1	1	1	1
Strategy 4	Alteration	2	2	2	2	2	2	6	3	3	1	2	2	4	4	2	2	2	3	2	4	6
	l-diversity	5	5	4	4	5	4	6	6	7	4	4	5	2	3	5	5	6	3	3	4	6
	t-closeness	6	6	4	5	6	3	6	6	4	5	5	4	6	5	4	5	4	6	6	3	4
Strategy 5	Alteration	7	7	7	7	7	7	7	7	7	7	7	7	7	7	7	7	7	7	7	7	7
	l-diversity	1	1	7	7	7	7	7	7	4	7	7	7	7	7	7	7	7	7	7	7	7
	t-closeness	1	1	7	7	7	7	7	7	7	7	7	7	7	7	7	7	7	7	7	7	7
Strategy 6	Alteration	4	4	6	6	6	6	4	5	5	5	5	5	5	5	5	6	5	5	5	5	5
	l-diversity	2	3	2	1	1	1	2	1	1	6	3	6	6	6	1	2	2	5	6	3	3
	t-closeness	4	3	2	2	1	1	2	1	1	2	2	1	2	4	1	1	2	2	2	2	6
Strategy 7	Alteration	6	6	4	4	4	4	2	4	4	4	4	3	3	3	4	4	4	4	4	2	3
	l-diversity	3	4	3	3	3	3	4	3	4	2	2	4	5	2	3	3	3	2	2	5	2
	t-closeness	2	4	3	3	3	4	3	3	3	3	3	6	3	2	3	3	3	3	3	6	2

(a) Strategies ranking for *alteration*, *l*-diversity and *t*-closeness

(b) Color gradient based on the deviation from the mean

Fig. 6. Comparison of the optimization strategies for different data distributions

With these two sets of experiments, we show that we can improve the privacy of published data preserving data utility for further analyzes.

7   Conclusion

In this paper, we looked for *k*-anonymous tables which are good trade-offs between data alteration, *l*-diversity and *t*-closeness. Firstly, we detailed the optimization process to obtain *k*-anonymous tables that limits the information loss with respect to a metric and we justified our choice of $NLLM$ as information loss metric. Then, we expressed *l*-diversity and *t*-closeness as quality measures of a *k*-anonymous table (thanks to the l_{div} and t_{close} values). Next, we implemented seven optimization strategies to integrate into a greedy anonymization algorithm and that mix data alteration, *l*-diversity and *t*-closeness. By applying these strategies to the *Adult Data Set*, we noticed that guiding the choice of merging with the alteration and *l*-diversity in the same time is a good compromise to keep an interesting level of *l*-diversity and *t*-closeness while limiting the data alteration. Later in our research, we will investigate how the sensitive values' distribution can be used to adapt the optimization of the *k*-anonymization process to provide better quality of the data in the PPDP context. As future works, we now consider the optimization process itself since our greedy algorithm does not give guarantees on the optimality of the *k*-anonymous tables it produces.

References

1. Kenthapadi, K., Mironov, I., Thakurta, A.G.: Privacy-preserving data mining in industry. In: Proceedings of the Twelfth ACM International Conference on Web Search and Data Mining, WSDM 2019, New York, NY, USA, pp. 840–841. Association for Computing Machinery (2019)
2. Fung, B.C.M., Wang, K., Fu, A.W.-C., Yu, P.S.: Introduction to Privacy-Preserving Data Publishing: Concepts and Techniques, 1st edn. Chapman & Hall/CRC (2010)
3. Dwork, C.: Differential privacy: a survey of results. In: Agrawal, M., Du, D., Duan, Z., Li, A. (eds.) TAMC 2008. LNCS, vol. 4978, pp. 1–19. Springer, Heidelberg (2008). https://doi.org/10.1007/978-3-540-79228-4_1
4. Dalenius, T.: Finding a needle in a haystack or identifying anonymous census records. J. Off. Stat. **2**(3), 329 (1986)
5. Lambert, D.: Measures of disclosure risk and harm. J. Off. Stat.-Stockholm- **9**, 313 (1993)
6. Sweeney, L.: k-anonymity: a model for protecting privacy. Int. J. Uncert. Fuzzin. Knowl.-Based Syst. **10**(05), 557–570 (2002)
7. Samarati, P.: Protecting respondents identities in microdata release. IEEE Trans. Knowl. Data Eng. **13**(6), 1010–1027 (2001)
8. Machanavajjhala, A., Kifer, D., Gehrke, J., Venkitasubramaniam, M.: l-diversity: privacy beyond k-anonymity. ACM Trans. Knowl. Discovery Data (TKDD) **1**(1), 3-es (2007)
9. Li, N., Li, T., Venkatasubramanian, S.: t-closeness: privacy beyond k-anonymity and l-diversity. In: 2007 IEEE 23rd International Conference on Data Engineering, pp. 106–115. IEEE (2007)
10. Mauger, C., Le Mahec, G., Dequen, G.: Modeling and evaluation of k-anonymization metrics. In: PrivacyPreserving Artificial Intelligence Workshop of AAAI 2020 (2020)
11. Bender, M.A., Farach-Colton, M., Pemmasani, G., Skiena, S., Sumazin, P.: Lowest common ancestors in trees and directed acyclic graphs. J. Algorithms **57**(2), 75–94 (2005)
12. Li, J., Wong, R.C.-W., Fu, A.W.-C., Pei, J.: Achieving k-anonymity by clustering in attribute hierarchical structures, pp. 405–416 (2006)
13. Xu, J., Wang, W., Pei, J., Wang, X., Shi, B., Fu, A.W.-C.: Utility-based anonymization using local recoding. In: Proceedings of the 12th ACM SIGKDD International Conference on Knowledge Discovery and Data Mining, KDD 2006, New York, NY, USA, pp. 785–790. ACM (2006)
14. Byun, J.-W., Kamra, A., Bertino, E., Li, N.: Efficient *k*-anonymization using clustering techniques. In: Kotagiri, R., Krishna, P.R., Mohania, M., Nantajeewarawat, E. (eds.) DASFAA 2007. LNCS, vol. 4443, pp. 188–200. Springer, Heidelberg (2007). https://doi.org/10.1007/978-3-540-71703-4_18

15. UCIrvine. Machine Learning Repository (1987). https://archive.ics.uci.edu/ml/index.php. Accessed June 2019
16. Meyerson, A., Williams, R.: On the complexity of optimal k-anonymity. In: Proceedings of the Twenty-third ACM SIGMOD-SIGACT-SIGART Symposium on Principles of Database Systems, PODS 2004, New York, NY, USA, pp. 223–228. ACM (2004)
17. Xiao, X., Yi, K., Tao, Y.: The hardness and approximation algorithms for l-diversity. In: Proceedings of the 13th International Conference on Extending Database Technology, pp. 135–146 (2010)
18. Liang, H., Yuan, H.: On the complexity of t-closeness anonymization and related problems. In: Meng, W., Feng, L., Bressan, S., Winiwarter, W., Song, W. (eds.) DASFAA 2013. LNCS, vol. 7825, pp. 331–345. Springer, Heidelberg (2013). https://doi.org/10.1007/978-3-642-37487-6_26
19. LeFevre, K., DeWitt, D.J., Ramakrishnan, R.: Mondrian multidimensional k-anonymity. In 22nd International Conference on Data Engineering (ICDE 2006), pp. 25–25, April 2006
20. Cao, J., Karras, P., Kalnis, P., Tan, K.-L.: Sabre: a sensitive attribute bucketization and redistribution framework for t-closeness. VLDB J. **20**(1), 59–81 (2011)

ArchiveSafe: Mass-Leakage-Resistant Storage from Proof-of-Work

Moe Sabry[1][✉], Reza Samavi[2][✉], and Douglas Stebila[3][✉]

[1] McMaster University, Hamilton, Canada
alym2@mcmaster.ca
[2] Vector Institute, Ryerson University, Toronto, Canada
samavi@ryerson.ca
[3] University of Waterloo, Waterloo, Canada
dstebila@uwaterloo.ca

Abstract. Data breaches—mass leakage of stored information—are a major security concern. Encryption can provide confidentiality, but encryption depends on a key which, if compromised, allows the attacker to decrypt everything, effectively instantly. Security of encrypted data thus becomes a question of protecting the encryption keys. In this paper, we propose using *keyless encryption* to construct a *mass leakage resistant archiving system*, where decryption of a file is only possible after the requester, whether an authorized user or an adversary, completes a *proof of work* in the form of solving a cryptographic puzzle. This proposal is geared towards protection of infrequently-accessed *archival data*, where any one file may not require too much work to decrypt, decryption of a large number of files—mass leakage—becomes increasingly expensive for an attacker. We present a prototype implementation realized as a user-space file system driver for Linux. We report experimental results of system behaviour under different file sizes and puzzle difficulty levels. Our keyless encryption technique can be added as a layer *on top of* traditional encryption: together they provide strong security against adversaries without the key and resistance against mass decryption by an attacker.

1 Introduction

Attacks on information systems have become increasingly common. Whatever the attack vector, a frequent outcome is a *data breach*, in which a large volume of sensitive information is stolen from the victim organization. Archival data— stored indefinitely but not regularly accessed—has been targeted in many data breaches [4,14,18], leading to loss of privacy, loss of reputation, business setbacks, and costly remediation.

Modern IT security protection techniques focus on *defense-in-depth*, one component of which is encryption of data at rest to support confidentiality. However, encryption, even when implemented using secure, carefully implemented algorithms, is typically all-or-nothing: if the key is secure, the attacker learn virtually

© Springer Nature Switzerland AG 2020
J. Garcia-Alfaro et al. (Eds.): DPM 2020/CBT 2020, LNCS 12484, pp. 89–107, 2020.
https://doi.org/10.1007/978-3-030-66172-4_6

nothing, and the attack cannot succeed, but once the key is compromised, the attacker can decrypt everything, with minimal overhead.

Hardware-assisted cryptography, such as hardware security modules (HSMs), trusted computing, or secure enclaves like Intel SGX[1] or ARM TrustZone[2] may prevent keys from leaking if decryption is only ever done inside a trusted module, but many IT systems remain software-only without use of these technologies.

Scenario and Goals. Against these types of threats, we aim develop a *mass leakage resistant archiving system* with the goal of enhancing defense-in-depth for encryption. We aim to preserve confidentiality even in the presence of an adversary with full access to the system, including ciphertexts and decryption keys. While no system can provide full cryptographic security in the face of such a well-informed adversary, our goal is to increase the economic cost of *mass leakage*, which for our purposes is defined as an adversary obtaining the plaintexts of a large number of files or database records, not just one.

Unlike most applications of cryptography, we do not aim to achieve a difference in work factor between honest parties and adversaries. Rather, we assume that honest parties and adversaries have different *goals*, and we aim to change the economics of data breaches by achieving a difference in the cost of honest parties and adversaries achieving their goals. In our scenario, honest parties need to store a large number of files, but only access a small number of them. Consider for example a tax agency: after processing millions of citizens' tax returns each year, those files must be stored for several years in case an audit or further analysis is required, but only a small fraction of those records will end up actually being pulled for analysis. In contrast, an adversary breaching the tax agency's records may want to read a large number of files to identify good candidates for identity theft or other criminal actions.

1.1 Contributions

We design a system, called *ArchiveSafe*, where access to a resource is only possible after the requester—whether an honest user on adversary—has expended sufficient computational effort, in the form of solving a "moderately hard" proof-of-work or cryptographic puzzle [10]. Since we will not rely on the access control system nor any keys to be uncompromised, the decryption operation itself must be tied to the cryptographic puzzle. In our approach, while a proper cryptographic key is used to encrypt a file, the encryption key is not stored, even for legitimate users. Instead, the key is wrapped in a proof-of-work-based encryption scheme with a desired difficulty level, and all users—adversarial or honest—must perform the proof-of-work to recover the key and then decrypt the file.

Our main technical tool for building of ArchiveSafe is a new cryptographic primitive that we call *difficulty-based keyless encryption* (DBKE), which is an encryption scheme that does not make use of a stored key. We give a generic

---

[1] https://software.intel.com/en-us/sgx.
[2] https://developer.arm.com/ip-products/security-ip/trustzone.

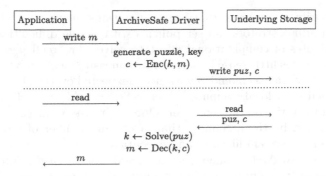

Fig. 1. High-level overview of ArchiveSafe, showing a write followed by a read.

construction for DBKE from a standard symmetric encryption scheme and a new tool called *difficulty-based keyless key wrap*, which wraps the symmetric encryption key in an encapsulation that can only be unwrapped by performing a sufficiently high number of operations, as in a proof-of-work scheme. Difficulty-based keyless key wrap can be achieved from many types of cryptographic puzzles, and we show one example based on hash function partial pre-image finding [11,12]. One interesting feature of using this form of hash-based puzzle, which to our knowledge is a novel observation on hash-based puzzles, is that the puzzle and ciphertext can be *degraded*—i.e., turned into a harder one—essentially for free. We use the reductionist security methodology to formalize the syntax and security properties of difficulty-based keyless encryption and keyless key wrap and show that our hash-based construction achieves these properties.

Figure 1 gives a high-level overview of how an application interacts with the ArchiveSafe system. The two main operations performed by the ArchiveSafe system are (i) creating a puzzle and encrypting during writes, and (ii) solving the puzzle and decrypting during reads. ArchiveSafe could be used in a variety of data storage architectures: on a local computer; on a file server; or in a cloud architecture. In a file server or cloud scenario, an IT system may be set up so the file server enforces that all files are protected by ArchiveSafe during writes by centralizing puzzle creation and encryption, but leaves puzzle solving and decryption to clients. Since puzzle creation and encryption in our system is cheap, this avoids bottlenecks on the file server. Individual client applications occasionally reading a small number of files have to do a moderate, but not prohibitive, amount of work to solve the puzzle to obtain the key to decrypt.

We build a prototype implementation showing the use of ArchiveSafe on a local computer. Our prototype is implemented as a filesystem-in-userspace (FUSE) driver on Linux. A FUSE driver can be used to intercept I/O operations in certain directories (mount points) before reading/writing to disk. This allows us to implement ArchiveSafe in a manner that is transparent to the application, as well as transparent to the underlying storage mechanism, which could be a local disk (with normal disk encryption enabled or not), or a network share mounted locally. We validate the performance of our prototype implementation, focusing primarily on ensuring that write operations incur minimal overhead. (Since system administrators can set policies with puzzle difficulties requiring seconds or minutes of computational effort to solve, slow read performance is *intended*, and there is little sense in performance measurements on reads, beyond checking that they scale as intended with no unexpected overhead.) We envision that, when used on a local computer, ArchiveSafe would be applied only to a subset of the directories on the computer. One might use ArchiveSafe to protect documents created by the user more than a certain number of days ago, but would not use it on system libraries and executables.

We highlight that ArchiveSafe is meant to add *defense-in-depth* to confidentiality: one would typically not rely on ArchiveSafe alone, but combine it with traditional encrypted file system or database encryption. In this combination, traditional encryption using strong algorithms and keys, provides a high level of security if the keys are not compromised, but we still have the difficulty-based keyless encryption of ArchiveSafe as a bulwark if the keys are compromised. To succeed under this setup, the adversary must compromise the traditional encryption keys in addition to solving a large number of DBKE puzzles corresponding to the files in the archive.

1.2   Related Work

Filesystem Encryption. Blaze [6] introduced the Cryptographic File System (CFS). CFS uses a different key for each directory, and the user is required to enter the key in every session to access the directory and its contents. Subsequent proposals include the Transparent Cryptographic File System (TCFS) [7], Cryptfs [24] and Ncryptfs [23]. In recent years, encrypted filesystems have become widespread, and all major operating systems provide implementations, often enabled by default (FileVault on Apple's macOS[3], BitLocker on Microsoft Windows[4], and a range of options on Linux such as Linux Unified Key Setup (LUKS)[5]). The common practice in these technologies is to use a single master key from which multiple keys are derived per-file, per-directory, or per-sector; the master key is usually stored on the device itself, encrypted under the user's password. Once the user has logged in, the filesystem transparently and automatically decrypts files.

Over the past decade, there has been much research on encrypted databases (e.g., [13,15,16]) that retain some functionality for legitimate users, for example using order-preserving encryption so that sorting a column of ciphertexts yields approximately the same order as if the plaintexts were sorted. This increased functionality comes at the cost of information leakage, and there is an extensive debate in the literature about these techniques.

---

[3] https://support.apple.com/en-ca/HT204837.

[4] https://docs.microsoft.com/en-us/windows/security/information-protection/ bitlocker/bitlocker-overview.

[5] https://guardianproject.info/archive/luks/.

Proof-of-Work Systems. Dwork and Naor [10] introduced client puzzles to control junk email: recipients would only accept emails if the sender was able to solve a puzzle. It should be "moderately hard" for the sender to solve the puzzle, but easy for recipient to check whether a solution is valid. This was the first example of a proof-of-work system, which in general grants access to a resource dependent on the requester being able to demonstrate proof that they have performed some work, typically in the form of solving a puzzle. Client puzzles were for many years suggested as a means to prevent denial of service attacks in a range of contexts [2,8,12,17,20,22], but have seen renewed interest as a building block for cryptocurrencies and blockchains. Client puzzles are generally classified either based on their limiting factors in solving the puzzle (CPU-bound versus memory-bound) or based on whether the operations required to solve the puzzle is parallelizable. The simplest CPU-bound puzzles are based on cryptographic hash functions, such as: finding a preimage of a hash given a hint (e.g., a part of the preimage) [11,12]; or finding an input whose hash starts with a certain number of zero bits [3]. Non-parallelizable CPU-bound puzzles often rely on a number of theoretical approaches. For example, [19] uses repeated squaring modulo an RSA modulus. Memory-bound puzzles [1,9] use techniques for which the best known solving algorithm involves a large number of memory accesses; it is argued that memory access time varies less than CPU speed between small and large computing platforms, and that building customized hardware is more expensive for memory-bound puzzles.

Proof-of-Work Systems for Confidentiality. In [19], time-lock encryption was proposed as a way of "sending information into the future", and focused specifically on hiding keys or data in a proof-of-work system that had a predictable wall-clock time for solving, thus focusing on puzzles for which the best known solving algorithm is inherently sequential. Vargas et al. [21] designed a database encryption system called "Dragchute" based on time-lock encryption, aiming to provide both confidentiality and the ability to demonstrate compliance with retention laws. Each ciphertext in this system is accompanied by an authentication tag which contains a non-interactive zero-knowledge proof. Solving the puzzle will yield a valid decryption key for the ciphertext; moreover, the proof can be checked much more efficiently than the full work required to solve and decrypt the ciphertext. A simpler database encryption scheme relying on hash-based client puzzles, without any efficient verification of well-formedness, was proposed by Moghimifar [13].

2   Requirements

In this section, we discuss the functionality and security requirements for a mass leakage resistant archiving system, which informs our construction and evaluation in subsequent sections.

2.1 Design Criteria

Confidentiality in the Face of Compromised Keys. The system should achieve some level of confidentiality even if all stored keys are compromised. This means we assume that an adversary can learn a symmetric key or a private key corresponding to a public key stored for later use in decrypting a ciphertext, even if the key is stored in a separate key management service, trusted computing or secure enclave environment, or separate tamper-resistant device.

Cooperation with Traditional Encryption. It should be possible to use the system in conjunction with the traditional encryption mechanisms applied to storage systems (folder/disk encryption, database encryption, etc.), so that strong confidentiality is achieved if keys are not compromised, but some confidentiality is retained in the face of compromised keys.

Reliance on Industry Standard Cryptographic Algorithms. Deployed IT systems should rely only on well-vetted, standardized cryptographic algorithms. But all such algorithms for achieving confidentiality—public key or symmetric—require a secret key, seemingly conflicting with the first design criteria of confidentiality in the face of compromised keys. Our construction builds a mechanism for confidentiality without keys while still relying on standard cryptographic algorithms like AES for symmetric encryption: while a proper cryptographic key is used to encrypt data, that key is not kept, even by authorized users. Instead, the key is wrapped in a proof-of-work-based encryption scheme with a desired difficulty level, and users must solve the proof-of-work to recover the key and then decrypt the data. We introduce difficulty-based keyless encryption in Sect. 3 which formalizes this idea and generically construct it from standard cryptographic algorithms such as AES and Argon2.

Imposing a Significant Cost to Access a Large Number of Files While Maintaining Acceptable Cost to Access One File. Since we do not have a key that gives honest users an advantage over the adversary, we should look at things from the viewpoint of typical honest behaviour—periodically accessing a small number of files—versus adversary behaviour—accessing a large number of files in a data breach. Proof-of-work and related techniques have long been used to achieve security goals from that viewpoint, whether in password hardening or client puzzles for denial of service resistance.

Customizing File Access Cost. It should be possible for a system administrator or user to control the cost incurred by the adversary or honest user for accessing a file. This may be set as a system-wide policy or a file-by-file basis, depending on the desired access control paradigm. This is achieved in our system by varying the difficulty level of the puzzle wrapping the decryption key.

A related design criteria is the ability to customize file access cost *over time*. Demand for access to records may change over time; for example, records older than 5 years may be accessed much less frequently than more recent records. Our system allows the file access cost to be increased with minimal effort, through a process we call *puzzle degradation*, that could be performed as part of regular system maintenance. This is a novel feature available from some types of puzzle constructions but not others, and in particular not from the number-theoretic repeated squaring non-parallelizable constructions used in time-lock puzzles [19] and the Dragchute database encryption system [21].

2.2   Choice of Puzzle

One of the major design decisions for our system is which type of puzzles to use: sequential versus parallelizable, and CPU-bound versus memory-bound.

As our design criteria focus on mass leakage adversaries trying to decrypt *many* files, and since we think of cost in a general economic sense, we do not have to restrict to proof-of-work mechanisms that are sequential/non-parallelizable. Concerned with an adversary trying to decrypt many files who has parallel computing resources available to them, it does not matter whether they choose to deploy their parallel resources to sequentially decrypt each file quickly or in parallel decrypt many files more slowly. Overall, they will decrypt the same number of files with the same resources. We also need not worry about the variability of puzzle solving time for individual instances, only the expected puzzle solving time for many instances. These design choices are, for example, significantly different from those of the Dragchute system for database confidentiality and integrity from proof-of-work. Moreover, parallelization permits honest users to reduce the latency in occasional access of files by taking advantage of short, on-demand use of cloud servers (see Table 3).

Whereas sequential versus parallelizable puzzles is a qualitative choice for our scenario, CPU-bound versus memory-bound is a quantitative choice with respect to the economic cost. To achieve a given dollar-cost-for-adversary, it is possible to pick appropriate parameters for both CPU-bound and memory-bound puzzles under appropriate cost and puzzle-solving assumptions. So, a priori, either can be used in our constructions. For our prototype we choose simple hash-based CPU-bound puzzles because puzzle creation is cheaper (thereby achieving extremely low overhead on write operations) and because they allow us to obtain novel useful functionality such as puzzle degradation (Sect. 3.3), but with the hash function being Argon2 which is designed to be resistant to GPU and ASIC optimization. Picking appropriate difficulty levels for puzzles is something an adopter must do as a function of the tolerable cost for honest users to access data, the perceived risk of a data breach, and the anticipated value of the information to an adversary. We do not aim to study such economic calculations exhaustively, but we provide one worked example in Sect. 4.4 and Table 3.

2.3   Threat Model

ArchiveSafe is a software system with one target asset, the data files. The security goal for the target asset is confidentiality. As shown in Fig. 1, information flows from the user application through the ArchiveSafe driver to the underlying storage during writes, and in the reverse direction during reads.

$\text{Exp}_{\Delta,d}^{\text{db-ind}}(\mathcal{A})$:	$\text{Exp}_{\Pi}^{\text{ind}}(\mathcal{A})$:	$\text{Exp}_{\Sigma,d}^{\text{key-ind}}(\mathcal{A})$:
1. $(m_0, m_1, st) \leftarrow_\$ \mathcal{A}(1^d)$	1. $(m_0, m_1, st) \leftarrow_\$ \mathcal{A}()$	1. $(k_0, w) \leftarrow_\$ \Sigma.\text{Wrap}()$
2. $b \leftarrow_\$ \{0,1\}$	2. $k \leftarrow_\$ \mathcal{K}$	2. $k_1 \leftarrow_\$ \mathcal{K}$
3. $c \leftarrow_\$ \Delta.\text{Enc}(d, m_b)$	3. $b \leftarrow_\$ \{0,1\}$	3. $b \leftarrow_\$ \{0,1\}$
4. $b' \leftarrow_\$ \mathcal{A}(c, st)$	4. $c \leftarrow_\$ \Pi.\text{Enc}(k, m_b)$	4. $b' \leftarrow_\$ \mathcal{A}(w, k_0, k_1)$
5. return $(b' = b)$	5. $b' \leftarrow_\$ \mathcal{A}(c, st)$	5. return $(b' = b)$
	6. return $(b' = b)$	

Fig. 2. Security experiments for (*left*) indistinguishability of difficulty-based keyless encryption scheme Δ at difficulty level d; (*centre*) one-time indistinguishability of symmetric encryption scheme Π; and (*right*) indistinguishability of difficulty-based keyless key wrap scheme Σ with keyspace $\mathcal{K}$ and difficulty level d.

An adversary could access the system either via the same mechanism as an honest user application (i.e., mediated by the ArchiveSafe driver), or may have direct access to the underlying storage. We aim to achieve confidentiality against a strong adversary that can bypass the ArchiveSafe driver during read operations (e.g., because they are untrusted server administrators, or because they have compromised the kernel using privilege escalation), or who can directly read from the underlying storage (e.g., an untrusted cloud storage provider, or physical theft of a hard drive). We do not consider in our threat model an adversary who undermines the write operation to intercept data during a write operation or who prevents the ArchiveSafe technique from being applied when saving files. We assume operations by honest parties are performed on a trusted and uncompromised system that faithfully deletes keys from memory once an operation is completed.

3   Difficulty-Based Keyless Encryption

A difficulty-based key encryption scheme is similar to a symmetric encryption scheme, except that no secret key is kept for use between the encryption and decryption algorithm.

Definition 1 (Difficulty-Based Keyless Encryption). *A difficulty-based keyless encryption (DBKE) scheme Δ for a message space $\mathcal{M}$ with maximum difficulty $D \in \mathbb{N}$ consists of two algorithms:*

- *$\Delta.\text{Enc}(d, m) \s\to c$: A (probabilistic) encryption algorithm that takes as input difficulty level $d \leq D$ and message m and outputs ciphertext c.*
- *$\Delta.\text{Dec}(c) \to m'$: A deterministic decryption algorithm that takes as input ciphertext c and outputs message m' or an error $\perp \notin \mathcal{M}$.*

A DBKE Δ is *correct* if, for all messages $m \in \mathcal{M}$ and all difficulty levels $d \leq D$, we have that $\Pr[\Delta.\text{Dec}(\Delta.\text{Enc}(d, m)) = m] = 1$, where the probability is taken over the randomness of $\Delta.\text{Enc}$.

The desired security property for a DBKE is semantic security in the form of ciphertext indistinguishability. Since there is no persistent secret key, there is no need to consider security notions incorporating chosen plaintext or chosen ciphertext attacks: each plaintext is protected by independent randomness. The security experiment $\mathrm{Exp}_{\Delta,d}^{\mathrm{db\text{-}ind}}(\mathcal{A})$ for an adversary $\mathcal{A}$ trying to break indistinguishability of DBKE scheme Δ at difficulty level d is shown in Fig. 2. We define the advantage of such an adversary in the security experiment as $\mathrm{Adv}_{\Delta,d}^{\mathrm{db\text{-}ind}}(\mathcal{A}) = \left| 2 \cdot \Pr\left[\mathrm{Exp}_{\Delta,d}^{\mathrm{db\text{-}ind}}(\mathcal{A}) \Rightarrow \mathbf{true}\right] - 1 \right|$. Useful forms of $\mathrm{Adv}_{\Delta,d}^{\mathrm{db\text{-}ind}}(\mathcal{A})$ will relate the amount of work done by the adversary, the difficulty level, and the adversary's success probability.

3.1 Generic Construction of DBKE

Our main construction of DBKE, as shown in Fig. 3, generically combines a traditional symmetric encryption scheme with a "keyless key wrap", which is difficulty-based form of key wrapping: there is no "master key" wrapping the session key, instead the session key is recovered via some difficulty-based operation. In this subsection we present the generic building blocks we use to construct DBKE. In Sect. 3.2 we show how to instantiate the keyless key wrap.

Definition 2 (Symmetric encryption scheme). *A symmetric encryption scheme Π with secret key space $\mathcal{K} = \{0,1\}^\lambda$ and message space $\mathcal{M}$ consists of two algorithms:*

- *$\Pi.\mathrm{Enc}(k, m) \mathrel{\$}\to c$: A (probabilistic) encryption algorithm that takes as input key $k \in \mathcal{K}$ and message $m \in \mathcal{M}$ and outputs ciphertext c.*
- *$\Pi.\mathrm{Dec}(k, c) \to m'$: A deterministic decryption algorithm that takes as input key $k \in \mathcal{K}$ and ciphertext c and outputs message $m' \in \mathcal{M}$ or an error $\perp \notin \mathcal{M}$.*

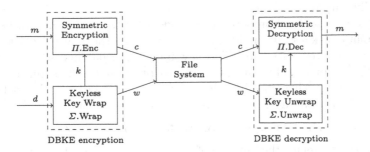

Fig. 3. Architectural diagram for generic construction of a difficulty-based keyless encryption scheme $\Gamma = \Gamma[\Pi, \Sigma]$ from a difficulty-based keyless key wrap scheme Σ and a symmetric encryption scheme Π.

$\Gamma.\text{Enc}(d, m)$:	$\Gamma.\text{Dec}((c, w))$:
1. $(k, w) \leftarrow_\$ \Sigma.\text{Wrap}(d)$	1. $k' \leftarrow \Sigma.\text{Unwrap}(w)$
2. $c \leftarrow_\$ \Pi.\text{Enc}(k, m)$	2. $m' \leftarrow \Pi.\text{Dec}(k', c')$
3. return (c, w)	3. return m'

Fig. 4. Generic construction of a difficulty-based keyless encryption scheme $\Gamma = \Gamma[\Pi, \Sigma]$ from a difficulty-based keyless key wrap scheme Σ and a symmetric encryption scheme Π.

Correctness is defined in the obvious way. For our purposes, a sufficient security property will be one-time semantic security, in the form of ciphertext indistinguishability. As above, we will not need to consider security notions incorporating chosen plaintext or chosen ciphertext attacks, since our system will use a key only once. The security experiment $\text{Exp}_\Pi^{\text{ind}}(\mathcal{A})$ for an adversary $\mathcal{A}$ trying to break indistinguishability of symmetric encryption scheme Π is shown in Fig. 2. We define the advantage of such an adversary in the security experiment as $\text{Adv}_\Pi^{\text{ind}}(\mathcal{A}) = \left| 2 \cdot \Pr \left[\text{Exp}_\Pi^{\text{ind}}(\mathcal{A}) \Rightarrow \texttt{true} \right] - 1 \right|$.

The second building block for our construction is a keyless key wrap scheme.

Definition 3 (Keyless key wrap scheme). *A keyless key wrap scheme Σ for a key space $\mathcal{K} = \{0, 1\}^\lambda$ with maximum difficulty level $D \in \mathbb{N}$ consists of two algorithms:*

- *$\Sigma.\text{Wrap}(d) \; \$\rightarrow (k, w)$: A (probabilistic) key wrapping algorithm that takes as input difficulty level $d \leq D$ and outputs key $k \in \mathcal{K}$ and wrapped key w.*
- *$\Sigma.\text{Unwrap}(w) \rightarrow k'$: A deterministic key unwrapping algorithm that takes as input wrapped key w and outputs key $k \in \mathcal{K}$ or an error $\bot \notin \mathcal{K}$.*

Correctness, again, is defined in the natural way: applying Unwrap to a wrapped key w output by Wrap should yield, with certainty, the same key k as originally output by Wrap.

The desirable security property for a keyless key wrap scheme will be indistinguishability of keys: given the wrapped key, can the adversary learn anything about the key within it? The key indistinguishability security experiment $\text{Exp}_{\Sigma, d}^{\text{key-ind}}$ for an adversary $\mathcal{A}$ trying to break key indistinguishability of a keyless key wrap scheme at difficulty level d is shown in Fig. 2. We define the advantage of such an adversary in the security experiment as $\text{Adv}_{\Sigma, d}^{\text{key-ind}}(\mathcal{A}) = \left| 2 \cdot \Pr \left[\text{Exp}_{\Sigma, d}^{\text{key-ind}}(\mathcal{A}) \Rightarrow \texttt{true} \right] - 1 \right|$. As with DBKE security, useful forms of $\text{Adv}_{\Sigma, d}^{\text{key-ind}}(\mathcal{A})$ will relate the amount of work done by the adversary, the difficulty level, and the adversary's success probability.

As noted above, we generically construct a difficulty-based keyless encryption scheme by combining a traditional symmetric encryption scheme with a keyless key wrap scheme, as outlined in Fig. 3. Let Π be a symmetric encryption scheme with key space $\mathcal{K} = \{0, 1\}^\lambda$, and let Σ be a keyless key wrap scheme for key space $\mathcal{K}$ with maximum difficulty level D. Construct the difficulty-based keyless encryption scheme $\Gamma[\Pi, \Sigma]$ from Π and Σ as outlined in Fig. 3 and specified in Fig. 4.

Our DBKE scheme Γ is secure, in the sense of Fig. 2, under the assumption that the building blocks are secure. The proof follows from a straightforward game-hopping argument; details are omitted due to space constraints and appear in the full version.[6]

Theorem 1. *If Σ is a key-indistinguishable difficulty-based keyless key wrap scheme, and Π is a one-time indistinguishable symmetric encryption scheme, then $\Gamma = \Gamma[\Pi, \Sigma]$ is a secure difficulty-based keyless encryption scheme. More precisely, let $d \leq D$ and let $\mathcal{A}$ be a probabilistic algorithm. Then there exists algorithms $\mathcal{B}_1$ and $\mathcal{B}_2$, such that $\mathrm{Adv}_{\Gamma,d}^{\mathsf{db\text{-}ind}}(\mathcal{A}) \leq 2 \cdot \mathrm{Adv}_{\Sigma,d}^{\mathsf{key\text{-}ind}}(\mathcal{B}_1^{\mathcal{A}}) + \mathrm{Adv}_{\Pi}^{\mathsf{ind}}(\mathcal{B}_2^{\mathcal{A}})$. Moreover, $\mathcal{B}_1^{\mathcal{A}}$ and $\mathcal{B}_2^{\mathcal{A}}$ have about the same runtime as $\mathcal{A}$.*

3.2 Hash-Based Construction of Difficulty-Based Keyless Key Wrap

We now show how to construct our difficulty-based keyless key wrap using a hash-based puzzle. The idea is simple: a random seed r is chosen, and the key and a checksum of the seed are derived from the seed using hash functions. The wrapped key consists of the checksum of the seed and the seed with *some of its bits removed*; the number of bits removed corresponds to the difficulty of the puzzle. This is similar to the sub-puzzle construction of Juels and Brainard [12] or partial inversion proof of work by Jakobsson and Juels [11]. Such a puzzle is solved by trying all possibilities for the missing bits, in any order and with or without using parallelization.

In particular, let $\lambda \in \mathbb{N}$, and let $H_1, H_2 : \{0,1\}^\lambda \to \{0,1\}^\lambda$ be independent hash functions. Define keyless key wrap scheme $P = P[H_1, H_2]$ as in Fig. 5 (left). The notation $r[\lambda - d : \lambda]$ on line 2 of P.Wrap denotes taking the substring of r corresponding to indices $\lambda - d$ up to λ, removing the first d bits of r.

P.Wrap(d):	P.Unwrap$(w = (h, \bar{r}))$:	$\Gamma[\Pi, P]$.Degrade$(\hat{c}, d')$:
1. $r \leftarrow\!\!\$ \{0,1\}^\lambda$	1. $d \leftarrow \lambda - |\bar{r}|$	1. parse $\hat{c}$ as $(c, w = (h, \bar{r}))$
2. $\bar{r} \leftarrow r[\lambda - d : \lambda]$	2. for $i \in \{0,1\}^d$:	2. $d \leftarrow \lambda - |\bar{r}|$
3. $h \leftarrow H_1(r)$	3. $r' \leftarrow i\|\bar{r}$	3. abort if $d' < d$
4. $k \leftarrow H_2(r)$	4. $h' \leftarrow H_1(r')$	4. $\bar{r}' \leftarrow \bar{r}[d' - d : |\bar{r}|]$
5. $w \leftarrow (h, \bar{r})$	5. if $h' = h$:	5. $w' \leftarrow (h, \bar{r}')$
6. return (k, w)	6. $k \leftarrow H_2(r')$	6. return (c, w')
	7. return k	
	8. return $\perp$	

Fig. 5. *Left:* Construction of a hash-based keyless key wrap scheme $P = P[H_1, H_2]$ from hash functions H_1, H_2. *Right:* Degradation algorithm for DBKE $\Gamma = \Gamma[\Pi, P]$ constructed using generic construction Γ of Fig. 4 using hash-based keyless key wrap scheme P of left.

---

[6] https://arxiv.org/abs/2009.00086.

The following theorem shows the key indistinguishability security of our hash-based keyless key wrap scheme P in the random oracle model. The proof consists of a query counting argument in the random oracle model; details are omitted due to space constraints and appear in the full version.

Theorem 2. *Let H_1 and H_2 be random oracles. Let $\lambda \in \mathbb{N}$ and let $d \leq \lambda$. Let $P = P[H_1, H_2]$ be the keyless key wrap scheme from Fig. 5 (left). Let $\mathcal{A}$ be an adversary in key indistinguishability experiment against P which makes q_1 and q_2 distinct queries to its H_1 and H_2 random oracles, respectively. Then $\mathrm{Adv}_{P,d}^{\mathrm{key\text{-}ind}}(\mathcal{A}) \leq \frac{q_1}{2^{d-1}} + \frac{2}{2^d - q_1}$.*

Puzzle Granularity. The partial pre-image puzzle construction used in Fig. 5 does not allow for fine-grained control of difficulty: removing each additional bit increases the expected computational cost by a factor of 2. Higher granularity can be achieved similar to how the puzzle difficulty in Bitcoin is set, by giving a hint that narrows the range of data from 2^d to some smaller subset.

3.3   Puzzle Degradation

We now introduce an additional feature of difficulty-based keyless encryption that emerges naturally from our hash-based keyless key wrap construction: *puzzle degradation*. Abstractly, puzzle degradation is a process that takes a DBKE ciphertext and increases the difficulty of decrypting it, preferably without needing to decrypt and then re-encrypt at a higher difficulty level.

In the context of the ArchiveSafe long-term archiving system, this may be used to gradually increase the difficulty of files that have not been accessed for a certain period of time. For example, a monthly maintenance process could apply degradation to stored files to gradually increase the cost (to both an attacker and an honest party) of accessing increasingly older files.

The DBKE system Δ from Definition 1 is augmented with the algorithm:

– $\Delta.\mathrm{Degrade}(c, d') \twoheadrightarrow c'$: A (possibly probabilistic) algorithm that takes as input ciphertext c and target difficulty level $d' \leq D$, and outputs updated ciphertext c'.

Correctness is extended to demand that a ciphertext output by $\Delta.\mathrm{Enc}$ then degraded any number of times is still correctly decrypted by $\Delta.\mathrm{Dec}$ (although decryption may take longer).

Security with the degraded algorithm included should mean, intuitively, that a ciphertext degraded any number of times can be decrypted only using the required amount of work at the new difficulty level.

We capture both correctness and security of degradation formally by demanding that, for all $d \leq d' \leq D$ and all $m \in \mathcal{M}$, we have that $\Delta.\mathrm{Enc}(d', m) \equiv \Delta.\mathrm{Degrade}(d', \Delta.\mathrm{Enc}(d, m))$; in other words: the distribution of ciphertexts produced by encrypting at difficulty d' is identical to the distribution of ciphertexts produced by encrypting at difficulty d and then degrading to difficulty d'.

We can achieve degradation in DBKE $\Gamma = \Gamma[\Pi, P]$ constructed from our hash-based keyless key wrap P in a trivial way: by removing $(d' - d)$ more bits from the puzzle hint $\bar{r}$. This clearly requires no decryption and re-encryption, only a constant-time edit to the metadata stored containing the wrapped key. The procedure Γ.Degrade is stated in Fig. 5 (*right*). Degraded ciphertexts are identically distributed to ciphertexts freshly generated at the target difficulty level, as removing additional bits of the partial seed $\bar{r}$ is associative. An adversary who possess a copy of the metadata from an earlier version of the archive prior to degradation can solve puzzles and decrypt at the earlier, non-degraded difficulty level.

3.4   Additional Considerations

Outsourcing Puzzle Solving. The generic DBKE construction Γ of Fig. 4 allows the key unwrapping and ciphertext decryption to be done separately, so the expensive key unwrapping could be outsourced to a cloud server. In the example of the hash-based keyless key wrap scheme P of Fig. 5, the user could give the wrapped key $w = (h, \bar{r})$ to the cloud server who unwraps and returns the key k, which the user then locally uses to decrypt the ciphertext c.

This does mean that the cloud server learns the encryption key k. However, this can be avoided with the following adaption to the construction P of Fig. 5. During wrapping, the algorithm generates an additional *salt* value $s \leftarrow_\$ \{0, 1\}^\lambda$ and computes $k \leftarrow H_2(r\|s)$; s is stored in the wrapped key w. When outsourcing the unwrapping to the cloud server, the user only sends h and $\bar{r}$, but not s. The cloud server is still able to use the checksum h with the partial seed $\bar{r}$ to recover the full seed r, but lacks the salt s and thus the cloud server alone cannot compute the decryption key k. Theorem 2 still applies to this adaptation.

Combining Keyless and Keyed Encryption. As previously mentioned, our keyless encryption approach can (and should) be used in conjunction with traditional keyed encryption mechanisms using a different set of keys. Traditional keyed encryption gives honest parties a (conjecturally exponential) work factor advantage over adversaries if keys remain uncompromised, while keyless encryption slows adversaries if the traditional encryption keys are compromised. The two schemes can be layered in one of two ways: first applying keyless encryption DBKE and encrypting the result using keyed symmetric encryption Sym (i.e., $c \leftarrow$ Sym.Enc(k, DBKE.Enc(d, m))) or in the order, with keyless encryption on the outer layer (i.e., $c \leftarrow$ DBKE.Enc(d, Sym.Enc(k, m))). Either approach yields robust confidentiality, but we recommend the latter method as it facilitates the puzzle degradation process described in Sect. 3.3.

4   Evaluation

We evaluate ArchiveSafe by measuring its performance against other systems through real life experiment. The goals of the experiment are to: (1) measure the overhead ArchiveSafe introduces on adversaries and honest users, and (2) verify that puzzle solving difficulty scale according to the theoretical system design.

4.1   Prototype Implementation

To run the evaluation experiment, we implemented a prototype of ArchiveSafe.[7] In terms of instantiating the difficulty-based keyless encryption using the generic construction from Sect. 3.1, our proof-of-concept uses AES-128 in CBC mode for the symmetric encryption scheme. The hash functions H_1 and H_2 in the hash-based keyless key wrap scheme are both instantiated with Argon2id [5] with a prefix byte acting as a domain separator between H_1 and H_2, with the following parameters: parallelism level: 8; memory: 102,400 KiB; iterations: 2; output length: 128 bits. We did not parallelize puzzle solving in Unwrap to avoid locking other system operations, but it is easily parallelized.

The ArchiveSafe prototype is implemented as a Linux Filesystem in Userspace (FUSE) using a Python toolkit[8] to simplify implementation. Our Python FUSE driver relies on the OpenSSL library for encryption and decryption, and Ubuntu's `argon2` package. In a real deployment in the context of a filesystem, ArchiveSafe would be implemented as a kernel module, likely written in C, for improved performance and reliability.

Our prototype has a tuneable difficulty level, which we label in this section as D1, D2, D3, etc. Difficulty Dx corresponds to hash-based keyless key wrap scheme P of Fig. 5 with difficulty parameter $d = 4x$; in other words, D1 removes 4 bits of the seed, D2 removes 8 bits of the seed, etc. We chose a 4-bit step between difficulty levels to focus on how system behaviour scales across difficulty levels; finer gradations could be chosen by users.

4.2   Experimental Setup

The experiment measures ArchiveSafe's performance at three difficulty levels (D1, D2, D3) compared to an unencrypted file system (denoted UN) and Linux's built-in folder encryption using eCryptfs[9] (denoted FE) and disk encryption (denoted DE) on read and write tasks at different file sizes. When running the ArchiveSafe experiments, the ArchiveSafe FUSE driver was writing its files to an unencrypted file system.

Measurements. For each storage system being evaluated, we measure *read* and *write* times for files of sizes 1 KB, 100 KB, 1 MB, 10 MB, and 100 MB. Performance is measured at the application level, from the time the file is opened until the time the read/write operation is completed. For folder and disk encryption,

---

[7] Our prototype is available at https://github.com/moesabry/ArchiveSafe.
[8] https://github.com/skorokithakis/python-fuse-sample.
[9] https://www.ecryptfs.org/.

this includes the filesystem's encryption operations. For ArchiveSafe, we instrumented the driver to record the total time as well times for different sub-tasks (encryption, puzzle solving, decryption, file system I/O).

Test Environment. Measurements were performed on a single-user Linux machine with no other processes running. The computer was a MacBook Pro running Ubuntu Linux 18.04 LTS with an 4-core Intel Core i7-4770HQ processor with base frequency 2.2 GHz, bursting to 3.4 GHz. The computer had 16 GiB of RAM. The hard drive was a 256 GiB solid state drive with 512-byte logical sectors and 4096-byte physical sectors. The disk encryption was done using Linux Unified Key Setup system version 2.0, and folder encryption was done using the Enterprise Cryptographic Filesystem (eCryptfs) version 5.3.

Execution. For each storage system and file size, we performed many repetitions of the following tasks. A file was created with randomly generated alphanumeric characters using a non-cryptographic random number generator. Read and write operations were measured as indicated above. For file sizes of 1 KB, 100 KB, 1 MB, and 10 MB, we collected data for 1000 writes and reads; for 100 MB files, we ran 200 writes and reads, due to extensive time of operations at this size.

4.3   Results

Table 1 shows average read and write times for the file systems under consideration at different file sizes. Since read operations in the ArchiveSafe system become increasingly expensive with difficulty, we show in Table 2 the average time of sub-tasks of ArchiveSafe read operations at different file sizes and difficulties: the puzzle solving time (which should scale with puzzle difficulty), the system file read time plus decryption time (which should scale with file size), and the overhead from other file system driver operations (which includes puzzle read and system file open times). As the partial pre-image puzzle used in ArchiveSafe leads to highly variable solving times, Fig. 6 shows the average time and standard deviation for puzzle solving at difficulties D1, D2, and D3.

Table 1. Average read and write times in milliseconds

File system	Read					Write				
	1 KB	100 KB	1 MB	10 MB	100 MB	1 KB	100 KB	1 MB	10 MB	100 MB
Unencrypted (UN)	0.526	0.550	1.70	10.1	110	0.07	0.25	0.85	6.76	97.82
Disk Encryption (DE)	0.737	0.924	3.15	10.5	160	0.08	0.25	0.83	6.63	97.97
Folder Encryption (FE)	0.737	0.961	3.42	10.9	190	0.12	0.50	3.31	29.07	319.88
ArchiveSafe D1	630	630	630	650	860	141.05	141.67	146.09	221.73	848.30
ArchiveSafe D2	7070	7080	7310	7180	7290	141.25	141.43	145.08	223.50	847.02
ArchiveSafe D3	112140	111760	107390	114530	107630	141.01	140.98	145.74	222.40	846.06

Table 2. Read sub-tasks average times in milliseconds

Diff.		1 KB	100 KB	1 MB	10 MB	100 MB
D1	Puzzle Solve	510	510	510	510	500
	Decryption	5.42	5.71	7.25	20	150
	Other	0.387	0.373	0.378	0.384	0.363
D2	Puzzle Solve	6960	6980	7210	7050	6930
	Decryption	5.58	6.12	7.89	20	140
	Other	0.357	0.373	0.376	0.374	0.335
D3	Puzzle Solve	112040	111730	107280	114410	107270
	Decryption	5.56	5.94	7.96	20	140
	Other	1.075	1.216	0.971	1.195	1.045

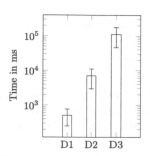

Fig. 6. Puzzle solving time in milliseconds (average, standard deviation)

4.4 Discussion

The results show consistent behaviour across different file sizes. The larger files consumed more time in decrypting and reading. We also observed that the time consumed is roughly the same for smaller file sizes (1 KB and 100 KB) where operation cost is dominated by overhead.

As expected, the read speeds decrease with the difficulty level because the system must solve the puzzle before reading the file and the puzzle solving effort scales with the difficulty level. As per Table 2, puzzle solve times on average scale by a factor of 13.6–14.1× between D1 and D2 and a factor of 14.9–16.2× between D2 and D3, roughly in line with the theoretical scaling factor of 16×.

Evaluating the overhead added by ArchiveSafe for write operations, we see in Table 1 that ArchiveSafe incurs a baseline overhead related to setting up the puzzle (which involves 2 Argon2 calls), then scales with the file size due to the cost of AES encryption and writing. Note that ArchiveSafe uses a different encryption library (user-space calls to OpenSSL) compared with disk and file encryption (kernel encryption via dm-crypt), so symmetric encryption/decryption performance is not directly comparable, but we see similar scaling.

The short summary of performance is that ArchiveSafe adds a 140–520 ms overhead when writing a file, and a customizable overhead when reading a file, ranging from 510 ms at difficulty D1, 7 s at D2, or 110 s at D3. But recall that adding computational overhead at read time is exactly the purpose of ArchiveSafe! What an acceptable difficulty level—and hence acceptable computational overhead at read time for honest users—is a policy choice by the system administrator. As noted earlier, choosing the difficulty level depends on the tolerable cost for honest users to access data, the perceived risk of a data breach, and the anticipated value of the information to an adversary, and is a calculation that must be left to the adopter. Note that honest users need not solely rely on sequential operations on their own computer: as described in Sect. 3.4 an ArchiveSafe installation could be configured so that honest users offload their puzzle solving tasks to private or commercial clouds which are spun

Table 3. Dollar cost and computation time required to unlock ArchiveSafe files

	D3	D4	D5	D6
Honest user decrypting 1 file				
Local machine, threaded 4 cores, 2.2 GHz	0.5 min	7.3 min	2 h	31 h
Cloud server c5.metal, spot pricing	≪$0.01	<$0.01	$0.05	$0.73
Adversary decrypting 1 million files				
Cloud server c5.metal	8 days	130 days	5.7 yrs	91.4 yrs
Cloud server c5.metal, spot pricing	$178	$2,852	$45,648	$730,364

up on demand with large amounts of parallelization to reduce the wall clock time before they can access a file.

Table 3 shows examples of costs at higher difficulty levels. To provide further interpretation to these costs, we look not only at the computation time required for an honest user on our test platform to decrypt a file, but also at the real-world cost for an adversary, based on the cost of renting computation time on Amazon Web Services (AWS) Elastic Cloud Compute (EC2) platform. EC2 has many machine types available; Argon2 is designed to not be substantially accelerated by more sophisticated architectures, GPUs, or ASICs. As such we choose for our pricing example an EC2 instance that minimizes cost per core-GHz-hour; the c5.metal EC2 instance type has 96 Intel Xeon cores running at 3.6 GHz at a cost of USD$0.9122 per hour using Amazon's cheapest spot pricing model.[10]

We can see, for example, that at difficulty D5, an honest user can unlock an archived file with about 2 h of work on a local machine, or about 3 min of c5.metal rental costing 4.5 cents at spot pricing (20 cents on-demand pricing). However, an adversary trying to decrypt 1 million such files from a data breach would need 5.7 years of c5.metal rental at a spot pricing cost of USD$45,648.

5   Conclusion

ArchiveSafe, using difficulty-based keyless encryption, can add defense-in-depth to confidentiality of archived data and change the economics of mass leakage attacks via data breaches. We expect that most uses of ArchiveSafe would be in addition to, not as a replacement for, traditional keyed encryption; full crypto-graphic security would be achieved if encryption keys are properly managed and kept safe, but ArchiveSafe provides a residual level of protection if traditional encryption keys are also breached. This means the key management service is no longer a single point of failure.

One target application is IT systems which retain large amounts of archival data, most of which will be rarely or perhaps never again accessed by legiti-mate users. Although honest users have no advantage in difficulty-based decryp-

---

[10] https://aws.amazon.com/ec2/instance-types/, https://aws.amazon.com/ec2/spot/pricing/; prices as of April 23, 2020.

tion compared to an adversary on a file-by-file basis, if their operational goals are different—an honest user decrypting 1 file occasionally, versus an adversary decrypting thousands or millions of files quickly—their costs are different.

Our approach can be applied in a variety of system architectures: local storage and execution (as demonstrated by our prototype), local storage with private or public cloud assistance for puzzle solving, or remote (file server/cloud) storage with local or assisted puzzle solving. Our approach can also apply to different storage paradigms, including file systems, cloud "blob" storage, and databases.

Puzzle difficulty can be set as a system-wide or with higher granularity based individual records' sensitivity. A novel features of our construction is the ability to degrade puzzle difficulty effectively for free, which could be built into periodic maintenance or through a heuristic system based on suspicious activity.

Acknowledgements. This work grew out of earlier discussions on use of puzzles for database encryption with Farhad Moghimifar, Suriadi Suriadi, and Ernest Foo at the Queensland University of Technology. R.S. is supported by Natural Sciences and Engineering Research Council of Canada (NSERC) Discovery grant RGPIN-2016-06062. D.S. is supported by NSERC Discovery grant RGPIN-2016-05146 and NSERC Discovery Accelerator Supplement grant RGPIN-2016-05146.

References

1. Abadi, M., Burrows, M., Manasse, M., Wobber, T.: Moderately hard, memory-bound functions. ACM Trans. Internet Technol. **5**(2), 299–327 (2005)
2. Aura, T., Nikander, P., Leiwo, J.: DOS-resistant authentication with client puzzles. In: Christianson, B., Malcolm, J.A., Crispo, B., Roe, M. (eds.) Security Protocols 2000. LNCS, vol. 2133, pp. 170–177. Springer, Heidelberg (2001). https://doi.org/10.1007/3-540-44810-1_22
3. Back, A.: Hashcash: a denial of service counter-measure (2004). http://www.hashcash.org/docs/hashcash.html
4. BBC: Adobe hack: at least 38 million accounts breached (2013). https://www.bbc.com/news/technology-24740873
5. Biryukov, A., Dinu, D., Khovratovich, D.: Argon2: new generation of memory-hard functions for password hashing and other applications. In: IEEE EuroS&P (2016)
6. Blaze, M.: A cryptographic file system for UNIX. In: ACM CCS (1993)
7. Cattaneo, G., Catuogno, L., Del Sorbo, A., Persiano, P.: The design and implementation of a transparent cryptographic file system for UNIX. In: USENIX Technical Conference, FREENIX Track (2001)
8. Dean, D., Stubblefield, A.: Using client puzzles to protect TLS. In: USENIX Security Symposium, vol. 42 (2001)
9. Dwork, C., Goldberg, A., Naor, M.: On Memory-bound functions for fighting spam. In: Boneh, D. (ed.) CRYPTO 2003. LNCS, vol. 2729, pp. 426–444. Springer, Heidelberg (2003). https://doi.org/10.1007/978-3-540-45146-4_25
10. Dwork, C., Naor, M.: Pricing via processing or combatting junk mail. In: Brickell, E.F. (ed.) CRYPTO 1992. LNCS, vol. 740, pp. 139–147. Springer, Heidelberg (1993). https://doi.org/10.1007/3-540-48071-4_10
11. Jakobsson, M., Juels, A.: Proofs of work and bread pudding protocols (extended abstract). In: IFIP TC6/TC11 Joint Working Conference on Secure Information Networks: Communications and Multimedia Security, pp. 258–272 (1999)

12. Juels, A., Brainard, J.: Client puzzles: a cryptographic countermeasure against connection depletion attacks. In: NDSS (1999)
13. Moghimifar, F.: Securing database using client puzzles. Master's report, Queensland University of Technology, November 2015
14. NBC News: Ameritrade warns 200,000 clients of lost data (2005). http://www.nbcnews.com/id/7561268.XeryPuhKiMo
15. Poddar, R., Boelter, T., Popa, R.A.: Arx: a strongly encrypted database system. IACR Cryptology ePrint Archive (2016)
16. Popa, R.A., Redfield, C., Zeldovich, N., Balakrishnan, H.: CryptDB: protecting confidentiality with encrypted query processing. In: Proceedings of the Twenty-Third ACM Symposium on Operating Systems Principles, pp. 85–100. ACM (2011)
17. Rangasamy, J., Stebila, D., Boyd, C., González-Nieto, J.M., Kuppusamy, L.: Effort-release public-key encryption from cryptographic puzzles. In: ACISP (2012)
18. Reuters: Bank of NY... (2008). https://www.reuters.com/article/bankofnymellon-breach-idUSWNAB863220080828
19. Rivest, R.L., Shamir, A., Wagner, D.A.: Time-lock puzzles and timed-release crypto. Technical report, MIT, March 1996. https://people.csail.mit.edu/rivest/pubs/RSW96.pdf
20. Suriadi, S., Stebila, D., Clark, A., Liu, H.: Defending web services against denial of service attacks using client puzzles. In: ICWS (2011)
21. Vargas, L., et al.: Mitigating risk while complying with data retention laws. In: ACM CCS (2018)
22. Waters, B., Juels, A., Halderman, J.A., Felten, E.W.: New client puzzle outsourcing techniques for DoS resistance. In: ACM CCS (2004)
23. Wright, C., Martino, M., Zadok, E.: NCryptfs: a secure and convenient cryptographic file system. In: USENIX Technical Conference, General Track, pp. 197–210 (2003)
24. Zadok, E., Badulescu, I., Shender, A.: Cryptfs: a stackable vnode level encryption file system. Technical report CUCS-021-98, CS Department, Columbia University (1998)

DPM Workshop: Obfuscation, Contact Tracing and Engineering

Joint Obfuscation for Privacy Protection in Location-Based Social Networks

Behnaz Bostanipour$^{(\boxtimes)}$ and George Theodorakopoulos

Cardiff University, Cardiff, UK
behnaz.bostanipour@gmail.com, theodorakopoulosg@cardiff.ac.uk

Abstract. In recent years, location-based social networks (LBSNs) such as Foursquare have emerged that enable users to share with each other, their (geographical) locations together with the semantic information associated with their locations. The semantic information captures the type of a location and is usually represented by a semantic tag. Semantic tag sharing increases the threat to users' *location privacy* which is already at risk because of location sharing. The existing solution to protect the location privacy of users in such LBSNs is to obfuscate the location and the semantic tag independently of each other in a so called disjoint obfuscation approach. More precisely, in this approach, the semantic tag is obfuscated i.e., replaced by a more general tag. Also, the location is obfuscated i.e., replaced by a generalized area (called *the cloaking area*) made of the actual location and some of its nearby locations. However, since in this approach the location obfuscation is performed in a semantic-oblivious manner, an adversary can still increase his chance to infer the actual location by detecting semantic incompatibility between the locations in the cloaking area and the obfuscated semantic tag. In this work, we address this issue by proposing a *joint obfuscation approach* in which the location obfuscation is performed based on the result of the semantic tag obfuscation. We also provide a formal framework for evaluation and comparison of our joint approach with the disjoint approach. By running an experimental evaluation on a dataset of real-world user mobility traces, we show that in almost all cases (i.e., for different values of the obfuscation parameters), the joint approach outperforms the disjoint approach in terms of location privacy protection. We also study how different obfuscation parameters can affect the performance of the obfuscation approaches. In particular, we show how changing these parameters can improve the performance of the joint approach.

Keywords: Privacy · Social networks · Location-based services · Semantics

1 Introduction

In location-based social networks (LBSNs) such as Foursquare and Facebook, users can share with each other, their (geographical) locations together with the

© Springer Nature Switzerland AG 2020
J. Garcia-Alfaro et al. (Eds.): DPM 2020/CBT 2020, LNCS 12484, pp. 111–127, 2020.
https://doi.org/10.1007/978-3-030-66172-4_7

Fig. 1. A check-in to a burger joint called "Whitmans" on Foursquare. The location and the semantic tag of the venue are highlighted by the red bounding boxes. (Color figure online)

semantic information associated with their locations. For instance, by checking-in to venue "Whitmans" on Foursquare, a user implicitly accepts to share with her friends, the address of the venue together with its type (category), which is represented in the form of a semantic tag "burger joint" (See Fig. 1). A venue's semantic tag usually belongs to a predefined set of tags, where the set of tags form a hierarchical tree in which the "burger joint" tag could be a descendant of the "restaurant" tag and the "restaurant" tag could be a descendant of the "food" tag, and so forth [1,5].

It is known that by disclosing their locations in LBSNs and in location-based services (LBSs), users put their *location privacy* at risk. In fact, an adversary (e.g., a curious service provider) can use a collection of users' disclosed locations to re-identify their pseudonymous location traces or to infer their locations at given time instants [20,23,24]. As shown in [1], revealing semantic tags together with locations, creates a still more powerful threat to the users' location privacy. Intuitively, this is because the mobility of users have some regular semantic patterns (e.g., people usually go to the movies after dining in a restaurant), which can be learned and exploited to better track their locations [1,5].

One way to protect the privacy of users is to build *privacy-aware LBSNs* in which users only share obfuscated versions of their locations and semantic tags. Thus, when a user checks-in to a venue on a privacy-aware LBSN, the venue's name, its exact location and its semantic tag are not disclosed to anyone. Instead, an obfuscated version of the location and an obfuscated version of the semantic tag are sent to the service provider and then shared with the user's friends on the LBSN. The existing solution in the literature to build such privacy-aware LBSNs consists of obfuscating the location and the semantic tag independently of each other in a so called *disjoint semantic tag-location obfuscation approach* [1]. Figure 2.a illustrates a toy example of this approach, where a geographical area is partitioned into four square regions (locations) and each region is identified by a number. Let us assume that a user Alice wants to check-in to venue "Super Duper Burger" on a privacy-aware LBSN. Thus, in the semantic tag obfuscation process, her location's semantic tag (i.e., "burger joint") is replaced by a more

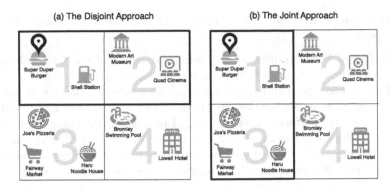

Fig. 2. Toy Examples of the obfuscation approaches.

general tag "restaurant". Also, in the location obfuscation process, her location (i.e., region 1) is replaced by a generalized area (also called a *cloaking area*) made of regions 1 and 2.[1] The problem with this approach is that an adversary (e.g., a curious service provider) who knows the semantic tags of the venues in the map can easily filter out region 2 from the cloaking area and infers that Alice is located in region 1. The reason is that region 2 is not *semantically compatible* with the "restaurant" tag i.e., it has no venue whose semantic tag is equal to the "restaurant" tag or is a descendant of the "restaurant" tag in the tag hierarchy.

In this work, we introduce a *joint semantic tag-location obfuscation approach* for building privacy-aware LBSNs. This approach aims to overcome the drawbacks of the disjoint approach by performing the location obfuscation based on the result of the semantic tag obfuscation. More precisely, in the location obfuscation process, the cloaking area is defined so that it has the maximum number of semantically compatible regions with the obfuscated semantic tag among the existing potential cloaking areas. Figure 2.b illustrates a toy example of this approach. Similar to the toy example of Fig. 2.a, in this example a user Alice wants to check-in to venue "Super Duper Burger" on a privacy-aware LBSN. Thus, in the semantic tag obfuscation process, her location's semantic tag (i.e., "burger joint") is replaced by a more general tag "restaurant". However, in the location obfuscation process, her location (i.e., region 1) is replaced by a cloaking area made of regions 1 and 3. The advantage of merging region 1 with region 3 instead of merging region 1 with region 2, is that region 3 is semantically compatible with the "restaurant" tag since it has two venues (i.e, "Joe's Pizzeria" and "Haru Noodle House") whose semantic tags (i.e., "pizza place" and "noodle house") are descendants of the "restaurant" tag in the tag hierarchy, respectively. Hence, the adversary cannot filter out the region 3 by knowing the "restaurant" tag. Thus, the resulting cloaking area has two semantically compatible regions with the "restaurant" tag, which is the maximum number of semantically compatible

---

[1] For simplicity's sake, in this work we consider only obfuscation by *generalization*, both for locations and semantic tags.

regions that can be achieved for the "restaurant" tag and the cloaking area size of two regions.

Contributions. We introduce a joint semantic tag-location obfuscation approach for privacy protection in LBSNs (and in LBSs, in general). We also provide a formal framework that can be used for evaluation and comparison of our approach with the disjoint obfuscation approach. Using a dataset of real-world user mobility traces, we perform an experimental evaluation for comparison of the joint and the disjoint approaches. The evaluation results show that in almost all cases (i.e., for different values of the obfuscation parameters), the joint approach outperforms the disjoint approach in terms of location privacy protection. We also study the impact of different obfuscation parameters on the performance of the obfuscation approaches. In particular, we show how changing these parameters can improve the performance of the joint approach. The most important contribution of our work is introducing *joint obfuscation* as a new type of obfuscation, in which some private attributes of a user are obfuscated based on the result of the obfuscation of some of her other private attributes. Accordingly, our work can be used as a model for more advanced obfuscation schemes that jointly obfuscate a greater number of private attributes.

Road Map. The remainder of the paper is organized as follows. In Sect. 2, we describe the system model and introduce some definitions. In particular, we present a privacy protection mechanism that can be defined to use one of the joint or disjoint obfuscation approaches. We also present an adversary model and describe the adversary's knowledge and attack. In Sect. 3, we introduce an implementation of the adversary's attack based on dynamic bayesian networks. In Sect. 4, we present the location privacy metric. In Sect. 5, we perform an experimental evaluation to compare the joint and the disjoint approaches in terms of location privacy protection and we discuss the results. In Sect. 6, we discuss the related work. Finally, we conclude the paper in Sect. 7.

2   System Model

In this section, we present the system model. Our model is built upon the framework proposed in [20,23,24] and its extension in [1].

Regions and Semantic Tags. We assume that the users move in a geographical area that is partitioned into a finite set $\mathcal{R}$ of distinct regions. We use the terms *region, geographical location* and *location* interchangeably. Each region has a unique identifier and contains a set of venues. A venue is characterized by its type, which is represented in the form of a semantic tag. The semantic tag of a venue belongs to a set $\mathcal{S}$ of all possible semantic tags. We assume that $\mathcal{S}$ can be represented as a tree data structure where each node is a semantic tag and the parent of a given node is a more general semantic tag with respect to a specified tag hierarchy. Below, we present some definitions that capture the semantic characteristics of venues and regions.

- Let v be a venue in a region in $\mathcal{R}$ and s be a semantic tag in $\mathcal{S}$. Then, we say v is *semantically compatible* with s, if v's semantic tag is equal to s or descendant of s in the semantic tag tree.
- Let r be a region in $\mathcal{R}$ and s be a semantic tag in $\mathcal{S}$. Then, $NV_S(r)$ denotes the number of venues in r whose semantic tags are equal to s. Similarly, $NDV_S(r)$ denotes the number of venues in r whose semantic tags are descendants of s in the semantic tag tree. Finally, $NCV_S(r)$ denotes the number of venues in r that are semantically compatible with s. Thus, $NCV_S(r){=}NV_S(r){+}\ NDV_S(r)$.
- Let r be a region in $\mathcal{R}$ and s be a semantic tag in $\mathcal{S}$. Then, we say that r is *semantically compatible* with s if r contains at least one venue which is semantically compatible with s, i.e., $NCV_S(r) > 0$.

Time. Time is discrete and the set of time instants when the users may be observed is $\mathcal{T} = \{1, ..., T\}$. The set $\mathcal{T}$ is called *the observation interval.*

Users. We assume a finite set of users, where each user has a unique identifier. The mobility of a user is characterized by her events and her traces. More specifically, the fact that a user u is at location r with semantic tag s at time t, can be represented by a tuple $<u, r, s, t>$. We call this tuple an *event*. Note that the semantic tag of location of u at time t refers in fact to the semantic tag of the location's venue where u is located at time t. The location trace and the semantic tag trace of user u can then be obtained based on the set of her events over the entire observation interval. Thus, *the location trace* of u is defined as $r_u^{1:T} \triangleq \{r_u^1, ..., r_u^T\}$, where r_u^t with $t \in \mathcal{T}$, denotes the location of u at time t. We assume that r_u^t is an instantiation of random variable R_u^t that takes values in $\mathcal{R}$. Moreover, *the semantic tag trace* of u is defined as $s_u^{1:T} \triangleq \{s_u^1, ..., s_u^T\}$, where s_u^t with $t \in \mathcal{T}$, denotes the semantic tag of location of u at time t. We assume that s_u^t is an instantiation of random variable S_u^t that takes values in $\mathcal{S}$.

Privacy Protection Mechanism (PPM). The privacy-protection mechanism (also called PPM) obfuscates user's locations and their corresponding semantic tags before reporting them to the online service provider. More precisely, PPM transforms each actual event $<u, r, s, t>$ to an *obfuscated event* $<u, \tilde{r}, \tilde{s}, t>$, where $\tilde{r}$ and $\tilde{s}$ are the obfuscated versions of r and s, respectively.

The obfuscation of r is achieved through *the location obfuscation* process of the PPM. The resulting pseudo-location $\tilde{r}$ is an instantiation of random variable $\widetilde{R}_u^t$ that takes values in set $\widetilde{\mathcal{R}}$, where $\widetilde{\mathcal{R}}$ is the power set of $\mathcal{R}$. We use the terms *pseudo-location* and *obfuscated location* interchangeably. In the literature, there exist various types of location obfuscation (see Sect. 6). In this work, we assume that the PPM performs a type of location obfuscation called *location generalization*. Thus, r is merged with its nearby regions to form an extended region (also called *a cloaking area* (CA)) that is represented by $\tilde{r}$. We also assume the existence of a parameter o_{loc} called *the location obfuscation level*. In this work, o_{loc} defines the number of regions in $\tilde{r}$. Thus, formally, $\tilde{r}$ represents a set that is composed of r and the other merged regions and has a cardinality of o_{loc}.

The obfuscation of s is achieved through *the semantic tag obfuscation* process of the PPM. The resulting pseudo-semantic tag $\tilde{s}$ is an instantiation of random variable $\widetilde{S}_u^t$ that takes values in set $\mathcal{S}$. We use the terms *pseudo-semantic tag* and *obfuscated semantic tag* interchangeably. In this work, we assume that the PPM performs a type of semantic tag obfuscation called *semantic tag generalization*, in which s is replaced by a more general semantic tag in the semantic tag tree. The level of generalization is defined by a parameter o_{sem} called *the semantic tag obfuscation level*. Thus, formally, $\tilde{s}$ is the ancestor of s that is o_{sem} level(s) above s in the semantic tag tree.

Based on what we have described, the location obfuscation and the semantic tag obfuscation can each be modeled by a probability distribution function. Thus, formally, a PPM is defined as a pair (f, g) where f and g are probability distribution functions that model the semantic tag obfuscation and the location obfuscation, respectively. By applying these functions on a user's events over time, the PPM creates *the obfuscated traces* of the user from her actual traces. Thus, *the obfuscated location trace* of a user u is defined as $\tilde{r}_u^{1:T} \triangleq \{\tilde{r}_u^1, ..., \tilde{r}_u^T\}$, where $\tilde{r}_u^t$ with $t \in \mathcal{T}$, denotes the pseudo-location of u at time t and is an instantiation of $\widetilde{R}_u^t$. Moreover, *the obfuscated semantic tag trace* of user u is defined as $\tilde{s}_u^{1:T} \triangleq \{\tilde{s}_u^1, ..., \tilde{s}_u^T\}$, where $\tilde{s}_u^t$ with $t \in \mathcal{T}$, denotes the pseudo-semantic tag of location of u at time t and is an instantiation of $\widetilde{S}_u^t$. The definition of f and g functions depends on the obfuscation approach used by the PPM. In the following, we introduce two obfuscation approaches and give the definition of the probability distribution functions for each approach.

- **Disjoint semantic tag-location obfuscation approach.** In this approach, the location obfuscation and the semantic tag obfuscation are performed independently of each other. Thus, the probability distribution functions in this approach are defined as follows [1].

$$f_u(s, \tilde{s}) = \Pr\left(\widetilde{S}_u^t = \tilde{s} \mid S_u^t = s\right) \tag{1}$$

$$g_u(r, \tilde{r}) = \Pr\left(\widetilde{R}_u^t = \tilde{r} \mid R_u^t = r\right) \tag{2}$$

- **Joint semantic tag-location obfuscation approach.** In this approach, the location obfuscation is performed based on the result of the semantic tag obfuscation. Thus, first $\tilde{s}$ is obtained from s by applying the semantic tag obfuscation process. Then, in the location obfuscation process, the merging of r with nearby locations is performed in a way that the resulting $\tilde{r}$ has the maximum number of semantically compatible regions with $\tilde{s}$. Formally this can be expressed as follows. Let $\mathcal{C}(r)$ be the set of potential cloaking areas for region r and $NCR_{\tilde{s}}(.)$ denote the number of regions that are semantically compatible with $\tilde{s}$ in a given cloaking area. Then, an element $\tilde{r}$ of $\mathcal{C}(r)$ has the maximum number of semantically compatible regions with semantic tag $\tilde{s}$ if $NCR_{\tilde{s}}(\tilde{r}) \geq NCR_{\tilde{s}}(\tilde{\rho})$ for $\forall \tilde{\rho} \in \mathcal{C}(r)$. Based on what we have described, the probability distribution functions in this approach are defined as follows.

$$f_u(s, \tilde{s}) = \Pr\left(\widetilde{S}_u^t = \tilde{s} \mid S_u^t = s\right) \tag{3}$$

$$g_u(r, \tilde{r}, \tilde{s}) = \Pr\left(\widetilde{R}_u^t = \tilde{r} \mid R_u^t = r, \widetilde{S}_u^t = \tilde{s}\right) \tag{4}$$

Adversary. Typically, the adversary is a curious service provider or an observer who observes the obfuscated traces of the users and wants to infer the locations of users at given time instants. We model the adversary by his *knowledge* and his *attack*.

- **Adversary's Knowledge.** The adversary has full knowledge of regions (including their venues and their semantic tags) and the semantic tag tree. He knows which obfuscation approach is used by the PPM and also knows the semantic tag obfuscation function (f) and the location obfuscation function (g) of PPM in both disjoint and joint approaches. We assume that the adversary performs his attack *a posteriori*, meaning that the adversary has access to the obfuscated traces of the users over the complete observation interval. In addition, he has access to some of the past semantic tag traces and past location traces of the users. We refer to this as his *prior information*.
- **Adversary's Attack.** The adversary performs the location-inference attack against users. In this attack, the goal of the adversary is to find the location of a user u at time t, given the obfuscated location trace and the obfuscated semantic tag trace of u. The attack can be formalized as finding the following posterior probability distribution over set $\mathcal{R}$ of regions:

$$\Pr\left(R_u^t = r \mid \tilde{r}_u^{1:T}, \tilde{s}_u^{1:T}\right) \tag{5}$$

3 Implementation of the Attack

To implement the attack, the adversary first builds a *dynamic bayesian network* (*DBN*) model for each user based on his knowledge. Roughly speaking, the DBN model for a user encodes the probabilistic dependencies between the random variables involved in the inference attack against that user. Once a DBN is built for a user, the adversary can perform his attack against the user by applying an existing DBN inference algorithm (such as junction tree algorithm or loopy belief propagation algorithm [11,16,17]) on the DBN built for the user. In the following, we discuss the DBN models.

3.1 The Dynamic Bayesian Network (DBN) Models

Based on his knowledge, the adversary builds a *dynamic bayesian network* (*DBN*) model for each user. A DBN is a probabilistic graphical model. It belongs to a wider class of probabilistic graphical models known as *bayesian networks* (*BNs*). In fact, a DBN is a BN which is used to model time series, sequential data [11,16].

The DBN of a user u presents a joint distribution over the random variables $R_u^{1:T}$, $S_u^{1:T}$, $\widetilde{R}_u^{1:T}$, $\widetilde{S}_u^{1:T}$, where $R_u^{1:T} \triangleq \{R_u^1, ..., R_u^T\}$, $S_u^{1:T} \triangleq \{S_u^1, ..., S_u^T\}$, $\widetilde{R}_u^{1:T} \triangleq$

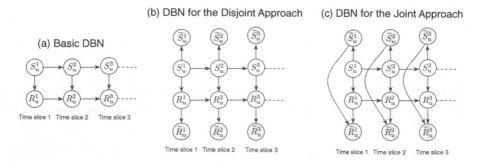

Fig. 3. The Dynamic Bayesian Network (DBN) Models.

$\{\widetilde{R}_u^1, ..., \widetilde{R}_u^T\}$ and $\widetilde{S}_u^{1:T} \triangleq \{\widetilde{S}_u^1, ..., \widetilde{S}_u^T\}$. These random variables can be divided into two categories: (1) *Observed variables*. These are the variables that are directly observed and whose values are known by the adversary. They include $\widetilde{R}_u^{1:T}$ and $\widetilde{S}_u^{1:T}$; (2) *Unobserved variables* (also called *hidden variables*). These are the variables that are not directly observed and whose values are supposed to be inferred from the observed variables. They include $R_u^{1:T}$ and $S_u^{1:T}$. The graphical structure of the DBN specifies all probabilistic dependencies between the hidden variables, between the hidden and the observed variables and between the observed variables.

The probabilistic dependencies between the hidden and the observed variables as well as between the observed variables themselves, depend on the obfuscation approach used by the PPM. Thereby, the DBN of a user in the case where the disjoint obfuscation approach is used differs from her DBN in the case where the joint approach is used. However, in both cases the probabilistic dependencies between the hidden variables remain the same. Thus, in the following we first present a basic DBN for a user u that encodes only the probabilistic dependencies between the hidden variables. Then, we present the DBNs of u for the disjoint and the joint obfuscation cases. These DBN models are made by adding the corresponding observed variables of each case to the basic DBN.

3.1.1   The Basic DBN

This model encodes the probabilistic dependencies between the hidden variables associated to user u, namely $R_u^{1:T}, S_u^{1:T}$ (see Fig. 3.a). The basic DBN models the mobility of u. The adversary builds this model based on the following assumption on user mobility: to move to the next location, a user first decides on the type (i.e., semantic tag) of the next location based on the type (i.e., semantic tag) of her current location [1]. Once the next location type is decided, the user can choose her next (geographical) location based on her current (geographical) location and the next location type [1]. For instance, a user is in a restaurant and decides to go to the movies, as she usually does after going to a restaurant. Thus, considering her current geographical location, she chooses the movie theater that is most convenient to her (e.g., the closest movie theater to the restaurant) [1].

Let us take a closer look at the model. Since a DBN is a type of bayesian network (BN), the model exhibits the general properties of BNs. More precisely, it is a directed acyclic graph in which nodes represent random variables and the edges represent conditional dependencies between variables. In addition, each node has a conditional probability distribution (CPD) associated to it, which is the CPD of the variable represented by the node, given the parent variables of the node (by parent variables of a node, we mean the variables that are represented by the parent nodes of that node in the graph) [14]. For instance, in each time slice t of Fig. 3.a, to represent the fact that S_u^t depends on S_u^{t-1}, an edge connects the corresponding nodes and the associated CPD is $\Pr(S_u^t \mid S_u^{t-1})$. The model has also some properties that are specific to DBNs. Firstly, it has a structure which is repeated over time. Secondly, the model is *first order Markovian*, i.e., the random variables in each time slice t are independent of all random variables from time slices 1 to $t-2$, given the random variables in time slice $t-1$. Finally, the model is *time-invariant*, i.e., the CPDs of the model do not change as a function of time. As a consequence of the Markov and the time-invariance properties of the model, $R_u^{1:T}$ and $S_u^{1:T}$ each form a time-invariant first order Markov chain.

Parameters. The model is fully specified by the following probability distributions.

- **The transition distributions: $\Pr(S_u^t \mid S_u^{t-1})$ and $\Pr(R_u^t \mid S_u^t, R_u^{t-1})$.**
  These are the CPDs that define the transition between any two consecutive time slices $t-1$ and t in the model. According to [1], the distribution $\Pr(R_u^t \mid S_u^t, R_u^{t-1})$ can be computed as follows:

$$
\Pr(R_u^t = r \mid S_u^t = s, R_u^{t-1} = r') = \begin{cases} 0, & \text{if } NV_S(r) = 0 \\ \alpha \dfrac{\Pr(R_u^t = r \mid R_u^{t-1} = r')}{\sum\limits_{\rho \in \mathcal{E}} \Pr(R_u^t = \rho \mid R_u^{t-1} = r')} & \text{otherwise} \\ +(1-\alpha) \cdot \Pr(R_u^t = r \mid S_u^t = s), \end{cases}
$$
(6)

where $\mathcal{E} = \{\rho \in \mathcal{R} : NV_S(\rho) > 0\}$ and α is a real-valued parameter that is used to set the weight of each term in the equation. The distributions $\Pr(S_u^t \mid S_u^{t-1})$ and $\Pr(R_u^t \mid R_u^{t-1})$ can be learned from the prior traces by applying maximum likelihood estimation (if the traces are complete) or by using algorithms such as Gibbs sampling (if the traces have missing locations or if they are noisy) [6,20,23]. The distribution $\Pr(R_u^t \mid S_u^t)$ can also be learned from the prior traces. More precisely, $\Pr(R_u^t = r \mid S_u^t = s)$ can be estimated by counting in the user's prior traces, the number of visits to a region r given the semantic tag s [1]. Note that in the experimental evaluation in [1], Ağir et al. set $\alpha = 0.5$ to accord the same importance to both terms of the equation. In this paper, we also set $\alpha = 0.5$ for the experimental evaluation.
- **The initial state distributions: $\Pr(R_u^1 \mid S_u^1)$ and $\Pr(S_u^1)$.** These are the distributions associated to the nodes of the first time slice of the model. For

the estimation of $\Pr\left(R_u^1 \mid S_u^1\right)$, we refer the reader to the previous point, where we discuss the estimation of $\Pr\left(R_u^t \mid S_u^t\right)$ from the prior traces (recall that the model is time-invariant). Moreover, we assume that $\Pr\left(S_u^1\right)$ is equal to the stationary distribution of the Markov chain $S_u^{1:T}$. Accordingly, it can be found based on $\Pr\left(S_u^t \mid S_u^{t-1}\right)$, which is the transition distribution of the chain. We refer the reader to the previous point where we discuss the estimation of $\Pr\left(S_u^t \mid S_u^{t-1}\right)$ from the prior traces.

3.1.2   The DBNs for the Obfuscation Approaches

Figure 3.b depicts the DBN built for user u in the case where the PPM uses the disjoint obfuscation approach. Also, Fig. 3.c depicts the DBN built for user u in the case where the PPM uses the joint obfuscation approach. Each of these DBNs is made by adding the observed variables $\widetilde{R}_u^{1:T}$ and $\widetilde{S}_u^{1:T}$ to the basic DBN, where the observed variables correspond to the obfuscation approach used by the PPM. Note that in the DBN model built for the joint approach, to represent the fact that in the joint obfuscation, $\widetilde{R}_u^t$ depends also on $\widetilde{S}_u^t$, an edge connects the corresponding nodes in each time slice t of the model (See Fig. 3.c).

Parameters. Each of these models is fully specified by the parameters of the basic DBN plus *the observation distributions*. The observation distributions of a model are the CPDs that define the probabilistic dependencies between the hidden and the observed variables in any time slice t in that model. The observation distributions of a model are defined based on the obfuscation approach used by the PPM. So, we have:

- **The observation distributions for the disjoint obfuscation case:** $\mathbf{Pr}\left(\widetilde{S}_u^t \mid S_u^t\right)$ and $\mathbf{Pr}\left(\widetilde{R}_u^t \mid R_u^t\right)$. These are in fact the obfuscation functions of the PPM in the disjoint obfuscation approach (see Eqs. 1 and 2), and hence known by the adversary.
- **The observation distributions for the joint obfuscation case:** $\mathbf{Pr}\left(\widetilde{S}_u^t \mid S_u^t\right)$ and $\mathbf{Pr}\left(\widetilde{R}_u^t \mid R_u^t, \widetilde{S}_u^t\right)$. These are in fact the obfuscation functions of the PPM in the joint obfuscation approach (see Eqs. 3 and 4), and hence known by the adversary.

4   Location Privacy Metric

The location privacy of a user u a time t is measured by the expected error of the adversary when performing the location-inference attack [23]. The expected error of the adversary is computed as:

$$\sum_{r \in \mathcal{R}} \Pr\left(R_u^t = r \mid \tilde{r}_u^{1:T}, \tilde{s}_u^{1:T}\right) \cdot d_{loc}(r, r_u^t) \tag{7}$$

where $\Pr\left(R_u^t = r \mid \tilde{r}_u^{1:T}, \tilde{s}_u^{1:T}\right)$ over set $\mathcal{R}$, is the output of the location-inference attack defined in Sect. 2 and $d_{loc}(\cdot,\cdot)$ denotes a distance function on the set $\mathcal{R}$ of regions. Here, we assume that $d_{loc}(\cdot,\cdot)$ is *the Haversine distance* between the centers of the two regions [14].

5   Experimental Evaluation

Using a dataset of real-world user mobility traces, we perform an experimental evaluation to compare the performance of the joint approach with the performance of the disjoint approach in terms of location privacy protection. We also study the impact of different obfuscation parameters on the performance of these approaches. More precisely, we first obfuscate the user traces under the disjoint and the joint approaches using different combinations of the obfuscation parameters. Then, we perform the location-inference attack on the obfuscated traces and measure the location privacy of users in both approaches based on the results of the attack.

5.1   Evaluation Setup

In this section, we describe the evaluation's setup.

5.1.1   Dataset and Space Discretization

We use the dataset that is introduced and described in [1]. It comprises the semantically-annotated location traces of Foursquare check-ins of 1065 users distributed across six large cities in North America and Europe [1]. The location information in the traces is presented as GPS coordinates. The dataset also contains a snapshot of Foursquare category tree at the time of data collection [1].

Regarding the space discretization, we use the same space discretization described in [1]. More precisely, within each city in the dataset, a geographical area of size ~2.4 km × 1.6 km that contains the largest number of check-ins is selected. Then, each selected area is partitioned into 96 locations (cells) by using a 12 × 8 regular square grid. Each grid cell has a unique ID. Once the partitioning is done, the GPS coordinates in user traces are mapped to the location, that is, the grid cell, they fall into. Moreover, for each grid cell, the Foursquare semantic tags of the venues that are located in that cell are identified and stored in an associative array. Thus, the associative array contains the key-value pairs, where in each pair the key is a grid cell ID and the value is the set of the semantic tags of the venues located in that cell.

5.1.2   Obfuscation

In the following, we first introduce the obfuscation algorithms used in our evaluation. We then describe the process of building the obfuscated traces from the real traces using these algorithms. In practice, these algorithms are implemented in Python.

Semantic Tag Obfuscation Algorithm. The semantic tag obfuscation in both disjoint and joint obfuscation approaches is performed by the semantic tag obfuscation algorithm described as below. The algorithm gets as input a set S of semantic tags that form a semantic tag tree, a semantic tag s in S and a semantic tag obfuscation level o_{sem}. It returns as output a pseudo-semantic tag

$\tilde{s}$, where $\tilde{s}$ is the ancestor of s that is o_{sem} level(s) above s in the semantic tag tree. In the case where the depth of semantic tag s in the semantic tag tree is smaller than o_{sem}, the algorithm returns the root of the semantic tag tree as $\tilde{s}$.

Location Obfuscation Algorithm. The location obfuscation in both disjoint and joint obfuscation approaches is performed by the location obfuscation algorithm. The algorithm takes as input a grid that we call the main grid for the sake of precision, a cell r of the main grid, a location obfuscation level o_{loc} and an obfuscation approach. In the case of joint obfuscation, in addition to what has been described, the following inputs should also be provided: the semantic tag tree that is used as input by the semantic tag obfuscation algorithm, the pseudo-semantic tag $\tilde{s}$ that is output by the semantic tag obfuscation algorithm and an associative array that contains key-value pairs where in each pair the key is a main grid cell ID and the value is the set of the semantic tags of the venues located in that cell. The algorithm returns as output a cloaking area $\tilde{r}$ for r.

The main idea behind the algorithm is to first find a set of potential cloaking areas for r and then based on the obfuscation approach, select an area among the potential cloaking areas and return it as $\tilde{r}$. The algorithm finds the potential cloaking areas by building a set of cloaking grids. A cloaking grid is an alternative tessellation for the same surface presented by the main grid. It has two properties: (1) each cell of a clocking grid is made of o_{loc} distinct cells of the main grid; (2) the number of rows and the number of columns of a cloaking grid are factors of the number of rows and the number of columns of the main grid, respectively. Each cloaking grid can be used to find a potential cloaking area for r. More precisely, the cell of a cloaking grid that contains r, is a potential clocking area for r and can be added to the set of potential cloaking areas.

Once the potential cloaking areas are found, an area among them is selected and returned as $\tilde{r}$. The selection is made based on the obfuscation approach. More precisely, in the case of the disjoint obfuscation, the algorithm selects an area uniformly at random among the potential cloaking areas and returns it as $\tilde{r}$. In the case of the joint obfuscation, the algorithm first looks for the areas with the maximum $NCR_{\tilde{s}}$ value among the potential cloaking areas. The results are then stored in the set $CAsWithMaxNCR$. If only one area with the maximum $NCR_{\tilde{s}}$ value is found (i.e., $|CAsWithMaxNCR| = 1$), the algorithm returns it as $\tilde{r}$. Otherwise, the algorithm looks for the areas with the maximum $SumNCV_{\tilde{s}}$ value among the elements of $CAsWithMaxNCR$. The results are then stored in the set $CAsWithMaxSumNCV$. Note that the $SumNCV_{\tilde{s}}$ of an area is in fact the sum of $NCV_{\tilde{s}}$ values over all the main grid cells in that area. If only one area with the maximum $SumNCV_{\tilde{s}}$ value is found (i.e., $|CAsWithMaxSumNCV| = 1$), the algorithm returns it as $\tilde{r}$. Otherwise, the algorithm selects an area uniformly at random among the elements of $CAsWithMaxSumNCV$ and returns it as $\tilde{r}$.

Note that, selecting the area with the maximum $SumNCV_{\tilde{s}}$ value among the areas with the maximum $NCR_{\tilde{s}}$ value is an additional mechanism that we use to enhance the resistance of the joint obfuscation against the privacy attacks. Intuitively, by selecting the clocking area with the maximum $NCR_{\tilde{s}}$ value (i.e., the area with the maximum number of semantically compatible locations), we decrease the number of locations that can be filtered out by the adversary from the cloaking area and by selecting the cloaking area with the maximum $SumNCV_{\tilde{s}}$ value (i.e., the area with the maximum number of semantically compatible venues), we increase the number of locations and semantic tags that can be guessed by the adversary as the actual location and semantic tag.

Building the Obfuscated Traces. For each city in the dataset, we choose the location traces and the semantic tag traces of 20 randomly chosen users. These traces are then obfuscated under the disjoint and the joint obfuscation approaches using the obfuscation algorithms. To better capture the fact that the users do not share their locations and their corresponding semantic tags all the time on LBSNs, we apply the obfuscation algorithms with an additional *hiding process*. Thus, we assume that at each time instant in the observation interval, both the user's location and its semantic tag can be hidden from the LBSN with *the hiding probability* λ or shared on the LBSN (and accordingly obfuscated by the algorithms under the disjoint and the joint approaches) with the probability $1 - \lambda$. The hidden locations and the hidden semantic tags are appeared in the obfuscated traces as *hidden*, denoted by $r_\perp$ and $s_\perp$ symbols, respectively. To build the obfuscated traces for each approach, we use all combinations of the following parameters: the location obfuscation level (o_{loc}), the semantic tag obfuscation level (o_{sem}) and the hiding probability (λ), where $o_{loc} \in \{1, 2, 4, 8, 16\}$ and $o_{sem} \in \{0, 1, 2\}$ and $\lambda \in \{0, 0.2, 0.4, 0.6, 0.8\}$. Note that, in what follows, we use the term *the obfuscation parameters* to refer to these parameters.

5.1.3   Attack and Privacy Evaluation

We implement the DBN models in Python by using *the pomegranate package* [19] and the Bayesian Belief Networks library [3]. For the attack, we apply the loopy belief propagation inference algorithm [17]. We perform the attack for the observation interval of length 3. We then use the metric defined in Sect. 4 to measure the location privacy of the users.

5.2   Experimental Results

In this section we present the results for different values of the obfuscation parameters. In this way, we can compare the performance of the two obfuscation approaches in terms of location privacy under different values of these parameters and also show how changing these parameters can affect the performance of the approaches. Note that in addition to the location privacy metric presented in Sect. 4, to discuss the results, we use the following additional metric:

- **Ratio of the location privacy means** (denoted by *loc-priv-ratio*). This is the ratio of the location privacy mean obtained for the joint approach to the location privacy mean obtained for the disjoint approach.

The evaluation results are depicted by Fig. 4 and Fig. 5. More precisely, Fig. 4 represents the location privacy results in the form of boxplots (i.e., first quartile,

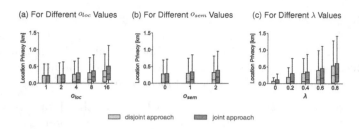

Fig. 4. Location privacy results.

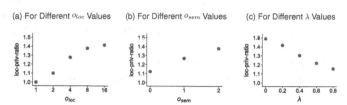

Fig. 5. *loc-priv-ratio* for different values of the obfuscation parameters.

median, third quartile and outliers). Note that the location privacy in Fig. 4 is expressed in kilometres. Also, Fig. 5 represents the ratios of the location privacy means in the form of scatterplots. Each figure has three subfigures (a), (b) and (c). Each subfigure represents the aggregated results for different values of a given obfuscation parameter, where the aggregation is performed over the results obtained for all users, all values of the obfuscation parameters and all cities. We have three main observations regarding these results. Thus, in the following we first describe the observations. Then, we describe the reason behind the observations.

1. As the values of o_{loc}, o_{sem} and λ increase, the median location privacy for the both obfuscation approaches increases (see subfigures (a),(b),(c) of Fig. 4).
2. Under all values of o_{loc}, o_{sem} and λ, the median location privacy obtained for the joint approach is higher than the median location privacy obtained for the disjoint approach (see subfigures (a),(b),(c) of Fig. 4). The only exception to this observation is the case where $o_{loc} = 1$ (See Fig. 4.a). In this case, no location obfuscation is performed and hence, the median location privacy is the same for the both obfuscation approaches.
3. As the values of o_{loc} and o_{sem} increase, the value of *loc-priv-ratio* also increases (see Fig. 5.a and Fig. 5.b). However, as the value of λ increases, the value of *loc-priv-ratio* decreases (see Fig. 5.c).

To explain these observations, we apply the following reasoning. As the value of o_{loc} increases, the number of regions (locations) in the cloaking area increases. Thus, by increasing o_{loc}, the median location privacy for the both approaches increases. Also, as the value of o_{sem} increases, the number of semantic tags that can be semantically compatible with the obfuscated semantic tag increases. This, in turn, increases the chance of having more semantically compatible regions with the obfuscated semantic tag in every potential cloaking area. Thus, by increasing o_{sem} the median location privacy for the both approaches increases. Moreover, we observe that by increasing o_{loc} and o_{sem}, the value of *loc-priv-ratio* also increases. Roughly speaking, this means that the joint approach shows a much better performance in terms of location privacy protection compared to the disjoint approach under higher values of o_{loc} and o_{sem}. In fact, as the value of o_{loc} increases, the number of candidate regions for being in the clocking area also increases. This, in turn, increases the chance that a greater number of the candidate regions are semantically compatible with the obfuscated semantic tag. Similarly, as the value of o_{sem} increases, the chance that a greater number of candidate regions are semantically compatible with the obfuscated semantic tag increases. The joint approach takes advantage of this increase, i.e., as the number of semantically compatible candidate regions increases, the joint approach selects a cloaking area with a greater number of semantically compatible regions and semantically compatible venues, whereas the disjoint approach is oblivious to the concept of semantic compatibility. Accordingly, the performance of the disjoint approach does not improve as much as the performance of the joint approach by increasing the values of o_{loc} and o_{sem}. We also observe that as the value of λ increases, the median location privacy for the both approaches increases. However, by increasing λ, the value of *loc-priv-ratio* decreases. Roughly speaking, this means that by increasing λ, the difference between the performance of the both approaches becomes less significant. Intuitively, this is because by increasing λ, we increase the number of hidden locations and hidden semantic tags compared to the number of the obfuscated locations and the obfuscated semantic tags in the obfuscated traces. This, in turn, increases the location privacies resulting for the both approaches but it also decreases the importance of the obfuscation approach in defining the amount of the resulting location privacies.

6   Related Work

The problem of protecting location privacy of users in LBSNs (and in LBSs, in general) has been extensively studied in the literature and various protection mechanisms are proposed. Many of the location privacy protection mechanisms apply location obfuscation. The popularity of the location obfuscation lies in the fact that it does not require changing the infrastructure, as it can be performed entirely on the user's side [25]. There exist different methods to obfuscate a location, for instance, by *hiding the location* from the LBS [4,8], by *perturbing the location* (e.g., by adding noise to the location coordinates) [2], by *generalizing the location* (e.g., by merging the location with nearby locations using a cloaking algorithm) [9,10,15,26] and by *adding fake (dummy) locations to the actual location* [6,7,12,27] (See [13,21,22] for detailed surveys on location obfuscation methods). Our work differs from these works by the fact that it considers not only the obfuscation of location but also the obfuscation of the semantic information to protect the location privacy. In addition, the location obfuscation in our work is performed with respect to the obfuscated semantic information, whereas the location obfuscation in these works is semantic-oblivious.

The disjoint obfuscation approach discussed in this paper, was originally introduced in [1]. Our work is close to the work presented in [1], in the sense that it assumes a similar system model and adversary model. In fact, our work and the work in [1] are both built upon the Shokri's framework for quantifying location privacy [20,23,24]) and they both rely on bayesian network models for implementing the inference attacks. However, as already discussed, in this paper we try to improve the work in [1], by proposing a joint obfuscation approach. Another difference between this paper and the work presented in [1] is the fact that, in [1], the authors study the impact of the location obfuscation and the semantic tag obfuscation on both location privacy and the semantic location privacy of users, whereas in this paper we only discuss the impact of the location obfuscation and the semantic tag obfuscation on location privacy. We intend to discuss the impact on semantic location privacy in a future work.

7   Conclusion

In this paper, we have introduced a joint semantic tag-location obfuscation approach for privacy protection in LBSNs. This approach aims to overcome the drawbacks of the existing disjoint approach, by performing the location obfuscation based on the result of the semantic tag obfuscation. We provided a formal framework for evaluation and comparison of the joint approach with the disjoint approach. Then, using a dataset of real-world user mobility traces, we performed an experimental evaluation. The evaluation results show that in almost all cases (i.e., for different values of the obfuscation parameters), the joint approach outperforms the disjoint approach in terms of location privacy protection. We also studied the impact of changing different obfuscation parameters on the obfuscation approaches. In particular, we showed that compared to the disjoint approach, the joint approach can take better advantage of higher values of location obfuscation level and semantic tag obfuscation level and exhibits even more satisfactory performance under higher values of these parameters.

Acknowledgements. This research is partially funded by a UNIL/CHUV postdoc mobility grant disbursed by University of Lausanne and Lausanne University Hospital. We also thank Berker Ağir for his comments and help regarding the disjoint obfuscation approach.

References

1. Ağir B., Huguenin, K., Hengartner, U., Hubaux, J.-P.: On the privacy implications of location semantics. In: PoPETs Journal (2016)
2. Andrés, M.E., Bordenabe, N.E., Chatzikokolakis, K., Palamidessi, C.: Geo-indistinguishability: differential privacy for location-based systems. In: ACM SIGSAC 2013 (2013)
3. eBay/BBN library.https://github.com/eBay/bayesian-belief-networks
4. Beresford, A., Stajano, F.: Location privacy in pervasive computing. In: IEEE Pervasive Computing (2003)

5. Bilogrevic, I., Huguenin, K., Mihaila, S., Shokri, R., Hubaux, J.-P.: Predicting users motivations behind location check-ins and utility implications of privacy protection mechanisms. In: NDSS 2015 (2015)
6. Bindschaedler, V., Shokri, R.: Synthesizing plausible privacy-preserving location traces. In: S& P 2016 (2016)
7. Chow, R., Golle, P.: Faking contextual data for fun, profit, and privacy. In: ACM WPES 2009 (2009)
8. Freudiger, J., Shokri, R., Hubaux, J.-P.: On the optimal placement of mix zones. In: PETS 2009 (2009)
9. Gedik, B.: Location privacy in mobile systems: a personalized anonymization model. In: ICDCS 2005 (2005)
10. Kalnis, P., Ghinita, G., Mouratidis, K., Papadias, D.: Preventing location-based identity inference in anonymous spatial queries. In: IEEE TKDE (2007)
11. Koller, D., Friedman, N.: Probabilistic Graphical Models: Principles and Techniques. The MIT Press, Cambridge (2009)
12. Krumm, J.: Realistic driving trips for location privacy. In: IEEE PerCom 2009 (2009)
13. Krumm, J.: A survey of computational location privacy. In: Personal Ubiquitous Computer (2009)
14. Olteanu, A.-M., Huguenin, K., Shokri, R., Humbert, M., Hubaux, J.-P.: Quantifying interdependent privacy risks with location data. IEEE Trans. Mob, Comput (2017)
15. Mokbel, M., Chow, C., Aref, W.: The new casper: query processing for location services without compromising privacy. In: VLDB 2006 (2006)
16. Murphy, K.P.: Dynamic Bayesian Networks: Representation, Inference and Learning. Ph.D. Thesis, UC Berkeley (2002)
17. Murphy, K.P., Weiss. Y., Jordan, M.: Loopy belief propagation for approximate inference: an empirical study. In: UAI (1999)
18. Pearl, J.: Probabilistic Reasoning in Intelligent Systems: Networks of Plausible Inference. M. Kaufmann (1988)
19. Pomegranate. https://pomegranate.readthedocs.io/en/latest/
20. Shokri, R.: Quantifying and Protecting Location Privacy. PhD. Thesis, EPFL (2012)
21. Shokri, R., Freudiger, J., Jadliwala, M., Hubaux, J.-P.: A distortion-based metric for location privacy. In: ACM WPES 2009 (2009)
22. Shokri, R., Freudiger, J., Hubaux, J.-P.: A unified framework for location privacy. In: HotPETs 2010 (2010)
23. Shokri, R., Theodorakopoulos, G., Le Boudec, J.-Y., Hubaux, J.-P.: Quantifying location privacy. In: IEEE S& P 2011 (2011)
24. Shokri, R., Theodorakopoulos, G., Danezis, G., Le Boudec, J.-Y., Hubaux, J.-P.: Quantifying location privacy: the case of sporadic location exposure. In: PETS 2011 (2011)
25. Shokri, R., Theodorakopoulos, G., Troncoso, C.: Privacy Games Along Location Traces: A Game-Theoretic Framework for Optimizing Location Privacy. In: ACM Trans. Priv, Secur (2016)
26. Xu, T., Cai, Y.: Feeling-based location privacy protection for location-based services. In: CCS 2009 (2009)
27. You, T., Peng, W., Lee, W.: Protecting moving trajectories with dummies. In: IEEE MDM 2007 (2007)

Modeling and Analyzing the Corona-Virus Warning App with the Isabelle Infrastructure Framework

Florian Kammüller[1,2(✉)] and Bianca Lutz[1,2(✉)]

[1] Middlesex University London, London, UK
f.kammueller@mdx.ac.uk, bianca.lutz@campus.tu-berlin.de
[2] Technische Universität Berlin, Berlin, Germany

Abstract. We provide a model in the Isabelle Infrastructure framework of the recently published German Corona-virus warning app (CWA). The app supports breaking infection chains by informing users whether they have been in close contact to an infected person. The app has a decentralized architecture that supports anonymity of users. We provide a formal model of the existing app with the Isabelle Infrastructure framework to show up some natural attacks in a very abstract model. We then use the security refinement process of the Isabelle Infrastructure framework to highlight how the use of continuously changing Ephemeral Ids (EphIDs) improves the anonymity.

1 Introduction

The German Chancellor Angela Merkel has strongly supported the publication of the mobile phone Corona-virus warning app (CWA; [14]) by publicly proclaiming that "this App deserves your trust" [2]. Many millions of mobile phone users in Germany have downloaded the app with 6 million on the first day. CWA is one amongst many similar applications that aim at the very important goal to "break infection chains" by providing timely information to users of whether they have been in close proximity to a person who tested positive for COVID-19.

The app was designed with great attention on privacy: a distributed architecture [15] has been adopted that is based on a very clever application design whereby clients broadcast highly anonymized identifiers (ids) via Bluetooth and store those ids of people in close proximity. Infected persons report their infection by uploading their ids to a central server, providing all clients the means to assess exposure risk locally, hence, stored contact data has never to be shared.

The Isabelle Infrastructure framework [11] allows modeling and analyzing architecture and scenarios including physical and logical entities, actors, and policies within the interactive theorem prover Isabelle supported with temporal logic, Kripke structures, and attack trees. It has been applied for example to Insider analysis in airplanes [12], privacy in IoT healthcare [4], and recently also to blockchain protocols [10].

© Springer Nature Switzerland AG 2020
J. Garcia-Alfaro et al. (Eds.): DPM 2020/CBT 2020, LNCS 12484, pp. 128–144, 2020.
https://doi.org/10.1007/978-3-030-66172-4_8

The technical advantage of modeling an application in the Isabelle Insider framework lies in (a) having explicit representations of infrastructures, actors and policies in a formal model that (b) allows additional automated verification of security properties with CTL, Kripke structures and Attack Trees within the interactive theorem prover Isabelle.

The app now in use in Germany has been developed based on a protocol proposed by the DP-3T project [16]: A sophisticated security concept conceived by experts in the field that has strong claims with regard to mathematical support [17] [p2]. However, there has, as of yet, to our knowledge no formal verification been involved. Even if a "post-production" formal specification seems pointless, it allows revealing weak points of the architecture, show that the measures that have been conceived are suitable to cover those weak points, or to what extent trade-offs have to be made due to inherent vulnerabilities. The protocol implemented by the framework CWA resembles only the most basic of the three protocols proposed by the DP-3T project. Hence, a formal verified model that stresses the impact or limits of certain security measures might give more weight to appeals like [19] to adopt the more sophisticated protocols.

The contributions of this paper are (a) formal re-engineering of CWA (b) providing an additional security and privacy analysis with interactive theorem proving certification of a novel view on the system architecture including actors, locations, and policies, (c) a formal definition of a security refinement process that allows improving a system based on attacks found by the attack tree analysis and (d) an application of the refinement to improve security of the CWA specification.

In this paper, we first provide some background in Sect. 2: we give a brief overview of related works and the protocol of CWA (Sect. 2.1). We then introduce the Isabelle Infrastructure framework (Sect. 2.2). Next, we present our model (Sect. 3) and analysis of privacy and attacks (Sect. 3.4). The found attack on the first abstract specification motivates refinement. The formal definition of refinement for the Isabelle Infrastructure framework is introduced and illustrated on CWA (Sect. 4) before drawing some conclusions (Sect. 5).

The formal model in the Isabelle insider framework is fully mechanized and proved in Isabelle (sources available [8]).

2 Background and Related Work

2.1 DP-3T and PEPP-PT

We are mainly concerned with the architecture and protocols proposed by the DP-3T (*Decentralized Privacy-Preserving Proximity Tracing*) project [16]. The main reason to focus on this particular family of protocols is the *Exposure Notification Framework* (ENF), jointly published by Apple and Google [1], that adopts core principles of the DP-3T proposal. This API is not only used in CWA but has the potential of being widely adopted in future app developments that might emerge due to the reach of players like Apple and Google.

There are, however, competing architectures noteworthy, namely protocols developed under the roof of the *Pan-European Privacy-Preserving Proximity Tracing* project (PEPP-PT) [21], e.g. PEPP-PT-ROBERT [22], that might be characterized as centralized architectures.

Neither DP-3T nor PEPP-PT are synonymous for just one single protocol. Each project endorses different protocols with unique properties in terms of privacy and data protection.

There is a variety of noteworthy privacy and security issues. The debate among advocates of centralized architectures and those in favor of a decentralized approach in particular yields a lot of interesting material detailing different attacks and possible mitigation strategies: [18,20,23].

In terms of attack scenarios, we focus on, what might be classified as deanonymization attacks: Tracking a device (see [18][p9], [23][p8]) and identifying infected individuals ([18][p5], [23][p9]).

Basic DP-3T Architecture. Upon installation, the app generates secret daily seeds to derive so-called *Ephemeral Ids* (EphIDs) from them. EphIDs are generated locally with cryptographic methods and cannot be connected to one another but only reconstructed from the secret seed they were derived from.

During normal operation each client broadcasts its EphIDs via Bluetooth whilst scanning for EphIDs broadcasted by other devices in the vicinity. Collected EphIDs are stored locally along with associated meta-data such as signal attenuation and date. In DP-3T the contact information gathered is never shared but only evaluated locally.

If patients test positive for the Corona-virus, they are entitled to upload specific data to a central backend server. This data is aggregated by the backend server and redistributed to all clients regularly to provide the means for local risk scoring, i. e., determining whether collected EphIDs match those broadcasted by now-confirmed Corona-virus patients during the last, e. g., 14, days.

In the most simple (and insecure) protocol proposed by DP-3T this basically translates into publishing the daily seeds used to derive EphIDs from. The protocol implemented by ENF and, hence, CWA adopts this low-cost design [15]. DP-3T proposes two other, more sophisticated protocols that improve privacy and data protection properties to different degrees but are more costly to implement. Figure 1 illustrates the basic system architecture along with some of the mitigation measures either implemented in CWA or proposed by DP-3T.

2.2   Isabelle Infrastructure Framework

The Isabelle Infrastructure is built in the interactive generic theorem prover Isabelle/HOL [13]. As a framework, it supports formalization and proof of systems with actors and policies. It originally emerged from verification of insider threat scenarios but it soon became clear that the theoretical concepts, like temporal logic combined with Kripke structures and a generic notion of state transitions were very suitable to be combined with attack trees into a formal

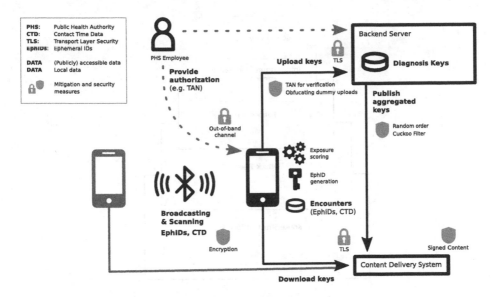

Fig. 1. Decentralized privacy-preserving proximity tracing protocol of CWA

security engineering process [3] and framework [7]. Figure 2 gives an overview of the Isabelle Infrastructure framework with its layers of object-logics – each level below embeds the one above showing the novel contribution of this paper in blue on the top.

Kripke Structures, CTL, and Attack Trees. The Isabelle framework has now after various case studies become a general framework for the state-based security analysis of infrastructures with policies and actors. Temporal logic and Kripke structures build the foundation. Meta-theoretical results have been established to show equivalence between attack trees and CTL statements [4]. This foundation provides a generic notion of state transition on which attack trees and temporal logic can be used to express properties. The main notions used in this paper are:

- Kripke structures and state transitions:
  Using a generic state transition relation $\rightarrow$, Kripke structures are defined as a set of states reachable by $\rightarrow$ from an initial state set, for example,

  `Kripke {t. ∃ i ∈ I. i →* t} I`

  where $\rightarrow^*$ is the reflexive transitive closure over $\rightarrow$.
- CTL statements:
  For example, we can write

  `K ⊢ EF s`

  to express that in Kripke structure K there is a path on which the property s (a set of states) will eventually hold.

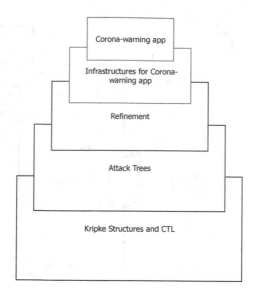

Fig. 2. Generic Isabelle Infrastructure framework applied to CWA.

– Attack trees:
   The datatype of attack trees has three constructors: $\oplus_\vee$ creates or-trees and
   $\oplus_\wedge$ creates and-trees. And-attack trees $l\oplus_\wedge^s$ and or-attack trees $l\oplus_\vee^s$ consist
   of a list of sub-attacks – again attack trees. The third constructor creates a
   base attack as a pair of state sets written $\mathcal{N}_{(I,s)}$. For example, a two step
   and-attack leading from state set I via si to s is expressed as

   $$\vdash [\mathcal{N}_{(I,si)}, \mathcal{N}_{(si,s)}]\oplus_\wedge^{(I,s)}$$

– Attack tree refinement, validity and adequacy:
   Attack trees have their own refinement (not to be mixed up with the system
   refinement presented in this paper as introduced in the next section). An
   abstract attack tree A of type α attree over an arbitrary state type σ may
   be refined by spelling out the attack steps until a valid attack is reached:
   $\vdash A :: (\sigma :: \text{state})$ attree.
   The validity is defined constructively (code is generated from it) and its adequacy with respect to a formal semantics in CTL is proved and can be used to
   facilitate actual application verification as demonstrated here in the stepwise
   system refinements.

Instantiation of Framework. The formal model of CWA uses the Isabelle
Infrastructure framework instantiating it by reusing its concept of *actors* for
users and smartphones whereby locations correspond to physical locations.
The Ephemeral Ids, their sending and change is added to infrastructures by
slightly adapting the basic state type of infrastructure graphs and accordingly the semantic rules for the actions move, get, and put. The details of the

newly adapted infrastructure are presented in Sect. 3. Technically, an Isabelle theory file `Infrastructure.thy` builds on top of the theories for Kripke structures and CTL (`MC.thy`), attack trees (`AT.thy`), and security refinement (`Refinement.thy`). Thus all these concepts can be used to specify the formal model for CWA, express relevant and interesting properties, and conduct interactive proofs (with the full support of the powerful and highly automated proof support of Isabelle). All Isabelle sources are available online [8].

Refinement. An additional feature that has been integrated into the Isabelle Infrastructure framework motivated by security engineering formal specifications for IoT healthcare system is an extension of the formal specification process introducing refinement of Kripke structures [7,11]. It refines a system model based on a formal definition of a combination of trace refinement and structural refinement (or datatype refinement). The definition allows proving property preservation results crucial for an iterative development process. The refinements of the system specification can be interleaved with attack analysis while security properties can be proved in Isabelle. In each iteration security qualities are accumulated while continuously attack trees scrutinize the design. One of the contributions of this paper is to explore different concepts of refinement: the formal expression of refinement, enables to pin down (i.e. exemplify) different concepts of refinement (data refinement, action refinement, trace refinement (aka spec refinement) and combinations thereof with concrete attack scenarios.

3   Modeling and Analyzing CWA

3.1   Infrastructures, Policies, and Actors

The Isabelle Infrastructure framework supports the representation of infrastructures as graphs with actors and policies attached to nodes. These infrastructures are the *states* of the Kripke structure.

The transition between states is triggered by non-parameterized actions `get`, `move`, and `put` executed by actors. Actors are given by an abstract type `actor` and a function `Actor` that creates elements of that type from identities (of type `string` written `''s''` in Isabelle). Actors are contained in an infrastructure graph type `igraph` constructed by its constructor `Lgraph`.

```
datatype igraph =
      Lgraph (location × location)set
             location ⇒ identity set
             identity ⇒ (string set × string set × efid)
             location ⇒ string × (dlm × data) set
             location ⇒ efid set
             actor ⇒ location ⇒ (identity × efid) set
```

In the current application of the framework to the CWA case study, this graph contains a set of location pairs representing the topology of the infrastructure as a graph of nodes and a function that assigns a set of actor identities to each node (location) in the graph. The third component of an `igraph` assigns the credentials to each actor: a triple-valued function whose first range component is a set describing the credentials in the possession of an actor and the second component is a set defining the roles the actor can take on; most prominently the third component is the `efid` assigned to the actor. This is initially just a natural number of type `nat` mapped by the constructor `Efid` to the new datatype `efid` but will be refined to actually represent lists of Ephemeral Ids later when refining the specification.

datatype `efid = Efid nat`

The fourth component of the type `igraph` assigns security labeled data to locations, a feature not used in the current application. The second to last component assigns the set of efids of all currently present smart phones to each location of the graph. The last component finally denotes the knowledge set of each actor for each location: a set of pairs of actors and potential ids.

Corresponding projection functions for each of the components of an infrastructure graph are provided; they are named `gra` for the actual set of pairs of locations, `agra` for the actor map, `cgra` for the credentials, `lgra` for the data at that location, `egra` for the assignment of current efids to locations, and `kgra` for the knowledge set for each actor for each location.

In CWA, the initial values for the `igraph` components use two locations `pub` and `shop` to define the following constants (we omit the data map component `ex_locs`).

```
ex_loc_ass ≡ (λ x. if x = pub then {''Alice'', ''Bob'', ''Eve''}
                else (if x = shop then {''Charly'', ''David''}
                else {}))
ex_creds ≡ (λ x. if x = ''Alice'' then ({}, {}, Efid 1) else
                (if x = ''Bob'' then   ({},{}, Efid 2) else
                (if x = ''Charly'' then ({},{}, Efid 3) else
                (if x = ''David'' then ({},{}, Efid 4) else
                (if x = ''Eve'' then ({},{}, Efid 5)
                else ({},{},Efid 0))))))
ex_efids ≡ (λ x. if x = pub then {Efid 1, Efid 2, Efid 5}
                else (if x = shop then {Efid 3, Efid 4} else {}))
ex_knos ≡ (λ x. (if x = Actor ''Eve'' then (λ l. {} else (λ l. {})))
```

These components are wrapped up into the following `igraph`.

```
ex_graph ≡
     Lgraph {(pub, shop)} ex_loc_ass ex_creds ex_locs ex_efids ex_knos
```

Infrastructures are given by the following datatype that contains an infrastructure graph of type `igraph` and a policy given by a function that assigns local policies over a graph to all locations of the graph.

datatype `infrastructure = Infrastructure igraph`
```
                              [igraph, location] ⇒ policy set
```

There are projection functions `graphI` and `delta` when applied to an infrastructure return the graph and the local policies, respectively. The function `local_policies` gives the policy for each location x over an infrastructure graph G as a pair: the first element of this pair is a function specifying the actors y that are entitled to perform the actions specified in the set which is the second element of that pair. The local policies definition for CWA, simply permits all actions to all actors in both locations.

```
local_policies G ≡
        (λ x. if x = pub then  {(λ y. True, {get,move,put})}
        else (if x = shop then {(λ y. True, {get,move,put})} else {}))
```

For CWA, the initial infrastructure contains the graph `ex_graph` with its two locations pub and shop and is then wrapped up with the local policies into the infrastructure `Corona_scenario` that represents the "initial" state for the Kripke structure.

```
Corona_scenario ≡ Infrastructure  ex_graph local_policies
```

3.2   Policies, Privacy, and Behaviour

Policies specify the expected behaviour of actors of an infrastructure. They are given by pairs of predicates (conditions) and sets of (enabled) actions. They are defined by the `enables` predicate: an actor h is enabled to perform an action a in infrastructure I, at location l if there exists a pair (p,e) in the local policy of l (`delta I l` projects to the local policy) such that the action a is a member of the action set e and the policy predicate p holds for actor h.

```
enables I l h a ≡ ∃ (p,e) ∈ delta I l. a ∈ e ∧ p h
```

The Privacy protection goal is to avoid deanonymization. That is, an attacker should not be able to disambiguate the set of pairs of real ids and EphIDs. This is abstractly expressed in the predicate `identifiable`.

```
identifiable eid A ≡ is_singleton{(Id,Eid). (Id, Eid) ∈ A ∧ Eid = eid}
```

The predicate `identifiable` is used to express as the global policy 'Eve cannot deanonymize an Ephemeral Id eid using the gathered knowledge':

```
global_policy I eid ≡
            ¬(identifiable eid
                ((∩ (kgra(graphI I)(Actor ''Eve'')'(nodes(graphI I))))
                - {(x,y). x = ''Eve''}))
```

3.3   Infrastructure State Transition

The state transition relation uses the syntactic infix notation I → I' to denote that infrastructures I and I' are in this relation. We will use this state transition to define the dynamic behaviour of the system including actors' movements and the evolution of their knowledge. This allows representing attacks as sequences of state transitions leading to states in which the global policy is violated. To give an intuitive motivating idea before the formal presentation in Sect. 3.4: the attack will consist of the state transitions of Eve getting available EphIds at the location pub, Alice moving to shop, Eve following her and again getting the EphIds at shop.

So, one relevant rule for the state transition is the one for move that defines the state transition relation expressing state changes when actors move across the infrastructure.

```
move: G = graphI I ⟹ a @_G l ⟹ a ∈ actors_graph(graphI I) ⟹
    l ∈ nodes G ⟹ l' ∈ nodes G ⟹ enables I l' (Actor h) move ⟹
    I' = Infrastructure (move_graph_a a l l' (graphI I))(delta I)
    ⟹ I → I'
```

The semantics of this rule is embedded in the function move_graph_a that adapts the infrastructure state so that the moving actor a is now associated to the target location l' in the actor map agra and not any more at l and also the association of efids is updated accordingly.

```
move_graph_a n l l' g ≡
  Lgraph (gra g)
          (if n ∈ ((agra g) l) ∧  n ∉ ((agra g) l') then
            ((agra g)(l := (agra g l) - {n}))(l' := (insert n (agra g l'))))
          else (agra g))
          (cgra g)(lgra g)
          (if n ∈ ((agra g) l) ∧  n ∉ ((agra g) l') then
              ((egra g)(l := (egra g l) - {efemid (cgra g n)}))
                      (l' := (insert (efemid (cgra g n))(egra g l'))))
          else egra g)
          (kgra g)
```

Another action relevant for the deanonymization attack describes how an actor gets information. This is defined by the rule of the state transition for the action get. Initially, this rule expresses that an actor that resides at a location l (a @_G l) and is enabled by the local policy in this location to "get" can combine all ids at the current location (contained in egra G l) with all actors at the current location (contained in agra G l) and add this set of pairs to his knowledge set kgra G using the function update f(l := n) redefining the function f for the input l to have now the new value n.

```
get_data: G = graphI I ⟹ a @_G l ⟹ enables I l (Actor a) get ⟹
    I' = Infrastructure
            (Lgraph (gra G)(agra G)(cgra G)(lgra G)(egra G)
              ((kgra G)((Actor a) := ((kgra G (Actor a))(l:=
```

```
                {(x,y). x ∈ agra G l ∧ y ∈ egra G l})))))
        (delta I)
  ⟹ I → I'
```

Based on this state transition and the above defined `Corona_scenario`, we define the first Kripke structure.

```
corona_Kripke ≡ Kripke { I. Corona_scenario →* I } {Corona_scenario}
```

3.4 Attack Analysis

For the analysis of attacks, we negate the security property that we want to achieve, usually the global policy.

Since we consider a predicate transformer semantics, we use sets of states to represent properties. The invalidated global policy is given by the set `scorona`.

```
scorona ≡ {x. ∃ n. ¬ global_policy x (Efid n)}
```

The attack we are interested in is to see whether for the scenario

```
Kripke_scenario ≡  Infrastructure ex_graph local_policies
```

from the initial state `Icorona` ≡{`corona_scenario`}, the critical state `scorona` can be reached, that is, is there a valid attack (`Icorona`,`scorona`)?

For the Kripke structure `corona_Kripke` we first derive a valid and-attack using the attack tree proof calculus.

$$
\vdash\ [\mathcal{N}_{(\text{Icorona},\text{Corona})},\mathcal{N}_{(\text{Corona},\text{Corona1})},\mathcal{N}_{(\text{Corona1},\text{Corona2})},\\
\mathcal{N}_{(\text{Corona2},\text{Corona3})},\mathcal{N}_{(\text{Corona3},\text{scorona})}]\oplus_{\wedge}^{(\text{Icorona},\text{scorona})}
$$

The sets `Corona`, `Corona1`, `Corona2`, `Corona3` are the intermediate states where `Bob` moves to shop and `Eve` follows him collecting the Ephemeral Ids in each location. The collected information enables identifying Bob's Ephemeral Id.

The attack tree calculus [4] exhibits that an attack is possible.

```
corona_Kripke ⊢ EF scorona
```

We can simply apply the Correctness theorem `AT_EF` [4,5]

```
⊢ A ⟹ attack A = (I,s)
⟹ Kripke {s . ∃ i ∈ I. (i →* s) } I ⊢ EF s
```

to immediately prove this CTL statement. This application of the meta-theorem of Correctness of attack trees saves us proving the CTL formula tediously by exploring the state space in Isabelle proofs. Alternatively, we could use the generated code for the function `is_attack_tree` in Scala (see [4]) to check that a refined attack of the above is valid.

4   Refinement

Intuitively, a refinement changes some aspect of the type of the state, for example, replaces a data type by a richer datatype or restricts the behaviour of the actors. The former is expressed directly by a mapping of datatypes, the latter is incorporated into the state transition relation of the Kripke structure that corresponds to the transformed model. In other words, we can encode a refinement within our framework as a relation on Kripke structures that is parameterized additionally by a function that maps the refined type to the abstract type. The direction "from refined to abstract" of this type mapping may seem curiously counter-intuitive. However, the actual refinement is given by the refinement that uses this function as an input. The refinement then refines an abstract to a more concrete system specification. The additional layer for the refinement can be formalized in Isabelle as a refinement relation $\sqsubseteq_{\mathcal{E}}$. This relation, called **refinement**, is typed as a relation over triples – a function from a threefold Cartesian product to **bool**, the type containing true and false only. The type variables σ and σ' input to the type constructor **Kripke** represent the abstract state type and the concrete state type. Consequently, the middle element of the triples selected by the relation **refinement** is a function of type $\sigma' \Rightarrow \sigma$ mapping elements of the refined state to the abstract state. The expression in quotation marks after the type is again the infix syntax in Isabelle that allows the definition of mathematical notation instead of writing **refinement** in prefix manner. This nicer infix syntax is already used in the actual definition. Finally, the arrow $\Longrightarrow$ is the implication of Isabelle's meta-logic while $\longrightarrow$ is the one of the *object* logic HOL. They are logically equivalent but of different types: within a HOL formula, for example, within the below $\forall$s' $\in$ states K'...., only the implication $\longrightarrow$ can be used.

```
refinement :: (σ Kripke × (σ' ⇒ σ) × σ' Kripke) ⇒ bool ("_ ⊑(_) _")
   K ⊑ε K' ≡ ∀ s' ∈ states K'. ∀ s ∈ init K'.
               s →*σ' s' ⟶ E(s) ∈ init K ∧ E(s) →*σ E(s')
```

The definition of K $\sqsubseteq_{\mathcal{E}}$ K' states that for any state s' of the refined Kripke structure that can be reached by the state transition in zero or more steps from an initial state s of the refined Kripke structure, the mapping $\mathcal{E}$ from the refined to the abstract model's state must preserve this reachability, i.e., the image of s must also be an initial state and from there the image of s' under $\mathcal{E}$ must be reached within 0 and n steps.

4.1   Property Preserving System Refinement

A first direct consequence of this definition is the following lemma where the operator ` in $\mathcal{E}$`(init K') represents function image, i.e., $\{\mathcal{E}(x) \mid x \in \text{init K'}\}$.

lemma init_ref: K $\sqsubseteq_{\mathcal{E}}$ K' $\Longrightarrow$ $\mathcal{E}$`(init K') $\subseteq$ init K

A more prominent consequence of the definition of refinement is that of property preservation. Here, we show that refinement preserves the CTL property of EF*s* which means that a reachability property true in the refined model K' is already true in the abstract model. A state set s' represents a property in the predicate transformer view of properties as sets of states. The additional condition on initial states ensures that we cannot "forget" them.

theorem prop_pres:
  K $\sqsubseteq_{\mathcal{E}}$ K' $\implies$ init K $\subseteq$ $\mathcal{E}$'(init K') $\implies$
  $\forall$ s' $\in$ Pow(states K'). K' $\vdash$ EF s' $\longrightarrow$ K $\vdash$ EF ($\mathcal{E}$'(s'))

It is remarkable, that our definition of refinement by Kripke structures entails property preservation and makes it possible to prove this as a theorem in Isabelle once for all, i.e., as a meta-theorem. However, this is due to the fact that our generic definition of state transition allows explicitly formalizing such sophisticated concepts like reachability. For practical purposes, however, the proof obligation of showing that a specific refinement is in fact a refinement is rather complex justly because of the explicit use of the transitive closure of the state transition relation. In most cases, the refinement will be simpler. Therefore, we offer additional help by the following theorem that uses a stronger characterization of Kripke structure refinement and shows that our refinement follows from this.

theorem strong_mt:
  $\mathcal{E}$'(init K') $\subseteq$ init K $\land$ s $\rightarrow_{\sigma'}$ s' $\longrightarrow$ $\mathcal{E}$(s) $\rightarrow_{\sigma}$ $\mathcal{E}$(s')
  $\implies$ K $\sqsubseteq_{\mathcal{E}}$ K'

This simpler characterization is in fact a stronger one: we could have $s \rightarrow_{\sigma'} s'$ in the refined Kripke structure K' and $\neg(\mathcal{E}(s) \rightarrow_{\sigma} \mathcal{E}(s'))$ but neither s nor s' are reachable from initial states in K'. For cases, where we have the simpler one-step proviso and also reachability from initial states we provide a slightly weaker version of **strong_mt**.

theorem strong_mt':
  $\mathcal{E}$'(init K') $\subseteq$ init K $\land$ ($\exists$ s0 $\in$ init K'. s0 $\rightarrow^*$ s)
  $\land$ s $\rightarrow_{\sigma'}$ s' $\longrightarrow$ $\mathcal{E}$(s) $\rightarrow_{\sigma}$ $\mathcal{E}$(s') $\implies$ K $\sqsubseteq_{\mathcal{E}}$ K'

This idea of property preservation coincides with the classical idea of trace refinement as it is given in process algebras like CSP. In this view, the properties of a system are given by the set of its event traces. Now, a refinement of the system is given by another system that has a subset of the event traces of the former one. Although the principal idea is similar, we greatly extend it since our notion additionally incorporates data refinement. Since we include a state map $\sigma' \Rightarrow \sigma$ in our refinement map, we additionally allow structural refinement: the state map generalizes the basic idea of trace refinement by traces corresponding to each other but allows additionally an exchange of data types. As we see in the application to the case study, the refinement steps may sometimes just specialize the traces: in this case the state map $\sigma' \Rightarrow \sigma$ is just identity.

In addition, we also have a simple implicit version of *action refinement*. In an action refinement, traces may be refined by combining consecutive system events into atomic events thereby reducing traces. We can observe this kind of refinement in the second refinement step of CWA considered next.

4.2   Refining the Specification

Clearly, fixed Ephemeral Ids are not really ephemeral. The model presented in Sect. 3 has deliberately been designed abstractly to allow focusing on the basic system architecture and finding an initial deanonymization attack. We now introduce "proper" Ephemeral Ids and show how the system datatype can be refined to a system that uses those instead of the fixed ones.

For the DP-3T Ephemeral Ids [17], for each day t a seed SK_t is used to generate a list of length $n = 24 * 60/L$, where L is the duration for which the Ephemeral Ids are posted by the smart phone

```
EphID1 || ... || EphIDn = PRG(PRF(SKt,''broadcast key''))
```

"where PRF is a pseudo-random function (e.g., HMAC-SHA256), "broadcast key" is a fixed, public string, and PRG is a pseudorandom generator (e.g. AES in counter mode)" [17].

From a cryptographic point of view, the crucial properties of the Ephemeral Ids are that they are purely random, therefore, they cannot be guessed, but, at the same time, if – after the actual encounter between sender and receiver – the seed SK_t is published, it is feasible to relate any of the EphIDi to SK_t for all $\mathtt{i} \in \{1, \ldots, n\}$. For a formalization of this crucial cryptographic property in Isabelle it suffices to define a new type of list of Ephemeral Ids efidlist containing the root SK_t (the first efid), a current efid indicated by a list pointer of type nat, and the actual list of efids.

```
datatype efidlist = Efids "efid" "nat" "efid list"
```

We define functions for this datatype: efidsroot returning the first of the three constituents in an efidlist (the root SK_t of type efid); efids_index giving the second component of type nat, that is, the index of the current efid; efids_inc_ind applied to an efidlist increments the index; efids_cur returning the current efid from the list and efids_list for the entire list (the third component of type efid list).

The first step of refinement replaces the simple efid in the infrastructure type by the new type efidlist. Note, that in the new datatype igraph this change affects only the third component, the credentials to become

```
identity ⇒ (string set × string set × efidlist)
```

The last two components, the set of currently present efids, and the knowledge set, remain the same and still operate on the simple type efid. The refined state transition relation implements the possibility of changing the Ephemeral Ids by the rule for the action put that resembles very much the rule for get.

The important change to the infrastructure state is implemented in the function
put_graph_efid that increases the current index in the efidlist in the credential component cgra g n for the "putting" actor identity n and inserts the
current efid from that credential component into the egra component, the set
of currently "present" Ephemeral Ids at the location l.

```
put_graph_efid n l g  ≡
  Lgraph (gra g)(agra g)
         ((cgra g)(n := (credentials (cgra g n), roles (cgra g n),
                          efids_inc_ind(efemid (cgra g n)))))
         (lgra g)
         ((egra g)(l := insert (efids_cur(efemid (cgra g n)))(egra g l)))
         (kgra g)
```

We can now apply the refinement by defining a datatype map from the refined
infrastructure type InfrastructureOne.infrastructure to the former one
Infrastructure.infrastructure.

```
definition refmap :: InfrastructureOne.infrastructure ⇒
                       Infrastructure.infrastructure
where refmap I =
  Infrastructure.Infrastructure
    (Infrastructure.Lgraph
       (InfrastructureOne.gra (graphI I))
       (InfrastructureOne.agra (graphI I))
       (λ h. repl_efr
          (InfrastructureOne.cgra (graphI I)) h)
          (InfrastructureOne.lgra (graphI I))
          (InfrastructureOne.egra (graphI I))
          (λ a. λ l.
  (λ (x,y).(x, efids_root(efemid(InfrastructureOne.cgra (graphI I) x))))
                   '(InfrastructureOne.kgra (graphI I)) a l))
```

This is then plugged into the parameter $\mathcal{E}$ of the refinement operator allowing
to prove corona_Kripke ⊑_refmap corona_Kripke0 where the latter is the refined
Kripke structure.

Surprisingly, we can still prove corona_Kripke0 ⊢ EF scorona0 by using the
same attack tree as in the abstract model: if Bob moves from pub to shop[1], he is
vulnerable to being identifiable as long as he does not change the current efid.
So, if Eve moves to the shop as well and performs a get before Bob does a put,
then Eve's knowledge sets permit identifying Bob's current Ephemeral Id as his.

Second Refinement Step. The persistent attack can be abbreviated informally by the action sequence [get,move,move,get] performed by actors Eve,
Bob, Eve, and Eve again, respectively. How can a second refinement step avoid
that Eve does the last get by imposing that after the first move of Bob a put

---

[1] That is, if he moves alone: if all others from pub go to shop with him his anonymity
remains intact.

action must happen before Eve can do another get? A very simple remedy to exclude this attack is to bind a put action after every move. We can implement that change by a minimal update to the function move_graph_a (see Sect. 3) by adding an increment (highlighted in the code snippet in bold letters) of the currently used Ephemeral Id before updating the egra component of the target location.

```
move_graph_a n l l' g ≡ ...
  (l' := insert (efids_cur( efids_inc_ind(efemid (cgra g n))))(egra g l))...
```

This is an action refinement because the move action is changed. It is a refinement, since any trace of the refined model can still be mapped to a trace in the more abstract model just omitting a few steps (the refinement relation is defined using the reflexive transitive closure $\rightarrow^*$).

5   Summary and Discussion of Relevance of the Approach

We can establish in our formal framework an attack that even a system using changing Ephemeral ids can be broken if the attacker physically follows a victim. This is a basic attack on anonymity: a user's connection between his Ephemeral Ids and personal details (Iphone MAC or name) is revealed to the attacker. The protection goal of privacy is thereby destroyed.

When establishing the attack we start from a simplistic scenario that does not use Ephemeral Ids but fixed ids. In this (over)simplified model the attack is established. We then define a formal refinement calculus for the Isabelle Infrastructure framework to refine the attack to a system with Ephemeral Ids that change in fixed time intervals obfuscating the relationship between user and his pseudonym[2].

Now, the refinement shows that although the Ephemeral Ids change regularly the same attack that has been identified on the very abstract level (fixed ids) persists. The refinement allows refining the datatype (Id $\mapsto$ EphID) but also delivers the usual trace refinement (behaviours of the refined systems are a subset of the traces of the abstract system). This persistence of the attack precisely shows which part of the system behaviour is responsible for the attack. In a second refinement step using action refinement based on this insight from the (repeated) attack, we can exclude the dangerous attack trace.

Clearly, the abstract attack we establish is obvious on an informal level but the persistence of the attack on the refined system is less obvious. The remedy by a second refinement step is an evident restriction of the system behaviour which gives a clear specification of a system secured against this attack. The use of formal methods therefore lies not in the discovery of an obvious attack on a simplified system but in showing how a formal specification including security refinement can lead to a stepwise improvement that is accompanied by formal

---

[2] We identify the smartphone and the user which might be also recognized by his appearance (face).

proof in the Isabelle Infrastructure framework. The solution to exclude the attack in the second refinement step binds the action move together with a put action. This shows that besides datatype refinement and trace refinement our refinement calculus also entails action refinement. This action refinement is implemented implicitly by changing the effects of the actions in the semantic state transition relation. In future work, we could think about making the action refinement more explicit by considering a relationship between semantic rules or by refining the refinement notion to a more explicit layer of protocol steps – similar to what has been done in previous applications of the Isabelle Infrastructure framework for example to Auction protocols [9] or the Quantum Key Distribution [6].

The security refinement in general might seem pointless, as in the first step of refinement the attack persists and even though the second refinement gets rid of this specific attack, it doesn't exclude the reachability of the attack goal altogether (if the attacker Eve gets Bob on his own in a location she can map all used EphIDs to him). However, the refinement makes the system relatively more secure in that for a larger number of traces the abstract attack does not work anymore[3]. It is important to emphasize that security refinement is a cyclic process that improves security but does not usually terminate (like a loop) with a fixed point of 100% secure system. In a refined model new detail may give rise to new attack possibilities. These additional attacks can be identified using the Attack Tree calculus and trigger further refinement steps.

References

1. Apple and Google. Exposure notification framework (2020). https://www.google.com/covid19/exposurenotifications/
2. Bundesregierung, D.: Die Corona-Warn-App: Unterstützt uns im Kampf gegen Corona, 2020. German government announcement and support of Coronavirus warning app. https://www.bundesregierung.de/breg-de/themen/corona-warn-app
3. CHIST-ERA. Success: Secure accessibility for the internet of things (2016). http://www.chistera.eu/projects/success and https://github.com/success-iot
4. Kammüller, F.: Attack trees in Isabelle. In: Naccache, D., et al. (eds.) ICICS 2018. LNCS, vol. 11149, pp. 611–628. Springer, Cham (2018). https://doi.org/10.1007/978-3-030-01950-1_36
5. Kammüller, F.: Formal modeling and analysis of data protection for GDPR compliance of IoT healthcare systems. In: IEEE Systems, Man and Cybernetics, SMC 2018. IEEE (2018)
6. Kammüller, F.: Attack trees in Isabelle extended with probabilities for quantum cryptography. Comput. Secur. **87**, 101572 (2019)
7. Kammüller, F.: Combining secure system design with risk assessment for IoT healthcare systems. In: Workshop on Security, Privacy, and Trust in the IoT, SPTIoT 2019, colocated with IEEE PerCom. IEEE (2019)
8. Kammüller, F.: Isabelle infrastructure framework with IoT healthcare S&P application and corona-virus warn app (2020). https://github.com/flokam/IsabelleAT

---

[3] Adding probabilities as in [6] enables quantifying this.

9. Kammüller, F., Kerber, M., Probst, C.: Insider threats for auctions: formal modeling, proof, and certified code. J. Wirel. Mob. Netw. Ubiquit. Comput. Dependable Appl. (JoWUA) 8(1), 44–78 (2017). Special Issue on Insider Threat Solutions - Moving from Concept to Reality
10. Kammüller, F., Nestmann, U.: Inter-blockchain protocols with the Isabelle Infrastructure framework. In: Formal Methods for Blockchain, 2nd International Workshop, Co-located with CAV 2020. Open Access series in Informatics, vol. 84. Dagstuhl Publishing (2020)
11. Kammüller, F.: A formal development cycle for security engineering in Isabelle (2020). Cornell University, arxive.org https://arxiv.org/abs/2001.08983
12. Kammüller, F., Kerber, M.: Applying the Isabelle Insider framework to airplane security (2020). Cornell University, arxive.org https://arxiv.org/abs/2003.11838
13. Nipkow, T., Wenzel, M., Paulson, L.C. (eds.): Isabelle/HOL – A Proof Assistant for Higher-Order Logic. LNCS, vol. 2283. Springer, Heidelberg (2002). https://doi.org/10.1007/3-540-45949-9
14. The Corona-Warn-App Project (2020). https://github.com/corona-warn-app
15. The Corona-Warn-App Project. Corona-warn-app solution architecture (2020). https://github.com/corona-warn-app/cwa-documentation/blob/master/solution_architecture.md
16. The DP-3T Project. Decentralized Privacy-Preserving Proximity Tracing (2020). https://github.com/DP-3T
17. The DP-3T Project. Decentralized privacy-preserving proximity tracing - White Paper (2020). https://github.com/DP-3T/documents/blob/master/DP3TWhitePaper.pdf
18. The DP-3T Project. Privacy and security risk evaluation of digital proximity tracing systems (2020). https://github.com/DP-3T/documents/blob/master/Securityanalysis/PrivacyandSecurityAttacksonDigitalProximityTracingSystems.pdf
19. The DP-3T Project. README: Apple/Google Exposure Notification (2020). https://github.com/DP-3T/documents
20. The DP-3T Project. Response to 'Analysis of DP3T: Between Scylla and Charybdis' (2020). https://github.com/DP-3T/documents/blob/master/Securityanalysis/Responseto'AnalysisofDP3T'.pdf
21. The PEPP-PT Project. Pan-European Privacy-Preserving Proximity Tracing (2020). https://github.com/PEPP-PT
22. The ROBERT Project. ROBust and privacy-presERving proximity Tracing protocol (2020). https://github.com/ROBERT-proximity-tracing
23. Vaudenay, S.: Analysis of DP3T: Between Scylla and Charybdis (2020). https://eprint.iacr.org/2020/399.pdf

Extracting Speech from Motion-Sensitive Sensors

Safaa Azzakhnini[1]($\boxtimes$) and Ralf C. Staudemeyer[2]

[1] Faculty of Sciences, Mohammed V University, Rabat, Morocco
safae.azzakhnini@gmail.com
[2] Schmalkalden University of Applied Sciences, Schmalkalden, Germany
r.staudemeyer@hs-sm.de

Abstract. The increasing presence of wireless sensor networks and the blanket re-use of the resulting data volumes by AI-based systems raises pressing ethical questions about the impact of these technologies on our society. One of the commonly used technologies are Smart Phones and similar mobile communication devices which attract people to improve their quality of life. These devices are equipped with rich sensors that provide an advanced and comprehensive user experience. However, it is a well known problem that the presence of numerous sensors is of major concern to the privacy of users and their social environment. Specifically previous studies already revealed that motion-sensitive sensors actually react to human speech. In this regards Deep Neural Networks (DNN) proved very successful to model high-level abstractions in data. Our main focus is highlighting (i) the potential risks related to these sensors leaking private information about speech and (ii) the ethical implications of advances in (deep) machine learning as a threat to privacy. In this paper we showcase a simple attack in which collected data from accelerometer and Vibration Energy Harvester (VEH) sensors can be used to eavesdrop on speech. We propose a multistage stacked auto-encoder model that learns the distinctive time and frequency characteristics independently without user interaction. We demonstrate the efficiency of our model with poor quality data and a very low sampling rate. We investigated three classification tasks: gender identification (i), hotwords detection (ii), and (iii) recognition of simple phrases selected from a previously well investigated dataset. Our experiments demonstrate the efficiency of our model and confirm that motion-sensitive sensors are a rich source of personal data, from which highly sensitive and private information about people in close proximity to the sensor emerges.

Keywords: Mobile devices · Users privacy · Deep neural networks · Data fusion

1 Introduction

Privacy is increasingly a concern in today's digitally connected world. Personal data is being collected and stored in several daily used devices such as smartphones, mobile devices and wearables. These devices are often equipped with

© Springer Nature Switzerland AG 2020
J. Garcia-Alfaro et al. (Eds.): DPM 2020/CBT 2020, LNCS 12484, pp. 145–160, 2020.
https://doi.org/10.1007/978-3-030-66172-4_9

sensors to provide services based on the according sensor readings, like location, movement, temperature, and alike. The data from such sensors, however, can also be used for other purposes. Meanwhile, machine learning is a field of research that became a core component of many real-world applications in many domains including health, transportation, energy, education, banking, biometrics to cite a few. The diverse and large availability of data, coupled with rapid technological advances in machine learning algorithms (which learn from data), is changing society markedly. Although it enables the development of many tools with the potential of bringing good to society, their misuse might also generate or inflate risks that harm society and the private life of individuals [4,7,26]. In this work, we address the privacy concern raised when the combination of unprotected data collection and advanced learning algorithms may lead to non-transparent inferences. We mainly focus on data collected from sensors built-in mobile and wearable devices. We investigate how data created by a movement sensor and an energy harvesting component can be used to extract information about human voice communication.

Sensor data has already received remarkable attention from the security research community, as to better understand the potential impact of this data on user privacy. Projects have investigated opportunities to identify and track users [3,11,18,22]. This was investigated in particular with the acceleration sensor [8,14,24,27,30,31,33,37]. These studies did also show that the motion sensors included in smartphones are sufficiently sensitive to allow the identification of acoustic information based on the readings induced by sound waves. An according investigation of data provided by gyroscopes was performed by [23]. This paper was inspired by works discussing such effects of acoustics on gyroscope measurements [9,12,13]. The authors there demonstrated by a rich experimental study that gyroscope data is sufficiently sensitive to extract information about the original audio signal. This included the identification of the speaker's gender as well as an isolated hot-word. In [36] the authors investigate accelerometer data for hot-word detection. The main motivation is to enable accurate low-energy and low-cost implementation of voice control by using the accelerometer instead of the microphone. The obtained accuracies were competitive with voice control applications such as "Google Now" and "Samsung S Voice". However, mobile operating systems limit the sampling rate (usually 200 Hz). Low sampling rates pose a hard limit on the available data and therefore are a significant challenge to speech reconstruction. To overcome this challenge, a recent work [17] has proposed an eavesdropping attack by leveraging a distributed form of time-interleaved analog-digital-conversion to approximate a higher sampling rate. Combining the data provided by a geophone, an accelerometer, and a gyroscope they were able to reconstruct intelligible speech. A threat analysis of extracting speech signals from motion sensors of smartphones is provided by [1]. The authors there examined the presence of speech information in accelerometer and gyroscope data by studying many possible attack scenarios and analysing the behaviour of these sensors. Furthering this track of investigations a recent publication explored vibration energy harvesters (VEH) and whether they can be used like a sensor [19]. VEHs convert physical movement into electric energy, often to extend battery life. Because of the high availability of vibration sources, VEHs are considered an effective energy harvesting option for low-power mobile devices, like for the Internet of Things (IoT). The authors there also notice that VEHs can be sensitive enough to detect hot-words in speech. In other recent works, the authors propose an eavesdropping attack based on accelerometer readings. The authors in [2] studied an accelerometer-based speech recognition under the setup that the accelerometer is on the same smartphone as the speaker. Moreover, the authors in [5] design a deep learning-based framework to recognize and reconstruct speech signals only from accelerometer measurements.

Contributions. In this paper, we propose to use DNNs on sensor data to increase the accuracy in recognising voice patterns. We want to determine the potential risks related to privacy when such data is not protected. Here we focus on the data collected from a VEH and an accelerometer while users were speaking as collected in a preceding study by [19]. Our intentions are twofold: Firstly we want to highlight the improved ability to extract acoustic patterns from sensors not primarily used for acoustic information by using DNNs. Secondly, we want to explore if the combination of data from different sensors can significantly improve the detection rates. We perform an experiment by using a DNN based on a stacked auto-encoder upon the collected data. Our model extracts acoustic features by exploring both time and frequency representations. The extracted features are then used in supervised classification to identify the speaker's gender, detect a simple hot-word, and distinguish it from short sample phrases. We show how the combination of the data provided by the VEH with the data of the acceleration sensor significantly improves the recognition rates in comparison to [19]. To that end we train the DNN with both sources. To the best of our knowledge the effect of speech on motion sensors has so far only been performed using manual feature extraction techniques [1,2,17,19,23,36] or using only one-way sensor [5]. We, therefore, assume our approach of using deep neural networks with different types of information in this context is novel.

Threat Model. When sensor readings expose voice communication additional threats to privacy become apparent. The threat model changes as an attacker then only needs access to sensor readings instead of the microphone directly. The attack vector thereby is extended to any application having access to the readings of relevant sensors, as for example on the user's device in Fig. 1.

The attacker here can identify acoustic patterns in the accelerometer and VEH readings. With the sensors used in the experiment, the user needs to be physically close to the device [19]. However, this seems very likely when using a mobile phone or a smart watch, which also happen to be the devices where accelerometer and VEHs are (to be) used. Furthermore, the attacker does not necessarily require direct access to the sensor data. We assume that access to locally cached sensor readings may be sufficient to allow offline attacks. We consider two scenarios in our study: In the first scenario, the attacker only has access to the data of one source. With the available data, we can compare having

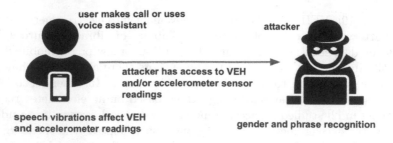

Fig. 1. Example for an attack scenario

access to only the accelerometer or only the VEH. We determine how well the DNN identifies the speaker's gender, detect the hot-word, and identify short sample phrases for each of those data sets. In the second scenario, we assume the attacker to have access to both, the accelerometer and the VEH. Here we combine the data sets of the accelerometer and the VEH to train the DNN. We can compare the results with those derived by using a single data source.

2 Background

This section describes the design of the investigated sensors and provides background information about the typical architecture of an auto-encoder and the corresponding learning algorithm.

Vibration Energy Harvester (VEH). A VEH is a transducer that converts kinetic energy from vibrations to electrical power. For low-power electronic devices in specific environments, they can harvest enough energy to operate the device [10,15,29]. A VEH can be seen as having three parts: the transducer to convert the kinetic to electrical energy, a power-electronic interface, and some electrical energy storage, like a battery [28]. Common VEH transducers are piezoelectric, as this type has shown the highest potential for harvesting energy [21,35]. Suitable vibration sources are diverse, as for example human motion, waves, wind, or vibrations of machinery. A typical piezoelectric element as used in VEHs is illustrated in Fig. 2 where one end of a cantilever beam is fixed to the device, while the other is set free to oscillate (vibrate). When the piezoelectric is affected by vibrations, an AC voltage is generated by the accumulation of positive and negative charges on the two opposing sides. The AC voltage generated in general is proportional to the applied stress.

Acoustic Effect. Sound waves, when emitted, are moving through air and cause pressure on the cantilever beam. Experiments [19] have demonstrated this effect by having a person shout three times while physically near to the piezoelectric part. The generated signal (see Fig. 3) shows how the VEH's voltage peaked with each shout.

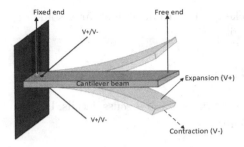

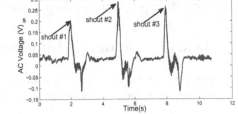

Fig. 2. Piezoelectric transducer [19]

Fig. 3. Effect of shouting on VEH piezoelectric cantilever beam [19]

Accelerometer. Accelerometers turn acceleration into an electrical signal based on the same operating principles as VEHs. The acceleration in different dimensions can be translated to changing positions. Raw gyroscope data consist of three values indicating the acceleration along the x-axis, y-axis, and z-axis (usually corresponding to the up-down, right-left, and front-back movement respectively).

Acoustic Effect. Recent work [36] showed that accelerometers are sensitive enough to draw conclusions about human speech. The authors there recorded sensor output while a speaker was spelling the vowel "A". The spectrum analysis of the output signal shows a considerable variation of the accelerometer readings during speech. They reported that the human voice has sufficient sound pressure to have detectable impact on smartphone accelerometers.

Stacked Auto-encoders. An auto-encoder (AE) is a type of artificial neural network (ANN) for unsupervised learning. The learning objective of the AE is to map the data of the input layer to the output layer in the way it is desired. The result is an approximation of the so-called identity function, where the output is a representation of the input. The architecture of an AE divides the ANN into an encoder and a decoder. The encoder takes the data at the input neurons and creates a "restricted" representation of it at the hidden layer. Since the hidden layer is smaller than the input layer it learns only the most relevant aspects of the input. The decoder then tries to reconstruct the original input from the representation in the hidden layer. This produces a higher-level representation from the lower-level representation of the input [6].

A stacked auto-encoder (SAE) is an ANN consisting of multiple hidden layers creating a deep neural network architecture. The SAE applies the so-called greedy layer-wise pre-training strategy which addresses the error-causing vanishing gradient problem. In SAEs the input layer is the encoded layer trained on the raw input. The output then is used as input to the next AE to obtain the next encoded layer and this process is repeated for subsequent layers. Stacking layers like this can then lead to deep stacked auto-encoders that carry some of the interesting properties of deep models [6].

3   Learning Acoustic Information

Here we present an overview of our proposed approach and discuss details, before presenting the experiments in the next chapter.

Classification Task. Classification tasks are tied into information representation. The learning process on how to represent data is a critical step that on the one hand should preserve as much information as possible from the input data. On the other hand this process should eliminate redundancies to foster the extraction of structures and properties. Motion sensors are designed to respond to movement. Their output signals originate from physical movement of an accordingly designed part of the sensor. They are particularly used for tasks related to motion recognition, such as identifying physical activity. Modelling motion sensor data to perform sound recognition is an especially challenging task, because the sensor's sensitivity is optimised towards such movements and not sound.

The artificial learner requires preprocessed data in form of features to learn from. A feature is a measurable property fed to the learning algorithm. These are normally manually extracted relying on knowledge of a human expert. This expertise is domain- and/or sensor-specific and is required for each new dataset or sensor modality in order to engineer the suitable features for a specific application. Therefore, the use of manual feature extraction is very limited. Furthermore it cannot be generalised across different application domains. As accelerometer and VEH sensors are of a non-acoustic nature, we do not benefit from a prior knowledge about useful measurements to apply in order to extract the acoustic information. To deal with this issue, we propose an unsupervised deep learning approach to automatically learn suitable features without relying on hand-crafted features. Here features are automatically extracted from data through layers were each successive layer acts as a feature extractor and is hypothesized to represent the data in a more abstract way. This process is unsupervised, which means that it is independent to a specific classification task. To this end we propose a SAE to discover relevant complex structures underlying speech and to learn a deep and high-level representation robust to intra-class variability including the sensor direction and the speaker speaking. An architectural overview of our approach is illustrated in Fig. 4. It is divided into two main phases: unsupervised feature learning, where we added the combination of the data-sources as well, and supervised classification.

Feature Learning. In this step, we investigate time and frequency data separately to train a bimodal representation from each sensor. We perform Fourier transformations on the frequency data. Then we use the greedy layer-wise training for the SAE. Therein, the features learned in a hidden layer are used as input

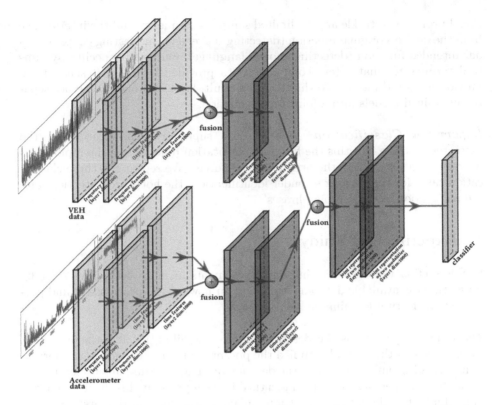

Fig. 4. The figure shows the whole network architecture. The two inputs are the frequency and time representation of the VEH and the accelerometer data. Each layer correspond to the hidden layer encoded using the autoencoder. The layers are stacked using layer wise training strategy. The last layer represents the classifcation step performed after the unsupervised features learning from previous layers.

to the next AE in order to produce a new representation of the data. By representing the data through layers we enable learning of complex patterns across data variations. After extracting the features separately from each source, that is time and frequency, we combine them into a joined time-frequency representation. This joint representation leads to a shallow model, thereby making it difficult for a single hidden layer model to directly find correlations between representations that have been joined. We, therefore, again apply greedy layer-wise training to improve discovery of high-level correlations across the two representations.

Data From Multiple Sources. With the assumed availability of different sensors, we then have separate types of data sources about a given moment. The machine learning community assumes potential in improved learning algorithms to specifically exploit such multi-modal data to form a unified picture [25]. Modelling speech recognition from data of non-acoustic sensors is challenging. Additional problems to tackle are the limited sampling frequency and the interference from the device's original function (detecting movement, harvesting energy) with our intended function (detecting spoken language). Our study specifically aims to determine to what extent combining data provided by different sensors can provide improved results. To that end, our multi-layer approach combines separately trained models into a joint representation.

Supervised Classification. We then use supervised classification on the extracted features. For this the fused representation functions as the input, thus providing features across the original data sources. We repeat the three classification tasks for the speaker's gender identification, the hot-word detection, and the recognition of the sample phrases.

4 Experimental Study

In this section we are describing our experiments in more detail. We start by presenting the available data and then explain how we pre-processed it and performed the feature learning and classification.

Data. The dataset we used is described in more detail in [19]. It is the only work we are aware of that already studied the potential of detecting acoustic information from VEH data. It contains the data for both, a VEH and an accelerometer, while different persons performed identical tasks repeatedly. Involved were eight individuals, four being male and four female, and the experiments were performed with two different orientations of the devices (horizontal and vertical). The devices were positioned close to the persons (3 cm) and the experiments repeated 30 times for the hot-word "Ok Google" and at least ten times for the phrases "Good morning", "how are you", and "fine thank you". Overall the data-set contains 1155 samples. Figure 5, represents the accelerometer and VEH sensor outputs while a person spoke the four phrases.

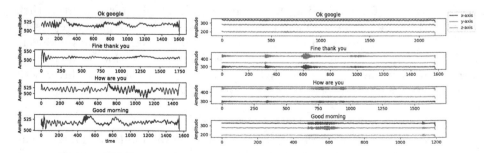

Fig. 5. The VEH signal (left) and the accelerometer outputs (x axis, y-axis, z-axis on right) while the user is speaking the four phrases ("good morning", "okay google", "fine thank you" and "how are you")

Preprocessing. In the pre-processing we apply our domain knowledge to address the specifics of the different data sources. As we face varying lengths of the samples, we started by interpolating all the samples in the data to the mean length. We separately handle the temporal and frequency representations. To minimise the signal-to-noise ratio we filter the input signals and normalise them. On the frequency representation we apply a fourier transformation and calculate the magnitude of the obtained complex values, which we then also normalised. For the accelerometer data, we down-sample the signal to 200 Hz. This is the limit on sampling frequency as posed by the mobile operating systems Android and iOS. We then interpolate the samples to their mean length and normalize the data. After first learning features for each axis (x, y, and z), we then compute the magnitude over the dimensions to obtain an overall feature vector. The three acceleration channels were combined as one using square summing to obtain the magnitude acceleration, which is orientation independent.

Feature Learning and Classification. The training procedure for time and frequency representations each is executed for 50 epochs, using a mini-batch size of 30 and learning rate of 0.001. The RMSprop variant of the stochastic gradient descent is used as the optimization algorithm. For the feature learning step, the used number of hidden units for the first layer is 1200 and for the second layer is 1000. For the classification we used and compared three common learning algorithms in order to select the good learner that can find out the relevant patterns from the obtained features from the Autoencoder. Principaly, Support Vector Machine (SVM) using the RBF kernel with $\gamma = 0.01$ and $C = 100$, K-nearest neighbours (KNN) with $K = 3$ and Neural Network Classifier (NN) with 2 hidden layers containing 100 units. The optimal hyperparameters were optimized by cross-validated grid-search over a parameter grid.

Evaluation. In the evaluation we used a k-fold cross-validation with $k = 10$. For this we divided the data into k equal folds (portions). We then trained the model on the $k - 1$ folds and test it against the remaining folds. That process was repeated $k = 10$ times. The final performance after that corresponds to the average of the obtained values. We used cross-validation analysis to ensure that all data was used for both, training and test. The classification of the proposed framework was performed using the four metrics accuracy, precision, recall, and F-measure.

5   Results and Discussion

In this section we present the results from our experiments in detail.

Single Data-Sets. We first evaluate the results from using the data of the accelerometer or VEH on their own, each. Tables 1, 2 present the classification performance for each of our metrics, that is accuracy (acc), precision (prec), recall (rec) and F-measure (f-score), as determined for each of the classifications

Table 1. The obtained results (%) using only VEH data

alg.	rep	Hot-word detection				Gender identification				Sentences recognition			
		acc	prec	rec	f-score	acc	prec	rec	f-score	acc	prec	rec	f-score
KNN	time	74	76	74	74	71	72	71	70	62	62	62	60
	freq	69	69	69	69	76	77	76	76	55	55	55	53
	our model	75	76	75	75	79	80	79	79	64	65	64	62
SVM	time	71	72	71	71	70	71	70	69	63	64	63	61
	freq	69	70	69	69	76	77	76	76	54	54	54	53
	our model	75	76	75	75	80	80	80	80	64	65	64	64
NN	time	70	72	70	70	62	64	62	61	61	62	61	60
	freq	65	68	65	63	72	74	72	72	54	54	54	51
	our model	75	76	75	75	77	79	77	77	65	65	65	64

Table 2. The obtained results (%) using only accelerometer data

alg.	rep	Hot-word detection				Gender identification				Sentences recognition			
		acc	prec	rec	f-score	acc	prec	rec	f-score	acc	prec	rec	f-score
KNN	time	71	72	71	71	83	83	83	83	58	59	58	56
	freq	55	55	55	55	64	65	64	63	42	38	42	37
	our model	77	77	77	77	83	83	83	83	65	65	65	63
SVM	time	58	60	58	54	80	80	80	80	48	31	48	33
	freq	58	58	58	58	71	72	71	71	41	39	41	39
	our model	76	76	76	76	86	86	86	86	65	65	65	64
NN	time	53	55	53	48	61	65	61	58	47	23	47	30
	freq	54	56	54	50	66	68	66	65	45	35	45	34
	our model	68	70	68	67	80	81	80	79	54	57	54	50

(gender identification, hot-word detection, and phrase recognition) for each of the used learning algorithms KNN, SVM, and NN (alg) for each of the data representations time-only, frequency-only, and our model. These allow us to see how our model compares to using only the time- or only the frequency-data. On the hot-word classification the KNN and SVM algorithms with our model both achieved an accuracy of 75% when used on the VEH data and 76% when used on the accelerometer data, in all cases out-performing the use of only time- or frequency representations. For gender identification results, the best classification performance was achieved by our model in combination with SVM, having an accuracy of 86% using the accelerometer data and near 80% using the VEH data, again out-performing the use of only one data-representation. The accuracy of our model in recognizing the phrases was in the range of 64–65% for all combinations but using NN on the accelerometer data and once more out-performed the use of single data representations in all combinations. The F-score shows comparable values. Therefore, we can conclude that features learned from the joint representation of time and frequency information leads to a considerable improvement of the classifications. Both, frequency and time representations, contain important information that can be combined for better results here.

We assume that more abstract features have been learned in the process. We highlight that sufficient information about the original activity of shouting can already be extracted with relevant accuracy even when using only one of the data sources.

Table 3. The obtained results (%) combining the VEH and the Accelerometer data

alg.	rep	Hot-word detection				Gender identification				Sentences recognition			
		acc	prec	rec	f-score	acc	prec	rec	f-score	acc	prec	rec	f-score
KNN	time	78	79	78	78	81	81	81	81	69	69	69	67
	freq	69	70	69	69	79	80	79	79	55	55	55	52
	our model	83	83	83	83	88	88	88	88	73	74	73	72
SVM	time	76	76	76	76	79	79	79	79	66	66	66	64
	freq	73	73	73	73	81	82	81	81	59	59	59	58
	our model	86	86	86	86	91	92	91	91	77	78	77	77
NN	time	68	69	68	67	73	74	73	73	61	64	61	59
	freq	71	72	71	71	79	80	79	79	59	59	59	57
	our model	81	82	81	80	88	89	88	88	74	75	74	74

Combination of Data-Sets. Next we examine if access to multiple data sources further increases the classifications. For this we repeated the training using both, the VEH and the accelerometer data, as described above. The results are—formatted as the previous tables—shown in Table 3. Combining the data-sources has significantly increased the accuracy of the classifications across the board by around 10%. The highest F-scores of 91%, 85%, and 77% for gender identification, hot-words detection and recognition of phrases respectively, were achieved when using the SVM classifier with our model. The increase was higher for our model than if using only the time or the frequency representation. In each of its levels, the ANN must have learned additional correlations between the data variables across frequency and time representations. Overall, the joint representation has lead to remarkably improved accuracy.

In Table 4 we compare our model with the results from the original work from [19] which only used the VEH data. The authors there compared results for different positions of the VEH. Recognising the importance of positioning, we specifically wanted the DNN to cope with this, as we hardly can influence the positioning in the scenario of spying. This way our results should be better suited to assess the practicality of an according attack vector. Moreover, we applied our model to the gyroscope data used by [23] for isolated words recognition. We compare our results with those obtained by the authors for the user independent case. The results show that our model provided better accuracy than the state of the art works, that were based on manual features.

The results show that our deep auto-encoder approach can improve the recognition of acoustic patterns from non-acoustic sensors, here acceleration and voltage readings. We do not claim that the proposed approach represents a direct

Table 4. comparison with state of the art methods

Method	Accuracy
Hot-words detection using VEH in a horizontal position [19]	73%
Hot-words detection using VEH in a vertical position [19]	63%
Hot-words detection using VEH invariant to sensor orientation (our model)	75%
Hot-words detection combining VEH with accelerometer (our model)	**86%**
Isolated words recognition (11 words) using gyroscope with SVM (Speaker-independent) [23]	10%
Isolated words recognition (11 words) using gyroscope (our model) Speaker-independent case	**25%**

substantial risk to privacy, yet, as the data-set is small and was derived in a very specific setting. However, mobile sensors beyond the obvious microphone and camera could become targeted by attackers as they—as of today—are often less protected. Despite the fact that the data provided by such sensors is always cluttered due to their main purpose, it still is possible to draw conclusions on audio information from them by using two main approaches. The first is to combine data from multiple sources by considering a multimodal architecture. This will exploit the complementary between multiple modalities (information obtained from multiple sensors) and will lead to more accurate results. The second is to include a de-noising component in the autoencoder. In fact, de-noising data is one of the areas where auto-encoders have been most successful [34].

Discussion. Considering that such sensors might generally not be considered as sensitive and therefore be less protected, they could rise to become popular attack surfaces in the future. Based on our results an attacker with access to the readings of multiple sensors must be regarded as dangerous, even if the primary function of the sensors seem harmless at first. With today's mobile devices many people already carry a multitude of sensors around and the trend seems to be for *even more.*

The findings compiled show that motion data are a rich source of personal data. The misuse of such data using learning algorithms that can extract visible and invisible patterns and correlations from it can lead to leakage of sensitive information such as the individual's speech. Furthermore, by combining different data sources we can learn more than from one source independently. Thus, more accurate information can be inferred from a combined analysis (in the studied case the accuracy has increased by 10%), which increases the risk of the privacy breach. Recognizing the speech does not only give information about what a speaker says, but also its attitude toward the listener and the topic under discussion, and the speaker own current state of mind as well. Many works have discussed the inferences that can be drawn from human speech extracted from audio data [20]. Therefore, the inferred speech information from motion sensors, in turn, can be used to deduce more non-transparent insights about individuals and manipulation about their private life [7]. Several examples of data breaches were revealed where personal information was exploited for many purposes, including political purposes [16], and others [32]. Therefore, the misuse of such data can seriously affect an individual's relationships, employability, or financial status, or lead to negative consequences for essential rights and social values such as freedom of expression, respect for private life. The privacy threat of unexpected inferences from unprotected data sources is not limited to those discussed in this paper. The problem of undesired inferences goes far beyond motion sensors and the deduced insights are related to the samples present in the used dataset. Thus, a larger database will contain a variety of characteristics from personal attributes in addition to gender and identity or age. Such attributes may include, emotions, personality traits, sexual orientation, ethnicity, religious and political views to cite a few. This diversity of data will allow discovering other correlations and obtaining more analysis. In sum, the aim of the paper is mainly to raise awareness about the ethical and privacy implications of the advancement of learning algorithms coupled with the growing availability of data. This is achieved by demonstrating how machine learning can be used as a tool for privacy breach and manipulation. Advances in technology change how personal information is collected and analysed, and therefore create new privacy risks. Thus the continued debate is needed to guide the development not only of technology but also of the policies that enable its use. And governments need to be more serious about finding a solution to limit the power that larger companies have over citizens.

6   Conclusions and Future Work

In this paper, we investigate the technical feasibility of speech inference from motion data using advanced machine learning models. We explore how non-acoustic sensor readouts can be used in uni-/multi-modal attacks. We propose a multi-level time-frequency based deep neural network to extract acoustic patterns from an accelerometer sensor and an energy harvesting component. Our model detects gender, single hot-words and spoken phrases with an accuracy of up to 91%, 85%, and 77% respectively. This findings show that motion sensors data are a rich source of personal data. They can be sufficient to obtain information about a device holder's speech especially when used data is combined from multiple sensors. By combining data sources we can learn more than would be the case from analysing single source independently, and more accurate predictions may be inferred which increases issues about privacy or decreases the privacy guarantee. An attacker with access to an accelerometer and some sensitive energy harvesting module is able to eavesdrop on human speech and draw conclusions about its content. Therefore, they could be considered private data in the same sense as audio data. The privacy of mobile device and wearables users, is a concern of growing importance. The zero permission nature of embedded motion sensors make acquiring the data easier. The collection of such data combined with a misuse of machine learning algorithms (which learn from data) can lead to a serious privacy risks and leakage of sensitive inferences about the user including his speech. The problem of undesired inferences goes far beyond motion sensors data and needs to be addressed for other data sources as well. Therefore, further research is required into the privacy implications of unprotected data collection taking into account the evolving state of the art in machine learning algorithms. Furthermore, a continued debate is needed not only about control over all sensor data, but also to guide the development of technology and of the policies that enable its use.

We consider the contents of this article to be early work on this topic. An interesting next step would be to examine the attack vector under real-world conditions. For further experiments a larger annotated data-set including more sensors as found in smartphones and a possibly large set of recorded situations would be needed. Only then would it be possible to realistically judge the threat that for example is posed by smartphones today, when installed applications are allowed access to sensors without care. Many factors usually do affect sensors and different sensors each have their specifics in how they are affected. This provides a large variety of possible experiments from recording and annotating data to performing analyses on that data then. Concerning the neural network it might be beneficial to use recurrent neural networks with long-short-term-memory to capture the temporal relationships in the data.

References

1. Anand, S.A., Saxena, N.: Speechless: analyzing the threat to speech privacy from smartphone motion sensors. In: 2018 IEEE Symposium on Security and Privacy (SP), pp. 116–133 (2018)
2. Anand, S.A., Wang, C., Liu, J., Saxena, N., Chen, Y.: Spearphone: a speech privacy exploit via accelerometer-sensed reverberations from smartphone loudspeakers. arXiv preprint arXiv:1907.05972 (2019)
3. Aviv, A.J., Sapp, B., Blaze, M., Smith, J.M.: Practicality of accelerometer side channels on smartphones. In: Proceedings of the 28th Annual Computer Security Applications Conference, pp. 41–50. ACM (2012)
4. Azencott, C.A.: Machine learning and genomics: precision medicine versus patient privacy. Philos. Trans. Roy. Soc. A Math. Phys. Eng. Sci. **376**(2128), 20170350 (2018)
5. Ba, Z., et al.: Learning-based practical smartphone eavesdropping with built-in accelerometer. In: Proceedings of the Network and Distributed Systems Security (NDSS) Symposium, pp. 23–26 (2020)
6. Baldi, P.: Autoencoders, unsupervised learning, and deep architectures. In: Proceedings of ICML Workshop on Unsupervised and Transfer Learning, pp. 37–49 (2012)
7. Berendt, B.: Privacy beyond confidentiality, data science beyond spying: from movement data and data privacy towards a wider fundamental rights discourse. In: Naldi, M., Italiano, G.F., Rannenberg, K., Medina, M., Bourka, A. (eds.) APF 2019. LNCS, vol. 11498, pp. 59–71. Springer, Cham (2019). https://doi.org/10.1007/978-3-030-21752-5_5
8. Cai, L., Chen, H.: Touchlogger: inferring keystrokes on touch screen from smartphone motion. HotSec **11**, 9–9 (2011)
9. Castro, S., Dean, R., Roth, G., Flowers, G.T., Grantham, B.: Influence of acoustic noise on the dynamic performance of mems gyroscopes. In: ASME 2007 International Mechanical Engineering Congress and Exposition, pp. 1825–1831. American Society of Mechanical Engineers (2007)

10. Choi, S., Seong, M., Kim, K.: Vibration control of an electrorheological fluid-based suspension system with an energy regenerative mechanism. Proc. Inst. Mech. Eng. Part D J. Automobile Eng. **223**(4), 459–469 (2009)
11. Das, A., Borisov, N., Caesar, M.: Tracking mobile web users through motion sensors: attacks and defenses. In: NDSS (2016)
12. Dean, R.N., et al.: On the degradation of mems gyroscope performance in the presence of high power acoustic noise. In: 2007 IEEE International Symposium on Industrial Electronics, pp. 1435–1440. IEEE (2007)
13. Dean, R.N., et al.: A characterization of the performance of a MEMS gyroscope in acoustically harsh environments. IEEE Trans. Industr. Electron. **58**(7), 2591–2596 (2010)
14. Dey, S., Roy, N., Xu, W., Choudhury, R.R., Nelakuditi, S.: Accelprint: imperfections of accelerometers make smartphones trackable. In: NDSS (2014)
15. Donelan, J.M., Li, Q., Naing, V., Hoffer, J., Weber, D., Kuo, A.D.: Biomechanical energy harvesting: generating electricity during walking with minimal user effort. Science **319**(5864), 807–810 (2008)
16. The Economist: The cambridge analytica scandal - britain moves to rein in data-analytics (2018). https://www.economist.com/britain/2018/03/28/britain-moves-to-rein-in-data-analytics
17. Han, J., Chung, A.J., Tague, P.: Pitchin: eavesdropping via intelligible speech reconstruction using non-acoustic sensor fusion. In: Proceedings of the 16th ACM/IEEE International Conference on Information Processing in Sensor Networks, pp. 181–192. ACM (2017)
18. Han, J., Owusu, E., Nguyen, L.T., Perrig, A., Zhang, J.: Accomplice: location inference using accelerometers on smartphones. In: 2012 Fourth International Conference on Communication Systems and Networks (COMSNETS 2012), pp. 1–9. IEEE (2012)
19. Khalifa, S., Hassan, M., Seneviratne, A.: Feasibility and accuracy of hotword detection using vibration energy harvester. In: World of Wireless, Mobile and Multimedia Networks (WoWMoM), 2016 IEEE 17th International Symposium on A, pp. 1–9. IEEE (2016)
20. Kröger, J.L., Lutz, O.H.-M., Raschke, P.: Privacy implications of voice and speech analysis – information disclosure by inference. In: Friedewald, M., Önen, M., Lievens, E., Krenn, S., Fricker, S. (eds.) Privacy and Identity 2019. IAICT, vol. 576, pp. 242–258. Springer, Cham (2020). https://doi.org/10.1007/978-3-030-42504-3_16
21. Lan, G., Xu, W., Khalifa, S., Hassan, M., Hu, W.: Veh-com: demodulating vibration energy harvesting for short range communication. In: 2017 IEEE International Conference on Pervasive Computing and Communications (PerCom), pp. 170–179. IEEE (2017)
22. Matyunin, N., Szefer, J., Katzenbeisser, S.: Zero-permission acoustic cross-device tracking. In: 2018 IEEE International Symposium on Hardware Oriented Security and Trust (HOST), pp. 25–32. IEEE (2018)
23. Michalevsky, Y., Boneh, D., Nakibly, G.: Gyrophone: recognizing speech from gyroscope signals. In: USENIX Security, pp. 1053–1067 (2014)
24. Miluzzo, E., Varshavsky, A., Balakrishnan, S., Choudhury, R.R.: Tapprints: your finger taps have fingerprints. In: Proceedings of the 10th International Conference on Mobile Systems, Applications, and Services, pp. 323–336. ACM (2012)
25. Ngiam, J., Khosla, A., Kim, M., Nam, J., Lee, H., Ng, A.Y.: Multimodal deep learning. In: Proceedings of the 28th International Conference on Machine Learning (ICML 2011), pp. 689–696 (2011)

26. Nissim, K., Wood, A.: Is privacy privacy? Philos. Trans. Roy. Soc. A Math. Phys. Eng. Sci. **376**(2128), 20170358 (2018)
27. Owusu, E., Han, J., Das, S., Perrig, A., Zhang, J.: Accessory: password inference using accelerometers on smartphones. In: Proceedings of the Twelfth Workshop on Mobile Computing Systems & Applications, p. 9. ACM (2012)
28. Rao, Y., Cheng, S., Arnold, D.P.: An energy harvesting system for passively generating power from human activities. J. Micromech. Microeng. **23**(11), 114012 (2013)
29. Rome, L.C., Flynn, L., Goldman, E.M., Yoo, T.D.: Generating electricity while walking with loads. Science **309**(5741), 1725–1728 (2005)
30. Simon, L., Anderson, R.: Pin skimmer: inferring pins through the camera and microphone. In: Proceedings of the Third ACM workshop on Security and Privacy in Smartphones & Mobile Devices, pp. 67–78. ACM (2013)
31. Song, C., Lin, F., Ba, Z., Ren, K., Zhou, C., Xu, W.: My smartphone knows what you print: exploring smartphone-based side-channel attacks against 3D printers. In: Proceedings of the 2016 ACM SIGSAC Conference on Computer and Communications Security, pp. 895–907. ACM (2016)
32. Swinhoe, D.: The 14 biggest data breaches of the 21st century (2020). https://www.csoonline.com/article/2130877/the-biggest-data-breaches-of-the-21st-century.html
33. Van Goethem, T., Scheepers, W., Preuveneers, D., Joosen, W.: Accelerometer-based device fingerprinting for multi-factor mobile authentication. In: Caballero, J., Bodden, E., Athanasopoulos, E. (eds.) ESSoS 2016. LNCS, vol. 9639, pp. 106–121. Springer, Cham (2016). https://doi.org/10.1007/978-3-319-30806-7_7
34. Vincent, P., Larochelle, H., Lajoie, I., Bengio, Y., Manzagol, P.A.: Stacked denoising autoencoders: learning useful representations in a deep network with a local denoising criterion. J. Mach. Learn. Res. **11**(12), 3371–3408 (2010)
35. Vullers, R., van Schaijk, R., Doms, I., Van Hoof, C., Mertens, R.: Micropower energy harvesting. Solid- State Electron. **53**(7), 684–693 (2009)
36. Zhang, L., Pathak, P.H., Wu, M., Zhao, Y., Mohapatra, P.: Accelword: energy efficient hotword detection through accelerometer. In: Proceedings of the 13th Annual International Conference on Mobile Systems, Applications, and Services, pp. 301–315. ACM (2015)
37. Zhang, Y., Xia, P., Luo, J., Ling, Z., Liu, B., Fu, X.: Fingerprint attack against touch-enabled devices. In: Proceedings of the second ACM workshop on Security and Privacy in Smartphones and Mobile Devices, pp. 57–68. ACM (2012)

PDP-ReqLite: A Lightweight Approach for the Elicitation of Privacy and Data Protection Requirements

Nicolás E. Díaz Ferreyra[1]([✉]), Patrick Tessier[2], Gabriel Pedroza[2], and Maritta Heisel[1]

[1] Department of Computer Science and Applied Cognitive Science, University of Duisburg-Essen, Oststr. 99, 47057 Duisburg, Germany
nicolas.diaz-ferreyra@uni-due.de, maritta.heisel@uni-due.de
[2] Department of System and Software Engineering, CEA LIST, P.C. 174, 91191 Gif-sur-Yvette, France
patrick.tessier@cea.fr, gabriel.pedroza@cea.fr

Abstract. With the introduction of the EU General Data Protection Regulation (GDPR), concerns about compliance started to arise among software companies inside and outside Europe. In order to achieve high compliance, software developers must consider those privacy and data protection goals defined across the different legal provisions in the GDPR. Prior work has introduced methods to systematically extract taxonomies of privacy requirements out of the GDPR's legal provisions. That is, a hierarchy of meta-requirements that can be instantiated for each specific software project. Particularly, ProPAn is a requirements elicitation method which leverages such taxonomies with the aim of achieving high levels of compliance. However, despite of its benefits, the method presents a high documentation overhead and redundancy across the artifacts it generates. In this work, we introduce a lightweight method named PDP-ReqLite initially inspired from ProPAn that introduces new artifacts for the documentation of personal data and information flows in a system-to-be. The purpose of PDP-ReqLite is to improve usability and applicability by reducing documentation overhead and complexity, and by introducing means to automate tasks, *e.g.*, automated requirements elicitation. In particular, this improved method provides additional features for incorporating new meta-requirements thus enlarging existing taxonomies.

Keywords: GDPR · Privacy requirements engineering · Data protection

1 Introduction

Nowadays, developing privacy-aware software systems has become a challenge of public interest. Legal frameworks such as the EU General Data Protection

© Springer Nature Switzerland AG 2020
J. Garcia-Alfaro et al. (Eds.): DPM 2020/CBT 2020, LNCS 12484, pp. 161–177, 2020.
https://doi.org/10.1007/978-3-030-66172-4_10

Regulation (GDPR) [17] have triggered major concerns about how information systems should implement data-protection functionalities and safeguard the privacy rights of their users. Privacy engineering is a discipline that has taken care of these challenges through methods, techniques and tools that allow software developers to build and incorporate privacy-related functionalities in their projects. Particularly, there is a growing understanding that privacy must be considered as a primary aspect in every system and software development process. That is, it must be considered right from the early stages of a systems' design process and throughout its whole life cycle. Therefore, under this premise, an adequate elicitation of privacy requirements results critical for developing software systems that guarantee the data protection rights of their end-users.

Privacy requirement engineering methods seeks to define, and document requirements related to privacy and data protection for their later implementation. Overall, these methods define a set of privacy and data protection goals like transparency or integrity which guide the elicitation process of such requirements. Furthermore, many of them introduce conceptual elements extracted from current standards or legal provisions in order to achieve high levels of compliance. Such is the case of ProPAn, a model-driven method for the elicitation of privacy requirements that incorporates principles introduced by well-established data protection frameworks and standards. Particularly, ProPAn comprises a collection of meta models (or requirements taxonomies) that are systematically extracted from the body of the EU GDPR and the ISO 29100. Such meta models guide the elicitation process of privacy requirements taking as input a collection of functional requirements that the system-to-be is expected to meet.

All in all, requirements engineering methods use different notations for the specification of requirements (e.g. textual, UML, use-case diagrams), and modelling languages for representing the system (or system-to-be) under consideration (e.g. BPMN, data-flow diagrams). In the particular case of ProPAn, functional requirements are specified using Jackson's Problem Frames notation. Such approach consists of describing the contextual elements with which the system-to-be must interact. In principle, this approach is suitable for the systematic elicitation of functional requirements. Nevertheless, it does not provide adequate means for a fine-grained documentation of the personal information that the system under consideration is expected to process. Hence, the method introduces a considerable amount of documentation overhead in order to document and analyze the information flows of the system and, thereby, generate the corresponding privacy and data protection requirements. Furthermore, even when such requirements are successfully generated, a high level of compliance cannot be ensured after their incorporation since the meta requirements used by the method do not cover all the legal provisions stated in the GDPR.

This paper introduces PDP-ReqLite, a lightweight method for the elicitation of privacy and data protection requirements. Particularly, PDP-ReqLite seeks to overcome the drawbacks identified in ProPAn regarding documentation overhead and compliance through new elicitation artifacts and requirements meta models. Such artifacts consist of data-flow and personal information diagrams that are independent from the Problem Frame notation employed by ProPAn but allow capturing the necessary information for the generation of privacy requirements. On the other hand, PDP-ReqLite introduces the possibility of defining additional meta requirements and models for achieving a broader scope and compliance with legal provisions and standards. Furthermore, a protocol for the systematic elicitation of such meta requirements is also introduced and illustrated alongside the different steps of PDP-ReqLite.

The rest of the paper is structured as follows. Section 2 gives the related work. The Sect. 3 introduces the theoretical background necessary to understand the proposed approach. The PDP-ReqLite method is presented in Sect. 4. The method applicability is demonstrated relying upon a Smart Grid case study in Sect. 5. The conclusions and perspectives finally come in Sect. 6.

2   Related Work

So far, several methods have been proposed for the generation of privacy and data protection requirements in software projects, each employing different notations and modelling languages [1,3–5,8]. Generally speaking, these methods consider privacy as a quality attribute or soft-goal that must be refined into a set of functional requirements [12]. For example, Dennedy et al. [5] propose to model a system-to-be through use cases and business activity diagrams enhanced with metadata related to the actors and information being processed by such system. In this approach, patterns (i.e. generic use cases) are used in combination with interpretation guidelines of the OECD privacy principles to identify and instantiate privacy use cases. Such instances guide the selection of Privacy Enhancing Technologies (PETs) which are prescribed by the method for each OECD principle. In line with this, Hoepman et al. [7] and Colesky et al. [3] elaborated a set of privacy patterns for the development of software architectures considering certain levels of privacy protection. Particularly, Colesky et al. [3] identified a set of privacy protection needs from the body of the GDPR and other legal frameworks like the Privacy Shield Agreement and refined them into a collection of privacy design tactics. Such tactics are then linked to specific privacy patterns (represented in natural language) and PETs for their later application in the design of software architectures.

Privacy regulations and the obligation to comply with privacy laws are driving factors for considering privacy as a software quality [12]. Privacy principles and goals are often introduced in requirement engineering methods to make these obligations more accessible and comprehensible for practitioners in the computer science domain. Furthermore, many of these approaches have been coined under the principles and premises of model-driven software engineering [12]. This is the case of ProPAn, a method for the systematic elicitation of privacy and data protection requirements which is driven by legal provisions and privacy goals related to transparency and intervenability, among others. Particularly, ProPAn is grounded in the provisions and guidelines included in the EU GDPR [17] and the ISO 29100 standard [9]. Nevertheless, the method exhibits extension points that makes it adaptable to other privacy legislations and data protection standards. Regarding data representation, text-based approaches like PRIPARE [14] are easier to adapt in the practice since users are not required to learn a specific modelling notation or formal language. Moreover, Meis et al. [12] show in a literature review on requirement engineering methods for privacy, that a large number of methods rely solely on textual documentation. However, informal notations make automation and consistency checking harder to perform, hence, a model-driven approach is preferable for these purposes.

3   Theoretical Background

In this section, we describe the theoretical foundations upon which PDP-ReqLite is elaborated. Particularly, a brief introduction to ProPAn and its most salient software artifacts is given in the following subsections. Alongside, an analysis of the benefits and drawbacks of this method is conducted in order to identify potential areas of improvement.

3.1   The ProPAn Approach

ProPAn [1] is a systematic method that helps identifying the privacy needs of a software system based on a set of functional requirements. Particularly, one of the core characteristics of ProPAn is the elicitation of functional requirements using *problem diagrams*. Such diagrams where introduced by Michael Jackson [10] as an approach to describe the environment in which a system-to-be must operate and the problem it must solve. In Jacksons' approach, software development consists of building a *Machine* (i.e. the system-to-be) that must be integrated in a certain environment represented by a collection of *Domains* (e.g. humans, technical devices, data representations, etc.) connected by interfaces through which they exchange certain *Phenomena* (i.e. events, actions, messages, and operations). Overall, the ProPAn method consists of two phases: *Identification of Privacy-Relevant Information Flows* and *Generation of Privacy Requirements*. In the first phase, the functional requirements of the system-to-be are identified and expressed through a collection of problem diagrams. In addition, the phenomena specified in such diagrams is further analysed and described in terms of personal information and data flows. For this, ProPAn introduces elicitation instruments additional to the ones proposed by Jackson with the purpose of documenting the personal information being processed by the system along with their corresponding data subjects (or system stakeholders) and data flows. These Functional Requirement Artifacts (FRAs) generated during the first stage of ProPAn become the input for the method's second stage.

In the second stage of the method, privacy requirement candidates are generated using a set of taxonomies that reflect privacy principles included in the GDPR and the ISO 29100 [9]. Overall, requirement candidates are generated for different privacy goals. Particularly, ProPAn follows the privacy protection goals introduced by Hansen [6], namely confidentiality, integrity, availability, unlinkability, transparency, and intervenability [1]. For each goal, the method provides a taxonomy (i.e. a metamodel) of privacy requirements and a collection of semantic templates with placeholders for their documentation. For example Fig. 1 depicts the taxonomy corresponding to the privacy goal unlinkability and the semantic template used to generate undetectability requirements. As it can be observed, the information available in the taxonomy (i.e. the attribute values) is leveraged by the semantic template to instantiate the corresponding requirement.

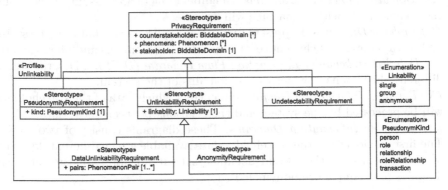

Fig. 1. Unlinkability requirements taxonomy (up) and semantic template for undetectability requirements (down) [13]

The second stage of ProPAn consists of four steps which are *Requirement Information Deduction*, *Generation of Privacy Requirement Candidates*, *Adjust Privacy Requirements*, and *Validate Privacy Requirements*. In the first step, the information necessary to instantiate the taxonomy of a particular privacy goal is deduced from the FRAs of the first stage. For instance, to generate unlikability requirements one must know which information from a stakeholder S should be undetectable for a counter-stakeholder C. This can be deduced by analysing the data flows and stakeholder information obtained during the first stage of ProPAn [12]. Once this information is deduced, a set of requirement candidates can be derived by instantiating the taxonomy and semantic templates of the privacy goal under consideration (Step 2). Since requirement candidates may be incomplete or result too strong/weak for the system-to-be under analysis, the user must review, complete and adjust the generated requirement candidates manually (Step 3). For instance, it may happen that an undetectability requirement must be relaxed and replaced with a confidentiality one. Once these adjustments are done, privacy requirement candidates are validated to check whether they remain consistent with the flow and availability of personal data at the different domains of the system-to-be (Step 4). Depending on the outcome of this validation activity, some requirements will be accepted and others may need to be adjusted.

3.2   Requirements Elicitation Artifacts

As described in Sect. 3.1, the first phase of ProPAn offers a collection of FRAs that allow software engineers to capture and document privacy-relevant knowledge of a system-to-be. More precisely, the software artifacts generated during this phase are:

- *(1) Context Diagram*: Describes the domains interacting with the machine, their corresponding interfaces, and exchanged phenomena.
- *(N) Domain Knowledge Diagrams*: Documents facts and assumptions about the context in which the machine will operate.
- *(N) Problem Diagrams*: Represent functional requirements that must be satisfied by the contextual elements of the machine (i.e. domains and phenomena).
- *(1) Detailed Stakeholder Information Flow Diagram (DSIFD)*: Describes how different phenomena flow across the domains of the system.
- *(N) Personal Information Diagrams*: Identifies which data of the stakeholders will be processed by the system and the relations between these data.
- *(N) Available Information Diagrams*: These diagrams consist of two views. The first one identifies the stakeholder data available at the different domains of the system, and the second documents their linkability nature at such domains (e.g. simple or anonymous).

from which only the DSIFD is generated automatically and the rest must be elaborated manually by engineers and privacy experts. To a certain extent, many of these artifacts are introduced to refine the information captured by the problem diagrams into data flows. This is because the phenomena represented in such diagrams describe mainly events and not the information that such events enclose. Hence, this approach can result in large amounts of documentation, particularly in software projects of middle and large size. Consequently, the integration of ProPAn into an Agile development process may be difficult because of its documentation overhead. Moreover, the jargon adopted by the method (i.e. words like "domains" and "phenomena") may alienate those who are not familiar with it and, consequently, hinder the method's usability.

4   PDP-ReqLite: A Lightweight Method for Privacy Requirements Engineering

All in all, ProPAn counts on multiple artifacts for capturing and documenting privacy-relevant information flows in a system-to-be. Such artifacts provide key input for conducting privacy analyses and, ultimately, for generating privacy requirements. However, their high syntactical correspondence with Jackson's terminology can jeopardize their usability for average software developers. Moreover, the overall documentation overhead in ProPAn can impact the development process of the system-to-be under analysis and eventually delay its commissioning. Hence, we introduce PDP-ReqLite, a lightweight method for the elicitation of privacy and data protection requirements which incorporates new artifacts for the documentation and analysis of privacy-relevant information flows. Alongside, we describe a protocol for the systematic elicitation of privacy and data protection taxonomies for achieving a broader scope and compliance with legal provisions and privacy standards to come.

4.1 Method Overview

Figure 2 illustrates the proposed requirement elicitation method named PDP-ReqLite. As it can be observed, this method keeps similarities with the second phase of ProPAn. Hence, to keep compatibility, PDP-ReqLite can receive as input either a set of software artifacts like the ones generated in the first phase of ProPAn (i.e. problem diagrams, domain knowledge, DSIFD, etc.), or alternative ones containing the same information. Particularly, our new lightweight method introduces two software artifacts as an alternative to the ones from ProPAn. The first one is a Requirements Data-Flow Diagram (RDFD) that describes requirements related to data processing and storage and the information flows between such requirements. Such a diagram resembles many aspects of ProPAn's DSIFD and AID but remains independent from the Problem Frames notation (i.e. it is not specified in terms of *phenomena* or *domains*). The other artifact introduced in this new approach is a Personal Information Diagram (PID). As described in Sect. 3.2, such a diagram is already present in ProPAn and, like the DSIFD, it its expressed through the jargon of Problem Frames. Conversely, this new PID is expressed in terms of stakeholders, data, and the linkability relations between them. Thereby, we look to overcome the issues related to usability and documentation overhead of the original method.

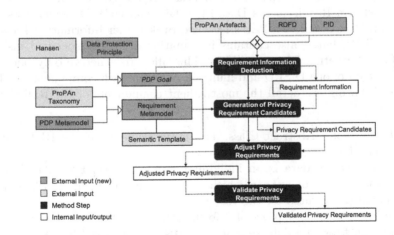

Fig. 2. PDP4E requirement elicitation method

Another element introduced by the PDP-ReqLite corresponds to the meta-models used to generate privacy and data protection requirements. As we described in Sect. 3.1, privacy requirements in ProPAn are derived using requirement taxonomies and semantic templates. Such taxonomies and templates are created by conducting an analysis of the GDPR and the ISO 29100. Such analysis is performed through the lens of the Hansen's privacy goals. That is, both law and standard are parsed into a set of taxonomies and semantic templates that represent each of the Hansen's goals. Nevertheless, expressing GDPR requirements only in terms of a limited set of principles (e.g., intervenability, unlikability and transparency) introduces a risk of methodological bias related to the choice of such principles. For this reason, we introduce two conceptual artifacts to achieve coverage and correctness during requirements elicitation. The first one is a protocol for extracting legal notions from the GDPR to capture in a structured vocabulary those concepts that can help us modelling Data Protection Principles (such protocol is described in Sect. 4.2). The second one is the possibility of adding new taxonomies or meta-requirements to the ones already introduced by ProPAn in order to achieve full coverage and avoid any potential bias. This is done by adding the extension point "Privacy and Data Protection Goal" (PDP Goal) in the requirement elicitation method of Fig. 2, which considers the incorporation of new data protection principles complementary to the goals of Hansen. Therefore, we consider the new PDP-ReqLite taxonomies as Requirement Meta-models and propose representing new data protection principles through PDP Meta-models. Such PDP Meta-models follow the same principle of the taxonomies introduced by ProPAn but instead of being associated with a privacy goal, they are associated to a privacy principle and defined using the vocabulary of legal notions.

Requirements Data-Flow Diagram (RDFD). Figure 3 (left) describes the meta-model of a Requirements Data-Flow Diagram (RDFD) which was introduced to replace mainly ProPAn's Detailed Stakeholder Information Flow Diagram (DSIFD), but it also contains information originally specified inside an Available Information Diagram (AID). This allow to generate only one global RDFD instead of one DISFD and multiple AIDs for each component inside the DISFD. Following, we detail the most salient components of the RDFD meta-model:

- *RDFD_Element*: Abstract Class. The main elements of the RDFD inherit from this class.
- *Data*: A piece of data is an individual unit of information. All data in a system-to-be has an **origin** which is the RDFD element in which it was originated (i.e. created for the very first time).
- *Record*: A record is a piece of information which has associated a certain **retention_time** in a data storage. Records are composed by data.
- *Data Record Requirement (DRR)*: It represents a requirement related to data storage. Particularly, it represents information structures that are implemented later on in a data base. A DRR is composed by a list of data records (**records_list**) which are pieces of information which have associated a cer-

tain retention time. The attribute `traceability` is a list of the functional requirements that the DRR contributes to.

- *Data Process Requirement (DPR)*: Represents activities that are performed over data records. Similar to a DRR, a DPR is also contains a list of the data (`data_list`) it is required to process. However, unlike DRRs, such data does not have a specific retention time associated. That is, it will be retained in memory during the processing time. In addition, a DPR has a `requestor_list` of the stakeholders that are allowed to execute it.
- *Data Flow Requirement (DFR)*: This element represents the exchange of information between RDFD elements. The attribute `data_list` represents the data flowing from one element to another.

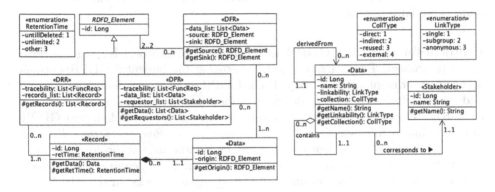

Fig. 3. RDFD metamodel (left) and PID metamodel (right).

Personal Information Diagram (PID). As it can be observed, the RDFD merges into one documentation artifact the information which was originally spread across ProPAn's DSIFD and AIDs. This improves the overall documentation navigability and interpretability. Figure 3 (right) introduces the metamodel of a Personal Information Diagram (PID) which is a simplified version of the one from ProPAn. The purpose of this new PID is also the documentation of the stakeholders' personal data that the system must process. The most salient components of the PID meta-model are:

- *Stakeholder*: An individual whose data is processed by the system-to-be.
- *Data*: An individual unit of information that has a `name`, `linkability` and `collection` type. Both, `linkability` and `collection` type have the same semantic as in ProPAn. A piece of data can be `derived_from` or `contain` other pieces of data.

The attribute `linkability` can adopt the values *single*, *subgroup*, or *anonymous*. The value *single* indicates that the data can only identify the individual it belongs to, *subgroup* when it identifies a potential subgroup of individuals, and *anonymous* when it does not provide any link to the data subject. On the other hand, `collection` can be *direct, indirect, reused,* or *external.* The value *direct* indicates that the stakeholder provides the information herself, the value *indirect* when the information is collected by observing the stakeholder's behaviour, *reused* when the data has been previously collected for another purpose (e.g. another project), and *external* in cases where the data is gathered through third parties.

4.2   Elicitation of Requirement Candidates

The automated elicitation of requirements is composed by two fundamental blocks: a protocol for covering GDPR directives and an algorithm for requirement candidates generation.

Protocol for Covering GDPR Directives. The protocol leverages several MDE techniques. First, a meta-model capturing fundamental GDPR notions and privacy principles was developed. The GDPR meta-model defines a language and syntax which is a basis to define so named meta-requirement categories. A meta-requirement is a pattern that results from translation of plain-text GDPR directives into predicates of the form *Pre-conditions* ⇒ *Post-conditions. Pre* and *Post-conditions* define the pattern that can be instantiated according to a given system model. As shown in the example bellow, the meta-requirements include placeholders to be filled according to the information included in the RDFD and PID model instance.

IF   process   *<self.processPD.size()*   greater   than   0>   processes   personal Data   of   *<self.processPD>*   **THEN**   the   Process   *<self>*   shall   be   lawful *<self.principles<LawFul>* (self.processPD. DataSubject) ⇒ .value=true>

The protocol followed to create the set of meta-requirements and the respective categories is as follows. First, a GDPR paragraph is taken as input and the goal is to translate it as a meta-requirement relying upon (1) the GDPR meta-model structure and contents and (2) the *Pre* and *Post-conditions* syntax. If the meta-model is not sufficient to do so, then it is extended by integrating the missing GDPR terms, notions and relationships. Once extended and the respective meta-requirement created, a new GDPR paragraph or principle is targeted. This iterative process is repeated till the coverage of GDPR articles and principles is ensured. This protocol ensures the introduction of new privacy principles coming, for instance, from updates or new regulations. Not having any dependency with existing privacy principles, the protocol prevents any bias whereas still achieves a good balance between legal and technical jargon.

Generation of Privacy Requirements Candidates. The generation is done by leveraging the information inside the RDFD and the PIDs. To illustrate how

```
List<UndetectReq> computeUndetectReq(Stakeholder S, Stakeholder C)
{
  List<UndetectReq> reqList = new List<UndetectReq>();
  List<Data> personalData = new List<Data>();

  List<Data> stakeholderData = getStakeholderData(PID,S);
  List<DPR> processList= getProcesses(RDFD,C);

  foreach(p in processList)
  {
    personalData.add(getProcessData(p));
  }

  List<Data> undetectableData = stakeholderData - personalData;

  foreach(u in undetectableData)
  {
    reqList = new UndetectReq(S,C,u);
  }

  return reqList;
}
```

```
The <C> shall not be able to sufficiently distinguish whether the
     personal information <u> of the <S> exist or not.
```

Fig. 4. Snippet for computing undetectability requirements (up) and the corresponding textual template (down)

this can be achieved, we analyse the generation of undetectability requirements. Basically, Pfitzmann et al. [16] define the undetectability of an information item as an attacker's inability to identify if such item exists or not. In other words, if some personal information PI of a stakeholder S is not accessible to another stakeholder C (and PI does not contain any other personal information accessible to C), then we assume that PI is undetectable to C. Note that we consider C as a stakeholder but also as a potential attacker. That is, as a "counter-stakeholder". Such analysis is described in the snippet of Fig. 4 and starts with the generation of an empty list of requirements (reqList) and another of personal data (personalData). Additionally, it creates a list of all the personal data of S which is kept inside the system-to-be. Such list is computed by the function getStakeHolderData with the help of the information inside the PID. Following, a list of all the processes in the RDFD for which C appears as requester is computed by the function getProcesses and stored inside processList. Next, algorithm iterates over the elements of this list, gathers all personal data involved in each process and adds it to personalData. Then, it proceeds to compute a list of undetectable data for C (undetectableData) by subtracting the elements inside personalData from stakeholderData. Finally, for each element inside undetectableData it generates a new undetectability requirement using and adds it to reqList and returns it afterwards. The text template of Fig. 4 is used for instantiating undetectability requirements. As one can observe, the generation of privacy requirements becomes smooth thanks to the privacy-relevant information captured across PDP-ReqLite's software artifacts.

4.3   Implemented Method

The PDP-ReqLite method is implemented as summarized in the following items:

S1. Specify functional requirements. In this phase, the engineer should specify the requirements associated to the functions to be covered by the system (functional requirements). To do so, the engineer can rely on well-known methods as suggested by the International Council of Systems Engineering (INCOSE), e.g., consider [18]. The specification is written in natural language, following good practices like for instance "one single sentence per system function". This step is a mean to simplify the next phase in the elicitation process. In particular, the encapsulation of functional requirements via minimal statements eases their correct transformation into a RDFD model.

S2. Transform functional requirements into a RDFD. In this phase, each functional requirement is transformed into a Requirement Process in the model which includes input/output data and the respective function tasks (i.e., the RDFD). Modelling the involved data types is an activity conducted in parallel. The data are required not only for completing the specification of the Requirement Process elements but also for identifying and labelling Personal Data (i.e., the PID). This phase of the elicitation process should be conducted manually since the expert should examine the form and contents of the functional requirements, and refine/adapt them, prior to transform them into the RDFD.

S3. Validation of the RDFD model and improvement. The validation phase yields outcomes regarding the model completeness and correctness. Model completeness is validated considering the language and syntax defined at meta-model level and determined by mandatory/optional attributes, their multiplicity and the associations types. Model correctness is validated by crosschecking the contents within and between RDFD and PID and the consistency between their attributes. Pre-defined rules are implemented to help the engineer to conduct an assessment validation and infer the solutions in case of conflicts. Indeed, the validation results essentially come as warnings and errors including a description of the issue. Then, the engineer can fix and improve the model so as to make it acceptable for the next phase. Since the process is iterative, going back to previous phases may be necessary.

S4. Privacy and GDPR requirements generation. Once the RDFD and PID model has been validated and accepted, according to the engineer evaluation, the specific privacy and GDPR requirements can be automatically generated: the generation is performed at the push of a button. All the GDPR and privacy principles instantiated either as meta-requirements or as meta-privacy patterns are considered during the generation. The respective algorithms are already implemented as built-in features of the PDP-ReqLite tool. They allow to obtain one requirement per meta-pattern including a full description. The requirements candidates should be validated by the engineer prior to follow other phases of the development cycle.

5   Automated Support for PDP-ReqLite Application

A tool support has been developed in the scope of the PDP4E project [15]. The
PDP-ReqLite tool is developed on top of Papyrus [2] and covers the different
modeling and analysis phases of the method as specified in Sect. 4.3. The tool
addresses different aspects regarding the need for automation during requirements generation, usability and re-usability of industry-size models. The main
features of the tool are demonstrated in the analysis of a Smart Grid case study.

5.1   Application to a Smart Grid Case Study

To illustrate the PDP-ReqLite implementation described in Sect. 4.3, we apply
it to analyze a Smart Grid case study. As shown in Fig. 5, the Smart Grid
design is described by a model composed by seven functions. The GDPR and
privacy requirements analysis mainly targets the *Billing* function. The resulting functional path includes the following dependencies. The *Measurement of
Consumption* function samples and provides electricity measures which are later
gathered by the *Grid Management* including the meter ID and client ID. Overall
electricity consumption over time per client are then computed and stored by
the *Consumption Data Processing* function. The information are finally accessed
by the *Billing* function to generate and submit an invoice relying upon personal
data of consumers. Further details of the Smart Grid architecture are provided
in this paper [11]. The model in Fig. 5 is used to specify the functional requirements the system should satisfy (Step 1, Sect. 4.3). The PDP-ReqLite modeling
features support the engineer to map the functional requirements into a RDFD
as shown in Fig. 6 (Step 2, Sect. 4.3). The model covers the functional path in
the Smart Grid system going from consumption measuring up to generation
of the customer bill. The rounded rectangles represent `ProcessRequirements`
whereas the normal rectangles represent the `DataStores`. These elements are
connected by directed edges representing data flows. The ports attached to the
`ProcessRequirements` are typed with conveyed data. Referred types are mod-
elled and structured in a dedicated PID view. The Fig. 7 shows an overview of the
PID used to model the data involved in the Billing processing. The PID includes

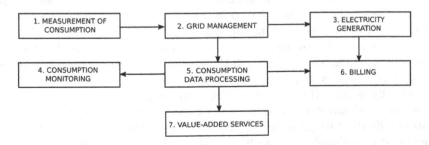

Fig. 5. Reference functions of the Smart Grid System

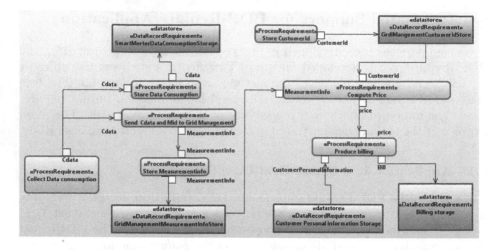

Fig. 6. RDFD model of the billing process within the Smart Grid System

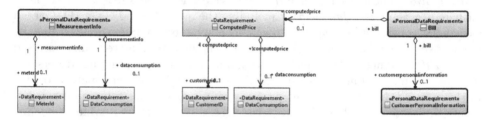

Fig. 7. Model view showing the PID of the Smart Grid System

composite structures that contain information about the electricity measurements (meter ID, consumption), the computed price per customer, and the final bill. More importantly, the PDP-ReqLite tool comes with dedicated types that can be used to identify personal information what is crucial to correctly elicit GDPR and privacy requirements. Once a first version of the RDFD and PID model was achieved, a round of validation and debugging was conducted (Step 3, Sect. 4.3). The resulting warnings and errors contain plain text messages that rely upon the syntax and rules defined in the GDPR meta-model. They indicate model discrepancies thus pointing out concerned elements by name and details on the specific issue. So, the completeness and correctness of the model were thus accordingly ensured. The final step in the method application generates the set of GDPR and privacy requirements (Step 4, Sect. 4.3). The requirements are automatically generated since the GDPR meta-requirement categories and the generation algorithm introduced in Sect. 4.2 have been implemented as built-in features of the PDP-ReqLite tool. As shown in Fig. 8, the generated requirements become part of the model and can be reused in other phases of the system development cycle. For instance, during the design phase, requirements are supposed to be satisfied by elements within the design model and validated through tests

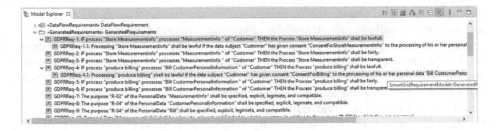

Fig. 8. Overview of the GDPR generated requirements

or similar validation instances. Last yet note the least, since there is no hard link between generated requirements and the RDFD and PID model, an update of the later may demand an iteration in order to obtain an updated version of requirements.

6   Conclusions and Perspectives

In this paper we have introduced a lightweight method named PDP-ReqLite to guide and support engineers during the elicitation of GDPR and privacy requirements in systems and software projects. The method has been proposed given that existing approaches impose certain restrictions mainly regarding the coverage of the GDPR regulation and certain biases potentially introduced during requirements elicitation. In this context, we have considered ProPAn as a reference method. By doing so, its main salient features and limitations have been assessed. So far, it has been concluded that ProPAn presents a high documentation overhead, complexity and redundancy across the artifacts it generates. It has been also identified a potential risk of bias since the method relies upon a limited set of principles (e.g., intervenability, unlikability and transparency) what reduces the choices the engineer has during the interpretation of GDPR directives. Overall, certain key ProPAn features, like the usage of privacy taxonomies and a generation algorithm, have been considered to develop extension points in the new method. As novelties of PDP-ReqLite, we can mention the following. The method only requires two modeling artifacts as inputs, the RDFD and PID, what significantly reduces overhead and complexity. The PDP-ReqLite method also introduces and implements a protocol that ensures full coverage of GDPR directives whereas still avoids the need for mapping them into existing privacy principles. The protocol produces GDPR taxonomies composed by meta-requirements which are predicate patterns defined in terms of GDPR directives and principles. The meta-requirements are instantiated during the requirements elicitation process. These feature also facilitates the integration of updates or even forthcoming privacy regulations. A tool support for the PDP-ReqLite method has been also implemented. The tool leverages several model-driven engineering techniques thus supporting RDFD and PID modelling and also automatic generation of candidate requirements. The method an tool features were finally demonstrated by analyzing a Smart Grid case study.

As work perspectives, we need to improve the automation of GDPR texts processing during the creation of meta-requirements since this task is for now human-based and highly time consuming. Since a high number of requirements can be obtained, even for simple system models, we should consider methods to structure, prioritize and treat them. To consolidate the approach, other privacy regulations can be targeted. Since the PDP-ReqLite method is positioned within a development life cycle, the interfaces with other cycle phases, like design, still need to be developed and consolidated.

Acknowledgements. This work was supported by the H2020 European Project No. 787034 "PDP4E: Privacy and Data Protection Methods for Engineering".

References

1. Beckers, K., Faßbender, S., Heisel, M., Meis, R.: A problem-based approach for computer-aided privacy threat identification. In: Preneel, B., Ikonomou, D. (eds.) APF 2012. LNCS, vol. 8319, pp. 1–16. Springer, Heidelberg (2014). https://doi.org/10.1007/978-3-642-54069-1_1
2. CEA-LIST: The Eclipse Papyrus project. https://www.eclipse.org/papyrus/ (2020)
3. Colesky, M., Hoepman, J.H., Hillen, C.: A critical analysis of privacy design strategies. In: 2016 IEEE Security and Privacy Workshops (SPW), pp. 33–40. IEEE (2016)
4. Deng, M., Wuyts, K., Scandariato, R., Preneel, B., Joosen, W.: A privacy threat analysis framework: supporting the elicitation and fulfillment of privacy requirements. Requirements Eng. **16**(1), 3–32 (2011). https://doi.org/10.1007/s00766-010-0115-7
5. Dennedy, M., Fox, J., Finneran, T.: The Privacy Engineer's Manifesto: Getting from Policy to Code to QA to Value. Apress, New York (2014)
6. Hansen, M., Jensen, M., Rost, M.: Protection goals for privacy engineering. In: 2015 IEEE Security and Privacy Workshops, pp. 159–166. IEEE (2015)
7. Hoepman, J.-H.: Privacy design strategies. In: Cuppens-Boulahia, N., Cuppens, F., Jajodia, S., Abou El Kalam, A., Sans, T. (eds.) SEC 2014. IAICT, vol. 428, pp. 446–459. Springer, Heidelberg (2014). https://doi.org/10.1007/978-3-642-55415-5_38
8. Howard, M., Lipner, S.: The security development lifecycle, vol. 8. Microsoft Press. Google Scholar Google Scholar Digital Library Digital Library, Redmond (2006)
9. Information Technology-Security Techniques-Privacy Framework. Standard ISO/IEC 29100:2011, International Organization for Standardization, Geneva, CH, December 2011. https://www.iso.org/standard/45123.html
10. Jackson, M.: Problem Frames: Analysing and Structuring Software Development Problems. Addison-Wesley, New York (2001)
11. Laakkonen, J., Annala, S., Jäppinen, P.: Abstracted architecture for smart grid privacy analysis. In: 2013 International Conference on Social Computing, pp. 637–646 (2013)

12. Meis, R.: Problem-Based Privacy Analysis (ProPAn): A Computer-aided Privacy Requirements Engineering Method. Ph.D. thesis, DuEPublico: Duisburg-Essen Publications [online], University of Duisburg-Essen, Germany, October 2018. https://doi.org/10.17185/duepublico/47797

13. Meis, R., Heisel, M.: Computer-aided identification and validation of privacy requirements. Information **7**(2), 28 (2016)

14. Notario, N., et al.: Pripare: integrating privacy best practices into a privacy engineering methodology. In: 2015 IEEE Security and Privacy Workshops, pp. 151–158. IEEE (2015)

15. PDP4E: The PDP4E Project. https://www.pdp4e-project.eu/ (2020)

16. Pfitzmann, A., Hansen, M.: A Terminology for Talking about Privacy by Data Minimization: Anonymity, Unlinkability, Undetectability, Unobservability, Pseudonymity, and Identity Management, August 2010. http://dud.inf.tu-dresden.de/literatur/Anon_Terminology_v0.34.pdf, v0.34

17. Regulation, G.D.P.: Regulation (Eu) 2016/679 of the European parliament and of the council of 27 April 2016 on the protection of natural persons with regard to the processing of personal data and on the free movement of such data, and repealing directive 95/46. Official J. Eur. Union (OJ) **59**(1–88), 294 (2016)

18. Ryan, M., Wheatcraft, L., Zinni, R., Dick, J., Baksa, K.: Guide for writing requirements. INCOSE, California, USA (2017)

Towards Multiple Pattern Type Privacy Protection in Complex Event Processing Through Event Obfuscation Strategies

Saravana Murthy Palanisamy[(✉)]

University of Stuttgart, Stuttgart, Germany
saravanamurthypalanisamy@gmail.com

Abstract. For a Complex Event Processing (CEP) system to be widely accepted, mitigating leaks of private information is paramount. In CEP systems, often private information are revealed through patterns instead of single events. There are very few mechanisms that protect privacy at the level of patterns. However these mechanisms consider only sequential patterns, one of the common pattern types in CEP. But this is highly confined since there are other common pattern types like conjunction, negation etc. So as a first step towards multiple pattern type privacy protection, in this paper we present a hybrid pattern level privacy protection mechanism that considers three common pattern types: sequence, conjunction and negation. Our approach is based on three event obfuscation strategies: event reordering, event suppression and introduction of fake events to conceal private patterns on the one hand, while minimizing impact on useful non-sensitive information required by IoT services to provide a certain Quality of Service (QoS) on the other hand. Our evaluations over real-world datasets show that our algorithms are effective in maximizing QoS while preserving privacy.

Keywords: Privacy · Complex event processing · Event obfuscation

1 Introduction

The Internet of Things (IoT) envisions a world with billions of networked sensors connected to the internet. Studies show that over 2.5 quintillion bytes of data are produced every day from these sensors[14]. These data are often raw sensor values and need to be processed into meaningful information in order to be useful for IoT applications like smart homes, e-health etc. Complex Event Processing (CEP) is a famous state-of-the-art paradigm for processing streams of such raw basic events into meaningful information (called "complex events") using a set of processing rules [11]. For example, a fitness tracker can infer the activity "doing sports" via basic events: $speed > 10\,km/h$ and $heart\ rate > 100\,bpm$.

The challenges while inferring meaningful information is a double-edged sword. On one side meaningful information is required to offer a certain *Quality of Service* (QoS). There is loss in QoS if a CEP system does not detect

© Springer Nature Switzerland AG 2020
J. Garcia-Alfaro et al. (Eds.): DPM 2020/CBT 2020, LNCS 12484, pp. 178–194, 2020.
https://doi.org/10.1007/978-3-030-66172-4_11

some events that originally existed (false negatives) or detects some non-existing events (false positives). On the other side some complex events might be privacy-sensitive. Though a user needs complex events to be detected accurately, he/she might not want to share any privacy-sensitive events. Thus a privacy protection mechanism is necessary for users to conceal private events while preserving QoS.

Access control is one prominent technique for privacy protection in CEP. However, most access control mechanisms protect privacy only at the level of single attributes of data [2,16]. But sensitive information is often revealed through complex data *patterns* that usually span several attributes. For example, heart rate and blood pressure might not reveal any useful information when analysed separately, but might reveal a disease when combined. We call these privacy-sensitive patterns in the event stream that a user or data owner wants to protect *private patterns*, while those patterns that are necessary for CEP applications to offer services and are not privacy-sensitive *public patterns*. Hence a pattern-level access control mechanism is required with which private patterns can be *obfuscated* while preserving as many public patterns as possible (maximum QoS).

Pattern-based access control strategy for CEP systems were proposed in [13,18]. However both these mechanisms only deal with patterns defined as a sequence of events. Although a sequence operator is one of the most common operator types in CEP, there are other common types like conjunction, negation etc.[5]. Also there can be more than one type of private pattern appearing at the same time which a user wants to conceal. For instance, on a weekday a user has taken a day off from work and is shopping. In the area of location privacy, this scenario can be viewed as two private patterns: a) "shopping" deduced by a series of location events [17] which is a sequence pattern; b) "not at work" which is a negation pattern. A user might want both these patterns to be concealed.

So as a first step towards multiple operator privacy protection in this paper, we introduce *Multi-Operator Privacy Protection component* (MOP) based on Integer Linear Programming (ILP) that considers all three commonly used CEP operator types namely sequence, conjunction and negation. Our MOP is based on three event obfuscation strategies: event suppression, event reordering and introduction of fake events, to conceal private patterns while maximizing QoS.

Overall, we make the following contributions in this paper: (1) We propose a baseline event obfuscation approach MOP, to maximize the utility of obfuscated event stream. (2) We introduce two extensions of the baseline approach working against two different adversary models. (3) For the evaluation of these approaches, we define the two adversary models that consider background knowledge of event distributions etc. gained from event histories.

The rest of this paper is organized as follows. In Sec. 2 we discuss related works followed by system model and problem statement in Sec. 3. In Sec. 4, we present our event obfuscation approaches that strive to maximize the utility of obfuscated event streams. In Sec. 5, we describe how an adversary uses observations learned from history data to reveal event obfuscations and describe our evaluation results, before concluding the paper in Sec. 6.

2   Related Works

Various access control mechanisms have been proposed to ensure privacy in event processing systems. However most of these works protect privacy at the level of attributes, ensuring that certain attributes in the event stream are only accessible to authorized parties [2,10]. However this is highly confined, since some attributes are either accessible or not at all, irrespective of whether it is part of a private or public pattern.

Another branch of privacy protection in event processing systems is differential privacy [4,8] and zero-knowledge privacy guarantees [15]. Though these mechanisms promise provable privacy guarantees, these works either protect privacy at the level of individual events/attributes or they protect privacy for individual users whose data are part of a dataset from a large population of users. The goal of our work is different in the sense that we try to achieve pattern-level privacy, considering data from a single user rather than a population of users.

Very few works [7,18] have been published that protect privacy at the level of patterns for CEP systems. Wang et al. [18] proposed a pattern-based access control strategy based on event suppression for sequence patterns. This approach conceals patterns by suppressing events that are part of private patterns while maximizing utility. In [13], Palanisamy et al. proposed an approach based on event reordering rather than suppression, but again only for sequence patterns. To the best of our knowledge there are not any research works that ensure pattern level privacy for CEP systems that consider multiple pattern types.

3   System Model and Problem Statement

In this section, we introduce our system model, which also includes our assumptions about the adversary who tries to detect private patterns. Moreover, we use the utility metric defined in [13] that defines the utility of an obfuscated event stream, which is then used as an objective in our problem statement.

3.1   System Model

Our system consists of the following components (cf. Figure 1): producers, consumers, CEP middleware in addition to Multi-Operator Privacy protection.

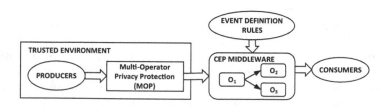

Fig. 1. CEP System + Multi-operator privacy protection component

Like in a typical CEP system [11], *Producers* generate basic events as input to the system. A CEP system could have multiple producers, but for this paper we assume that event streams from different producers are merged together into a single event stream in the order of timestamps like in [18]. Of course it is not possible for the users to know the exact event patterns that reveal sensitive information. Thus a separate system to translate the privacy requirements of a user into event patterns is necessary and this is a separate area of research [12]. For our work we assume that the user uses such a system to provide the necessary event patterns to be concealed. The *CEP middleware* extracts high level information (complex events) from basic events which are then forwarded to the *consumers* (e.g. an IoT service provider). We use a standard CEP middleware [6] which is a set of interconnected operators (O_x in Fig. 1). Operators are computing nodes that transforms input event stream into one or more outgoing event streams based on a set of predefined rules. The cooperative processing of several such operators result in a complex event. Generally, operators do not consider the complete (theoretically infinite length) event stream, instead process the event stream in smaller frames within a limited time or length called *windows*.

In this paper we consider three common operator types: *sequence, negation,* and *conjunction* [5]. A sequence operator captures a pattern in which a set of events arrive in a specific order in a window. An example sequence pattern denoting unhealthy behaviour of a diabetes patient (i.e., a private pattern) that should be hidden to an untrusted party (say health insurance company of the user) could be: $SEQ(Eating\_Sugar, High\_Blood\_Sugar\_Level, Insulin\_Intake)$. A conjunction operator queries the occurrence of a set of events within a window in any order and an example private pattern for the same user could be: $AND(Eating\_Sugar, No\_Insulin\_Intake)$. A negation operator queries the absence of a particular event within a specified window and an example private pattern could be: $NOT(Insulin\_Intake)$.

Like in [13,18], we also assume that the CEP middleware and the consumers are untrusted and are operated by another party other than the user (e.g., an IoT service provider). So private patterns from producers should be concealed before they are forwarded to the CEP or consumer. Thus we place our *Multi-Operator Privacy Protection component* (MOP) between producers and CEP and forward all producer events via MOP as shown in Fig. 1. The MOP performs three obfuscation strategies namely event reordering, event suppression and introduction of fake events to hide sequence, conjunction and negation type private patterns respectively. Both, producers and MOP, run in a trusted execution environment (e.g. smart phone of a user, private fog node etc.).

It is also important to specify the assumptions about the adversary that tries to compromise the privacy of users by detecting private patterns. We assume a "honest-but-curious" adversary which is a common model in privacy. In other words, one of the non-trusted components (CEP middleware or consumer) might be the adversary. In this case, the adversary is not able to observe the original event stream, but can observe the whole obfuscated event stream as sent by the

MOP. We also assume that the adversary has some background knowledge about the original event stream learned from external sources (say publicly available event streams).

3.2 Problem Statement

Informally, the problem solved by our approach is to preserve privacy by performing the three obfuscations while maximizing QoS. This is not a trivial problem, since there might be different combinations of obfuscations each having varying impact on QoS. We measure QoS in terms of false positive patterns (public patterns introduced by obfuscations that never happened) and false negative patterns (actual public patterns destroyed by obfuscations). In order to define the impact of obfuscations more precisely, we use the *utility metric* proposed in [13] as given in Equ. 1. However for our work the three terms of this utility metric now include all three pattern types as opposed to only sequence type patterns in case of [13]. The utility metric (U) is given as follows:

$$U = \Sigma_{i=1}^{\#\ of\ matched\ true\ public\ Patterns} w_i \quad - \quad \Sigma_{j=1}^{\#\ of\ matched\ false\ positives} w_j$$
$$-\Sigma_{k=1}^{\#\ of\ matched\ private\ patterns} w_k \tag{1}$$

The second term in the equation is to introduce a negative penalty for each false positive. Negative penalties for false negatives are deducted already, since they are not included in matched public patterns thus reducing the actual utility metric. Thus, the first two terms increase the utility for each true positive match of a public pattern and decrease the utility for each false positive or false negative match. The weights w_i and w_j shown in Equ. 1 show the relative importance of different public patterns onto QoS. Matched private patterns are considered in the third term. Including private patterns in the utility metric rather than making it a hard constraint (no private pattern matches) enables us to obtain a trade-off between privacy and QoS, i.e., revealing some private information for more public pattern matches. Here, weight w_k of a private pattern k is given as:

$$w_k = (\Sigma w_i + 1) * cp_k \tag{2}$$

Tuning parameter cp_k enables to leverage privacy for QoS by specifying a criticality percentage for private pattern k. If we set the private pattern criticality to 100%, i.e., $cp_k = 1$, then a single match of that private pattern k would outweigh the effect of all public pattern matches such that, no private patterns of that type will be revealed (100% privacy). For $cp_k = 0$ that type of private pattern is always revealed. The problem now is to find a strategy that performs the three obfuscations and maximizes utility while making it (ideally) impossible for the adversary to detect concealed private patterns. Solving this problem requires some assumptions about the background knowledge of the adversary to understand what possibilities the adversary has to detect event obfuscations. We consider two kinds of adversary model: deterministic and probabilistic.

Deterministic Adversary model: This type of adversary requires 100% "confidence" that a private pattern is concealed. One example for such an adversary could be a car manufacturer who is curious to detect a concealed private pattern (say bad driving behaviour of the user) that caused damage to the vehicle, with 100% confidence to deny a warranty claim. The adversary in this case employs three attacks one for each obfuscation mechanism.

Causal order constraint attacks rely on knowledge about causal relationship between events. We say the order of two events e_1 and e_2 is causally constrained if e_2 must never happen before e_1. Reordering e_1 and e_2 could immediately be detected as a violation of this constraint known to the adversary.

Periodic event constraint attacks rely on knowledge about periodic events. For instance, in a e-health scenario the event "blood sugar level" is recorded every 30 mins. Suppressing such events could be detected immediately as a violation of this constraint.

Infeasible event constraint attacks are based on knowledge about events that are impossible to happen in a window. For example, the location event "at mall" is infeasible after closing hours. Introducing such fake events could be detected immediately as a constraint violation.

Probabilistic Adversary model: Here, it is sufficient for the adversary to detect a concealed private pattern with a confidence $(\gamma) < 100\%$. An example adversary could be a car insurance company who might increase the insurance premium, even if a concealed private pattern about the user's bad driving behaviour is revealed with 80% confidence. The adversary in this model employs statistical attacks, in addition to those from the deterministic adversary.

Statistical attacks consider the inter-arrival time distribution of events, either between same or different types of events. For instance, by analysing a publicly available data set, an adversary might know that, in 90% of all cases the time between two insulin injections for patients is around 2 h. Suppressing an "insulin injection" event would lead to a difference of 4 h between two injections indicating the adversary that an event has been suppressed with 90% confidence. Thus, besides maximizing utility, obfuscations are to be performed such that it is unlikely to detect event obfuscations performed with 100% confidence for deterministic adversaries and below a certain confidence threshold (γ) for probabilistic adversaries.

4   Event Obfuscation Approaches

In this section, we present our two event obfuscation approaches: Counter Deterministic Attack (CDA) and Counter Probabilistic Attack (CPA) obfuscation strategies that conceals private patterns against deterministic and probabilistic adversaries respectively. Both the approaches are extensions of a *baseline approach* based on Integer Linear Programming (ILP) which we will present first in the next sub-section followed by the two extensions.

4.1 Baseline ILP Approach

The primary goal of this ILP approach is to find an optimal combination of the three event obfuscation strategies that maximizes utility as defined by Equ. 1. The ILP is invoked on a full window of events, whenever this window contains at least one private pattern of any type. Of course, those windows without private patterns can be forwarded as it is. The problem of finding an optimal combination of the event obfuscation strategies is translated as an ILP with the utility metric as objective.

ILP Formulation:- Parameters: We now derive the parameters to formulate our ILP.

Table 1. ILP parameters

Parameters	Parameter description
$\mathcal{N}$	Number of events in the window
$\mathcal{T}_N$	Set of timestamps of event instances in the window
$\mathcal{N}_{TQ}^S, \mathcal{N}_{TQ}^C, \mathcal{N}_{TQ}^N, \mathcal{N}_{FQ}^S, \mathcal{N}_{FQ}^C, \mathcal{N}_{FQ}^N$	Set of true and false positives for sequence, conjunction and negation type *public* patterns
$\mathcal{N}_{TP}^S, \mathcal{N}_{TP}^C, \mathcal{N}_{TP}^N, \mathcal{N}_{FP}^S, \mathcal{N}_{FP}^C, \mathcal{N}_{FP}^N$	Set of true and false positives for sequence, conjunction and negation type *private* patterns
$\mathcal{W}_{TQ}^S, \mathcal{N}_{TQ}^C, \mathcal{N}_{TQ}^N, \mathcal{W}_{FQ}^S, \mathcal{N}_{FQ}^C, \mathcal{N}_{FQ}^N$	Set of weights for true and false positives for sequence, conjunction and negation type *public* patterns
$\mathcal{W}_{TP}^S, \mathcal{N}_{TP}^C, \mathcal{N}_{TP}^N, \mathcal{W}_{FP}^S, \mathcal{N}_{FP}^C, \mathcal{N}_{FP}^N$	Set of weights for true and false positives for sequence, conjunction and negation type *private* patterns

We define $\mathcal{N}$ as number of events in the window on which our ILP is invoked. We introduce another parameter set $\mathcal{T}_N$ of size $\mathcal{N}$ representing arrival timestamps of event instances in that window. $\mathcal{N}_{TQ}^S$, $\mathcal{N}_{TQ}^C$, and $\mathcal{N}_{TQ}^N$ represent list of matched sequence, conjunction, and negation type *true positive* public patterns in the window before obfuscation. $\mathcal{N}_{FQ}^S$, $\mathcal{N}_{FQ}^C$, and $\mathcal{N}_{FQ}^N$ represent list of sequence, conjunction and negation type *false positive* public patterns. Here TQ and FQ represent true and false positive public patterns. Similar to public patterns, we have $\mathcal{N}_{TP}^S$, $\mathcal{N}_{TP}^C$, $\mathcal{N}_{TP}^N$, $\mathcal{N}_{FP}^S$, $\mathcal{N}_{FP}^C$, and $\mathcal{N}_{FP}^N$ representing list of true and false positive private patterns for the three operator types. Here, TP and FP represent true and false positive private patterns. The above 12 parameters are collectively called *pattern parameters*. As described in Equ. 1, we require positive weights signifying relative importance between public patterns and negative weights for false positives and private patterns. Thus we define 12

Table 2. ILP variables

Variables	Variable description
$\mathbf{V}^S_{TQ}, \mathbf{V}^C_{TQ}, \mathbf{V}^N_{TQ}, \mathbf{V}^S_{FQ}, \mathbf{V}^C_{FQ}, \mathbf{V}^N_{FQ}$	Set of decision variables for true and false positives for sequence, conjunction and negation type *public* patterns
$\mathbf{V}^S_{TP}, \mathbf{V}^C_{TP}, \mathbf{V}^N_{TP}, \mathbf{V}^S_{FP}, \mathbf{V}^C_{FP}, \mathbf{V}^N_{FP}$	Set of decision variables for true and false positives for sequence, conjunction and negation type *private* patterns
$\mathbf{O}_{NN}$	Matrix for all $\mathcal{N} \times \mathcal{N}$ ordered pairs in the window
$\mathbf{X}_N$	Set of variables representing change in timestamps
$\mathbf{E}_N$	Set of decision variables representing event suppressions
$\mathbf{I}_I$	Set of decision variables representing event introductions

sets of parameters representing weights $(\mathcal{W}^Y_{XX})$ for all three pattern types that correspond to each of the pattern parameters as shown in the last two rows of Table 1. These weights are the objective coefficients of our ILP.

Variables: We now define variables required for our ILP formulation (cf. Table 2). We define 3 sets of binary decision variables: $\mathbf{V}^S_{TQ}$, $\mathbf{V}^C_{TQ}$, and $\mathbf{V}^N_{TQ}$, one for each pattern type and each variable in a set represent a match for a true positive public pattern of that type. Similarly $\mathbf{V}^S_{TP}$, $\mathbf{V}^C_{TP}$, and $\mathbf{V}^N_{TP}$ represent match for true positive private patterns. Similarly for false positives, we introduce another 6 sets of decision variables representing matched false positive public and private patterns for each operator type: $\mathbf{V}^S_{FQ}$, $\mathbf{V}^C_{FQ}$, $\mathbf{V}^N_{FQ}$ and $\mathbf{V}^S_{FP}$, $\mathbf{V}^C_{FP}$, $\mathbf{V}^N_{FP}$. Among the false positive variables, those that represent sequence and conjunction patterns are positive integer variables. This is because there might be multiple false positive matches for the same pattern after obfuscation (since there can be multiple instances of the same event type) which is not known a priori in case of sequence and conjunction patterns which in turn should be considered for determining the optimal solution. However it is sufficient to define binary variables for false positive negation type patterns since there cannot be multiple false positive matches for the same negation type pattern in a window. The sizes of these 12 variable sets are determined by the cardinality of their corresponding *pattern parameters* as given in Table 1.

All the binary decision variables mentioned above have a common interpretation and a sample interpretation is given as: $\mathbf{V}_{TQ}^S[i] = 1$ if i^{th} pattern is matched in that window and 0 otherwise (Here $i \in \{1, 2, ... |\mathcal{N}_{TQ}^S|\}$). Similarly all integer decision variables have the same interpretation and a sample interpretation is given as $\mathbf{V}_{FQ}^S[j]$ is ≥ 1, one for every match of that pattern and 0 if that pattern has no match at all in that window (Here $j \in \{1, 2, ... |\mathcal{N}_{FQ}^S|\}$).

The linear combination of the weights and above mentioned decision variables form the utility function and is also the objective function of our ILP. For clarity, we group these 12 decision variable sets into 4 sets $\mathbf{V}_{TQ}, \mathbf{V}_{FQ}, \mathbf{V}_{TP}, \mathbf{V}_{FP}$ representing true positive public & private and false positive public & private patterns by grouping variables of all three pattern types together into one. The weight parameters are also similarly grouped: $\mathcal{W}_{TQ}, \mathcal{W}_{FQ}, \mathcal{W}_{TP}, \mathcal{W}_{FP}$. Now the objective function is written as:

$$maximize \sum_{i=1}^{|\mathcal{N}_{TQ}|} \mathcal{W}_{TQ} * \mathbf{V}_{TQ} + \sum_{j=1}^{|\mathcal{N}_{FQ}|} \mathcal{W}_{FQ} * \mathbf{V}_{FQ} +$$

$$\sum_{k=1}^{|\mathcal{N}_{TP}|} \mathcal{W}_{TP} * \mathbf{V}_{TP} + \sum_{m=1}^{|\mathcal{N}_{FP}|} \mathcal{W}_{FP} * \mathbf{V}_{FP} \tag{3}$$

We will now describe the auxiliary variables necessary for our ILP. For a sequence pattern (say SEQ(A,B,C)) to be matched in a window, all ordered event pairs [SEQ(A,B), SEQ(B,C)] of that pattern should be matched. An ordered event pair is said to be matched if the two events occur in the same sequence after obfuscation. Thus we introduce a binary variable matrix $\mathbf{O}_{NN} \in \{0, 1\}^{\mathcal{N} \times \mathcal{N}}$ that represent whether the ordered pairs are matched in the window, and a set of bounded integer variables $\mathbf{X}_N$ of size $\mathcal{N}$ that represents the change in arrival timestamps after obfuscation for all event instances in that window. The relation between these two variables is written as a constraint given by:

$$\mathbf{O}_{NN}[i][j] = \begin{cases} 1 \to \text{if } \mathcal{T}_N[j] + \mathbf{X}_N[j] > \mathcal{T}_N[i] + \mathbf{X}_N[i] \\ 0 \to \text{otherwise} \end{cases} \tag{4}$$

where $i, j \in \{1, 2, ... \mathcal{N}\}$. This means that if an event instance e_i happens before e_j, then $\mathbf{O}_{NN}[i][j] = 1$.

For a conjunction pattern to be matched in a window, all instances of event types that constitute a conjunction pattern should occur in that window. Thus, we define a set of binary variables $\mathbf{E}_N$ of size $\mathcal{N}$ such that $\mathbf{E}[i] = 0$ if i^{th} event instance in that window is suppressed and is 1 otherwise (Here $i \in \{1, 2, ... \mathcal{N}\}$).

For a negation pattern to match, no event instance of that event type in the negation pattern should occur in the window. To conceal a negation private pattern, it is necessary to introduce a fake event instance of the event type that constitutes the pattern. Thus we define another binary decision variable set $\mathbf{I}_I$ of size $|\mathcal{N}_{TP}^N|$ for each negation type private pattern in addition to $\mathbf{E}_N$ defined above. $\mathbf{I}_I$ is interpreted as $\mathbf{I}_I[i] = 1$ if that i^{th} event is introduced fake and 0 otherwise here $i \in \{1, 2, ... |\mathcal{N}_{TP}^N|\}$. This means that additional events might be introduced in the window and so we extend $\mathbf{O}_{NN}$ to $\mathbf{O}_{NN}^*$, whose size will then be $(\mathcal{N} + |\mathcal{N}_{TP}^N|) \times (\mathcal{N} + |\mathcal{N}_{TP}^N|)$. Also $\mathcal{T}_N$ and $\mathbf{X}_N$ are changed to $\mathcal{T}_N^*$ and $\mathbf{X}_N^*$ whose sizes are now changed to $\mathcal{N} + |\mathcal{N}_{TP}^N|$.

Constraints: Now, we will explain the constraints, that translate the requirement for the event obfuscation problem. We classify these constraints into three categories: sequence, conjunction, and negation constraints.

Sequence constraints ensure that a sequence pattern is matched only if all ordered pairs of that pattern are matched. Here, all true positive sequence patterns (both public & private) have similar constraints and a sample constraint is given by

$$\forall \mathcal{N}_{TQ}^S : \quad IF(AND(\mathbb{M}_{TQ}^S[i])) \ THEN \ (\mathbf{V}_{TQ}^S[i] = True) \tag{5}$$

where $\mathbb{M}_{TQ}^S[i] \subset \mathbf{O}_{NN}$ consists set of all ordered pairs that correspond to i^{th} sequence pattern in $\mathcal{N}_{TQ}^S$. For false positive sequence patterns (both public and private), since we do not know a priori the number of matches, it is necessary to consider all possible combinations of ordered pairs that might lead to a match. A sample constraint for a false positive sequence pattern is given as:

$$\forall \mathcal{N}_{FQ}^S : \quad \mathbf{V}_{FQ}^S[i] = \sum_{j=1}^{|\mathbb{M}_{FQ}^S[i]|} AND(\mathbb{M}_{FQ}^S[i][j]) \tag{6}$$

where $\mathbb{M}_{FQ}^S[i]$ contains list of all ordered pair combination sets of the ith sequence pattern in $\mathcal{N}_{FQ}^S$ and $\mathbb{M}_{FQ}^S[i][j] \subset \mathbf{O}_{NN}^*$. The above two constraints ensure correctness of sequence pattern matches in terms of ordered pairs. Since we might also perform suppression, when a suppressed event is part of a sequence pattern, that sequence pattern is also suppressed. Thus to ensure correctness of a sequence pattern match in terms of suppressed events, we add another set of constraints for all sequence patterns, and a sample constraint is given as:

$$\forall \mathcal{N}_{TQ}^S : \quad IF(AND(\mathbb{U}_{TQ}^S[i]) \ THEN \ (\mathbf{V}_{TQ}^S[i] = True) \tag{7}$$

where $\mathbb{U}_{TQ}^S[i] \subset (\mathbf{E}_N \cup \mathbf{I}_I)$ consists set of all events that are part of sequence pattern i. $\mathbb{U}$ contains set of all events for every true positive sequence pattern and list of all sets of event combinations for every false positive sequence pattern.

Conjunction constraints ensure that a conjunction pattern is matched only if all event instances of that conjunction pattern are not suppressed. For true positive conjunction patterns a sample constraint is given by:

$$\forall \mathcal{N}_{TQ}^C : \quad IF(AND(\mathbb{U}_{TQ}^C[i])) \ THEN \ (\mathbf{V}_{TQ}^C[i] = True) \tag{8}$$

where $\mathbb{U}_{TQ}^C[i] \subset \mathbf{E_N}$ contains set of all events that are part of the conjunction pattern i. This constraint is common for all true positive conjunction patterns (both private and public). For false positive conjunction patterns (both public and private) a sample constraint is given by:

$$\forall \mathcal{N}_{FQ}^C : \quad \mathbf{V}_{FQ}^C[i] = \sum_{j=1}^{|\mathbb{U}_{FQ}^C[i]|} AND(\mathbb{U}_{FQ}^C[i][j]) \tag{9}$$

where $\mathbb{U}_{FQ}^C[i]$ contains list of all event combination sets that correspond to the ith conjunction pattern in $\mathcal{N}_{FQ}^C$ and $\mathbb{U}_{FQ}^C[i][j] \subset (\mathbf{E_N} \cup \mathbf{I}_I)$.

Negation constraints ensure that a negation pattern is matched only if an event instance of a particular event type does not occur in that window. It is not necessary for any additional constraints for true positive negation type public patterns since those events will not be introduced. Only those events that are part of true positive negation type private patterns might be introduced. Thus the constraint for negation type private patterns is given by:

$$\forall \mathcal{N}_{TP}^N : \quad IF(\mathbf{I}_I[i] == True) \ THEN \ (\mathbf{V}_{TP}^N[i] = False) \tag{10}$$

Event suppression might introduce a false positive negation pattern. Formally for a false positive negation pattern to be true, it is necessary that all event instances of that event type that define the negation pattern are suppressed. A sample constraint for a negation type false positive pattern is given as:

$$\forall \mathcal{N}_{FQ}^N : \quad IF(NOT(OR(\mathbb{U}_{FQ}^N[i]))) \ THEN \ (\mathbf{V}_{FQ}^N[i] = True) \tag{11}$$

where $\mathbb{U}_{FQ}^N[i] \subset \mathbf{E_N}$ contains set of all event instances of that event type that constitute i^{th} negation pattern. The above constraint is common for all false positive negation patterns (both public and private).

The baseline approach described above aims at maximizing utility but does not consider all adversarial impacts. In the next subsections we will describe how this baseline approach is extended to the CDA and CPA obfuscation strategies that protect against deterministic and probabilistic adversaries respectively.

4.2   Counter Deterministic Attack Obfuscation (CDA)

To ensure protection against the deterministic adversary, it is sufficient if the approach does not perform any impossible obfuscations. So in this approach we introduce constraints such that our ILP neither reorders causally ordered pairs nor suppresses periodic events nor introduces fake infeasible events.

4.3   Counter Probabilistic Attack Obfuscation (CPA)

Probabilistic adversaries consider statistical attacks in addition to attacks of deterministic adversaries. Thus it is necessary to reduce the confidence level of the adversary below a certain confidence (γ) as described in Sect. 3. We propose such an approach that reduces adversary confidence by introducing fake event-obfuscations analogous to real ones such that obfuscations performed for concealing private patterns become indistinguishable from the *pseudo-obfuscations*. To achieve this, it is necessary to consider three factors:

1. *Introduce pseudo-obfuscations*: To introduce pseudo-obfuscations, we define pseudo-private patterns similar (but not exactly the same) to real private patterns. This is done by defining pseudo-private patterns with a combination of events that are predominantly part of real private patterns. We add these pseudo-patterns to the list of private patterns to conceal in addition to actual private patterns. The ILP, thus treats both pseudo and real private patterns in the same manner and hence the output obfuscations introduced are indistinguishable and thus the confidence of the adversary is reduced.

2. *Number of pseudo-obfuscations to be introduced*: To reduce the confidence of the adversary below γ, by proportionality principle it is necessary to introduce atleast $\kappa = ((\rho/\gamma) - 1)\%$ obfuscations where ρ is the *prior probability* the adversary has, before we introduce pseudo-obfuscations. If ρ is below the confidence threshold, it is not necessary to introduce any pseudo-obfuscations.

3. *Selection of windows for pseudo-obfuscations*: For selecting windows to introduce pseudo-obfuscations one simple way is to uniformly distribute the pseudo-private patterns over all the windows. But utility of those windows that already contain private patterns might get affected. This is because higher the number of private patterns to be concealed, higher the probability that concealing a private pattern would also affect a public pattern. So those windows that do not have any private pattern matches are selected for introducing pseudo-private patterns.

Overall, the idea is to introduce pseudo-private patterns along with real private patterns only to selected windows such that the obfuscations are revealed with less than $\gamma\%$ confidence.

5   Evaluation Results

In this section, we evaluate our two obfuscation approaches with respect to their ability to achieve indistinguishability against adversaries with minimum impact onto public patterns (preserving QoS). As all state-of-the-art approaches are based on single operator types, it is not fair to compare our approach in terms of either privacy or utility for our evaluations. This is because utility and privacy are no longer the same between single and multi operator approaches even for the same window of events. Moreover, obfuscating one operator type pattern might introduce false positives or negatives of a different pattern type. Such interdependencies do not exist in case of single operator approaches.

5.1 Evaluation Setup

For the performance evaluation, we used a commodity server with AMD Ryzen 5-2500U processor (6 cores at 2.0 GHz) and 16 GB RAM. We implemented our obfuscation algorithms in Python using Gurobi as the ILP solver.

Datasets: To evaluate our approach we used two publicly available real-world datasets. The first dataset is an online retail dataset [3] that contains all transactions between 01/12/2010 and 09/12/2011 of a UK based online retailer selling all-occasion gifts. It includes 20,000 transactions and 500,000 purchased items from among 3,200 different products with timestamps and customer ids. We selected 50 most popular sequence, conjunction (of length 2 to 4) and negation patterns altogether as public and private patterns of varying length (e.g. A user hosting a Christmas Party deduced by the pattern: AND(Party Cone Christmas Decoration, Traditional Christmas Ribbons, Party invites Christmas)). The window size for these patterns vary from 5–800 events.

The second dataset is a msbnc web page visit dataset [1]. The dataset includes anonymous web page visits of users who visited msnbc.com in September 1999. Each window in the dataset corresponds to page views of a user during that day. Each event in the window corresponds to a user's request for a web page. We use the page visits of 20000 users. Similar to the e-commerce dataset, we searched and selected 25 most popular sequence, conjunction and negation patterns of varying length. Window size is the number of page visits of a user in a day and it varies between 3 and 400 pages. Such a dataset might reveal private information about the user like travel destinations, favourite TV-shows etc.

5.2 Adversary Model

To evaluate the effectiveness of our approaches in protecting privacy, we first need to elaborate on the two adversary models. In our system model (Sec. 3), we have assumed that the deterministic adversary has information about causal, periodic and infeasible event constraints. We also assumed that the probabilistic adversary has background knowledge about statistical information about true (typical) inter-arrival time distribution of events on the modified event stream.

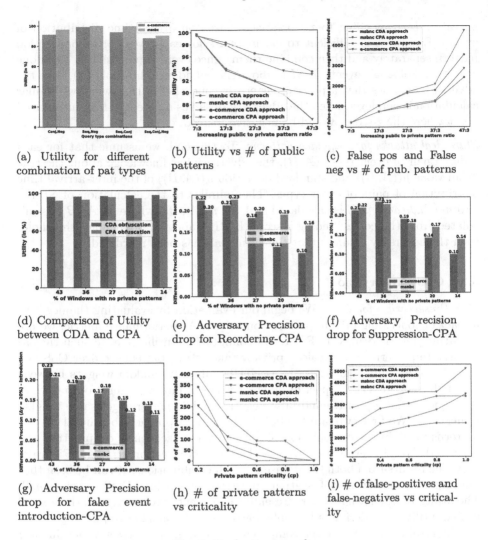

(a) Utility for different combination of pat types

(b) Utility vs # of public patterns

(c) False pos and False neg vs # of pub. patterns

(d) Comparison of Utility between CDA and CPA

(e) Adversary Precision drop for Reordering-CPA

(f) Adversary Precision drop for Suppression-CPA

(g) Adversary Precision drop for fake event introduction-CPA

(h) # of private patterns vs criticality

(i) # of false-positives and false-negatives vs criticality

Fig. 2. Evaluations results

Statistical attacks: We assume that from publicly available data the adversary knows the true mean value $\mu(A)$ and true standard deviation $\sigma(A)$ of the inter-arrival time distribution for events of event types say A, B, C, etc. So now from observing the obfuscated event stream, for an event instance say A_i, the adversary can calculate the so-called *z-score* [9] $z(A_{i-1}, A_i) = \frac{t(A_i)-t(A_{i-1})-\mu((A))}{\sigma((A))}$, i.e., the number of standard deviations by which the observed inter-arrival time is below or above the true mean inter-arrival time. When the adversary observes a potentially suppressed event say A_i in the event stream, he calculates the *Suppression Indicator (SI)* $= 1 - p_z(A_{i-1}, A_{i+1})$ where p_z is the probability value corresponding to the z-score of that event instance $(z(A_{i-1}, A_{i+1}))$.

p_z values corresponding to z-scores vary based on arrival-time distribution of events. Besides it is sufficient to calculate *SI* for each event of a conjunction pattern separately and then combine them, since event suppression is also done at the level of single events. If *SI* is above the confidence threshold (γ), then the adversary assumes that a private pattern is concealed in that window. Similar calculation is employed when the adversary observes a potential fake introduced event where the z-scores would be negative instead.

Statistical attacks for Sequence patterns: To this end, we assume that for each ordered pair of event types (A, B), the adversary has knowledge about the true mean value $\mu((A, B))$ and standard deviation $\sigma((A, B))$ of the inter-arrival time distribution of pairs of event types. Then similar to the calculation of *SI*, the *Reorder Indicator (RI)* is calculated as $1 - p_z(A_i, B_j)$ where $p_z(A_i, B_j)$ is calculated from the corresponding z-score. If RI is above a pre-defined threshold, then the adversary assumes that the event pair has been reordered.

5.3   QoS Preservation

QoS Preservation for CDA: We begin our evaluation by evaluating the negative impact of concealing private patterns onto QoS. As performance metric, we use the utility metric defined in Eq. 1. We configure the utility metric such that a) no private patterns are revealed (privacy takes strict precedence over QoS i.e., $c_p = 1$); b) all public patterns are assigned uniformly random weights between 1 and 10 to express the impact of different types of public patterns onto QoS; c) consequently false positive and false negative public patterns get same weights in negative. We first evaluate the capability of our approach to conceal private patterns for different combination of pattern types (sequence, conjunction and negation). For this evaluation we use the CDA obfuscation strategy. Figure 2a show the results from both the datasets for all combinations. It can be seen that the impact of our event obfuscation approach onto utility (QoS) is very small. The utility value shown here is represented as percentage of maximum theoretical utility (utility considering only public patterns). The number of public patterns for the msnbc dataset is lesser compared to e-commerce dataset which in turn results in lesser false positives and false negatives and hence better utility.

Privacy-QoS trade-off: With increase in number of public patterns, there is a higher chance that an obfuscation to conceal a private pattern might also impact public patterns. In this respect we show the impact of our event obfuscation approaches with increase in the number of public patterns. Figure 2b shows the result for increasing number of public patterns with the number of private patterns unchanged for both the datasets. It can be seen that the number of public patterns indeed influence QoS. Besides we show the impact of increasing public patterns on the number of false positives and false negatives with the same setup for the two datasets. in Fig. 2c.

CPA Approach: The pseudo-obfuscations introduced by our CPA approach might affect some public patterns and hence there is a drop in utility at the expense of making our obfuscations indistinguishable. Here we compare the drop in utility with and without pseudo-obfuscations. We again use the setting such that the approaches do not reveal any private patterns. To evaluate the reduction in confidence achieved by our CPA approach, the required reduction in confidence $\rho - \gamma$ is set to 20%. Also we introduce pseudo-obfuscations only in windows that do not have any private pattern matches. Now for CPA approach, we calculate κ (cf. Sect. 4), generate 10 pseudo-private patterns for each operator type, distribute these 10 pseudo patterns κ times uniformly over the selected windows. Figure 2d shows that the utility comparison between CDA and CPA obfuscation strategies with decrease in size of selected windows for introducing pseudo-event reorderings for the e-commerce database and it can be seen that the drop in utility is negligible to achieve reduction in confidence of the adversary.

Robustness to probabilistic attacks: The confidence of the adversary is evaluated by his *precision* (correctly identified private patterns divided by the overall number of correctly or incorrectly identified private patterns). Figure 2e shows the achieved reduction in adversary precision using CPA approach compared to CDA approach with decrease in the number of selected windows for pseudo-obfuscations in case of reordering for both the datasets. We select those windows with no private patterns to introduce pseudo-private patterns for this evaluation. It can be seen from the figure that, if the number of selected windows for pseudo-obfuscations decreases, then the achieved reduction in confidence of adversary also decreases. Figure 2f and Fig. 2g shows the drop in adversary precision achieved using the CPA approach with the same setup with respect to suppression and introduction of fake events respectively for both datasets.

Till now, we only evaluated with a setup where privacy took precedence over QoS, i.e., with 0% revealed private patterns. Now, we evaluate the privacy-QoS trade-off. In order to realize this trade-off we tune the criticality percentage cp_k in Equ. 5. Figure 2h and Fig. 2i shows number of private patterns and number of false positives and false negatives over cp_k respectively. The figures show that increase in values of cp increase privacy while decreasing QoS.

6 Summary and Future Works

In this paper, we proposed a hybrid pattern-level access control component for three most commonly used CEP operators namely sequence, conjunction and negation. The approach conceals private patterns using three obfuscation strategies: event reordering, event suppression and introduction of fake events. The approach besides protecting privacy by concealing private patterns, also maximizes quality of service by preserving as many public patterns as possible. We presented two approaches that maximize utility while protecting against deterministic and probabilistic adversaries. For future work, the approach could be extended to include privacy protection for other CEP operators.

References

1. Cadez, I.V., Heckerman, D., Meek, C., Smyth, P., White, S.: Visualization of navigation patterns on a web site using model-based clustering. In: KDD (2000)
2. Cao, J., Carminati, B., Ferrari, E., Tan, K.L.: ACStream: enforcing access control over data streams. In: 2009 IEEE 25th International Conference on Data Engineering (2009)
3. Chen, D., Sain, S.L., Guo, K.: Data mining for the online retail industry: a case study of RFM model-based customer segmentation using data mining. J. Database Mark. Customer Strategy Manage. **19**(3), 197–208 (2012)
4. Chen, Y., Machanavajjhala, A., Hay, M., Miklau, G.: Pegasus: data-adaptive differentially private stream processing. In: Proceedings of the 2017 ACM SIGSAC Conference on Computer and Communications Security, CCS 2017, ACM (2017)
5. Cugola, G., Margara, A.: Processing flows of information. ACM Comput. Surv. **44**(3), 1–62 (2012)
6. Cugola, G., Margara, A.: Deployment strategies for distributed complex event processing. Computing **95**(2), 129–156 (2013). https://doi.org/10.1007/s00607-012-0217-9
7. He, Y., Barman, S., Wang, D., Naughton, J.F.: On the complexity of privacy-preserving complex event processing. In: Proceedings of the 30th symposium on Principles of database systems of data - PODS 2011. ACM Press (2011)
8. Kellaris, G., Papadopoulos, S., Xiao, X., Papadias, D.: Differentially private event sequences over infinite streams. Proc. VLDB Endowment **7**(12), 1155–1166 (2014)
9. Kreyzig, E.: Advanced Engineering Mathematics, 4th edn. Wiley, New York (1979)
10. Lindner, W., Meier, J.: Securing the borealis data stream engine. In: 2006 10th International Database Engineering and Applications Symposium (IDEAS 2006) (2006)
11. Luckham, D.: The power of events: an introduction to complex event processing in distributed enterprise systems. In: Bassiliades, N., Governatori, G., Paschke, A. (eds.) RuleML 2008. LNCS, vol. 5321, pp. 3–3. Springer, Heidelberg (2008). https://doi.org/10.1007/978-3-540-88808-6_2
12. Mindermann, K., Riedel, F., Abdulkhaleq, A., Stach, C., Wagner, S.: Exploratory study of the privacy extension for system theoretic process analysis (STPA-Priv) to elicit privacy risks in eHealth. In: 2017 IEEE 25th International Requirements Engineering Conference Workshops (REW) (September 2017)
13. Palanisamy, S.M., Dürr, F., Tariq, M.A., Rothermel, K.: Preserving privacy and quality of service in complex event processing through event reordering. In: Proceedings of the 12th ACM International Conference on Distributed and Event-based Systems - DEBS 2018, ACM Press (2018)
14. Petrov, C.: 25+ impressive big data statistics for 2020 (July 2020). https://techjury.net/blog/big-data-statistics/#gref
15. Quoc, D.L., Beck, M., Bhatotia, P., Chen, R., Fetzer, C., Strufe, T.: Privacy preserving stream analytics: The marriage of randomized response and approximate computing. CoRR abs/1701.05403 (2017)
16. Schilling, B., Koldehofe, B., Rothermel, K., Ramachandran, U.: Access policy consolidation for event processing systems. In: 2013 Conference on Networked Systems. IEEE (March 2013)
17. der Spek, S.V., Schaick, J.V., Bois, P.D., Haan, R.D.: Sensing human activity: GPS tracking. Sensors **9**(4), 3033–3055 (2009). https://doi.org/10.3390/s90403033
18. Wang, D., He, Y., Rundensteiner, E., Naughton, J.F.: Utility-maximizing event stream suppression. In: Proceedings of the 2013 International Conference on Management of data - SIGMOD 2013, ACM Press (2013)

GPS-Based Behavioral Authentication Utilizing Distance Coherence

Tran Phuong Thao[✉] and Rie Shigetomi Yamaguchi

Graduate School of Information Science and Technology, University of Tokyo,
Tokyo, Japan
tpthao@yamagula.ic.i.u-tokyo.ac.jp, yamaguchi.rie@i.u-tokyo.ac.jp

Abstract. Current user authentication systems are based on PIN code, password, or biometrics traits, which can have some limitations in usage and security. Lifestyle authentication has become a new research approach in which the promising idea is to use the location history since it is relatively unique. Even when people live in the same area or have occasional travel, it does not vary from day to day. For Global Positioning System (GPS) data, previous work used the longitude, latitude, and timestamp as the classification features. In this paper, we investigate a new approach utilizing distance coherence, which can be extracted from the GPS itself without the need to require other information. We applied three ensemble classifications, including RandomForest, ExtraTrees, and Bagging algorithms. The experimental result showed that our approach could achieve 99.42%, 99.12%, and 99.25% of accuracy, respectively.

Keywords: Smartphone location-based authentication · Lifestyle authentication · Global Positioning System (GPS) · Biometrics authentication

1 Introduction

"Society 5.0" [4] has become a well-known buzzword which was introduced by the Japanese government in 2011[1]. Society 5.0 focuses on two critical keywords, **human-centered** and **smart** society with the support of Artificial Intelligent (AI), Internet of Things (IoT), big data, and cutting-edge technologies.

Let's consider an example of the electronic payment system. In 1871, Western Union debuted the electronic fund transfer (EFT), allowing people to send money to pay for goods and services without necessarily having to be physically present at the point-of-sale. In 1946, John Biggins invented the first bank-issued credit card to replace paper money (the concept of using a card for purchases and the term credit card was described in 1887 by Edward Bellamy). In 2011, Google launched a mobile wallet project to replace physical cash and credit cards.

---

[1] Society 5.0 follows Society 1.0 (the hunting society), Society 2.0 (agricultural society), Society 3.0 (industrial society), and Society 4.0 (information society).

© Springer Nature Switzerland AG 2020
J. Garcia-Alfaro et al. (Eds.): DPM 2020/CBT 2020, LNCS 12484, pp. 195–215, 2020.
https://doi.org/10.1007/978-3-030-66172-4_12

Nowadays, the cashless payment system has become a new trend. Many digital wallet services appeared, such as Apple Pay (from 2014), Google Pay (from 2015 as Android Pay and 2018 as Google Pay), Rakuten Pay (from 2016), etc. The biggest challenge is how to authenticate the users. The current approach relies on the mobile phones' authentication using PIN code, password, biometrics (i.e., fingerprinting, iris, face, etc.), or multi-factor method, which combines more than one form of authentication from independent categories of credentials.

Attacks and Vulnerabilities in Current Smartphone Authentication. Many sophisticated attacks in smartphone authentication have appeared. First, *PIN code/password-guessing attack* [15,16] tries to recover the password plaintext from its hashed form using a brute force search, which systematically checks every combination of letters, symbols, numbers and dictionary attack which uses a dictionary of common words. Second, *biometric spoofing* tries to generate synthetic or fake biometric traits of legal users to fool the capture sensors including *facial spoofing* which utilizes printed facial photographs and digital video [21] or a 3D mask [22], *fingerprinting spoofing* [23] which utilizes artificial replicas with different materials such as gelatin, latex, play-doh or silicone, and *iris spoofing* [17] which utilizes an image forging natural iridal texture characteristics [18] or even cosmetic contact lenses [19,20], and the combination of all these three spoofing types [24]. Third, *smudge attack* tries to guess the graphical password pattern in touch screen phones by analyzing the epidermal oils and smears left on the device's screen by the user's fingers [25]. Fourth, *shoulder-surfing attack* [26] uses social engineering techniques to steal the victim's personal information such as PIN code and password by looking over the victim's shoulder or by eavesdropping on sensitive information being spoken and heard or keystrokes on a device. Finally, a large number of users themselves do not lock their smartphones. [11] analyzed over 150 smartphone users and showed that 33% of the users do not use any screen lock. [12] conducted face-to-face qualitative interviews with 28 participants. 29% of the users responded that they did not lock their devices with three common reasons, including emergency personnel not identifying them, not having the devices returned if lost, and not believing they worth data. [13] run an online survey with 260 participants and a field study with 52 participants to analyze smartphone users' risk perception and behaviors. They showed that 40.9% of users use slide-to-unlock, and 16.2% of users do not use any screen lock.

Location-Based Behavioral Authentication. There are some research questions in constructing a smarter and securer mobile-based authentication. First, for mitigating the attacks above, is there an additional mobile-based authentication for supporting the conventional authentication using PIN code, password, and biometric traits (i.e., fingerprints, face, iris)? Second, imaging the scenario that a user is on the way to going to a coffee shop. Before he arrives, the coffee shop can predict that he will arrive 15 min later with a high probability, prepare in advance his usual order, and automatically subtract the charge from his account. The user then does not need to wait for the order and payment process.

So, the question is: is it possible to authenticate and predict the location (for example, the coffee shop) that the users are likely going to? Last but not least, in the situation of the COVID-19, the current smartphone-based cashless payment can reduce the chance of using cash or card, but still, the user needs to touch the smartphone screen to show the bar code to the cashier. The final question is whether the user can pay for goods when only bringing the smartphone without touching the screen?

An idea to answer the questions is using behavioral-based information. This new research's main challenge is how to decide useful behavioral information for authentication. Inspirited from L. Fridman (MIT) et al. [5], just in 2016, GPS location history is a promising approach because "It is relatively unique to each individual even for people living in the same area of a city. Also, outside of occasional travel, it does not vary significantly from day to day. Human beings are creatures of habit, and in as much as location is a measure of habit". At this time, single behavioral authentication is used as an additional method to support the conventional authentication or to combine with other behavioral authentications. In the future, if we can construct a payment system such that (i) the users do not need to bring devices, (ii) the security and privacy are ensured, and (iii) the conventional biometrics authentication can be replaced entirely, it is a step closer to Society 5.0.

Motivation. A system can achieve a high authentication accuracy when it can collect multiple factors as much as possible. However, in the users' viewpoint, a convenient system should not bring strong privacy concerns to the users by requiring too much information. From the GPS, most of the previous work utilized the longitude, latitude, and timestamp as the features for the user authentication. Given the limited information, if we can obtain metadata that carries extra independent information from the GPS itself, we can improve the accuracy. An example of GPS-based self-enhancement is [7] in which they extracted the address from the pair of longitude and latitude using a reverse geocoding.

Contribution. In this paper, we propose an idea to extract the distance coherence features from the GPS itself without any other information besides the GPS. The locations at close time clocks may have some closer correlation in physical distance than the locations at far time clocks for each user. The idea is inspired by the fact that a human needs time to move from one location to another. Since this concept can reflect a movement "lifestyle" of the users, we hypothesized that it might improve the accuracy. Although it may be not 100% correct when the user goes forward and then backward within the considered period of time, we combine the proposed distance coherence features with the previous ones. To evaluate how feasible the approach is, we collected 107,637 GPS records from 348 users. We applied three ensemble machine learning classification (RandomForest, ExtraTrees, and Bagging) on a total of 13 features, including the distance coherences features. The experimental result showed that our approach outperforms the approach without the distance coherence features with the accuracy of 99.42% (for RandomForest), 99.12% (for ExtraTrees), 99.25% (for Bagging).

Considering its reasonability, it may raise a question. Since we infer the distance coherence from the GPS and timestamp, whether the distance coherence's entropy is the same as that of the GPS and timestamp? In other words, whether the distance coherence gives no additional information to the GPS and timestamp. However, for each sample, the corresponding distance coherence is computed from a sample and other samples with a close timestamp with the considered sample. Therefore, the GPS, timestamp, and distance coherence are independent variables. Of course, we can improve the model if we combine the GPS and timestamp with other factors such as Wifi information, web browser log, etc. However, this paper aims to clarify whether the distance coherence extracted from the GPS and the timestamp can improve the classification model. We thus excluded other factors to make the comparison clean.

Roadmap. The rest of this paper is organized as follows. The related work is introduced in Sect. 2. The proposed method is described in Sect. 3. The experiment is presented in Sect. 4. The threat model is presented in Sect. 5. The discussion about future work is shown in Sect. 6. Finally, the conclusion is drawn in Sect. 7.

2   Related Work

This section presents related work focusing on multimodal authentication using human-smartphone interactions and other factors. The term *multimodal* (not *multimodel*) is used to indicate the biometrics authentication using multiple biometric data. It is the opposite with *unimodal*, which uses only a single biometric data.

2.1   Multimodal Authentication for Smartphone

L. Fridman et al. [5] analyzed four modal behavioral data from active mobile devices, including text stylometry typed on a soft keyboard, application usage patterns, web browsing behavior, and physical location of the device from GPS (outdoor) and Wifi (indoor). They collected the data from 200 users in more than 30 d. The authors proposed a parallel binary decision-level fusion architecture for classifiers based on four biometric modalities. A. Alejandro et al. [8] analyzed multimodal data from four biometric data channels (including touch gestures, keystroking, accelerometer, and gyroscope) and three behavior profiling (including WiFi, GPS location, and app usage). They obtained the data during the natural human-smartphone interaction of 48 users, on average, ten days per user. They proposed two authentication models named the one-time approach that uses all the channel information available during one session, and an active approach that uses behavioral data from multiple sessions by updating a confidence score. W. Shi et al. [6] proposed an authentication framework that enables continuous and implicit user identification service for a smartphone. They collected the data from four sensor modalities, including voice, GPS location, multitouch, and locomotion. They conducted a preliminary empirical study with a small set of users (seven). The result showed that the four modalities are enough for mobile user identification. R. Valentin et al. [10] analyzed multimodal sensing modalities with mobile devices when the GPS, accelerometer, and audio signals are utilized for human recognition. They collected the data from four existing datasets which consist of 491 users. They applied four variants of deep learning for interpreting user activity and context as captured by multi-sensor systems. M. Upal et al. [14] investigated user authentication methods using the first non-commercial multimodal data, which focuses on three smartphone sensors (front camera, touch sensor, and location service). They collected the data from 48 users for two months. Their benchmark results for face detection, face verification, touch-based user identification, and location-based next place prediction showed that more robust methods fine-tuned to the mobile platform are needed to achieve satisfactory verification accuracy. T. Thao et al. [7] extracted the addresses given the longitudes and latitudes from the GPS records. They then applied the text mining on the addresses. They collected the data from 50 users for about four months. Their experimental result showed that the combination between the text features and the GPS data could improve the classification accuracy. B. Aaron et al. [9] proposed a wallet repository that can store biometric data using multiple layers: a biometric layer, a genomic layer, a health layer, a privacy layer, and a processing layer. They used the processing layer to determine and track the user location, the speed when the user is moving using GPS data.

2.2   Other Multimodal Authentication

Besides using human-smartphone interactions, multimodal authentication also uses other factors. T. Kaczmarek et al. [27] investigated a new hybrid biometric based on a human user's seated posture pattern in an average office chair throughout a typical workday. Their experimental results on a population of 30 users showed that the posture pattern biometric could capture a unique combination of physiological and behavioral traits and can authenticate the users with 91% of accuracy. M. Ivan et al. [28] proposed an approach which combines the PIN code and the pulse-response. For the experiment process, they collected biometric information from 10 users. The result showed that each human body exhibits a unique response to a signal pulse applied at the palm of one hand and measured at the other's palm. The experimental result for user authentication achieved 88% of accuracy when taking the records weeks apart. W. Louis et al. [30] and R. Alejandro et al. [32] constructed a continuous authentication system based on electrocardiogram (ECG) and electroencephalogram (EEG). Their approaches achieved 1.57% and 0.82% of the false-negative rate, respectively. E. Simon et al. [29] extracted distinct patterns from eye movement (it is different from iris) with 21 features for user authentication. The data was collected from 30 users in 2 weeks with three scenarios (no prior knowledge, the knowledge gained through description, and knowledge gain through observation). The experimental result achieved 3.98% of equal error rate.

3   Proposed Approach

This section describes our proposed method, including data collection, feature extraction and selection, and our learning method.

3.1   Data Collection

We created a navigation application named MITHRA (Multi-factor Identification/auTHentication ReseArch) in the project of the University of Tokyo to collect the users' GPS information. The application is available on both iOS and Android smartphones. We developed the application run in the background. We collected the data from 348 users with 107,637 GPS records, including pairs of longitude and latitude for four months from January 11 to April 26 in 2017[2]. Compared to the existing works (see Sect. 2), the number of users in our dataset is higher than most of the papers and is only lower than [10], which could collect the information from 491 users. We recruited the participants randomly. The users live and work in random areas. The GPS data was measured every minute. The value of the longitudes and latitudes were collected with the precision up to 6 decimal places (e.g., 36.xxxxxx) corresponding to 0.1 m.

Privacy Consent. The privacy consent is shown to the users during the installation process. The installation can only be done if the users accept the terms and conditions agreement. Even after successfully installing the application, the users can choose to start or stop using the application anytime. Any personal information of the users such as name, age, gender, race, ethnicity, income, education, etc. is not collected. We collected only the email addresses the user identity used to distinguish the users from each other. Although the application collects the GPS information, the users do not need to disclose their home location, office location, etc. Our project was reviewed by the Ethics Review Committee of the Graduate School of Information Science and Technology, the University of Tokyo. Finally, all the users who installed the application agreed to participate in our project.

3.2   Feature Extraction and Selection

We categorized the features into two groups: (i) the features extracted from the GPS and the timestamp, and (ii) the features using the distance coherence score.

---

[2] Although we collected the GPS from smartphones in this project, we can also collect the GPS from many smaller devices such as smartwatches or smartbands nowadays.

GPS and Datetime. There are seven features in this group. Two features were extracted from the GPS, including the latitudes and the longitudes represented by float numbers. The valid ranges for the latitudes and the longitudes are the continuous range $[-90, +90]$ and $[-180, +180]$, respectively. Five features were extracted from the timestamp, including month, day, hour, minute, and day of a week (i.e., seven days from Monday to Sunday) represented by integer numbers. The valid ranges for these features are the intervals $[1, 12]$, $[1, 31]$, $[0, 23]$, $[0, 59]$, and $[1, 7]$, respectively. We did not extract the year as a feature because all the data samples were collected in the same year (2017).

Distance Coherence. There are α features in this group (we will soon explain how to choose α). Each z-th feature ($z \in [1, \alpha]$) represents the distance coherence (similarity score) between each data sample with the average of all the other samples in the dataset that belong to the same user and that occur before or after p hours for every $p \in [0, z]$ with the considered sample. $p = 0$ is when the other samples occur in the same hour with the considered sample.

More concretely, the features are computed as follows (see Fig. 1). Let $\{dc_z\}$ denote the set of α features where $z \in [1, \alpha]$. Let s_i denote each sample in the dataset where $i \in [1, n]$ and n denotes the number of samples (in our dataset, $n = 107,637$). For each feature dc_z, let $K_z = \{s'_j\}$ (where $j \in [1, n]$ and $j \neq i$) denotes the set of all the other samples such that s_i and s'_j belong to the same user U_t (where $t \in [1, 348]$). State differently, s_i and s'_j have the same label U_t. Let $lat(s_i)$ and $lat(s'_j)$, $lon(s_i)$ and $lon(s'_j)$, and $hour(s_i)$ and $hour(s'_j)$ denote the latitude, the longitude, and the hour features for s_i and s'_j, respectively. For each dc_z, K_z is chosen such that:

$$hour(s_i) = hour(s'_j) \pm p \quad \text{for } \forall p \in [1, z] \tag{1}$$

The average coordinate s''_j is determined from all the samples s'_j in K_z such as:

$$lat(s''_j) = \mathsf{average}(lat(s'_j)) \quad \forall s'_j \in K_z \tag{2}$$

$$lon(s''_j) = \mathsf{average}(lon(s'_j)) \quad \forall s'_j \in K_z \tag{3}$$

The features are finally calculated as the distance between s_i and s''_j:

$$dc_z(s_i) = \sqrt[2]{(lat(s_i) - lat(s''_j))^2 + (lon(s_i) - lon(s''_j))^2} \tag{4}$$

From Eq. 1, we can observe that K_z chosen for dc_z is a subset of $K_{z'}$ chosen for $dc_{z'}$ for all $z, z' \in [1, \alpha]$ such that $z' > z$. It may raise the question that whether all the α features have a correlation. However, the averages from even correlated sets are completely different (for example, $\mathsf{average}(1, 2, 3) = 2$ which is different from $\mathsf{average}(1, 2, 3, 4) = 5$). All the features dc_z are thus independent variables. A numeric example for how to calculate the distance coherence features will be given in Appendix A.

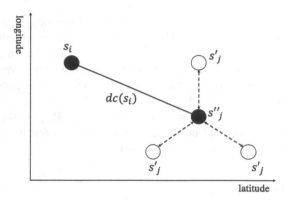

Fig. 1. Distance coherence (similarity score)

We now explain how the concrete value for α is. In our approach, we use three advanced classification machine learning algorithms, which are Random-Forest, ExtraTrees, and Bagging (explained in more detail in Sect. 3.3). We experimented with every α from 1 and increased it gradually. We found that the best α for RandomForest, ExtraTrees, and Bagging is 3, 4, and 5, respectively, at which the algorithms reach the peak performance (Sect. 4.3). Since α reflects the movement lifestyle of the users, it is reasonable for α to be not large. For instance, the GPS (latitude, longitude) of a user U_t at 15:00 may have some physical distance coherence with the GPS records at 14:00 and 16:00 than the GPS records at 13:00 and 17:00. In the rest of this paper, we use α-DC to denote the approach in which α distance coherence features are used, and $\{$lat, lon, mon, day, hour, min, weekday, $dc_1, dc_2, \cdots, dc_6\}$ to denote the set of the thirteen features related to both the GPS and timestamp and the distance coherence.

Feature Distribution. We describe the distribution statistics for the features in Table 1, including the mean, standard error, median, standard deviation, Kurtosis score, skewness score, min value, and max value. A normal distribution check for the features is not necessary [31]. The negative and positive values in the latitude and the longitude in the "Min" and "Max" columns indicate that the users who used to commute in Japan might travel abroad during the data collection. This kind of data can create noises during the training and testing processes. However, we did not remove it because the data reflects the users' natural behavior. Although the noises may lower the accuracy, we want to measure how practical the approach is when using real data without being manipulated.

Table 1. Feature distribution

Feature	Mean	SE	Median	SD	Kurtosis	Skewness	Min	Max
lat	35.262	0.014	35.376	4.554	151.722	−10.935	−36.858	43.907
lon	136.783	0.034	137.846	11.165	248.09	−15.101	−121.979	174.799
month	3.321	0.002	3.000	0.753	−0.260	−0.777	1.000	4.000
day	17.328	0.026	19.000	8.600	−1.075	−0.285	1.000	31.000
hour	13.421	0.019	14.000	6.388	−0.820	−0.417	0.000	23.000
min	28.919	0.053	29.000	17.357	−1.186	0.038	0.000	59.000
weekday	3.986	0.006	4.000	1.966	−1.215	−0.016	1.000	7.000
dc_1	4,104.198	137.84	191.318	45,214.683	976.703	27.756	0.000	2,545,473.711
dc_2	4,359.489	137.598	239.163	45,140.323	988.797	27.801	0.000	2,548,301.562
dc_3	4,586.805	140.910	259.640	46,228.488	995.124	27.895	0.000	2,549,190.471
dc_4	4,678.671	140.658	272.654	46,147.07	978.139	27.653	0.004	2,554,832.383
dc_5	4,781.704	141.784	276.978	46,516.486	1,002.699	28.001	0.048	2,567,773.385
dc_6	4,822.694	143.361	284.604	47,033.864	1,013.685	28.284	0.017	2,568,234.888

SE (Standard Error), SD (Standard Deviation), DC: Distance Coherence

3.3 Learning

This section explains the machine learning algorithms chosen for our model and the evaluation method. In the dataset, each user has a different label. Each label has a different set of records.

Average Ensemble Classifications. The dataset contains 107,637 samples with a large number of labels (348 users). Instead of using the traditional algorithms, we use *average ensemble classifications* to get better performance. The average ensemble algorithms build several base estimators independently and produce one optimal predictive estimator by averaging all the base estimators' predictions. The combined estimator is better than any single base estimator by reducing the variance to control over-fitting. The common algorithms include:

- RandomForest [1]: implements a meta estimator that fits some decision tree classifiers on various randomized sub-samples and uses averaging to create the best predictive estimator. When each estimator is built, a bootstrap is created by randomly sampling the dataset with replacement. The sub-samples' size is set to be the same as the size of the original input sample. A decision tree is usually trained by recursively splitting the data (converting the non-homogeneous parent into the two most homogeneous child nodes). The algorithm selects an optimal split on the features selected at every node.
- ExtraTrees [2]: produces the best predictive estimator in a way like RandomForest. However, there are some differences. While RandomForest uses the optimal split, ExtraTrees uses the random split. While RandomForest sets the *bootstrap = True* by default, ExtraTrees sets the *bootstrap = False* by default. It means that while RandomForest supports drawing sampling with replacement, ExtraTrees supports drawing sampling without replacement.

– Bagging (Bootstrap Aggregating) [3]: uses all the features for splitting a node while RandomForest and ExtraTrees select only a subset of randomized features for splitting a node.

Stratified K-Fold. We shuffled the data at first and then used a k-fold cross validation. Since the numbers of samples of the users are imbalanced, using the normal k-fold cross validation can lead to the following problem. There may exist a class c_k ($k \in \{1, 2, \cdots, 348\}$) in which all the samples belong to the test set; and the training set does not contain any samples. The classifier, therefore, cannot learn about the class c_k. To solve this problem, we used *Stratified k-fold* cross-validation object, which is a variation of k-fold and can deal with imbalanced data in each class. As presented in Fig. 2, it splits the data in the train and the test sets. It returns stratified folds made by preserving the percentage of samples for each class.

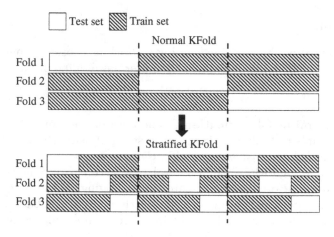

Fig. 2. A stratified KFold

Evaluation Metrics. To evaluate our approach, we measure the following metrics:

$$accuracy = \frac{tp + tn}{tp + fp + fn + tn}, \quad precision = \frac{tp}{tp + fp}, \quad recall = \frac{tp}{tp + fn} \quad (5)$$

$$F1 = 2 \times \frac{recall \times precision}{recall + precision}, \quad FPR = \frac{fp}{fp + tn}, \quad FNR = \frac{fn}{fn + tp} \quad (6)$$

where tp, tn, fp, fn denote the true positive, true negative, false positive, and false negative values, respectively. FPR and FNR denote the false positive rate and false-negative rate, respectively. The accuracy is a good metric when the distribution for each label is almost similar. However, for an imbalanced dataset, F1-score is the better metric.

4   Experiment

This section presents the experimental setup, the results obtained after applying the classification, and how to find the best α for each algorithm.

4.1   Experimental Setup

We implemented the program using Python 3.7.4 on a computer MacBook Pro 2.8 GHz Intel Core i7, RAM 16 GB. The machine learning algorithms are executed using *scikit-learn*[3] library version 0.22.

For each ensemble algorithm, the number of base estimators $n\_estimators$ is set to 100. The k value in the stratified k-fold cross validation is set to $k = 10$. Since the categorical labels are represented in text strings (such as 'user001', 'user002', etc.), the labels are transformed to numerical values using the *label encoding*. While the *ordinal encoding* encodes a label to an integer array and the *one-hot encoding* encodes it to a one-hot numeric array, the *label encoding* encodes it to the values between 0 and $q - 1$ where q is the number of distinct labels of all the classes. The label encoding is the most lightweight method and uses less disk space. Since the data is imbalanced, to avoid the situation that F1 is not between precision and recall, we calculate the three metrics (precision, recall, and F1 score) for each label and find their average weight by the number of true instances of each class. This process can be done by setting the parameter $average = weighted$ in the *sklearn.metrics*. For the accuracy, this parameter is not necessary. Since the values of the distance coherence features are small, we scaled them up to $\times 10^4$. For each of the three algorithms (RandomForest, ExtraTrees, and Bagging), we experimented with different α's. We applied the classification 107,637 samples with 348 labels, which correspond to 348 users.

4.2   Main Result

The main result is presented in Table 2. In the table, NoDC represents the approach not using distance coherence features, while α-DC represents the approach using α distance coherence features. As proved later in Sect. 4.3, RandomForest, ExtraTrees, and Bagging reach the best performance at $\alpha = 3$, $\alpha = 4$ and $\alpha = 5$, respectively. Thus, we chose 3-DC, 4-DC, and 5-DC to compare with NoDC in this table (although only 1-DC can already beat NoDC (see Sect. 4.3)).

The result shows that our approach α-DC outperforms NoDC in all the cases. Comparing all the algorithms using NoDC only with each other, Bagging

---

[3] https://scikit-learn.org/stable/.

gives the best result with 98.69% of F1 score with 0.02% of false-negative rate. Comparing all the algorithms using our approach with each other, RandomForest gives the best result with 99.42% of F1 score and merely 0.01% of false-negative rate even though RandomForest just reaches $\alpha = 3$ (which is less than $\alpha = 4$ for ExtraTrees and $\alpha = 5$ for Bagging). Comparing the improvement between α-DC and NoDC, ExtraTrees gives the best result when 2.34% of F1 score is increased ($\triangle = +2.34$) and 0.04% of false-negative rate is reduced ($\triangle = -0.04$).

Table 2. Result for distance coherent with different ensemble algorithms

Measure	RandomForest			ExtraTrees			Bagging		
	NoDC	3-DC	$\triangle$	NoDC	4-DC	$\triangle$	NoDC	5-DC	$\triangle$
F1	97.95	99.42	+1.47	96.77	99.11	+2.34	98.69	99.24	+0.55
Accuracy	97.97	99.42	+1.45	96.80	99.12	+2.32	98.69	99.25	+0.56
Precision	98.05	99.45	+1.40	96.90	99.15	+2.25	98.75	99.28	+0.53
Recall	97.97	99.42	+1.45	96.80	99.12	+2.32	98.69	99.25	+0.56
FPR	0.00	0.00	0.00	0.00	0.00	0.00	0.00	0.00	0.00
FNR	0.03	0.01	-0.02	0.05	0.01	-0.04	0.02	0.01	-0.01

NoDC: the approach without distance coherence features,
α-DC ($\alpha = 3, 4, 5$): the approach using distance coherence features,
$\triangle$: the improved score between α-DC and NoDC.

4.3   Best Alpha (α) for Each Algorithm

This section explains the experiment to find the best α for each algorithm. First, α is set to 1 and is then gradually increased until the performance becomes convergent or reduced after reaching the peak. The result and its graphs are presented in Table 3 and Fig. 3. The proposed approach using RandomForest, ExtraTrees, and Bagging got the best performance at $\alpha = 3$, $\alpha = 4$, and $\alpha = 5$, respectively. Figure 3 shows that in all the algorithms, the graph almost has the cone shape (the result is gradually increased, gets the peak, and then is reduced or becomes convergent), not a zigzag shape (in which we cannot predict where is the peak). The result also shows that by even just using 1-DC ($\alpha = 1$), our approach can already beat NoDC.

4.4   Computation Time

For the best algorithms (5-DC using Bagging, 4-DC using ExtraTrees, and 3-DC using RandomForest), the average computational time for the training and cross-validation processes from 5 execution times is 2,272 s (38 min), merely 270 s (4.5 min), and 596 s (10 min) respectively. It is not a big deal for the server. When the number of users is much more increased (e.g., to thousands), it is not complicated to transform the current model from the one-class classification to a multi-class classification where each user has a different classifier with binary labels representing whether or not a sample belongs to that user.

Table 3. Result for each alpha

		1-DC	2-DC	3-DC	4-DC	5-DC	6-DC
RandomForest	F1	99.11	99.41	99.42	99.38	99.36	99.31
	Accuracy	99.11	99.42	99.42	99.38	99.37	99.31
	Precision	99.15	99.44	99.45	99.41	99.39	99.35
	Recall	99.11	99.42	99.42	99.38	99.37	99.31
	FPR	0.00	0.00	0.00	0.00	0.00	0.00
	FNR	0.01	0.01	0.01	0.01	0.01	0.01
ExtraTrees	F1	97.27	98.90	98.98	99.11	99.11	99.11
	Accuracy	97.30	98.91	98.99	99.12	99.12	99.11
	Precision	97.40	98.95	99.03	99.15	99.15	99.15
	Recall	97.30	98.91	98.99	99.12	99.12	99.11
	FPR	0.00	0.00	0.00	0.00	0.00	0.00
	FNR	0.04	0.02	0.02	0.01	0.01	0.01
Bagging	F1	99.03	99.07	99.10	99.14	99.24	99.23
	Accuracy	99.04	99.07	99.10	99.14	99.25	99.23
	Precision	99.07	99.11	99.14	99.18	99.28	99.26
	Recall	99.04	99.07	99.10	99.14	99.25	99.23
	FPR	0.00	0.00	0.00	0.00	0.00	0.00
	FNR	0.01	0.01	0.01	0.01	0.01	0.01

5 Threat Model

This section presents the threat model, including the focused attack, the adversary's probability, and the assumptions.

5.1 Targeted Attack

Most of such authentication systems, not just our approach but other previous biometrics-based authentication, focus on protecting against insider threats in which the adversary tries to impersonate the authentication of an authorized user in the system. As mentioned in Sect. 1, at this time, the behavioral-based authentication should be used as an additional approach to support the conventional PIN code, password, or biometric authentications. So let's run an example in which our approach is combined with PIN code-based authentication. Let Pr_A denote the probability that the adversary A can break the system. Pr_A is defined as:

$$Pr_A = Pr_{guess} \cdot Pr_{forge} \tag{7}$$

where Pr_{guess} and Pr_{forge} denote the probability that A can correctly guess the PIN code and the average probability that A can fool the classifier, respectively. Pr_{forge} is the false-negative rate which is the percentage of identification

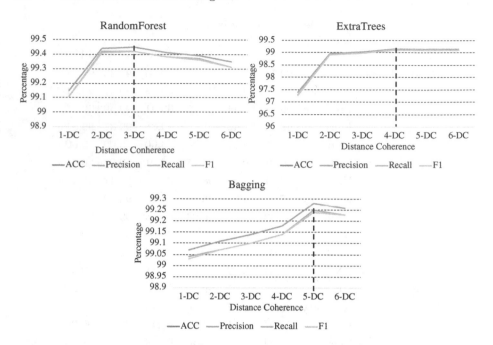

Fig. 3. Different alpha's for distance coherence

instances in which the unauthorized users are incorrectly accepted. Table 2 shows that all the 3-DC, 4-DC, and 5-DC approaches corresponding to the three different algorithms have the same 0.01% of false-negative rate. Thus, $Pr_{forge} = 10^{-4}$. Let τ and σ denote the number of digits in the PIN code and the number of guessing candidates for each PIN code digit. If $\mathcal{A}$ has n_t tries before the device is locked with many wrong PIN codes, we have $Pr_{guess} = \frac{n_t}{\sigma^\tau}$. Therefore:

$$Pr_{\mathcal{A}} = 10^{-4} \cdot \frac{n_t}{\sigma^\tau} \tag{8}$$

Most of the new smartphone operation systems nowadays require six digits for PIN code. Typically, there are ten digits of candidates from 0 to 9 for each digit. The users often have 4 to 6 PIN code tries for Android and iOS before the device is locked. Therefore, $Pr_{\mathcal{A}} \simeq 4 \cdot 10^{-10}$ to $6 \cdot 10^{-10}$.

Suppose the attacker can guess the PIN code after shoulder surfing and then robs the user's smartphone. Since the application is designed such that every GPS record is sent to the server in realtime and the GPS history is not stored in the user smartphone, the attacker cannot see the log from the robbed phone to imitate the user's behavior. Also, there is no function of downloading the GPS log from the server to the smartphone because it is a doubtable action from a (suspicious) user. The only action that the attacker can manipulate on the GPS tracking application is to turn it on/off or uninstall it. If the attacker continues to use the smartphone without being able to search for the history log from the smartphone application), the probability for the attacker $Pr_{\mathcal{A}}$ is now 0.01%.

Even though it is not 0% for the best case, it is still much better than 100% for $\mathcal{A}$ to break the system without our approach. Similarly, if the *collusion attack* in which an authorized user shares his/her PIN code to others occurs, $Pr_{\mathcal{A}}$ is also 0.01%. If the colluded user tells others his/her personal location history, every single continuous GPS record cannot be imitated. It is why we investigated the idea of using behaviors (especially long-term and continuous).

The model assumes that the server storing the GPS cannot be accessed or corrupted by the adversary. The data is encrypted, and only the trusted server can decrypt it. The data is transmitted via a secure network. Each smartphone is used by only a unique user. The smartphone and the server are protected against the side-channel attack collecting the user data via timing information, power consumption, electromagnetic leaks, or sound. Finally, we assumed that the users are honest in sending their data to the server, which performs the classification.

5.2   Security Scenario Discussion

In this section, we discuss other security scenarios from using smartphones.

What if Two Users Live and Work in the Same Areas? As mentioned in Sect. 3.1, since our project recruited the users randomly, the users live and work in random areas. Even if in the rare case, when two users live and work in the same area, they cannot have the same GPS tracking for every single hour. Each user has many activities at different timestamps, not just at home and office (such as shopping, outdoor exercising, picking children at schools, etc.). Furthermore, we can collect indoor positioning inside the home and the office building besides the GPS such as WiFi or Bluetooth beacons. Since this paper aims to investigate the benefit of the extra information (i.e., the distance coherence) from the GPS itself, we do not consider to collect indoor location information. However, it is entirely possible since we can collect the GPS and the indoor location information independently. Let's consider the case when legal users have the same trajectory within a period of time (e.g., older people in a senior home have daily activities confined to the surroundings). Since the longitude and latitude values have 6 decimal places (see Sect. 3.1), the precision is 0.1 m. With this precision, two users cannot have the same movement log in a long period.

How Does the System Work When Individuals Are Outside Their Routine or When the Attacker Follows (imitates) the User's Behavior? Since these questions are not just for the GPS-based location authentication but the general behavioral-based authentication, we discuss from the general to specific perspectives. We emphasize that a single-factor behavioral-based authentication is used to support (not to replace) the conventional approaches such as password or biometrics; or it is combined with other behavioral factors to build up a multi-factor behavioral-based authentication. Suppose a user is outside his/her routine or the attacker tries to imitate the user's behavior. In that case, the password/biometric or other routines are used to lower the false rejection and false acceptance rates. Although behavioral-based authentication has not yet been commonly used, researchers proved that this new but promising research is possible for real applications. For instance, Google has launched the Project Abacus [33] in 2016 to collect smartphone sensor signals (i.e., front-facing camera, touchscreen and keyboard, gyroscope, accelerometer, magnetometer, ambient light sensor, etc.). They demonstrated that human kinematics could convey important information about user identity and serve as a valuable component of multi-modal authentication systems. Among many behaviors, location is a typical factor in identifying users. Human beings are creatures of habit, and in as much as location is a measure of habit [5]. Also, the location is easy to collect since it is available in most modern smartphones.

Is It a Problem When a User Gets a New Phone? It has no problem since the smartphone is just the device/tool, not the method. The user can register a location-based authentication system with an account and its application installed in his smartphones. As long as the user does not share his account with others and an account can only log in one smartphone at a specific timestamp, his unique GPS data can be collected regardless of how many smartphones are used and whether the user shares his smartphones with others.

6   Future Work

This section describes an idea for future work based on the separation of daily and weekly distance coherences. In our current approach, for each sample s_i, the distance coherence features are calculated by grouping the other samples, which have the corresponding clock hours close to the clock hour of s_i regardless of the dates. We thus call it daily distance coherence. An example is given in the first chart of Fig. 4. We can calculate the features chosen for the sample s_i at the timestamp 7:00 April 10, 2020 (Friday) using the samples at $7{:}00 \pm \alpha$ on any date of the same user.

However, another promising method may improve the accuracy or F1 score. For each sample s_i, we can calculate the distance coherence features by grouping the other samples, which have the clock hours close to the clock hour of s_i on only the days with the same day of the week. We thus call it weekly distance coherence. We consider the example in the second chart of Fig. 4. Suppose s_i occurred at 7:00 April 10, 2020 (Friday); we can calculate the featured chosen for s_i from the samples at $7{:}00 \pm \alpha$ on every Friday such as April 03, 2020, or April 17, 2020, etc. These features may reflect the lifestyle of the users that we are aiming for in this paper. For example, a worker goes to work every weekday but goes to the usual supermarket every Saturday around 10:00; a student has a training course at a usual stadium every Thursday around 15:00. The weekly distance coherence can measure these habits. Remark that the weekly distance coherence features are not covered in the daily ones. Each feature is computed

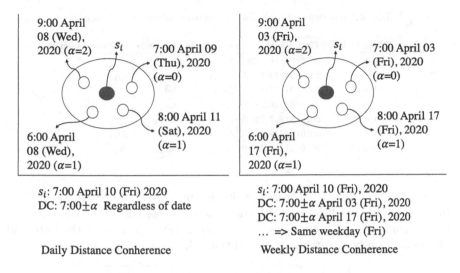

Fig. 4. Daily and weekly distance coherence

from the average of all the samples chosen for the main sample. Even though the set of the samples selected for the weekly case is a subset of the set, their averages are different in the daily case.

7 Conclusion

This paper has shown that using the distance coherence score as the additional features can improve user authentication. We collected 107,637 GPS records, including longitude, latitude, and timestamp from 348 users in Japan. The three average ensemble algorithms, including RandomForest, ExtraTrees, and Bagging, are applied to the classification and are evaluated using stratified k-fold. The experimental result showed that our approach outperforms the approach without the distance coherence in all the cases. The accuracy can reach up to 99.42%, 99.12%, and 99.25% using RandomForest, ExtraTrees, and Bagging, respectively. The F1 score can be improved even 2.34%, and the false-negative rate can be reduced by 0.04% using ExtraTrees.

Appendix

A   Numeric Example (for Distance Coherence Extraction)

In this section, we give a numeric example for the distance coherence extraction in Sect. 3.2. Suppose the data consists of 7 samples $\{s_1, s_2, \cdots, s_7\}$ from 2 users $\{user1, user2\}$ as showed in Table 4. We explain how to calculate the distance coherence for each sample $\{dc_{11}, dc_{12}, dc_{13}, dc_{21}, dc_{22}, dc_{23}, dc_{24}\}$. Suppose α (the number of distance coherence feature) is set to $\alpha = 1$.

Table 4. Numeric example for calculating distance coherence

Sample ID	User/class	Timestamp	Longitude	Latitude	Distance coherence
1	User1	2020/01/16 10:55	lon_{11}	lat_{11}	dc_{11}
2	User1	2020/01/17 11:55	lon_{12}	lat_{12}	dc_{12}
3	User1	2020/01/17 12:50	lon_{13}	lat_{13}	dc_{13}
4	User2	2020/01/16 21:30	lon_{21}	lat_{21}	dc_{21}
5	User2	2020/01/17 22:10	lon_{22}	lat_{22}	dc_{22}
6	User2	2020/01/18 21:45	lon_{23}	lat_{23}	dc_{23}
7	User2	2020/01/19 20:10	lon_{24}	lat_{24}	dc_{25}

For s_1, the hour extracted from the timestamp is $hour(s_1) = 10$. We find all the samples s_i that belong to the same class ($user1$) and have $hour(s_i)$ such that $(hour(s_1) - \alpha) \leq hour(s_i) \leq (hour(s_1) + \alpha)$ regardless of the date and the second. Only s_2 satisfies the conditions (i.e., $hour(s_2) = 11$). Thus:

$$dc_{11} = \sqrt[2]{(lon_{11} - lon_{12})^2 + (lat_{11} - lat_{12})^2} \tag{9}$$

– For s_2, $hour(s_2) = 11$. s_i from $user1$ that satisfy $(hour(s_2) - \alpha) \leq hour(s_i) \leq (hour(s_2) + \alpha)$ are s_1 and s_3 ($hour(s_1) = 10, hour(s_3) = 12$). Thus:

$$dc_{12} = \sqrt[2]{(lon_{12} - \frac{lon_{11} + lon_{13}}{2})^2 + (lat_{12} - \frac{lat_{11} + lat_{13}}{2})^2} \tag{10}$$

– For s_3, $hour(s_3) = 12$. s_i from $user1$ that satisfies $(hour(s_3) - \alpha) \leq hour(s_i) \leq hour(s_3) + \alpha)$ is only s_2 ($hour(s_2) = 11$). Thus:

$$dc_{13} = \sqrt[2]{(lon_{13} - lon_{12})^2 + (lat_{13} - lat_{12})^2} \tag{11}$$

– For s_4, $hour(s_4) = 21$. s_i from $user2$ that satisfy $(hour(s_4) - \alpha) \leq hour(s_i) \leq (hour(s_4) + \alpha)$ are s_5, s_6, and s_7 ($hour(s_5) = 22, hour(s_6) = 21, hour(s_7) = 20$). Thus:

$$dc_{21} = \sqrt[2]{(lon_{21} - \frac{lon_{22} + lon_{23} + lon_{24}}{3})^2 + (lat_{21} - \frac{lat_{22} + lat_{23} + lat_{24}}{3})^2} \tag{12}$$

– For s_5, $hour(s_5) = 22$. s_i from $user2$ that satisfy $(hour(s_5) - \alpha) \leq hour(s_i) \leq (hour(s_5) + \alpha)$ are s_4 and s_6 ($hour(s_4) = hour(s_6) = 21$). Thus:

$$dc_{22} = \sqrt[2]{(lon_{22} - \frac{lon_{21} + lon_{23}}{2})^2 + (lat_{22} - \frac{lat_{21} + lat_{23}}{2})^2} \tag{13}$$

– For s_6, $hour(s_6) = 21$. s_i from $user2$ that satisfy $(hour(s_6) - \alpha) \leq hour(s_i) \leq (hour(s_6) + \alpha)$ are s_4, s_5, and s_7 ($hour(s_4) = 21, hour(s_5) = 22, hour(s_7) = 20$). Thus:

$$dc_{23} = \sqrt[2]{(lon_{23} - \frac{lon_{21} + lon_{22} + lon_{24}}{3})^2 + (lat_{23} - \frac{lat_{21} + lat_{22} + lat_{24}}{3})^2} \tag{14}$$

– For s_7, $hour(s_7) = 20$. s_i from $user2$ that satisfy $(hour(s_7) - \alpha) \leq hour(s_i) \leq (hour(s_7) + \alpha)$ are s_4 and s_6 $(hour(s_4) = hour(s_6) = 21)$. Thus:

$$dc_{24} = \sqrt[2]{(lon_{24} - \frac{lon_{21} + lon_{23}}{2})^2 + (lat_{24} - \frac{lat_{21} + lat_{23}}{2})^2} \qquad (15)$$

References

1. Breiman, L.: Random Forests. Mach. Learn. **45**(1), 5–32 (2001)
2. Geurts, P., Damien, E., Wehenkel, L.: Extremely randomized trees. Mach. Learn. **63**(1), 3–42 (2006)
3. Louppe, G., Geurts, P.: Ensembles on random patches. In: European Conference on Machine Learning and Principles and Practice of Knowledge Discovery in Databases (ECML PKDD 2012), pp. 346–361 (2012)
4. Cabinet Office, the Government of Japan, Society 5.0. https://www8.cao.go.jp/cstp/english/society5_0/index.html. Accessed 26 Apr 2020
5. Fridman, L., Steven, W., Rachel, G., Moshe, K.: Active authentication on mobile devices via Stylometry, application usage, web browsing, and GPS location. IEEE Syst. J. **11**(2), 513–521 (2016)
6. Shi, W., Yang, J., Jiang, Y., Yang, F., Xiong, Y.: SenGuard: passive user identification on smartphones using multiple sensors. In: IEEE 7th International Conference on Wireless and Mobile Computing, Networking and Communications (WiMob 2011), pp. 141–148 (2011)
7. Thao, T.P., Irvan, M., Kobayashi, R., Yamaguchi, R.S., Nakata, T.: Self-enhancing GPS-based authentication using corresponding address. In: Singhal, A., Vaidya, J. (eds.) DBSec 2020. Self-enhancing GPS-Based Authentication Using Corresponding Address, vol. 12122, pp. 333–344. Springer, Cham (2020). https://doi.org/10.1007/978-3-030-49669-2_19
8. Alejandro, A., Aythami, M., Vera-Rodriguez, R., Julian, F., Ruben, T.: Multi-Lock: mobile active authentication based on multiple biometric and behavioral patterns. In: International Workshop on Multimodal Understanding and Learning for Embodied Applications (MULEA 2019), pp. 53–59 (2019)
9. Aaron, B., Christopher, D., Barry, G., David, K.: System and method for real world biometric analytics through the use of a multimodal biometric analytic wallet. US patent, US20180276362A1 (2018). https://patents.google.com/patent/US20100050253. Accessed 26 Apr 2020
10. Valentin, R.: Multimodal deep learning for activity and context recognition. In: Publication: Proceedings of the ACM on Interactive, Mobile, Wearable and Ubiquitous Technologies (IMWUT 2018), (2018) Article no. 157
11. Dirk, B., Shu, L., Mitch, K., Aaron, S., Charles, C., John, D.: Modifying smartphone user locking behavior. In: 9th Symposium on Usable Privacy and Security (SOUPS 2013), pp. 1–14 (2013). article no. 10
12. Egelman, S., Jain, S., Portnoff, R., Liao, K., Consolvo, S., Wagner, D.: Are you ready to lock?. In: 21st ACM Conference on Computer and Communications Security (CCS 2014), pp. 750–761 (2014)
13. Harbach, M., Zezschwitz, E., Fichtner, A., Luca, A., Smith, M.: It's a hard lock life: a field study of smartphone (un) locking behavior and risk perception. In: 10th USENIX Conference on Usable Privacy and Security (SOUP 2014), pp. 213–230 (2014)

14. Upal, M., Sayantan, S., Vishal, P., Rama, C.: Active user authentication for smart-phones: a challenge data set and benchmark results. In: 8th International Conference on Biometrics Theory, Applications and Systems (BTAS 2016) (2016)
15. Hashcat - Advanced Password Recovery. https://hashcat.net/hashcat/. Accessed 27 Apr 2020
16. John the Ripper password cracker. https://www.openwall.com/john/. Accessed 27 Apr 2020
17. Marsicoa, M.D., Michele, N., Daniel, R., Wechsler, H.: Mobile iris challenge evaluation (MICHE)-I, biometric iris dataset and protocols. Pattern Recogn. Lett. **57**, 17–23 (2015)
18. Venugopalan, S., Savvides, M.: How to generate spoofed irises from an iris code template. IEEE Trans. Inf. Forensics Sec. **6**(2), 385–395 (2011)
19. Bowyer, K.W., Doyle, J.S.: Cosmetic contact lenses and iris recognition spoofing. Computer **47**(5), 96–98 (2014)
20. Daksha, Y., Naman, K., James, S.D., Richa, S., Mayank, V., Kevin, W.B.: Unraveling the effect of textured contact lenses on iris recognition. IEEE Trans. Inf. Forensics Secur. **9**(5), 851–862 (2014)
21. Chingovska, I., Anjos, A., Marcel, S.: On the effectiveness of local binary patterns in face anti-spoofing. In: IEEE International Conference of Biometrics Special Interest Group (BIOSIG 2012) (2012)
22. Erdogmus, N., Marcel, S.: Spoofing in 2D face recognition with 3D masks and anti-spoofing with Kinect. In: IEEE 6th International Conference on Biometrics: Theory Applications and Systems (VISAPP 2013), pp. 1–6 (2013)
23. Anthony, R.: System for and method of securing fingerprint biometric systems against fake-finger spoofing. US Patent US7505613B2 (2009). https://patents.google.com/patent/US7505613B2/en. Accessed 27 Apr 2020
24. David, M., et al.: Deep representations for iris, face, and fingerprint spoofing detection. IEEE Trans. Inf. Forensics Secur. **10**(4), 864–879 (2015)
25. Adam, J.A., Katherine, G., Evan, M., Matt, B., Jonathan, M.S.: Smudge attacks on smartphone touch screens. In: 4th USENIX Conference on Offensive Technologies (WOOT 2010), pp. 1–7 (2010)
26. Malin, E., Mohamed, K., Emanuel, V.Z., Heinrich, H., Florian, A.: Understanding shoulder surfing in the wild: stories from users and observers. In: ACM CHI Conference on Human Factors in Computing Systems, pp. 4254–4265 (2017)
27. Kaczmarek, T., Ercan, O., Gene, T.: Assentication: user deauthentication and lunchtime attack mitigation with seated posture biometric. In: 16th Conference on Applied Cryptography and Network Security (ACNS 2018), pp. 616–633 (2018)
28. Ivan, M., Kasper, R., Marc, R., Gene, T.: Authentication using pulse-response biometrics. Commun. ACM **60**(2), 108–115 (2017)
29. Simon, E., Kasper, B.R., Vincent, L., Ivan, M.: Preventing lunchtime attacks: fighting insider threats with eye movement biometrics. In: 22nd Annual Network and Distributed System Security Symposium (NDSS 2015) (2015)
30. Louis, W., Komeili, M., Hatzinakos, D.: Continuous authentication using one-dimensional multi-resolution local binary patterns (1dmrlbp) in ECG biometrics. IEEE Trans. Inf. Forensics Secur. **11**(12), 2818–2832 (2016)
31. Thao, T.P., et al.: Human factors in exhaustion and stress of Japanese nursery teachers: evidence from regression model on a novel dataset. In: 13th International Conference on Advances in Computer-Human Interactions (ACHI 2020), pp. 124–129. http://www.tpthao.com/pdf/2020_ACHI.pdf

32. Alejandro, R., Stephen, D., Ivan, C., Giulio, R.: STARFAST: a wireless wearable EEG/ECG biometric system based on the ENOBIO sensor. In: International Workshop on Wearable Mycro and Nanosystems for Personalised Health (pHealth 2008) (2008)
33. Neverova, N., et al.: Learning human identity from motion patterns. IEEE Access **4**, 1810–1820 (2016)

DPM Workshop: Short Papers

Short Paper: Integrating the Data Protection Impact Assessment into the Software Development Lifecycle

Christopher Irvine(✉) ⓘD, Dharini BalasubramaniamⓘD,
and Tristan Hendersonⓘ

School of Computer Science, University of St. Andrews, St. Andrews KY16 9SX, UK
{cai3,dharini,tnhh}@st-andrews.ac.uk
https://www.st-andrews.ac.uk/computer-science/

Abstract. Recent years have seen many privacy violations that have cost both the users of software systems and the businesses that run them in a variety of ways. One potential cause of these violations may be the ad hoc nature of the implementation of privacy measures within software systems, which may stem from the poor representation of privacy within many Software Development LifeCycle (SDLC) processes. We propose to give privacy a higher priority within the SDLC through the creation of a confederated *Privacy-Aware* SDLC (PASDLC) which incorporates the Data Protection Impact Assessment (DPIA) lifecycle. The PASDLC brings stakeholders of the software system closer together through the implementation of multiple interception points, whilst prompting the stakeholders to consider privacy within the software system. We consider many challenges to the creation of the PASDLC, including potential communication issues from confederating the processes of a SDLC and the effective measurement of privacy as an attribute of a software system.

Keywords: Privacy · Software architecture · Software engineering lifecycle · Data protection impact assessment

1 Introduction

Recent years have seen several privacy breaches and violations. For example, on the 5th of March 2020, Virgin Media admitted a database, containing the personal details of 900,000 people, was left unsecured and accessible online for 10 months, during which this data was accessed "on at least one location" [4]. In 2019 a major breach was reported by Capital One impacting 106 million people which compromised social security numbers and bank accounts [3]. Other examples include Google ignoring user privacy preferences [23] and recent concerns that Zoom has been sharing user data with Facebook without user consent [12]. These privacy breaches and violations are all described as accidental or avoidable [3,4], which suggests there is a procedural issue with privacy in software development.

© Springer Nature Switzerland AG 2020
J. Garcia-Alfaro et al. (Eds.): DPM 2020/CBT 2020, LNCS 12484, pp. 219–228, 2020.
https://doi.org/10.1007/978-3-030-66172-4_13

At the time of writing, the NHS COVID-19 contact-tracing app is under investigation regarding a lack of consideration of privacy [8] and deploying the system without an approved Data Protection Impact Assessment (DPIA) [24]. The DPIA is a legal requirement under the European Union General Data Protection Regulation (EU GDPR) [10, Article 35] and the UK's Data Protection Act (2018)(DPA) [33]. A recent survey on DPIAs, performed by the European Unions Protection Supervisor, revealed that data protection officers who took part in the surveyed DPIAs believed that the DPIA processes would benefit from greater awareness and more internal support, additionally the process itself could be simpler. A recent survey of Data Protection Officers found that DPIA processes were promising, but would benefit from greater awareness, internal support and a simplification of the process itself [11].

One potential cause of a privacy breach or violation is the ad hoc nature of implementing privacy measures into software systems [17,25] due to the poor representation of privacy within the Software development LifeCycle (SDLC) [5,25]. We aim to bring clarity to the SDLC by prompting stakeholders to consider privacy as an attribute of the software system before, during and after implementation. To achieve this aim, we propose a *Privacy-Aware* SDLC (PASDLC) that combines the DPIA Lifecycle[1] with the SDLC.

The PASDLC takes into consideration legal requirements, such as those set out in the GDPR and the DPA, by regularly prompting consideration and review of the data processing that occurs within the software system being designed. To achieve this, the normally loosely related stages of a SDLC are confederated into a single governing structure where each lifecycle or process will intercept others at multiple stages, bringing the stakeholders of the software system closer together. This structure brings together both the law and computing; it has often been argued that such a multidisciplinary approach is required to address the potential harm from technology, for instance through Lessig's "pathetic dot" [21, ch. 7]. Bringing multiple disciplines together, however, may also cause communication and consistency issues impacting the overall quality of the implemented software system [19]. We discuss these challenges and how we approach them in the initial design of the PASDLC which revolves around the early processes of the SDLC, namely requirements engineering, software architecture design and implementation.

2   Background

2.1   Software Development Lifecycle

Software engineering is governed by various lifecycles and processes which guide stakeholders in developing a software system that satisfies requirements and constraints. These processes allow multiple teams of stakeholders to work on the same software system with minimal disruption [31, ch. 2]. A generic SDLC can be found in Fig. 1. Each stage within a SDLC consists of processes and lifecycles such as requirements engineering or software engineering methodologies.

---

[1] As developed by the Information Commissioner's Office [14].

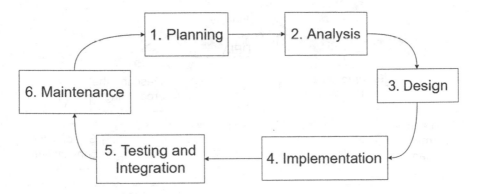

Fig. 1. A graphical representation of a software development lifecycle.

2.2 Software Architecture

Software architecture is a high level model capturing significant design decisions relating to the structure and behaviour of a software system and providing guidance to developers on how to implement and maintain the system, including details such as software components and the interactions among them [32]. Software architecture is created using design processes such as Attribute-Driven Development (ADD) [35] and evaluation processes such as the Architecture-Tradeoff Analysis Method (ATAM) [18]. Privacy is not well represented within these processes, except from using Unified Modelling Language (UML) diagrams to document privacy requirements as stated in the requirements specification [26].

2.3 Data Protection Impact Assessment

Software systems that involve the processing of personal data of EU residents are governed by the GDPR[2]. More specifically, some systems, for instance those that use automated processing that cause legal effects, or systematically monitor publicly accessible areas at a large scale, must preform a DPIA. To aid in this process, the Information Commissioner's Office (ICO) has created a suggested lifecycle for completing and updating a DPIA (Fig. 2) [14].

To be an effective impact assessment tool, the DPIA must be completed before any processing of sensitive data by the software system or any future iterations of the software system which change how data is processed.

From a software engineering perspective, the most interesting stages of the DPIA lifecycle are 7, 8 and 9. Stages 1 to 6 involve stakeholders with technical expertise from multiple disciplines who compile the DPIA document which is then signed off by the Data Protection Officer (DPO), who may be a non-engineer, in stage 7. Once the DPIA has been approved, the technical stakeholders will execute stages 8 and 9. Without a pre-established common vocabulary,

---

[2] We focus on the GDPR, but other similar regulations are appearing in other jurisdictions such as the California Consumer Privacy Act.

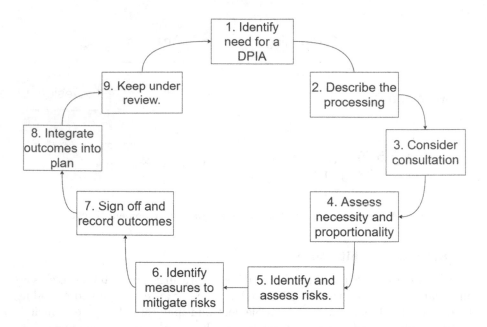

Fig. 2. A graphical representation of a data protection impact assessment lifecycle

the DPO may not fully understand the content of the DPIA leading to privacy measures being approved or rejected incorrectly.

2.4   Related Work

Privacy engineering aims to create techniques that decrease privacy risks and increase effective privacy controls within software systems [9], integrating Privacy Enhancing Technologies (PETs) such as anonymisation. Software engineers who use the PASDLC will be able to use Privacy Engineering techniques to implement the planned privacy measures during the implementation and design stages of the PASDLC.

Privacy by Design (PbD) [7] and Data Protection by Design (DPbD)[3] serve as principles to guide the development activities of software engineers towards creating software systems with increased privacy awareness. Hadar et al. find that developers may be actively discouraged from PbD processes due to organisational norms or lack of knowledge [13]. We propose to integrate the DPIA (and DPbD) into the organisation through the PASDLC.

Some PbD/DPbD activities encourage stakeholders to integrate privacy into the architectural specification [29]. This is done either by integrating specific privacy enhancing methods into the architectural specification [20] or the creation of specific software architectural privacy views. Sion proposed that DPbD should

---

[3] Data Protection by Design is specific to GDPR (Article 25).

have a dedicated architectural view supported by data flow diagrams to instruct engineers how to model the flow of data between software components [30].

To test whether the PASDLC improves privacy within a software system, we need to be able to measure privacy. There are multiple privacy metrics available which measure different data ranging from the estimated effort required for a third party to breach a database to the gain the third party would receive for completing the breach [34]. Each metric is individually useful to the stakeholders, however, there is no overall measurement of privacy within a software system. Zhao and Wagner recommend combining metrics into a *metric suite*, which is specific to the software system, as a method of measuring overall privacy of the software system [36].

Sedano et al. and Sievi-Korte et al. note communication issues have been amplified by the rising level of outsourcing in the software engineering industry, resulting in increased design deviations [27, 28]. Current solutions revolve around categorising the causes of the communication issues – such as time zones and response delays – and then creating a mitigation strategy for each category. These strategies often rely on the use of third party instant messaging, video conferencing and organisation tools [16], which, as the Berlin data protection authority outlines, may themselves introduce data protection risks [6].

Whilst this research is concerned with the ICO's methodology for generating and maintaining a DPIA, we note that other methods may be used, such as the model-based approach proposed by Ahmadian in [1].

3   Approach

We hypothesise that a confederated PASDLC which combines the SDLC and the DPIA lifecycles, as discussed in Sect. 2, can improve privacy within the developed software system. The PASDLC goes beyond integrating the DPIA lifecycle into regular procedure, providing multiple intersection points between each of the stages within the PASDLC that allow stakeholders of the software system to address concerns mid-iteration.

At this point our focus is on the initial stages of developing the PASDLC: requirements engineering, software architecture design & evaluation and implementation to act as a proof of concept. See Fig. 3 for a high level view of the PASDLC.

Using the NHS COVID-19 contact-tracing app as a case study (see Sect. 1) we discuss the PASDLC further. The requirements will be agreed with the clients, the NHS and the UK Government, and the need for a DPIA is established due to the sensitive health and location data processed by the app [10, Article 35]. The stakeholders will describe in detail the processing necessary for the app to function. At this point external consultants may be employed, such as data protection lawyers, to assist with the DPIA risk assessment later in the process. Once the requirements engineering processes have ended, the necessity and proportionality of the processing is assessed to ensure it is vital to the functionality of the software system. For the contact-tracing app, processing

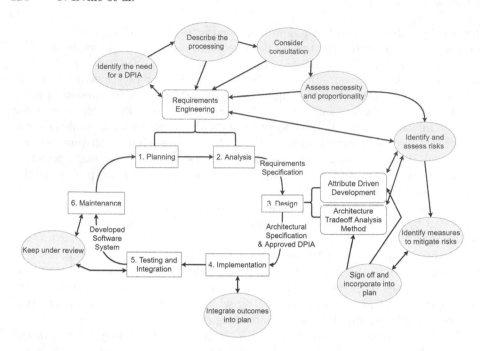

Fig. 3. A high level view of the PASDLC; the steps of the DPIA are in grey ovals, and the steps of the SDLC are in white rectangles, with suggested processes for the design step in rectangles with rounded corners. The arrows signify the order in which processes should be carried out by stakeholders.

sensitive data is vital to the functionality, therefore the DPIA process moves on to the risk assessment stages.

During the design stage of the PASDLC a variety of methodologies to develop (ADD) and evaluate (ATAM) a software architecture can be used. Regardless of the methodology used, as part of the DPIA, a privacy risk assessment will be performed by the stakeholders of the software system. An example risk for the app may be an unauthorised access to the NHS patient records which could affect millions of people. Risk mitigation methods are then integrated into the requirements and software architecture specifications, for example, limiting the data access to the NHS patient records to only COVID-19 related data.

The software system is implemented using the approved requirements and architecture specifications controlled by the software engineering methodology the stakeholders choose. A primary goal when testing the software system will be to ensure that the software system adheres to the approved DPIA by checking that all implementable privacy measures have been implemented. After passing the testing processes, the software system is deployed and remains in the maintenance stage of the PASDLC until new features are added. Requiring the approval of the DPO before the implementation stage of the PASDLC reduces the risk of deploying a software system or integrating a new feature into an existing software system without an approved DPIA, as was the case for the contact-tracing app. By integrating both and making it clear that this is an ongoing and repeated lifecycle, we also hope to prevent a mismatch between DPIA and released system, as was also the case for the NHS app, with a DPIA only being released for an initial pilot test and not for the final system.

In lower level views of the PASDLC, specific processes, such as scrum or waterfall (for the S.D. 4), ADD and ATAM (for S.D. 3) and requirements engineering (for S.D. 1 and 2), will be inserted into the corresponding stage of the PASDLC. Each activity within these processes will be mapped to the appropriate DPIA activities, providing an easy to use framework for engineers and non-engineers alike to follow the development of a *Privacy-Aware* software system.

The PASDLC will become an engineering privacy tool box which will not only be compatible with PETs, PbD/DPbD and standards such as ISO/IEC 29110 [15,22] or the generally accepted privacy principles [2], it will prompt to the user to consider the inclusion of relevant standards, processes or technologies at the appropriate points. The PASDLC will not prescribe to the user any one given standard, technology or processes and will encourage the user to research the best standard, technology or process for the software system being developed.

This research will address three main challenges: measuring privacy, managing communication issues and evaluating the PASDLC proof of concept. As discussed in Sect. 2.4, Metric suites may be the solution to measuring privacy within software systems and evaluating the effectiveness of the PASDLC.

Requiring stakeholders from different disciplines to work closer together through the non-linear nature of the PASDLC may exacerbate existing communication issues – such as the DPO not understanding technical terminology within the DPIA – or create new ones. Part of this research will investigate the potential for communication issues and explore mitigation techniques, such as establishing a common vocabulary or defining system documentation, that can be utilised by stakeholders to counter their adverse effects on the software system. Successful mitigation techniques will be incorporated into the PASDLC either as a step (such as in the case of establishing a common dictionary) or highlighting existing steps to encourage users of the PASDLC to deploy the appropriate mitigation technique.

The final challenge is the evaluation of the PASDLC proof of concept. Case studies will have their software architecture redeveloped using the PASDLC processes. The amount of privacy in both the original and redeveloped architectures will be measured where we expect to see an increase in privacy within the redeveloped architecture.

4   Conclusion

This work aims to address the insufficient privacy measures implemented into software systems, potentially caused by the poor representation of privacy within many SDLC processes. We hypothesise that this problem can be addressed by integrating the DPIA lifecycle with the SDLC creating the PASDLC.

We will evaluate the developed PASDLC proof of concept by redeveloping the software architectures of case studies using the PASDLC where we expect to see an increase in privacy in the redeveloped architecture as measured by privacy metrics. We will further investigate the PASDLC for potential communication issues. Strategies to mitigate these issues will be developed to reduce consistency problems across multiple artefacts and stakeholders of the software system.

The next steps are the development and evaluation of the proof of concept PASDLC which will expand into the creation of an engineering privacy toolbox which is both compatible and promotes the use of privacy standards, practices and technologies.

Through the creation of an effective PASDLC we hope to see a reduction in privacy breaches and violations that can cause financial and reputational harm to the stakeholders of software systems which process sensitive data.

References

1. Ahmadian, A.S., Strüber, D., Riediger, V., Jürjens, J.: Supporting privacy impact assessment by model-based privacy analysis. In: Proceedings of the ACM Symposium on Applied Computing, pp. 1467–1474 (2018). https://doi.org/10.1145/3167132.3167288
2. American Institute of Certified Public Accountants, Inc. and Canadian Institute of Chartered Accountants: Generally Accepted Privacy Principles and Criteria (August), pp. 1–84 (2009). http://www.aicpa.org/InterestAreas/InformationTechnology/Resources/Privacy/GenerallyAcceptedPrivacyPrinciples/DownloadableDocuments/GAPP_PrinciplesandCriteria.pdf
3. BBC News: Capital One data breach: Arrest after details of 106m people stolen - BBC News. https://www.bbc.co.uk/news/world-us-canada-49159859 (2019)
4. BBC News: Virgin Media data breach affects 900,000 people - BBC News. https://www.bbc.co.uk/news/business-51760510 (2020)
5. Beckers, K.: Comparing privacy requirements engineering approaches. In: Proceedings - 2012 7th International Conference on Availability, Reliability and Security, ARES 2012, pp. 574–581 (2012). https://doi.org/10.1109/ARES.2012.29
6. Berliner Beauftragte für Datenschutz und Informationsfreiheit: Hinweise für Berliner Verantwortliche zu Anbietern von Videokonferenz-Diensten. https://www.datenschutz-berlin.de/fileadmin/user_upload/pdf/orientierungshilfen/2020-BlnBDI-Hinweise_Berliner_Verantwortliche_zu_Anbietern_Videokonferenz-Dienste.pdf, July 2020
7. Cavoukian, A., et al.: Privacy by design: The 7 foundational principles. Information and privacy commissioner of Ontario, Canada 5 (2009)
8. Dearden, L.: Coronavirus: NHS contact-tracing app must not be released to public without privacy protections, MPs say — The Independent. https://www.independent.co.uk/news/uk/home-news/coronavirus-nhs-contact-tracing-app-covid-19-uk-release-date-privacy-protection-a9503321.html
9. Dennedy, M.F., Fox, J., Finneran, T.R., Bonabeau, E.: The Privacy Engineer's Manifesto: Getting from Policy to Code to QA to Value. Apress, Berkely (2014)
10. EU: Regulation (EU) 2016/679 of the European Parliament and of the Council of 27 April 2016 on the protection of natural persons with regard to the processing of personal data and on the free movement of such data, and repealing Directive 95/4. Official J. European Union (OJ) **59**, 1–88 (2016)

11. European Data Protection Supervisor: EDPS Survey on Data Protection Impact Assessments under Article 39 of the Regulation 1, 1–31 (2020). https://edps.europa.eu/data-protection/our-work/publications/reports/edps-survey-data-protection-impact-assessments-under

12. Foltyn, T.: Zoom's privacy and security woes in the spotlight (2020). https://www.welivesecurity.com/2020/04/03/zoom-privacy-security-spotlight/

13. Hadar, I., Hasson, T., Ayalon, O., Toch, E., Birnhack, M., Sherman, S., Balissa, A.: Privacy by designers: software developers' privacy mindset. Emp. Softw. Eng. **23**(1), 259–289 (2017). https://doi.org/10.1007/s10664-017-9517-1

14. Information Commissioner's Office: Data protection impact assessments — ICO (2018). https://ico.org.uk/for-organisations/guide-to-data-protection/guide-to-the-general-data-protection-regulation-gdpr/accountability-and-governance/data-protection-impact-assessments/

15. ISO/IEC 29110-2-1:2015: Software engineering - Lifecycle profiles for Very Small Entities (VSEs) - Part 2-1: Framework and taxonomy. Standard, International Organization for Standardization, November 2015

16. Jaanu, T., Paasivaara, M., Lassenius, C.: Effects of four distances on communication processes in global software projects. In: Proceedings of the 2012 ACM-IEEE International Symposium on Empirical Software Engineering and Measurement, pp. 231–234 (2012)

17. Kalloniatis, C., Kavakli, E., Gritzalis, S.: Dealing with privacy issues during the system design process. In: Proceedings of the Fifth IEEE International Symposium on Signal Processing and Information Technology 2005, pp. 546–551 (2005)

18. Kazman, R., Klein, M., Clements, P.: Atam: method for architecture evaluation. Tech. Rep. CMU/SEI-2000-TR-004, Software Engineering Institute, Carnegie Mellon University, Pittsburgh, PA (2000). http://resources.sei.cmu.edu/library/asset-view.cfm?AssetID=5177

19. Khan, A.A., Basri, S., Dominc, P.: A proposed framework for communication risks during RCM in GSD. Procedia Soc. Behav. Sci. **129**, 496–503 (2014). https://doi.org/10.1016/j.sbspro.2014.03.706

20. Kung, A.: PEARs: Privacy Enhancing ARchitectures. Lecture Notes in Computer Science (including subseries Lecture Notes in Artificial Intelligence and Lecture Notes in Bioinformatics) **8450**, 18–29 (2014). https://doi.org/10.1007/978-3-319-06749-0_2

21. Lessig, L.: C o d e, 2nd edn. New York, New York, USA (2006)

22. Morales-Trujillo, M.E., Garcia-Mireles, G.A.: Extending ISO/IEC 29110 basic profile with privacy-by-design approach: A case study in the health care sector. Proceedings - 2018 International Conference on the Quality of Information and Communications Technology, QUATIC 2018, pp. 56–64 (2018). https://doi.org/10.1109/QUATIC.2018.00018

23. Nakashima, R.: AP Exclusive: Google tracks your movements, like it or not (2018). https://apnews.com/828aefab64d4411bac257a07c1af0ecb

24. Page, C.: Test and trace initiative faces legal challenge in the U.K. over data collection (2020). https://www.forbes.com/sites/carlypage/2020/06/01/nhs-faces-legal-challenge-over-rushed-test-and-trace-initiative/#73c74e2f673f

25. Peixoto, M., Ferreira, D., Cavalcanti, M., Silva, C., Vilela, J., Araújo, J., Gorschek, T.: On understanding how developers perceive and interpret privacy requirements research preview. In: Madhavji, N., Pasquale, L., Ferrari, A., Gnesi, S. (eds.) REFSQ 2020. LNCS, vol. 12045, pp. 116–123. Springer, Cham (2020). https://doi.org/10.1007/978-3-030-44429-7_8

26. Sachitano, A., Chapman, R.O., Hamilton, J.A.: Security in software architecture: a case study. In: Proceedings fron the Fifth Annual IEEE System, Man and Cybernetics Information Assurance Workshop, SMC, pp. 370–376. IEEE, West Point, NY, USA (2004). https://doi.org/10.1109/iaw.2004.1437841

27. Sedano, T., Ralph, P., Péraire, C.: Software development waste. In: 2017 IEEE/ACM 39th International Conference on Software Engineering (ICSE), pp. 130–140 (2017)

28. Sievi-Korte, O., Richardson, I., Beecham, S.: Software architecture design in global software development: An empirical study. J. Syst. Softw. **158** (2019). https://doi.org/10.1016/j.jss.2019.110400

29. Sion, L., Van Landuyt, D., Yskout, K., Joosen, W.: Sparta: security privacy architecture through risk-driven threat assessment. In: 2018 IEEE International Conference on Software Architecture Companion (ICSA-C), pp. 89–92 (2018)

30. Sion, L., et al.: An architectural view for data protection by design. In: Proceedings - 2019 IEEE International Conference on Software Architecture, ICSA 2019, pp. 11–20. No. i, IEEE, Hamburg, Germany (2019). https://doi.org/10.1109/ICSA.2019.00010

31. Sommerville, I.: Software engineering (10th edition) (2016)

32. Taylor, R.N., Medvidovic, N., Dashofy, E.: Software Architecture: Foundations, Theory and Practice (2010)

33. UK Government: Data Protection Act 2018 (2018)

34. Wagner, I., Eckhoff, D.: Technical privacy metrics: a systematic survey. ACM Comput. Surv. **51**(3) (2018). https://doi.org/10.1145/3168389

35. Wojcik, R., et al.: Attribute-driven design (add), version 2.0. Technical report, CARNEGIE-MELLON UNIV PITTSBURGH PA SOFTWARE ENGINEERING INST (2006)

36. Zhao, Y., Wagner, I.: Using metrics suites to improve the measurement of privacy in graphs. IEEE Trans. Dependable Secure Comput. pp. 1 (2020). https://doi.org/10.1109/tdsc.2020.2980271

Citizens as Data Donors: Maximizing Participation Through Privacy Assurance and Behavioral Change

(Short Paper)

Mohamad Gharib[✉]

University of Florence, Florence, Italy
mohamad.gharib@unifi.it

Abstract. Data are the infrastructure of science, and for some scientific studies, a vast amount of data might be needed. One way to obtain such data is through Citizen Science (CS), a research technique that enlists the public in gathering data. Although citizens themselves can be the source of such data, most of the citizens' participation in CS so far focused on providing data concerning almost everything except themselves. In particular, citizens can participate as data donors (Citizens as Data Donors (CaDD)), where they allow professionals to have access to their personal data for the purposes of the public good. However, personal data cannot be used without citizens' consent as such data are protected by various privacy laws. In this paper, a method for maximizing citizens' participation as data donors by understanding and addressing their privacy requirements taking into consideration the perceived benefits and ease of the donation behavior is proposed. The method is illustrated with an example concerning an Ambient-Assisted Living (AAL) System.

Keywords: Data donation · CaDD · Privacy requirements · Behavioral change · Citizen Science

1 Introduction

Citizen Science (CS) is a research technique that enlists the general public (citizens) in collecting and/or processing data as part of a scientific inquiry [1]. CS has been successfully used to provide solutions to real-world problems in several different domains such as climate, medicine, computer science, genetics, engineering, etc. [1,2]. Although citizens' personal data might be of great importance for CS, most of the citizens' participation in CS so far did not target such data. In other words, citizens can participate as data donors (e.g., Citizens as Data Donors (CaDD)), where they allow professionals to collect and/or have access to their personal data for the public good (e.g., research).

Personal data can be of great value for research especially in the medical domain, where such data can be used for improving health and social care on a

© Springer Nature Switzerland AG 2020
J. Garcia-Alfaro et al. (Eds.): DPM 2020/CBT 2020, LNCS 12484, pp. 229–239, 2020.
https://doi.org/10.1007/978-3-030-66172-4_14

large scale [3]. However, most developed countries enacted various laws and regulations to govern the use of personal data (e.g., GDPR in the EU [4], HIPAA [5] for the healthcare domain in the USA, etc.). Failing to comply with privacy laws may result in huge direct costs as well as indirect consequences such as damaging customers' trust, loyalty, etc. [6]. Accordingly, privacy became a main concern when collecting, storing, and managing personal data [7], since personal data cannot be used without citizens' (legal owners/data subject) consent/approval.

According to Skatova et al. [8], we know very little about citizens' motivations to share their personal data freely for the purposes of the public good. Yet a considerable number of citizens donate their blood, organs, stem cells, etc., and they may donate their organs or their whole body after death [3]. Although donating personal data is not like donating blood or organs because it might endanger citizens' privacy, understanding and tackling citizens' privacy needs and concerns shall increase their participation as data donors.

On the other hand, several behavioral change theories have been proposed with a main objective of understanding, explaining, and/or predicting why and how humans' behavior changes (e.g., [9,10]). Usually, these theories rely on environmental, personal, behavioral characteristics, ability, motivations, etc. as the main factors that derive behavioral change. Behavioral change theories have been successfully applied in several domains, e.g., medical, criminology, education to mention a few. However, applying these theories to a novel behavior such as the donation of personal data for the purposes of public good has not been deeply investigated yet. To this end, a method for maximizing citizens' participation as data donors by understanding and tackling their privacy requirements taking into consideration the perceived benefits and ease of the donation behavior is proposed. Such a method shall advances research in different areas that rely on personal data by making such data available for researchers.

The rest of the paper is organized as follows; Sect. 2 outlines the foundations of this research, and Sect. 3 presents an example to illustrate this work. Section 4 presents the problem statement and research challenges, and the method is presented in Sect. 5. Section 6 discusses the advantages of this work, and Sect. 7 concludes the paper and discusses future work.

2   Research Baseline

2.1   Citizen Science

Haklay [11] classified CS projects based on the level/type of citizens' participation into four levels (shown in Fig. 1): **Level 1. (L1)** *Crowdsourcing:* participation is limited to the provision of data [11]. **L2.** *Distributed intelligence:* participation focuses on collecting data and performing some basic activities [11]. **L3.** *Participatory science:* participants might be involved in the definition of the problem and data collection method besides their role in data collection and analysis [11]. **L4.** *Extreme science:* participants heavily participate in problem definition, data collection and analysis.

Citizens as Data Donors (CaDD) may occur at any of the previously mentioned levels, i.e., citizens' participation can range from data provision to heavily involved in problem definition. Unlike other forms of CS, citizens need to allow professionals/scientists to collect and/or have access to their personal data for the purposes of the public good. Therefore, understanding and addressing citizens' privacy requirements is essential for the success of CaDD projects.

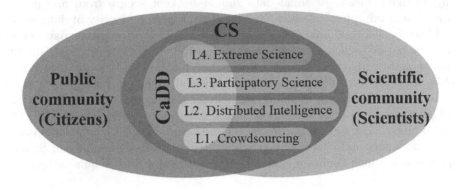

Fig. 1. Venn diagram showing the levels of citizens' participation in CS projects

2.2 Behavioral Change Theories

Several behavioral change theories have been developed with the main objective of understanding, explaining, and predicting why and how humans' behavior changes (e.g., Theory of Planned Behavior (TPB) [9], Transtheoretical model [10]). In particular, most of these theories try to analyze a specific behavioral change by identifying key constructs that might influence human attitude toward such behavioral change, i.e., accepting and/or participating in a specific behavior.

The TPB has been adopted since it has been proven to be a useful tool in explaining, predicting and changing many health behaviors [12]. Figure 2 shows a representation of the TPB, where a human intention is driven by three factors: 1- *attitudes toward the behavior* refer to the degree that a person has a favorable or unfavorable evaluation of the behavior, 2- *subjective norms* refer to the perceived social pressure to perform or not to perform the behavior, and 3- *perceived behavioral control* refers to the perceived ease or difficulty of performing the behavior. These three factors can be analyzed relying on *behavioral, normative* and *control beliefs* respectively. Then, *intentions* is formulated based on these three factors, and given a sufficient degree of actual control over the *behavior*; people are expected to carry out their *intentions*.

It worth mentioning that the TPB was a foundation for the Technology Acceptance Model (TAM) [13] that models how individuals come to accept and use a certain new technology. In this context, the TBP matches well the individual nature of CaDD as it has to do with perceived usefulness, ease of use and subjective norms.

2.3   Privacy Requirements

Privacy is a vague concept to grasp, and numerous attempts have been made to clarify this concept by linking it to more refined concepts. In [6], an extensive ontology for privacy requirements has been proposed, which has been mined through a systematic literature review[1]. This ontology provides the required concepts and relationships for analyzing five main privacy requirements, namely: 1- *Confidentiality*, means personal data should be kept secure from any potential leaks and improper access, 2- *Anonymity*, means the identity of data owner should not be disclosed unless it is strictly required, 3- *Notice*, means data owner should be notified when its data is being collected, 4- *Transparency*, means the owner should be able to know who is using her/his data and for what purposes, and 5- *Accountability*, means information owners should have a mechanism available to them to hold data users accountable for their actions concerning data.

This ontology can be used to facilitate and improve the design of CaDD projects since it can reduce the vagueness and terminological confusion between project designers and citizens by providing a shared understanding of privacy requirements, which facilitate capturing and addressing such requirements.

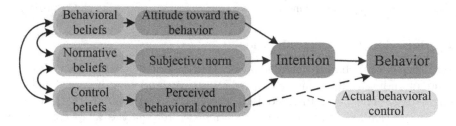

Fig. 2. The diagram of the theory of planned behavior [9]

3   Illustrative Example: Ambient-Assisted Living (AAL) System

AAL systems have been proposed as a solution to decrease the costs of health care services as well as the workload of medical practitioners especially in the case of chronic diseases (e.g., diabetes, obesity, cancer, etc.).

Our example concerns a person called Jack that suffers from diabetes. Jack lives in a home that is equipped with an AAL system, which depends on several sensors to collect Jack's vital signs, insulin levels, location, activities, etc. Such data is transmitted to a nearby caring center, where a nurse can monitor the data, detect unusual situations and react accordingly. The nurse may also share Jack's data with a medical professional depending on Jack's situation. The exact same data that is being collected and processed for assessing and supporting

---

[1] A detailed information about the systematic literature review can be found at [7].

Jack's life can be used for the purposes of the public good, i.e., advancing a wide spectrum of medical research concerning diabetes. However, most of these data are personal and cannot be used without Jack's concern. Therefore, Jack's privacy requirements are key factors that need to be understood and tackled to facilitate his participation as a data donor.

4   Problem Statement and Research Challenges

Considering the previous example, Jack's data cannot be collected nor processed without his consent. Therefore, we need to investigate how we can maximize the acceptance of citizens for donating their personal data. Applying the TPB can solve this problem, but it has not deeply investigated for such behavior yet. To tackle this problem, we need to tackle the following Research Challenges (RCs):

RC1: *How can we capture citizens' privacy concerns/requirements for donating their personal data for the purpose of public good?*

RC2: *How can we capture the main constructs of the TPB (attitudes, subjective norms, perceived behavioral control, and intentions) with respect to citizens' privacy requirements?*

RC3: *How significant is the impact of citizens' attitudes, subjective norms, perceived behavioral control on their intentions for donating their personal data?*

RC4: *How citizens' actual behavior concerning the donation of their personal data can be captured?*

RC5: *How well do citizens' intentions for the donation of their personal data conform to their actual behavior?*

RC6: *How can we derive citizens' requirements for the donation of their personal data?*

5   Towards a Method for Deriving Citizens' Requirements for Donating Their Personal Data

The process underlying the method (shown in Fig. 3) has been developed based on the TPB with special emphasis on privacy requirements. The process aims at assisting CaDD project designers while deriving citizens' requirements for donating their personal data, and it is composed of eight steps that aim at tackling the research challenges:

Step 1. Defining the behavior of interest: the behavior should be clearly defined in terms of its actions, context, and time frame. Concerning our example, the citizens' behavior of interest is allowing the collection and processing of their medical and activities related data. Moreover, we need to identify a list of citizens' personal data that are subject to the behavior, which includes: her/his vital signs, insulin levels, physical activities and treatment data.

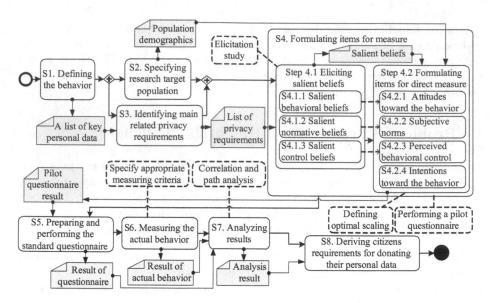

Fig. 3. A process for deriving citizens' requirements for donating their personal data

Step 2. Specifying the research target population: the target population of this research can be any individual that suffers from diabetes. In case of a minor, their legal guardian can provide the consent on behalf of them. Note that some techniques form crowdsourcing can be adopted for specifying the diversity, largeness and suitability of the research target population. Moreover, the population demographics should be captured at this step since it will be used in Step 4.2.

Step 3. Identifying main related privacy requirements: based on the list of personal data that have been identified in step one, a set of privacy requirements can be formulated at this step taking into consideration the privacy requirements presented in Sect. 2. More specifically, we identify all privacy requirements (e.g., confidentiality, anonymity, transparency, notice, accountability) that can be applied to tackle privacy concerns related to the identified personal data.

Step 4. Formulating items for measure: at this step, we formulate items to be used for assessing the main constructs of the TPB: *attitudes, subjective norms, perceived behavioral control,* and *intentions.* Basically, this step is composed of two sub-steps:

  Step 4.1 Eliciting salient beliefs: three types of salient beliefs (also called accessible beliefs) should be elicited: *behavioral, normative,* and *control* to formulate items for direct measure of *attitudes, subjective norms,* and *perceived behavioral control* respectively. This can be done by conducting an *elicitation study* by providing open-ended questions about the behavior of interest to sample participants, and the most frequently mentioned beliefs are used as salient beliefs. Following [9,14], examples of how such beliefs can be elicited are provided as follows:

Salient behavioral beliefs can be elicited by asking the participants questions like *What do you believe are the advantages/disadvantages of donating your personal data for the purpose of the public good?* We can be more specific by asking directly about the potential disadvantages of donating personal data with respect to the privacy concerns/requirements presented in Sect. 2. For instance, we can list these privacy concerns (e.g., confidentiality, anonymity, transparency, etc.) along with their definitions and ask participants questions like *What do you believe are the disadvantages of donating your personal data for the purpose of research with respect to the list of privacy concerns?* To assure a more complete set of privacy concerns and their corresponding disadvantages, we can ask questions like *Do you believe there are other privacy concerns for donating your personal data that is not covered by the provided list?, If yes, please list privacy concerns as well as any disadvantages of donating your personal data with respect to them.*

Concerning *salient normative beliefs*, first we identify relevant referent individuals/groups (e.g., family, friends) that might influence the participants' decision. Then, we capture the participant's motivation to comply with what their referent thinks by asking questions like *How much do you want to do what your referent thinks you should do?* Also, we can be more specific by asking direct questions like *Are there any referent who would approve/disapprove your decision for donating your personal data for the purpose of research if the confidentiality, anonymity, transparency, etc. of such data was assured/not assured?*

Salient control beliefs can be elicited with respect to privacy concerns by asking questions like *What kind of privacy concerns might demotivate you for donating your personal data?* Or we can make these questions more specific by including examples of potential privacy concerns and asking participants whether such concerns might negatively influence their decisions. Moreover, we need to understand whether addressing such concerns will facilitate the donation behavior by asking questions like *What kind of privacy protection mechanisms might motivate you for donating your personal data for the purpose of the public good?* Similarly, we can make such questions more specific by including examples of the potential privacy protection mechanisms and asking participants whether such protection mechanisms might positively influence their decisions.

Step 4.2 Formulating items for direct measure: this can be done through a pilot questionnaire that includes items to measure each of the obtained salient beliefs on optimal scaling (e.g., 7 points Likert scale) to select reliable and valid items for the direct measure. Following [9,14], examples on how to formulate potential direct measures are provided: Consider that one of the identified advantages of donating personal data is improving research in your chronic disease domain; a measure of attitude toward this behavior could take the following form: *On a scale of*

1 o 7, where 7 is the highest, donating your personal data for advancing research in the area of your chronic disease can be:

Worthless 1 2 3 4 5 6 7 Valuable

Consider that the identified referent is family and one of the *normative beliefs* is complying with what my family believes; a potential direct measure of *subjective norms* toward the *behavior* could take the following form:

My family whose opinion I value would:

Approve/Encourage 1 2 3 4 5 6 7 Disapprove/Discourage

my decision for donating my personal data for advancing research.

Consider that one of the identified *control beliefs* (e.g., a privacy concern) of donating personal data is losing confidentiality; a potential direct measure of *perceived behavioral control* could be formulated as follows: *Donating my personal data for research without protecting my confidentiality would be:*

Impossible 1 2 3 4 5 6 7 Possible

Finally, a potential direct measure of *Intentions* can be formulated based on [9] as follows:

I intend/plan to donate my personal data for the purpose of research?

Extremely unlikely 1 2 3 4 5 6 7 Extremely likely

Based on the result of the pilot questionnaire, we can formulate direct measures for the constructs of the TPB.

Step 5. Preparing and performing the standard questionnaire: after formulating the items for the direct measure, we can prepare the questionnaire to be used in the study. Moreover, we need to define the procedure to be followed including how the questionnaire will be available for participants and for how long. When the questionnaire procedure is consolidated, the questionnaire can be performed.

Step 6. Measuring the actual behavior: clear criteria for measuring the actual behavior should be defined. Concerning our example, the actual behavior can be easily measured by contacting the participants after a specific period of time (e.g., two/three months) and asking them whether they had agreed to donate their personal data for research.

Step 7. Analyzing results: we analyze the results of the questionnaire and the actual behavior trying to identify significant correlations between the variables of the study. The TPB model can be revised based on the result of the analysis by removing variables that do not have significant relationships (e.g., path analysis). We also identify the control variables that are significantly correlated with at least one of the main constructs of the TPB.

Step 8. Deriving citizens' requirements for donating their personal data: based on the result of the analysis, we will have the final TPB model that contain the main TPB constructs, which can be used to predict/explain citizens' *intentions* as well as how such *intentions* might maximize the *behavior*. This knowledge can be used to derive citizens' requirements for donating their personal data. For instance, we may find that assuring the anonymity (one of the privacy requirements) of citizens' data may positively contribute to their attitudes, which contributes to their intentions and in turn to their actual behavior. Similarly, we may find that assuring the notice concern may positively contribute to citizens' perceived behavioral control that contributes to their intentions and in turn to their actual behavior.

6   Discussion

The main objective of this paper is to highlight the importance of citizens' participation as data donors, and it is intended to be a starting point for understanding and tackling citizens' requirements for donating their personal data for the public good concerning their privacy concerns. Such requirements can be derived from our TPB based method, after identifying which are the main constructs that can be used to maximize citizens' intentions to participate as data donors and in turn their actual participation. This would constitute a great step forward in improving research in vast areas by making personal data available to be used by researchers. The method also captures beliefs that influence the main TPB constructs, which can be used to gain a better understanding of how we can influence citizens' decisions starting from their beliefs. Although the method focused on the medical domain, it can be applied to other domains.

CaDD may solve several existing problems in other forms of CS such as the quality and trustworthiness of collected data [15], since data is collected and managed only by professionals, who can apply appropriate protocols for ensuring the quality and trustworthiness of collected data. Moreover, collected data can be used for various projects if the purpose of such projects is complaint with the citizens' privacy requirements, i.e., researchers can avoid the burden of collecting the data they require for their work, they only need to be compliant with the specified privacy requirements. This can save the time and effort of many researchers by allowing them to focus on their scientific contributions rather than on collecting data and paperwork.

7   Conclusion and Future Work

In this paper, the importance of citizens' participation as data donors for research was discussed. Several research challenges to be tackled in order to identify citizens' participation requirements were listed and discussed. Then, a method to be followed for deriving citizens' participation requirements was presented. The method has been developed based on the TPB with special emphasis on privacy requirements, and examples from the medical domain to illustrate its usability and usefulness were used.

This is still a research-in-progress, which provide opportunities for future research. In particular, the proposed method is yet to be refined aiming to have a consolidated version of it, which can be reliably used for CaDD projects. The method will be validated by deploying it to real CaDD studies from different domains. Also, investigating how influencing some of the citizens' beliefs to increase their participation as data donors is on the agenda for future work. Additionally, it is planned to develop a Goal-Oriented Requirements Engineering (GORE) framework [16] that allows for modeling and analyzing citizens' requirements for the donation of their personal, which may facilitate the adoption of our proposed method. GORE can accommodate well the main constructs of the TPB as well as their main interrelationships since it allows for capturing citizens' requirements in their social and organizational context.

Acknowledgment. The author would like to thank Prof. Raian Ali for his comments, advice and useful discussions.

References

1. Phillips, T., et al.: Citizen science: a developing tool for expanding science knowledge and scientific literacy. Bioscience **59**(11), 977–984 (2009)
2. Silvertown, J.: A new dawn for citizen science. Trends Ecol. Evol. **24**(9), 467–471 (2009)
3. Krutzinna, J., Taddeo, M., Floridi, L.: Enabling posthumous medical data donation: an appeal for the ethical utilisation of personal health data. Sci. Eng. Ethics **25**(5), 1357–1387 (2018). https://doi.org/10.1007/s11948-018-0067-8
4. European Parliament: GDBR - Regulation (EU) 2016/679 on the protection of natural persons with regard to the processing of personal data and on the free movement of such data, and repealing Directive 95/46/EC, vol. 59, pp. 1–88 (2016)
5. The health insurance portability and accountability act of 1996 (HIPAA), vol. 25, no. 1 (1996)
6. Gharib, M., Giorgini, P., Mylopoulos, J.: Towards an ontology for privacy requirements via a systematic literature review. In: Mayr, H.C., Guizzardi, G., Ma, H., Pastor, O. (eds.) ER 2017. LNCS, vol. 10650, pp. 193–208. Springer, Cham (2017). https://doi.org/10.1007/978-3-319-69904-2_16
7. Gharib, M., Giorgini, P., Mylopoulos, J.: Ontologies for Privacy Requirements Engineering: A Systematic Literature Review. preprint arXiv:1611.10097 (2016)
8. Skatova, A., Ng, E., Goulding, J.: Data Donation: Sharing Personal Data for Public Good? Application of Digital Innovation, pp. 8–10, December 2014
9. Ajzen, I.: The Theory of Planned Behavior. Organizational Behavior & Human Decision Processes **50**(2) (91) 179 (1991)
10. Prochaska, J., Colleen, R., Evers, K.: The Transtheoretical Model and Stages of Change. Jossey-Bass, San Francisco (2002)
11. Haklay, M.: Citizen science and volunteered geographic information: overview and typology of participation. In: Sui, D., Elwood, S., Goodchild, M. (eds.) Crowdsourcing Geographic Knowledge, pp. 105–122. Springer, Dordrecht (2013). https://doi.org/10.1007/978-94-007-4587-2_7

12. Sault, K.: Understanding organ donation attitudes and behaviour from a theory of planned behaviour perspective. University of Chester, pp. 1–28 (2011)

13. Davis, F.D., Bagozzi, R.P., Warshaw, P.R.: User acceptance of computer technology: a comparison of two theoretical models. Manag. Sci. **35**(8), 982–1003 (2008)

14. Ajzen, I.: Constructing a theory of planned behavior questionnaire. Technical report, Amherst, MA (2006)

15. Hunter, J., Alabri, A., Van Ingen, C.: Assessing the quality and trustworthiness of citizen science data. Concurr. Comput. Pract. Exp. **25**(4), 454–466 (2013)

16. Yu, E.S.K.: Modelling strategic relationships for process. Ph.D. thesis, University of Toronto (1995)

Tracking the Invisible: Privacy-Preserving Contact Tracing to Control the Spread of a Virus

Didem Demirag[1]([⊠]) and Erman Ayday[2,3]

[1] Concordia University, Montreal, QC, Canada
d_demira@encs.concordia.ca
[2] Case Western Reserve University, Cleveland, OH, USA
exa208@case.edu
[3] Bilkent University, Ankara, Turkey

Abstract. Today, tracking and controlling the spread of a virus is a crucial need for almost all countries. Doing this early would save millions of lives and help countries keep a stable economy. The easiest way to control the spread of a virus is to immediately inform the individuals who recently had close contact with the diagnosed patients. However, to achieve this, a centralized authority (e.g., a health authority) needs detailed location information from both healthy individuals and diagnosed patients. Thus, such an approach, although beneficial to control the spread of a virus, results in serious privacy concerns, and hence privacy-preserving solutions are required to solve this problem. Previous works on this topic either (i) compromise privacy (especially privacy of diagnosed patients) to have better efficiency or (ii) provide unscalable solutions. In this work, we propose a technique based on private set intersection between physical contact histories of individuals (that are recorded using smart phones) and a centralized database (run by a health authority) that keeps the identities of the positively diagnosed patients for the disease. Proposed solution protects the location privacy of both healthy individuals and diagnosed patients and it guarantees that the identities of the diagnosed patients remain hidden from other individuals. Notably, proposed scheme allows individuals to receive warning messages indicating their previous contacts with a positively diagnosed patient. Such warning messages will help them realize the risk and isolate themselves from other people. We make sure that the warning messages are only observed by the corresponding individuals and not by the health authority. We also implement the proposed scheme and show its efficiency and scalability via simulations.

1 Introduction

A pandemic, which typically occurs due to uncontrollable spread of a virus, is a major threat for the mankind. It may have serious consequences including

---

An extended version of this work is available at: https://arxiv.org/pdf/2003.13073v2.pdf.

© Springer Nature Switzerland AG 2020
J. Garcia-Alfaro et al. (Eds.): DPM 2020/CBT 2020, LNCS 12484, pp. 240–249, 2020.
https://doi.org/10.1007/978-3-030-66172-4_15

people losing their lives and economical devastation for countries. To decrease the severity of such consequences, it is crucial for countries to track the spread of a virus before it becomes widespread.

Main threat during such a spread is the individuals that had close contact with the carriers of the disease (i.e., people carrying the virus before they are diagnosed with the disease or before they start showing symptoms). Thus, it is very beneficial to identify and warn individuals that were in close contact with a carrier right after the carrier is diagnosed. If a country can identify who had close contact with the already diagnosed patients, by sending warnings to its citizens and telling them to self-quarantine themselves, the spread of the virus can be controlled. By doing so, individuals that receive such warnings (that they had close contact with one or more diagnosed patients) can take self-measures immediately. This is also economically preferred instead of completely shutting down a country.

However, implementing such an approach is not trivial due to privacy reasons. First of all, due to patient confidentiality, identities of diagnosed patients cannot be shared with other individuals. Similarly, healthy individuals do not want to share sensitive information about themselves (e.g., their whereabouts) with the authorities of the country.

In this work, we propose a privacy-preserving technique that allows individuals receive warnings if they have been in close proximity of diagnosed patients in the past few weeks (that is determined based on the incubation period of the virus). We propose keeping the (physical) contact histories of individuals by using communication protocols in their smart phones. These contact histories are then used to determine if an individual was in close contact with a diagnosed patient in the past few weeks, and if so, the individual receives a warning. In order to do this in a privacy-preserving way, the proposed system uses private set intersection (PSI) on the background as the cryptographic building block (between the local contact histories of the individuals and database keeping the identities of the diagnosed patients). Even though PSI consumes more resources, it provides more privacy for the involving parties. By utilizing PSI, we aim to mitigate the privacy vulnerabilities of existing schemes.

The proposed scheme guarantees that (i) identities or the whereabouts of the diagnosed patients are not revealed to any other individuals, (ii) contact histories of the individuals are not shared with any other parties, (iii) warning received by an individual (saying that they were in close proximity of a diagnosed patient) is only observed by the corresponding individual and no one else, and (iv) the individual that receives a warning can anonymously share their demographics with the healthcare officials only if they want to. Furthermore, we also propose an extension of the proposed scheme against malicious individuals that may try to tamper their local contact histories in order to learn the diagnosis of some target individuals. We also implement and evaluate the proposed technique to show its efficiency and practicality.

The rest of the paper is organized as follows. In the next section, we summarize the related work. In Sect. 3, we describe the proposed solution in detail.

In Sect. 4, we implement and evaluate the proposed scheme. Finally, in Sect. 5, we conclude the paper.

2   Related Work

The importance of disease surveillance (without considering the privacy) has been studied by [4,5]. Privacy considerations in existing contact tracing mobile apps for COVID-19 are addressed in [6]. Authors show that none of the existing apps and schemes (except for private messaging systems which lack scalability) can protect the privacy of diagnosed patients and other exposed individuals at the same time.

Most of the current proposed systems are Bluetooth-based. Covid Watch [2] is an open source project that relies on Bluetooth for contact tracing and also uses anonymized GPS data to detect high-risk areas. Furthermore, Epione [13] is a PSI-CA based system, where a new semi-honest PSI-CA primitive for asymmetric sets is used. While Epione is very similar to our proposed work, we published our initial idea [8] on arxiv simultaneously with Epione.

A privacy-preserving Bluetooth protocol for contact tracing is proposed in [3]. Users receive the information about diagnosed people from a diagnosis server and the matching is done locally on the user's device. In a similar system proposed in [14], users keep their local contact histories by broadcasting their ephemeral, pseudo-random IDs from their smart phones and recording the IDs of other users that are in close proximity. The risk of a person for contracting the disease is computed locally on their phone. However, this system is not robust against a malicious user that may try to identify the infected individuals by observing (or modifying) their contact history.

Some apps, including [10,11] track individuals' location and save it in a local database. However, such an approach compromises location privacy of diagnosed patients as location information is gathered by the health authorities. As opposed to these approaches, in this work, we propose a scheme that protects the privacy of diagnosed individuals as well as the healthy ones.

Some other works incorporate different building blocks as well. In [12], a secure multiparty computation-based approach is proposed. Another solution utilizes trusted execution environment (TEE) [1]. Here, users share encrypted location history and also the test status. The system uses private computation to determine the people who were in contact with a diagnosed person. Finally, in [15], authors introduce BeepTrace, which is a blockchain-enabled approach.

3   Proposed Solution

In this section, we first introduce our system and threat models and then, we describe the proposed solution in detail.

3.1 System Model

The proposed system includes healthy (or not yet diagnosed) individuals with smart phones, diagnosed patients for the disease, and a health authority (e.g., ministry of health or NIH). Individuals interact with the database of the health authority. In the following, we will describe the proposed scheme assuming a single database for the health authority. For the sake of generality, one can also assume multiple local databases for the health authority (e.g., located in different geographical regions).

The health authority keeps the identities of the diagnosed patients and it does not want this information to be learnt by other parties. Individuals keep their local (physical) contact histories in their smart phones and they do not want this information to be observed by other parties (including the health authority). Also, when an individual receives a warning about a contact with a diagnosed patient, the individual wants to make sure that no other party can observe this warning.

3.2 Threat Model

We consider a semi-honest attacker model for the parties that involve in the protocol. That is, each party in the system follows the protocol honestly but they may be curious to learn sensitive information of the other parties. On the other hand, individuals may try to learn the identities of diagnosed patients or the health authority may try to learn the contact histories of the individuals. As we will discuss in detail later, the proposed algorithm protects the parties against these threats. Finally, we assume all communications between parties (between smart phones of two individuals or between an individual and the database of the health authority) are encrypted, and hence robust against eavesdroppers.

In the following, we provide a list of possible attacks against the proposed system.

1. A curious user trying to infer contact information or diagnosis belonging to a target user.
2. A curious user trying to introduce fake contacts in the contact list,
3. The server colluding with a curious user to infer contact information or diagnosis belonging to another target user.

3.3 Keeping the Contact History at Local Devices

Each individual keeps a vector in their local smart phone for their physical contact history. When an individual A spends some amount of time within the close proximity of an individual B, their phone records the ID of person B. For IDs of the individuals, we propose using the hash of their User ID (UID), which is generated by the application. To measure the proximity between the individuals, we propose using the Bluetooth signals on their devices. Thus, to add individual A as a contact, B needs to spend at least t seconds within r radius of A. This process is also illustrated in Fig. 1. As a result of this interaction, the new record in the contact history of A is the ID of B. Each individual may also separately keep the time and the duration of the contact (to have more insight about their risk, as will be discussed later).

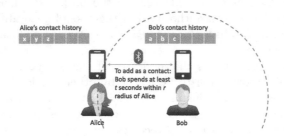

Fig. 1. Keeping and updating local contact histories of the individuals.

It has been shown that the strengths of Bluetooth signals can be used to approximate the distance between two devices [9,16]. Alternatively, one can also use (i) just the Bluetooth coverage (e.g., when two devices are in the range of each other for more than t seconds, they can update their local contact histories with each others' IDs), (ii) GPS information (when two devices are within their Bluetooth coverage, they can exchange GPS information to measure their distance more accurately and update their local contacts if they spend more than t seconds within a close range of each other), or (iii) NFC signal coverage (when the devices are within NFC signal coverage of each other, which is about 3 feet maximum, for more than t seconds, they can update their local contact histories with each others' IDs). Since this part is not the main contribution of the paper, we do not go into the details of establishing the contact histories.

It is important to make sure that an individual cannot add a contact in their contact list aiming to learn whether a target person has positive diagnosis or not. For instance, knowing the UID of a target person, an attacker may construct its local contact list only from the ID of that target, and hence learn the diagnosis of the target. To prevent such an attack, we consider two options: (i) make sure the local contact histories of individuals are stored in such a way that data cannot be accessed or modified by the individuals (e.g., the local contact history can be encrypted in the device by the key of the health authority or the contact history can be stored in a storage for which the individual does not have read/write permission). Or, (ii) each new contact B of an individual A also includes a digital signature that is signed by a centralized authority (e.g., the telecom operator). To do so, if individuals A and B spend a certain amount of time within close proximity of each other (measured as discussed before), they both send the contact request to the operator, the operator signs and sends back the signed contact record to both parties, and each party keeps the contact records and the corresponding signature together. This way, an attacker cannot fake new contacts in its local contact history. The validity of these signatures are then verified when the local contact history of an individual is compared with the diagnosed patients in the health authority's database.

Using either of these techniques, the developed algorithm makes sure that the contact history cannot be tampered by the individual. Note that if the storage of the local contact list would be an overhead, it is also possible to store the local contacts of an individual at a cloud server (encrypted by individual's key) and update the local contacts periodically. Current Bluetooth based solutions, such as [3] do not let the users access their contact histories (that is stored on their mobile devices). Even if the user can access their contact history, tampering with this list can be avoided by using digital signatures and encryption, as explained in this section.

3.4 Keeping the IDs of Diagnosed Patients at a Centralized Database

When an individual is diagnosed (e.g., by a hospital) with the disease, the User ID (UID) of the positively diagnosed patient is stored in the database of the health authority (e.g., ministry of health), as shown in Fig. 2. It is important to note that only the hospital and the health authority know the ID of the diagnosed individual.

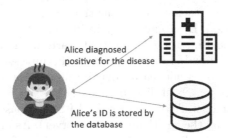

Fig. 2. Updating the database of the health authority with the IDs of the diagnosed patients.

3.5 Private Set Intersection to Identify the Individuals at Risk

The application on an individual's smart phone sends queries to the health authority's database following a random schedule. This schedule can be determined by the system to avoid an overload to the database. It is also important not to allow the individual to send queries at any time in order to control the system's bandwidth.

An individual A uses their contact history to query the database of the health authority and the goal is to identify whether there is an intersection between the local contact history of the individual and the IDs of the diagnosed patients in the authority's database (as shown in Fig. 3). Size of this intersection reveals the number of diagnosed people with whom A had been in close proximity in the previous a few weeks. As the size of the intersection increases, the risk of individual A being infected also increases. The proposed algorithm provides the result of this intersection to individual A as a warning message. Using the warning, the individual may take early precautions (e.g., have a test or quarantine themselves).

Fig. 3. Privacy-preserving interaction between an individual and the database of the health authority.

To compute this intersection in a privacy-preserving way, we use the private set intersection cardinality (PSI-CA) protocol, in which parties that are involved in the protocol obfuscate their inputs (sensitive information) and compute the result of this intersection. Eventually, only individual A learns the result of the intersection and the health authority does not learn any information about the contact history of individual A or the result of the intersection. We also make sure that individual A does not learn anything about the database content of the health authority (e.g., IDs of diagnosed patients).

Here, we explain the details of the proposed PSI-CA based protocol between an individual (client) and the health authority (server). As input to the protocol, client has its local contact list and server has the list of positively diagnosed patients.

Client masks its input with the random exponent R_c' and obtains the list of a_i-s and computes $X = g^{R_c}$ (X is similar to an ElGamal public key). Client sends the list of a_i values and X to the server.

Server permutes its input list and applies $H(.)$ on the list. Server masks a_i values with its random exponent R_s', shuffles the resulting list, and computes $Y = g^{R_s}$, which is a public-key like value. Server creates the list of ts_j-s by applying the one-way function $H(.)$ over the multiplication of X^{R_s} and exponentiation of hs_j-s to random value R_s'. Server sends shuffled and masked a_i values, Y, and ts_j-s to the client.

As the last step, client does the matching between the list of ts_j-s that it received from the server and its own list of tc_i-s. tc_i-s are obtained by applying the one-way function $H(.)$ over the multiplication of Y^{R_s} and the shuffled a_i-s, which are stripped of the random value R_c'. At the end of the protocol, client only learns the cardinality of the intersection. At the last step, a notification is generated based on the output of PSI-CA.

3.6 Further Steps to Track the Spread

Once an individual receives a warning as a result of the proposed algorithm, they can choose to (i) provide (anonymous) information back to the health authority to help the authority to track the spread and/or (ii) share their local contact history with the health authority to get further information about their risk.

In (i), the individual shares their demographics, the size of intersection they obtain as a result of the proposed algorithm, and their location with the health authority. Using such information received from different individuals, the health authority can have a clear idea about how the virus spreads in the population. In (ii), the health authority, using the local contact history of the individual and further details about the contacts of individual (duration and location of each contact), can provide a more detailed risk information to the individual (e.g., if the duration of the contact with a diagnosed patient is long, then the risk of individual also increases). As discussed before, such contact details (i.e., duration or location) are not used in the proposed privacy-preserving algorithm; they can be collected and kept by the individual and may be shared with the health authority to get more insight about the risk.

4 Evaluation

We implemented and evaluated the proposed privacy-preserving search algorithm. We ran our experiments on macOS High Sierra, 2.3 GHz Intel Core i5, 8 GB RAM, and 256 GB hard disk. We used MD5 as the hash function to hash the UIDs of individuals in the local contact lists and in the health authority's database. We used the implementation of PSI-CA in [7], in which q and p are 160 and 1024 bits, respectively. We ran each experiment for 20 times and reported the average.

We show the results of the evaluation of PSI-based solution in Tables 1 and 2. In Table 1, we set the size of client's local contact list to $1,000$ and vary the size of server's database. In Table 2, we set the size of server's database to $100,000$ and vary the size of client's local contact list. Our results show that the online phase of the protocol can be efficiently completed by the parties even when the input sizes of both parties are significantly large. Note that the server does not need to run the offline part of the algorithm for each client separately. Instead, the server can use the same offline computation during its interaction with every client. Also, a client can conduct its offline steps as it generates its local contact list.

Complexity of the proposed algorithm is linear in the size of the two sets. Let the cardinality of server's set be w and client's set be v. Client performs $2(v + 1)$ exponentiations with $|q|$-bit (short) exponents modulo $|p|$-bit and v modular multiplications. Server performs $(v + w)$ modular exponentiations with

Table 1. Offline and online run-times for PSI-based protocol (in milliseconds) at the client (individual) and server (health authority) with varying size for server's database. Size of client's contact list is set to 1,000.

Size of server's database	Offline time (ms)	Online time (ms)
1,000	Client: 210.6	Client: 100.85
	Server: 388.05	Server: 107.5
10,000	Client: 201.2	Client: 978.7
	Server: 2213.5	Server: 1003.8
100,000	Client: 202.95	Client: 9766.1
	Server: 20054.1	Server: 9925.6
1,000,000	Client: 202.4	Client: 96685.8
	Server: 194289.6	Server: 98631.1

Table 2. Offline and online run-times for PSI-based protocol (in milliseconds) at the client (individual) and server (health authority) with varying size for client's local contact list. Size of server's database is set to 100,000.

Size of client's contact list	Offline time (ms)	Online time (ms)
10	Client: 2.7	Client: 9852.95
	Server: 20012.75	Server: 9560.8
100	Client: 22.6	Client: 9854.2
	Server: 20218.1	Server: 9968.65
1,000	Client: 202.3	Client: 9817.5
	Server: 20448	Server: 9979.75
10,000	Client: 1990.4	Client: 9787.45
	Server: 20246.45	Server: 9970.65

short exponents and w modular multiplications. The resulting communication overhead is $2(v+1)$ $|p|$-bit and w κ-bit values, where κ is the security parameter. It can be deduced from these results that the protocol does not incur a significant overhead for a smart phone. Security and correctness of the proposed algorithm depends on the security and correctness of the original PSI-CA algorithm. We refer to [7] for details.

5   Conclusion

In this paper, we have proposed a privacy-preserving technique to control the spread of a virus in a population. The proposed technique is based on private set intersection between physical contact histories of individuals (that are recorded using smart phones) and a centralized database (run by a health authority) that keeps the identities of the positively diagnosed patients for the disease. We have shown that individuals can receive warning messages indicating their previous contacts with a positively diagnosed patient as a result of the proposed technique. While doing so, neither of the parties that involve in the protocol obtain any sensitive information about each other. We believe that the proposed scheme can efficiently help countries control the spread of a virus in a privacy-preserving way, without violating privacy of their citizens.

References

1. COVID-19 self-reporting with privacy (2020). https://github.com/enigmampc/safetrace. Accessed 11 Apr 2020
2. COVID watch (2020). https://www.covid-watch.org/article. Accessed 11 Apr 2020
3. Privacy-preserving contact tracing (2020). https://www.apple.com/covid19/contacttracing. Accessed 10 Apr 2020

4. Bhatia, S., et al.: Big brother is watching-using digital disease surveillance tools for near real-time forecasting. Int. J. Infect. Dis. **79**, 27 (2019)
5. Carneiro, H.A., Mylonakis, E.: Google trends: a web-based tool for real-time surveillance of disease outbreaks. Clin. Infect. Dis. **49**(10), 1557–1564 (2009)
6. Cho, H., Ippolito, D., Yu, Y.W.: Contact tracing mobile apps for COVID-19: privacy considerations and related trade-offs. arXiv preprint arXiv:2003.11511 (2020)
7. De Cristofaro, E., Gasti, P., Tsudik, G.: Fast and private computation of cardinality of set intersection and union. In: Pieprzyk, J., Sadeghi, A.-R., Manulis, M. (eds.) CANS 2012. LNCS, vol. 7712, pp. 218–231. Springer, Heidelberg (2012). https://doi.org/10.1007/978-3-642-35404-5_17
8. Demirag, D., Ayday, E.: Tracking and controlling the spread of a virus in a privacy-preserving way. arXiv preprint arXiv:2003.13073 (2020). https://arxiv.org/pdf/2003.13073v1.pdf
9. Jung, J., Kang, D., Bae, C.: Distance estimation of smart device using Bluetooth. In: The Eighth International Conference on Systems and Networks Communications, pp. 13–18 (2013)
10. Moyal, O.S.: "Hamagen" Application – Fighting the Corona Virus, March 2020. https://medium.com/proferosec-osm/hamagen-application-fighiting-the-corona-virus-4ecf55eb4f7c. Accessed 26 Mar 2020
11. Raskar, R., et al.: Apps gone rogue: maintaining personal privacy in an epidemic. arXiv preprint arXiv:2003.08567 (2020)
12. Reichert, L., Brack, S., Scheuermann, B.: Privacy-preserving contact tracing of COVID-19 patients. IACR Cryptol. ePrint Arch. **2020**, 375 (2020)
13. Trieu, N., Shehata, K., Saxena, P., Shokri, R., Song, D.: Epione: lightweight contact tracing with strong privacy. arXiv preprint arXiv:2004.13293 (2020)
14. Troncoso, C., et al.: Decentralized privacy-preserving proximity tracing. https://github.com/DP-3T/documents/blob/master/DP3T%20White%20Paper.pdf. Accessed 3 Apr 2020
15. Xu, H., Zhang, L., Onireti, O., Fang, Y., Buchanan, W.B., Imran, M.A.: BeepTrace: blockchain-enabled privacy-preserving contact tracing for COVID-19 pandemic and beyond. arXiv preprint arXiv:2005.10103 (2020)
16. Zhou, S., Pollard, J.K.: Position measurement using Bluetooth. IEEE Trans. Consum. Electron. **52**(2), 555–558 (2006)

Privacy Policy Classification with XLNet
(Short Paper)

Majd Mustapha$^{(\boxtimes)}$ ⓘ, Katsiaryna Krasnashchok ⓘ, Anas Al Bassit ⓘ,
and Sabri Skhiri ⓘ

EURA NOVA, 1435 Mont-Saint-Guibert, Belgium
{majd.mustapha,katherine.krasnoschok,anas.albassit,
sabri.skhiri}@euranova.eu

Abstract. Popularization of privacy policies has become an attractive
subject of research in recent years, notably after General Data Protection Regulation came into force in the European Union. While GDPR
gives Data Subjects more rights and control over the use of their personal data, length and complexity of privacy policies can still prevent
them from exercising those rights. An accepted way to improve the interpretability of privacy policies is through assigning understandable categories to every paragraph or segment in said documents. Current state
of the art in privacy policy analysis has established a baseline in multi-
label classification on the dataset containing 115 privacy policies, using
BERT Transformers. In this paper, we propose a new classification model
based on the XLNet. Trained on the same dataset, our model improves
the baseline F1 macro and micro averages by 1–3% for both majority vote
and union-based gold standards. Moreover, the results reported by our
XLNet-based model have been achieved without fine-tuning on domain-
specific data, which reduces the training time and complexity, compared
to the BERT-based model. To make our method reproducible, we report
our hyper-parameters and provide access to all used resources, including
code. This work may therefore be considered as a first step to establishing
a new baseline for privacy policy classification.

Keywords: Privacy policy · Multi-label classification · Deep learning

1 Introduction

Despite the rising importance of how personal data is managed and protected,
people still routinely skip privacy policy contracts, due to their complexity and
length. A simple word count on privacy policies of the biggest digital companies
shows that after GDPR came into force in 2018, the length of privacy policy
contracts has increased by over 25% on average, peaking at 94% for Wikipedia
[13]. With the increase of number of digital services we use, it became less and
less enticing to try to understand what is seemingly an endless block of text.

The recent research works have made a considerable progress in helping scientists and end users make sense of the conditions described in privacy policies,

© Springer Nature Switzerland AG 2020
J. Garcia-Alfaro et al. (Eds.): DPM 2020/CBT 2020, LNCS 12484, pp. 250–257, 2020.
https://doi.org/10.1007/978-3-030-66172-4_16

by classifying their segments into understandable pre-defined categories, that users can refer to and compare between policies. These efforts resulted in the creation of several datasets of various detail level, containing diverse categories describing the policies from different aspects, depending on the objective.

This work is developed within the ASGARD project[1], in particular, its RUNE track, whose objective is supporting the automation of privacy by design. One of the primary tasks of the track is translation of privacy policies, data processing agreements and contracts into a machine-readable format. Such task requires a trustworthy dataset for extraction of policy attributes. We experiment with the OPP-115 dataset [16], which is an accepted gold-standard containing 115 annotated privacy policies. To the best of our knowledge, this is the most detailed and widely used privacy policy dataset in the research community, despite being somewhat outdated and incomplete for usage in the GDPR-specific context [6].

In this paper, we present a privacy policy classification model based on XLNet [17] and showcase its performance in comparison to the baseline, established by Najmeh Mousavi Nejad et al.[2] [10] using BERT on OPP-115 dataset with two gold standards: majority vote and union-based. Our goal is to strengthen the baseline results using the latest advancements in Deep Learning and Natural Language Processing, as well as to demonstrate the performance of pre-trained XLNet in legal domain. Our approach of applying XLNet for privacy policy classification outperforms the state of the art in terms of macro/micro average F1-scores by 2%/1% for the majority vote and 3%/3% for the union-based gold standard. This result has been achieved without fine-tuning our XLNet-based model on domain-specific data, comparing to the fine-tuned BERT-based model in [10]. We make sure to guarantee reproducibility of our results through keeping the same splits as the baseline [10] and sharing the hyperparameters and code[3]. This work may therefore be considered as a first step to establishing a new baseline for privacy policy classification with OPP-115 dataset.

The paper is structured as follows: in Sect. 2 we lay out the research efforts in privacy policy analysis; in Sect. 3 we describe the model and how it differs from the BERT-based baseline model; Sect. 4 reports our results in privacy policy classification; we discuss our findings in Sect. 5; finally, Sect. 6 concludes the paper and outlines our plans for the future work.

2   Related Work

After GDPR has been enforced EU-wide, interest towards privacy policy analysis has increased significantly, which is evident by the great number of privacy and GDPR-related research projects in the EU and worldwide. Among the most prominent of them, the Usable Privacy Policy Project[4], started long before the

---

[1] Supported and funded by the Walloon region, Belgium.
[2] To be published in the proceedings of The 35th International Conference on ICT Systems Security and Privacy Protection (2020).
[3] https://github.com/euranova/privacy-policy-classification-xlnet.
[4] https://usableprivacy.org/.

GDPR, aims to benefit users through demystifying privacy policies. OPP-115 dataset [16] has been created in the context of the project, and became the first of its kind, with fine-grained annotations on paragraph level. Several other useful datasets have also been released for the same project [12,18]. In our work we make use of OPP-115, as it is the most used dataset in the privacy policy research, due to its detail level and rigorous annotation procedure.

Another outstanding project in the field of improving interpretability of privacy policies is Polisis [7] – a framework that categorizes, visualizes, and explains the contents of a policy to an end user in an interactive manner. The authors have trained their classification model on OPP-115, and reported their results. In this paper we do not compare our model to Polisis' CNN-based model, since the current BERT-based state of the art already outperforms it.

Beyond the research community, we can note "Terms of Service; Didn't Read" (ToS;DR)[5] project, which utilizes crowd-sourcing efforts to evaluate and classify terms of service and privacy policy documents in the context of their fairness to the users and how much concern they raise for data privacy and security. The ratings given to various services and websites help end users grasp the overall meaning and important notions in the policies, though the categories are less detailed than the ones the OPP-115 dataset presents.

When it comes to classification of textual data, until very recently, state of the art relied mostly on the variations of Recurrent Neural Networks [3,8]. However, the inherent sequential nature of recurrent models is what limits their ability to process long sentences and stands in the way of faster parallel training. Attention mechanism [2] confronted the problem by modeling dependencies regardless of the distance between the sequence elements. Consequently, Transformers [14] were designed to speed up the training for neural machine translation, through reducing sequential computation with multiple self-attention heads. The Bidirectional Encoder Representations from Transformers (BERT) [5] improved upon the limitations of existing work in pre-trained contextual representations [9,11] by using deeply bidirectional contextualization. BERT was the first generic representation model that achieved state-of-the-art performance on a large array of sentence-level and token-level tasks, outperforming many task-specific models [5]. In the context of our work, the latest and best reported performance on the OPP-115 dataset until now has been achieved by Najmeh Mousavi Nejad et al. [10] with a model based on fine-tuned BERT, which we adopt as a baseline.

3   XLNet Privacy Policy Classification Model

In order to compare fairly to the state of the art, we use the OPP-115 datatset with the same splits as in [10], on which we train our classifier, consisting of a pre-trained XLNet[6,7] and a dense layer for classification. In this Section, we lay

---

[5] https://tosdr.org/about.html.

[6] https://github.com/huggingface/transformers.

[7] https://github.com/kaushaltrivedi/fast-bert.

out the background and justify the decisions made for our classification model, by discussing the differences between XLNet and BERT.

3.1 Transformer-XL and XLNet

A limitation of vanilla Transformers is in stateless computations that put an upper limit on the distance of relationships they can model [1]. The Transformer-XL [4] is an extension of the Transformer that overcomes this shortcoming by caching the hidden states of the previous sequence and passing them as keys/values when processing the current sequence. It also introduces relative positional embeddings that encode relative distances between words and allow the model to compute the attention score for words that are before and after the current word.

XLNet [17] changed the way a language modeling problem is approached. It is an auto-regressive language model that outputs the joint probability of a sequence of tokens with recurrence. It calculates the probability of a word, conditioned on all possible permutations of words in a sentence, as opposed to just those to the left or the right of the target word. The model achieves state-of-the-art performance on the GLUE benchmark [15], trained on a large corpus.

3.2 XLNet vs BERT

Despite its strong performance across the multitude of tasks, BERT has attracted criticism due to the following flaws [17]:

- In the Transformer architecture the model can acquire context information exclusively within the boundaries of the maximum input sequence length, so a longer document would be divided into independently processed segments.
- BERT suffers a discrepancy between fine-tuning and pre-training, when it comes to predicting masked tokens: during pre-training, tokens are replaced with the [MASK] symbol, though, it never appears in downstream tasks.
- When predicting masked tokens, BERT disregards the dependencies between them, thus reducing the number of dependencies it can learn at once.

The sequence length constraint is tackled by XLNet due to the features of Transformer-XL, whose Recurrence Mechanism and Relative Positional Encoding help capture long-term dependencies for longer documents. The model caches the hidden state sequence, computed from the previous segment, and reuses it as an extended context, when processing the next segment. This additional input allows the network to exploit historical information, and still keep the gradient within a segment. While BERT encodes context positions statically, Relative Positional Encoding of Transformer-XL allows for the encoding of positions in a relative distance from the current token at each attention module. The aim is to accommodate the Recurrence Mechanism and avoid having tokens from different positions with the same positional encoding.

Transformer-XL only holds unidirectional context, predicting current token based on sequential context on its left or its right. However, it solves the issue by introducing the Permutation Language Modeling objective: instead of predicting tokens in sequential order, it follows a random permutation order. Only the last tokens in a factorization order are chosen for training to reduce optimization difficulty that comes from working with permutations.

Building on the information above, we believe that applying XLNet to the downstream task of privacy policy classification holds the potential of improving the current baseline results achieved with the BERT-based model in [10].

4   Evaluation

To evaluate our approach, we follow Najmeh Mousavi Nejad et al. [10] and train our XLNet-based classifier on the Online Privacy Policies (OPP-115) dataset. A comprehensive description of the dataset and its categories can be found in [16], and the gold standards with their label distributions are presented in [10]. Thus, here we briefly mention the key aspects of the dataset that are necessary for the interpretation of the results.

OPP-115 consists of 115 privacy policies, manually annotated on a para-graph level, resulting in 3 792 paragraphs, 10 high-level classes and 22 distinct attributes. Like the majority of previous works, we are only considering the high-level categories for classification, 12 exactly[8]. Therefore, we have a 12-class multi-label classification task at hand. In order to establish a firm comparison to the state-of-the-art results, we apply the same splits used by Najmeh Mousavi Nejad et al. [10]: the authors reported that they randomly partitioned splits, according to Machine Learning best practices, into a ratio of 3:1:1 for train, validation and test, respectively. For the same purpose, we also evaluate on the two gold standards, considered by the baseline model: the majority vote and union-based. We report the resulting F1 values of our XLNet-based model in Table 1, in comparison to BERT-based model performance reported in [10].

Table 1 shows that XLNet improves both baselines - BERT and BERT fine-tuned - without the need of fine-tuning on the domain-specific data. These improvements can be explained by the architectural differences between XLNet and BERT, mentioned in Sect. 3, and additionally, by the fact that XLNet has been trained on a bigger corpus, that includes the training data of BERT. There-fore, it works with bigger vocabulary and moreover, it generalizes better. Another factor that we believe affected the performance for the better, is Transformer-XL's Recurrence Mechanism and Relative Positional Encoding, that help capture long-term dependencies for long documents and sentences. This feature is espe-cially important in analysis of legal documents, such as privacy policies, which tend to have long and complicated sentence and paragraph structure. As evident from Table 1, in total, our XLNet-based model outperforms the state of the art by 2%/1% for the majority vote gold standard and 3%/3% for the union-based gold standard, for macro/micro F1 average scores, respectively, while keeping the tendency for micro- to outperform macro-averages, mentioned also in [10].

---

[8] We follow the baseline [10], where the *Other* category was broken down into its 3 underlying attributes.

Table 1. F1 values in % for 2 baseline models from [10] models and our model (in bold) on the two gold standards with a threshold $= 0.5$ (V - validation; T - test)

Labels	Majority-vote gold standard						Union-based gold standard					
	BERT		BERT FT		**XLNET**		BERT		BERT FT		**XLNET**	
	V	T	V	T	V	T	V	T	V	T	V	T
First Party Collection & Use	87	88	88	91	89	90	83	84	87	86	85	87
Third Party Sharing & Collection	86	85	87	90	89	88	79	82	83	86	83	89
User Access, Edit and Deletion	82	63	77	73	81	76	54	49	56	65	70	73
Data Retention	40	33	54	56	62	64	36	68	62	71	75	73
Data Security	87	82	54	56	89	81	71	80	73	76	76	78
International/Specific Audiences	94	81	87	80	95	84	87	93	92	92	90	90
Do Not Track	80	100	95	83	80	100	80	60	100	92	80	93
Policy Change	80	88	80	100	89	89	75	78	77	80	70	84
User Choice/Control	75	81	85	90	81	77	64	63	66	65	64	69
Introductory/Generic	75	76	78	79	82	81	74	68	73	67	67	74
Practice Not Covered	18	32	35	35	56	42	44	46	45	48	45	56
Privacy Contact Information	79	80	79	78	84	80	75	71	83	78	80	83
Macro Averages	74	74	77	79	81	**81**	68	70	75	76	77	**79**
Micro Averages	81	82	83	85	86	**86**	73	74	77	77	78	**80**

If we compare to base BERT, the difference is more remarkable, encoding the performance gap between "pure" BERT and XLNet: 7%/5% for the majority vote and 9%/6% for union-based gold standard (macro/micro F1).

5 Discussion

Looking at the F1 values per label, we can note that XLNet outperforms both BERT and BERT fine-tuned on most of the categories, with an impressive increase in certain cases. A good example is *Data Retention* class, whose F1 metric improved greatly (from 56% to 64%) for majority-vote gold standard, but not so much for the union-based, where we had more than twice as much training examples[9]. Another category that exhibited poor performance for the BERT-based models is *Practice Not Covered*: as noticed by the authors, this class covers broad range of topics and vocabulary, which makes it harder for the classification model to learn. Interestingly, XLNet improves F1 values on this class significantly in both gold standards, while still demonstrating better performance on union-based label set. From these examples we can conclude that XLNet has the potential of improving classification results for the underrepresented or "tough to learn" classes, even with small amount of examples to learn from.

As we noted before, for this paper we did not consider fine-tuning XLNet (which would take considerable time and resources in preparation and training) as the pre-trained version has already given us the desired improved performance, comparing even to fine-tuned BERT, let alone the base one. However, we have

---

[9] For the label distribution in the two gold standards see [10].

reasons to believe that, just like with BERT, fine-tuning XLNet on the domain-specific data (a big set of privacy policies) should result in even higher F1 values. Currently, we leave this step for the future work.

Additionally, we would like to point out that the training of our model did not require any significant resources or time, in fact, the training configuration is the same as for the BERT-based model, for the most part. Hence, the improved results have been achieved without a sacrifice in training resources.

6   Conclusion and Future Work

In this paper, we demonstrated the performance of recently released XLNet model in legal/privacy domain, where this kind of model has not been applied, to the best of our knowledge. We evaluated an XLNet-based multi-label classification model on the OPP-115 dataset, with the goal of establishing a new baseline for privacy policy analysis. Our experiments with a pre-trained XLNet showed that it outperforms BERT on this particular domain-specific task, and moreover, it does so without the need to be fine-tuned on the domain-specific data.

In terms of the future work, we plan to experiment with fine-tuning XLNet on a large set of privacy policies, and we expect this step to further improve the results. As for the next phases in terms of the ASGARD project, we intend to use the model and the classification results to translate privacy policies into a machine-readable representation, to be used in the downstream applications, such as compliance checking and access control for business requests. For this purpose, the dataset and annotations will need to be enriched with missing concepts, including GDPR-specific attributes, such as various legal basis terms. It becomes increasingly important to be able to extract legal basis, as the majority of new and updated policies mention it for the purpose of being GDPR-compliant, yet the current version of the dataset contains only a subset of the legal bases mentioned in the GDPR. Therefore, our future work will focus on improving both the classification model and the dataset, in order to obtain the high quality representations of policies and contracts.

References

1. Al-Rfou, R., Choe, D., Constant, N., Guo, M., Jones, L.: Character-level language modeling with deeper self-attention. CoRR abs/1808.04444 (2018)
2. Bahdanau, D., Cho, K., Bengio, Y.: Neural machine translation by jointly learning to align and translate. In: 3rd International Conference on Learning Representations, ICLR 2015, Conference Track Proceedings (2015)
3. Chung, J., Gulcehre, C., Cho, K., Bengio, Y.: Empirical evaluation of gated recurrent neural networks on sequence modeling. In: NIPS 2014 Workshop on Deep Learning (2014)

4. Dai, Z., Yang, Z., Yang, Y., Carbonell, J.G., Le, Q.V., Salakhutdinov, R.: Transformer-XL: attentive language models beyond a fixed-length context. In: Proceedings of the 57th Conference of the Association for Computational Linguistics, ACL 2019, Volume 1: Long Papers, pp. 2978–2988. ACL (2019). https://doi.org/10.18653/v1/p19-1285

5. Devlin, J., Chang, M., Lee, K., Toutanova, K.: BERT: pre-training of deep bidirectional transformers for language understanding. In: Proceedings of the 2019 Conference of the North American Chapter of the Association for Computational Linguistics: Human Language Technologies, Volume 1 (Long and Short Papers), pp. 4171–4186. ACL (2019). https://doi.org/10.18653/v1/n19-1423

6. Gallé, M., Christofi, A., Elsahar, H.: The case for a GDPR-specific annotated dataset of privacy policies. In: AAAI Symposium on Privacy-Enhancing AI and HLT Technologies (2019)

7. Harkous, H., Fawaz, K., Lebret, R., Schaub, F., Shin, K.G., Aberer, K.: Polisis: automated analysis and presentation of privacy policies using deep learning. In: 27th {USENIX} Security Symposium, {USENIX} Security 2018, pp. 531–548 (2018)

8. Hochreiter, S., Schmidhuber, J.: Long short-term memory. Neural Comput. **9**, 1735–80 (1997). https://doi.org/10.1162/neco.1997.9.8.1735

9. Howard, J., Ruder, S.: Universal language model fine-tuning for text classification. In: Proceedings of the 56th Annual Meeting of the Association for Computational Linguistics, ACL 2018, Melbourne, Australia, 15–20 July 2018, Volume 1: Long Papers, pp. 328–339. ACL (2018). https://doi.org/10.18653/v1/P18-1031

10. Mousavi, N., Jabat, P., Nedelchev, R., Scerri, S., Graux, D.: Establishing a strong baseline for privacy policy classification. In: IFIP International Conference on ICT Systems Security and Privacy Protection (2020)

11. Peters, M., et al.: Deep contextualized word representations. In: Proceedings of the 2018 Conference of the North American Chapter of the Association for Computational Linguistics: Human Language Technologies, Volume 1 (Long Papers), pp. 2227–2237. ACL, New Orleans (2018). https://doi.org/10.18653/v1/N18-1202

12. Sathyendra, K.M., Wilson, S., Schaub, F., Zimmeck, S., Sadeh, N.M.: Identifying the provision of choices in privacy policy text. In: Proceedings of the 2017 Conference on Empirical Methods in Natural Language Processing, EMNLP 2017, pp. 2774–2779. ACL (2017)

13. Sobers, R.: The average reading level of a privacy policy (2020). https://www.varonis.com/blog/gdpr-privacy-policy/

14. Vaswani, A., et al.: Attention is all you need. In: Advances in Neural Information Processing Systems 30, pp. 5998–6008. Curran Associates, Inc. (2017)

15. Wang, A., Singh, A., Michael, J., Hill, F., Levy, O., Bowman, S.R.: GLUE: a multitask benchmark and analysis platform for natural language understanding. arXiv preprint arXiv:1804.07461 (2018)

16. Wilson, S., et al.: The creation and analysis of a website privacy policy corpus. In: Proceedings of the 54th Annual Meeting of the Association for Computational Linguistics (Volume 1: Long Papers), pp. 1330–1340 (2016)

17. Yang, Z., Dai, Z., Yang, Y., Carbonell, J.G., Salakhutdinov, R., Le, Q.V.: XLNet: generalized autoregressive pretraining for language understanding. In: Advances in Neural Information Processing Systems 32: Annual Conference on Neural Information Processing Systems 2019, NeurIPS 2019, pp. 5754–5764 (2019)

18. Zimmeck, S., et al.: MAPS: scaling privacy compliance analysis to a million apps. PoPETs **2019**(3), 66–86 (2019). https://doi.org/10.2478/popets-2019-0037

Every Query Counts: Analyzing the Privacy Loss of Exploratory Data Analyses

Saskia Nuñez von Voigt[1]([⊠]), Mira Pauli[2], Johanna Reichert[2],
and Florian Tschorsch[1]

[1] Distributed Security Infrastructure Group, Technische Universität Berlin,
Straße des 17. Juni 135, 10623 Berlin, Germany
{saskia.nunezvonvoigt,florian.tschorsch}@tu-berlin.de
[2] anacision GmbH, Albert-Nestler-Straße 19, 76131 Karlsruhe, Germany
{mira.pauli,johanna.reichert}@anacision.de

Abstract. An exploratory data analysis is an essential step for every
data analyst to gain insights, evaluate data quality and (if required)
select a machine learning model for further processing. While privacy-
preserving machine learning is on the rise, more often than not this initial
analysis is not counted towards the privacy budget. In this paper, we
quantify the privacy loss for basic statistical functions and highlight the
importance of taking it into account when calculating the privacy-loss
budget of a machine learning approach.

1 Introduction

One of the most prevalent barriers of machine learning involve data management
in general and information security and privacy in particular. This is especially
relevant for sensitive data sets that, for example, include medical and financial
data items. In order to overcome the barriers, the area of privacy-preserving
machine learning (PPML) gained attention [2,11]. It is concerned with providing
an infrastructure for secure and privacy-preserving data access as well as privacy-
preserving model generation.

While PPML reduces the risk of data leaks, particularly the risk of model
inversion attacks, one aspect is often overlooked: In order to decide which type
of model should be trained and how it should be parametrized, a data analyst
performs a preceding exploratory data analysis (EDA). The EDA consists of
querying the data for a number of statistics and metrics. The goal is to gain
insights on the data quality, as well as the relationships between the variables to
initiate data preprocessing *before* a model is created. To do so, the data analyst
has typically full data access and is not restricted in her queries.

In this paper, we evaluate the privacy loss of performing an EDA. To this end,
we assume that an analyst obtains differentially-private answers [4] to preserve
information privacy. We quantify the privacy loss for basic analysis steps, which
can be used to make decisions on how to clean the data, select features, and
to select a model. Based on our evaluation, we discuss the implications of the

© Springer Nature Switzerland AG 2020
J. Garcia-Alfaro et al. (Eds.): DPM 2020/CBT 2020, LNCS 12484, pp. 258–266, 2020.
https://doi.org/10.1007/978-3-030-66172-4_17

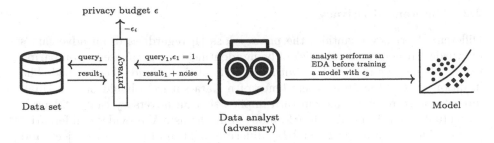

Fig. 1. System model.

resulting privacy loss and conclude that an interactive EDA is not feasible in a privacy-preserving setting.

At the same time, we compare the accuracy of an interactive approach with the generation of differentially-private synthetic data. Our results underline that the privacy loss can be mitigated by determining which functions are needed such that they can be answered as correlated queries. The generation of synthetic data is a generalization of this approach. Accordingly, we recommend to develop standardized sets of EDA functions to reduce the privacy loss and/or increase accuracy. In all cases, however, the privacy loss inevitably increases with the amount of information requested and should be considered for EDAs in general.

This paper is organized as follows. In Sect. 2 and Sect. 3, we describe our system model and introduce a basic set of EDA functions, respectively. In Sect. 4, we evaluate the privacy loss and discuss the feasibility of a differentially-private interactive EDA, before concluding this paper in Sect. 5.

2 Background

2.1 System and Adversary Model

An EDA is typically performed before a machine learning model is created in order to obtain a basic understanding of variable distributions, data quality, and the relationship between variables. By querying this information, a data analyst can determine the necessary steps for data cleaning and a suitable model.

In this paper, we consider the data analyst as an adversary, who should not be able to reveal information about individuals. That is, we assume an interactive query-response setting, which is visualized in Fig. 1. The analyst (internal or external) is allowed to query a data set and request aggregated data to perform the EDA and afterwards train a model. In order to mitigate re-identification attacks, noise is added to the results, which satisfy the definition of differential privacy (see below). A privacy budget tracks the privacy loss generated by the queries. It decreases with each query until it is spent and no further queries are answered. The system model captures the privacy-utility trade-off inherent to the notion of information privacy. We believe that the requirement of an EDA is often overlooked when it comes to creating privacy-preserving models.

2.2 Differential Privacy

Differential privacy quantifies the privacy loss [4] regardless of an adversary's knowledge. It determines the risk of being identified in a database by comparing results of querying the database with and without the individual concerned. The intuition is that the absence/existence of a data subject should have a small impact on the results, which in turn implies that an adversary cannot identify individuals from the result. More formally, a mechanism $\mathcal{K}$ provides ϵ-differential privacy if for all data sets D_1 and D_2, differing on at most one data subject, and all $S \subseteq \text{Range}(\mathcal{K})$ satisfy

$$P[\mathcal{K}(D_1) \in S] \leq e^\epsilon \cdot P[\mathcal{K}(D_2) \in S]. \tag{1}$$

Differential privacy ensures that the result of an analysis changes by at most a multiplicative factor e^ϵ when a record is included in the data set or not. For $\epsilon = 0$, the result of an analysis is exactly the same whether a record is included or not and thus provides perfect privacy. With $\epsilon = 0$, however, we cannot obtain meaningful results. In contrast, higher ϵ provide lower privacy guarantee. It is therefore necessary to find a balance between ϵ and the accuracy of the results.

Any mechanism guaranteeing differential privacy is robust under composition [10]. If we apply the mechanisms $\mathcal{K}_i$, each providing ϵ_i-differential privacy, several times to the same data, the sequence of queries gives ϵ-differential privacy with $\epsilon = \sum_i \epsilon_i$. In other words, the maximum privacy loss is bounded by the privacy budget ϵ, which in turn is reduced by ϵ_i for each query. As soon as the budget is spent, no further queries are answered. The parallel application of mechanisms $\mathcal{K}_i$ for D_i, an arbitrary disjoint subset of the input domain D, each providing ϵ_i-differential privacy, gives ϵ-differential privacy with $\epsilon = \max(\epsilon_i)$.

In an EDA, a data analyst queries interactively. Wile a query might depend on the results of previous queries, they are yet unknown in advance. We therefore simply assume random queries. Consequentially, we apply the differential privacy mechanism for each query and calculate the required privacy budget ϵ according the composition theorems.

To satisfy differential privacy for numeric queries, commonly random noise drawn from a Laplace distribution is added to the numerical output $f(X)$ [4]. The magnitude of noise is calibrated according to the sensitivity of a function. The sensitivity Δf is the maximum difference that an output can change by removing or adding a record. For example, a simple counting query, i.e., how many rows have a specific variable value, has $\Delta f = 1$. Differential privacy is then provided by $f(X) + \text{Lap}(\Delta f / \epsilon)$.

3 Exploratory Data Analysis

An EDA is an essential step in any data science application. Generally, an EDA includes different methods and can be an exhaustive analysis within itself. Moreover, the process is not standardized and depends on the objective of the analysis.

Table 1. Privacy loss for statistical functions of a basic EDA.

| Information | Statistical function | | Privacy loss |
	Numerical (NUM)	Categorical (CAT)	
Distribution (DIST)	Range, Q_1, Q_2, Q_3	Value counts	$\epsilon_i \cdot (5 \cdot n + c)$
Missing values (MISS)	Count	Value counts	$\epsilon_i \cdot n$
Outliers (OUTL)	Count outside cut-off	Value counts	$\epsilon_i \cdot n$
Correlation (CORR)	Spearman's correlation	Cramer's V	$\epsilon_i \cdot \left(\binom{n}{2} + \binom{c}{2} \right)$

In the following, we select some basic statistical functions that serve as minimum set of queries, which we derived from literature as well as our own practice in the field. The selected statistical functions for this basic EDA are listed in Table 1. Even if we limit our EDA to certain functions, we still assume that the queries performed by the analyst are not known in advance and are sent interactively depending on the results. Since some analyses depend on the data type, we differentiate functions between categorical and numerical variables.

Distribution. The distribution of the data is important to understand the data. For numerical variables, the range and quantiles provide information about the validity of the data and a sense of the range of the data. For categorical variables, a data analyst retrieves the unique variable values, especially the number of observations of each variable value. Variables with a discrete uniform distribution, for example, are not suitable to identify meaningful patterns. Variables that show this behavior need to be cleaned or removed for the training process.

Missing Values. The number of missing values indicates whether steps for data cleaning are necessary. There are different options such as case deletions or imputation with a vast body of literature discussing these options and their implications for later analysis steps [1].

Outliers. Machine learning models can be influenced by outliers, thus an analyst should be aware of their presence in the data set. There are many sophisticated tools to detect outliers, that mostly come with a high degree of privacy loss. Therefore, we resort to a simple box plot approach, where the cutoff point for outliers is defined as the upper and lower quantiles (Q_1 and Q_3) and a tolerance of $1.5 \cdot (Q_3 - Q_1)$ [6]. We then count all values that lie above or below that cutoff point. In this univariate outlier detection context, categorical variables are not covered, as rare values have already become visible from the distribution.

Correlation. The results of the correlation between variables mainly contribute to feature selection, where certain variables may be excluded from the model or combined with each other. Correlated variables are problematic for the interpretation of a model [14]. Furthermore, the relationship between independent variables may imply that dimensionality reduction methods can be applied to the data set to improve model performance. Based on this motivation, we include Spearman's correlation matrix for numerical data and a Cramer's V for categorical variables in our basic set of EDA functions.

4   Privacy Loss and Accuracy Impact Assessment

In Table 1, we quantify the privacy loss of the functions of our basic EDA. The privacy budget required to compute the respective functions is cumulated by the privacy loss of each query. It depends on the privacy loss per query ϵ_i, the number of categorical variables c, and the number of numerical variables n.

For the numerical distribution a data analyst queries the min, max, Q_1, Q_2, and Q_3. In other words, to obtain the information an analyst needs to query the data five times. Since each record is contained in each variable, an analyst spends $5 \cdot \epsilon_i \cdot n$ of its privacy budget for this statistical function. The categorical distribution can be investigated by the counts per variable value that are queried only once per variable and the required budget increases by ϵ_i and c.

The missing values as well as the outliers of categorical variables are visible from the value counts. Therefore, the privacy budget only increases by the numerical variables for both the missing values and the outliers.

We quantify the relationship between two variables using Spearman's correlation for numerical and Cramer's V for categorical variables. Since both measures are symmetrical, the privacy budget increases by the number of permutations

4.1   Privacy Loss

We determine the privacy budget for some data sets from the UCI Machine Learning Repository[1]. The data sets differ in size and number of variables. Common values for ϵ comprise 0.01, 0.1, 1, $\ln(2)$, or $\ln(3)$ [5]. Therefore we fixed the privacy guarantee for each query to $\epsilon_i = 0.01$, as this is the smallest value.

Figure 2 shows the cumulative privacy loss by conducting all statistical functions from our basic EDA. We observe an increasing and high privacy loss. For computing all functions, the adult data set requires the smallest privacy budget. The prime cause of this difference is the small number of variables in total. Indeed, the magic04 data set has less variables in total but more numerical variables. Since an analyst sends an additional query for numerical variables to determine the missing values or outliers, the privacy loss increases and is thus higher than for categorical variables.

The correlation leads to the highest privacy loss, since the budget increases by the binomial coefficient $\binom{n}{2}$ and $\binom{c}{2}$.

Note that the privacy budget increases linearly with the number of queries. With a lower privacy guarantee, i.e., $\epsilon_i > 0.01$, the total privacy budget would exceed the privacy budget of $\epsilon = 3$, which yields a 20 times higher chance (e^3) to be compromised. With a smaller ϵ_i, we can reduce the privacy loss and therefore the total required privacy budget. However, this leads to an accuracy loss.

---

[1] http://archive.ics.uci.edu/ml.

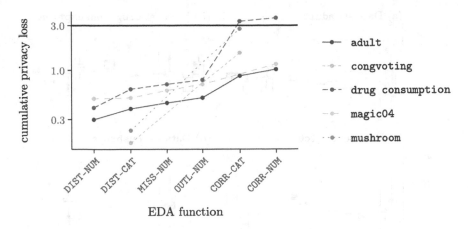

Fig. 2. Cumulative privacy loss with $\epsilon_i = 0.01$ for different datasets.

4.2   Accuracy

Due to the order of queried information the answers of our queries cannot be re-used. In order to reduce the privacy budget, numerous approaches aggregate queries and determine correlations between queries [7–9,12,13]. This allows estimating results from other noisy answers without spending its privacy budget. The results of these mechanisms can also be treated as differentially-private synthetic data that support the original working method of a data analyst.

In this section, we evaluate the accuracy of a differentially-private EDA and compare the interactive setting with differentially-private synthetic data sets. For data sets with numeric variables, we remove some values from a variable to have a numerical variable with 10% missing values.

We apply the Laplace mechanism for each query and generate differentially private synthetic data sets using the correlated mode of DataSynthesizer[2] that learns a Bayesian network with a degree of four. For comparison, we generate synthetic data with the same privacy budget that is required to investigate the correlation in an interactive setting. For example for the `adult` synthetic data set, with an $\epsilon_i = 0.01$ per query in an interactive setting, we set $\epsilon = 51 \cdot 0.01 = 0.51$.

We measure the accuracy of our basic EDA using the relative error of each query. Figure 3 reports the relative error for each statistical function visualized as box plot containing the relative error for each query. Overall, the synthetic data sets have a smaller relative error compared to the interactive setting. However, the relative error of the synthetic data sets for the numerical correlation is higher compared to the interactive setting. For the data set `magic04` (Fig. 3c), we observe a similar effect for the outliers. The high error occurs in the synthetic data sets due to the high range of some numerical variables. Remarkably, we obtain a high error for outliers for the interactive setting. This demonstrates that the relative error for the variables varies.

---

[2] Available for download at https://github.com/DataResponsibly/DataSynthesizer.

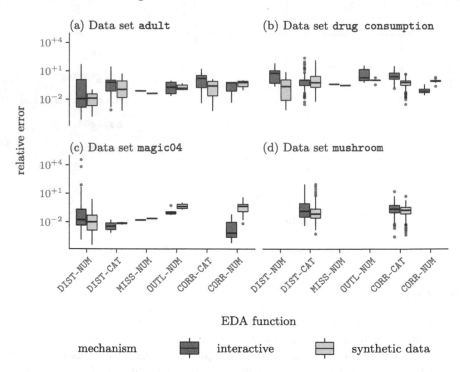

Fig. 3. Accuracy of statistical functions given by the relative error.

4.3 Discussion

The results show that even basic investigations of an EDA require a high privacy budget in an interactive setting. Therefore, an interactive analysis with both acceptable accuracy and an acceptable privacy guarantee seems not possible.

Non-interactive mechanisms, such as differentially-private synthetic data sets, can be used to increase accuracy and/or reduce the privacy budget. Notably, the synthetic data set can be used directly to train a model without dividing the privacy budget among EDA and model generation. However, the expressiveness of non-interactive mechanisms is limited to the correlations used for generating the output. Therefore, these mechanisms are not applicable for an interactive setting with random or unknown queries [3].

In an EDA, information is queried interactively, where one query depends on the results of previous queries. Grouping or limiting the queries to certain statistics, a differentially-private EDA might become feasible, though. We therefore appeal to data analysts to agree on widely applicable statistics that show the information necessary for model generation. With our basic EDA, we made a first attempt to create such a collection of statistics.

Please note however that further research is necessary. In particular, evaluating the *utility loss*, i.e., the usability of the results for inferring information (in contrast to the accuracy of individual queries) requires more attention in the future. We however believe that a standardized set of statistical functions used in an EDA could be optimized to balance the privacy-utility trade-off.

5   Conclusion

In this paper we demonstrate the increase of the privacy loss and thus the required budget for an interactive differentially-private analysis. We argue that the EDA should be considered in privacy-preserving models, as it is an essential step in machine learning. In order to address the privacy-utility trade-off, we propose to agree on standardized sets of EDA functions and use the remaining privacy budget for model creation.

Acknowledgement. This work was supported by the Federal Ministry of Education and Research of Germany (project number 16KIS0909).

References

1. Acuña, E., Rodriguez, C.: The treatment of missing values and its effect on classifier accuracy. In: Banks, D., McMorris, F.R., Arabie, P., Gaul, W. (eds.) Classification, Clustering, and Data Mining Applications, pp. 639–647. Springer, Berlin (2004)
2. Al-Rubaie, M., Chang, J.M.: Privacy-preserving machine learning: threats and solutions. IEEE Secur. Priv. **17**(2), 49–58 (2019)
3. Dankar, F.K., Emam, K.E.: Practicing differential privacy in health care: a review. Trans. Data Priv. **6**(1), 35–67 (2013)
4. Dwork, C.: Differential privacy. In: 33rd International Colloquium on Automata, Languages and Programming, ICALP 2006, pp. 1–12 (2006)
5. Dwork, C.: Differential Privacy: a survey of results. In: Agrawal, M., Du, D., Duan, Z., Li, A. (eds.) TAMC 2008. LNCS, vol. 4978, pp. 1–19. Springer, Heidelberg (2008). https://doi.org/10.1007/978-3-540-79228-4_1
6. Laurikkala, J., Juhola, M., Kentala, E., Lavrac, N., Miksch, S., Kavsek, B.: Informal identification of outliers in medical data. In: Fifth International Workshop on Intelligent Data Analysis in Medicine and Pharmacology, vol. 1, pp. 20–24 (2000)
7. Leoni, D.: Non-interactive differential privacy: a survey. In: International Workshop on Open Data, WOD 2012, pp. 40–52. ACM (2012)
8. Li, C., Hay, M., Rastogi, V., Miklau, G., McGregor, A.: Optimizing linear counting queries under differential privacy. In: 29th ACM Symposium on Principles of Database Systems, PODS 2010, pp. 123–134 (2010)
9. Li, C., Miklau, G.: An adaptive mechanism for accurate query answering under differential privacy. Proc. VLDB Endow. **5**(6), 514–525 (2012)
10. McSherry, F., Talwar, K.: Mechanism design via differential privacy. In: Proceedings of the 48th Annual IEEE Symposium on Foundations of Computer Science, FOCS 2007, pp. 94–103 (2007)
11. Mohassel, P., Zhang, Y.: Secureml: A system for scalable privacy-preserving machine learning. In: IEEE Symposium on Security and Privacy, SP 2017, pp. 19–38 (2017)
12. Roth, A., Roughgarden, T.: Interactive privacy via the median mechanism. In: 42nd ACM Symposium on Theory of Computing, STOC 2010, pp. 765–774 (2010)

13. Yaroslavtsev, G., Cormode, G., Procopiuc, C.M., Srivastava, D.: Accurate and efficient private release of data cubes and contingency tables. In: 29th IEEE International Conference on Data Engineering, ICDE 2013, pp. 745–756 (2013)
14. Zuur, A.F., Ieno, E.N., Elphick, C.S.: A protocol for data exploration to avoid common statistical problems. Methods Ecol. Evol. 1(1), 3–14 (2010)

CBT Workshop: Transactions, Mining, Second Layer and Inter-bank Payments

TxChain: Efficient Cryptocurrency Light Clients via Contingent Transaction Aggregation

Alexei Zamyatin[1]([envelope]), Zeta Avarikioti[2], Daniel Perez[1],
and William J. Knottenbelt[1]

[1] Imperial College London, London, UK
azamyatin@imperial.ac.uk
[2] ETH Zurich, Zurich, Switzerland

Abstract. Cryptocurrency *light-* or *simplified payment verification* (SPV) clients allow nodes with limited resources to efficiently verify execution of payments. Instead of downloading the entire blockchain, only block headers and selected transactions are stored. Still, the storage and bandwidth cost, linear in blockchain size, remain non-negligible, especially for smart contracts and mobile devices: as of April 2020, these amount to 50 MB in Bitcoin and 5 GB in Ethereum.

Recently, two improved *sublinear* light clients were proposed: to validate the blockchain, NIPoPoWs and FlyClient only download a polylogarithmic number of block headers, sampled at random. The actual verification of payments, however, remains costly: for each verified transaction, the corresponding block must too be downloaded. This yields NIPoPoWs and FlyClient only effective under low transaction volumes.

We present TxCHAIN, a novel mechanism to maintain efficiency of light clients even under high transaction volumes. Specifically, we introduce the concept of *contingent transaction aggregation*, where proving inclusion of a single contingent transaction implicitly proves that n other transactions exist in the blockchain. To verify n payments, TxCHAIN requires a only single transaction in the best ($n \leq c$), and $\lceil \frac{n}{c} + log_c(n) \rceil$ transactions in the worst case ($n > c$), where c is a blockchain constant. We deploy TxCHAIN on Bitcoin without consensus changes and implement a hard fork for Ethereum. To demonstrate effectiveness in the cross-chain setting, we implement TxCHAIN as a smart contract on Ethereum to efficiently verify Bitcoin payments.

1 Introduction

With decentralized cryptocurrencies finding more and more applications in industry, the need to deliver digital payments on resource-constrained devices, such as mobile phones, wearable- and Internet-of-things (IoT) devices, is steadily increasing. Even within the cryptocurrency ecosystem, the need for efficient payment verification is becoming imminent. One example are multi-currency wallets, which track the state of multiple cryptocurrencies and hence face high

© Springer Nature Switzerland AG 2020
J. Garcia-Alfaro et al. (Eds.): DPM 2020/CBT 2020, LNCS 12484, pp. 269–286, 2020.
https://doi.org/10.1007/978-3-030-66172-4_18

storage and bandwidth requirements. Another are the growing number of cross-cryptocurrency applications [1,11,12]. Here, verification of correct payments happens cross-chain and is often executed by smart contracts, where storage and bandwidth is priced by the byte.

In this paper, we present TxChain, a novel scheme to improve the efficiency of transaction verification, which improves upon recent work on optimized light clients [2,7]. Thereby, we do not rely on complex cryptographic schemes, but rather leverage the security properties offered by the consensus of decentralized cryptocurrencies – making TxChain compatible with the majority of existing systems.

Blockchain and Light Clients (SPV). Most widely-used cryptocurrencies, such as Bitcoin and Ethereum, maintain an append-only transaction ledger, the *blockchain*. The blockchain consists of a sequence of blocks chained together via cryptographic hashes. Each block thereby consists of a *block header* and a batch of valid transactions. The block header contains a pointer to the previous block, (ii) a vector commitment over all included transactions, and (iii) additional metadata (e.g. timestamp, version, etc.). Each block is uniquely identifier by a hash over its block header.

Vector commitments are employed by users to verify transactions without downloading the entire blockchain. For example, Simplified Payment Verification (SPV) clients in Bitcoin [9] only maintain a copy of the block headers of the longest (valid) proof-of-work chain, where each header includes the root of a Merkle tree that contains the identifier's of the block's transactions as leaves. To verify a transaction is included in a block, an SPV client requires (i) the block header of the block that contains the transaction (to extract the Merkle root), and (ii) the Merkle tree path to the leaf containing the transaction identifier (given the Merkle root). The size of the Merkle path, i.e., the number of hashes, is thereby logarithmic to the number of transactions in the block.

Sublinear Light Clients. Recently, two proposals for so-called *sublinear* light clients were made: *non-interactive proofs of proof-of-work* (NIPoPoW) [7] and FlyClient [2]. In contrast to naïve SPV clients, NIPoPoWs and FlyClient only require to download a fraction of the block headers to verify that a given chain is the valid chain[1]. Both mechanisms sample a subset of block headers *at random*, such that a fake chain produced by an adversary corrupting at most 33% of consensus participants or total computational power will be detected with overwhelming probability – and hence rejected.

NIPoPoWs [7] sample block headers which exceed the minimum Proof-of-Work target – the so-called *superblocks*. Due to the design of PoW, statistically, $1/2$ of the generated blocks will exceed the minimum target (level-1 superblocks), $1/4$ will exceed the target by a higher number (level-2 superblocks), etc. By only sampling superblocks, the number of block headers NIPoPoW clients need to download is polylogarithmic in the blockchain size. Unless deployed as a non-backward compatible hard fork [13], NIPoPoWs require block headers to

---

[1] The chain with the most accumulated Proof-of-Work in PoW blockchains.

contain an additional *interlink* data structure (pointers to previous superblocks) for secure verification of the valid chain.

FlyClient [2] samples block headers based on an optimized heuristic, which takes as input a random number, e.g. generated using the latest PoW block hash. Similarly to NIPoPoWs, a backward compatible deployment of FlyClient requires additional data to be stored in block headers: the root of a Merkle Mountain Range commitment – an efficiently-updatable Merkle tree variant which supports logarithmic subtree proofs. The leaves of the MMR contain block hashes of all blocks generated so far.

Both protocols also provide mechanisms to verify that a block header, not sampled as part of the (poly)logarithmic valid chain proof, is indeed part of the valid chain. In NIPoPoWs, this is achieved via so-called *infix* proofs, which link the blocks in question to the sampled superblocks via the interlink structure. In FlyClient, this is achieved by a Merkle tree path from the MMR root to the leaf containing the hash of the block in question. Note that additional block inclusion checks are not necessary in naïve SPV clients, since all block headers are already downloaded.

Probabilistic Sampling Dilemma. To the best of our knowledge, all sublinear light client verification protocols only reduce the block-header data submitted to the client, i.e., the protocols provide efficient valid chain proofs. The ultimate goal of light clients, however, is not only to efficiently determine the valid (or "main") chain, but to verify the inclusion of transactions in the latter. As such, to prove the inclusion of n transactions in the blockchain, both super-block NIPoPoWs and FlyClient require n block headers and n Merkle tree membership proofs to be submitted to the client – on top of the valid chain proof. Therefore, for large n, transaction inclusion verification becomes the performance bottleneck of sublinear light clients. Considering the additional data stored in block headers, performance may even be worse than that of naïve SPV clients for high transaction volumes. We term this problem the *Probabilistic Sampling Dilemma*.

Our Contribution. In summary, this paper makes the following contributions:

- **Probabilistic Sampling Dilemma**. We introduce the Probabilistic Sampling Di-lemma and provide a formal analysis, deriving the expected overhead of payment verification in sublinear light clients (Sect. 3).
- **Aggregated Transaction Verification**. We introduce TxCHAIN as a new technique for compressing transaction inclusion proofs, leveraging the security assumptions of the underlying blockchain (Sect. 4). In particular, to prove the inclusion of n transactions, TxCHAIN creates $\lceil \frac{n}{c} \rceil$ *contingent* (on-chain) transactions, where c is a constant dependent on the block/transaction size of the blockchain. Contingent transactions are only valid if each of the referenced n transactions exist in the blockchain. Proving the inclusion of a contingent transaction hence proves inclusion of the n referenced transactions. To circumvent block size limitations, we further show how to construct hierarchies of contingent transactions. As a result, to prove the existence of n transactions, TxCHAIN requires a single contingent transaction in the best case ($n \leq c$) and $\lceil \frac{n}{c} + log_c(n) \rceil$ in the worst case ($n > c$).

- **Formal analysis.** We prove TxChain's security and formally analyze it's efficiency (Sect. 5). Under high transaction volumes, TxChain reduces the number of downloaded block headers by up to a factor of 977x for FlyClient, and 973x for NIPoPoWs, for $c = 1000$ as in Bitcoin. In terms of transaction inclusion proofs, TxChain achieves an improvement of up to 1190x across all types of light clients.
- **Light Client Implementations.** We show how TxChain can be deployed (i) in Bitcoin without requiring changes to the underlying protocol and as a soft fork, (ii) and as a hard fork in Ethereum. We show TxChain's performance improvement when added as an extension to NIPoPoWs, FlyClient and even naïve (linear) SPV clients (Sect. 6.1 and 6.2).
- **Cross-Chain Deployment.** To demonstrate effectiveness in resource constrained environments, we implement TxChain as a smart contract on Ethereum which efficiently verifies Bitcoin payments (Sect. 6.3)[2].

2 Model and Definitions

2.1 System Model

Our setting consists of three types of users: *miners*, full *nodes*, and light *clients*.

Miners participate in the consensus protocol that orders the blocks, e.g., in Proof-of-Work blockchains the miners are the users that create the blocks by solving the computationally difficult puzzles. The miners essentially determine which is the valid chain.

Full nodes verify and store a copy of the entire valid (honest) chain[3]. Since a blockchain is a distributed system, the valid chain is the one agreed by the honest miners. To verify that a blockchain is the valid chain, a user can download a copy of the entire chain from one full node (or miner, ideally multiple), and verify all blocks. However, this is quite costly, both in terms of space and computation.

Light clients allow for fast synchronization and transaction verification, under the assumption that the valid chain follows the rules of the network. Specifically, light clients only maintain the following: (i) the necessary data to verify chain validity, i.e., for SPV clients all block headers, while for sublinear light clients a (random) sample of block headers with cardinality polylogarithmic to the length of the valid chain, (ii) for each transaction to-be-verified, the corresponding block header to extract the vector commitment (and optionally a proof that this block header is indeed part of the valid chain), and an inclusion proof, e.g., for Bitcoin the Merkle tree root and path.

Assumptions. We make the usual cryptographic assumptions: all users are computationally bounded; cryptographically-secure communication channels, hash

---

[2] Full paper version and open source code available at https://github.com/txchain/txchain.

[3] Miners are also full nodes, while full nodes are miners with zero "voting power".

functions, signatures, and encryption schemes exist. Further, we assume the underlying blockchain maintains a distributed transaction ledger that has the properties of persistence and liveness as defined in [4]. Persistence states that once a transaction is included "deep" enough in an honest miner's valid chain it will be included in every honest miners' valid chain in the same block, i.e., the transaction will be "stable". We assume persistence is parametrized by a "depth" parameter k, meaning that we assume finality of transaction after k blocks. Liveness states that a transaction given as input to all honest miners for a "long" enough period will eventually become stable. Lastly, we note that TxChain does not require any synchrony assumptions since it is a non-interactive proof scheme. Hence, we assume the same network model of the underlying blockchain system. We note, however, that each client is assumed to be connected to at least one honest full node or miner and is hence not prone to eclipse attacks [6].

Threat Model. We assume a rushing and fully adaptive adversary, meaning that the adversary can reorder the delivery of messages, but cannot modify or drop them, and corrupt users on-the-fly. However, the proportion of corrupted miners (consensus participants) is bounded by the threshold necessary to ensure safety and liveness for the underlying system [3]. For Nakamoto consensus, we bound the fraction of computational power $\frac{\alpha}{1+\alpha}$ controlled by the adversary at any moment by $\frac{\alpha}{1+\alpha} \leq 1/3$ [4], where α is a security parameter. In Byzantine fault tolerant settings, e.g. Proof-of-Stake such as [8], the fraction of corrupted consensus participants f is bounded by $f < 1/3$.

Blockchain Notation. We denote a block header, i.e., a block without the included transactions, at position i in chain C as C_i. The genesis block header is, therefore, C_0, while C_h denotes the block header at the tip of the chain, where h is the current "length" (or height) of chain C. Each block header includes (at least) a vector commitment over the set of transactions included in block, and the hash of the previous block header in chain C. This hash acts as a reference to the previous block and thus the hash-chain is formed. The vector commitment, on the other hand, is a cryptographic accumulator over an ordered list of transactions or a *position binding* commitment, which can be opened at any position with a proof sublinear in the length of the vector.

We use T_{id} to refer to a transaction with identifier id. Furthermore, we denote by $\gamma_{(\cdot,\cdot)}$ the inclusion proof of a transaction in a block. Specifically, $\gamma_{(i,id)}$ denotes an inclusion proof of transaction T_{id} in the block at position i of the chain. If there exists a proof $\gamma_{(i,id)}$, we write $T_{id} \in C_i$ Typically, the transaction inclusion proof employs the vector commitment on the block header. We define as $\beta_{(C_i,C)}$ the inclusion proof of the block header C_i in chain C. A naïve block inclusion proof is the entire hash chain C: the hash-chain that includes the block C_i points back correctly to the genesis block C_0 (ground truth). Lastly, we denote as $\pi_{(C,C_h)}$ a chain validity proof: a proof that a chain C at some round ending in a specific block C_h at position h (the tip of the chain) is the valid chain, i.e, the chain agreed by the honest miners. We denote by $|S|$ the cardinality of a set S. Further, we abuse the block header notation C_i to also refer to the block.

2.2   Protocol Goals

We use the prover–verifier model from [7]. In TxChain, the prover (full node) wants to convince the verifier (client) that a set of transactions T are included in the valid chain C. To do so, the prover(s) must provide three types of proofs to the verifier:

1. *Chain validity proof* $\pi_{(\cdot,\cdot)}$: A proof that chain C is the valid chain. Both NIPoPoW and FlyClient provide succinct proofs that the given chain is valid.
2. *Transaction inclusion proofs* Γ: For each transaction in T, a proof of inclusion in a specific block $\gamma_{(\cdot,\cdot)}$.
3. *Block inclusion proofs* $\mathcal{B}$: For each block that contains a transaction of T, a proof of inclusion $\beta_{(\cdot,\cdot)}$ that the block is in the valid chain C. The structure of this proof is specific to the protocol used to verify that chain C is the valid chain.

These proofs are not necessarily distinct, meaning that the data the prover sends to the verifier for all three proofs may overlap. For instance, in an SPV client, the proof of block inclusion (3) requires no additional data since all block headers are stored and verified as part of the verification process of the chain validity. Therefore, if the block inclusion proof is already part of the chain validity proof, we do not send the data twice.

Desired Properties. Our goal is to design a protocol that is *secure* and *efficient*:

- *Security* in TxChain encapsulates the correctness of the protocol, meaning that a verifier only accept the proofs, i.e., terminates correctly, if the prover is honest and knows the valid chain. In other words, the verifier will terminate correctly if all transactions in T are included in the valid chain C.
- *Efficiency* captures the storage cost of the protocol, i.e., how much data must be sent to the verifier as part of the verification steps (1–3). To evaluate the efficiency of TxChain, we calculate these storage costs and compare them against existing solutions for different sets of transactions (increasing cardinality).

3   Probabilistic Sampling: Cure or Curse?

In this section, we highlight practical challenges of light clients based on probabilistic sampling. We demonstrate that these light clients offer only optimistic performance improvements when the transactions to-be-verified are many, and in the worst case, can perform worse than naïve SPV clients. We term this problem the *Probabilistic Sampling Dilemma*. We first provide an intuition, and then a formal analysis to measure efficiency.

3.1   Probabilistic Sampling Dilemma

Chain Validity Proof. Existing sublinear light clients, such as superblock NIPoPoWs [7] and FlyClient [2] use probabilistic sampling to reduce the number of block headers necessary to prove knowledge of the valid chain (chain validity proof). FlyClient relies on a pre-defined heuristic for sampling blocks, while superblock NIPoPoWs sample headers of blocks which exceed the minimum PoW difficulty. Due to the nature of Proof-of-Work (and specifically hash functions modeled as random oracles), the appearance of such blocks is considered random. In both cases, the prover cannot predict upfront which blocks to provide to the verifier as part of the requested chain validity proof. This property yields the probability of the prover defrauding the verifier with respect to the chain validity proof negligible, within our model as described in Sect. 2.

Block Inclusion Proof. In naïve SPV clients, the block inclusion proof is trivial, as the verifier already has the hash-chain for the chain validity proof. However, this is not the case in sublinear light clients that use probabilistic sampling: For a given set of transactions, the prover must provide to the verifier (a) the block headers and block inclusion proofs for the chain validity proof ((poly)logarithmic in cardinality), and (b) for any block including a transaction of the input set that is *not sampled* for the chain validity proof, the corresponding block header and block inclusion proof.

The reason for the additional block headers is that the probabilistic sample of block headers is independent of the transactions the client wants to verify. Therefore, in addition to the chain validity proof (e.g., NIPoPoW) and the transaction inclusion proof for every transaction, the prover must also persuade the verifier that the block header that corresponds to the transaction inclusion proof of each transaction is part of the valid chain. This implies that the cost of the probabilistic NIPoPoWs is also *dependent on the number of transactions to-be-verified and how they are distributed in the blockchain.*

Probabilistic Sampling Dilemma. An additional overhead of probabilistic NIPoPoW is the increase of the block header size – especially if deployed in the blockchain without major modification to the underlying consensus rules. This results in the following phenomenon: the storage and bandwidth cost of both superblock NIPoPoWs and FlyClient can exceed that of naïve SPV clients for high transaction volumes (as shown in the experimental evaluations in Sect. 6.1). In particular, in probabilistic sampling clients the cost is proportional to the number of different block headers (and block inclusion proofs) that are given to the verifier, multiplied by the block header size. If transactions are distributed across many different blocks of the chain, which are *not sampled* in the chain validity proof, the cost, i.e., the additive data for the three proofs (c.f. Section 2.2) sent to the verifier/light client, increases.

As a result, a dilemma arises for clients with constrained resources: Clients can either (a) anticipate a high transaction volume and use a naïve SPV client, accepting a higher cost for chain validity proofs, or (b) rely on a probabilistic sampling (NIPoPoWs, FlyClient), saving costs on downloaded block headers under low transaction volumes, but under high transaction volumes end up with overall higher storage and bandwidth costs. We call this the *Probabilistic Sampling Dilemma*.

3.2 Analysis

In this section, we show that given a set of transactions to-be-verified T, the cost of probabilistic sampling light clients grows proportionally to the number of transactions $n = |T|$ and sublinear to the length of the chain. As such, when the number of transactions is large, the costs of the protocol is dominated by the cost of the block inclusion proofs, instead of the chain validity proof.

To that end, suppose $C_1, \ldots, C_\sigma$ is the set of blocks sampled for the chain validity proof. The selected set is expressed via a random variable X which follows the probability distribution defined in the light client protocol – e.g. uniformly-random distribution with respect to the length of the chain in Fly-Client. This means, that $X_i = 1$ if the block header C_i is chosen to be part of the chain validity proof. Now, suppose σ is the size of the probabilistic sample and h the length of the valid chain, then if X follows a discrete uniform distribution, it holds that $Pr[X_i = 1] = \frac{\sigma}{h}$, for all $i \in \{0, 1, \ldots, h-1\}$. As mentioned in Sect. 3, we assume the prover cannot influence or bias this random variable for security reasons.

On the other hand, we define the discrete random variable $Y_{i,j} = 1$ if transaction $\textsc{t}_j \in T$ is included in block C_i. For the purpose of our analysis, we assume $Y_{i,j}$ follows a discrete uniform distribution on the length of the chain h as well. Thus, $Pr[Y_{i,j} = 1] = \frac{1}{h}$, for all $i \in \{0, 1, \ldots, h-1\}$ and $j \in \{1, 2, \ldots, n\}$. We further define the discrete random variable Y_i to express if a block contains at least one of the transactions in T; $Y_i = 1$ if for any $j \in \{1, 2, \ldots, n\}$, $Y_{i,j} = 1$. Each trial is independent as a transaction's inclusion in a block has no influence on which block will contain another transaction (for block size large enough) Therefore, $Pr[Y_i = 1] = 1 - Pr[Y_{i,1} = 0] \cdot Pr[Y_{i,2} = 0] \ldots Pr[Y_{i,n} = 0] = 1 - \left(1 - \frac{1}{h}\right)^n$. For every block that includes at least one transaction from T, the prover must provide to the verifier the block header and a block inclusion proof, even if this block is not sampled for the chain validity proof. To determine the overhead on the cost, we have to count the number of blocks that include at least one transaction and are not sampled for the chain validity proof. To that end, we define $Z_i = 1$ if $Y_i = 1 \wedge X_i = 0$. Since Y_i and X_i are independent random variables, $Pr[Z_i = 1] = Pr[Y_i = 1] \cdot Pr[X_i = 0] = \left(1 - (1 - \frac{1}{h})^n\right) \cdot \left(1 - \frac{\sigma}{h}\right)$. Thus, the expected number of additional block headers are

$$\mathbb{E}(Z) = \mathbb{E}\left(\sum_{i=0}^{h-1} Z_i\right) = h \cdot Pr[Z_i = 1] = (h - \sigma) \cdot \left(1 - (1 - \frac{1}{h})^n\right) \geq \left(1 - \frac{\sigma}{h}\right) \cdot n$$

We observe that the smaller the sample for the chain validity proof, the larger the expected number of additional transactions. Furthermore, we notice that for a given chain length and sample size, the expected number of additional blocks grows with the number of transactions to-be-verified.

4   TxChain Design

In this section we present the design of TxChain. We first define the concept of contingent transactions and then present how this mechanism can be used to circumvent the Probabilistic Sampling Dilemma.

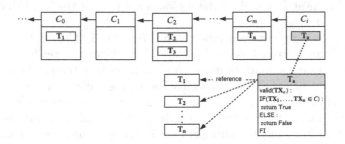

Fig. 1. Visualization of TxChain: a contingent transaction T_a is only valid and can hence be included in the valid chain C at index i if all referenced transactions $\mathrm{T}_1, \ldots, \mathrm{T}_n$ are included in C, and hence are valid. The inclusion proof $\gamma_{(i,a)}$ for T_a is hence also proves inclusion of $\mathrm{T}_1, \ldots, \mathrm{T}_n$.

4.1   Contingent Transactions

Smart contracts in blockchains allow us to define under which conditions a transaction can be included in the underlying ledger, i.e., specify when the transaction becomes valid under the blockchain's consensus rules. In TxChain, we leverage a fairly simple type of smart contracts: contingent payments (or transactions). Thereby, a transaction T_a is constructed such that it becomes valid – and hence can be included in the underlying ledger – if and only if a set of transactions $T = \mathrm{T}_1, \ldots, \mathrm{T}_n$ was already included in the underlying ledger. Formally,

Definition 1 (Contingent Transaction). *A transaction* T_a *is contingent on a set of transactions* $T = \mathrm{T}_1, \ldots, \mathrm{T}_n$ *if* T_a *can only be included in* C_i *if* C *already contains* $\mathrm{T}_1, \ldots, \mathrm{T}_n$. *Formally:* $\mathrm{T}_a \in C_i \implies \forall j \in \{1, 2, \ldots, n\}\ \exists m \in \{0, \ldots, i\} s.t. \mathrm{T}_j \in C_m$.

When checking validity of a contingent transaction T_a, *full nodes* look up the referenced transactions $\mathrm{T}_1, \ldots, \mathrm{T}_n$ in their local copy of the full valid chain, and only accept T_a if all transactions were indeed found, as illustrated in Fig. 1.

4.2   TxChain: Contingent Transaction Aggregation

We now apply the concept of contingent transactions to reduce the storage and bandwidth requirements of light clients when verifying n transaction inclusion proofs. Consider the following setting: A prover wants to convince a verifier that a set of transactions $T = \text{T}_1, \ldots, \text{T}_n$ was included in the valid chain C. The transactions are thereby distributed across h different blocks, $h <= n$. In TXCHAIN, the prover creates a *contingent transaction* T_a, referencing transactions $\text{T}_1, \ldots, \text{T}_n$ and includes it in the blockchain at position i, i.e., $\text{T}_a \in C_i$. Following Definition 1, by convincing the verifier that $\text{T}_a \in C_i$ the prover also proves that for every $\text{T}_1, \ldots, \text{T}_n$ there is a block C_m ($m \in \{0, \ldots, h\}$) that includes the transaction, and all these blocks are part of the valid chain C (i.e., $\forall m \in \{0, \ldots, h\}\ \exists \beta_{(C_m, C)}$).

Specifically, the prover has a valid chain of $h+1$ blocks $C_0, \ldots, C_h$ and receives a query for a set of transactions $T = \text{T}_1, \ldots, \text{T}_n$ from the verifier. The prover creates transaction T_a, contingent on T and includes it in the valid chain in block C_i ($i > h$). Once included, the prover computes the valid chain proof $\pi_{(C, C_{i+k})}$, the block inclusion proof $\beta_{(C_i, C)}$ and the transaction inclusion proof $\gamma_{(i,c)}$ and sends these proofs to the verifier, alongside T_a. The verifier checks the provided proofs and that T_a is indeed contingent on T. Once T_a has k confirmations, the verifier accepts T_a as proof that transactions T are in the valid chain.

4.3   Hierarchical TXCHAIN

So far, we have assumed that a single transaction T_a can be contingent on an arbitrary number n of pre-existing transactions. Including references to $T = \{\text{T}_1, \ldots, \text{T}_n\}$ in T_a, however, comes at a cost: each additional reference means additional data must be attached to T_a. However, blockchains typically exhibit block or transaction size limits due to network latency concerns: the larger a transaction, the slower it will be propagated across the network, and the more susceptible it is to double-spending attacks [5].

Depending on the size of these identifiers, which in turn depends on the design of the underlying blockchain as well as the means of deployment of TXCHAIN (c.f. Section 6), the number of transactions referenced by a single contingent transaction T_a can be limited. We capture this by a constant $c > 1$. As long as $n \leq c$, verifying n transactions requires only a single contingent transaction.

Consider, however, a scenario where $n > c$, i.e., a prover wants to convince the verifier that a large number of transactions are included, but cannot reference them all within a single contingent transaction. To circumvent this problem, the prover splits transactions $\text{T}_1, \ldots, \text{T}_n$ across multiple contingent transactions $\text{T}_{a(1)}, \ldots, \text{T}_{a(n/c)}$. Next, the prover constructs an *hierarchical* dependency across the "first-layer" contingent transactions by creating transactions $\text{T}_{a(n/c)}, \cdots \text{T}_{a(n/c^2)}$. In simple terms, the prover creates a *N-arry* tree of contingent transactions, where each node is a contingent transaction acting as inclusion proof for c nodes (transactions) in that branch.

As a result, the prover can apply TXCHAIN to an arbitrary number of transactions, at the cost of including in the blockchain and sending to the verifier $\frac{n}{c} + \lceil log_c(n) \rceil$ contingent transactions. For example, for $n = 1000$ and $c = 100$, the number of contingent transactions would be 11. This yields a 91x reduction in the required transaction and block inclusion proofs. If $c \geq n$ (e.g. $c = 1000$), the reduction in the example is 1000x. That is, the number of transactions c that can be referenced by a contingent transactions directly impacts the improvement offered by TxChain.

5 Security and Efficiency Analysis

In this section we show how TxChain achieves the two protocol goals: *security* and *efficiency* (see Sect. 2.2).

5.1 Security Analysis

TxChain achieves security when the verifier terminates correctly if and only if the prover is honest.

> [⇒] If the prover is honest then, all transactions are included in the valid chain C, and the proofs are generated according to the protocol specifications. Therefore, the verification of all proofs will be successful by the verifier and thus will terminate correctly.
>
> [⇐] For the opposite direction, we will prove the statement by contradiction. Let us assume the verifier terminates correctly but the prover is malicious. This implies that the prover deviated from the protocol specification. Given that the verifier terminated, the verifier received the corresponding proofs from the prover. Since the security of the generation of the proofs is guaranteed by the underlying light client verification protocol, the prover must have deviated from the protocol during the creation of the contingent transaction. However, the verifier has the block inclusion proof for the contingent transaction and also the last k blocks headers of the chain; therefore, the prover can only deviate during the creation of the contingent transaction. However, during the verification of the transaction inclusion proof the verifier ensures that all requested transaction identifiers are tied to this transaction. Thus, the prover cannot create an incorrect contingent transaction. Contradiction. We conclude that TxChain achieves security.

Hierarchical TxChain. The security of the hierarchical TxChain construction follows from recursively applying the security analysis of TxChain. See full paper version for detailed discussion (See footnote 2).

5.2 Efficiency Analysis

We now discuss how TxChain achieves *efficiency* by comparing the storage costs of naïve (SPV) and sublinear (NIPoPoWs and FlyClient) light clients *with* and *without* applying TxChain. We assume a secure hash function H and denote its size $|H|$. We analyze the cost of each proof (see Sect. 2) below.

Valid Chain Proofs: The size of the valid chain proof in naïve SPV is linear in h. The size of the valid chain proof in sublinear light clients depends on two parameters: (i) λ which defines the probability $2^{-\lambda}$ of a verifier terminating correctly on an invalid proof, (ii) α which defines the strength of the adversary $\alpha/(1 + \alpha)$, e.g. the hash rate in PoW blockchains , and (iii) the "depth" parameter k. The NIPoPoW $\pi_{(C,C_h)}$ size [2,7] is given by $log_{1/\alpha}(2)\lambda \cdot ((log_2(h) + 1) \cdot C + log_2(h) \cdot \lceil log_2(log_2(h)) \rceil \cdot |H|)$. The FlyClient $\pi_{(C,C_h)}$ size [2] is given by $\lambda log_{1/\alpha}(2)ln(h) \cdot (C + |H|)$. Note the increased block header size due to additionally required number of hashes $|H|$ in NIPoPoWs (interlink structure) and FlyClient (MMR root).

Block Inclusion Proofs ($\mathcal{B}$): Since naïve SPV clients store all block headers, no extra block inclusion proofs $\beta_{(\cdot,\cdot)}$ are required. Both NIPoPoW and FlyClient require block inclusion proofs for blocks not sampled as part of $\pi_{(C,C_h)}$ – for both mechanisms, the size of $\beta_{(\cdot,\cdot)}$ is $log(h) \cdot |H|$ per block header.

Transaction Inclusion Proofs (Γ): A transaction inclusion proof $\gamma(i, id)$ is a list of hashes (Merkle tree path), logarithmic in the number of transactions contained in block C_i. Hence, the size of each proof is $log(t) \cdot |H|$, where t is the total number of transactions included in the block containing a transaction of T.

TxChain Efficiency. In Sect. 3, we determined the expected number of additional block headers and block inclusion proofs $\mathbb{E}(|\mathcal{B}|)$ required in NIPoPoW and FlyClient to verify the inclusion of n transactions for any given blockchain size h: $\mathbb{E}(|\mathcal{B}|) = (h - \sigma) \cdot (1 - (1 - \frac{1}{h})^n)$, where σ is the number of blocks sampled for the chain validity proof. When applying TxChain to such probabilistic sampling clients, this number decreases to: $\mathbb{E}(|\mathcal{B}'|) = \frac{\mathbb{E}(|\mathcal{B}|)}{c} + log_c(\mathbb{E}(|\mathcal{B}|))$. We observe that the improvement achieved by TxChain is most significant for large c, since $lim_{c \to \infty}\mathbb{E}(|\mathcal{B}'|) = 1$.

To evaluate the theoretical improvement we can achieve in TxChain, we apply TxChain as an extension to both NIPoPoW and FlyClient. Figure 2 overviews the expected number of (a) additional block inclusion proofs (and hence block headers) and (b) required transaction inclusion proofs, *before* and *after* applying TxChain, for blockchain size $h = 100000$ and $c = 1000$. A more detailed cost breakdown is provided in the full paper version[2]. We observe that as expected, TxChain becomes more effective as n increases, up until $n = |T| = h$. Statistically, given a blockchain size of 100000 and 50000 to-be-verified transactions, FlyClient on average requires the submission of 39120 block inclusion proofs and block headers, on top of the blocks sampled as part of the chain validity proof. NIPoPoWs, which sample 40% more blocks as part of the chain validity proof [2], require 39000 additional block headers. If we apply TxChain's contingent transaction aggregation to FlyClient and NIPoPoWs, assuming a realistic $c = 1000$ (e.g. corresponds to a transaction with 1000 inputs in Bitcoin), we only need to download 42 additional block headers, achieving an improvement factor of 931x over FlyClient and 928x over NIPoPoWs.

TxChain achieves even higher improvement factors for higher values of $\Gamma = n$ in FlyClient and NIPoPoW, since $\mathbb{E}(|\mathcal{B}|) \leq n$. For 50000 to-be-verified transactions and a blockchain size of 100000, the use of TxChain improves over both "Vanilla" FlyClient and NIPoPoW by a factor of 1190x: instead of 50000, we require only 42 transaction inclusion proofs. It is worth mentioning that the same improvement identically applies to naïve SPV clients, as visualized in Fig. 2(b).

We note the actual improvement in terms of storage and bandwidth costs depends on how TxChain, and specifically contingent transactions, are implemented in the underlying blockchain, as we discuss in Sect. 6.

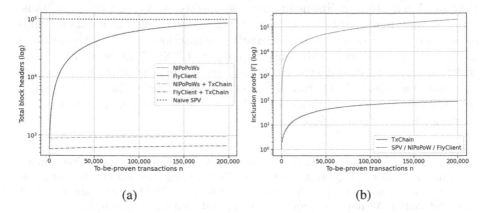

(a)   (b)

Fig. 2. Effects of applying TxChain to FlyClient and NIPoPoWs. (a) Total number of block headers required for verification of n transactions $(\pi_{(C,C_h)} + \mathbb{E}(|\mathcal{B}|))$. (b) Number of transaction inclusion proofs Γ in light clients before and after applying TxChain (logarithmic y-axis). Numbers $h = 100000$ and $c = 1000$.

Limitations. While the design of TxChain is simple and avoids complex cryptographic schemes, making it compatible with the majority of existing blockchain systems, it also exhibits limitations. The requirement of including additional transactions in the blockchain results in additional transaction fees for the prover (c.f. Section 6.1). Further, TxChain may not be applicable in times of high network congestion, i.e., if a prover is unable to reliably include a contingent transaction in the blockchain. This in turn, in the worst case, may yield TxChain not applicable to instant or day-to-day payments. Summarizing, TxChain is most effective in settings where the storage and especially bandwidth requirements of the verifier are the main bottleneck of a protocol, or even priced by byte – as is the case when verification is performed in on-chain smart contracts, as we show in Sect. 6.3.

6 Deploying TxChain in Practice

In this section we discuss how TxChain can be added to light clients of the two major blockchains Bitcoin and Ethereum and evaluate the achieved improvements. Note: we evaluate both NIPoPoW and FlyClient under constant difficulty, since NIPoPoW currently does not support variable difficulty [2, 7].

6.1   Fork Free Deployment

We first discuss how TxCHAIN can be deployed in a fully backward compatible manner without requiring forks in Bitcoin (and similar systems). In blockchains like Ethereum, which rely on an account-based model, TxCHAIN requires a soft or hard fork.

Bitcoin: Dust Output Spending. Bitcoin operates a so-called Unspent Transaction Output model (UTXO). Each new transaction consists of inputs and outputs, where inputs *spend* outputs of existing transactions. Outputs specify rules for how the coins *locked* in the unspent output (UTXO) can be spent, i.e. via smart contracts. In Bitcoin, these contracts are written in Script, a stack-based scripting language. UTXOs can only be spent as a whole. As of this writing, the only way to create conditional relation across transactions in Bitcoin is by creating *spending* relationships.

Table 1. Storage and bandwidth costs of naïve SPV, Flyclient and NIPoPoWs, *without* ("Vanilla") and with a *fork-free deployment* of TxChain, for different numbers of to-be-verified transactions n, for blockchain size $h = 630000$ (as of 5 May 2020) and $c = 1000$. FlyClient/NIPoPoW numbers provided for soft and hard fork deployment.

n	naïve SPV Vanilla in mB	TxCHAIN in mB	Impr. factor	FlyClient Soft Fork Vanilla in mB	TxCHAIN in mB	Impr. factor	FlyClient Hard Fork Vanilla in mB	TxCHAIN in mB	Impr. factor	Superblock NIPoPoWs Soft Fork Vanilla in mB	TxCHAIN in mB	Impr. factor	Superblock NIPoPoWs Hard Fork Vanilla in mB	TxCHAIN in mB	Impr. factor
1	50.4	50.4	1.0	0.51	0.51	1.0	0.1	0.1	1.0	0.77	0.77	1.0	0.15	0.15	1.0
10	50.41	50.4	1.0	0.52	0.51	1.02	0.1	0.1	1.04	0.78	0.77	1.01	0.15	0.15	1.03
100	50.49	50.4	1.0	0.62	0.51	1.21	0.15	0.1	1.5	0.88	0.77	1.14	0.2	0.15	1.33
1000	51.32	50.4	1.02	1.61	0.51	3.16	0.59	0.1	6.03	1.88	0.77	2.43	0.64	0.15	4.33
10000	59.58	50.42	1.18	11.51	0.53	21.58	5.05	0.11	44.04	11.77	0.8	14.81	5.1	0.16	30.97
50000	96.3	50.66	1.9	54.42	0.8	68.11	24.67	0.36	69.17	54.67	1.06	51.56	24.72	0.41	60.8
100000	142.2	51.39	2.77	105.69	1.5	70.68	48.84	1.03	47.61	105.92	1.76	60.31	48.89	1.08	45.46

To deploy TxCHAIN in Bitcoin *without* consensus changes we can use *dust output* spending for the creation of contingent transactions. When creating transactions $T_1, \ldots, T_n$ the prover includes an additional output in each transaction, containing at least the minimum possible value transferable in Bitcoin ($54.60 \cdot 10^{-6}$ BTC which is approx. USD 0.4 as of 5 May 2020). The contingent transaction T_a then spends outputs of $T_1, \ldots, T_n$ and, due to Bitcoin's consensus rules, can hence only be included in the blockchain if all spent UTXOs already exist.

A practical limitation is that the prover must be able to spend from the outputs of transactions $T_1, \ldots, T_n$ when creating T_a. In the simplest case, the prover is the author of $T_1, \ldots, T_n$ (i.e., controls the signing keys), and can hence spend from the corresponding outputs. For the case where $T_1, \ldots, T_n$ are authored by different users, we outline two simple coordination schemes. A straightforward approach is for the prover to publicly announce his public key, e.g. on a public bulletin board (can also be Bitcoin or Ethereum), such that users can create dust outputs spendable via the prover's signing key. The value accumulated from the dust outputs can thereby serve as means to cover the prover's costs for broadcasting T_a. An approach without additional communication overhead is to use *anyone-can-spend* outputs and allow miners to aggregate $T_1, \ldots, T_n$ when claiming the dust outputs as fees. In both cases, the dust outputs of $T_1, \ldots, T_n$ can be supplemented with pre-defined timelocks, allowing transaction aggregation, e.g. only once every 6 h. This contributes to provers/miners aggregating multiple transactions, rather than spending from each $T_1, \ldots, T_n$ as they are broadcast by users. Other, more complex and costly designs involving HTLCs and zero-knowledge contingent payments are left to future work.

Evaluation. In our evaluation, we use Bitcoin P2WPKH transactions. In Bitcoin, $C = 80$ bytes and $|H| = 32$ bytes. The average transaction size in 2019 was 534 bytes, while the average size of the coinbase transaction was 259 bytes, the average depth of the transaction Merkle tree was 12. The coinbase transaction is the first transaction of every block and is used by NIPoPoWs and FlyClient to include the interlink data / MMR root required for block inclusion proofs, when deployed as a backward-compatible soft or velvet instead of a hard fork [13]. Summarizing, each block inclusion proof in NIPoPoW and FlyClient requires additionally $259 + 12 \cdot |H| = 643$ bytes, and each transaction inclusion proof 384 bytes - avoidable when applying TxCHAIN. However, multi-input Bitcoin transactions using by TxCHAIN come at a cost: 93 bytes per input and 45 bytes flat per contingent transaction (assuming one P2WPKH output). Thereby, Bitcoin full nodes will relay transactions of up to 100kb (github.com/bitcoin/bitcoin/blob/eb7daf4/src/policy/policy.h#L24), thus $c \approx 1000$.

We overview the storage and bandwidth costs of naïve SPV, FlyClient and NIPoPoWs with and without TxCHAIN in Table 1, for a Bitcoin block height $h = 630000$ (as of 5 May 2020) and $c = 1000$. We observe that with TxCHAIN the storage and verification costs under remain *nearly constant*, offering a significant improvement over "Vanilla" light client implementations, e.g. achieving an improvement factor of 71x for FlyClient and 60x for NIPoPoWs for $n = 100000$. However, fork-free deployment comes at a cost: dust outputs increase the size of contingent transactions by 93 bytes per referenced input - hence, preventing TxCHAIN from achieving the theoretical improvements outlined in Sect. 5.2. The costs for including a transaction with $c = 1000$ inputs in Bitcoin, at a fee of $3 \cdot 10^{-6}$ BTC per byte, amount to USD 21.2 (as of 5 May 2020).

6.2   Deployment via Soft or Hard Forks

Considering both FlyClient and NIPoPoWs require a soft or hard fork to be deployed in Bitcoin and Ethereum, the minor modifications to transaction validity rules necessary for TxCHAIN could arguably be added in parallel – if FlyClient or NIPoPoW are indeed deployed in practice. In both Bitcoin and Ethereum, TxCHAIN can be deployed as a hard fork by introducing a new

TXEXISTS instruction with the following semantics: (i) Pop one argument, representing the hash of a transaction, from the stack, (ii) push 1 to the stack if the transaction was found or 0 otherwise. Interestingly, Bitcoin allows re-purposing of unused instructions ("OpCodes"), enabling deployment via a soft fork.

Bitcoin: Soft Fork by Re-purposing OP_NOP. Bitcoin allows to introduce new instructions by re-purposing "reserved" OpCodes, e.g. OP_NOP10. These OpCodes are currently ignored during execution, allowing to add additional rules without causing conflicts between upgraded and non-upgraded nodes. Specifically TXEXISTS can be implemented using the following sequence: OP_PUSHDATA1 20 <TXID> OP_NOP10 OP_VERIFY.

On non-upgraded nodes, OP_NOP10 will be ignored and OP_VERIFY will evaluate to true, as the top element of the stack will be non-empty/non-zero (the transaction ID). On upgraded nodes, OP_NOP10 will be interpreted as TXEXISTS, popping the transaction ID from the stack and pushing back 1 if the transaction exist or 0 otherwise. Therefore, OP_VERIFY will fail if and only if the node has been upgraded and the transaction ID does not exist, which enables a soft fork deployment.

A soft fork deployment in Bitcoin avoids the requirement to actually spend UTXOs in contingent transactions. This not only simplifies coordination for provers (no construction needed for the prover to spend from UTXOs), but also reduce the costs per referenced transaction / UTXO from 93 bytes (per input) to 32 bytes per transaction identifier (SHA256 hash) plus 4 bytes for the OpCode flags. This results in an expected 2.8x improvement over the fork-free deployment of TxChain (detailed numbers provided in the full paper version[2]). However, considering the simple deployment of TxChain in Bitcoin without consensus changes, we defer the implementation of TXEXISTS to future work.

Ethereum: New Instruction (Hard Fork). Unlike Bitcoin which uses the UTXO model, Ethereum does not provide a native way of implementing transaction dependencies. Furthermore, the ID of a transaction cannot be accessed from within smart contracts, making it impossible to implement TXEXISTS purely as a smart contract. To deploy TxChain on Ethereum, we hence propose a hard fork introducing TXEXISTS as a new instruction. We implement TXEXISTS in Geth (v1.9.15), the most commonly used Ethereum implementation, using Go 1.14.4 and construct a Solidity (v0.6.7) smart contract to perform TxChain transaction verification using the newly added instruction: the contract takes as input n transaction identifiers and returns true if all are in the valid chain, and reverts otherwise. This way, the (contingent) transaction calling the contract will only succeed, if the n to-be-verified transactions are indeed in the main chain. In Geth, Ethereum transactions are already indexed by hash: checking the existence of a transaction does not require any further indexing, but only a single random read in the underlying LevelDB database. This is equivalent to EXCODESIZE or BALANCE in terms of IO access [10]. However, given that the total number of transactions is vastly higher than the number of addresses, chances of cache miss are higher with TXEXISTS than with BALANCE. Therefore, we assign a conservative price of 2000 gas to the instruction, i.e., more than twice as expensive as the 900 gas of `EXCODESIZE` and `BALANCE`. Finding an optimal pricing would require further benchmarking and is left to future work.

Evaluation. Using the our Geth client, we measure the cost of a transaction contingent on $c = 1147$ other transactions - deriving a conservative value for c by assuming a block gas limit of 5 million [10], i.e., 50% of the block gas limit. Given the 168.01 USD/ETH exchange rate as per 24 April 2020 and a 5 Gwei gas, this results in an upper limit of $\approx$ USD 12.6 per (full) contingent transaction. In more detail, the base costs for the contingent transaction amount to 26,633 gas (0.022 USD) and every additional referenced transaction adds 4,333 gas (0.0036 USD) to the cost. To measure the overall storage and bandwidth improvements when applied to NiPoPoWs and FlyClient, we assume the 2019 average Ethereum transaction size of 499 bytes. We note that storing a single hash in a smart contract on Ethereum, necessary to include the interlink data (NIPoPoW) or MMR root (FlyClient) in a block, requires a 167 byte transaction. Given Ethereum's block height $h = 10000000$ (as of 4 May 2020), $n = 100000$ transactions and $c = 1147$, TxChain achieves a 24x improvement over a soft fork deployment of FlyClient (28x for a hard fork) and a 17x improvement over a soft fork deployment of NIPoPoWs (20x for a hard fork). We provide a detailed breakdown of the storage and bandwidth costs in the full paper version (See footnote 2).

6.3   Case-Study: TxChain for Cross-Chain Transactions

Reducing the number of downloaded block headers and transaction inclusion proofs can be especially useful in the cross-chain setting, where storage and bandwidth costs are priced by the byte. To showcase the applicability of TxChain, we use contingent transactions to verify Bitcoin transactions on Ethereum, e.g. useful in protocols such as XCLAIM [12]. Specifically, we extend BTC-Relay[4], a Bitcoin SPV client implemented as an Ethereum Solidity smart contract, with the TxChain functionality as described in Sect. 4.2 using the fork-free deployment in Bitcoin as presented in Sect. 6.1.

We compare the gas costs when verifying multiple transactions using BTC-Relay before and after applying TxChain: we are able to save up to 66.94% on the Ethereum gas costs. A detailed breakdown of the costs and improvements over the naïve SPV BTC Relay are given in the full paper version; the code is available as open source (See footnote 2). The measured cost improvements are thereby limited by Ethereum's memory pricing function: the costs are linear only up to 724 bytes (equiv. to T_a with $n = 16$ contingent transactions), after which polynomial pricing is applied. Also, we are only able to parse T_a with up to 90 contingent transactions in the smart contract due to Ethereum's block gas limit. As such, the savings achieved by TxChain can be even higher on blockchain platforms with alternative memory pricing models and better support for Bitcoin primitives[5]. Furthermore, applying TxChain to cross-chain SPV

---

[4] github.com/interlay/BTC-Relay-Solidity.

[5] e.g. Polkadot (polkadot.network), RSK (rsk.co) or Liquid (blockstream.com/liquid/).

clients supporting FlyClient or NIPoPoWs - which, at the time of writing, do not yet exist - would further increase the cost savings, as discussed in Sect. 5.

References

1. Back, A.: Enabling blockchain innovations with pegged sidechains (2014). https://blockstream.com/sidechains.pdf. Accessed 05 Jul 2016
2. Bünz, B., Kiffer, L., Luu, L., Zamani, M.: Flyclient: super-light clients for cryptocurrencies. In: 2020 IEEE Symposium on Security and Privacy (SP), IEEE (2020)
3. Fuzzati, R.: A formal approach to fault tolerant distributed consensus. PhD thesis (2008)
4. Garay, J., Kiayias, A., Leonardos, N.: The Bitcoin backbone protocol: analysis and applications. In: Oswald, E., Fischlin, M. (eds.) EUROCRYPT 2015. LNCS, vol. 9057, pp. 281–310. Springer, Heidelberg (2015). https://doi.org/10.1007/978-3-662-46803-6_10
5. Gervais, A., Ritzdorf, H., Karame, G.O., Capkun, S.: Tampering with the delivery of blocks and transactions in bitcoin. In: Proceedings of the 22nd ACM SIGSAC Conference on Computer and Communications Security, pp. 692–705. ACM (2015)
6. Heilman, E., Kendler, A., Zohar, A., Goldberg, S.: Eclipse attacks on bitcoin's peer-to-peer network. In: 24th USENIX Security Symposium (USENIX Security 15), pp. 129–144 (2015)
7. Kiayias, A., Miller, A., Zindros, D.: Non-interactive proofs of proof-of-work. In: Bonneau, J., Heninger, N. (eds.) FC 2020. LNCS, vol. 12059, pp. 505–522. Springer, Cham (2020). https://doi.org/10.1007/978-3-030-51280-4_27
8. Kiayias, A., Russell, A., David, B., Oliynykov, R.: Ouroboros: a provably secure proof-of-stake blockchain protocol. In: Katz, J., Shacham, H. (eds.) CRYPTO 2017. LNCS, vol. 10401, pp. 357–388. Springer, Cham (2017). https://doi.org/10.1007/978-3-319-63688-7_12
9. Nakamoto, S.: Bitcoin: a peer-to-peer electronic cash system (December 2008). https://bitcoin.org/bitcoin.pdf. Accessed 01 July 2015
10. Perez, D., Livshits, B.: Broken metre: Attacking resource metering in EVM. In: Network and Distributed System Security Symposium (NDSS) (2020)
11. Zamyatin, A., et al.: Sok: Communication across distributed ledgers. Technical report, IACR Cryptology ePrint Archive **2019**, 1128 (2019)
12. Zamyatin, A., et al.: Xclaim: trustless, interoperable, cryptocurrency-backed assets. In: 2019 IEEE Symposium on Security and Privacy (SP), pp. 193–210. IEEE (2019)
13. Zamyatin, A., Stifter, N., Judmayer, A., Schindler, P., Weippl, E., Knottenbelt, W.J.: A wild velvet fork appears! inclusive blockchain protocol changes in practice. In: Zohar, A. (ed.) FC 2018. LNCS, vol. 10958, pp. 31–42. Springer, Heidelberg (2019). https://doi.org/10.1007/978-3-662-58820-8_3

VRF-Based Mining Simple Non-outsourceable Cryptocurrency Mining

Runchao Han[1,2]([⊠]), Haoyu Lin[3,4], and Jiangshan Yu[1]

[1] Monash University, Melbourne, Australia
runchao.han@monash.edu
[2] CSIRO-Data61, Sydney, Australia
[3] Bytom Foundation, Singapore, Singapore
[4] ZenGo X, Tel Aviv, Israel

Abstract. This paper introduces VRF-based mining, a simple and effective way of making pooled mining impossible. Instead of using hash functions, VRF-based mining uses Verifiable Random Functions (VRFs) for Proof-of-work (PoW)-based consensus. As VRF binds an output with a secret key, a pool operator should reveal its secret key to outsource the mining process to miners, and miners can anonymously steal cryptocurrency in the pool operator's wallet.

We revisit the definition of *non-outsourceability* in existing research, and identify two properties, namely *punish-mining-reward* and *stealing-unlinkability*. *Punish-mining-reward* specifies that if a pool operator outsources mining to a miner, then the miner can steal mining reward. *Stealing-unlinkability* specifies that the pool operator cannot identify miners stealing mining reward. We show that VRF-based mining satisfies *punish-mining-reward*, but not *stealing-unlinkability*. Nevertheless, the pool operator should take extra effort – which makes maintaining mining pools expensive – to identify mining reward stealers and transfer mining reward before being stolen. In addition, we discuss several considerations on instantiating VRFs for VRF-based mining. Moreover, we experimentally show that VRF-based mining is simple to implement and introduces negligible overhead compared to hash-based mining.

1   Introduction

Bitcoin [27] started the era of cryptocurrency. In Bitcoin, each participant maintains its own ledger. The ledger is structured as a blockchain, i.e., a chain of blocks of transactions. Participants keep executing Proof-of-Work (PoW)-based consensus to agree on blocks and append them to the blockchain. In PoW-based consensus, each participant keeps trying to solve a computationally hard PoW puzzle [16]. Once solving the puzzle, the participant appends its block to the blockchain and gets some coins as reward. By adaptively adjusting the difficulty of PoW puzzles, PoW-based consensus can ensure only one participant solves

© Springer Nature Switzerland AG 2020
J. Garcia-Alfaro et al. (Eds.): DPM 2020/CBT 2020, LNCS 12484, pp. 287–304, 2020.
https://doi.org/10.1007/978-3-030-66172-4_19

the puzzle for each time period with high probability. Participants of PoW-based consensus are also known as miners, the process of solving PoW puzzles is known as mining, and the computation power used for mining is known as mining power.

Due to the limited rate of producing blocks, a miner's reward can be highly volatile if it chooses to mine by himself. To stabilise mining rewards, miners usually choose to join mining pools. A mining pool allows miners to mine on blockchain in the name of the pool operator, and the pool operator distributes the mining reward to solo miners in a fine-grained way. While miners are willing to participate in mining pools, mining pools lead to mining power centralisation. Nowadays, four largest mining pools control more than 51% Bitcoin mining power [5], which can be a lurking threat to blockchain ecosystem. However, mining power centralisation contradicts Bitcoin's design objective – decentralisation, and weakens PoW-based consensus' security [17,27]. To avoid this, researchers have been working on re-decentralising mining power, mainly by non-outsourceable mining [21,26] and decentralised mining pools [15,24,33]. However, existing approaches are either inefficient or ineffective, which will be discussed in Sect. 9 later.

This paper introduces *VRF-based mining*, a surprisingly simple but effective approach to make pooled mining impossible. VRF-based mining replaces hash functions in PoW-based consensus with Verifiable Random Functions (VRFs) [25]. VRF requires a miner to input its secret key to compute the output, so a pool operator should reveal its secret key to miners in order to outsource mining. Thus, any miner can steal mining reward of a block owned by the pool operator anonymously. Our contributions are as follows.

We Analyse the Non-outsourceability of VRF-Based Mining. Miller et al. [26] first formalises the *non-outsourceability* of mining in PoW-based consensus. We find *non-outsourceability* consists of two orthogonal properties, namely *punish-mining-reward* and *stealing-unlinkability*. *Punish-mining-reward* specifies that miners can steal mining reward if the pool operator outsources mining. *Stealing-unlinkability* specifies that the pool operator cannot know who steals mining reward. We then show that VRF-based mining achieves *punish-mining-reward*, but not *stealing-unlinkability*. Nevertheless, the pool operator should take extra effort – which makes maintaining mining pools expensive – to identify mining reward stealers and transfer mining reward before being stolen.

We Discuss Considerations for Instantiating VRF-Based Mining. VRF has four customisable components, namely the elliptic curve, two hash functions between strings and elliptic curve elements, and a normal hash function. We discuss considerations on choosing them for VRF-based mining.

We Evaluate Feasibility of VRF-Based Mining. We implement Elliptic curve-based VRF specified in [19] using Go programming language, and compare its performance with three mainstream mining algorithms SHA256D, Scrypt and CryptoNight. Our results show that VRF-based mining is easy to implement and introduces negligible overhead compared to hash-based mining.

We Show that Partial Outsourcing is Unrealistic. Partial outsourcing is that, a pool operator interactively outsources computation that does not need the secret key to miners. We show that partial outsourcing is unprofitable, as it's both computation-intensive and I/O-intensive.

This paper is organised as follows. Section 2 and Sect. 3 describes preliminaries and the construction of VRF-based mining, respectively. Section 4 revisits the definition of non-outsourceability, and shows VRF-based mining achieves better non-outsourceability than existing proposals. Section 5 discusses concerns of instantiating VRFs for VRF-based mining. Section 6 provides an experimental analysis on the practicality of VRF-based mining. Section 7 discusses why partial outsourcing in VRF-based mining is unprofitable. Section 8 discusses potential problems in VRF-based mining and their solutions. Section 9 summaries related work, and Sect. 10 concludes this paper. We attach the pseudocode of the standardised EC-VRF construction [19] in Appendix.

2   Preliminaries

2.1   PoW-Based Consensus and Mining

Miners participate in PoW-based consensus by *mining*, which works as follows. Given the blockchain's latest view, the miner creates a block template t, which consists of transactions to include, hash of the last block, and other metadata. The miner then tries to solve a PoW puzzle that, the miner should find a nonce n such that $H(t||n)$ is smaller than a difficulty parameter T. Note that $H(\cdot)$ is a one-way hash function, and the miner can only try different nonces until finding a valid one. Once the miner find a valid nonce, it can assemble this nonce and t to a block, and append this block to the blockchain. The miner will get some coins as the reward of mining. By adaptively adjusting T, the rate of new blocks remains stable. If miners mine too many blocks in a previous time period, the protocol will increase T so that miners will mine slower. Otherwise, the protocol will decrease T.

2.2   Mining Pools

As the rate of new blocks is limited, the mining reward of miners is highly volatile, especially for miners with less powerful hardware. To stabilise mining reward, miners usually participate in mining pools. Mining pools enable miners to mine collaboratively and distribute reward in a fine-grained way. A mining pool usually relies on a centralised pool operator. All miners mine in the name of the pool operator, and the pool operator distributes rewards in proportion to miners' contribution.

Concretely, a mining pool works as follows. First, a pool operator specifies the pool difficulty PT—a difficulty lower than the blockchain network—and a search interval $[n_1, n_m]$ of nonces. Then, the pool operator sends the block template t, PT, n_1 and n_m to the miner, and the miner starts to find a nonce in

$[n_1, n_m]$ which satisfies PT. Once finding a valid nonce n_k, the miner sends n_k back to the pool operator. The pool operator then verifies whether n_k produces a hash satisfying PT, and records the miner's contribution (a.k.a. a share) if valid. After a time period (say 24 h), the pool operator calculates the total contribution of each miner, and distributes the mining reward to miners according to their submitted shares. As PT is easier to solve, calculating the mining power of a miner using shares is more fine-grained than using blocks. In this way, each miner is rewarded in a more fine-grained way, so more stably.

2.3 Verifiable Random Functions

Verifiable Random Function (VRF) [25] is a public-key version of cryptographic hash function. In addition to the input string, VRF requires a pair of a secret key and a public key. Given an input string and a secret key, one can compute an output. Anyone knowing the associated public key can verify the correctness of the output, and can also verify the output is generated by the owner of the secret key. Formally, a VRF consists of four algorithms: VRFKeyGen, VRFHash, VRFProve and VRFVerify.

- VRFKeyGen$(1^\lambda) \rightarrow (sk, pk)$: On input security parameter 1^λ, outputs a secret/public key pair (sk, pk).
- VRFHash$(sk, \alpha) \rightarrow \beta$: On input sk and an arbitrary-length string α, outputs a fixed-length output β.
- VRFProve$(sk, \alpha) \rightarrow \pi$: On input sk and α, outputs the proof of correctness π for β.
- VRFVerify$(pk, \alpha, \beta, \pi) \rightarrow \{True, False\}$: On input pk, α, β, π, outputs the verification result $True$ or $False$.

Informally, VRF should preserve the following three security properties [19]:

- *Uniqueness*: Given a secret key sk and an input α, VRFHash(sk, α) produces a unique valid output.
- *Collision Resistance*: It is computationally hard to find two inputs α and α' that VRFHash(sk, α) = VRFHash(sk, α').
- *Pseudorandomness*: It is computationally hard to distinguish the output of VRFHash(sk, α) from a random string if not knowing the corresponding public key pk and proof π.

Algorithm 3 in Appendix A describes the Elliptic-curve-based VRF (EC-VRF) construction standardised in draft-goldbe-vrf [19].

3 VRF-Based Mining

Instead of using a hash function, VRF-based mining uses a VRF to produce outputs that satisfy the difficulty requirement. VRF takes both an input and a secret key to produce an output. The owner of this secret key can produce a proof proving the ownership of its output. Thus, to outsource the mining process,

---

Algorithm 1: Work(sk, pk, tpl, T).

---

  while $nonce+ = 1$ **do**   ▷ Refresh the nonce
     | $blk \leftarrow$ ConstructBlock($tpl, nonce$)   ▷ Assemble block
     | $out \leftarrow$ VRFHash(sk, blk)   ▷ Produce VRF output
     | **if** $out < T$ **then**   ▷ If meeting difficulty
     | | break   ▷ Mining successful
     | **end**
  end
  $\pi \leftarrow$ VRFProve(sk, blk)   ▷ Produce the proof
  $B \leftarrow (blk, pk, out, \pi)$ ▷ Assemble the complete block
  return B

Algorithm 2: Verify(B, T)

  $(blk, pk, out, pi) \leftarrow B$ ▷ Disassemble block
  Require B's coinbase tx is binding to pk
  require($out < T$)   ▷ Check if satisfying diff
  /* Here VRFVerify($\cdot$) ensures: */
  /* 1. out is generated by the owner of sk */
  /* 2. out is a valid output of VRFHash(sk, blk)   */
  require(VRFVerify(pk, blk, out, π))
  ... ▷ Verify other fields
  ... ▷ Verify transactions

---

the pool operator has to reveal its secret key to miners. However, with the secret key, any miner in the mining pool can steal all mining rewards.

Cryptocurrency mining consists of two components, namely mining blocks and verifying blocks. We call the process of mining a block Work($\cdot$), and the process of verifying a block Verify($\cdot$). Algorithm 1 and 2 describe Work($\cdot$) and Verify($\cdot$) of VRF-based mining, respectively.

Work. In Work($\cdot$), the miner - with secret key sk and block template tpl - keeps searching for a *nonce* that can make the VRF output *out* of the block *blk* to meet the blockchain difficulty T. Once finding a valid *nonce* that makes $out < T$, the miner produces proof π, assembles *blk*, *pk*, *out*, π to the complete block B. The miner then broadcasts B to the network.

Verify. Upon a new block B, the verifier runs Verify($\cdot$) to verify B's validity. In addition to verification rules in hash-based mining, Verify($\cdot$) specifies three extra rules. First, the VRF output *out* should be smaller than the difficulty parameter T. Second, B's coinbase transaction should be binding to pk. If the transaction's output stores the public key, then it should equal to pk. If the transaction's output stores the address – which is usually a digest of the public key, then it should equal to the digest of pk. Last, the verifier should run VRFVerify($\cdot$) to check if 1) *out* is produced by the owner of pk, and 2) *out* is a valid VRF output of *blk*.

4 Non-outsourceability Analysis

In this section, we revisit existing definitions on *non-outsourceability*, and show that VRF-based mining achieves strong *non-outsourceability*.

4.1 Revised Definitions

Miller et al. [26] first formalise cryptocurrency mining as *scratch-off puzzles*, and formally define two levels of *non-outsourceability*, namely *weak non-outsourceability* and *strong non-outsourceability*.

- *Weak non-outsourcability*: If the pool operator outsources the mining process, miners can always steal the reward of mining.
- *Strong non-outsourcability*: In addition to *weak non-outsourcability*, the pool operator cannot link the stolen mining reward with the miner who steals it.

Weak non-outsourceability defines the punishment of outsourcing, while *strong non-outsourceability* covers both the punishment and the anonymity of the stealer. We call the property defining the punishment of outsourcing *punish-mining-reward*. The anonymity of stealers defined in [26] is a special case of *transaction unlinkability* [32]: Given two arbitrary transactions, it is hard to know whether their outputs belong to the same secret key. To steal the mining reward in [26], the miner should create a transaction, of which the input is the mining reward and the output points to its address. Finding out who steals the mining reward is equivalent to finding out the address holding the output, and we call the property making such attempt infeasible *stealing-unlinkability*.

4.2 Non-outsourceability of VRF-Based Mining

VRF-based mining achieves *punish-mining-reward*, but not *stealing-unlinkability*. To outsource mining to a miner, the pool operator should share a secret key with it. This enables the miner to steal the mining reward, so VRF-based mining achieves *punish-mining-reward*. The pool operator can give a new secret key and a block template to each miner at every height. If a miner steals mining reward, the pool operator can identify the stealer by the secret key in the transaction stealing the reward. Thus, VRF-based mining does not satisfy *stealing-unlinkability*.

Nevertheless, VRF-based mining makes maintaining mining pools quite expensive. First, the pool operator should monitor stealing behaviours by examining new blocks' coinbase transactions all the time. In addition, every time the pool operator's miners mine a block, the pool operator should transfer mining reward to its own wallet before a miner steals it.

5 Instantiating VRF

In order to implement VRF-based mining, one needs to first instantiate the VRF. VRF in Algorithm 3 has four configurable components, including the elliptic curve and three hash functions. Three hash functions are: $H_1(\cdot)$ mapping an arbitrary-length string into an elliptic curve element, $H_2(\cdot)$ mapping an elliptic curve element into a fixed-length string, and $H_3(\cdot)$ mapping an arbitrary-length string into a fixed-length string. We discuss considerations on choosing these four components for VRF-based mining.

5.1 Elliptic Curve

As neither blockchains and VRF limits the choice of elliptic curves, any elliptic curve can be adapted. For example, among prominent elliptic curves, Edwards25519 [10] can be a promising choice. First, Edwards25519 works on a prime field with the prime number $2^{255} - 19$, which provides sufficient enumeration space for VRF. Second, Edwards25519 supports Ed25519, a fast and secure digital signature algorithm. Last, Edwards25519 is compatible with existing blockchains, as numerous blockchains and projects using VRF adapt Edwards25519 as their underlying elliptic curve [3,4,6].

5.2 Hashing a String to an Elliptic Curve Point $H_1(\cdot)$

The first hash function $H_1(\cdot)$ hashes a string to an elliptic curve point. A standardisation document [28] specifies several hash-to-curve functions [11,14,20,31] that fit into different elliptic curves and satisfy our requirements. Within these functions, Elligator2 [11] is the recommended one for Edwards25519.

5.3 Hashing an Elliptic Curve Point to a String $H_2(\cdot)$

The second hash function $H_2(\cdot)$ hashes an elliptic curve point to a fixed-length string. It can be divided to two steps: 1) encoding an elliptic curve point to a string, and 2) hashing the string using a normal hash function. The encoding step can be bidirectional and unencrypted, so can be done simply by converting a big integer to a string. The hashing step should be cryptographically secure, so can adapt any existing cryptographically secure hash functions.

5.4 Normal Hash Function $H_3(\cdot)$

The third hash function $H_3(\cdot)$ hashes an arbitrary string to a fixed-length string. It is only used in VRFProve($\cdot$) and VRFVerify($\cdot$) i.e., producing and verifying proofs of VRF outputs. The overhead of proving and verification should be minimised, so fast and cryptographically secure hash functions such as Keccak [12] and BLAKE [9] are suitable for $H_3(\cdot)$.

5.5 Memory-Hard Mining

Some PoW-based blockchains—such as Ethereum [36] and Monero [4]—employ memory-hard hash functions in order to minimise advantage of specialised mining hardware and achieve better decentralisation. Different from normal hash functions, the performance of computing memory-hard hash functions is bounded by memory access rather than arithmetic operations in processors. As memory access is much harder to optimise compared to arithmetic operations in processors, high-end hardware cannot outperform low-end hardware greatly in terms of memory-hard functions.

To make VRF-based mining memory-hard, VRFHash($\cdot$) should be memory-hard. VRFHash($\cdot$) of the standardised VRF consists of one $H_1(\cdot)$ hashing, one scalar-point multiplication and one $H_2(\cdot)$ hashing. By making $H_1(\cdot)$ or $H_2(\cdot)$ memory-hard, VRF-based mining will be memory-hard. This can be achieved by embedding a memory-hard hash function such as Ethash [35] and CryptoNight [29] in $H_1(\cdot)$ or $H_2(\cdot)$.

6 Practicality of VRF-Based Mining

In this section, we benchmark VRFs and compare their performance with existing hash functions for mining. The experimental results show that VRF-based mining is easy to implement and introduces negligible overhead compared to hash-based mining.

6.1 Experimental Setting

We implement the standardised EC-VRF in Algorithm 3 using Go programming language, without any optimisation. We use Edwards25519 [10] as the underlying elliptic curve, Elligator2 [11] as $H_1(\cdot)$, SHA-3 as the hash function. Edwards25519, SHA-3 and the encoding of points on Edwards25519 are supported by Go's standard library. We use open-source implementations of SHA256D[1], Scrypt[2], and CryptoNight[3]. All experiments run on a MacBook Pro with a 2.2 GHz Intel Core i7 Processor and a 16 GB DDR4 RAM. Each group of experiments consists of ten runs, and we take the average value of ten values as the result.

6.2 VRF v.s. Existing Mining Algorithms

We compare the performance of VRF with existing mining algorithms. Figure 1a shows the runtime of VRF and other algorithms. SHA256D is much faster than other algorithms, as SHA256D is simply executing SHA256 twice. In addition, VRFVerify($\cdot$) is slightly slower than VRFProve($\cdot$), and VRFProve($\cdot$) is slightly slower than VRFHash($\cdot$). Last, although without optimisation, all functions of VRF are much faster than Scrypt and CryptoNight.

---

[1] https://github.com/seehuhn/sha256d.
[2] https://github.com/elithrar/simple-scrypt.
[3] https://github.com/Equim-chan/cryptonight.

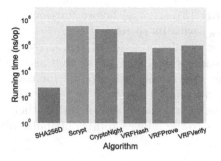
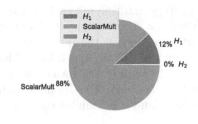

(a) Comparing the runtime of VRF and other mining algorithms.

(b) Runtime breakdown of VRFHash($\cdot$).

Fig. 1. Evaluation of VRF.

6.3 Runtime Breakdown of VRF

We profile VRFHash($\cdot$) by evaluating its runtime of each step. Figure 1b shows that, the elliptic curve scalar multiplication $\gamma \leftarrow h^{sk}(\cdot)$ takes 88% of VRFHash($\cdot$)'s running time. This is because we use SHA-3 as the hash function in $H_1(\cdot)$ and $H_2(\cdot)$, and SHA-3 is designed to be fast. Meanwhile, we calculate the elliptic curve scalar multiplication using the trivial double-and-add method without any optimisation, thus is much slower than $H_1(\cdot)$ and $H_2(\cdot)$. There have been optimisation techniques for elliptic curve scalar multiplication, and some miners may exploit them for accelerating mining. This may be unfair to other miners. To avoid this, we suggest to replace $H_1(\cdot)$ and/or $H_2(\cdot)$ with slow hash functions such as Scrypt and CryptoNight.

7 Profitability of Partial Outsourcing

The pool operator may still have opportunity to partially outsource mining. The mining function VRFHash consists of three steps: 1) $h \leftarrow H_1(\alpha)$, 2) $\gamma \leftarrow h^{sk}$ and 3) $\beta \leftarrow H_2(\gamma)$. Non-outsourceability is from the second step $\gamma = h^{sk}$, as it requires the knowledge of the pool operator's secret key sk. The pool operator can outsource the first step $h = H_1(\alpha)$ and the last step $\beta = H_2(\gamma)$ by distributing different αs and γs to miners, respectively. However, we show that such partial outsourcing is very inefficient and unprofitable compared to outsourcing in hash-based mining, due to the computing and I/O overhead.

7.1 Partial Outsourcing

In VRF-based mining, the pool operator can outsource $H_1(\cdot)$ or $H_2(\cdot)$. To outsource $H_1(\cdot)$, the pool operator generates a series of nonces $\{n_1, \ldots, n_m\}$, then sends the series and the block template t to a miner. Then, the miner computes $H_1(n_i)$ for each $i \in [1, m]$, then sends back all $h_i = H_1(\cdot)$ hashes to the pool operator. The pool operator should verify $\{h_1, \ldots, h_m\}$ before starting the second step—multiplying each of $\{h_1, \ldots, h_m\}$ with its secret key sk.

After the second step, the pool operator obtains a series of $\{\gamma_1, \ldots, \gamma_m\}$. To outsource $H_2(\cdot)$, the pool operator first sends $\{\gamma_1, \ldots, \gamma_m\}$ as well as the pool difficulty PT to the miner. Then, the miner calculates $H_2(\gamma_i)$ for each $i \in [1, m]$, compare the hashes with PT, and sends back γs that satisfy the difficulty (denoted as Γ). Upon receiving these γs, the pool operator verifies their correctness and accumulates the mined shares to the miner's total contribution.

7.2   First Obstacle: Overhead of Verification

The first obstacle of partial outsourcing is verifying hashes from miners. For outsourcing $H_1(\cdot)$, the pool operator should verify all of $\{h_1, \ldots, h_m\}$. For outsourcing $H_2(\cdot)$, The pool operator should verify σs satisfying PT. Such verification overhead is even more than the pool operator mining by himself. Thus, partial outsourcing unprofitable.

7.3   Second Obstacle: Overhead of I/O

To bypass the first obstacle, the pool operator and the miners can trust each other and omit the verification. This is possible as pooled mining is beneficial for them: the pool operator can earn some fees from the miners, while miners can stabilise their mining reward.

However, partial outsourcing can still be unprofitable even without the verification. VRF-based mining is extremely I/O intensive, and the network bandwidth of the pool operator's server is limited. To outsource a single $H_1(\cdot)$, the pool operator should at least receive a $H_1(\cdot)$ hash from the miner. To outsource a single $H_2(\cdot)$, the pool operator should at least send a σ to the miner.

Assume a pool operator with bandwidth BW (in bytes/s), and the pool operator can achieve optimal bandwidth utilisation on mining. Assume each the pool operator should transfer N bytes for outsourcing each mining attempt. Then, the maximum hashrate that the pool operator can achieve is

$$\text{Maximum hashrate} = \frac{BW}{N}$$

Either a $H_1(\cdot)$ hash or a γ (a point on the elliptic curve) is at least 32 bytes. If outsourcing both $H_1(\cdot)$ and $H_2(\cdot)$, the maximum hashrate the pool operator can support is Maximum Hashrate $= \frac{BW}{64}$ (h/s). If outsourcing only one of them, the maximum hashrate is Maximum Hashrate $= \frac{BW}{32}$ (h/s).

Figure 2 shows relationship between the server's network bandwidth and the maximum hashrate the server can achieve. The result shows that, existing servers can only achieve limited hashrate on partial outsourcing. On AWS [1], I3EN Metal is the server with most bandwidth, which is 3,500 MB/s. However, I3EN Metal can support hashrate less than $\frac{1}{10}$ of Monero's total mining power. Within those mainstream cryptocurrencies, Monero's hashrate is the least. Even

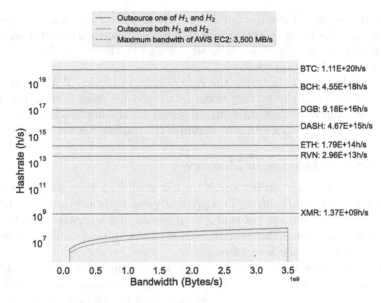

Fig. 2. Server bandwidth v.s. maximum hashrate. Data of server bandwidth and hashrate were fetc.hed from AWS [1] and CoinWarz [2] at 01/03/2020, respectively.

if the pool operator rents a cluster of I3EN Metal machines for more bandwidth, I3EN Metal is quite expensive (10.848 USD per hour), leading to high expense of maintaining a mining pool. Therefore, partial outsourcing in VRF-based mining is costly and unrealistic.

8   Discussions

While eliminating mining pools can improve decentralisation, it also introduces new problems. We discuss two problems and their possible solutions, namely 1) high reward variance and 2) secret key leakage in memory.

8.1   Weaker Security Guarantee of PoW-Based Consensus

The reason of miners joining mining pools is that, miners may not obtain stable income via solo mining. Miners may be discouraged to mine if their rewards are highly volatile. With weaker incentive of mining, fewer miners will join the blockchain. The blockchain will then attract less mining power, which weakens the security of PoW-based consensus.

This problem can be addressed by making the mining reward fine-grained. Miller et al. [26] proposes the *multi-tier reward scheme*. In multi-tier reward scheme, the mining difficulty is divided into different levels, and miners can mine blocks satisfying different difficulty levels arbitrarily. In this way, mining reward is distributed in a fine-grained way, so lowers the reward variance.

StrongChain [30] introduces the notion of *Collaborative PoW*, where miners are encouraged to mine blocks together and the mining reward is distributed in proportion to miners' contributions. Bobtail [13] and HotPoW [22] further explore the Collaborative PoW approach.

Another solution is to increase the rate of mining blocks. With more blocks mined in a time unit, the mining reward can also be more stable. For example, although of independent interest, protocols for scaling blockchains such as sharding [34] and DAG [23] can also stabilise the mining reward variance.

8.2   Secret Key Leakage in Memory

VRF-mining requires the secret key, so a miner should keep its secret key in plaintext in memory *all the time*. This gives adversaries opportunity to steal the secret key from the memory. For example, if the mining software has a bug that enables hackers to access the memory space of the mining software, then the hacker can easily steal the secret key.

For VRF-based mining, keeping secret keys in memory is inevitable. To achieve *non-outsourceability*, the secret key should be combined to the mining process. As long as mining does not stop, the secret key should be kept in plaintext in memory. This applies to all protocols that execute frequently and require secret keys, such as TLS.

There have been several different ways to protect in-memory secret keys. First, the miner can isolate the scalar multiplication to a software or hardware enclave. Note that the encalves are unnecessary to be general-purpose. Second, the process of the mining software can destroy itself once detecting anomalous memory access attempts. Third, the miner can isolate mining from the blockchain node. For example, it can run the mining process independently with its blockchain node process. In this way, if an adversary compromises its node but not the operating system, the adversary still cannot read the secret key in another process. Fourth, it can run the mining process in an offline machine that can only communicate with its blockchain node. Fifth, Oblivious RAM (ORAM) is a promising primitive to protect sensitive data in memory. ORAM allows CPUs to access data in memory while the data in memory is encrypted and the access pattern is hidden. Last, the miner can use a new secret key for each block, so that leaking a secret key only affects the reward of a single block.

9   Related Work

We review related research on preventing mining pools, and compare them with VRF-based mining. We classify related research to two types, namely pooled-mining-unfriendly mining protocols and decentralised mining pools.

9.1   Mining Protocols

There are two mining protocols aiming at discouraging or breaking mining pools: the *non-outsourceable scratch-off puzzle* [26] and the *Two Phase Proof-of-Work* (*2P-PoW*) [21]. Table 1 summarises our comparisons.

Table 1. Comparison between mining protocols. NSP is short for non-outsourceable scratch-off puzzle.

	VRF-based mining	NSP-1	NSP-2	2P-PoW
Punish-mining-reward	✓	✓	✓	✓
Stealing-unlinkability	✗†	✗	✓	✗
No partial outsourcing	✓	✓	✓	✗
Support randomised signatures	✓	✓	✓	✗
No complex cryptography	✓	✓	✗	✓

†The pool operator should take non-negligible effort to deanonymise stealing behaviours.

Table 2. Comparison with decentralised mining pools.

	VRF-based mining	P2Pool	SmartPool	BetterHash
Complexity	-	Blockchain	Smart contract	-
Decentralisation	Mining	Mining	Mining	Select txs

Non-outsourceable Scratch-Off Puzzle. Miller et al. [26] formalises mining as *scratch-off puzzles*, defines *non-outsourceability*, and proposes two *non-outsourceable scratch-off puzzles*. One achieves *weak non-outsourceability*—miners can steal the mining reward, and the other achieves *strong non-outsourceability*—miners can steal the mining reward anonymously.

The weak non-outsourceable scratch-off puzzle works as follows. First, the miner randomly generates a Merkle tree. Second, the miner randomly chooses a nonce, samples some leaves of the Merkle tree according to the nonce, and hashes their Merkle proofs together to a single hash. If this hash meets the difficulty requirement, then the nonce is valid. Last, the miner binds the valid nonce and its block template together to a valid block.

In order to outsource the mining process, the mining pool should distribute the search space of nonces to miners. A miner can steal the mining reward by binding valid nonces it finds with its own block template. However, this stealing process is not anonymous. Unlike existing PoW-based consensus where miners can choose both nonces and block templates, the weak non-outsourceable scratch-off puzzle only allows miners to choose nonces, so all miners share the same search space of nonces. Thus, the pool operator can link the nonce in the stolen block with the miner who is assigned with the search space covering this nonce. To achieve *strong non-outsourceability*, the strong non-outsourceable scratch-off puzzle replaces the plaintext nonce in the block with a Zero Knowledge Proof proving the statement "I know a valid nonce".

As discussed in Sect. 4, while being simpler and more efficient than non-outsourceable scratch-off puzzle, our VRF-based mining achieves *strong non-outsourceability*.

2P-PoW. Eyal and Sirer proposes 2P-PoW [21], a mining protocol that discourages pooled mining. In 2P-PoW, mining consists of two phases, and each phase has a difficulty parameter. A miner should find a nonce that makes the block to pass two phases: 1) the SHA256D hash of the block meets the first difficulty, 2) the SHA256 hash of the signature of the block meets the second difficulty. As the second requirement requires the secret key, pool operators cannot outsource the second phase.

Compared to VRF-based mining that makes pooled mining impossible, 2P-PoW is partially outsourceable by outsourcing the first phase. In addition, 2P-PoW requires the digital signature algorithm to be deterministic, while commonly used digital signatures such as ECDSA rely on randomisation. If the signature is randomised, the pool operator can make use of all nonces from miners that meet the first phase but fail the second phase. Given a nonce meeting the first difficulty, the pool operator repetitively generates signatures to meet the second requirement. Moreover, how to adjust two difficulties still remains unknown and requires some simulations.

9.2   Decentralised Mining Pools

Decentralised mining pool is a type of mining pools that work in a decentralised way: miners mine in the name of themselves and share reward in a fine-grained way. In this way, miners are rewarded stably while mining power is not controlled by pool operators. Table 2 summarises the comparison between VRF-based mining with decentralised mining pools.

P2Pool [33] is a decentralised mining pool for Bitcoin. Instead of using a centralised server, P2Pool uses a blockchain called *share-chain* to receive shares from miners. All miners in P2Pool participate in the PoW-based consensus of share-chain. Once a miner finds a share on Bitcoin, it appends a block to the share-chain. The block consists of the share and a coinbase transaction that rewards miners in proportion to their shares. Once a miner mines a block that also satisfies Bitcoin's difficulty, it submits this block to the Bitcoin blockchain, and miners are rewarded according to the coinbase transaction. P2Pool suffers from several limitations. First, handling the difficulty of mining shares is hard. If the difficulty is high, miners' reward will still be volatile. If the difficulty is low, there will be numerous low-difficulty shares, which introduces huge overhead on broadcasting and receiving shares. Second, shares on share-chain are much more frequent than blocks on Bitcoin blockchain, and the share-chain suffers from high orphan rate. Last, existing research shows that P2Pool is vulnerable to temporary dishonest majority [37].

SmartPool [24] is another decentralised mining pool. Instead of using a blockchain, SmartPool employs smart contracts to track shares from miners. This implies that SmartPool cannot work on blockchains without smart contracts. In addition, as blockchains achieve limited throughput, blockchains can only handle a limited number of shares for each time unit. In this way, distributing mining reward may also be delayed, especially when a large number of miners participate in the SmartPool. Moreover, as the SmartPool smart contract should verify the validity of blocks, miners should submit the entire block—including transactions—to the SmartPool. Verifying blocks introduces non-negligible computing overhead and transaction fee, and storing blocks in smart contracts also introduces non-negligible overhead on storage.

BetterHash [15] is another decentralised mining protocol, which has been integrated into *Stratum V2* [8], the next generation of the *Stratum* [7] pooled mining protocol. In *BetterHash*, the block operator allows miners to choose transactions and construct blocks in its name, rather than constructing block templates by himself. Thus, *BetterHash* only contributes to the decentralisation of constructing blocks, but does not improve the decentralisation of mining power.

10   Conclusion and Future Work

In this paper, we propose VRF-based mining, that can make pooled mining in Proof-of-work-based consensus impossible. VRF-based mining is simple and intuitive: miners produce digests of blocks using VRFs rather than hash functions, so that a pool operator should reveal its secret key to outsource the mining process to other miners. We show that VRF-based mining achieves good *non-outsourceability* guarantee. In addition, we discuss considerations of instantiating VRF-based mining. Moreover, we experimentally proves that VRF-based mining is simple to implement and introduces negligible overhead.

Adding *stealing-unlinkability* to VRF-based mining remains as an open problem. The key – as discussed by Miller et al. [26] – is to exclude everything that the pool operator can exploit to track miners from mining. A possible construction can be excluding Merkle root from mining and replacing VRF with *Anonymous VRF* [18] – a VRF variant where VRF outputs cannot be linked to any secret key. We consider concrete construction as future work.

Acknowledgement. We thank Mikerah, Omer Shlomovits, Silur, John Trump, Cheng Wang and anonymous reviewers for insightful discussion and feedback.

A   The Standardised Elliptic-Curve-Based VRF

Algorithm 3 describes the Elliptic-curve-based VRF (EC-VRF) construction standardised in draft-goldbe-vrf [19].

Algorithm 3: The Elliptic-curve-based VRF (EC-VRF) construction standardised in draft-goldbe-vrf [19].

Preliminaries:
- G is a cyclic group of prime order q with generator g.
- $H_1(\cdot)$ hashes an arbitrary-length string into an element in G.
- $H_2(\cdot)$ hashes an element in G into a fixed-length string.
- $H_3(\cdot)$ hashes an arbitrary-length string into a fixed-length string.
- random($[x, y]$) uniformly and randomly picks a number in $[x, y]$.

Algorithm VRFKeyGen(1^λ):
  $sk = \mathsf{random}([0, q-1])$
  $pk = g^{sk}$
  return (sk, pk)
Algorithm VRFHash(sk, α):
  $h = H_1(\alpha)$
  $\gamma = h^{sk}$
  $\beta = H_2(\gamma)$
  return β
Algorithm VRFProve(sk, α):
  $h = H_1(\alpha)$
  $\gamma = h^{sk}$
  $k = \mathsf{random}([0, q-1])$
  $c = H_3(g, h, g^{sk}, h^{sk}, g^k, h^k)$
  $s = k - c \cdot sk \pmod{q}$
  $\pi = (\gamma, c, s)$
  return π
Algorithm VRFVerify(pk, α, β, π):
  $u = pk^c \cdot g^s$
  $h = H_1(\alpha)$
  if $\gamma \notin G$ **then return** 0
  $v = \gamma^c \cdot h^s$
  if $c \neq H_3(g, h, pk, \gamma, u, v)$ **then return** 0
  return 1

References

1. Amazon EBS-Optimized Instances. https://docs.aws.amazon.com/AWSEC2/latest/UserGuide/ebs-optimized.html
2. Cryptocurrency Mining Profitability Calculator. https://www.coinwarz.com/cryptocurrency
3. Home — ethereum.org. https://ethereum.org/
4. Monero - Secure, Private, Untraceable. https://www.getmonero.org
5. Pool Stats - btc.com. https://btc.com/stats/pool. Accessed 24 Nov 2019
6. Tendermint. https://tendermint.com/
7. Stratum Mining Protocol - Bitcoin Wiki (2015). https://en.bitcoin.it/wiki/Stratum_mining_protocol. Accessed 08 Dec 2019
8. Stratum v2 — The Next Generation Protocol for Pooled Mining (2019). https://stratumprotocol.org/. Accessed 08 Dec 2019

9. Aumasson, J.P., Henzen, L., Meier, W., Phan, R.C.W.: Sha-3 proposal blake. Submiss. NIST **92** (2008)
10. Bernstein, D.J., Duif, N., Lange, T., Schwabe, P., Yang, B.Y.: High-speed high-security signatures. J. Cryptogr. Eng. **2**(2), 77–89 (2012)
11. Bernstein, D.J., Hamburg, M., Krasnova, A., Lange, T.: Elligator: elliptic-curve points indistinguishable from uniform random strings. In: Proceedings of the 2013 ACM SIGSAC Conference on Computer & Communications Security, pp. 967–980. ACM (2013)
12. Bertoni, G., Daemen, J., Peeters, M., Van Assche, G.: Keccak. In: Johansson, T., Nguyen, P.Q. (eds.) EUROCRYPT 2013. LNCS, vol. 7881, pp. 313–314. Springer, Heidelberg (2013). https://doi.org/10.1007/978-3-642-38348-9_19
13. Bissias, G., Levine, B.N.: Bobtail: improved blockchain security with low-variance mining. In: ISOC Network and Distributed System Security Symposium (2020)
14. Brier, E., Coron, J.-S., Icart, T., Madore, D., Randriam, H., Tibouchi, M.: Efficient indifferentiable hashing into ordinary elliptic curves. In: Rabin, T. (ed.) CRYPTO 2010. LNCS, vol. 6223, pp. 237–254. Springer, Heidelberg (2010). https://doi.org/10.1007/978-3-642-14623-7_13
15. Corallo, M.: Betterhash mining protocol(s) (2019). https://github.com/TheBlueMatt/bips/blob/betterhash/bip-XXXX.mediawiki. Accessed 08 Dec 2019
16. Dwork, C., Naor, M.: Pricing via processing or combatting junk mail. In: Brickell, E.F. (ed.) CRYPTO 1992. LNCS, vol. 740, pp. 139–147. Springer, Heidelberg (1993). https://doi.org/10.1007/3-540-48071-4_10
17. Eyal, I., Sirer, E.G.: Majority is not enough: bitcoin mining is vulnerable. Commun. ACM **61**(7), 95–102 (2018)
18. Ganesh, C., Orlandi, C., Tschudi, D.: Proof-of-stake protocols for privacy-aware blockchains. In: Ishai, Y., Rijmen, V. (eds.) EUROCRYPT 2019. LNCS, vol. 11476, pp. 690–719. Springer, Cham (2019). https://doi.org/10.1007/978-3-030-17653-2_23
19. Goldberg, S., Papadopoulos, D., Vcelak, J.: Draft-goldbe-vrf: Verifiable random functions (2017)
20. Icart, T.: How to hash into elliptic curves. In: Halevi, S. (ed.) CRYPTO 2009. LNCS, vol. 5677, pp. 303–316. Springer, Heidelberg (2009). https://doi.org/10.1007/978-3-642-03356-8_18
21. Ittay, E., Sirer, Gün, E.: How to disincentivize large bitcoin mining pools (2014). http://hackingdistributed.com/2014/06/18/how-to-disincentivize-large-bitcoin-mining-pools/
22. Keller, P., Böhme, R.: HotPoW: finality from proof-of-work quorums. arXiv preprint arXiv:1907.13531 (2019)
23. Li, C., Li, P., Zhou, D., Xu, W., Long, F., Yao, A.: Scaling nakamoto consensus to thousands of transactions per second. arXiv preprint arXiv:1805.03870 (2018)
24. Luu, L., Velner, Y., Teutsch, J., Saxena, P.: SmartPool: practical decentralized pooled mining. In: 26th {USENIX} Security Symposium ({USENIX} Security 17), pp. 1409–1426 (2017)
25. Micali, S., Rabin, M., Vadhan, S.: Verifiable random functions. In: 40th Annual Symposium on Foundations of Computer Science (Cat. No. 99CB37039), pp. 120–130. IEEE (1999)
26. Miller, A., Kosba, A., Katz, J., Shi, E.: Nonoutsourceable scratch-off puzzles to discourage bitcoin mining coalitions. In: Proceedings of the 22nd ACM SIGSAC Conference on Computer and Communications Security, pp. 680–691. ACM (2015)
27. Nakamoto, S., et al.: Bitcoin: a peer-to-peer electronic cash system (2008)

28. Scott, S., Sullivan, N., Wood, C.A.: Hashing to elliptic curves. Tech. rep., Internet-Draft draft-irtf-cfrg-hash-to-curve-03. Internet Engineering Task (2019)
29. Seigen, M.J., Nieminen, T.: Neocortex, and antonio m. juarez. cryptonight hash function. cryptonote (March 2013)
30. Szalachowski, P., Reijsbergen, D., Homoliak, I., Sun, S.: Strongchain: transparent and collaborative proof-of-work consensus. arXiv preprint arXiv:1905.09655 (2019)
31. Ulas, M.: Rational points on certain hyperelliptic curves over finite fields. arXiv preprint arXiv:0706.1448 (2007)
32. Van Saberhagen, N.: Cryptonote v 2.0 (2013)
33. Voight, F.: P2Pool: decentralized, dos-resistant, hop-proof pool (2011)
34. Wang, J., Wang, H.: Monoxide: scale out blockchains with asynchronous consensus zones. In: 16th {USENIX} Symposium on Networked Systems Design and Implementation ({NSDI} 19), pp. 95–112 (2019)
35. Wiki, E.: Ethash. GitHub Ethereum Wiki (2017). https://github.com/ethereum/wiki/wiki/Ethash
36. Wood, G., et al.: Ethereum: a secure decentralised generalised transaction ledger. Ethereum Proj. Yellow Pap. **151**(2014), 1–32 (2014)
37. Zamyatin, A.: Decentralized mining pools: security and attacks. https://www.alexeizamyatin.me/files/Decentralized_Mining-Security_and_Attacks.pdf

On the Selection of the LN Client Implementation Parameters

Luis E. Oleas-Chávez[1]([envelope]), Cristina Pérez-Solà[2,3],
and Jordi Herrera-Joacomartí[1,3]

[1] Department of Information Engineering and Communications,
Universitat Autònoma de Barcelona, Bellaterra - Cerdanyola, Spain
luis.oleas@e-campus.uab.cat, jordi.herrera@uab.cat
[2] Internet Interdisciplinary Institute (IN3), Universitat Oberta de Catalunya,
Barcelona, Spain
cperezsola@uoc.edu
[3] CYBERCAT - Center for Cybersecurity Research of Catalonia, Barcelona, Spain

Abstract. The Lightning Network (LN) is a payment network deployed on top of Bitcoin. In the LN, the payer and the payee do not need to have an open direct channel to transact: they can transact through channels by means of other users of the network, that act as intermediaries for the payments. The parameters of the contracts being used in these multihop payments determine the level of security offered, but also the usefulness of the LN as a payment network. In this paper, we evaluate the impact of tuning the parameters of the contracts for the security and performance of the payment network, and provide recommendations on the values for those parameters, taking into account the trade-off between network utility and security.

Keywords: Lightning network · Payment channel networks · Bitcoin · Blockchain · Security

1 Introduction

The Lightning Network is a P2P network built on top of Bitcoin protocol. Its main feature is to allow two users to transact with each other with all the benefits that payment channels offer, but without having to open a direct channel between themselves. The mechanism implemented is by creating multihop routes, that carry payments through other LN users.

Multihop payments in the LN are performed in two stages: on the first stage, a set of contracts (HTLCs) are created, and the funds to satisfy these contracts are locked; on the second stage, either the payment becomes effective or the contracts are cancelled. In either way, funds are unlocked, and become available again in the LN.

Users pay fees to nodes in the middle of multihop payments, to compensate for their work. However, if a multihop payment is cancelled in the second stage,

J. Garcia-Alfaro et al. (Eds.): DPM 2020/CBT 2020, LNCS 12484, pp. 305–318, 2020.
https://doi.org/10.1007/978-3-030-66172-4_20

such fees are not paid. This introduces a vector of attack: an attacker can lock
users' funds in the network by performing the first stage of the payment, and
then cancelling the payment. Moreover, attackers can try to hold payments in the
first stage for a long time, increasing the economical damage to the participants.

Previous studies [13] show that the cost of this attack is low when LN nodes
use default configuration values for several key parameters. The cost of the attack
can be increased by adjusting the parameters of HTLCs negotiation. However,
such parameters also impact on the performance of the payment network, since
the same values that can mitigate the attack can also reduce the performance
in terms of multihop payment availability.

In this paper, we tune two different parameters of the LN implementations:
cltv_expiry_delta and *locktime_max*. The goal is to define a proper value for
those parameters that maximizes the performance of the LN in terms of payment
success rate while minimizing the damages of an attack.

The rest of the paper is organized as follows. Section 2 provides the required
background of the LN to understand the performed analysis. In Sect. 3, we define
the two sets of metrics used to evaluate the parameters, regarding both the
performance of the LN (in terms of payment success) and resilience to security
attacks. Section 4 describes how we setup the experiment scenario and Sect. 5
provides the results of our findings. Finally, Sect. 6 concludes the paper and
provides some guidelines for further research.

2   Background

After its initial proposal in 2016 and its first stable release in 2018, the research
community laid down its attention on LN. The reason lies on that LN's solution
overcomes the scaling and instant payment issues that deter to Bitcoin as a viable
payment method. The exchange of Bitcoins on this peer-to-peer (P2P) network
takes place outside of the blockchain by means of payment channels created
by nodes that deploy any version of a LN client [5], being either: LND [16],
c-lightning [7] or eclair [6]. A node that runs any of those clients can connect to
other LN nodes as well as to a node in the Bitcoin P2P network. This connectivity
structure is essential to exchange Bitcoin transactions without setting them down
on the blockchain, i.e. payment channels are the fundamental element of LN.

To open the aforementioned payment channel, a peer sends a funding transaction to the blockchain to create the channel with a fixed *capacity*. On the contrary, to close it, the peer sends a settlement transaction. Once peers establish
the channel, they can exchange transactions, which last a fraction of time because
of its non-essential update on the blockchain. Any single transaction, between a
couple of peers, shifts the *balance* when processing the mutually signed commitment transaction. The commitment transaction contains the payment amount
and the fee charged.

However, to provide a more extended service, the LN allows multihop approach, in which a node can perform a payment from a source to a target that
does not share a direct payment channel. Hence, a payment route is a bond by

which a transaction traverses a defined path through nodes with sufficient funds charging a nominal fee.

On most LN implementations, the source node, which performs the payment, constructs a path using a route discovery through the maintenance of an up-to-date topology structure of the LN network. Although, a LN implementation can provide to source node a suitable route, with the number of hops and their charged fees, toward a certain target node, that source node might compute a payment route as needed with the information available on this P2P environment.

Hashed Timelock Contracts (HTLC) [3] enforces an atomic exchange among the nodes on the route, i.e. all the hop payments succeed or none will proceed to redeem the funds. HTLC creates a bond between a pair of nodes, sender A and receiver B, to perform payments, in which B can redeem the bitcoins deposited by A only if B provides both a preimage of hash value and a digital signature. As a conceptualization of a contract, the sender A settles an expiration date to the deposit performed in the payment. In case, the receiver B does not commit a preimage on time, A can provide a digital signature to retrieve the deposit. On a route payment, with two or more hops, the target node sends to the source node a computed hash value $h(x)$, in which x is a generated random value. For instance, let us assume that node A performs a payment to node B through node C, i.e. $A \leftrightarrow B \leftrightarrow C$. Node A, which receives $h(x)$ from C, generates a HTLC to route the payment to B, which later routes a generated HTLC with the same $h(x)$ to C. Then, C, which generated x, reveals the preimage to B to redeem the transaction. Likewise, B reveals x to A to redeem the payment.

Under the basic concepts described above and following the categorization on [2], payment channels maintain an operational cycle with the following steps:

- **channel funding**: a node sends a funding transaction to the blockchain at the time it opens a payment channel.
- **payment execution**: channel peers reflect the new balance when a node sent a commitment transaction.
- **channel closing**: a node sends the last commitment transaction to the blockchain when any of the channel peers wants to close it.
- **unbalancing** results at the moment when either a node reaches a zero balance or performs payments on the channel following a single direction.
- **multihop payment** is essential when a direct channel does not exist between peers. HTLC enforces a via to achieve a payment from a source node to a target node. However, the contract may incur on any of the following states: a source node creates a HTLC that has to reach to the target node through intermediate nodes (HTLC Establishment); a target node forwards a revealed preimage through the intermediate nodes, which will redeem their corresponding payment, to the source node (HTLC Fulfillment); and a source node or intermediate nodes do not receive the revealed preimage and the timelock in the contract expires (HTLC Failure).

Even though the LN exhibits the properties of a P2P network, its connectivity could fall upon against target attacks [1,11]. Therefore, it is important to analyse the robustness of the LN. On [10], authors simulated attacks, such as the case an attacker destroys nodes with the high degree of connectivity, and possible countermeasures, as a defender that re-establish connectivity by adding nodes to the network. Furthermore, proposals such as [19] aim to enhance routing throughput by leaving the payment channel balanced after performing a transaction.

2.1 Parameters that Define Multihop Routes

Let us consider the next scenario, $A_1 \rightarrow A_2 \rightarrow \cdots \rightarrow A_i \rightarrow \cdots \rightarrow A_n$, in which node A_i may not proceed with the payment due to an unknown reason. In that case, locks will arise among the hops performed between nodes A_1 and A_i. The reason comes from the policy taken by A_1 that sets a time that bounds the total locking time, known as the absolute expiration block height θ. On the event of an unsuccessful payment, θ sets the time to release the amount involved on a locked payment route. Therefore, as nodes route the payment to their subsequent nodes, the value of θ decreases after each hop. The value by which the total timelock is decreased at each hop is advertised by each node of LN, and is known as $cltv\_expiry\_delta$ [18] (δ), i.e. δ defines the tolerated difference in blocks specified by each node along the route. It is worth to mention that the value of δ may differ depending on the direction that a transfer traverses the same channel, because each node sets that value. With regard to the target node, the $min\_final\_cltv\_expiry$ [17] value comes into play instead of δ.

On the other hand, the public data released by each node allows to create a route from a source node to a target node. The source node provides the initial θ value, that is decreased at each hop on the route. For a payment path to be valid, the last hop must still be able to set a timelock he agrees to, that is, at least $(\theta_0 - \sum_{i=2}^{n} \delta_i) > 0$. Although, this mechanism allows to source node to limit the duration of a locktime over a payment, a malicious node could try to lock indefinitely the funds of intermediate nodes by setting an initial large θ. Moreover, among the LN implementations, the δ value can be set by default to either 40 blocks or 144 blocks.

Moreover, to avoid long timeouts, nodes set their $locktime\_max$ (T_{max}), the maximum time they allow for HTLC expiration values in outgoing payments on the channel. In consequence, the relation $\theta < T_{max}$ must always hold, to provide a node the option to accept a payment as an intermediate node on that route. Otherwise, the intermediate node must refuse to route the payment and the source node must compute a different path. Besides the maximum hop limit (set to at most 20 hops), δ and T_{max} form part of the parametric consideration taken by a source node to create a payment route.

Despite the parameters explained above, an intermediate node goal is to make a profit from routing payments. Whence, at the time a source node constructs a route, it must gather specific information about fees or minimum payment amount that each intermediate node will charge or agree to transfer during using its channel. As part of that information, nodes propagate the minimum amount payment, in millisatoshi, that will agree to transfer, known as *htlc_minimum_msat* [18]. Additionally, a node reveals a couple of values related to fees: *fee_base_msat* [17], fee comprised on each HTLC as the constant amount charged by a node that performs a transfer, and *fee_proportional_millionths* [17], fee that increases proportionally per amount transferred.

This paper is focused on multihop payments. We intend to provide recommendations on the optimum values of *cltv_expiry_delta* and T_{max} configuration parameters, to provide the best trade-off between the efficiency of the network and its resilience to attacks.

Detailed explanations of the main concepts about the LN can be found in the literature [4,12,14]. The BOLTs [15] also provide a more technical description of LN specifications.

3   Metrics

In order to determine the most appropriate values for the parameters that we want to assess, we define two different sets of metrics. Such metrics are somehow opposite since the extreme values for one of the sets produce poor results in the other one, so a trade-off between both values has to be achieved.

3.1   Metrics to Evaluate Performance

Lightning Network (LN) is meant to perform payments between users. With this general objective in mind, we could measure the performance of the LN based on the possibility that two different users of the network would be able to perform a payment between them. However, as we point out in Sect. 2, not all pairs of nodes in the LN share a channel so the majority of payments between nodes are performed through multihop routes. *A* may perform a payment to *B* if there is a path between both users with enough funds, and the configuration parameters of the implementations allow to do so.

We measure the performance by repeatedly picking two random nodes in the lightning network and trying to perform a payment between them. For each chosen pair, payments of different amounts are attempted, from 1 to 4294967 satoshis (the maximum payment commonly allowed in the LN implementations), tacking as intermediate amounts all base 2 possible values between those limits. Performance is measured, for each amount, as the percentage of successful payments from the total number of attempts.

Notice that path availability is a feature that depends on different parameters. First of all, it depends on the topology of the LN, defined by each of the channels created in the network. A path must exist between *A* and *B* to allow a payment between them. However, such basic requirement is not the only one needed. Capacity of each channel that the payment traverses must be bigger that the payment amount itself. In fact, even this condition is not enough since the channel capacity must be properly distributed and the balance of each member of each channel has to be greater than the payment (in the right direction of the payment).

Nevertheless, none of the above requirements to perform a payment between two users depends on the parameters that we want to evaluate. An intermediate node in a path may refuse to route a payment if the proposed HTLC expiration time does to meet his requirements, either because it is to high (higher than his T_{max}) or because it is too low (and thus can not ensure a difference of δ with the next hop's HTLC expiration time). For his reason, lowering T_{max} or increasing δ configuration values in the LN clients may reduce the probability that a random payment can be successfully performed in the network.

3.2 Metrics to Evaluate Security

Recently, security of the LN has been analyzed in different research papers and some attacks have been presented. One of those attacks [13] may lock the funds of a victim by performing payments through that node that take longer to finish than needed. The attack takes advantage of the multihop ability and the possibility to loop a single route multiple times through a single user. The severity of the attack can be measured with two different parameters (as defined in [13]): the Attack Effort Ratio (AER) and the $\Delta(b)$ function.

Definition 1. *The **Attack Effort Ratio** (AER) is the ratio between the capacity needed to perform the attack and the capacity that the attack blocks, i.e.,*

$$AER = \frac{C_{attack}}{C_{blocked}}$$

AER measures the profitability of the attack. The lower the AER, the more efficient the attack is in economic terms, and thus the higher the incentive for the adversary to perform such attack.

To measure the time during which the balance is locked, the Δ function can be defined.

Definition 2. *The $\Delta(b)$ **function** is a time based decreasing function that measures the total capacity blocked w.r.t. the time during which the attack has been conducted. The block generation count, b, is used as the time unit for this function.*

For instance, $\Delta(0) = C_{blocked}$ since it provides the total capacity blocked at the initial time of the attack, when no new block is yet generated. Eventually, $\Delta(b) = 0$ for a large b, since the blocking effectiveness of the attack decreases when more blocks are generated.

Since the attack is performed through multiple payments, the $\Delta(b)$ function is computed taking into account the expiration values of each payment that forms the attack[1]. If we define $\Delta_i(b)$ as the capacity blocked by payment i during b blocks, then $\Delta(b) = \sum_i \Delta_i(b), \forall i \in attack$.

For comparison purposes, we define two single value metrics that compress the $\Delta(b)$ function: Total Blocked Time and Normalized Total Blocked Time.

---

[1] See [13] for further details.

Total Blocked Time, TBT, of the attack is the sum of the $\Delta(b)$ values:

$$TBT = \sum_{b=0}^{\infty} \Delta(b)$$

The **normalized** TBT, $\widetilde{TBT}$, is defined as:

$$\widetilde{TBT} = \frac{TBT}{C_{blocked} \cdot \max\{T_{max}\}},$$

where $\max\{T_{max}\}$ is the maximum default value of T_{max} used in all the experiments. Therefore, $0 < \widetilde{TBT} \leq 1$, and the ideal attack with $\widetilde{TBT} = 1$ would be blocking $C_{blocked}$ capacity during 5000 blocks, that is, more than 34 days.

4   Experiment Setup

The goal of the experiments is to evaluate the impact the values of δ and T_{max} have on both the security of the network and its performance, using the metrics defined in Sect. 3.

The experiments consist on a set of simulations where the parameters δ and T_{max} are adjusted for all the nodes in the network. Then, on the one hand, performance is evaluated over the resulting graph (as described in Sect. 3.1) and, on the other hand, a lockdown attack [13] is simulated over the network and the effectiveness and cost of the attack are also evaluated (using the metrics described in Sect. 3.2).

Specifically, each of the experiments is performed in the following way:

1. A LN mainnet graph describing nodes and the existing channels is obtained from a lightning client.
2. Balances are assigned randomly using different probability distributions, and taking into account the capacity of each channel as described in the LN graph.
3. All nodes of the network are configured to simulate their behaviour assuming a certain pair of (δ, T_{max}) values.
4. Evaluation of the performance of the payment network (enforcing the restrictions given by δ and T_{max} values, and taking into account existing channels and their balances).
5. A lockdown attack is simulated over the network.
6. The cost and effectiveness of the attack is evaluated using the AER and normalized TBT metrics.

The following sections describe the LN graph, the balances assignation procedure, and the tested values of the (δ, T_{max}) pair.

4.1 LN Payment Channel Graph and Balances

Our simulations will assess the effectiveness of the attack given the actual topology of the network. We base our simulations on the attack algorithm described in [13]. The simulations are made on a snapshot of the LN running on top of the bitcoin mainnet and taken on the 12nd of January, 2020.

Both to execute an attack on the network and to evaluate its performance, we need to complement the information of the LN graph with additional data, specifically, the balance of each channel in the network.

The LN does not publicly disclose channels' balances: each user only knows the balances of the channels he participates into them. One alternative to retrieve such balances will be to execute an attack on the network (as described in [9]). However, instead of performing such attack, we have assigned the balances of each channel using different statistical distributions, trying to reproduce the different scenarios that could be found in the network. In order to assign balances to channels, we proceed in the following way: for each channel, first the balance of one of the nodes is randomly selected using one of the selected distributions, and taking the capacity of the channel as the maximum possible value to generate. Then, the balance of the other node in the channel is set as the remaining balance (that is, the capacity minus the balance). Five different distributions are used to assign balances to channels: *deterministic, uniform, normal, exponential,* and *beta.* The *deterministic* distribution always assigns half of the capacity of the channel to each of the nodes; the *normal* distribution is used with $\mu = 0.5$ and $\sigma = 0.2$; the *exponential* distribution uses $\lambda = 1$; and the *beta* distribution $\alpha = \beta = 0.25$.

4.2 δ and T_{max} Values

We have simulated the network with 16 combinations of δ and T_{max} values. In particular, we have tested all combinations of $T_{max} \in \{432, 1008, 2016, 5000\}$ and $\delta \in \{14, 40, 144, 288\}$.

The tested values include the ones found in the most popular LN client implementations (see Table 1), as well as one additional value for each parameter: a value of 432 (three times 144) for T_{max} and a value of 288 for δ (the double of the maximum default value in any implementation) are also tested. This allows us to test scenarios for which the T_{max}/δ ratio is less than 2, and thus restricts multihop payments.

Table 1. δ and T_{max} values found in the most popular LN clients.

	lnd (old)	lnd (new)	c-lightning	eclair
T_{max}	5000	5000	2016	1008
δ	144	40	14·	144

5   Experiment Results

This section summarizes the results of the experiments. For each of the probability distributions, the same experiment is repeated 10 times, and the averages of the results are presented here.

5.1   Performance

Figure 1 shows the performance results when using a normal distribution to generate channel balances. Each of the individual heatmaps shows the percentage of random payments for which there are valid multihop paths for a specific amount of satoshis.

To understand these results it is important to note that the diameter of the graph is 7. Moreover, regardless of any restrictions imposed by the configuration parameters of the nodes (δ and T_{max}), only 21% of the payments between any two random nodes on the graph can be executed (due to the structure of the graph itself). For the payments that can indeed be done, the median number of hops is between 3 and 4 (depending on the specific configuration of balances), with an average around 3.75.

Configurations for (δ, T_{max}) with values $(288, 432)$, $(288, 1008)$ and $(144, 432)$ have a T_{max}/δ ratio lower than the graph's diameter. Therefore, their results differ significantly from all the other configurations.

- Regardless of the amount, payments with (δ, T_{max}) = $(288, 432)$ always fail. This is because this configuration of parameters does not allow any multihop route, and thus payments may succeed only if two randomly selected nodes have a direct channel.
- Configurations $(288, 1008)$ and $(144, 432)$ have a T_{max}/δ ratio of 3.5 and 3, respectively. These values are close to the median of the paths found. This is why there is a performance decay when using these two configurations (with respect to those that have a ratio higher than the graph's diameter). As expected, the percentage of successful payments decreases with the increase of the payment amount, since available balances limit payments.
- All other configurations have similar performance, regardless of the specific (δ, T_{max}) values. Again, the percentage of successful payments decreases with the increase of the payment amount, going from 21% for lower amounts, down to 1.9% for payments of the maximum amount.

For space constraints, we have not included the results for the other four distributions. However, the results are very similar, and the same conclusions can be extrapolated to them.

5.2   Security

Table 2 shows the values of the metrics used to evaluate security (AER and the normalized TBT, $\widetilde{TBT}$) again for instances where balances were assigned using a normal distribution.

The general trend that can be observed is that increasing δ and/or decreasing T_{max} makes the attack more difficult for the attacker. Specifically, increasing δ and/or decreasing T_{max} results in:

– higher (or, on some specific configurations, equal) AER values. This implies the attacker needs to be in possession of more bitcoins in order to perform the attack, because more capacity in the channels the attacker creates for the attack is needed. The bitcoins spent in capacity can be recovered once the attack is finished, but the attacker must have them as long as the attack lasts.
– more (or, on some specific configurations, equal) channels needed. This implies a higher economic cost for the attacker which needs to pay more bitcoins in fees to open those channels. The attacker needs to spend these bitcoins (that is, he does not get the bitcoins back once the attack has finished).
– lower (or, on some specific configurations, equal) $\widetilde{TBT}$ values, which means the attacker is able to block the victim during shorter amounts of time.

There are a couple of exceptions to the previous tendencies. On the one hand, for the configuration $(\delta, T_{max}) = (288, 432)$ the attacker is not able to block the victim, because no multihop payments can be done with these parameters. Therefore, the attack has no cost for the attacker (since no capacity is blocked). On the other hand, for $(\delta, T_{max}) = (144, 2016)$ the tendency for $\widetilde{TBT}$ deviates from the rest. The reason is that the higher amount of resources spent by the attacker (more channels and capacity) allow for longer blocking times.

Table 2. Attack metrics results for different tested parameters with a normal distribution balance.

T_{max}	δ	EAR	Blocked capacity	Channels needed	$\widetilde{TBT}$
432	14	0.138	95.92%	34.2	0.04
432	40	0.274	95.84%	66.9	0.02
432	144	0.840	75.88%	179.0	0.02
432	288	0.000	0.00%	0.0	0
1008	14	0.138	95.92%	34.2	0.15
1008	40	0.138	95.92%	34.2	0.07
1008	144	0.528	95.88%	127.9	0.08
1008	288	0.890	85.34%	201.5	0.07
2016	14	0.138	95.92%	34.2	0.34
2016	40	0.138	95.92%	34.2	0.26
2016	144	0.187	95.98%	46.4	0.06
2016	288	0.528	95.88%	127.9	0.15
5000	14	0.138	95.92%	34.2	0.92
5000	40	0.138	95.92%	34.2	0.83
5000	144	0.138	95.92%	34.2	0.51
5000	288	0.154	95.92%	38.1	0.17

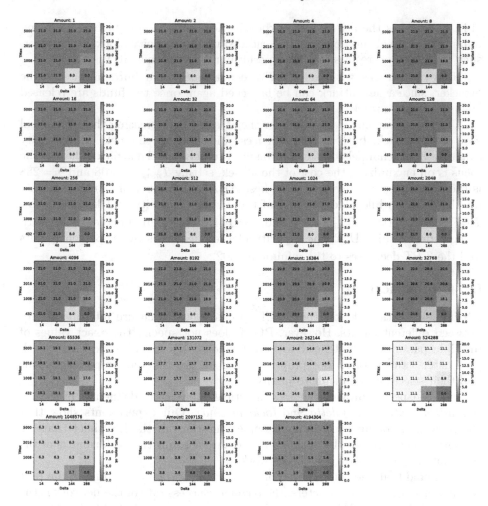

Fig. 1. Payment performance for different (δ, T_{max}) pairs

5.3   Discussion

From the perspective of the performance of the payment network, any (δ, T_{max}) configuration except for the three most restrictive ones $((288, 432), (288, 1008)$ and $(144, 432))$ offers similar results. Therefore, we should focus on the security properties offered by these similar configurations in order to choose the best pair of values without affecting the performance of the payment network.

Depending on the security metric chosen to evaluate the success of the attack, different pairs of values could be chosen.

If the focus is on minimizing the time the attacker is able to lock funds, then $(40, 432)$ and $(144, 432)$ are the best choices, since they both minimize $\widetilde{TBT}$.

(144, 432) makes the attack more expensive for the attacker (higher AER and number of channels needed) and less successful (less capacity blocked), however, such configuration results in a poor performance as we show in Fig. 1.

However, attacks with low $\widetilde{TBT}$ are not much of a burdensome for the attacker, since a new attack can be launched again once the funds are released from a previous attack.

Therefore, one may want to hinder the attacker by increasing the economical cost of the attack, both in terms of fees paid to open channels and capacity available in his channels that has to be used to perform the attack. Then, if the focus is on maximizing the cost of the attack, setting $T_{max} = 1008$ and $\delta = 288$ is the best choice: it provides the highest AER and number of channels needed for the attack, while blocking 85% of the victim's capacity and keeping a low $\widetilde{TBT}$ (0.07). Setting $T_{max} = 432$ and $\delta = 144$ is also a good choice, since with a slight decrease in AER, the capacity blocked decreases by 10 percent points and the $\widetilde{TBT}$ decreases to the minimum, 0.02.

6 Conclusion

LN implementations follow the BOLT specifications to ensure interoperativity between different clients. However, BOLT does not specify the exact values of multiple parameters that need to be set when a LN client is executed. Such parameter setup is often not proper defined for the different implementations and their selection is difficult to justify.

In this paper we provide the first analytical approach to define two of the LN parameters: *cltv_expiry_delta* and *locktime_max*. Our experiments show that the parameters defined in the main implementations of the LN client that are currently in use are not the optimal, taking into account the performance of the payments and the security of the network.

We found that the combination of $T_{max} = 432$ and $\delta = 40$ is one of the best to choose. With these parameters, the payment success rate of the network is the same than the main LN implementations, but the metrics related to the attacks reflect a worse scenario for the attacker: the total time that an attacker can lock the funds of a victim ($\widetilde{TBT}$) is reduced, at least, by a factor of 4 with respect to the parameters used by other implementations, maintaining at the same time, the funds needed to perform the attack (EAR) in a moderate level.

This paper has focused on the impact of two parameters, that affect the timeout of HTLCs, in both the security and the performance of the network. Regarding security, we have focused on protecting the network from lockdown attacks, that attempt to freeze the LN funds of the victims. Further work could try to assess how the network responds to other kinds of attacks, for instance, attacks trying to flood the blockchain by closing multiple channels at the same time [8]; or to consider other metrics when evaluating network performance, for instance, not only the ability to make payments but also their cost in fees.

Acknowledgment. This work was supported in part by the Spanish Government, under Grant RTI2018-095094-B-C22 "CONSENT".

References

1. Albert, R., Jeong, H., Barabási, A.L.: Error and attack tolerance of complex networks. Nature **406**(6794), 378–382 (2000)
2. Conoscenti, M., Vetrò, A., De Martin, J.C.: Hubs, rebalancing and service providers in the lightning network. IEEE Access **7**, 132828–132840 (2019)
3. Decker, C., Wattenhofer, R.: A fast and scalable payment network with bitcoin duplex micropayment channels. In: Pelc, A., Schwarzmann, A.A. (eds.) SSS 2015. LNCS, vol. 9212, pp. 3–18. Springer, Cham (2015). https://doi.org/10.1007/978-3-319-21741-3_1
4. Di Stasi, G., Avallone, S., Canonico, R., Ventre, G.: Routing payments on the lightning network. In: 2018 IEEE International Conference on Internet of Things (iThings) and IEEE Green Computing and Communications (GreenCom) and IEEE Cyber, Physical and Social Computing (CPSCom) and IEEE Smart Data (SmartData), pp. 1161–1170. IEEE (2018)
5. Donet Donet, J.A., Pérez-Solà, C., Herrera-Joancomartí, J.: The bitcoin P2P network. In: Böhme, R., Brenner, M., Moore, T., Smith, M. (eds.) FC 2014. LNCS, vol. 8438, pp. 87–102. Springer, Heidelberg (2014). https://doi.org/10.1007/978-3-662-44774-1_7
6. Eclair: A scala implementation of the lightning network (2020). https://github.com/ACINQ/eclair
7. Elements Project: C-lightning - a lightning network implementation in C (2019). https://github.com/ElementsProject/lightning
8. Harris, J., Zohar, A.: Flood & loot: a systemic attack on the lightning network. arXiv preprint arXiv:2006.08513 (2020)
9. Herrera-Joancomartí, J., Navarro-Arribas, G., Ranchal-Pedrosa, A., Pérez-Solà, C., Garcia-Alfaro, J.: On the difficulty of hiding the balance of lightning network channels. In: Proceedings of the 2019 ACM Asia Conference on Computer and Communications Security, Asia CCS 2019, pp. 602–612. ACM, New York (2019). https://doi.org/10.1145/3321705.3329812, http://doi.acm.org/10.1145/3321705.3329812
10. Lee, S., Kim, H.: On the robustness of lightning network in bitcoin. Pervasive Mob. Comput. **61**, 101108 (2020)
11. Lin, J.H., Primicerio, K., Squartini, T., Decker, C., Tessone, C.J.: Lightning network: a second path towards centralisation of the bitcoin economy. arXiv preprint arXiv:2002.02819 (2020)
12. McCorry, P., Möser, M., Shahandasti, S.F., Hao, F.: Towards bitcoin payment networks. In: Liu, J.K.K., Steinfeld, R. (eds.) ACISP 2016. LNCS, vol. 9722, pp. 57–76. Springer, Cham (2016). https://doi.org/10.1007/978-3-319-40253-6_4
13. Pérez-Solà, C., Ranchal-Pedrosa, A., Herrera-Joancomartí, J., Navarro-Arribas, G., Garcia-Alfaro, J.: LockDown: balance availability attack against lightning network channels. In: Bonneau, J., Heninger, N. (eds.) FC 2020. LNCS, vol. 12059, pp. 245–263. Springer, Cham (2020). https://doi.org/10.1007/978-3-030-51280-4_14
14. Poon, J., Dryja, T.: The bitcoin lightning network: scalable off-chain instant payments (2016)
15. Samokhvalov, A., Poon, J., Osuntokun, O.: Basis of lightning technology (BOLTs) (2018). https://github.com/lightningnetwork/lightning-rfc
16. Samokhvalov, A., Poon, J., Osuntokun, O.: The lightning network daemon (2018). https://github.com/lightningnetwork/lnd
17. Samokhvalov, A., Poon, J., Osuntokun, O.: Lightning network in-progress specifications. BOLT 11: Invoice protocol for lightning payments (2018). https://github.com/lightningnetwork/lightning-rfc

18. Samokhvalov, A., Poon, J., Osuntokun, O.: P2P node and channel discovery. BOLT 7: Onion routing protocol (2018). https://github.com/lightningnetwork/lightning-rfc
19. Sivaraman, V., et al.: High throughput cryptocurrency routing in payment channel networks. In: 17th {USENIX} Symposium on Networked Systems Design and Implementation ({NSDI} 20), pp. 777–796 (2020)

Privacy Preserving Netting Protocol
for Inter-bank Payments

Hisham S. Galal$^{(\boxtimes)}$ and Amr M. Youssef

Concordia Institute for Information Systems Engineering, Concordia University,
Montréal, QC, Canada
H_galal@encs.concordia.ca

Abstract. Banks transfer money and securities instantaneously on a
gross basis by utilizing Real-Time Gross Settlement (RTGS) systems.
Central banks are in charge of managing and operating RTGS systems,
and they require each local inter-bank payment instruction to be processed by them. Accordingly, contemporary RTGS systems face many
challenges including unconditional trust and privileges given to the central banks, and the inherent single point of failure vulnerability associated with centralized systems. To address these challenges, some financial institutions are starting to embrace blockchain technology. Project
Jasper and Project Ubin are two successful preliminary attempts. However, these projects do not preserve participants' privacy, and more
importantly, they lack liquidity saving mechanisms to resolve the frequently occurring gridlock state. An efficient way to resolve gridlock is
to settle payment instructions on a netting basis. In this paper, we propose a decentralized netting protocol that ensures the correctness of the
netting result, while hiding the transferred amounts and preserving recipients' privacy. We evaluate the protocol's performance on Ethereum and
show that the proposed protocol achieves its desired security properties
while being feasible to deploy in practice.

Keywords: Netting · zkSNARK · Ethereum · Smart contract

1 Introduction

Traditionally, banks use Real-Time Gross Settlement (RTGS) systems [1] to
settle inter-bank payment instructions. The country's central bank is the sole
operator of its RTGS system. It enforces each bank to have a local account
with liquidity above a certain limit. To settle a payment instruction, the central
bank debits the instruction's amount from the sender account while crediting
the same amount to the recipient atomically. The settlement process is instantaneous (i.e., in real-time) if the sender has sufficient liquidity. Otherwise, the
payment instruction is pushed to an outgoing queue associated with the sender's
account. The outgoing queue is a priority queue where higher priority payment
instructions are pushed ahead of lower ones. Moreover, payment instructions
that have the same priority level are settled according to a "First In First Out"

© Springer Nature Switzerland AG 2020
J. Garcia-Alfaro et al. (Eds.): DPM 2020/CBT 2020, LNCS 12484, pp. 319–334, 2020.
https://doi.org/10.1007/978-3-030-66172-4_21

(FIFO) policy. Once the sender's liquidity becomes sufficient, the highest priority pending outgoing payment instructions are settled automatically.

Gridlock refers to the state when pending payment instructions cannot be settled on a gross basis due to insufficient liquidity. Therefore, to resolve the gridlock state, RTGS systems utilize a Liquidity Saving Mechanism (LSM) [2] to settle payment instructions on a netting basis. To illustrate the gridlock resolution, consider the scenario shown in Fig. 1 where the RTGS system is initially in a gridlock state because none of the banks has sufficient liquidity to settle its outgoing payment instruction. Although banks can borrow some funds from the central bank to resolve gridlock, the available credit may still be insufficient to settle payment instructions. Therefore, banks prefer to utilize LSM before resorting to credit. Central banks perform LSM since they have a global view on all pending payment instructions.

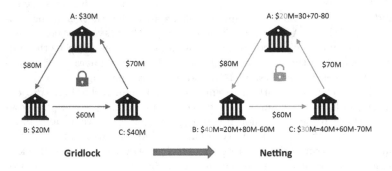

Fig. 1. An example for resolving gridlock state in RTGS

With the growing volume of inter-bank payments, contemporary RTGS systems face many security challenges. Most importantly, central banks have privileges on all payment instructions, and they require unconditional trust to maintain the ledgers in RTGS. Moreover, RTGS as centralized systems are vulnerable to the inherent single point of failure problem. To face these challenges, some RTGS operators are beginning to embrace the blockchain technology. Project Jasper [3] and Project Ubin [4] are some of such successful attempts to utilize blockchain. Blockchain alone is not a silver bullet to solve all of the above problems, however, one can build cryptographic protocols utilizing it to provide the required functionality in a trustless manner while preserving participants' privacy (e.g., see [5–7]). More specifically, the migration of traditional RTGS to the blockchain requires an efficient decentralized netting method to resolve gridlock while delivering better privacy for participants.

Contributions. The contributions of this paper are two-fold:

1. We design a decentralized netting protocol that provides confidential payments while preserving recipients' privacy.
2. We evaluate the protocol's performance on Ethereum.

The rest of this paper is organized as follows. Section 2 presents a brief review of some related work on utilizing blockchain in RTGS systems. Section 3 presents the cryptographic primitives utilized in our protocol. In Sect. 4, we describe the netting problem and show a decentralized protocol to solve it. Section 5 provides the design of the proposed protocol. In Sect. 6, we evaluate the performance of our protocol when implemented on top of Ethereum. Finally, in Sect. 7, we present our conclusions.

2 Related Work

Project Jasper [3] and Project Ubin [4] are two successful deployed projects that investigate the advantages of migrating traditional RTGS to the blockchain. They managed to resolve the single point of failure issue while achieving an immediate gross settlement. However, they do not include LSM functionality, which is an important requirement in RTGS systems.

Wang *et al.* [8] introduced an end-to-end prototype based on Hyperledger Fabric enterprise blockchain platform [9]. The prototype supports gross settlement, gridlock resolution, and reconciliation for inter-bank payment business. Gridlocks are resolved through a timestamp-based algorithm, which shares enough information among participants without the risk of privacy violation. The prototype relies on a central party to check the correctness of the netting result. Furthermore, while it hides the amounts in payment instructions, it reveals the net amounts.

Cao *et al.* [10] proposed a decentralized netting protocol that guarantees netting correctness. The participants submit their local settlements to a smart contract. The protocol hides payment amounts using Pedersen commitments and utilizes extensive zero-knowledge range proofs. Furthermore, to obfuscate the links between senders and recipients, participants can send payment instructions with empty amounts. Obviously, these empty instructions are also associated with zero-knowledge proofs, which add extra overhead to the protocol.

3 Preliminaries

3.1 Notations

Let $\mathbb{G}$ denote an elliptic curve group with a generator $\mathcal{G}$ of prime order q defined over a field $\mathbb{F}_p$. We assume the Decisional Diffie Hellman (DDH) holds in $\mathbb{G}$. Let λ denote a security parameter. We denote lists by bold symbols such as $\boldsymbol{x} = [x_1, \ldots, x_n] = [x_i]_1^n$ of size $n = |\boldsymbol{x}|$. Let $[N]$ denote the list of integers $\{1, \ldots, N\}$. Let $r \leftarrow_\$ \mathbb{Z}_q$ denote randomly and uniformly sampling a value r in $\mathbb{Z}_q$. We denote a zero-knowledge proof of knowledge statement by $\mathbf{PoK}\{(x; w) : \mathcal{R}(x, w)\}$, where x is a public input, w is a witness, and $\mathcal{R}(x, w)$ is a binary decidable relation. Let H be a cryptographic collision resistant hash function, and the symbol $||$ denote the concatenation operator.

3.2 ElGamal Encryption over Elliptic Curve

We utilize ElGamal encryption scheme over the elliptic curve [11] group $\mathbb{G}$. Let $f : \mathbb{Z}_q \rightarrow \mathbb{G}$ be an efficient bijective function that maps message values in $\mathbb{Z}_q$ to points in group $\mathbb{G}$. The encryption scheme consists of the following a probabilistic polynomial-time (PPT) algorithms:

- $(x, \mathcal{Y}) \leftarrow \mathcal{K}(1^\lambda)$. It generates a secret key $x \leftarrow_\$ \mathbb{Z}_q$ and a public key $\mathcal{Y} \leftarrow x\mathcal{G}$.
- $\mathcal{C} = (\mathcal{C}_1, \mathcal{C}_2) \leftarrow \mathcal{E}(m, \mathcal{Y})$. It encrypts a message $m \in \mathbb{Z}_q$ using the public key $\mathcal{Y}$, and outputs a ciphertext $\mathcal{C} = (r\mathcal{G}, f(m) + r\mathcal{Y})$, where $r \leftarrow_\$ \mathbb{Z}_q$.
- $m \leftarrow \mathcal{D}(\mathcal{C}, x)$. It decrypts the ciphertext $\mathcal{C}$ using the secret key x, and outputs $m \leftarrow f^{-1}(\mathcal{C}_2 - x\mathcal{C}_1)$.

Note that we assume the function $f : \mathbb{Z}_q \to \mathbb{G}$ is additively homomorphic such that $f(m_1) + f(m_2) = f(m_1 + m_2)$. Accordingly, the encryption scheme becomes additively homomorphic as well. For example, given two ciphertext $\mathcal{C}_a = (r_a\mathcal{G}, f(m_a) + r_a\mathcal{Y})$ and $\mathcal{C}_b = (r_b\mathcal{G}, f(m_b) + r_b\mathcal{Y})$ encrypted by the same public key, we can get a ciphertext for $m_a + m_b$ as $\mathcal{C}' = \mathcal{C}_a + \mathcal{C}_b = (r_a\mathcal{G} + r_b\mathcal{G}, f(m_a) + f(m_b) + r_a\mathcal{Y} + r_b\mathcal{Y}) = ((r_a + r_b)\mathcal{G}, f(m_a + m_b) + (r_a + r_b)\mathcal{Y})$.

3.3 zkSNARK

Let $\mathcal{R} = (x, w)$ be a polynomial-time decidable binary relation where x refers to a statement instance, and w refers to a witness. Let $\mathcal{L}$ be the NP language corresponding to the relation $\mathcal{R}$. We say that Ψ is a publicly verifiable zero-knowledge Succinct Non-interactive Argument of Knowledge (zkSNARK) [12] for $\mathcal{L}$ if Ψ contains the following three PPT algorithms:

1. $crs \leftarrow \mathcal{K}(1^\lambda)$. It take the security parameter λ as input, and runs a setup routine to generate a Common Reference String (CRS) $crs = (pk, vk)$ along with a trapdoor td, where pk and vk denote the *proving key* and *vk verification key*, respectively.
2. $\pi \leftarrow \mathcal{P}(pk, x, w)$. It generates a proof π to prove that $\mathcal{R}(x, w)$ holds.
3. $\{0, 1\} \leftarrow \mathcal{V}(vk, x, \pi)$. It verifies the proof π for the instance x and returns either 0 (reject) or 1 (accept).

If the trapdoor td is leaked, then the prover can generate fraudulent proof that will be accepted by the verifier. Similarly, the verifier can exploit td to extract information about the witness. Therefore, the common reference string generation algorithm $\mathcal{K}$ is either run by a trusted third party, or by utilizing a Multi-Party Computation (MPC) protocol [13] when the former option is not viable.

   In this paper, we utilize one of the most efficient construction [14] as it generates the smallest proof (i.e., two elements in $\mathbb{G}_1$ and one element in $\mathbb{G}_2$, where $\mathbb{G}_1$ and $\mathbb{G}_2$ are asymmetric bilinear groups). To verify a proof, the verifier needs to perform three pairing operations before deciding whether to accept or reject the proof. It is worth mentioning that the proof verification operation has to take into account the public inputs and performs some operations on them before checking the zkSNARK proof. More precisely, for each public input encoded as $\mathbb{F}_p$ element, the verifier performs two operations: scalar point multiplication and point addition.

4   The Netting Problem

We follow the notations defined in [10] to illustrate the netting problem. Let N denote the number of participants and P_i refer to the ith participant. Let $\boldsymbol{Q}$ denote the list of all outgoing payment queues, which is defined as:

$$\boldsymbol{Q} = [\boldsymbol{Q}_1, \ldots, \boldsymbol{Q}_N]$$
$$\boldsymbol{Q}_i = [Q_{i,1}, \ldots, Q_{i,n_i}] \text{ where } n_i = |\boldsymbol{Q}_i|$$
$$Q_{i,k} = (Rec_{i,k}, V_{i,k}) \text{ where } V_{i,k} > 0$$
$$Rec_{i,k} \in \{P_j\}_{j=1,\ j \neq i}^{N}$$

A payment instruction $Q_{i,k}$ consists of two fields: a recipient denoted by $Rec_{i,k}$ and an outgoing amount denoted by $V_{i,k}$. Note that, if there are multiple payment instructions to the same recipient, then they are aggregated in a single payment instruction $Q_{i,k}$, where $V_{i,k}$ is the total amount. Furthermore, for each payment queue $\boldsymbol{Q}_i$, we define a settlement indicator $\boldsymbol{x}_i$ as:

$$\boldsymbol{x} = [\boldsymbol{x}_1, \ldots, \boldsymbol{x}_N]$$
$$\boldsymbol{x}_i = [x_{i,1}, \ldots, x_{i,n_i}], \text{ where } x_{i,k} = \begin{cases} 1 & \text{if payment } Q_{i,k} \text{ will be settled} \\ 0 & \text{otherwise} \end{cases}$$

Given $\boldsymbol{x}$, we define the following functions for a participant P_i:

$$T_i(\boldsymbol{x}) = \sum_{k=1}^{n_i} x_{i,k}$$
$$S_i(\boldsymbol{x}) = \sum_{k=1}^{n_i} x_{i,k} V_{i,k}$$
$$R_i(\boldsymbol{x}) = \sum_{j=1}^{N} \sum_{k=1}^{n_i} x_{j,k} V_{i,k} \text{ where } Rec_{j,k} = P_i$$

where $T_i(\boldsymbol{x})$ denotes the number of payment instructions that will be settled, $S_i(\boldsymbol{x})$ denotes the total outgoing amount, and $R_i(\boldsymbol{x})$ denotes the total incoming amount. Let $\hat{B}_i$ and $\tilde{B}_i$ denote the ex-ante and ex-post balances of participant P_i (i.e., balance before and after netting, respectively). The balance relationship is defined as:

$$\tilde{B}_i = \hat{B}_i - S_i(\boldsymbol{x}) + R_i(\boldsymbol{x}) \tag{1}$$

The netting problem is to find the solution that satisfies the following constraints:

1. The **liquidity** constraint which dictates that the ex-post balance of each participant after netting must be non-negative.

$$\forall i \in [N] \ \tilde{B}_i \geq 0$$

2. The **sequence** constraint which requires payment instructions to be settled according to their priority order [15].

$$\forall i \in [N], \ k \in [n_i - 1] \ x_{i,k+1} \leq x_{i,k}$$

Let $h(\boldsymbol{x}_i)$ denote the index of lowest priority payment instruction in $\boldsymbol{Q}_i$ that will be settled, which is defined as:

$$h(\boldsymbol{x}_i) = \begin{cases} 0 & \text{if } \forall k \in [n_i] \ x_{i,k} = 0 \\ max(k) & \text{where } x_{i,k} = 1 \end{cases}$$

3. The **optimality** constraint which ensures settling the highest possible number of payment instructions by maximizing $\sum_{i=1}^{N} T_i(\boldsymbol{x})$.

4.1 Decentralized Netting Protocol

We describe the decentralized netting protocol introduced in [10] to resolve the gridlock over a variable number of rounds. The protocol assumes transparent communication between participants. In other words, this protocol does not provide any privacy, and participants have a global view on all payment instructions Q and settlement indicators x.

The protocol starts with the initial assumption that all payment instructions will be settled where

$$\forall i \in [N], \ k \in [n_i] \ x_{i,k} = 1,$$

Certainly, this assumption may be invalid, (i.e., some but not all payment instructions will be actually settled). Accordingly, for each round t, participants run Algorithm 1 to update their settlement indicators x^t. Eventually, the protocol stops when there are no further updates in the settlement indicators.

Algorithm 1. Updates the settlement indicator queue x_i^t for round t [10]

1: **function** UPDATEINDICATOR(x^{t-1}, Q)
2:     $x_i^t \leftarrow x_i^{t-1}$ ▷ Set the current indicator to the indicator of previous round
3:     $k \leftarrow h(x_i^t)$ ▷ Set k as the index of lowest priority payment
4:     **while** $k \geq 0$ **do**   ▷ Iterate from lowest priority payment to highest
5:         $\tilde{B}_i \leftarrow \hat{B}_i - S_i(x^{t-1}) + R_i(x^{t-1})$ ▷ Compute ex-post balance based on x^{t-1}
6:         **if** $\tilde{B}_i < 0$ **then**   ▷ If $\tilde{B}_i$ is negative, unsettle the lowest priority payment
7:             $x_{i,k}^t \leftarrow 0$
8:             $k \leftarrow k - 1$
9:         **else**
10:             **break**
11:         **end if**
12:     **end while**
13:     **return** $(x_i^t, \tilde{B}_i)$
14: **end function**

The main objective of Algorithm 1 is to iteratively unsettle lowest priority payment instructions until the three constraints are satisfied. In Line 6, the algorithm checks for non-negative ex-post balance, thus, enforcing the liquidity constraint. Furthermore, in Line 4, it enforces the sequence constraint by iterating over payment instructions from lowest to highest priority. Finally, the optimality constraint is satisfied in Line 10 by stopping the algorithm on the highest possible number of payment instructions that meet the liquidity and sequence constraints.

Eventually, the protocol halts when there is no further change in settlement indicators in the final round (i.e., $x^t = x^{t-1}$). The end result is either learning the netting solution or reaching a deadlock where the settlement indicator of each participant is $x_i^t = [0]_1^{n_i}$ (i.e., no participant can settle any payment instruction on a netting basis). In the former, participants can update their ex-post balance

$\tilde{B}_i$ of participants. Conversely, in the latter, participants have to inject more liquidity to resolve the deadlock and reset the protocol.

5 Privacy Preserving Netting Protocol Design

To protect the privacy of participants, we modify the decentralized netting protocol to (i) conceal payment amounts and (ii) hide links between senders and recipients. It is worth mentioning that participants in our context refer to banks not individuals. In particular, inter-bank payments are aggregates of individuals transactions. Hence, our protocol is designed to preserve the privacy of involved banks in inter-bank payments transactions. Our approach to fulfilling the first objective is to utilize ElGamal encryption. We did not use Pedersen commitments as followed in [10], mainly because the sender would have to open a communication link with the recipient to send the opening values, which can be leaked and compromise the recipient's privacy. When a participant sends a payment instruction to the smart contract, it sends an encrypted payment amount without including the recipient's identity. Subsequently, other participants will individually try to decrypt it locally using their own private keys. Certainly, only the intended recipient will successfully decrypt it. Consequently, no link is publicly established on the smart contract between senders and recipients, which fulfills our second objective.

Later on, after resolving the gridlock, each participant will send a zero-knowledge proof to the smart contract to prove the correctness of its ex-post balance based on ex-ante balance, outgoing amounts, and incoming amounts. However, since we removed recipients' identities from payment instructions, the smart contract cannot determine the incoming payment instruction for any participant. Nonetheless, we must ensure that participants do not use arbitrary ciphertext as their incoming amounts. In other words, each participant must prove that its incoming payment instructions are part of the list containing all payment instructions sent to the smart contract. To solve this challenge, the smart contract utilizes a Merkle tree to accumulate all payment instructions. Given the public state of the smart contract, participants can clearly see the paths in that tree. As a result, each participant can prove that it knows the Merkle tree paths for its incoming payment instructions without revealing them, which in turn effectively enforces the recipient's privacy (more detail in Sect. 5.6).

5.1 Overview of the Protocol

We briefly describe our protocol as follows:

1. The protocol starts with a Setup phase where an MPC protocol is used to generate the CRS for the zkSNARK proof system, and a smart contract is deployed on the blockchain.
2. Participants initialize their encrypted ex-ante balance on the smart contract.
3. Each participant submits its payment instructions to the smart contract and utilize zkSNARK to prove their correctness.
4. Participants scan the smart contract to learn their incoming amounts based on their success in decrypting the submitted payment instructions.

5. Participants begin to resolve the gridlock over a number of variable rounds as follows:
   (a) In the first round, they assume all payment instructions will be settled and set their settlement indicator $x_i^{t=1} = [1]^{n_i}$.
   (b) In subsequent round t, each participant P_i locally runs Algorithm 1 to update its settlement indicator from x_i^{t-1} to x_i^t, and send x_i^t to the smart contract.
   (c) If there are no changes (i.e., $x^t = x^{t-1}$), the smart contract builds a Merkle tree over payment instructions that will be settled; otherwise, participants repeat the above step again for the new round $t := t + 1$.
6. Participants send transactions to the smart contract containing their encrypted ex-post balance and a zkSNARK proof to prove its correctness.
7. Upon successful verification, the smart contract accepts the ex-post balance.

5.2   Setup

To promote a modular design, the protocol utilizes several smart contracts that are deployed on the blockchain.

1. **Registry**: It contains ElGamal public encryption keys of all participants.
2. **Serials**: The sole purpose of this smart contract is to prevent double-spending of incoming payment instructions by tracking the serial numbers (also known as nullifiers [16]) of the settled ones (more detail in Sect. 5.6).
3. **MerkleTree$_{pk}$**: It accumulates the public keys of all participants.
4. **MerkleTree$_s$**: It accumulates all payment instructions that will be settled after gridlock resolution.
5. **Verifier**: It verifies zkSNARK proofs submitted by participants, and it contains the verification key vk generated by zkSNARK setup algorithm.
6. **Main**: This is the main smart contract which handles the deposit of funds (i.e., ex-ante balance), controls the transitions between phases and rounds, and utilize the above smart contracts.

The security of this protocol depends mainly on the setup process of the zkSNARK proof system Ψ. Obviously, utilizing a trusted third party to generate the CRS is not acceptable in this context. Thus, we propose to run an MPC protocol [13] between participants to generate the CRS. As long as there is at least a single honest participant, then we can consider Ψ to be secure.

5.3   Initializing Ex-Ante Balance

To join the protocol, a participant P_i deposits its ex-ante balance B_i in Main as shown in Fig. 2. Initially, Registry checks whether the transaction sender is authorized based on its address and returns its public key on success. If this is the first deposit by the sender, then the sender's ex-ante balance is set to the encryption of the msg.value by the sender's public key and randomness $r = 0$. Otherwise, the deposit is to inject more liquidity into the sender's balance by utilizing the additively homomorphic property of ElGamal encryption.

Generally, in blockchains with a public state such as Ethereum, we cannot hide the deposit value of ex-ante balance. However, after resolving gridlock, participants will send their ex-post balances in encrypted form to Main.

```
Deposit():          require Registry.ContainsAddress(msg.sender)
                    𝒴 := Registry.GetPublicKey(msg.sender)
                    Let v := msg.value
                    Let 𝒞 := ℰ(v, 𝒴)
                    If Balance[msg.sender] is null
                            Balance[msg.sender] := 𝒞
                    Else
                            Let 𝒞^old := Balance[msg.sender]
                            Let 𝒞^new := (EC.Add(𝒞₁^old, 𝒞₁), EC.Add(𝒞₂^old, 𝒞₂))
                            Balance[msg.sender] := 𝒞^new
```

Fig. 2. Pseudocode for deposit function.

5.4   Submitting Payment Instructions

To submit payment instructions while hiding amounts and preserving recipient's privacy, a participant P_i sends a transaction to Main containing its outgoing payment queue Q_i without indicating recipients' identities (i.e., their public keys).

$$Q_i \leftarrow [\mathcal{C}_{i,1}, \ldots, \mathcal{C}_{i,n_i}]$$
$$\mathcal{C}_{i,k} \leftarrow \mathcal{E}(v_{i,k}, \mathcal{Y}_{i,k})$$
$$\mathcal{Y}_{i,k} \in [\mathcal{Y}_j]_{j=1, j \neq i}^{N}$$

P_i utilizes the zkSNARK proof system Ψ to prove that (i) the amounts encrypted in Q_i fall in range $[0, 2^l - 1]$ for a system parameter l, and (ii) the ciphertext are generated using public keys from the list $\mathcal{Y}$, which are accumulated in MerkleTree$_{pk}$ with $root_{pk}$ as its root. Technically speaking, P_i utilize zkSNARK proof system Ψ to generate a proof π_i for the following statement:

$$\mathbf{PoK}\{(Q_i, root_{pk}; \psi, v_i) : \forall \; \mathcal{C}_k \in Q_i \;\; \mathcal{C}_k = \mathcal{E}(v_k, \mathcal{Y}_k) \; \wedge \; v_{i,j} \in [0, 2^l - 1]$$
$$\wedge \; \mathtt{Merkle}.\mathcal{V}(root_{pk}, \mathcal{Y}_k, \psi_k) = 1\}$$

where ψ is the list of Merkle proof of membership for each public key $\mathcal{Y}_k$ used to encrypt payment instruction $\mathcal{C}_k$.

Main handles this transaction as shown in Fig. 3. It checks that the sender is one of the authorized participants. Subsequently, if it successfully verifies the proof π_i, then it stores Q_i in the list Out and initializes the settlement indicator by setting 1 in all indices (see Sect. 4.1) which gives the assumption that all payment amounts will be settled. Otherwise, it reverts the transaction.

Once the transaction is accepted by Main, each participant P_j, where $j \neq i \; \wedge \; j \in [N]$, will scan payment instructions in Main.Out$[P_i$.Address$]$ and try to decrypt them locally using its private key. Accordingly, P_j will learn if it is the intended recipient based on successful decryption.

```
Submit (Q_i, π_i):   require Registry.ContainsAddress(msg.sender)
                     root_pk := MerkleTree_pk.GetRoot()
                     require Verifier.Verify(Q_i, root_pk, π_i)
                     Out[msg.sender] := Q_i
                     Let n_i := |Q_i|
                     Indicator[msg.sender] := [1]^{n_i}
```

Fig. 3. Pseudocode for submit function.

5.5   Updating Settlement Indicators

In this phase, participants utilize decentralized netting protocol to resolve grid-lock over a variable number of rounds before converging to the netting solution. Main implements the transitions of rounds as shown in Fig. 4. An important caveat here is that smart contracts do not execute code unless they are instructed to do so via transactions. Hence, we require one of the participants P' to send transactions to Main to transit between rounds and states. The gridlock resolution proceeds as follow:

1. Participant P' submits a Start transaction to initiate the first round of decentralized netting protocol.
2. Each participant P_i runs Algorithm 1 to update its settlement indicator x_i and submits a Receive transaction within its predefined time-window.
3. Participant P' submits a Final transaction to determine the next state of this phase. More precisely, if there are changes in settlement indicators, then participants proceed to the next round and repeat Step 2. Otherwise, the protocol has either reached a deadlock state or it has successfully resolved the gridlock. In the former case, participants have to inject more liquidity by submitting Deposit transactions, then reset the current round in Step 2. Conversely, in the latter case, Main initializes MerkleTree_s to accumulate all payment instructions that will be settled according to the current indicators, and sets the flag Resolved to transit to next phase.

5.6   Updating Ex-Post Balance

After resolving the gridlock, each participant P_i utilizes the zkSNARK proof system Ψ to generate a proof π about the correctness of its encrypted ex-post balance $\tilde{B}$. Then, P_i submits an Update transaction containing the parameters π and $\tilde{B}$ as shown in Fig. 5. Informally speaking, the proof π shows that given the public input:

- $root_s$ of the MerkleTree_s.
- $\mathcal{Y}$ as the public key of P_i.
- S as the list of settled payment instructions according to indicator x_i.
- U as the highest priority unsettled payment instruction based on x_i.
- $\hat{B}$ and $\tilde{B}$ as the encryption of ex-ante and ex-post balances by the public key $\mathcal{Y}$, respectively.
- sn as the list containing serial numbers of incoming payment instructions.

```
Start ():      require START = false
               START := true
               t := 1
               updated := false

Receive(x_i): require START = true
               require ValidReceiveWindow(Block.Number)
               require Registry.ContainsAddress(msg.sender)
               If Indicator[msg.sender] ≠ x_i
                   Indicator[msg.sender] := x_i
                   updated := true
Final():       require ValidFinalWindow(Block.Number)
               If updated = true
                   t := t + 1
                   updated := false
               Else
                   If Indicator.AllZeros() = true
                   DEADLOCK := true
                   Else
                       Out_s := GetSettledOnly(Out,Indicator)
                       MerkleTree_s := MerkleTree(Out_s)
                       RESOLVED := true
```

Fig. 4. Pseudocode for updating indicators in `Main`

and the witnesses:

- x as the secret key corresponding to the public key $\mathcal{Y}$.
- $\boldsymbol{R}$ as the list of incoming payments instructions accumulated in `MerkleTree_s`.
- $\boldsymbol{\psi}$ as the list of Merkle proofs of membership for $\boldsymbol{R}$ in `MerkleTree_s`.
- $\boldsymbol{r}$ as the list of decrypted incoming payment amounts from $\boldsymbol{R}$.
- $\boldsymbol{s}$ as the list of outgoing payment amounts encrypted in $\boldsymbol{S}$.
- $\boldsymbol{\mathcal{Y}}_s$ as the list of public keys for recipients of payment instructions in $\boldsymbol{S}$.
- u as the decrypted payment amount from $\mathcal{U}$.
- $\mathcal{Y}_u$ as the public key of the recipient of $\mathcal{U}$.
- $\hat{b}$ and $\tilde{b}$ as the ex-ante and ex-post balances encrypted in $\tilde{B}$ and $\hat{B}$

that the *conjunction* of the following relations holds:

1. $\mathcal{Y} = x\mathcal{G}$
2. $\forall R_k \in \boldsymbol{R} \ \ \boldsymbol{r} = [r_k = \mathcal{D}(R_k, x)]$
3. $\forall R_k \in \boldsymbol{R} \ \ \boldsymbol{sn} = [sn_k = H(x\|R_k)]$
4. $\forall \psi_k \in \boldsymbol{\psi} \ \ \text{Merkle}.\mathcal{V}(root_s, R_k, \psi_k) = 1$
5. $\forall s_j \in \boldsymbol{s}, \mathcal{Y}_j \in \boldsymbol{\mathcal{Y}}_s \ \ \boldsymbol{S} = [S_j = \mathcal{E}(s_j, \mathcal{Y}_j)]$
6. $U = \mathcal{E}(u, \mathcal{Y}_u) \ \wedge \ \hat{B} = \mathcal{E}(\hat{b}, \mathcal{Y}) \ \wedge \ \tilde{B} = \mathcal{E}(\tilde{b}, \mathcal{Y})$
7. $\tilde{b} = \hat{b} - \sum \boldsymbol{s} + \sum \boldsymbol{r} \geq 0$
8. $\tilde{b} - u < 0$

The first relation indicates that the participant P_i knows the secret key x corresponding to the public key $\mathcal{Y}$. The second relation proves that r contains the incoming payment amounts decrypted from R by its secret key x. The third relation proves that the serial numbers in sn correspond to the hash of incoming payment instructions with the secret encryption key x. Accordingly, valid incoming payment instructions must have unique serial numbers to prevent double-spending. The fourth relation shows that P_i knows valid membership proofs ψ to prove that the payment instructions in R are accumulated in $\mathtt{MerkleTree}_s$. The fifth relation shows that the outgoing payment amounts in s are encrypted to ciphertext in S by the public keys in $\mathcal{Y}_s$. Note that in previous $\mathtt{Submit}$ transaction, the smart contract verifies that the public keys used to encrypt outgoing payment instructions are valid registered public keys of participants. Hence, there is no need to verify the correctness of public keys in $\mathcal{Y}_s$ once again. The sixth relation shows that $U, \hat{B}$, and $\tilde{B}$ are the ciphertext corresponding to $u, \hat{b}$, and $\tilde{B}$, respectively. The seventh relation ensure that the liquidity constraint holds. Finally, the last relation proves optimality constraints is satisfied by showing that the highest priority unsettled payment will result in negative ex-post balance. Thus, the optimal netting solution is to settle the outgoing payments in S.

```
Update(π, B̃, sn):   require Registry.ContainsAddress(msg.sender)
                     require RESOLVED = true
                     require Unique(sn)
                     require Serials.ContainsAny(sn) = false
                     Y := Registry.GetPublicKey(msg.sender)
                     root_s := MerkleTree_s.GetRoot()
                     B̂ := GetBalance(msg.sender)
                     S := GetSettledPayments(msg.sender)
                     U := GetHighestUnsettled(msg.sender)
                     require Verifier.verify(B̃, B̂, Y, root_s, S, U, sn, π)
                     Serials.append(sn)
                     Balance[msg.sender] := B̃
```

Fig. 5. Pseudocode for updating ex-post balance in $\mathtt{Main}$

6   Performance Evaluation

We evaluate the protocol's performance on Ethereum. The results show that the protocol is feasible and practical to deploy. Recently, Ethereum has gone through multiple planned hard-forks to upgrade its virtual machine (EVM) with new op-codes and features that will help Ethereum transit to Proof-of-Stake (PoS). One of these features is the support for running EC operations inside smart contracts. More specifically, the fork *Byzantium* [17] introduced two pre-compiled contracts: EIP-196 to perform point addition and multiplication operations, and EIP-197 for pairing checks on the curve *BN128*. Accordingly, smart contracts can efficiently verify many cryptographic proofs including zkSNARK [12]. However, the gas cost incurred by EC operations were relatively high which limited the feasibility of some cryptographic protocols on Ethereum. Therefore, the fork code-named *Istanbul* [18] made adjustments to the cost of EC operations. Strictly speaking, the gas cost of point addition, multiplication, and k pairing check got reduced from $500; 40000; 100000 + k \times 80000$ down to $150; 6000; 45000 + k \times 34000$, respectively.

6.1 Evaluations

We utilize the zkSNARK construction proposed in [14]. The major advantage of this construction is the small proof size 128-bytes and efficient verifier which requires three pairing checks. Using the gas adjustments brought by *Istanbul* fork in Ethereum, pairing checks cost 45000 gas in addition to 34000 gas for each check. Thus, the verification cost of zkSNARK proof is $147000 = 45000 + 3 \times 34000$ gas. Moreover, the verifier performs EC operations on the public input before verifying the proof. Specifically, for each public input encoded as $\mathbb{F}_p$ element, the verifier invokes two operations: point multiplication and point addition. Consequently, for a proof π with public input of size m elements in $\mathbb{F}_p$, the verification gas cost is $6150m + 147000$. The encoding of an ElGamal ciphertext, a public key, and a hash value are four, two, and one $\mathbb{F}_p$ elements, respectively.

To evaluate our protocol, we estimate the gas cost associated with the elliptic curve operations performed during zkSNARK proofs verification. Generally, participants send zkSNARK proofs in Submit and Update transactions. In Fig. 6, we report the gas cost for these transactions with respect the numbers of outgoing and incoming payment instructions n_i and m_i, respectively.

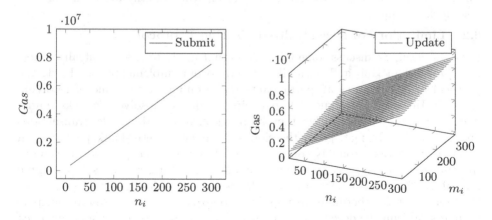

Fig. 6. Gas cost of zkSNARK proof verification for Submit and Update transactions

In the Submit transaction, the public input consists of a list of n_i ciphertext for payment instructions in Q_i, and a hash value for the root of MerkleTree$_{pk}$.

Accordingly, we can estimate the gas cost for proof verification as $6150(4n_i + 1) + 147000$ gas. Similarly, in the `Submit` transaction, the public input consists of seven parameters: three ciphertext $(\tilde{B}, \hat{B}, U)$, a list of n_i ciphertext for payment instructions in S, a public key $\mathcal{Y}$, a hash value for the root of `MerkleTree`$_s$, and a list of m_i serial numbers. Consequently, we can estimate the gas cost as $6150(15 + 4n_i + m_i) + 147000$.

Table 1 shows the size and cost in USD for `Submit` and `Update` transactions in the setting where $n_i = m_i = 10$. At the time of writing in August 2020, one Ether coin costs $\approx\$400$ USD, and the average gas price is $\approx 200\ Gwei = 200 \times 10^{-9}$ Ether. The gas cost of a transaction is computed as the incurred gas times gas price in Ether times Ether price in USD.

Table 1. Size and cost in USD for `Submit` and `Update` transactions

Transaction	Size (bytes)	Gas	Cost (USD)
Submit	1408	399150	$32
Update	2080	546750	$43.75

Based on the evaluation results, we believe the protocol is practical to deploy on Ethereum. For example, with the current block gas limit $\approx$ 10M gas on Ethereum, we find that the proof verification for `Submit` and `Update` transactions cost 3.9% and 5.4% of the block limit when the number of outgoing and incoming payment instructions $n_i = m_i = 10$, respectively. Furthermore, the protocol will perform much better on permissioned blockchain preferred by banks such as Corda [19] or Hyperledger [20] since there are neither lengthy block mining time nor block gas limit.

6.2   Limitations of Decentralized Netting Protocol

In this section, we discuss some limitations that apply to the decentralized netting protocol in [10], and naturally extend to our implementation. First, the protocol in [10] requires all participants to be online at the time of resolving gridlock. However, we argue that participants do not resolve gridlocks immediately once they occur, rather they keep aggregating individuals' transactions during the day. In fact, given the slow settlement of inter-bank payments in practice which takes roughly couple of days, banks can setup a specific time at the end of a business day to resolve gridlock. Therefore, we can safely assume that the online requirement is practically relaxed and does not cause in severe liveness issues. Furthermore, to improve the speed of gridlock resolution, participants can run the decentralized netting protocol off-chain to resolve gridlock without being controlled by the `Main` smart contract. Then, participants can submit correctness proofs and utilize `Main` for settlement only.

The second issue is that the protocol leaks some information about recipients that can be exploited in an extreme case to successfully break their anonymity. In particular, we are concerned with how updates to the settlement indicators in subsequent rounds can affect recipients' anonymity. Suppose, in rounds k and $k + 1$, s and r, that participants update their indicators, respectively. An observer can infer that the r participants are recipients to payments from the s senders since they updated their indicators in response to changes in s indicators. Consequently, as s increases, it becomes harder to link the r recipients. On the other hand, an extreme case, which is the major limitation of decentralized netting protocol, is when $s = 1$, then the observer can successfully link all r participants as recipients to the participant in previous round. One can solve this problem by requiring all participants to submit encrypted indicators with different randomness in each round, regardless of any changes in the underlying values. Note that, each individual element $x_{i,j}$ in indicator vector x_i is encrypted by the public key $\mathcal{Y}_j$ of the recipient P_j. Accordingly, the observer neither can determine whether individual values at $x_{i,j}$ have changed, nor can link recipients to senders since all participants are submitting encrypted indicators in each round. Therefore, the size of anonymity set for recipients becomes N, which is the total number of participants. Certainly, this requires modifying the zero-knowledge proof in the Update transaction which we leave for future work.

7   Conclusions

Financial institutions are embracing blockchain technology to address challenges in traditional RTGS. We designed a privacy preserving decentralized protocol that resolves gridlock in RTGS. Furthermore, we enhanced the privacy of participants by hiding the links between senders and recipients while providing confidentiality to payment amounts. To assess the feasibility and performance of our protocol, we estimate the proof verification gas cost when deployed on Ethereum which yielded promising results. For future work, we will investigate other proof systems with better proving time and transparent setup.

References

1. Kahn, C.M., Roberds, W.: Real-time gross settlement and the costs of immediacy. J. Monetary Econ. **47**(2), 299–319 (2001)
2. Norman, B.: Liquidity saving in real-time gross settlement systems: an overview. J. Payments Strategy Syst. **4**(3), 261–276 (2010)
3. Chapman, J., Garratt, R., Hendry, S., McCormack, A., McMahon, W.: Project jasper: are distributed wholesale payment systems feasible yet. Financ. Syst. **59**, 59 (2017)
4. Project ubin: central bank digital money using distributed ledger technology. https://www.mas.gov.sg/schemes-and-initiatives/Project-Ubin. Accessed 07 July 2020
5. Galal, H.S., Youssef, A.M.: Verifiable sealed-bid auction on the ethereum blockchain. In: Zohar, A., et al. (eds.) FC 2018. LNCS, vol. 10958, pp. 265–278. Springer, Heidelberg (2019). https://doi.org/10.1007/978-3-662-58820-8_18
6. Galal, H.S., Youssef, A.M.: Succinctly verifiable sealed-bid auction smart contract. In: Garcia-Alfaro, J., Herrera-Joancomartí, J., Livraga, G., Rios, R. (eds.) DPM/CBT -2018. LNCS, vol. 11025, pp. 3–19. Springer, Cham (2018). https://doi.org/10.1007/978-3-030-00305-0_1

7. Galal, H.S., Youssef, A.M.: Trustee: full privacy preserving vickrey auction on top of ethereum. In: Bracciali, A., Clark, J., Pintore, F., Rønne, P.B., Sala, M. (eds.) FC 2019. LNCS, vol. 11599, pp. 190–207. Springer, Cham (2020). https://doi.org/10.1007/978-3-030-43725-1_14

8. Wang, X., Xu, X., Feagan, L., Huang, S., Jiao, L., Zhao, W.: Inter-bank payment system on enterprise blockchain platform. In: 2018 IEEE 11th International Conference on Cloud Computing (CLOUD), pp. 614–621. IEEE (2018)

9. Cachin, C., et al.: Architecture of the hyperledger blockchain fabric. In: Workshop on Distributed Cryptocurrencies and Consensus Ledgers, vol. 310 (2016)

10. Cao, S., Yuan, Y., De Caro, A., Nandakumar, K., Elkhiyaoui, K., Hu, Y.: Decentralized privacy-preserving netting protocol on blockchain for payment systems. In: Bonneau, J., Heninger, N. (eds.) FC 2020. LNCS, vol. 12059, pp. 137–155. Springer, Cham (2020). https://doi.org/10.1007/978-3-030-51280-4_9

11. Koblitz, N.: Elliptic curve cryptosystems. Math. Comput. **48**(177), 203–209 (1987)

12. Ben-Sasson, E., Chiesa, A., Tromer, E., Virza, M.: Succinct non-interactive zero knowledge for a von Neumann architecture. In: 23rd USENIX Security Symposium (USENIX Security 2014), pp. 781–796 (2014)

13. Bowe, S., Gabizon, A., Green, M.D.: A multi-party protocol for constructing the public parameters of the pinocchio zk-SNARK. In: Zohar, A., et al. (eds.) FC 2018. LNCS, vol. 10958, pp. 64–77. Springer, Heidelberg (2019). https://doi.org/10.1007/978-3-662-58820-8_5

14. Groth, J.: On the size of pairing-based non-interactive arguments. In: Fischlin, M., Coron, J.-S. (eds.) EUROCRYPT 2016. LNCS, vol. 9666, pp. 305–326. Springer, Heidelberg (2016). https://doi.org/10.1007/978-3-662-49896-5_11

15. Soramaki, K., Bech, M.L.: Gridlock resolution in interbank payment systems (2001)

16. Sasson, E.B., et al.: Zerocash: decentralized anonymous payments from bitcoin. In: 2014 IEEE Symposium on Security and Privacy, pp. 459–474. IEEE (2014)

17. Byzantium hard fork changes. https://github.com/ethereum/wiki/wiki/Byzantium-Hard-Fork-changes. Accessed 07 July 2020

18. Eip 1108: Reduce alt_bn128 precompile gas costs. https://eips.ethereum.org/EIPS/eip-1108. Accessed 07 July 2020

19. Hearn, M.: Corda: a distributed ledger. Corda technical white paper, vol. 2016 (2016)

20. Androulaki, E., et al.: Hyperledger fabric: a distributed operating system for permissioned blockchains. In: Proceedings of the Thirteenth EuroSys Conference, pp. 1–15 (2018)

CBT Workshop: Signature Schemes, Formal Methods and Incentivization

Triptych: Logarithmic-Sized Linkable
Ring Signatures with Applications

Sarang Noether[✉] and Brandon Goodell

Monero Research Lab, London, UK
{sarangn.oether,surae.noether}@protonmail.com

Abstract. Ring signatures are a common construction used to provide signer ambiguity among a non-interactive set of public keys specified at the time of signing. Unlike early approaches where signature size is linear in the size of the signer anonymity set, current optimal solutions either require centralized trusted setups or produce signatures logarithmic in size. However, few also provide linkability, a property used to determine whether the signer of a message has signed any previous message, possibly with restrictions on the anonymity set choice. Here we introduce Triptych, a family of linkable ring signatures without trusted setup that is based on generalizations of zero-knowledge proofs of knowledge of commitment openings to zero. We demonstrate applications of Triptych in signer-ambiguous transaction protocols by extending the construction to openings of parallel commitments in independent anonymity sets. Signatures are logarithmic in the anonymity set size and, while verification complexity is linear, collections of proofs can be efficiently verified in batches. We show that for anonymity set sizes practical for use in distributed protocols, Triptych offers competitive performance with a straightforward construction.

1 Introduction

First introduced in [21] with respect to RSA groups, ring signatures permit the signing of messages using public key sets not fixed in advance, without the need of a trusted group manager. Earlier constructions lacked such flexibility, requiring either centralized key setup or the establishment of fixed signing sets. Later work [2] established more robust security models for unforgeability and anonymity, capturing realistic threat models where an adversary is permitted to corrupt keys, convince honest signers to include malicious anonymity set members, or obtain signatures in advance.

Since a ring signature has an anonymity set of public keys, one of which is the true signer, the detection of signing by the same key requires an additional property, linkability. A linkable ring signature [16] enables verifiers to determine whether the (unknown) signer of a message has signed other messages. Such a construction was proposed for election applications, where it is necessary to ensure that votes are anonymous, but voters are permitted to vote only once on a particular issue. The construction in [16], with a hash-trapdoor structure similar to that of [22], is of particular interest due to potential flexibility in linking; while

© Springer Nature Switzerland AG 2020
J. Garcia-Alfaro et al. (Eds.): DPM 2020/CBT 2020, LNCS 12484, pp. 337–354, 2020.
https://doi.org/10.1007/978-3-030-66172-4_22

its linking is limited to signer-selected but unchanging signer anonymity sets, it permits linking on a per-issue basis. Additional recent work in [1] introduces the property of linkable anonymity, using sets of signatures and establishing restrictions on key corruption. Other related interesting properties like traceability [8,9] imply stronger capabilities, where an attempt to sign two messages with the same key permits verifiers to identify the signer.

Linkable ring signatures have seen particularly useful applications in signer-ambiguous transaction protocols. In such an application, transactions are authorized by a ring signature whose signing anonymity set consists of previously-generated transaction outputs. A signature demonstrates that the signer controls the private key of one such output without revealing which is the signer, and linkability is used to assure verifiers that output has not been used in another signature (signifying a double-spend attempt).

A practical consideration for the use of linkable ring signatures in transaction protocols is how signature size and verification time scale with the size of the anonymity set. In common applied constructions like [10,19], signature size and verification time scale linearly with the size of the signing ambiguity set; since such signatures are typically included in a public distributed data structure like a blockchain, there is a balance between the size of the anonymity set and the requirements for storage and verification. Recent protocol work in this area mitigates the size restriction. For example, in [24], the authors introduce a confidential transaction protocol based on a proving system whose size scales logarithmically with the anonymity set size, and which includes a method for demonstrating amount balance; amount commitment range proving is offloaded to other constructions like [4]. In [15], the authors use a more general proving technique to accomplish a similar goal; however, the protocol offers further size benefits by integrating commitment range proofs into the proof structure directly, taking advantage of the logarithmic proof size.

Other signer-ambiguous transaction protocols not based on linkable ring signatures offer more competitive performance. For example, protocols like [13] produce maximal theoretical signer ambiguity through the use of zero-knowledge Merkle proofs (among others) that offer extremely small proofs with low verification time, but at the cost of a trusted structured setup process that arises from the underlying proving system [11]. Like this work, [14] is a transaction protocol also based on [12]; however, it is intended to operate on commitments similar to those used in [18] but with the inclusion of amounts, and has limitations on addressing and sender tracing.

1.1 Our Contribution

We produce a family of linkable ring signatures, which we call Triptych. The constructions are a linkable generalization of Groth's one-of-many commitment-to-zero proving system [12], with optimizations from Bootle [3] applied for improvements to proof size and verification complexity. In the simplest version of Triptych, the prover shows that it knows the opening of a commitment to zero within a commitment set, and also that it has constructed a linking tag using the same opening, producing a linkable ring signature construction. We then modify Groth's ring signature definitions to include linkability and a related property, non-frameability.

In an extension of Triptych, we include multiple independent sets of commitments. Here, the prover proceeds as before to show its knowledge of an opening to a commitment in one set, as well as the construction of the linking tag. However, the proof also shows that the prover knows an opening of a commitment at the same position in all other sets. This construction has immediate application; in some signer-ambiguous confidential transaction protocols, transaction inputs are commitments to zero, for which the signer shows it knows the opening. Each commitment comes equipped with another commitment to the amount of the input; by offsetting these commitments homomorphically and carefully choosing commitment randomness, the prover can show that a particular transaction balances.

We show that Triptych produces signatures with competitive performance to other modern linkable ring signatures for limited anonymity set sizes. We note that similar constructions also require linear verification time, meaning that the size of anonymity set used in practice is likely to be limited for performance reasons.

2   Preliminaries

2.1   Public Parameters

Let $\mathbb{G}$ be a cyclic group in which the discrete logarithm problem is hard, and let $\mathbb{F}$ be the scalar field of $\mathbb{G}$. Let $\mathcal{H} : \{0,1\}^* \to \mathbb{F}$ be a cryptographic hash function. Let G and H be generators of $\mathbb{G}$ with unknown discrete logarithm relationship. Let $N = n^m$ be a size parameter, where $n > 1$ and $m > 1$. Let $\{G_{j,i}\}_{j,i=0}^{m-1,n-1}$ be a set of generators of $\mathbb{G}$ with unknown discrete logarithm relationship to each other, to G, and to H. Let U be a generator of $\mathbb{G}$. Note that all generators may be produced using public randomness; for example, the use of a suitable hash function with domain separation may be appropriate. All such public parameters are assumed to comprise a global reference string known to all players; in particular, we exclude them from algorithm definitions and Fiat-Shamir transcript hashes for readability.

2.2   Pedersen Commitment

Let Com be a homomorphic commitment scheme that is perfectly hiding and computationally binding. In this work, we assume use of the Pedersen commitment scheme: for $x, r \in \mathbb{F}$, define $,(x,r) \equiv xG + rH$ to be the commitment of the value x with randomness r. This can be trivially extended to support matrix values; for $\{x_{j,i}\}, r \in \mathbb{F}$, define $,(x,r) \equiv rH + \sum_{j,i} x_{j,i} G_{j,i}$. Note in particular that Pedersen matrix commitments are similarly homomorphic.

2.3   Other Notation

For integers or field elements i, j, the Kronecker delta function $\delta(i, j)$ evaluates to 1 if $i = j$ and 0 otherwise, where the output is taken to be in the appropriate set.

We sometimes use index subscript notation of the form i_j to indicate the j digit of i, where such a decomposition of i is taken base n with padded length m:

$$\sum_{j=0}^{m} i_j n^j = i$$

This notation will be specified explicitly where confusion may occur.

3   Protocol: Linkable One-of-many Commitment

We wish to build a linkable ring signature construction, where a signer who knows the opening of a commitment may sign messages using an anonymity set containing other commitments for which the signer does not know openings. Included with the proof of knowledge, the signer also provides a linking tag that is the image of the signing commitment's opening under a verifiable pseudorandom function, using the method of [6] that has previously appeared in [15, 24]. Part of the soundness of the proving system relies on the proper construction of this linking tag. Upon receipt, a verifier can check whether the linking tag has previously appeared in any other valid proof; if it has not, injectivity assures the verifier that no other signature has been produced by the (unknown) signer.

More specifically, we modify the construction of Bootle [3], which itself is a generalization of a construction by Groth [12]. We produce a sigma protocol for the following relation:

$$\mathcal{R}_{\text{link}} = \left\{ \{M_i\}_{i=0}^{N-1} \subset \mathbb{G}, J \in \mathbb{G}; (l \in \mathbb{Z}, r \in \mathbb{F}) : M_l = rG \text{ and } U = rJ \right\}$$

Figs. 1 and 2 describe the protocol.

Observe that this protocol can be made non-interactive using the Fiat-Shamir heuristic, where the verifier challenge is produced using a collision-resistant hash function (modeling a random oracle) and the proof transcript [7].

We will show that the sigma protocol is complete, sound, and zero-knowledge, the precise definitions of which are common and found in [12]. Informally, we require the protocol be:

- *Perfectly complete*: Given knowledge of a witness to a statement in the proof relation, an honest prover can always convince an honest verifier of the validity of the witness.
- *Special sound*: Given a statement in the proof relation, if a prover can answer multiple verifier challenges correctly, then it is possible to extract a witness for this statement.

$\mathcal{P}_{\text{link}}(\{M_i\}, J; (l, r)):$

- Select random $r_A \in \mathbb{F}$ and $\{a_{j,i}\}_{i=1,j=0}^{n-1,m-1} \subset \mathbb{F}$. Set

$$\{a_{j,0}\}_{j=0}^{m-1} \equiv -\sum_{i=1}^{n-1} a_{j,i}$$

  and define $A \equiv \text{Com}(a, r_A)$.
- Define $\{\sigma_{j,i}\}_{i,j=0}^{n-1,j-1} \subset \mathbb{F}$ such that $\sigma_{j,i} \equiv \delta(l_j, i)$ (using our decomposition notation), and choose random $r_B \in \mathbb{F}$. Define $B \equiv \text{Com}(\sigma, r_B)$.
- Select random $r_C \in \mathbb{F}$, and define $C \equiv \text{Com}(a(1 - 2\sigma), r_C)$.
- Select random $r_D \in \mathbb{F}$, and define $D \equiv \text{Com}(-a^2, r_D)$.
- Define coefficients $\{p_{k,j}\}_{k,j=0}^{N-1,m-1}$ such that

$$p_k(x) \equiv \prod_{j=0}^{m-1} (\sigma_{j,k}x + a_{j,k}) = \delta(l, k) x^m + \sum_{j=0}^{m-1} p_{k,j} x^j$$

  for all $k \in [0, N)$ (using our decomposition notation).
- Select random $\{\rho_j\}_{j=0}^{m-1} \subset \mathbb{F}$.
- Define $\{X_j\}_{j=0}^{m-1} \subset \mathbb{G}$ such that:

$$X_j \equiv \sum_{k=0}^{N-1} p_{k,j} M_k + \rho_j G$$

- Define $\{Y_j\}_{j=0}^{m-1} \subset \mathbb{G}$ such that:

$$Y_j \equiv U \sum_{k=0}^{N-1} p_{k,j} + \rho_j J$$

$\mathcal{P} \to \mathcal{V}:$
$A, B, C, D, \{X_j\}, \{Y_j\}$

$\mathcal{V} \to \mathcal{P}:$
$\xi \in \{0, 1\}^*$

$\mathcal{P}(\xi):$

- Define $\{f_{j,i}\}_{i=1,j}^{n-1,m-1}$ such that $f_{j,i} \equiv \sigma_{j,i}\xi + a_{j,i}$.
- Define $z_A \equiv r_A + \xi r_B$ and $z_C \equiv \xi r_C + r_D$.
- Define $z \equiv r\xi^m - \sum_{j=0}^{m-1} \rho_j \xi^j$.

$\mathcal{P} \to \mathcal{V}:$
$\{f_{j,i}\}_{j=0,i=1}^{m-1,n-1}, z_A, z_C, z$

Fig. 1. Sigma protocol for $\mathcal{R}_{\text{link}}$

$\mathcal{V}_{\text{link}}(\{M_i\}, J):$

- For $0 \le j < m$, let $f_{j,0} \equiv \xi - \sum_{i=1}^{n-1} f_{j,i}$.
- Accept if and only if:

$$A + \xi B = \text{Com}(f, z_A) \tag{1}$$
$$\xi C + D = \text{Com}(f(\xi - f), z_C) \tag{2}$$

$$\sum_{k=0}^{N-1} M_k \left(\prod_{j=0}^{m-1} f_{j,k_j} \right) - \sum_{j=0}^{m-1} \xi^j X_j - zG = 0 \tag{3}$$

$$U \sum_{k=0}^{N-1} \left(\prod_{j=0}^{m-1} f_{j,k_j} \right) - \sum_{j=0}^{m-1} \xi^j Y_j - zJ = 0 \tag{4}$$

Fig. 2. Sigma protocol for $\mathcal{R}_{\text{link}}$ (continued)

- *Special honest-verifier zero knowledge*: Given any statement and verifier challenge, it is possible to simulate a transcript that is accepted by an honest verifier without knowledge of a corresponding witness.

Theorem 1. *The protocol listed in Figs. 1 and 2 is perfectly complete, special honest-verifier zero knowledge, and $(m + 1)$-special sound.*

Proof. The proof follows similarly to that of [3].

We first show perfect completeness. Suppose the verifier receives a proof generated by an honest prover. Equation 1 holds using the identity $\sum_{i=0}^{n-1} \sigma_{j,i} = 1$ for all $0 \le j < m$. Equation 2 follows similarly, using the identity $(\sigma_{j,i})^2 = \sigma_{j,i}$ for all $0 \le j < m$. To show Eq. 3 holds:

$$\sum_{k=0}^{N-1} M_k \left(\prod_{j=0}^{m-1} f_{j,k_j} \right) - \sum_{j=0}^{m-1} \xi^j X_j - zG$$

$$= \sum_{k=0}^{N-1} M_k p_k(\xi) - \sum_{j=0}^{m-1} \xi^j \left(\sum_{k=0}^{N-1} p_{k,j} M_k + \rho_j G \right) - zG$$

$$= \sum_{k=0}^{N-1} M_k \left(p_k(\xi) - \sum_{j=0}^{m-1} \xi^j p_{k,j} \right) - \sum_{j=0}^{m-1} \xi^j \rho_j G - zG$$

$$= \sum_{k=0}^{N-1} M_k \xi^m \delta(l, k) - \sum_{j=0}^{m-1} \xi^j \rho_j G - \left(r\xi^m - \sum_{j=0}^{m-1} \rho_j \xi^j \right) G$$

$$= \xi^m r G - \sum_{j=0}^{m-1} \xi^j \rho_j G - \xi^m r G + \sum_{j=0}^{m-1} \xi^j \rho_j G$$

$$= 0$$

Eq. 4 follows similarly:

$$U \sum_{k=0}^{N-1} \left(\prod_{j=0}^{m-1} f_{j,k_j} \right) - \sum_{j=0}^{m-1} \xi^j Y_j - zJ$$

$$= U \sum_{k=0}^{N-1} p_k(\xi) - \sum_{j=0}^{m-1} \xi^j \left(U \sum_{k=0}^{N-1} p_{k,j} + \rho_j J \right) - zJ$$

$$= U \sum_{k=0}^{N-1} \left(p_k(\xi) - \sum_{j=0}^{m-1} \xi^j p_{k,j} \right) - \sum_{j=0}^{m-1} \xi^j \rho_j J - zJ$$

$$= U \sum_{k=0}^{N-1} \xi^m \delta(l,k) - \sum_{j=0}^{m-1} \xi^j \rho_j J - \left(r\xi^m - \sum_{j=0}^{m-1} \rho_j \xi^j \right) J$$

$$= \xi^m U - \sum_{j=0}^{m-1} \xi^j \rho_j G - \xi^m rJ + \sum_{j=0}^{m-1} \xi^j \rho_j G$$

$$= 0$$

since $J = r^{-1}U$ in a valid proof. Hence the protocol is perfectly complete.

We next show that the protocol is special honest-verifier zero knowledge. To do so, we construct a simulator that, given a random verifier challenge ξ, can construct a proof transcript with identical distribution to a valid proof.

First, observe that the simulator presented in the proof of Lemma 1 in [3] translates identically to our setting. If the simulator chooses $B \in \mathbb{G}$ uniformly at random, the cited lemma assures us a valid simulation of the proof elements $A, C, D, z_A, z_C, \{f_{j,i\neq 0}^{(u)}\}$; we may compute each $f_{j,0}^{(u)}$ from this. Further, in a valid proof, B is independent and uniformly distributed as well.

The proof elements $\{X_j\}_{j=1}^{m-1}$ and $\{Y_j\}_{j=1}^{m-1}$ are independent and uniformly distributed in a valid proof since the set $\{\rho_j\}$ is random and the discrete logarithm problem in $\mathbb{G}$ is hard, so the simulator may choose these uniformly at random. The verification checks require that X_0 and Y_0 be uniquely determined by the other elements in the corresponding sets in both real proofs and by the simulator.

Finally, z is uniformly distributed in valid proofs given random ξ, so the simulator may choose it uniformly at random. Hence the construction is special honest verifier zero-knowledge.

It remains to show that the protocol is $(m+1)$-special sound, where $m > 1$. To show this, we construct an extractor that, given $m + 1$ valid responses to $m+1$ distinct verifier challenges for the same initial statement, produces a valid witness.

Suppose that for a given statement, we have a set of $m + 1$ distinct verifier challenges $\{\xi_e\}_{e=0}^m$ corresponding to unique valid responses of this form:

$$\left\{ \{f_{j,i}^{(e)}\}, \{z_e\} \right\}_{e=0}^m$$

From the 3-special soundness in [3] and $m > 1$ we have valid witness extractions $\{\sigma_{j,i}\}_{j,i=0}^{m-1,n-1}$ and $\{a_{j,i}\}_{j,i=0}^{m-1,n-1}$, and the Pedersen binding property ensures that (with high probability) we have:

$$f_{j,i}^{(e)} = \sigma_{j,i}\xi_e + a_{j,i}$$

for all $e \in [0, m]$. Using the extracted values, compute

$$p_k(\xi) \equiv \prod_{j=0}^{m-1} (\sigma_{j,k}\xi + a_{j,k})$$

for all $k \in [0, N)$. Extraction of $\{\sigma_{j,i}\}_{j,i=0}^{m-1,n-1}$ immediately yields the signing index l.

We have seen that p_k is of degree m only when $k = l$. Hence there exist coefficients $\{\overline{X}_j, \overline{Y}_j\}_{j=0}^{m-1}$, computed uniquely from the statement and extracted values, such that Eqs. 3 and 4 are of the following form:

$$\xi^m M_l + \sum_{j=0}^{m-1} \xi^j \overline{X}_j = zG$$

$$\xi^m U + \sum_{j=0}^{m-1} \xi^j \overline{Y}_j = zJ$$

Construct a Vandermonde matrix V where the e row is $(1, \xi_e, \ldots, \xi_e^m)$. Since all ξ_e are distinct, the rows of V span $\mathbb{F}^{m+1}$; hence there exist weights $\{\theta_e\}_{e=0}^m$ such that the resulting row linear combination produces the vector $(0, \ldots, 0, 1)$. That is, $\sum_{e=0}^m \theta_e \xi_e^j = \delta(j, m)$.

For each of the previous two equations, we can therefore build a linear combination over e. For the first:

$$M_l = \sum_{e=0}^m \theta_e \xi_e^m M_l + \sum_{e=0}^m \theta_e \left(\sum_{j=0}^{m-1} \xi_e^j \overline{X}_j \right) = \left(\sum_{e=0}^m \theta_e z_e \right) G$$

Hence we extract $r \equiv \sum_{e=0}^m \theta_e z_e$. For the second:

$$U = \sum_{e=0}^m \theta_e \xi_e^m U + \sum_{e=0}^m \theta_e \left(\sum_{j=0}^{m-1} \xi_e^j \overline{X}_j \right) = \left(\sum_{e=0}^m \theta_e z_e \right) J$$

This implies that $rJ = U$, as required. Hence the protocol is $(m + 1)$-special sound, which completes the proof.

4   Security: Linkable Ring Signature

Informally, a linkable ring signature is a construction permitting signatures on messages using a signer-selected anonymity set (called a *ring*) of possible signers.

A valid signature convinces a verifier that the signer knows (at least) one of the private keys to a ring member. The construction is linkable if it is possible to determine whether two signatures were generated using the same private key, regardless of the ring members used.

We use the security definitions in [12] as a starting point, directly adopting definitions for correctness and unforgeability that also appear in more recent work like [1]. However, we modify the definition of anonymity to account for linking tags, such that the adversary is required to differentiate between at least two possible honest signers that the adversary has not corrupted. To account for the linking properties desired in our construction, we use the clever linkability definition from [1], which uses a set-theoretic approach. We use a straightforward definition for non-frameability, where the adversary produces a target signature on an honest key after receiving signing and corruption oracle access, and must then produce a new signature that links.

More formally, a *linkable ring signature* (LRS) construction is a set of algorithms KeyGen, Sign, Verify, and Link satisfying certain properties. A set of public parameters is assumed to be available to each algorithm.

- KeyGen$(r) \rightarrow (x, X)$: Generates a secret key x and corresponding public key X, optionally using randomness r; if not specified, the secret key is sampled uniformly at random.
- Sign$(x, M, R) \rightarrow \sigma$: Generates a signature σ on a message $M \in \{0, 1\}^*$ with respect to the ring $R = \{X_1, \ldots, X_n\}$, provided that x is a secret key corresponding to some $X_i \in R$ generated by KeyGen.
- Verify$(\sigma, M, R) \rightarrow \{0, 1\}$: Verifies a signature σ on a message M with respect to the ring R. Outputs 0 is the signature is rejected, and 1 if accepted.
- Link$(\sigma, \sigma') \rightarrow \{0, 1\}$: Determines if signatures σ and σ' were signed using the same private key. Outputs 0 if the signatures were signed using different private keys, and 1 if they were signed using the same private key.

We require that an LRS have the properties of correctness, anonymity, unforgeability, linkability, and non-frameability.

Correctness requires that a signature generated honestly will always verify.

Definition 1 (Correctness). *Consider the following game between a challenger and a probabilistic polynomial-time adversary $\mathcal{A}$:*

- *The challenger runs KeyGen $\rightarrow (x, X)$ and supplies the keys to $\mathcal{A}$.*
- *The adversary $\mathcal{A}$ chooses a ring such that $X \in R$ and a message $M \in \{0, 1\}^*$, and sends them to the challenger.*
- *The challenger signs the message with Sign$(x, M, R) \rightarrow \sigma$.*

If $Pr[Verify(\sigma, M, R) = 1] = 1$, we say that the LRS is perfectly correct.

Note that we do not require any ring members (except for X) to have been generated by KeyGen. However, distributed applications may in practice place additional restrictions on public keys used in anonymity sets. This allows for the possibility that $\mathcal{A}$ maliciously chooses ring members.

Unforgeability requires that an adversary who does not control the private key to a ring member cannot generate a valid signature on any message using that ring.

Definition 2 (Unforgeability). *Consider the following game between a challenger and a probabilistic polynomial-time adversary* $\mathcal{A}$:

- *The adversary* $\mathcal{A}$ *is granted access to a public-key oracle GenOracle that (on the* i^{th} *invocation) runs KeyGen* $\rightarrow (x_i, X_i)$ *and returns* X_i *to* $\mathcal{A}$.
- *The adversary* $\mathcal{A}$ *is granted access to a corruption oracle CorruptOracle(i) that returns* x_i *if it corresponds to a query to GenOracle.*
- *The adversary* $\mathcal{A}$ *is granted access to a signing oracle SignOracle(X, M, R) that performs the query Sign(x, M, R)* $\rightarrow \sigma$ *and returns* σ *to* $\mathcal{A}$, *provided that* X *corresponds to a query to GenOracle and* $X \in R$.
- *Then,* $\mathcal{A}$ *outputs* (σ, M, R) *such that SignOracle was not queried with input* $(-, M, R)$, *all keys in* R *were generated by queries to GenOracle, and no key in* R *was corrupted by CorruptOracle.*

If $Pr[Verify(\sigma, M, R) = 1] \approx 0$, *then we say that the LRS is unforgeable with respect to insider corruption.*

Anonymity requires that as long as a ring contains at least two members that have not been corrupted, an adversary can do no better than guessing at determining the signer of an honest signature.

Definition 3 (Anonymity). *Consider the following game between a challenger and a probabilistic polynomial-time adversary* $\mathcal{A}$:

- *The adversary* $\mathcal{A}$ *is granted access to the public-key oracle GenOracle and the corruption oracle CorruptOracle.*
- *The adversary* $\mathcal{A}$ *chooses a message* $M \in \{0,1\}^*$, *a ring* R, *and indices* i_0 *and* i_1, *and sends them to the challenger. We require that* $X_{i_0}, X_{i_1} \in R$ *such that both keys were generated by queries to GenOracle, and neither key was queried to CorruptOracle.*
- *The challenger selects a uniformly random bit* $b \in \{0,1\}$, *generates a signature* $Sign(x_{i_b}, M, R) \rightarrow \sigma$, *and sends it to* $\mathcal{A}$.
- *The adversary* $\mathcal{A}$ *chooses a bit* $b' \in \{0,1\}$.

If $Pr[b' = b] \approx 1/2$ *and* $\mathcal{A}$ *did not make any corruption queries after receiving the challenge bit, we say that the LRS is anonymous.*

We observe that this definition permits the adversary to have corrupted or maliciously generated all but two keys in the ring. Some definitions allow the adversary to corrupt more keys, but we will see that this is inconsistent with our linkability construction, where an adversary in control of a ring member's private key can trivially determine if it was the signer by examining the linking tag associated to a signature.

Linkability requires that an adversary be unable to produce $k + 1$ non-linked signatures on a combined anonymity set of k public keys.

Definition 4 (Linkability). *Consider the following game between a challenger and a probabilistic polynomial-time adversary $\mathcal{A}$:*

- *For $i \in [0, k-1]$, the adversary $\mathcal{A}$ produces a public key X_i, message M_i, ring R_i, and signature σ_i.*
- *The adversary $\mathcal{A}$ produces another message M, ring R, and signature σ.*
- *All tuples $(X_i, M_i, R_i, \sigma_i)$ and (M, R, σ) are sent to the challenger.*
- *The challenger checks the following:*
  - *$|V| = k$, where $V \equiv \bigcup_{i=0}^{k-1} R_i$.*
  - *Each $X_i \in V$.*
  - *Each $R_i \subset V$.*
  - *$Verify(\sigma_i, M_i, R_i) = 1$ for all i.*
  - *$Verify(\sigma, M, R) = 1$.*
  - *For all $i \neq j$, we have $Link(\sigma_i, \sigma_j) = Link(\sigma_i, \sigma) = 0$.*
- *If all checks pass, $\mathcal{A}$ wins.*

If $\mathcal{A}$ wins with only negligible probability for all k, we say the LRS is linkable.

Non-frameability requires that an adversary be unable to generate a signature that links with an honest signature.

Definition 5 (Non-frameability). *Consider also the following game between a challenger and a probabilistic polynomial-time adversary $\mathcal{A}$:*

- *The adversary $\mathcal{A}$ is granted access to the public-key oracle GenOracle.*
- *The adversary $\mathcal{A}$ is granted access to the corruption oracle CorruptOracle.*
- *The adversary $\mathcal{A}$ is granted access to the signing oracle SignOracle.*
- *The adversary $\mathcal{A}$ chooses a public key X that was generated by a query to GenOracle, but was not presented as a query to CorruptOracle. It selects a message $M \in \{0,1\}^*$ and ring R such that $X \in R$. It queries $SignOracle(X, M, R) \to \sigma$.*
- *The adversary $\mathcal{A}$ then produces a tuple (M', R', σ') and sends (M', R', σ') to the challenger, along with (X, M, R, σ).*
- *If $Verify(\sigma', M', R') = 0$ or if σ' was produced using a query to SignOracle, the challenger aborts.*

If $Pr[Link(\sigma, \sigma') = 1] \approx 0$, we say that the LRS is non-frameable.

5   Application: Linkable Ring Signature

The constructions in [3, 12] describe how to use a similar sigma protocol to construct a simple ring signature scheme. Using our modifications, we can easily extend this to account for linkability and non-frameability. We briefly show how to do so.

Theorem 2. *The protocol in Fig. 3 is a linkable ring signature construction.*

KeyGen(r) :

- If not specified, select $r \in \mathbb{F}$ uniformly at random.
- Compute $R = rG$.
- Return $(x, X) = (r, R)$.

Sign(x, M, R) :

- Let $R = \{X_0, \ldots, X_{N-1}\}$ such that $X_l = x_l G$.
- Compute $J \equiv x_l^{-1} U$.
- Run $\mathcal{P}_{\text{link}}(R, J; (l, x_l)) \to a$ (up to the verifier challenge).
- Set $\xi \equiv \mathcal{H}(M, R, a)$.
- Run $\mathcal{P}_{\text{link}}(\xi) \to z$ (after the verifier challenge).
- Return $\sigma = (a, z, J)$.

Verify(σ, M, R) :

- Let $R = \{X_0, \ldots, X_{N-1}\}$ such that $X_l - x_l G$.
- Let $\sigma = (a, z, J)$.
- Set $\xi \equiv \mathcal{H}(M, R, a)$.
- Return $\mathcal{V}_{\text{link}}(R, J, a, z)$.

Link(σ, σ') :

- We implicitly assume that σ and σ' have been previously verified.
- Let $\sigma = (a, z, J)$ and $\sigma' = (a', z', J')$.
- If $J = J'$, return 1. Otherwise, return 0.

Fig. 3. Linkable ring signature using $\mathcal{R}_{\text{link}}$

Proof. Perfect correctness follows immediately from the perfect completeness of the proving system for $\mathcal{R}_{link}$.

Similarly, anonymity follows since the proving system is special honest-verifier zero knowledge, and therefore witness indistinguishable [5]. Any adversarial advantage in breaking anonymity must therefore arise from distinguishing either input commitments or linking tags in signatures. Since honestly-generated input Pedersen commitments are perfectly hiding, they are indistinguishable from elements of $\mathbb{G}$ selected uniformly at random; we assume by definition that at least two such commitments are present in such a signature. Further, honestly-generated linking tags are generated from a one-way pseudorandom function, and therefore in the random oracle model are independently uniformly distributed from other proof elements and input commitments.

The proof for unforgeability in [12] relies on the (special) soundness of the underlying sigma protocol; it applies directly to our modification for $\mathcal{R}_{link}$, and is not repeated here.

To show linkability, observe first that Link simply compares linking tags, so two signatures link if and only if they share a common linking tag. Suppose an adversary can win the linkability game with non-negligible probability for some $k > 1$. Since all provided signatures verify, soundness implies extraction of a witness x_i from signature σ_i for all i, and of a witness x from σ. Note that all $\{x_i\}$ and x are distinct. If $x_i = x_j$ for $i \neq j$, then the corresponding linking tags J_i and J_j are such that $x_i J_i = x_j J_j = U$; then $J_i = J_j$, which contradicts $\text{Link}(\sigma_i, \sigma_j) = 0$. The same reasoning holds to show x is similarly distinct. Soundness also implies that for all i, there exists $X_i \in R_i$ such that $x_i G = X_i$; similarly, there exists $X \in R$ such that $xG = X$. By assumption we have

$$\{X_0, \ldots, X_{k-1}, X\} \subset \left(\bigcup_{i=0}^{k-1} R_i \right) \cup R \subset V.$$

However, note that $|\{X_0, \ldots, X_{k-1}, X\}| = k + 1$, but that $|V| = k$, a contradiction.

Finally, we show non-frameability and assume that an adversary has a non-negligible advantage in breaking this property. Because $\text{Verify}(\sigma', M', R') = 1$, soundness implies extraction of a witness $x' \in \mathbb{F}$ such that $x'G \in R'$; we also have a witness x such that $xG \in R$ from the known signature σ. Since $\text{Link}(\sigma, \sigma') = 1$, the corresponding linking tags J and J' are equal by definition; hence by soundness $xJ = x'J' = U$, giving $x = x'$. However, the adversary did not query CorruptOracle with X, meaning it breaks the discrete logarithm problem non-negligibly.

6   Protocol: Parallel Linkable One-of-many Commitment

In this section, we describe a modification of the sigma protocol for $\mathcal{R}_{\text{link}}$ that permits us to prove knowledge of multiple commitments in $d > 1$ separate sets at the same index position, while retaining the linking property in the first commitment set only. This forms a version of Triptych with the same functionality as the d-linkable ring signature construction in [10], although the precise security model is a bit different. We later show how to apply such a construction to a signer-ambiguous transaction protocol that can demonstrate balance preservation.

We wish to produce a sigma protocol for the following relation, for some given vector dimension $d > 1$.

$$\mathcal{R}_{\text{par}} = \left\{ \{M_{i,\alpha}\}_{i,\alpha=0}^{N-1,d-1} \subset \mathbb{G}^d, J \in G; \left(l, \{r_\alpha\}_{\alpha=0}^{d-1} \right) : \right.$$

$$\left. \{M_{l,\alpha} = r_\alpha G\}_{\alpha=0}^{d-1} \text{ and } U = r_0 J \right\}$$

This requires only minor modifications to the protocol for $\mathcal{R}_{\text{link}}$, so we document only the modified proof elements constructed and verified in Fig. 4. All other proof elements are generated and verified identically.

Theorem 3. *The protocol in Fig. 4 is perfectly complete, special honest-verifier zero knowledge, and $(m + 1)$-special sound.*

Proof. In the random oracle model, extraction of a witness of the form $r_0 + \sum_\alpha \mu_\alpha r_\alpha$ implies knowledge of all $\{r_\alpha\}$ such that $r_\alpha G = M_{l,\alpha}$, similarly to the key-aggregation arguments in [17]. The same extraction gives

$$\left(r_0 + \sum_\alpha \mu_\alpha r_\alpha\right) J = U + \sum_\alpha \mu_\alpha K_\alpha,$$

which implies in particular that $r_0 J = U$, as required.

The rest of the proof follows with only trivial modifications from the proof for $\mathcal{R}_{\text{link}}$.

7 Application: Signer-Ambiguous Transaction Protocol

The parallel construction described in Fig. 4 can be used with $d = 2$ in a signer-ambiguous transaction protocol.

Suppose a user wishes to generate a transaction consuming W previously-generated outputs and generating T fresh outputs. The user shuffles the consumed outputs within a larger list of N outputs $\{M_{k,0}\}_{k=0}^{N-1}$, such that there exist indices $\{l_u\}_{u=0}^{W-1}$ where each $M_{l_u,0} = r_u$ for some known private key r_u. Further, assume each $M_{l_u,0}$ comes equipped with an amount commitment of the form $M_{l_u,1} \equiv, (a_u, s_u)$ for amount a_u and mask s_u. (All other $M_{k,0}$ also come equipped with a corresponding $M_{k,1}$, but the structure of these points is not relevant here.)

The user generates W auxiliary commitments $P'_u \equiv, (a_u, s'_u)$ to the same amounts, but with different masks $\{s'_u\}$ chosen uniformly at random from $\mathbb{F}$. Then, the user generates W spend proofs, each using the following prover inputs for $u \in [0, W)$:

$$\mathcal{P}_{par}(\{M_{k,0}\}_{k=0}^{N-1}, \{M_{k,1} - P'_u\}_{k=0}^{N-1}, r_u^{-1} U; (l_u, r_u, s_u - s'_u))$$

For $j \in [0, T)$, the user generates a fresh output of the form $Q_j \equiv, (b_j, t_j)$ for amount b_j and mask t_j. The masks are chosen such that for $j \in [1, T)$, we have t_j chosen uniformly at random from $\mathbb{F}$. We then choose

$$t_0 \equiv \sum_{u=0}^{W-1} s'_u - \sum_{j=1}^{T-1} t_j$$

and include all $\{P'_u\}$ auxiliary commitments in the transaction.

To verify such a transaction, the verifier first performs verification on each spend proof to ensure it is valid. Then, the verifier ensures that

$$\sum_{u=0}^{W-1} P'_u - \sum_{j=0}^{T-1} Q_j = 0$$

such that the transaction balances. This succeeds since the commitments sum to zero if and only if the difference of input and output amounts is zero, which holds since the Pedersen commitment construction is computationally binding.

8 Efficiency

Triptych proofs scale logarithmically with the size of the input anonymity set; this is the best asymptotic scaling known for ring signatures that do not require a trusted setup process over non-pairing groups. Related protocols based on the inner-product compression method of [4] include Omniring [15] and RingCT 3.0 [15]. However, it is challenging to directly compare these protocols' efficiency. Omniring includes all transaction input signatures, output range proofs, and balance within a single proof structure; however, it is not possible to verify a batch of proofs more efficiently by combining common generators. While an early version of RingCT 3.0 used separate input, range, and balance proofs, the most recent version merges all input and balance proofs together but outsources the range proofs to an efficient construction like [4]; this comes at the cost of requiring that the number of inputs be a power of two or otherwise carefully padded (affecting verification time). Therefore, for the purpose of comparison we modify slightly the earlier version of RingCT 3.0 with a soundness fix applied from the updated version, ignoring the size and verification cost of non-proof elements. Another more direct comparison is to CLSAG, a linear-sized linkable ring signature construction [10].

We now show size and verification comparisons of the parallel instantiation of Triptych with $d = 2$, the earlier (modified) version of RingCT 3.0, and 2-CLSAG. For verification scaling, we also account for the use of batching in Triptych and RingCT 3.0, where generators common to multiple proofs are used only once in verification. Further, since verification in both of these constructions reduces to checking whether several multiscalar multiplications are zero, we may apply random weighting such that verifying a batch of multiple proofs reduces to a single multiscalar multiplication. The use of efficient multiscalar multiplication algorithms like [20,23] means that an n-multiscalar multiplication evaluates as $O(n/\log n)$. This form of batching does not apply to CLSAG, where verification consists of a sequence of hash function evaluations.

Table 1 compares proof/signature sizes and verification complexity for these constructions as a function of the anonymity set size N and batch size B. Verification complexity is separated into the number of hash-to-$\mathbb{F}$ operations (denoted $\mathcal{H}$), hash-to-$\mathbb{G}$ operations (denoted $\mathbb{H}$), and i-multiscalar multiplication operations of size $k(i)$. We note that although RingCT 3.0 proofs are slightly smaller for large N, Triptych proofs are smaller for $N < 512$, a limited but reasonable range given practical verification times. We also note that the application of Triptych in a complete transaction protocol is not directly compared to RingCT 3.0 here, as the use of non-proof/signature auxiliary data in such a protocol may differ based on particular implementations.

$\mathcal{P}_{\text{par}}\left(\{M_{i,\alpha}\}, J; (l, \{r_\alpha\})\right):$

- Define $K_\alpha \equiv r_\alpha J$ for $\alpha \in (0, d)$.
- Define $\mu_\alpha \equiv \mathcal{H}\left(\alpha, \{M_{i,\alpha}\}, J, \{K_\alpha\}\right)$ for $\alpha \in (0, d)$.
- Define $\{X_j\}_{j=0}^{m-1} \subset \mathbb{G}$ such that:

$$X_j \equiv \sum_{k=0}^{N-1} p_{k,j}\left(M_{k,0} + \sum_{\alpha=1}^{d-1} \mu_\alpha M_{k,\alpha}\right) + \rho_j G$$

- Define $\{Y_j\}_{j=0}^{m-1} \subset \mathbb{G}$ such that:

$$Y_j \equiv \left(U + \sum_{\alpha=1}^{d-1} \mu_\alpha K_\alpha\right) \sum_{k=0}^{N-1} p_{k,j} + \rho_j G$$

$\mathcal{P} \to \mathcal{V}:$
$\{K_\alpha\}, \{X_j\}, \{Y_j\}$

$\mathcal{V} \to \mathcal{P}:$
$\xi \in \{0,1\}^*$

$\mathcal{P}(\xi):$

- Define $z \equiv \left(r_0 + \sum_{\alpha=1}^{d-1} \mu_\alpha r_\alpha\right)\xi^m - \sum_{j=0}^{m-1} \rho_j \xi^j.$

$\mathcal{P} \to \mathcal{V}:$
z

$\mathcal{V}_{\text{par}}(\{M_{i,\alpha}\}, J):$

- Define $\mu_\alpha \equiv \mathcal{H}\left(\alpha, \{M_{i,\alpha}\}, J, \{K_\alpha\}\right)$ for $\alpha \in (0, d)$.
- Accept if and only if:

$$\sum_{k=0}^{N-1}\left(M_{k,0} + \sum_{\alpha=1}^{d-1} \mu_\alpha M_{k,\alpha}\right)\left(\prod_{j=0}^{m-1} f_{j,k_j}\right) - \sum_{j=0}^{m-1} \xi^j X_j - zG = 0$$

$$\left(U + \sum_{\alpha=1}^{d-1} \mu_\alpha K_\alpha\right)\sum_{k=0}^{N-1}\left(\prod_{j=0}^{m-1} f_{j,k_j}\right) - \sum_{j=0}^{m-1} \xi^j Y_j - zJ = 0$$

Fig. 4. Sigma protocol (abbreviated) for $\mathcal{R}_{\text{par}}$

Table 1. Proof sizes and verification complexity, for anonymity set size N and batch size B

	Size ($\mathbb{G}$)	Size ($\mathbb{F}$)	Verification (batch total)
CLSAG [10]	2	$N+1$	$B(N+2)\mathcal{H} + BN\mathbb{H} + 2BNk(3)$
RingCT 3.0 [24]	$2\lg(N) + 9$	9	$k(B[2N + 2\lg(N) + 9] + 2N + 5)$
Triptych (this work)	$2\lg(N) + 6$	$\lg(N) + 3$	$k(B[2N + 2\lg(N) + 2] + 2\lg(N) + 3)$

References

1. Backes, M., Döttling, N., Hanzlik, L., Kluczniak, K., Schneider, J.: Ring signatures: logarithmic-size, no setup—from standard assumptions. In: Ishai, Y., Rijmen, V. (eds.) EUROCRYPT 2019. LNCS, vol. 11478, pp. 281–311. Springer, Cham (2019). https://doi.org/10.1007/978-3-030-17659-4_10

2. Bender, A., Katz, J., Morselli, R.: Ring signatures: stronger definitions, and constructions without random oracles. In: Halevi, S., Rabin, T. (eds.) TCC 2006. LNCS, vol. 3876, pp. 60–79. Springer, Heidelberg (2006). https://doi.org/10.1007/11681878_4

3. Bootle, J., Cerulli, A., Chaidos, P., Ghadafi, E., Groth, J., Petit, C.: Short accountable ring signatures based on DDH. In: Pernul, G., Ryan, P.Y.A., Weippl, E. (eds.) ESORICS 2015. LNCS, vol. 9326, pp. 243–265. Springer, Cham (2015). https://doi.org/10.1007/978-3-319-24174-6_13

4. Bünz, B., Bootle, J., Boneh, D., Poelstra, A., Wuille, P., Maxwell, G.: Bulletproofs: short proofs for confidential transactions and more. In: 2018 IEEE Symposium on Security and Privacy (SP), pp. 315–334. IEEE (2018)

5. Cramer, R., Damgård, I., Schoenmakers, B.: Proofs of partial knowledge and simplified design of witness hiding protocols. In: Desmedt, Y.G. (ed.) CRYPTO 1994. LNCS, vol. 839, pp. 174–187. Springer, Heidelberg (1994). https://doi.org/10.1007/3-540-48658-5_19

6. Dodis, Y., Yampolskiy, A.: A verifiable random function with short proofs and keys. In: Vaudenay, S. (ed.) PKC 2005. LNCS, vol. 3386, pp. 416–431. Springer, Heidelberg (2005). https://doi.org/10.1007/978-3-540-30580-4_28

7. Fiat, A., Shamir, A.: How to prove yourself: practical solutions to identification and signature problems. In: Odlyzko, A.M. (ed.) CRYPTO 1986. LNCS, vol. 263, pp. 186–194. Springer, Heidelberg (1987). https://doi.org/10.1007/3-540-47721-7_12

8. Fujisaki, E.: Sub-linear Size Traceable Ring Signatures without Random Oracles. In: Kiayias, A. (ed.) CT-RSA 2011. LNCS, vol. 6558, pp. 393–415. Springer, Heidelberg (2011). https://doi.org/10.1007/978-3-642-19074-2_25

9. Fujisaki, E., Suzuki, K.: Traceable ring signature. In: Okamoto, T., Wang, X. (eds.) PKC 2007. LNCS, vol. 4450, pp. 181–200. Springer, Heidelberg (2007). https://doi.org/10.1007/978-3-540-71677-8_13

10. Goodell, B., Noether, S., Blue, A.: Compact linkable ring signatures and applications. Cryptology ePrint Archive, Report 2019/654 (2019). https://eprint.iacr.org/2019/654

11. Groth, J.: On the size of pairing-based non-interactive arguments. In: Fischlin, M., Coron, J.-S. (eds.) EUROCRYPT 2016. LNCS, vol. 9666, pp. 305–326. Springer, Heidelberg (2016). https://doi.org/10.1007/978-3-662-49896-5_11

12. Groth, J., Kohlweiss, M.: One-out-of-many proofs: or how to leak a secret and spend a coin. In: Oswald, E., Fischlin, M. (eds.) EUROCRYPT 2015. LNCS, vol. 9057, pp. 253–280. Springer, Heidelberg (2015). https://doi.org/10.1007/978-3-662-46803-6_9

13. Hopwood, D., Bowe, S., Hornby, T., Wilcox, N.: Zcash protocol specification. Technical Report 2016-1.10. Zerocoin Electric Coin Company, Technical Report (2016)

14. Jivanyan, A.: Lelantus: Towards confidentiality and anonymity of blockchain transactions from standard assumptions. Cryptology ePrint Archive, Report 2019/373 (2019). https://eprint.iacr.org/2019/373

15. Lai, R.W.F., Ronge, V., Ruffing, T., Schröder, D., Thyagarajan, S.A.K., Wang, J.: Omniring: Scaling up private payments without trusted setup-formal foundations and constructions of ring confidential transactions with log-size proofs. Cryptology ePrint Archive, Report 2019/580 (2019). https://eprint.iacr.org/2019/580

16. Liu, J.K., Wei, V.K., Wong, D.S.: Linkable spontaneous anonymous group signature for Ad Hoc groups. In: Wang, H., Pieprzyk, J., Varadharajan, V. (eds.) ACISP 2004. LNCS, vol. 3108, pp. 325–335. Springer, Heidelberg (2004). https://doi.org/10.1007/978-3-540-27800-9_28

17. Maxwell, G., Poelstra, A., Seurin, Y., Wuille, P.: Simple Schnorr multi-signatures with applications to Bitcoin. Des. Codes Cryptogr. **87**(9), 2139–2164 (2019). https://doi.org/10.1007/s10623-019-00608-x

18. Miers, I., Garman, C., Green, M., Rubin, A.D.: Zerocoin: anonymous distributed e-cash from bitcoin. In: 2013 IEEE Symposium on Security and Privacy, pp. 397–411. IEEE (2013)

19. Noether, S., Mackenzie, A.: The Monero Research Lab. Ring confidential transactions. Ledger, vol. 1(0), pp. 1–18 (2016)

20. Pippenger, N.: On the evaluation of powers and monomials. SIAM J. Comput. **9**(2), 230–250 (1980)

21. Rivest, R.L., Shamir, A., Tauman, Y.: How to leak a secret. In: Boyd, C. (ed.) ASIACRYPT 2001. LNCS, vol. 2248, pp. 552–565. Springer, Heidelberg (2001). https://doi.org/10.1007/3-540-45682-1_32

22. Schnorr, C.P.: Efficient signature generation by smart cards. J. Cryptol. **4**(3), 161–174 (1991). https://doi.org/10.1007/BF00196725

23. Straus, E.G.: Addition chains of vectors (problem 5125). Am. Math. Mon. **70**(806–808), 16 (1964)

24. Yuen, T.H., et al.: RingCT 3.0 for blockchain confidential transaction: Shorter size and stronger security. Cryptology ePrint Archive, Report 2019/508 (2019). https://eprint.iacr.org/2019/508

Moderated Redactable Blockchains: A Definitional Framework with an Efficient Construct

Mohammad Sadeq Dousti[1]([✉]) and Alptekin Küpçü[2]

[1] Johannes Gutenberg University, Mainz, Germany
modousti@uni-mainz.de
[2] Koç University, İstanbul, Turkey
akupcu@ku.edu.tr

Abstract. Blockchain is a multiparty protocol to reach agreement on the order of events, and to record them consistently and immutably without centralized trust. In some cases, however, the blockchain can benefit from some *controlled* mutability. Examples include removing private information or unlawful content, and correcting protocol vulnerabilities which would otherwise require a *hard fork*. Two approaches to control the mutability are: *moderation*, where one or more designated administrators can use their private keys to approve a redaction, and *voting*, where miners can vote to endorse a suggested redaction. In this paper, we first present several attacks against existing redactable blockchain solutions. Next, we provide a definitional framework for moderated redactable blockchains. Finally, we propose a provable and efficient construct, which applies a single digital signature per redaction, achieving a much simpler and secure result compared to the prior art in the moderated setting.

Keywords: Blockchain · Bitcoin · Moderated redactable blockchain · Formal threat model · Signature scheme

1 Introduction

The concept of blockchain was pioneered by Bitcoin [16]. It is a distributed protocol that allows all honest parties to keep a ledger of event logs in a consistent manner and without any trust assumption. There are various incarnations of blockchains, which may relax or strengthen some of the conditions. The original blockchain is *permissionless*, meaning any party can participate in the protocol. *Permissioned* blockchains operate in an authenticated environment, where joining the network is subject to an administrative decision. A *private* blockchain is a specific type of permissioned blockchain, where every participant can view the ledger, but only an authorized set of entities can append. For further discussion, see [13].

© Springer Nature Switzerland AG 2020
J. Garcia-Alfaro et al. (Eds.): DPM 2020/CBT 2020, LNCS 12484, pp. 355–373, 2020.
https://doi.org/10.1007/978-3-030-66172-4_23

One of the most important properties of blockchain is the *immutability* of the ledger. After all, cryptocurrencies require that once a transaction is recorded, it cannot be undone. However, this desirable property has its downsides. Criminals have occasionally appended arbitrary contents to the ledger that is forbidden by national or international laws—such as child abuse [11,12] and malware [18]. Another use case is where some information about a user is stored in the ledger, and later the user requests them to be removed [15], exercising the "right to be forgotten" under privacy laws such as the General Data Protection Regulation (GDPR) [4]. A third case is when a massive fraud has been made possible due to a flaw in the blockchain protocol. In immutable blockchains, the only way to invalidate such fraudulent transactions is by updating the protocol and the software—a process known as a *hard fork*. The DAO Attack [3] is an example, which resulted in a hard fork in Ethereum [20] back in 2016. For further discussion, see [1].

To overcome the limitations associated with immutability, several researchers proposed solutions for *controlled* mutability. The literature has two approaches for controlling the mutability: *Moderated* [1,5,10], where redactions can only be applied by a designated set of users (known as the administrators), and *unmoderated* (or voting-based) [7,19] where suggested redactions are voted on, and applied only if they receive a quorum of votes within a specific period. Notice that the terms permissioned and moderated are orthogonal: In permissioned blockchains, users need administrative permission to join the network. In moderated blockchains, administrators must approve redactions (changes to the blocks in the ledger). Even in a blockchain that is both moderated and permissioned, the administrators in charge of admitting users can be different from the administrators in charge of approving redactions.

In this paper, four novel attacks are presented against existing redactable blockchains: Two attacks against moderated constructs, and two against the unmoderated ones. Learning from the attacks, we suggest the goals for a definitional framework for redactable blockchains, and put forward an adversarial model and a security definition satisfying those goals. Finally, two constructs of redactable blockchains are presented: The former serves as an instrumental example, and is proven incorrect and insecure. The latter resolves the issues, and we prove it both correct and secure in our definitional framework.

2   Previous Work

Moderated Redactable Blockchains. In their seminal work, Ateniese et al. [1] constructed the first redactable blockchain. They proposed a special primitive called an *enhanced chameleon hash function*. A chameleon hash function is a collision-resistant hash function, such that finding collisions is easy given a private (trapdoor) key. The *enhanced* version satisfies the additional property that finding collisions (without the private key) is hard, even if the adversary can get collisions for inputs of her choice from an oracle. The primitive is rather complex and involved: In the standard model, it requires a witness whose size is 18 group elements under the SXDH assumption, or 39 group elements under the DLIN assumption [1]. Derler et al. [6] extended the above idea above to attribute-based chameleon hashes. Instead of applying redactions freely at the block level, the administrators are bound by a fine-grained policy on what attributes they can change. They employ *ciphertext-policy attribute-based encryptions* and *chameleon hashes with ephemeral trapdoors*. Recently, Grigoriev and Shpilrain [10] proposed a simple construct based on textbook RSA. However, Sect. 4 shows that it is insecure.

Interestingly, none of the work listed above provides a security model/definition tailored specifically for redactable blockchains, and therefore their constructs have no security proofs: While [1,6] focus on proving the security of the underlying cryptographic primitives (e.g., the enhanced chameleon hash function), [10] has no rigorous proof of security. We also show that all constructs succumb to reversion attacks.

Unmoderated (Voting-based) Redactable Blockchains. Puddu et al. [19] defined an idea called μchain for enabling mutability for proof-of-work blockchains. The mutability is controlled by fiat, imposed by consensus, and is publicly verifiable. It can be used in both moderated and unmoderated settings: In the moderated setting, the sender can create multiple mutations of a transaction, and encrypt all but one (the active transaction). The decryption key is distributed between miners using a secret-sharing scheme. The sender also proposes a policy as to how other mutations can be activated, and by whom. If a mutation request is approved by this policy, miners decrypt the intended mutation by a multi-party decryption protocol. In the unmoderated setting, the mutation to be activated is voted on. Deuber et al. [7] discuss various issues with μchain. They also propose a distributed consensus protocol for redaction. Their protocol does not require heavy cryptographic operations or trusting a set of administrators. It starts when a participant proposes a redaction. If the proposed block satisfies the verification algorithm, it enters a voting phase. If enough miners vote for it within a certain period of time, the change is applied to the ledger.

In Sect. 4, we show that care must be taken when dealing with votes. In particular, if not properly designed and implemented, it is possible to redact a block containing a vote for some previous block, which may render the corresponding redactions invalid. Furthermore, we explore possible ways where a minority group can prevent a policy to be applied, or even go against the policy.

3 Preliminaries

Assignment Notation. Assignments are denoted as $x \leftarrow 2$. To say something holds by definition, we use $x \stackrel{\text{def}}{=} y$. The symbol $x = y$ is used for checking or asserting equality.

List Manipulation. Let $\mathcal{L} \stackrel{\text{def}}{=} [B_0, \ldots, B_\ell]$ be a list. The elements of the list can be addressed by their index: $B_i \stackrel{\text{def}}{=} \mathcal{L}[i]$ for $0 \leq i \leq \ell$. We use the following

---

1. GenSig(1^λ) is run to obtain pk and sk.
2. The adversary $\mathcal{A}$ is given pk and access to the signing oracle $\text{Sign}_{sk}(\cdot)$, and she returns a pair (m, σ). Let t be the number of queries $\mathcal{A}$ asks its oracle, and $Q \overset{\text{def}}{=} \{(m_i, \sigma_i)\}_{i=1}^t$ be the set of query-response pairs. That is, m_i is the ith query, and σ_i is the corresponding response from the oracle.
3. The adversary is said to win if VerifySig(pk, m, σ) = 1 and $(m, \sigma) \neq Q$. In this case, the experiment outputs 1. Otherwise, it outputs 0.

Experiment 1. The strong signature forgery experiment $\text{SSig-forge}_{\mathcal{A},\Pi}^{\text{cma}}(\lambda)$, where the adversary can mount a chosen-message attack.

notation to address sublists: For integers i, j with $0 \leq i \leq j \leq \text{len}(\mathcal{L})$, define $\mathcal{L}[i : j] \overset{\text{def}}{=} [B_i, \ldots, B_j]$. If $j < i$, the sublist is empty. If $\mathcal{L}_1$ and $\mathcal{L}_2$ are two list, their concatenation is denoted by $\mathcal{L}_1 + \mathcal{L}_2$.

Blocks. A block B is denoted by a tuple, such as (P, C, V, W), containing various components. Each component can be set to a default value, such as the empty string ε. Blockchains may add other or remove components of their choice to the block structure. Here is the description of the most common components: P is the prefix of the block. It is often a function of previous blocks in the ledger. C is the content of the block (in cryptocurrency nomenclature, it is the set of transactions). V is the version of the block. W is the witness of the block. It is used in redactions. We assume the existence of efficient algorithms Prefix(B), Content(B), Version(B), and Witness(W), which efficiently extract the relevant component from block B. If we are interested in a block except one of its components, we denote it by striking through that component: $B^{\cancel{W}}$ is block B except its W component.

sUF-CMA Secure Signatures. The main primitive used in our construct is a signature schemes *strongly* unforgeable under adaptive chosen-message attack (sUF-CMA). Let us define the syntax and security for this primitive.

Definition 1 (Syntax of Signature Schemes). *A signature scheme consists of three efficient algorithms* $\Pi \overset{\text{def}}{=} (\text{GenSig}, \text{Sign}, \text{VerifySig})$, *satisfying the following:*

- *On input the security parameter* 1^λ, *the key generation algorithm* GenSig *creates a pair of keys* (pk, sk). *We assume that* $|pk|, |sk| \geq \lambda$, *and* λ *can be inferred from each key.*
- *On input any message* m *in the message space, the signing algorithm generates a signature:* $\sigma \leftarrow \text{Sign}(sk, m)$.
- *On input any message* m *in the message space, and any signature* σ *created on* m *by the signing algorithm, the (deterministic) verification algorithm must return 1:* VerifySig($pk, m, \text{Sign}(sk, m)$) = 1.

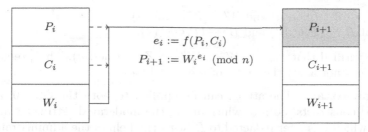

Fig. 1. The relationship between two consecutive blocks in the GS Construct. C_i is the content. W_i is the witness, which is picked uniformly from $\mathbb{Z}_n$ such that it does not to have order 2. The prefix P_{i+1} depends on all parts of block B_i via the relation $P_{i+1} \leftarrow W_i^{f(P_i,C_i)} \pmod{n}$, where n is an RSA modulus and f is an efficient integer-valued function.

The strong security of signature schemes is defined as follows:

Definition 2 (Strong Unforgeability of Signature Schemes). *A signature scheme* $\Pi \overset{\text{def}}{=} (\mathsf{GenSig}, \mathsf{Sign}, \mathsf{VerifySig})$ *is strongly unforgeable under adaptive chosen-message attack (sUF-CMA) if for every efficient adversary* $\mathcal{A}$ *taking part in Experiment 1, there exists a negligible function* negl, *such that*

$$\Pr[\mathsf{SSig\text{-}forge}^{\mathsf{cma}}_{\mathcal{A},\Pi}(\lambda) = 1] \leq \mathsf{negl}(\lambda).$$

The main assumption of this section is the existence of sUF-CMA secure signature schemes. There are efficient transformations that convert any UF-CMA secure signature to an sUF-CMA secure one [14]. Boneh et al. [2, p. 230] provide a list of many constructions of efficient sUF-CMA signatures in the literature, both in the standard and the random oracle models.

4 Novel Attacks on Previous Constructs

In this section, we explain several attacks against certain previous constructs, which carry over their desired security properties from immutable blockchain models [9,17], to the redactable setting. We stress that most attacks can be easily prevented by small modifications in the corresponding construct. However, the mere existence of the attacks in the face of security proofs shows that one should consider an adversarial model tailored for the redactable blockchains. Due to a lack of space, we only provide an overview of the attacks. The interested reader may refer to the full version of this paper [8] for further details.

Moderator Circumvention Attack: The attack is specific to the GS Construct [10], whose block relationship is depicted in Fig. 1. The attacker can craft two blocks B and B', append B to the ledger, and at any point in time replace it with B'. It works without administrator involvement, since the witness verification simply holds for both blocks. It works as follows:

1. Pick Z from $\mathbb{Z}_n$ uniformly at random. Retry this step if Z has order 2.
2. Let $e \leftarrow f(P, C)$ and $e' \leftarrow f(P, C')$.

3. Let $W \leftarrow Z^{e'} \pmod{n}$ and $W' \leftarrow Z^e \pmod{n}$.
4. Output $B \leftarrow (P, C, W)$ and $B' \leftarrow (P, C', W')$.

It can be verified that $P_{\text{next}} = W^e = W'^{e'} = Z^{e \cdot e'} \pmod{n}$. Thus, replacing B with B' does not affect the prefix of the next block.

Reversion Attack: The attack can be applied to both the GS [10] and the AMVA [1] constructs, both of which are in the moderated settings. Consider a block B, which was later redacted to B' with the help of the administrators. An adversary can simply revert a redacted block B' to its previous state B: Since no versioning scheme is in place, all versions of a block are valid.

Vote Erasure Attack: The vote erasure is a special kind of attack where a series of valid actions on the ledger puts it in an *inconsistent* state, meaning that at least one block is no longer valid. Erasing votes already collected for a redaction is only applicable to the voting (unmoderated) settings, like the DMTS Construct [7]. In this construct, a redaction B_i^* is suggested by a participant. After validating this block, a voting period starts. It comprises the next t blocks appended to the ledger. If at least a ρ fraction of these t blocks endorse this redaction, it is considered approved, and every (honest) participant applies the redaction. Miners who want to endorse this redaction must include the hash $H(B_i^*)$ in the content of blocks they mine. The authors use $t = 4$ and $\rho = 3/4$. This means that in the next four mined blocks, at least three must include $H(B_i^*)$, as illustrated below:

$$\cdots \rightarrow \underbrace{B_i}_{\text{redact to } B_i^*} \rightarrow \cdots \rightarrow \underbrace{B_\ell}_{\text{last block}} \rightarrow \boxed{\underbrace{B_{\ell+1} \rightarrow B_{\ell+2} \rightarrow B_{\ell+3} \rightarrow B_{\ell+4}}_{\text{voting period}}} \rightarrow \cdots$$

When the redaction B_i^* is suggested, the last block was B_ℓ. In the voting period, four blocks $B_{\ell+1}, \ldots, B_{\ell+4}$ are mined. If at least three of them include the hash $H(B_i^*)$ in their content, then the redaction is approved, and every honest participant updates its local ledger to include B_i^* instead of B_i.

For concreteness, assume that except for $B_{\ell+4}$, all other blocks in the voting period endorsed this redaction. An adversary can now propose a redaction $B_{\ell+1}^*$, which is identical to $B_{\ell+1}$, but does not include the hash $H(B_i^*)$. This suggestion goes through the voting period, and since nothing in the DMTS Construct forbids redacting "ballot blocks" it might be approved. However, removing the vote results in the ledger being in an inconsistent state: On the one hand, the ledger of honest participants includes B_i^*. On the other hand, the ledger now has only two votes for it, which means the redaction is not approved. Any joining party who receives a copy of the ledger and verifies it can observe this discrepancy.

It is easy to prevent this attack by designating the blocks including votes as special "ballot blocks." It must be required that ballot blocks are not redactable, or at least their redaction cannot remove the vote from the block.

Miner Corruption Attack: The attack is applicable to the DMTS Construct [7]. Let the approval quorum be $\rho \stackrel{\text{def}}{=} \frac{3}{4}$, as suggested by the paper: When a redaction is proposed, at least three out of the next four mined blocks should carry a vote approving the redaction. Consider an adversary who controls 49%

of the miners, all of whom *abstain* from endorsing any redactions. A simple combinatorial analysis shows that even if all honest miners vote in favor of all redactions, only $\binom{4}{3}(0.51)^3(0.49) + (0.51)^4 \approx 33\%$ of them are approved. Furthermore, for an adversarially suggested redaction, even if all honest miners refrain from voting, there is a $\binom{4}{3}(0.49)^3(0.51) + (0.49)^4 \approx 30\%$ chance of approval. Increasing ρ decreases the chance of honest redactions, while decreasing it increases the chance of adversarial redactions.

5   Defining Moderated Redactable Blockchain

5.1   Design Goals

Section 4 demonstrates that adapting existing models and definitions of immutable blockchains to the redactable setting is challenging, as mutability opens a variety of ways for an adversary to attack the blockchain. We propose decoupling the two notions: A challenger is introduced, who enforces most of the restrictions imposed by an immutable blockchain. On the other hand, we allow the adversary to control the participants in the network, receive an arbitrary number of redactions, and install an arbitrary number of blocks in the ledger. In designing our definitional framework, we pursued the following goals:

- **Bitcoin independence:** The framework should *not* impose Bitcoin protocol or data structures. For instance, the blockchain designer might opt not to include the hash of the previous block in the current block.
- **Consensus independence:** The framework should *not* impose a specific consensus mechanism, such as the proof of work (PoW) or the proof of stake (PoS). Rather, it should depend on an abstraction that provides consensus.
- **General content:** The framework should *not* assume that the content of each block includes a set of transactions. Rather, the content must be treated as an arbitrary bit string.
- **Simplicity:** The framework should be as simple as possible. With this aim, we abstract out the distributed nature of the network by a centralizing challenger.
- **Moderation:** The framework should support the moderated setting. This is by choice rather than merit, meaning a framework for the unmoderated setting is equally important, but is left as future work.
- **Operation segregation:** The framework should *not* combine operations which are semantically different. For instance, consider redaction and installation: When an administrator is asked for a redaction, he should merely return a redacted block, rather than installing the block in the ledger. The installation must be performed separately.
- **Allowing adversarial transformation:** The framework should allow the adversary to append any valid block at the end of the ledger. Also, she must be able to receive the redaction of as many blocks as she wants. Finally, she must be able to install any valid redaction.

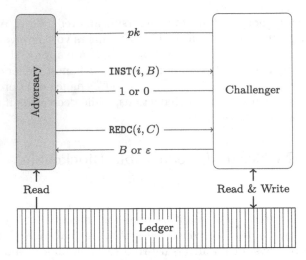

Fig. 2. The proposed adversarial model. The challenger creates a key pair and the ledger. It gives the public key pk to the adversary, and provides her with read-only access to the ledger. All write operations (installations) should go through the challenger's INST interface, by specifying the location i pointing to a valid block index in the ledger, and the block B to be installed. The challenger returns 1 if the installation is successful, and 0 otherwise. The adversary can also request redactions via the challenger's REDC interface. She provides the redaction location i, as well as the new block's content C. If the operation is successful, the challenger returns a redacted block B, which can then be installed using its INST interface. Otherwise, the challenger returns an empty block ε. The adversary is deemed successful if she installs a redacted block which is not obtained via the REDC interface.

- **Ledger consistency:** The ledger must remain consistent at all times. That is, there should not be a valid transformation that invalidates one or more blocks already installed in the ledger (cf. Sect. 4).

5.2   Informal Model

Figure 2 illustrates our definitional framework informally. Notice that it resembles a game between a challenger and a single adversary. It is as if she has total control over the participants in the blockchain: As long as she plays by the rules, she can append any valid block to the ledger, request any block content to be redacted to an arbitrary yet valid value, and install any valid redacted block. Furthermore, no modification is made to the chain without the adversary saying so. In fact, the challenger is an abstraction of an ideal consensus protocol. The goal of the adversary is to create a redacted block which is not provided by the administrators controlled by the challenger, and install it in the ledger.

Observe the similarity with the way signature schemes are modeled: Obtaining redactions for arbitrary content are akin to acquiring a signature on arbitrary messages (the adaptive chosen message attack). Furthermore, the security definition is similar: Any new redaction constitutes an attack, which is akin to existential forgery in signature schemes. In fact, as shown in Sect. 6, a strongly unforgeable signature scheme can be used to construct a secure redactable blockchain in our model.

In what follows, we abstract out a redactable blockchain as a tuple of efficient algorithms. The abstraction pertains to a centralized setting, where there is a challenger with a private key, playing against an adversary with the public key and read-only access to the ledger. The adversary can install blocks by asking the challenger, who accepts the request as long as the adversary abides by the rules. The verification algorithm distinguishes valid blocks from invalid ones. Contrary to previous work such as [1,7], which explicitly use the proof-of-work verification in their model, we let each construct decide on its own verification algorithm. For instance, a construct may use separate verification algorithms for normal and redacted blocks. This simplifies and generalizes the scheme. The adversary can also ask the challenger to redact block contents, in hope that she learns how to redact a block without the challenger's help. The adversary is deemed successful if she can generate a new redaction.

We realize that block versioning is useful, and therefore incorporate it into our formalization below. If a solution does not employ versioning, those parts in the definition may be ignored.

5.3 Definition

The blockchain storage (the ledger) is modeled as a list of blocks $\mathcal{L} \stackrel{\text{def}}{=} [B_0, B_1, \ldots, B_\ell]$. The list starts at index 0, and the block at $\mathcal{L}[0]$ is called the *genesis* block. This block is generated initially, and it helps in simplifying the presentation. We assume that the variable ℓ always keeps the number of real (non-genesis) blocks: $\ell \stackrel{\text{def}}{=} \mathsf{len}(\mathcal{L}) - 1$. Initially, $\ell \leftarrow 0$, as there is only one block in the ledger (the genesis block) Upon appending each new block, ℓ is incremented. The value ℓ is *not* an upper bound: $\mathcal{L}$ can grow to include any polynomial number of blocks. The ledger is published as a *read-only* list. The only way an adversary can modify $\mathcal{L}$ is via a call to the challenger's INST interface, as depicted by Fig. 2.

Definition 3 defines five efficient algorithms that constitute a moderated redactable blockchain scheme. We then express two syntactical requirements: Every block created correctly must be verifiable, and so is every block redacted correctly. Throughout, the following *transformation* is used: It expresses the effect of installing a block B at position i of ledger $\mathcal{L}$, where $1 \leq i \leq \ell + 1$:

$$\mathsf{Transform}(\mathcal{L}, i, B) \stackrel{\text{def}}{=} \mathcal{L}[0 : i - 1] + [B] + \mathcal{L}[i + 1 : \ell]. \tag{1}$$

Notice that Transform returns a new ledger, rather than changing $\mathcal{L}$. By list manipulation rules defined in Sect. 3, if $i + 1 > \ell$, the rightmost sublist $\mathcal{L}[i+1 : \ell]$ is empty. The resulting ledger has the same length as $\mathcal{L}$ if $1 \leq i \leq \ell$, and is longer than $\mathcal{L}$ by one block if $i = \ell + 1$.

Definition 3. *A* moderated redactable blockchain scheme *is a tuple of proba-bilistic polynomial-time algorithms* $\mathcal{RBC} \overset{\text{def}}{=}$ (Gen, Create, Verify, Redact, Install) *satisfying the following:*

1. *The* **key-generation algorithm** Gen(1^λ): *Takes as input a unary security parameter* 1^λ *and outputs* $(pk, sk, \mathcal{L})$, *where pk is the* public key, *sk is the* private key, *and* $\mathcal{L}$ *is the ledger. We assume that* $|pk|, |sk|$ *are polynomial in* λ, *and* λ *can be inferred from pk or sk.*
2. *The* **block-creator algorithm** Create($pk, \mathcal{L}, C$): *Takes as input the public key pk, the ledger* $\mathcal{L}$, *and a content* C. *It generates and returns a block* B *containing* C, *to be appended at the end of* $\mathcal{L}$.
3. *The* **block-verifier algorithm** Verify($pk, \mathcal{L}, i, B$): *Takes as input the public key pk, the ledger* $\mathcal{L}$, *a positive integer* $i \leq \ell+1$, *and a block* B. *It performs two verifications, denoted* Φ *and* Ψ, *which are specified as part of* Verify *description by the blockchain designer. Let:*

$$V \leftarrow \text{Version}(B), \tag{2}$$

$$\boldsymbol{V} \leftarrow \left[\text{Version}(\mathcal{L}[0]), \dots, \text{Version}(\mathcal{L}[\ell])\right], \tag{3}$$

$$\mathcal{L}^* \leftarrow \text{Transform}(\mathcal{L}, i, B). \tag{4}$$

Verify *returns 1 if and only if both* $\Phi(\boldsymbol{V}, i, V)$ *and* $\Psi(pk, \mathcal{L}^*)$ *return 1. Algorithm* Φ *prevents reversion attacks by comparing the version of* B *with (possibly all) existing block versions. Algorithm* Ψ *checks the the consistency of the ledger for* $\mathcal{L}^*$ *that results from installing* B *at position* i *of* $\mathcal{L}$.

4. *The* **redaction algorithm** Redact($sk, \mathcal{L}, i, C$): *Takes as input the private key sk, the ledger* $\mathcal{L}$, *a positive integer* $i \leq \ell$, *and a content* C. *It returns a block* B *containing* C, *to replace* $\mathcal{L}[i]$.
5. *The* **block-installer algorithm** Install($pk, \mathcal{L}, i, B$): *Takes as input the public key pk, the ledger* $\mathcal{L}$, *a positive integer* $i \leq \ell + 1$, *and a block* B. *If* Verify($pk, \mathcal{L}, i, B$) *is 0, it returns 0. Otherwise, it installs* B *at index* i *of* $\mathcal{L}$ *(replacing an existing block in case* $i \leq \ell$*), and returns 1. Formally, a successful installation of* B *at index* i *is denoted by* $\mathcal{L} \leftarrow$ Transform($\mathcal{L}, i, B$), *as defined by Eq. (1).*

For any moderated redactable blockchain scheme $\mathcal{RBC}$, the following correctness requirements must be satisfied.

Definition 4 (Correctness). *It is required that for every* λ, *every* $(pk, sk, \mathcal{L})$ *output by* Gen(1^λ), *and any valid content* C:

(a) **Anyone can create a valid block to be appended to the ledger:** *Let* $B \leftarrow$ Create($pk, \mathcal{L}, C$). *Then*

$$\text{Content}(B) = C \quad \wedge \quad \text{Verify}(pk, \mathcal{L}, \ell+1, B) = 1.$$

(b) **The administrator can change any block of the ledger to contain any valid content:** *For any positive integer* $i < \ell$, *let* $B \leftarrow$ Redact($sk, \mathcal{L}, i, C$). *Then*

$$\text{Content}(B) = C \quad \wedge \quad \text{Verify}(pk, \mathcal{L}, i, B) = 1.$$

1. $\mathsf{Gen}(1^\lambda)$ is run to obtain $(pk, sk, \mathcal{L})$. The set Hist $\leftarrow \emptyset$ is set to empty.
2. Adversary $\mathcal{A}$ is given pk, a read-only view of $\mathcal{L}$, and access to oracles $\mathsf{REDC}_{sk,\mathcal{L}}(\cdot, \cdot)$ and $\mathsf{INST}_{pk,\mathcal{L}}(\cdot, \cdot)$.
    - The REDC oracle responds to queries of the form (i, C) by returning a redacted block $B \leftarrow \mathsf{Redact}(sk, \mathcal{L}, i, C)$. It also adds (i, B) to the set Hist, i.e., Hist $\leftarrow$ Hist $\cup \{(i, B)\}$.
    - The INST oracle responds to queries of the form (i, B) by returning a bit $b \leftarrow \mathsf{Install}(pk, \mathcal{L}, i, B)$.
3. Finally, $\mathcal{A}$ outputs (i^*, B^*). She succeeds, and the experiment returns 1, if and only if all of the following conditions hold:
    (a) $0 < i^* < \ell$,   (b) $\mathsf{Verify}(pk, \mathcal{L}, i^*, B^*) = 1$,   (c) $(i^*, B^*) \notin$ Hist .

Experiment 2. The redaction experiment $\mathsf{Redact}_{\mathcal{A}, \mathcal{RBC}}(\lambda)$. The success conditions can be explained as: (a) The index i points to an *internal* block of the ledger (as otherwise it is not an attack), (b) The block B^* is valid for position i^*, and (c) The pair (i^*, B^*) is new, meaning that B^* is not received from the redaction oracle in response to a query for index i^*. A particular observation is that the adversary wins if B^* is received from REDC, but for another location $i' \neq i^*$.

Let $\mathcal{RBC}$ be a moderated redactable blockchain scheme per Definition 3, and consider Experiment 2 for an adversary $\mathcal{A}$ and security parameter λ.

Definition 5. *A redactable blockchain scheme $\mathcal{RBC}$ is* existentially unredactable under chosen-redaction attacks, *or just* secure, *if for all probabilistic polynomial-time adversaries $\mathcal{A}$ taking part in Experiment 2, there is a negligible function* negl *such that* $\Pr\left[\mathsf{Redact}_{\mathcal{A}, \mathcal{RBC}}(\lambda) = 1\right] \leq \mathsf{negl}(\lambda)$.

6   A Construct Based on Signature Schemes

In this section, we present Construct 1 which, based on a simpled assumption explained below, is proven secure under Definition 5. The interested reader may read Appendix A beforehand, which contains a simple construct which is proven both incorrect and insecure. It is not a prerequisite to the rest of this paper, but serves an illustrative purpose in explaining the inner working of the adversarial model.

The adversarial model completely delegates the blockchain functionality to the challenger of Fig. 2: Any write operation must go through the challenger. We are therefore not worried about keeping an immutable total ordering of the blocks. It is similar in nature to the ideal functionality in a hybrid multi-party setting, except that our model is game-based rather than simulation-based.

This construct uses the block structure $B \overset{\text{def}}{=} (C, V, W)$, where each block contains content C, version V, and witness W. The blocks do not have a prefix whatsoever, in which the hash of the previous block is included. This is because, as explained above, our adversarial model idealizes the total ordering of blocks in the ledger by preventing direct write access from the adversary.

The block content C is arbitrary, but the version V and witness W must follow some rules that might not seem obvious at first. Appendix A shows that a careless choice of protocol for determining these fields can lead to correctness and security issues.

Each block must have a unique version number: The jth block to be installed (be it appended or redacted) should carry version j. This guarantees the uniqueness of each block in the ledger.

The witness W is the empty string ε when the block is being appended. However, when the block is being redacted, the administrator uses the private key of the blockchain (which is also the private key of an sUF-CMA secure signature scheme) to sign the concatenation of three fields: The content of this block, the version of this block, and the version of the next block in the ledger.

If the next block is redacted later, its version number will change, effectively rendering any signature in the current block invalid. To prevent correctness issues, the signature is verified only when its block is newer than the next block. This check is easily conducted due to the unique versioning that we introduced: For any two consecutive blocks $B \overset{\text{def}}{=} (C, V, W)$ and $B' \overset{\text{def}}{=} (C', V', W')$ in the ledger, define:

$$\psi(pk, B, B') \overset{\text{def}}{=} \begin{cases} 1 & \text{if } V' > V, \\ \mathsf{VerifySig}(pk, C \parallel V \parallel V', W) & \text{if } V' < V. \end{cases} \tag{5}$$

As we will see, the algorithm Ψ calls ψ for each pair of blocks in the ledger, and returns the logical AND of their results.

Construction 1 (Secure). *The redactable blockchain* $\mathcal{RBC}_{\text{good}}$ *is defined as follows. The block structure is* $B \overset{\text{def}}{=} (C, V, W)$, *where each block contains content* C, *version* V, *and witness* W.

- $\mathsf{Gen}(1^\lambda)$ *simply calls the generator for the underlying signature scheme to obtain the public and private keys:* $(pk, sk) \leftarrow \mathsf{GenSig}(1^\lambda)$. *It sets* $\mathcal{L} \leftarrow [B_0]$, *where* $B_0 \leftarrow (\varepsilon, 1, \varepsilon)$.
- $\mathsf{Create}(pk, \mathcal{L}, C)$ *returns* $B \leftarrow (C, V, \varepsilon)$, *where* V *is larger than any version in the ledger (and is thus unique). Symbolically,* $V \leftarrow \mathsf{MaxV}(\boldsymbol{V})$, *where* $\boldsymbol{V}$ *is defined as in Eq. (3), and*

$$\mathsf{MaxV}(\boldsymbol{V}) \overset{\text{def}}{=} 1 + \max_{0 \leq i \leq \ell} \boldsymbol{V}[i]. \tag{6}$$

- $\mathsf{Verify}(pk, \mathcal{L}, i, B)$ *returns 1 if and only if all conditions below are satisfied:*
  - B *has correct structure, and* $0 < i \leq \ell + 1$.
  - $\Phi(\boldsymbol{V}, i, V)$ *returns 1: This happens if and only if* $V = \mathsf{MaxV}(\boldsymbol{V})$.
  - $\Psi(pk, \mathcal{L}^*)$ *returns 1: This happens if and only if for every pair* (B, B') *of subsequent blocks in* $\mathcal{L}^*$, *it holds that* $\psi(pk, B, B') = 1$, *as per Eq. (5).*
- $\mathsf{Redact}(sk, \mathcal{L}, i, C)$: *If* i *points to an internal block (i.e.,* $0 < i < \ell$), *it creates a block* $B \leftarrow (C, V, W)$ *using content* C, *where* $V \leftarrow \mathsf{MaxV}(\boldsymbol{V})$ *and*

$$W \leftarrow \mathsf{Sign}\left(sk, C \parallel V \parallel \mathsf{Version}(\mathcal{L}[i+1])\right).$$

– Install$(pk, \mathcal{L}, i, B)$: *Works exactly as specified in Definition 3.*

Notice that for redacting the block at $i = \ell$, the private key is not required. For any C, replacing the existing block $\mathcal{L}[\ell]$ with $B \leftarrow (C, \mathsf{MaxV}(\boldsymbol{V}), \varepsilon)$ is valid. This is because there is no next block B' for which $\psi(pk, B, B') = 1$ must hold. However, the ability to redact the last block without the private key does not constitute an attack. In our model (Experiment 2), the adversary succeeds only if she redacts a block inside the ledger (i.e., $0 < i < \ell$).

Theorem 1. $\mathcal{RBC}_{\mathrm{good}}$ *is correct per Definition 4.*

Proof. There are two conditions to check.

Condition (a): $\mathsf{Create}(pk, \mathcal{L}, C)$ returns $B \leftarrow (C, \mathsf{MaxV}(\boldsymbol{V}), \varepsilon)$. Clearly, the content of this block is C. Furthermore, if $\mathcal{L}$ is already a valid chain, so is $\mathcal{L}^* \leftarrow \mathcal{L} + [B]$. This is because the version of B is correctly computed as required by Φ. Moreover, ψ returns 1 on all pairs of blocks in $\mathcal{L}^*$ prior to the last pair (due to the validity of $\mathcal{L}$). Finally, for the last pair $(\mathcal{L}[\ell], B)$, since $\mathsf{Version}(\mathcal{L}[\ell]) < \mathsf{Version}(B)$, the return value of ψ is trivially 1. As a result, all block pairs verify, and Ψ returns 1 as well.

Condition (b): $\mathsf{Redact}(sk, \mathcal{L}, i, C)$ returns $B \leftarrow (C, \mathsf{MaxV}(\boldsymbol{V}), W)$. Clearly, the content of this block is C. Furthermore, if $\mathcal{L}$ is already a valid chain, so is $\mathcal{L}^* \leftarrow \mathsf{Transform}(\mathcal{L}, i, B)$. This is because the version of B is correctly computed as required by Φ. Moreover, ψ returns 1 on all pairs of blocks in $\mathcal{L}^*$, except perhaps the two *special* pairs involving B (the validity of other pairs is due to the validity of $\mathcal{L}$). We show that ψ also returns 1 on those special pairs, which involve B:

- The first special pair is $(\mathcal{L}[i-1], B)$. Since $\mathsf{Version}(\mathcal{L}[i-1]) < \mathsf{Version}(B)$, the return value of ψ is trivially 1.
- The second special pair is $(B, \mathcal{L}[i+1])$. Since $\mathsf{Version}(\mathcal{L}[i+1]) < \mathsf{Version}(B)$, algorithm ψ requires the block B to hold a proper witness. This holds due to the correctness of the underlying signature scheme.

As a result, all block pairs verify, and Ψ returns 1 as well. □

Theorem 2. *If the signature scheme* $(\mathsf{GenSig}, \mathsf{Sign}, \mathsf{VerifySig})$ *is strongly unforgeable under chosen-message attack* $(sUF\text{-}CMA)$*, then* $\mathcal{RBC}_{\mathrm{good}}$ *is secure per Definition 5.*

Proof. Let $\mathcal{A}$ be an adversary who, for infinitely many λ values, succeeds in the experiment $\mathsf{Redact}_{\mathcal{A}, \mathcal{RBC}_{\mathrm{good}}}(\lambda)$ with probability at least $\epsilon \stackrel{\mathrm{def}}{=} \epsilon(\lambda)$. We construct a forger algorithm $\mathcal{F}$ which, for infinitely many λ values, forges a signature with probability ϵ.

The forger $\mathcal{F}$ receives as input the public key pk of the signature scheme, as well as oracle access to the signing oracle $\mathsf{Sign}_{sk}(\cdot)$. It sets $\mathsf{Hist} \leftarrow \emptyset$, generates $\mathcal{L} \leftarrow [B_0]$ as in Construct 1, runs $\mathcal{A}(pk, \mathcal{L})$, and answers its queries as follows:

– **Installation queries** $\mathsf{INST}(i, B)$: The forger $\mathcal{F}$ simply calls $b \leftarrow \mathsf{Install}(pk, \mathcal{L}, i, B)$, and returns b.

– **Redaction queries** REDC(i, C): If $i \leq 0$ or $i \geq \ell$, the forger $\mathcal{F}$ returns ε. Otherwise, $\mathcal{F}$ creates block $B \leftarrow (C, V, W)$, where $V \leftarrow \mathsf{MaxV}(\boldsymbol{V})$, and W is computed by querying the signature oracle on $(C \parallel V \parallel \mathsf{Version}(\mathcal{L}[i+1]))$. It then adds (i, B) to Hist, and returns B.

If the adversary stops but does not succeed in outputting (i, B) as required in Experiment 2, the forger $\mathcal{F}$ outputs $\perp$ and halts. Otherwise, parse $B \overset{\mathrm{def}}{=} (C, V, W)$. Since B is verified, W is a valid signature on $m \leftarrow (C \parallel V \parallel V_{i+1})$, where $V_{i+1} \overset{\mathrm{def}}{=} \mathsf{Version}(\mathcal{L}[i+1])$. Subsequently, $\mathcal{F}$ outputs (m, W) as a forgery.

To show that the forgery is new, we must prove that W was never returned by the signing oracle in response to query m. Since $(i, B) \notin$ Hist, we consider the two remaining possibilities:

– $(i', B) \in$ Hist for some $i' \neq i$: Impossible because $\mathsf{Version}(\mathcal{L}[i+1])$, which constitutes a part of m, is unique due to the uniqueness of version numbers in our solution. Therefore, no other position i' may correspond to the same m.
– $(i, B') \in$ Hist for some $B' \neq B$, where B can be efficiently computed from $B' \overset{\mathrm{def}}{=} (C', V', W')$, and W' is valid on m: For this to happen, it must be the case that B and B' are identical except in their witnesses. Then, both W and W' are valid signatures on m. This constitutes a strong forgery on the signature scheme, and $\mathcal{F}$ can output (m, W) as a valid forgery.

We conclude that the success probability of $\mathcal{F}$ in producing a valid forgery is the same as the success probability of $\mathcal{A}$ in producing a valid redaction. □

7   Conclusion and Future Work

In this paper, we discussed two settings for redactable blockchains: The moderated setting, where redactions are handled by administrators, and the unmoderated setting, where redactions are voted on. Four novel attacks were discussed against previous constructs in both settings. We argued the attacks are the result of the lack of a definitional framework for redactable blockchains. We suggested the first attempt at such a framework, and explained our design decisions. A simple constructs based on signature schemes was proposed, and proven to be correct and secure.

The simple definitional framework of Sect. 5 can be extended in many ways, some of which are explored below.

Privacy. A desirable property is to make it impossible to show that a block was once in the ledger. For instance, consider Construct 1, where a redacted block B contains a signature on itself and the next block. Assume B is redacted to B'. While B no longer belongs to the ledger, anyone can verify its witness and conclude that it once belonged to the ledger, potentially violating users' privacy.

Distributed Administration. Currently, the model supports a single administrator. As in [1], one can conceive of a model where the key pair of the blockchain is jointly generated by several administrators, where each administrator receives a share of the private key. Redactions are applied by running a multiparty computation between the administrators. For instance, in our construct, a *threshold signature* can be used. An idea (novel in the context of redactable blockchains) is to allow the set of administrators to grow or shrink over time. The policies governing joining and leaving an administrator, as well as the redistribution of private key shares, are of particular interest.

Accountability. It might be beneficial to hold administrators accountable for redactions. That is, when a block is last redacted, how many times has it been redacted, and which subset of administrators approved the redaction (in the case of distributed administration).

Supporting Block Removals and Insertions. Currently, our model only supports block modifications. Ateniese et al. [1] show how block removals can be supported, by modifying the block before the one being removed. Removing blocks is beneficial in that it can shrink the ledger. It is also possible to add support block insertions. We extended our definitional framework to support both operations, and constructed a blockchain satisfying the corresponding security requirements. It will appear in the full version of this paper.

Multiparty Setting. In our model, a single adversary plays a game against a challenger. We think the model is elegant in its simplicity, which allowed us to find various attacks against [1,7,10] (as well as Construct 2 presented in Appendix A). It also idealizes modifications to the ledger by regulating writes through the challenger, effectively separating redactability from other properties of a blockchain. Furthermore, the model does not care about the underlying consensus mechanism, while prior models (for the immutable blockchains) are bound to the specific consensus protocol such as proof-of-work [9,17]. We stipulate that our model is good for quickly *proofread* a particular moderated redactable blockchain, but it is only a first step. Since there is no composition theorem for the game-based security proofs, one cannot simply replace the ideal functionality in the hybrid model with a real one, and hope the proof carries over to the real model. Furthermore, the simplified model might be unable to capture some attacks in the real world. For these reasons, we propose extending the ideas in this paper to the multiparty setting, where various parties are joining and leaving the network (as well as an adversary who can corrupt a minority of them).

Acknowledgment. The second author acknowledges support from TÜBİTAK, the Scientific and Technological Research Council of Turkey, under project number 119E088.

A   An Incorrect and Insecure Construct

In this appendix, we present a construct that is both incorrect and insecure, but helps in understanding the way our definitional framework works. Normal blocks do not include any information about each other (such as the hash of the previous block). Such information, necessary for the secure operation of an ordinary blockchain, is abstracted via the ideal functionality in the model: The adversary is not allowed to make any direct writes to the ledger, and therefore the challenger can keep the ledger blocks in their total order. The redactability is achieved with a signature scheme *strongly* unforgeable under adaptive chosen-message attack (sUF-CMA), denoted (GenSig, Sign, VerifySig): The challenger installs a redacted block only if its witness holds the signature of itself and the next block. The reversion attack (Sect. 4) is prevented by introducing version numbers in the block structure: Initially, each block carries version 1. Upon each redaction, the version number is incremented. The verification function of the blockchain checks whether the version of a redacted block is strictly greater than the version of the block being replaced. This way, the adversary cannot reinstall a previously valid block again.

Construction 2 (Insecure and Incorrect). *The redactable blockchain* $\mathcal{RBC}_{\text{bad}}$ *is defined as follows. The block structure is* $B \overset{\text{def}}{=} (C, V, W)$, *where each block contains content* C, *version* V, *and witness* W.

- Gen(1^λ) *simply calls the generator for the underlying signature scheme to obtain the public and private keys:* $(pk, sk) \leftarrow$ GenSig(1^λ). *It sets* $\mathcal{L} \leftarrow [B_0]$, *where* $B_0 \leftarrow (\varepsilon, 1, \varepsilon)$.
- Create($pk, \mathcal{L}, C$) *returns* $B \leftarrow (C, 1, \varepsilon)$.
- Verify($pk, \mathcal{L}, i, B$) *returns 1 if and only if all of the following conditions hold:*
  - B *has correct structure, and* $i \leq \ell + 1$ *is a positive integer.*
  - $\Phi(\boldsymbol{V}, i, V)$ *returns 1: This happens if and only if* $(i = \ell + 1) \wedge (V = 1)$ *(the block is being appended and has version 1), or* $(i \leq \ell) \wedge (\boldsymbol{V}[i] < V)$ *(an existing block is being redacted, and the new version is greater than the existing one to foil reversion attacks).*
  - $\Psi(pk, \mathcal{L}^*)$ *returns 1: This happens if and only if for every pair* (B, B') *of subsequent blocks in* $\mathcal{L}^*$, *if* Version(B) > 1 *(i.e., if* B *is redacted), then*

  $$\text{VerifySig}(pk, B^{\not{W}} \,||\, B', W) = 1, \tag{7}$$

  where $W \overset{\text{def}}{=}$ Witness(B), *and* $B^{\not{W}} \overset{\text{def}}{=} (C, V)$ *(i.e., block* B *except* W*). Put simply, this means that* W *is a valid signature on* $C \,||\, V \,||\, C' \,||\, V' \,||\, W'$.
- Redact($sk, \mathcal{L}, i, C$): *Creates* $B \leftarrow (C, V, W)$ *using content* C, *where* $V \leftarrow$ Version($\mathcal{L}[i]$) $+ 1$ *and* W *is a signature on the current block except* W *itself (denoted* $B^{\not{W}}$*), as well as the next block* $\mathcal{L}[i+1]$:

  $$W \leftarrow \text{Sign}(sk, B^{\not{W}} \,||\, \mathcal{L}[i+1]).$$

  Notice that incrementing the version number, as well as the computation of witness by signing the current and next blocks, are consistent with the requirements of Verify.
- Install($pk, \mathcal{L}, i, B$): *Works exactly as specified in Definition 3.*

Correctness Issues. A series of valid actions can put the ledger in a state that block creation for appending is no longer possible, violating the first requirement of Definition 4. For instance, let C_1, C_1' and C_2 be any valid contents, and consider the following actions, following $(pk, sk, \mathcal{L}) \leftarrow \mathsf{Gen}(1^\lambda)$:

$$B_1 \leftarrow \mathsf{Create}(pk, \mathcal{L}, C_1), \qquad \mathsf{Install}(pk, \mathcal{L}, 1, B_1)$$
$$B_1' \leftarrow \mathsf{Redact}(sk, \mathcal{L}, 1, C_1'), \qquad \mathsf{Install}(pk, \mathcal{L}, 1, B_1')$$
$$B_2 \leftarrow \mathsf{Create}(pk, \mathcal{L}, C_2), \qquad \mathsf{Install}(pk, \mathcal{L}, 2, B_2)$$

The first line creates and appends a block, the second line redacts it, and the third line tries to append a new block. The last $\mathsf{Install}$ fails as it calls Verify, which in turn calls Ψ: Since the version of B_1' is greater than 1, Ψ requires it to hold a signature containing information about the next block, as per Eq. (7), which is not the case.

The underlying reason is that, in this particular construct, it is meaningless for the last block of the ledger to be redacted, as there is no next block to sign. It is possible *not* to increase version number for redacting the last block, or disallow such redaction by requiring $i \neq \ell$ in designing Redact.

One can violate the second requirement of Definition 4 as well, by following a series of valid actions that put the ledger in a state where redaction of some blocks are impossible. Let $\mathcal{L} \leftarrow [B_0, B_1, B_2, B_3]$ be a ledger constructed by appending three blocks, and C_1' and C_2' be valid contents. Consider the following actions:

$$B_1' \leftarrow \mathsf{Redact}(sk, \mathcal{L}, 1, C_1'), \qquad \mathsf{Install}(pk, \mathcal{L}, 1, B_1')$$
$$B_2' \leftarrow \mathsf{Redact}(sk, \mathcal{L}, 1, C_2'), \qquad \mathsf{Install}(pk, \mathcal{L}, 1, B_2')$$

Again, the last install fails: For the pair (B_1', B_2'), algorithm Ψ requires B_1' to hold a signature on $B_1'^W \| B_2'$ (see Eq. (7)). However, B_1' is redacted prior to B_2': As a result, B_1' holds a signature on $B_1'^W \| B_2$, which becomes invalid after B_2 is redacted. Consequently, the second requirement of Definition 4 is violated.

The underlying reason is the indifference in the verification algorithms as to which block is newer. The next section shows how using unique versions can resolve this issue.

Security Issues. On the surface, it seems that the adversary cannot succeed in Experiment 2. An informal (and false) argument is as follows: We use an adversary who succeeds in the game as a subroutine, to forge a valid signature on an arbitrary message. The forger simulates the challenger. It gives the public key of the signature scheme to the adversary, and answers all redaction queries by using the *signing oracle*. When the adversary outputs a successful redaction (i, B), the witness W is a valid signature on the message $m \leftarrow B^W \| \mathcal{L}[i+1]$. The forger outputs (m, W) as a valid message-signature pair.

The fallacy in the above argument is that the forger must output a *new* pair (m, W), as required by sUF-CMA signature forgery. However, the informal proof does not show that this pair is new. In fact, as is explained below, it is easy for an adversary to succeed in the game without forging any signature.

Adversary $\mathcal{A}$ proceeds as follows: It creates a block $B \leftarrow (\texttt{"original"}, 1, \varepsilon)$, and appends it three times by calling the INST interface of the challenger on queries $(1, B)$, $(2, B)$ and $(3, B)$, respectively. At this point, $\mathcal{L} = [B_0, B, B, B]$.

Next, $\mathcal{A}$ queries the REDC interface of the challenger on $(1, \texttt{"modified"})$, and receives $B' \leftarrow (\texttt{"modified"}, 2, W)$, where W is a signature on $m \leftarrow B'^{\mathcal{W}} \parallel B$, where $B'^{\mathcal{W}}$ is $\texttt{"modified"} \parallel 2$.

While the redaction was requested for position 1, the adversary uses position 2: She outputs $(2, B')$, and halts.

At this point, $\mathsf{Hist} = \{(1, B')\}$, and therefore $(2, B')$ is new. Furthermore, B' is a valid redaction for position 2, since $\mathcal{L}[3] = \mathcal{L}[2] = B$. We conclude that the adversary breaks the security by outputting a successful reduction, without forging a new signature. The underlying reason for this attack is duplicate blocks in the ledger. Construct 1 in Sect. 6 resolved this issue by incorporating unique versioning.

References

1. Ateniese, G., Magri, B., Venturi, D., Andrade, E.: Redactable blockchain-or-rewriting history in bitcoin and friends. In: EuroS&P. IEEE (2017)
2. Boneh, D., Shen, E., Waters, B.: Strongly unforgeable signatures based on computational Diffie-Hellman. In: Yung, M., Dodis, Y., Kiayias, A., Malkin, T. (eds.) PKC 2006. LNCS, vol. 3958, pp. 229–240. Springer, Heidelberg (2006). https://doi.org/10.1007/11745853_15
3. CoinDesk: Understanding The DAO Attack (2016). https://tinyurl.com/dao-attack
4. Council of European Union: Regulation (EU) 2016/679: General Data Protection Regulation (GDPR) (2016). https://gdpr-info.eu
5. Derler, D., Ramacher, S., Slamanig, D., Striecks, C.: I Want to Forget: Fine-Grained Encryption with Full Forward Secrecy in the Distributed Setting. IACR Cryptology ePrint Archive (2019)
6. Derler, D., Samelin, K., Slamanig, D., Striecks, C.: Fine-Grained and Controlled Rewriting in Blockchains: Chameleon-Hashing Gone Attribute-Based. IACR Cryptology ePrint Archive (2019)
7. Deuber, D., Magri, B., Thyagarajan, S.A.K.: Redactable blockchain in the permissionless setting. In: Symposium on Security and Privacy. IEEE (2019)
8. Dousti, M.S., Küpçü, A.: Moderated Redactable Blockchains: A Definitional Framework with an Efficient Construct. IACR Cryptology ePrint Archive (2020)
9. Garay, J., Kiayias, A., Leonardos, N.: The bitcoin backbone protocol: analysis and applications. In: Oswald, E., Fischlin, M. (eds.) EUROCRYPT 2015. LNCS, vol. 9057, pp. 281–310. Springer, Heidelberg (2015). https://doi.org/10.1007/978-3-662-46803-6_10
10. Grigoriev, D., Shpilrain, V.: RSA and Redactable Blockchains. arXiv report 2001.10783 (2020)
11. Hargreaves, S., Cowley, S.: How Porn Links and Ben Bernanke Snuck Into Bitcoin's Code (2013). https://tinyurl.com/bitcoin-snuck
12. Hopkins, C.: If You Own Bitcoin, You Also Own Links to Child Porn (2020). https://tinyurl.com/bitcoin-child

13. Kolb, J., AbdelBaky, M., Katz, R.H., Culler, D.E.: Core concepts, challenges, and future directions in blockchain: a centralized tutorial. ACM Comput. Surv. **53**(1), 1–39 (2020)
14. Liu, J.K., Au, M.H., Susilo, W., Zhou, J.: Short generic transformation to strongly unforgeable signature in the standard model. In: Gritzalis, D., Preneel, B., Theoharidou, M. (eds.) ESORICS 2010. LNCS, vol. 6345, pp. 168–181. Springer, Heidelberg (2010). https://doi.org/10.1007/978-3-642-15497-3_11
15. Lumb, R.: Downside of Bitcoin: A Ledger That Can't Be Corrected (2016). https://tinyurl.com/btc-immutable
16. Nakamoto, S.: Bitcoin: A Peer-to-Peer Electronic Cash System (2009). http://www.bitcoin.org/bitcoin.pdf
17. Pass, R., Shi, E.: FruitChains: a fair blockchain. In: Symposium on Principles of Distributed Computing (2017)
18. Pearson, J.: The Bitcoin Blockchain Could Be Used to Spread Malware, INTERPOL Says (2015). https://tinyurl.com/bitcoin-malware
19. Puddu, I., Dmitrienko, A., Capkun, S.: μchain: How to Forget Without Hard Forks. IACR Cryptology ePrint Archive (2017)
20. Wood, G.: Ethereum: A Secure Decentralised Generalised Transaction Ledger. Ethereum Project yellow paper (2014)

Radium: Improving Dynamic PoW Targeting

George Bissias[(✉)]

College of Information and Computer Sciences, UMass Amherst, Amherst, USA
gbiss@cs.umass.edu
https://people.cs.umass.edu/~gbiss

Abstract. Most PoW blockchain protocols operate with a simple mechanism whereby a threshold is set for each block and miners generate block hashes until one of those values falls below the threshold. Although largely effective, this mechanism produces blocks at a highly variable rate and also leaves a blockchain susceptible to chain death, i.e. abandonment in the event that the threshold is set too high to attract any miners. A recent innovation called real-time block rate targeting, or RTT, fixes these problems by reducing the target throughout the mining interval. RTT exhibits much less variable block times and even features the ability to fully adjust the target after each block. However, as we show in this paper, RTT also suffers from a critical vulnerability whereby miners deviate from the protocol to increase their profits. We introduce the Radium protocol, which mitigates this vulnerability in RTT while retaining lower variance block times, responsive target adjustment, and lowering the risk of chain death. We also show that Radium's susceptibility to the doublespend attack and orphaned blocks remains similar to Bitcoin.

Keywords: Proof-of-work · Dynamic difficulty · Block time

1 Introduction

To date, the most popular consensus mechanism for public blockchains is proof-of-work (PoW) [7]. Under PoW, a blockchain (or simply *chain*) is secured by compelling participants to provide evidence of wasted computation or *work*. Every unit of work boosts a participant's odds of deciding the content of the next block. If any one individual or group controls the majority of work, then they are capable of deciding the majority of blocks, and it is possible for them to rewrite an arbitrarily long portion of the chain and censor future transactions. Indeed, even if one mining group produces only a significant fraction of the work, then it is still possible for them to rewrite short portions of the blockchain with relatively high probability. This allows for the group to reverse transactions, an activity known as *doublespending* [7,11]. For this reason, blockchain security is intimately tied to the aggregate work required to produce a block. The most popular PoW blockchains have attracted a large number of participants, who collectively expend a great deal of work. Maintaining a consistent level of work is critical both to maintaining attack protection as well as a stable block time.

© Springer Nature Switzerland AG 2020
J. Garcia-Alfaro et al. (Eds.): DPM 2020/CBT 2020, LNCS 12484, pp. 374–389, 2020.
https://doi.org/10.1007/978-3-030-66172-4_24

A specific kind of work is required for each blockchain, which we call its *PoW algorithm*. Typically, specialized hardware called an application specific integrated circuit (ASIC) is required for producing work relevant to a given PoW algorithm. As a result, it is common for multiple Blockchains to occupy the same *PoW market* where they compete for security. In order to attract participants to expend work, blockchains offer a subsidy for blocks produced. Recent research (Kwon et al. [5] and Bissias et al. [3]) has shown that the relative fiat exchange value of these subsidies, across blockchains in the same market, determines the distribution of work. The end result is that participants will frequently shift their work from one chain to another as the value of rewards fluctuate. These fluctuations can be devastating to minority work chains that can experience huge changes in aggregate work in relative terms. In the worst case, a drastic drop in the fiat exchange value for a minority work chain can remove all incentive for miners to allocate it any work. This causes what is called a *chain death spiral* [9].

In this paper, we analyze a recently introduced protocol called real-time block rate targeting, or RTT [4], whose intended purpose is improve responsiveness to changes in hash rate. We show that RTT currently suffers from a vulnerability due to misaligned miner incentives. We then describe a modification to the RTT protocol, which we call *Radium*, which fixes this problem. Radium retains the benefits of RTT including lower variance block times, a more responsive difficulty adjustment algorithm (DAA), and prevention of chain death. Not previously studied in the RTT paper, we also show that Radium maintains orphan rate and doublespend attack prevention similar to Bitcoin.

2   Background and Related Work

Under PoW, *miners* repeatedly perturb and hash the block header with frequency h, which is called the *hash rate*. Miners hope to hash a value that falls below a protocol-defined *target G*. When such a value is found, the block is added to the blockchain and the miner receives coins as a reward. Thus coin issuance is tied to block discovery, and so the protocol must adjust G periodically in order to maintain a steady rate of inflation. Closely related to the target and hash rate is *difficulty D*, which was shown by Ozisik et al. [8] to be equivalent to the expected number of hashes required to mine a single block whose hash falls below G. The authors further showed that $D = S/G$ where S is the size of the hash space. Accordingly, one can equivalently adjust the target by creating an inverse change in difficulty. Indeed, all of the most popular PoW blockchains employ some form of *difficulty adjustment algorithm* or DAA.

2.1   Difficulty Adjustment

Currently, all DAAs that we are aware of implement a feedback controller, which first forms a statistical estimate of recent hash rates by observing previous block times and then adjusts the difficulty so as to achieve a target block time T. When the difficulty is tuned so that the target block time is achieved, we say that the DAA is *at rest*. For example, every 2016 blocks, Bitcoin (BTC) scales the current difficulty according to

$$D' = DT/\overline{T}, \tag{1}$$

where $\overline{T}$ is the average actual block time over the previous 2016 blocks. This simple DAA works fairly well for BTC primarily because the blockchain enjoys more than 90% of the total available SHA256 hash rate. However, for blockchains with a small fraction of the available hash rate, such as Bitcoin Cash (BCH), simple feedback controllers is inadequate [12].

2.2 Conventional PoW Mining

The distribution of block inter-arrival time under conventional PoW is $\texttt{Expon}(\lambda)$ where $\frac{1}{\lambda} = T$, the target block time (see Rizun [10] and Ozisik et al. [8]). And, as described above,

$$D = S/G, \tag{2}$$

where D is the expected number of hashes required to mine a block, G is the target, and S is the size of the hash space. For fixed hash rate h we have by definition

$$H = hE[T], \tag{3}$$

where T and H are the actual block time and hashes per block, respectively. In particular, this implies that

$$D = hT, \tag{4}$$

when the DAA is at rest.

2.3 RTT Mining

Stone [12] was perhaps the first to suggest the notion of increasing the mining target *during* a single block interval in order to compensate for statistical tail events or a sudden loss of hash rate. Recently, Harding [4] introduced a new PoW consensus mechanism called RTT that leverages this idea. When mining a given block, instead of using a fixed target G, RTT varies the target as a function of the time since the last block. This small change is significant because it alters the statistics of the mining process.

Define the *instantaneous mining rate*, or expected blocks mined per second, for RTT as

$$\lambda(t) = at^{k-1}, \tag{5}$$

with security constant k and tuning constant a. Variable t represents the elapsed time since the last block. Let T be a random variable corresponding to the block inter-arrival time. Harding shows that, given instantaneous mining rate $\lambda(t)$,

$$T \sim \texttt{Weibull}(k, a), \tag{6}$$

where T has density function

$$f(t; k, a) = at^{k-1}e^{-at^k/k},$$

(7)

distribution function

$$F(t; k, a) = 1 - e^{-at^k/k},$$

(8)

and expected value

$$E[T] = \left(\frac{k}{a}\right)^{1/k} \Gamma\left(1 + \frac{1}{k}\right).$$

(9)

From Eq. 9, it is evident that, when targeting a block in expected time $\mathcal{T}$, the constant a should be defined as

$$a = k \left[\frac{\Gamma\left(1 + \frac{1}{k}\right)}{\mathcal{T}}\right]^k$$

(10)

RTT is designed to maintain compatibility with Bitcoin, which requires RTT to maintain conventional mining targets on the blockchain: G_i for each block i. This has the primary benefit of maintaining blockchain continuity before and after upgrade and the ancillary benefit of allowing for conventional difficulty adjustment. From conventional target G_i and instantaneous mining rate $\lambda_i(t)$, RTT requires a *subtarget* $g_n(t)$ such that the expected mining time for RTT under $g_n(t)$ is equal to target mining time $\mathcal{T}$. To mine block i, miners must find a block at some elapsed time t whose hash falls below $g_i(t)$.

Under conventional PoW, G_i implies an instantaneous block mining rate of

$$\lambda = 1/\mathcal{T}$$

(11)

blocks per second. Accordingly, the sub-target $g_i(t)$ is defined as

$$g_i(t) = G_i \frac{\lambda_i(t)}{\lambda},$$

(12)

which can be interpreted as normalizing G_n according to the variable block production rate of RTT.

3   Future Mining Attack on RTT

In this section we describe a *future mining* attack on RTT. Miner A, having fraction q of the total hash rate, chooses a future time t^* and allocates all of his hash rate to finding a block that meets sub-target $g(t^*)$ until t^* has expired. There are three mutually exclusive outcomes: *(i)* A mines a block prior to t^*; *(ii)* the remaining miners M, having fraction $1 - q$ of the hash rate, mine a block prior t^*; or *(iii)* a block is first mined after t^*. For outcome *(iii)*, we assume that A will revert to protocol-compliant mining, i.e. A will mine to actual time t provided that $t \geq t^*$. In this section we identify a value of t^* such that the probability of A mining a block before M exceeds q, which is his fair share.

3.1   Attacker Expected Block Time

Let T_A and T_M denote statistics corresponding to the time required for A and M, respectively, to mine their next blocks. And let $p(t^*)$ denote the probability that A mines a block before M when his future mining time is t^*. Note that

$$p(t^*) \geq P(T_A < t^*, T_M > t^*) = P(T_A < t^*)P(T_M > t^*). \tag{13}$$

Because A mines with a fixed target $g(t^*)$ for each block, T_A is exponentially distributed (as described in Sect. 2).

It is apparent from Eqs. 2–4 that if D is initially tuned for hash rate h and target G, but all miners instead mine according to the sub-target at time t^*, then they would expect a block to arrive in time

$$E[T] = \frac{S}{hg(t^*)} = \frac{G}{g(t^*)}\frac{S}{hG} = \frac{G}{g(t^*)}T. \tag{14}$$

For miner A, the expected block time is scaled by his fraction of the total hash rate q. Therefore, the expected block time for A is given by

$$E[T_A] = \frac{S}{qhg(t^*)} = \frac{G}{qg(t^*)}\frac{S}{hG} = \frac{G}{qg(t^*)}T. \tag{15}$$

3.2   Compliant Expected Block Time

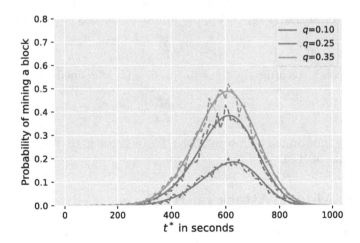

Fig. 1. Probability of successful future mining attack for various attacker shares of total hash rate (each curve) and future mining times (independent axis). Solid curves indicate theoretical probabilities and dashed curves indicate the results of a mining simulation with 500 trials per point, per curve.

From the discussion in Sect. 2.3, it is clear that T_M has Weibull distribution since miners M are assumed to be compliant. But they are missing fraction q of the hash rate, which we must account for in determining their expected mining time. It is difficult to reason directly about how Weibull mining time changes with a loss of hash rate, but straightforward to reason about the effect of such a change under conventional PoW.

Let T'_M be a random variable representing the mining time for miners M having fraction $p = 1 - q$ of the total hash rate under the assumption that they use conventional PoW, i.e. mining to fixed target G for each block. Reasoning similarly to Eq. 15, we have

$$E[T'_M] = \frac{S}{phG} = \frac{1}{p}\frac{S}{hG} = \frac{T}{p}. \tag{16}$$

Target G is a conventional PoW target, so we reason that mining in RTT with fraction p of the total hash rate is equivalent to *all miners* mining against initial target pG. The sub-target is related to G by $g(t) = G\lambda(t)/\lambda$. This implies that a sub-target adjusted for hash rate p would be

$$g_M(t) = pG\frac{\lambda(t)}{\lambda} = G\frac{p\lambda(t)}{\lambda} = G\frac{pat^{k-1}}{\lambda} = G\frac{\lambda_M(t)}{\lambda}, \tag{17}$$

where $\lambda_M(t) = pat^{k-1}$. Thus, according to Eqs. 5 and 6,

$$T_M \sim \texttt{Weibull}(k, pa). \tag{18}$$

Finally, we can produce the bound for $p(t^*)$ in Eq. 13 by multiplying the CDF for T_A, evaluated at t^* by the inverse-CDF for T_M, evaluated at t^*.

Figure 1 shows the associated probability of mining a block when future mining for many possible future times t^*. Each curve corresponds to a different fraction of the total hash rate for A. Solid lines are those predicted by the bound in Eq. 13 and dashed lines are the results of a mining simulation. The plot shows that for each hash rate, there exists a regime of values for t^* where the probability of mining a block is greater than the *fair* probability (equivalent to A's share of the hash rate).

4 Defacto Future Mining in RTT

In Sect. 3 we showed that the RTT protocol is vulnerable to future mining. This attack arises because miners are incentivized to mine to a fixed target in the future rather than adhere to the dynamic target established by the protocol. Therefore it seems that future mining is inevitable in RTT. Yet it seems possible that RTT could still be fair for all miners if they all future mine so as to maximize their individual profit. In this section, we show that there is a unique Nash equilibrium future mining time τ, depending on the chain's profitability relative to other chains, to which all miners will mine. Once this time expires, the Nash equilibrium behavior is to mine according to the compliant RTT sub-target.

4.1 Block Preemption

Future mining involves mining to a target $g(t^*)$ corresponding to a future time t^*. Because it is a probabilistic process, the miner will fail to mine a block in time t^* with some frequency. At this point, he must choose a new time $t^*|t$, given that t seconds have passed. This process continues until a block is mined.

There exists a risk/reward tradeoff in future mining related to the fact that a miner cannot release a block mined at a future time until that time arrives. Thus, if miner M mines to future time t^*, then the remaining miners M_- can mine to time $t^* - \epsilon$, $\epsilon > 0$, and all blocks mined by M can be preempted by any block mined by M_- prior to t^*. We call this process *block preemption*.

4.2 Game Theoretical Results

Assumptions. In our game theoretical model, we assume all miners follow a strategy where they will future mine whenever it is possible to do so without being preempted.

Miners typically have a choice where they direct their hash rate. Let ρ denote the (fixed) prevailing *reward rate*, which is the amount of fiat that can be gained per hash when miners mine on a competing blockchain. Furthermore, let $R(t^*)$ denote the reward rate when future mining to time t^* on the RTT chain. We assume that a rational miner will choose to direct all of his hash rate to a competing chain whenever $R(t^*) < \rho$. Thus, we imagine that miners choose t^* so as to maximize $R(t^*)$. We begin with the following result showing that the Nash equilibrium for t^* as a function of ρ.

Theorem 1. *There exists a unique Nash equilibrium for initial future mining time* $t^* = \tau$*, where* $R(\tau) = \rho$*.*

Proof. Consider the best response $t^*(M)$ for miner M given a known choice for $t^*(M_-) > \tau$ for the remaining miners M_-. By choosing $t^*(M) = t(M_-)^* - \epsilon$, for an infinitesimally small $\epsilon > 0$, M can be certain that his blocks will preempt those of M_- (ignoring block propagation delay). Moreover, M mines at effectively the same difficulty as M_- for each $t(M)^*$. Therefore, the expected profit per hash for M is strictly superior to that of M_-. Now consider the best response for M when M_- chooses $\mathbf{t}(M_-)^* = \tau$. If M chooses to mine to time $\tau - \epsilon$, then he will be mining at a loss relative to prevailing reward rate ρ. On the other hand, if M mines to future time $\tau + \epsilon$, then his blocks will be preempted by any blocks mined by M_-. Therefore, the best response for M is also to future mine to time τ. It follows that τ is a Nash equilibrium for t^*. □

Having established an equilibrium for the first future mining time, we turn now to subsequent times, which will be targeted in the event that no block is found by time $t^* = \tau$. Somewhat surprisingly, the Nash equilibrium for $t^*|t$ turns out to be equal to the current time t itself.

Theorem 2. *For any $t > \tau$, $t^*|t = t$ is a unique Nash equilibrium.*

Proof. Consider the best response for miner M given that M_- is mining to time $t^*(M_-)|t = t$, when $t > \tau$. M certainly wishes to mine on the RTT chain since $R(t) > \rho$ for $t > \tau$. But because t is not in the future, it is not possible for M to mine to a slightly earlier time. And if M was to mine to a future time $t + \epsilon$, for $\epsilon > 0$, then it would be possible for his blocks to be preempted. Therefore, the best response for M is to also mine to $t^*(M)|t = t$. It follows that $t^*|t = t$ is a Nash equilibrium. $\square$

Together, Theorems 1 and 2 show that all RTT miners will future mine to time τ until the actual time t exceeds τ at which point they will revert to (compliant) mining against target $g(t)$. There are three major issues with this behavior. First, at time τ, there is a significant chance that multiple miners will have already future mined a block, creating a block race and, inevitably, a higher block orphan rate. Second, suppose that on average fraction α of the total hash rate is devoted by all miners to future mining to τ, with the remaining $1 - \alpha$ being devoted to mining via dynamic target after τ. By future mining to $\tau - \epsilon$, attacker A can preempt any block future mined by other miners. So at arbitrarily small cost, A eliminates orphan risk for fraction α of his blocks. This makes both censoring and doublespending transactions easier for the attacker. A third drawback to defacto future mining is that target G no longer quantifies the actual security applied to the chain. Under conventional PoW, Eq. 2 can be used to determine D, which is equivalent to the expected number of hashes performed per block, a proxy for blockchain security. However, given defacto future mining on RTT, the target overshoots the actual hashes per block because miners never mine to a target greater than $g(\tau) < G$.

5   Radium Protocol

In this section we present the Radium protocol, which is an extension of RTT. The primary difference is that, in Radium, block reward is also scaled with inter-block time. This causes the reward per hash to remain uniform for a given block (much like conventional PoW), eliminating the profitability of future mining.

5.1   Mining

Radium targets a 600 s average block time like bitcoin, i.e. $\mathcal{T} = 600$. Like RTT, the mining target at each second t after the last block is given by sub-target $g_k(t)$ where $k = 2$. For a given target G, and combining Eqs. 10–12, we have

$$g_k(t) = G\frac{\lambda(t)}{\lambda} = G\frac{at^{k-1}}{1/\mathcal{T}} = G\mathcal{T}t^{k-1}k\left[\frac{\Gamma(1+\frac{1}{k})}{\mathcal{T}}\right]^k = kG\Gamma\left(1+\frac{1}{k}\right)^k\frac{t^{k-1}}{\mathcal{T}^{k-1}}.$$

$$(19)$$

Radium can use any PoW algorithm, for example SHA256. Mined blocks are rapidly propagated header-first to all other miners. If the timestamp of the block is drastically different than the time on the recipient's machine, then it is discarded. In practice the time difference can be as little as the maximum expected header propagation delay if miners use NTP to coordinate clocks. The use of NTP in the Bitcoin network has been discussed as a possibility in the past [1]. Note that NTP synchronized clocks are to aid compliant miners. **Radium does not rely on dishonest miners reporting accurate time.**

5.2 Rewards

Let $d(t) = S/g_k(t)$ be the *sub-difficulty*, where S is the size of the hash space. And define reward function $r(t) = C\frac{d(t)}{d(T)}$ for a block mined at elapsed time t, where C is nominal reward including conventional block subsidy and fees. By construction, $r(t)$ will pay out exactly C coins when a block is mined in target time, T seconds. And, by manipulating the block subsidy, it will pay out more or less than that if the block is mined, respectively, sooner or later. The appeal of using $r(t)$ is that the expected reward-per-hash for mining at any given sub-target $g_k(t^*)$ is constant: $\frac{C}{d(T)}$, which disincentivizes future mining.

One of the features of the RTT protocol is that the risk of entering a chain death spiral is eliminated because the difficulty will eventually approach zero as time progresses. The same is true for Radium, except that the reward payout also approaches zero. Thus, in relative terms, the reward per hash never increases in Radium. However, chain death remains highly unlikely because the difficulty will eventually drop so that a block can be mined quickly on a single CPU.

5.3 Difficulty Adjustment

Radium uses feedback control to adjust its difficulty in much the same way as conventional PoW protocols. In particular, it adopts the same mechanism used by RTT, which we describe and refine presently.

Mining amounts to successive draws of random variable T (representing block time) from a given distribution, while difficulty adjustment involves estimating the current scale of the block time distribution from T and moving that scale closer to the ideal. Therefore, difficulty adjustment is essentially parameter estimation from sample T. Rather than directly estimating the scale of Weibull distributed T, Harding [4] opts to transform T to an exponentially distributed random variable T' and estimate its scale instead. Because this transformation amplifies distortions due to hash rate fluctuations, he finds that a single sample is often sufficient to accurately update the difficulty.

Theorem 3. *A block with inter-arrival time T mined under the Radium protocol with target G would have inter-arrival time $T' = \frac{aT^k T}{k}$ if mined under conventional PoW with target G.*

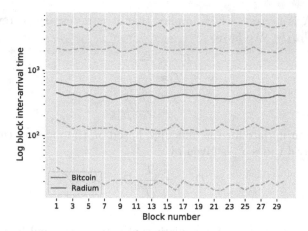

Fig. 2. Median block times for Bitcoin (red) and Radium (blue) across 1000 trials of a 30-block simulation (5th and 95th percentiles shown as dashed lines). After each block in the simulation, the difficulty is adjusted according to Eq. 1 for Bitcoin and Eq. 23 for Radium, with $\overline{T}$ being the mean of the previous two block times. (Color figure online)

Proof. Let T be a random variable drawn from $\mathtt{Weibull}(k, a)$ and having CDF $F(t; k, a)$ as defined in Eq. 8. The probability integral transform (PIT) dictates that random variable $U = F(T; k, a)$ has distribution $\mathtt{Uniform}(0, 1)$. Now define $H(x; \lambda) = 1 - e^{-\lambda x}$, the CDF of the distribution $\mathtt{Expon}(\lambda)$, where λ is defined in Eq. 11. We recover $T' \sim \mathtt{Expon}(\lambda)$ by applying the PIT in reverse using H^{-1}:

$$
\begin{aligned}
T' &= H^{-1}(U; \lambda) \\
&= -\frac{\ln(1-U)}{\lambda} \\
&= -\frac{\ln(1 - F(T; k, a))}{\lambda} \\
&= -\frac{\ln(1 - 1 - e^{aT^k/k})}{\lambda} \\
&= \frac{aT^k T}{k}.
\end{aligned}
\tag{20}
$$

□

Suppose that miners currently operate with hash rate h and that for block i, it happens that $T'_i \neq \mathcal{T}$. Being exponential, the actual inter-arrival time for block i, T'_i, is an unbiased estimator of its expected value, i.e. $T'_i \approx E[T'_i] = \frac{1}{\lambda_i}$. Now suppose that $T'_i \neq \mathcal{T}$. We seek to adjust G_{i+1} so that $T'_{i+1} = \mathcal{T}$. Note that, because D_i represents the expected number of hashes required to mine a block, $T'_i \approx 1/\lambda_i = D_i/h$. And, according to Eqs. 11 and 4,

$$
\frac{1}{\lambda_i} = \mathcal{T} = \frac{D_i}{h} = \frac{S}{G_i h}
\tag{21}
$$

when the DAA is at rest, which implies that it is necessary to revise G_{i+1} so that $\mathcal{T} = S/(G_{i+1}h)$. We have,

$$
\begin{aligned}
T_i' &\approx \frac{D_i}{h} \\
\Rightarrow \frac{at^k}{k}\mathcal{T} &\approx \frac{D_i}{h}. \\
\Rightarrow \mathcal{T} &\approx \frac{k}{at^k}\frac{D_i}{h} \\
&= \frac{D_i}{(at^k/k)h}.
\end{aligned}
\tag{22}
$$

It follows that an update for the difficulty, based on the mean of the previous n block inter-arrival times $\overline{T}$, is given by

$$
D_{i+1} = \frac{k}{a\overline{T}^k}D_i. \tag{23}
$$

Table 1. Block time statistics for simulations of both Bitcoin and Radium when the difficulty is adjusted every block based on the previous two block times. Statistics of the distribution $\texttt{Expon}(\mathcal{T})$, representing the best possible variability for Bitcoin, are provided for comparison. Each statistic reported is itself the result of the median over the 30-block simulation, with 1000 trials performed per block.

Statistic	5th percentile	Median	95th percentile
Two-sample Bitcoin	18 s	410 s	4994 s
Bitcoin Ideal	31 s	416 s	1797 s
Two-sample Radium	129 s	599 s	2114 s

5.4   Block Time Simulation

We ran a mining simulation in both Bitcoin and Radium that updated the difficulty in each according to Eq. 1 and Eq. 23, respectively, where $\overline{T}$ was the mean of the last two block times. Each trial of the simulation ran for 30 consecutive blocks for 1000 trials total. On a log scale, Fig. 2 shows the median and 5th and 95th percentiles for Bitcoin and Radium. Not surprisingly, Bitcoin block times (red) show large variability. However, Radium (blue) shows much better concentration of block times around the target of 600 s.

Table 1 quantifies the median (across the 30 blocks) of medians and 5th and 95th percentiles (each across the 1000 trials). It includes the same statistics for distribution $\texttt{Expon}(\mathcal{T})$, which corresponds to the best possible variability for Bitcoin, when the ideal difficulty is known. The table shows that the median block time for Radium is much closer to the target time of 600 s than either two-sample Bitcoin or the ideal. Also, the 5th percentile for two-sample Radium avoids producing extremely early blocks. Finally, the 95th percentile of block times for Radium stays within 18% of the 95th percentile of Bitcoin Ideal. In contrast, two-sample Bitcoin adjustment is almost 3 times the ideal. *Overall, we find that two-sample Radium difficulty adjustment performs nearly as well as the best possible Bitcoin difficulty adjustment algorithm.*

5.5   Reduction in Block Time Variance

A major feature of RTT is that its Weibull distributed block times have lower variance than exponentially distributed block times under conventional PoW. This affords RTT, and Radium by proxy, with more reliable block inter-arrival times. In this section, we calculate the variances of the Radium block time and compare it to that of the Bitcoin protocol.

We compare the variance in block time for Radium relative to the Bitcoin protocol when the expected block times are both equal to T. To that end, let X and Y_k be random variables representing the block times for Bitcoin and Radium (for given k), respectively. Section 2.2 explains that X is exponentially distributed with mean $T = 1/\lambda$. It is well known that the variance of the exponential distribution is equal to the square of its mean, i.e. $Var_T[X] = T^2$. On the other hand, Sect. 2.3 explained that block times have distribution $\texttt{Weibull}(k, a)$, with a is defined in Eq. 10. For the mean of the Weibull distribution we have $E[Y_k] = \gamma \Gamma(1 + 1/k)$, where

$$\gamma = \left(\frac{k}{a}\right)^{1/k} = \frac{T}{\Gamma(1 + 1/k)}. \tag{24}$$

Note that, by construction, $E[Y_k] = T$. Next, the variance of Y is given by

$$Var[Y_k] = \gamma^2 \left[\Gamma(1 + 2/k) - \Gamma(1 + 1/k)^2\right]. \tag{25}$$

Thus, when blocks are expected every T seconds, the variance is

$$Var[Y_k] = \left(\frac{T}{\Gamma(1 + 1/k)}\right)^2 \left[\Gamma(1 + 2/k) - \Gamma(1 + 1/k)^2\right]. \tag{26}$$

Finally, the *improvement* in variance when adopting Radium over Bitcoin is equal to

$$\frac{Var[Y_k]}{Var[X]} = \left(\frac{1}{\Gamma(1 + 1/k)}\right)^2 \left[\Gamma(1 + 2/k) - \Gamma(1 + 1/k)^2\right] = \frac{\Gamma(1 + 2/k)}{\Gamma(1 + 1/k)^2} - 1. \tag{27}$$

In particular, the improvement for $k = 2$ becomes

$$\frac{Var[Y_2]}{Var[X]} = \frac{\Gamma(2)}{\Gamma(3/2)^2} - 1 = \frac{4}{\pi} - 1 \approx 0.27. \tag{28}$$

5.6   Orphan Rate

Perhaps the only drawback of more reliable block times is an increase in the rate that *orphan* blocks are produced. An orphan occurs when two viable blocks are produced at roughly the same time. Miners will ultimately settle on one to form the tip of the blockchain, while the other will be discarded.

Fortunately, the orphan rate observed under the Radium protocol is not expected to be much worse than the orphan rate observed for Bitcoin. To demonstrate this, we ran a mining simulation of both the Bitcoin and Radium protocols for more than 850,000 blocks each. Any time two blocks were generated within the same three second time period, we incremented the orphan counter. A three second interval was chosen because it represents a realistic delay in today's Bitcoin network [6]. Our simulation showed that Bitcoin is expected to experience orphans approximately 0.22% of the time while Radium is expected to experience orphans about 0.36% of the time. Thus, Radium's orphan rate is approximately 63% greater than that of Bitcoin; yet the absolute rate remains low.

6   Radium Security Analysis

In this section, we analyze various aspects of Radium protocol security. Our primary focus is on incentivizing protocol compliance as well as mitigating the effects of common attacks on PoW blockchains.

6.1   Reward Function Exploitation

A major concern with using dynamic reward function $r(t)$ (defined in Sect. 5.2) over a constant reward function is that a miner with a large amount of hash rate might suddenly switch from one blockchain (say BTC) over to the Radium chain and mine a block at a very high difficulty so as to gain excessive reward. We call this behavior *switch-mining*. The following argument attempts to show the conditions under which miners can and cannot profit in this fashion. We find that when $k \leq 2$, there exists no advantage to switch-mining between Radium and another chain.

Suppose that for block 1, a miner from chain X suddenly increases the hash rate on the Radium chain by multiple $x > 1$. Equation 18 shows that the resulting block time distribution is `Weibull`(k, xa). Combining Eqs. 10 and 9 it follows that the expected block time $E[T_1]$ will be

$$E[T_1] = \Gamma(1 + 1/k)\left(\frac{k}{xa}\right)^{1/k} = \mathcal{T}x^{-1/k}. \tag{29}$$

Thus, the expected reward $E[R_1]$ amounts to

$$E[R_1] = C\frac{d(\mathcal{T}x^{-1/k})}{d(\mathcal{T})} = C\frac{g(\mathcal{T})}{g(\mathcal{T}x^{-1/k})} = C\frac{\mathcal{T}^{k-1}}{(\mathcal{T}x^{-1/k})^{k-1}} = Cx^{(k-1)/k}. \tag{30}$$

Of course, the DAA will respond by adjusting the target so that the increased hash rate yields a block in time $\mathcal{T}$. Next, suppose that, for block 2, the miners withdraw their hash rate. The affect of this withdrawal is inverse-symmetric to the affect of the increase; it follows by substituting $y = 1/x$ in the equations above. We have $E[T_2] = \mathcal{T}x^{1/k}$ and $E[R_2] = Cx^{-(k-1)/k}$.

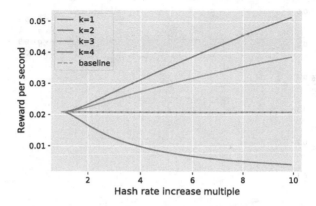

Fig. 3. Expected reward per second for a network of miners who switch-mine between Radium and another coin such as Bitcoin. Each curve corresponds to a different value of k from Eq. 10. The dashed line indicates reward per second if miners do not switch.

Figure 3 shows the reward-per-second as a function of hash rate increase multiples x for various values of k where $C = 12.5$. Because the attack takes two blocks to carry out, we measure aggregate reward over both blocks. The results are compared to *baseline*, where hash rate does not fluctuate. We can see from the figure that it is indeed possible for miners to profit, per-unit-hash, for values of k exceeding 2. However, when $k = 1$, miners actually lose profit, and for $k = 2$, there is no change in profitability.

6.2   Doublespend Attack Susceptibility

Bissias and Levine [2] argue that high variance is at the core of two of the most fundamental attacks on PoW blockchains: the doublespend and selfish mining. Their Bobtail protocol demonstrates that a lower variance block time can substantially mitigate both attacks. We can compare Radium's improvement in variance over Bitcoin (see Sect. 5.5) to that of Bobtail over Bitcoin.

Let Z_j be a random variable representing the block time using Bobtail with parameter j; i.e., there are j proofs per block. It has been shown [2] that the improvement in variance relative to Bitcoin is given by

$$\frac{Var[Z_j]}{Var[X]} = \frac{8j + 4}{6(j^2 + j)}. \tag{31}$$

Finally, we can determine the value of j for which Bobtail's improvement in variance is equivalent to RTT with $k = 2$ by solving

$$\frac{4}{\pi} - 1 = \frac{8j + 4}{6(j^2 + j)}. \tag{32}$$

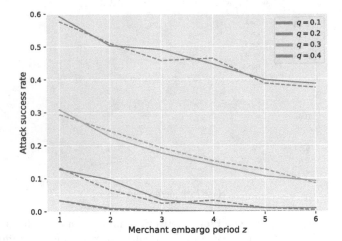

Fig. 4. Probability (dependent axis) that an attacker, having fraction q of the total hash rate (individual lines), succeeds in a doublespend attack when merchants impose an embargo period (independent axis) of z blocks. The solid and dashed lines indicate success probability in the Bitcoin and Radium protocols, respectively. Each point represents the success frequency over 1000 trials.

Solving for j we have

$$j = \frac{7\pi - 12 + \sqrt{144 - 72\pi + 25\pi^2}}{6(4 - \pi)} > 4. \tag{33}$$

Yet despite the fact that the reduction in variance for Radium is roughly equivalent to Bobtail with $j = 4$, it turns out that Radium has the same susceptibility to doublespend attacks as does Bitcoin. Figure 4 shows the result of a mining simulator that we ran for both Bitcoin (solid lines) and Radium (dashed lines). Each curve represents a different attacker hash power, ranging from 10% up to 40% of the total. Points along each curve correspond to the embargo period imposed by the coin receiver, a merchant for example. For an embargo period of length z, the merchant will not release goods purchased with a transaction in block i until z additional blocks have been mined after it. The figure shows that there are negligible differences between attacker success probability when comparing Bitcoin to Radium.

The results of our simulation suggest that there might be something fundamental about the doublespend protection afforded by protocols that use just one PoW sample per block. We formalize this conjecture below, but leave investigation to future work.

Conjecture 1. Mining a block under PoW amounts to sampling a sufficiently low statistic from a known distribution. For example, in Bitcoin, the statistic is a single exponential random variable. Let K be any mining statistic on a single sample per block, i.e. a single random variable is sampled once. And assume that

K is fair in the sense that a miner with fraction x of the hash rate receives fraction x of the rewards in expectation. Then the doublespend protection offered by a protocol using K is no better than that offered by a protocol using an exponential random variable for its statistic.

7 Conclusion

We have identified and analyzed a critical vulnerability in the real-time block rate targeting protocol (RTT). To mitigate this vulnerability, we introduced Radium, a refinement of RTT. Like RTT, Radium offers less variable block times, a more responsive DAA, and thwarts the chain death spiral that threatens minority hash rate blockchains. We have also shown that Radium maintains Bitcoin's robustness to the doublespend attack as well as its low orphan rate.

References

1. AddTimeData will never update nTimeOffset past 199 samples. https://github.com/bitcoin/bitcoin/issues/4521, July 2014
2. Bissias, G., Levine, B.N.: Bobtail: improved blockchain security with low-variance mining. In: ISOC Network and Distributed System Security Symposium (2020)
3. Bissias, G., Levine, B.N., Thibodeau, D.: Greedy but Cautious: Conditions for Miner Convergence to Resource Allocation Equilibrium. https://arxiv.org/pdf/1907.09883.pdf, July 2019
4. Harding, T.M.: Real-Time Block Rate Targeting. Ledger 5 (2020)
5. Kwon, Y., Kim, H., Shin, J., Kim, Y.: Bitcoin vs. bitcoin cash: coexistence or downfall of bitcoin cash? In: IEEE Symposium on Security and Privacy, pp. 935–951, February 2019
6. Nagayama, R., Shudo, K., Banno, R.: Identifying impacts of protocol and internet development on the bitcoin network. https://arxiv.org/pdf/1912.05208.pdf, December 2019
7. Nakamoto, S.: Bitcoin: A Peer-to-Peer Electronic Cash System, May 2009
8. Ozisik, A.P., Bissias, G., Levine, B.N.: Estimation of Miner Hash Rates and Consensus on Blockchains. Technical Report arXiv:1707.00082, University of Massachusetts, Amherst, MA, July 2017
9. Phanpp. Chain Death Spiral - A Fatal Bitcoin Vulnerability. http://bitcoinandtheblockchain.blogspot.com/2017/08/chain-death-spiral-fatal-bitcoin.html, August 2017
10. Rizun, P.R.: Subchains: a technique to scale bitcoin and improve the user experience: open review. Ledger 1 (2016)
11. Rosenfeld, M.: Analysis of hashrate-based double-spending. https://bitcoil.co.il/Doublespend.pdf, December 2012
12. Stone, G.A.: Tail Removal Block Validation. https://medium.com/@g.andrew.stone/tail-removal-block-validation-ae26fb436524, October 2017

Proof of No-Work: How to Incentivize Individuals to Stay at Home

Michael Bartholic$^{(\boxtimes)}$, Jianan Su, Ryosuke Ushida, Yusuke Ikeno,
Zhengrong Gu, and Shin'ichiro Matsuo

Georgetown University, Washington, D.C., USA
{mwb70,js4488,ru64,yi106,zg120,sm3377}@georgetown.edu

Abstract. The recent pandemic of novel coronavirus introduces a new challenge to balancing social welfare, the economy, and privacy while reducing contact among individuals. To reduce the reproduction rate without spoiling our economy, we need good incentive mechanisms to reduce the possibility of spreading the virus as well as good privacy enhancing techniques. Unfortunately, some of the recent approaches in contact tracing are not successful due to privacy concerns and a lack of sufficient incentive mechanisms to guide behavior instead of simply tracking infections. In this paper, we provide a design using smart contracts as an incentive mechanism with enhanced privacy of user location information. We utilize encrypted data calculated from a set of network routing information, and a plaintext equality test of a public key cryptosystem to estimate the duration one is present at the same location. By staying at the same location longer, a user can obtain greater rewards. We have implemented a proof concept of this scheme to evaluate its efficiency. We also discuss financial regulation and economic viewpoints.

Keywords: Smart contract · Blockchain · Incentive mechanism · Privacy protection

1 Introduction

1.1 Background

In the long history of computer science it has helped humans to make their lives and society more predictable, inclusive, and collaborative. It automates a multitude of business processes and communications, provides a high degree of future analysis, and realizes dynamic, border-less, multi-lateral and permissionless communications. These benefits provided by computer science dramatically enhance the social nature of human. COVID-19, which presents a tremendous challenge to our social nature, forces us to find new styles of human society. The good news is we already maintain a combination of Internet technologies and strong logistics; we are already holding online meetings and conducting everyday life by using the Internet amid the COVID-19 pandemic. Though we know staying

© Springer Nature Switzerland AG 2020
J. Garcia-Alfaro et al. (Eds.): DPM 2020/CBT 2020, LNCS 12484, pp. 390–406, 2020.
https://doi.org/10.1007/978-3-030-66172-4_25

at home and social distancing are a strong measures to reduce the reproduction rate of this disease, it is difficult to keep people following strict regulations with the reality of powerful economic pressures to maintain traditional life.

An existing attempt to reduce the reproduction rate is "contact tracing", which utilizes GPS and Bluetooth interaction data of citizens and notifies users of the system the possibility of contact with a person who is infected [6]. This may reduce the reproduction rate only when the individuals adequately distance themselves at home for enough time (e.g. 14 days). However, this idea has two major problems. The first is privacy issue that some organization may obtain the history of GPS data of a person. To solve this privacy concern, Apple and Google implement a privacy enhancing technique [9]. But, this attempt raises a debate on centralized solution versus decentralized solution to gather personal data used for social welfare. The second problem is it does not provide much incentive to use over the privacy concern. At the time of writing this paper, the number of installs is much lower than expected. For example, the rate of partic-ipation among citizens is about 30% in Singapore and 9% in Japan. A research study claims that a minimum 60% of participation rate is needed to make this technology effective to reduce the reproduction rate [8]. That is, unfortunately, this trial is currently unsuccessful due to the lack of enough incentive mecha-nisms. Because the nature of COVID-19 - low death rate, low incidence rate and long incubation period - it is needed to implement some incentive mechanism to staying at home or at the same place as long as possible, even for asymptomatic persons. Stimulus check may heal the loss caused by staying at home for a brief period, however, this does not incentivize individuals to stay at home for an extension amount of time. From the above, we need a new mechanism which can incentivize individuals staying at home as long as possible, while protecting personal data against some centralized organization.

1.2   Related Works

Apple and Google provides a platform for contact tracing with utilizes GPS data of smartphones [9]. Some country apply this platform to contact tracing application, and the other group of countries try to implement its own similar application like Tracetogether in Singapore [1] according to the nation's privacy policy. However, at the time of writing this paper, this direction has not been successful. This policy and realized application don't provide enough incentive to citizens to use it. There are many debates on this type of application regarding its governance model: centralized vs. decentralized [2,4,10]. There are many pros. and cons. for both, and there exist many statements on this topic.

Originally, the mathematics of Bitcoin is a great example of creating incen-tive mechanisms to maintain the public ledger. Likewise, smart contracts are also a platform to provide incentive to maintain some system/ecosystem sustainable. However, there is not so many research on the social sustainable incentive mecha-nisms based on permissionless blockchain and smart contract. [12] is an example to incentivize people to keep networked device secure to reduce the cost of cyber insurance.

1.3 Our Contribution

In this paper, we propose a scheme to provide rewards according to the time staying at the same place. To estimate the duration of time that a given person stays at the same location, we utilize a time-wise difference generated in part by the common traceroute utility. This data is encrypted on blockchain by an encryption scheme which permits plain-text equality tests. The data is recorded over a public blockchain as a publicly verifiable time-stamped "IP fingerprint". This construction keeps the actual IP address of a device secret to decentralized nodes, but anyone can calculate the duration of time the device keeps the same physical location. We discuss potential attack scenarios to fake the result of traceroute utility, and provide countermeasures. We also implemented the smart contract scheme over Ethereum platform and shows the result of implementation. We also discuss the security and privacy of our proposal, effectiveness of our proposal from economic point of view, and analysis from regulation viewpoints.

2 Stakeholders and Goals of Proposed Scheme

We consider three kinds of stakeholders in this system:

User. These are the individuals participating in the system for their own benefit and the benefit of the infection susceptible community. Users are those who are being incentivized to stay home/work whenever possible and to avoid social contact. Through passing time-wise location checks and engagement checks, each user can earn reward tokens that are associated with their individual UUID within the network and accessible from the mobile application. This process acts to go beyond contract tracing of infected individuals and reduce contact between individuals in the first place. We assume that users behave as follows:

- (Good) They are motivated to get rewards by staying home.
- (Bad) They want to get more reward than they are eligible.

Reward Organizations. These are the organizations that are offering rewards for those individuals willing to take action to combat the spread of infections. These organizations can be real-world organizations such as supermarkets, gas stations, and other similar establishments. We assume that the reward organizations have incentives as follows:

- (Good) Some retail stores, such as grocery stores, may want to offer discount to rewarded customers because they can hedge the infection risk in their stores.
- (Bad) They want to provide less reward due to their budget constraint.

Hosts. These are the organizations that operate host servers, run full node of blockchain, and provide client application in this system. The hosts can be both public and private entities and each function can be run by multiple organizations such as health authority and Internet service provider (ISP). Incentives structure is as below.

- (Good) Public entity such as public health authorities or NPO would have an incentive to run the hosts or provide financial supports to the hosts run by private companies because this system could serve for social benefits by preventing users from contracting the virus.
- (Bad) ISP offering home wifi service is considered a suitable operator of the host servers. But the ISP can be disincentivized by the operating costs.

The goals of the proposed scheme are as follows:

- **Correctness:** If a user stays at the same location, an appropriate reward is given to the user.
- **Security:** A user cannot obtain more reward than predefined amount by the rule. A reward organization is not allowed to pay less than predefined amount.
- **Good incentive mechanism:** The amount of reward provides enough incentive to a user to staying at the same location.
- **Privacy:** Any pair of location data and time for each user is kept secret.
- **Decentralized governance:** If the data and logic is controlled by a single organization, the organization could be a single point of failure and locking-in to the organization happens. This situation implies centralization of governance and spoils check and balance mechanism among stakeholders.

3   Design of Smart Contract for Incentives

3.1   System Model

The primary components and stakeholders of the system are illustrated in Fig. 1. The application component is an application installed on a user's device M_i which generates location proofs using their Wi-Fi connection information. Here, a mobile phone's local IP address is given by a home WiFi router W_j which has both internal local IP address range and global IP address IP_{W_j}. W_j transmits them to the system endpoint. Our construction is influenced by the assumption

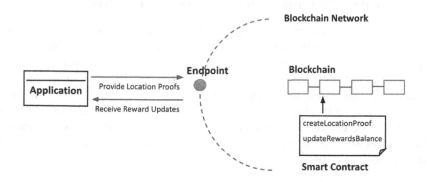

Fig. 1. System model of social distancing reward system

that M_i and W_j for all i, j have a Trusted Execution Environment (TEE) [11] to protect code and cryptographic keys loaded inside regarding to authenticity of data input to blockchain[1]. The endpoint is a set of 1 to n host servers that are responsible for user location checking and run full nodes in the blockchain network. The blockchain component is used to store validated location proofs of users and works together with smart contract to automate rewarding process.

3.2   Primary Processes

The proposed scheme consists of five key phases: register, check-engagement, check-route, calculate rewards, and redemption. The register phase only runs once per user who is participating in the system. The next two phases run in continual loops after the user has registered. The payout phase can take place at any interval and is event driven. Organizations who opt to take part in the system will have the ability to receive tokens and are expected to exchange them for some real life service, coupon, or reward.

Register: This phase consists of the process of initializing the user's device to take part in the system. The user will enroll themselves with the required information such as email address and password.

Check engagement: This phase is to ensure the user has their personal device with them and is not cheating by leaving the device at home or otherwise.

Check route: This phase is the application runs the custom traceroute configuration several times to obtain IP routes between the user and appointed host servers to estimate if the user stays at the same location across time. The application will store data used in the checking process on blockchain.

Calculate rewards: This phase is using result from check route phase to calculate rewards user should receive. Updated rewards balance of user will be stored on blockchain.

Payout: This process is where the user can exchange their accumulated tokens for real world coupons or prizes from the reward organizations.

3.3   Calculating Rewards - How to Provide Incentive

In order to adequately incentivize the behaviors that are known to be lower risk, we need a way to measure compliance with the system's goals. Most basically, this can be thought of as a measurement of how stationary someone is, and since one is unlikely to be able to spend a majority duration of their time at a location they do not live nor work, a way to measure how much socially isolated distanced behavior one is undertaking. There are several ways to calculate compliance with the system based on user location records, however effectively all techniques will be based around ideas of variability and the distribution of locations. We will discuss two rewards calculation protocols in this section.

---

[1] Usage of TEE at user device is not for operation of blockchain nodes.

3.3.1 A Scheme Using Shannon Entropy

A preferred calculation methodology makes use of Shannon Entropy and has several useful side effects. Namely, this method is simple with only one formula, is time independent, produces a single output value, possesses a well defined meaning, and places all scores on a bounded interval in which they can be directly compared. The minimum value of the interval will be $S = 0$, representing "entropy" of zero in the circumstance where all inputs are the same. Likewise, the maximum value of the interval will be $S = S_{max}$, a value determined by the total count of measurements in the interval (which is presumable fixed) that occurs when all inputs are distinct. Such a capacity for direct comparisons between individuals/groups or one's own performance over time also provides a useful measure for the gamification of the system.

Input:

- Location information (transformed IP address) as ciphertext
- NIST Randomness Beacon validated timestamp
- UUID of user: This is not used by any operation, but this process is done for one UUID at a time.

Parameters:

- I: **Interval of interest** Time interval that contains all of the proofs we care to be observing during this check. Should cover all of a user's typical routine "cycle" as well as backwards and forwards into the previous intervals. To check for consistency with the previous interval. I.e. 24 h of Wednesday, + final 12 h of Tuesday, + first 12 h of Thursday makes a 48 h interval of interest
- C: **uniformity check frequency** Should be more frequent and shorter in duration than the I. I.e. checks of a 48 h interval above could take place every 12 or 24 h. With the interval of interest shifting forward by C each time.
- S_{max}: **Maximum Valid Entropy** We can determine this empirically by creating example "intervals" and calculating what their entropy would be for acceptable and unacceptable examples. Theoretically S ranges from 0 to infinity. In this circumstance, S ranges from 0 to a finite max that is defined by every location in our interval being unique.
- X: **the collection of all location ciphertexts from the interval I** These ciphertexts will be sorted into categories X_i based on comparisons of plaintext equality.
- **Payout duration** Separately from deriving our entropy measure from the location information, we maintain another parameter for how often the system would execute payouts. This parameter is unrelated to the entropy calculation but will inform the systems reward procedure.

Process:

1. Use comparisons (equality) to sort the locations of each check into categories to count frequencies, that is make a histogram.[2]
2. Calculate the Shannon Entropy S given the these X_i using the formula, where $P(X_i)$ is the probability of apparent location i within all samples of X:

$$S(X) = -\sum_{i=1}^{n} P(X_i) log_2 P(X_i) \tag{1}$$

Steps:

1. Each X_i is defined by the unique categories determined as follows:
   (a) Using the plaintext equality comparison operation (will be discussed in Sect. 4) bin each sample in X into the relevant X_i by comparing each item with the existing bins.
   (b) If an item is equal to an example from a given bin, put it in that bin and move to the next sample.
   (c) If an item is not equal to an example from a given bin, try the next bin until all bins have been exhausted. If no existing bins match, create a new bin for this location.
   (d) When each sample has been binned, each location bin X_i will represent the frequency with which the user was at the given location. These frequencies will be used to calculate entropy in step 2.
2. Evaluate (1) to get S, make decisions based on choice of threshold:
   (a) If $S \leq S_{max}$, there is an acceptable level of variability in user locations. Therefore, the check passes and the user can be granted tokens for this interval.
   (b) The user is issued a payout using when their a token count surpasses a payout threshold. Done.
   (c) If $S < S_{max}$, there is an unacceptable level of variability in user locations. Therefore, the check fails and the user is not granted any validation.
   (d) The user is not issued tokens and receives no payout.

It is worth noting that there are a few assumptions required to use this scheme. For example, two long stretches (a qualitatively positive behavior) within an interval can appear with the same measure as a "tick-tock" behavior of switching between two locations (a qualitatively negative behavior) for the duration of the interval. Aside from this most extreme example, it is not difficult to generate other examples with the same derived measure. Generally, we do not find these collisions to be of particular concern as the adversarial option represents complex, tedious movements that are unlikely to be actualized physically. Nevertheless, we find that the benefits in simplicity and utility of

---

[2] One could very well stop after creating a histogram of the location distribution, but a user's performance is less clear when viewed categorically and hence we prefer to have a derived metric that greatly simplifies the act of comparing user performance.

this entropy measure to out-weight the required assumptions. Notably, if these assumptions are deemed unsatisfactory, one could easily apply additional heuristics to the input data such as only considering location checks with continuity of location between the point previous check and the subsequent check (effectively making the minimum viable location be "3 checks" long) and recording non-conforming measurements as distinct from all others.

3.3.2   A Scheme Using Tracking Duration at Location - Streaks

Another simple way to encourage users to get involved in social isolation is to reward users when they stay at the same place for a specific time duration (e.g. 5 h). To achieve this, we first count the intervals of time that a user continuously stays at a place. Every time when we get a validated proof, we compare it with the last proof (or set of proofs) recorded. We will increase N by 1 for each interval that the user stays in the same place if the fingerprints are equal. Repeating these steps, we know the time length of each place a user continuously stays. To calculate rewards a user will receive, we simply multiply the number of times duration of time satisfies predefined time duration condition and rewards received per time. This mechanism is both easy to compute and simpler for a user to understand, so in some ways it may be considered preferable to the more complex entropy measure. Considering that users may be at different places such as grocery stores and workplace, and they are not able to stay at a place all the time. Total rewards R a user received in a day is defined as

$$N = count(T \geq C) \tag{2}$$

for each streak of duration T in a day.

$$R = r \times N \tag{3}$$

where r is reward per valid interval, N is number of intervals of $T \geq C$, T is duration of each fixed location, and C minimum duration for reward threshold.

4   Proposed Scheme

4.1   Design of Privacy Protection

4.1.1   Privacy Goals

In contrast to many existing systems which require somewhat liberal data sharing, we're looking to exercise a minimalist approach with what information will be shared in this system. Systems oriented toward contact tracing such as Tracetogether or the Apple/Google contact tracing API are susceptible to accumulating excessive and reveling levels of person information even when done correctly [4]. Instead we look to share only what is absolutely necessary to encourage and incentivize individuals to take precautionary measures. In this way we strive to provide a system that prioritizes individual privacy while still creating a positive influence on

- Limit on-chain data to only what is strictly necessary: Following our minimalist system design we only want to share the minimum data necessary for operability and verification of the system. Instead of collecting a wealth of data and paring down to what is useful to track a user, we are only looking to record what is explicitly necessary and sufficient for the system to operate in its intended capacity.
- Limit size and weight of on-chain data for computational efficiency: To have a scalable system without ballooning computational requirements, we want to ensure computational complexity is not needless increased by any factor. High time complexity encryption schemes or work-based puzzles are therefore easily out of the question.
- Sufficiently protect on-chain data: Even the minimal data we are choosing to record to the blockchain must be protected in such a way that individual identities or institutional affiliations are not leaked.
- Limit off-chain data to reduce risk profile and increase inclusively: Beyond from the requirements of the blockchain and data privacy, it is also key to consider the information a user must divulge to enroll and participate. While limited information will be sorted in a mobile application off-chain, we also want to limit any personal information stored here. This will act to decrease the risk profile of the information stored on a user's device and also may increase user's willingness to participate if personal information need not be shared to join.

4.1.2   Fingerprinting Scheme with Public Plaintext-Equality Testing

Fingerprinting scheme enables parties to evaluate the equality of fingerprint or encrypted data without revealing any information about plaintext. It provides semantic security and prevents low-entropy messages from brute-force attack. The generation of fingerprints and the testing algorithm require keys can be either private or public. In our prototype system, we use secret fingerprinting and public testing of plaintext-equality. It prevents leakage of user private information such as their traceroute output and enables every entity in the blockchain network to evaluate the equality of user IP fingerprints at different time intervals. The protocol was first introduced in [3] and consists of four algorithms: KeyGen, LFingerprint, RFingerprint, and Test. KeyGen creates the left and right fingerprinting keys lk and rk as well as the public parameter pp. LFingerprint takes a left-fingerprinting key lk and a message m and outputs a left-fingerprint f_L. RFingerprint takes right-fingerprinting key rk and a message m' and outputs a right-fingerprint f_R. Test takes a left-fingerprint f_L and right-fingerprint f_R and reveals whether they correspond to the same message or not. Let $\mathcal{H}$ be a random oracle. Let $e : \mathbb{G}_1 \times \mathbb{G}_2 \rightarrow \mathbb{G}_T$ be a type-3 pairing with $\mathbb{G}_1, \mathbb{G}_2, \mathbb{G}_T$ of prime order p.

1. KeyGen: randomly draw $(g, \tilde{g}, x, y) \leftarrow \mathbb{G}_1 \times \mathbb{G}_2 \times \mathbb{Z}_p^2$, set $(X, \tilde{X}, Y, \tilde{Y}) \leftarrow (g^x, \tilde{g}^x, g^y, \tilde{g}^y)$, return $lk = X$, $rk = \tilde{X}$, and public parameter $pp = (g, Y, \tilde{g}, \tilde{Y})$.
2. LFingerprint(lk, m): draw $u \leftarrow \mathbb{Z}_p^*$, return $f_L = (g^u, (XY^{\mathcal{H}(m)})^u)$.

3. RFingerprint(rk, m'): draw $u \leftarrow \mathbb{Z}_p^*$, return $f_R = (\tilde{g}^u, (\tilde{X}\tilde{Y}^{\mathcal{H}(m')})^u)$.
4. Test(f_L, f_R): return 1 if $f_{L,1}, f_{R,1} \neq 1_{\mathbb{G}_1}$ and $e(f_{L,1}, f_{R,2}) = e(f_{L,2}, f_{R,1})$, else 0.

4.1.3   Data Management

– On-chain data
   - Quantity of Tokens associated with UUID: A measure of the current "credit" the user has earned in the system.
   - Verified timestamps of each proof operation: These timestamps can be drawn from a source that provides unpredictable nonce information such as the NIST Randomness Beacon.
   - Encrypted location fingerprints corresponding to each proof: These fingerprints are derived from information including the IP address of the user, a trace-route to given host servers, and possibly other factors that may increase the uniqueness and difficulty of spoofing. These fingerprints are encrypted using an scheme that preserves the plaintext equality operation such as that described in.
– Off-chain data (stored locally in mobile application only)
   - User's name: This is never shared on the blockchain and only required for redemption. However, it is locked into the application during registration to limit the ability to share with others, and remove the ability to be able to redeem someone else's work.
   - User's UUID: This is used to include with proofs, but of course is not private as the rest of the proof contents. This user's mobile device will maintain the only association between the given user and their UUID.

Derived measures such as the Shannon Entropy "performance index" of the user (i.e. the user's score in compliance with the system) during a given interval can be maintained either on-chain or off-chain depending on efficiency concerns and computational/storage capabilities of the network. The reward granting functionalities will derive and make use of these measures when determining user payouts using the information which is available on-chain. As such, no additional information is divulged by incorporating previous computations or intermediate values on-chain and there may be desirable performance benefits to be had from such a process.

4.2   Security Design

In this section, we discuss security requirements of our system. We assume that underlying permissionless blockchain is secure, that is, common prefix, chain quality, persistence and liveness [7] are assured. Hence, we concentrate on the oracle problem to assure the correctness of the input to blockchain. Two types of attacks we need to consider are as follows.

Security against malicious user: The malicious incentive of a user is obtaining more reward than the amount which is calculated from the actual time to stay at the same location. To prevent this kind of attack, the following characteristics are needed for each fingerprint's data.

1. Each fingerprint is bound to behavior of the user (authenticity)
2. Each fingerprint is bound to physical location of the user
3. Valid fingerprint is random and unpredictable from past valid fingerprint

Malicious activities could be conducted before and during the check-route phase and during the transmission of data from user's device to host server. User pretends staying at same place overtime by leaving registered device at a place to complete system protocols and goes to other places without keeping that device with him/her. To prevent this malicious activity, we implement asymmetric key based authentication protocol associated with a registered device per user. It is a way to achieve the first characteristics.

Even if the first is achieved, the authenticated device can output fingerprints with fixed routes regardless of physical location by using VPN services. To assure we meet the second requirement, we involve the global IP address of the WiFi router which provides local IP address with the data included into blockchain. A digital signature by the WiFi router is given to the data.

The third characteristics is associated with replay attack during the transmission of data from user's device to host server. The consequence of such attack could be victims receive less rewards even they follow the rewarding protocol and attackers receive rewards without doing any work. To prevent such an attack, a challenge and response protocol with randomness beacon is implemented. We use randomness beacon and EUF-CMA digital signature scheme and store randomness beacon and verification key on blockchain for public verification.

Security against malicious reward organization:
The reward organization might have an incentive to provide less reward than the amount which is calculated from the actual time to stay at the same location. How ever, we assume that records on reward over blockchain are not compromised. Thus, we can prevent and publicly verify such an malicious activity.

4.3   Protocol Description

Location proofs will be generated locally on the user's mobile device using information collected by the device itself. Only once the location fingerprints are generated and possibly revealing location information has be protected are proof contents written on chain. In general this process is as follows:

Registration: During registration, a secured communication channel between user's device and a host server will be set up first. A key pair signing key sk_i /verification key vk_i of M_i and a key pair lk_i/rk_i following the KeyGen in fingerprinting scheme are generated. These keys are managed by making use of TEE. When user signs up, the application will send user account information provided by user to the host server. Host server will verify user's account information then securely store them.

Check engagement: To involve a user interaction, user's cellphone will receive a notification which asks user to complete a verification on the application to prove that the user has registered device and does not simply leave the device somewhere while the user is elsewhere. If engagement check fails, user's current location will be determined as invalid.

Check route: This phase consists two steps. First, the application generates left and right fingerprints of user's current routes then signs the fingerprints and current time t using sk_i and a randomness beacon based on EUF-CMA digital signature scheme such as ECDSA.

Step 1: $lf_{i,t}$ = LFingerprint (lk_i, pp, IP): Application generates left-fingerprint f_L of user IP routes with lk and sends it to appointed host server.

Step 2: $rf_{i,t}$ = RFingerprint (rk_i, pp, IP): Application generates right-fingerprint f_R of user IP routes with rk and sends it to appointed host server.

Step 3: $Sig_{i,t} = Sig_{sk_i}\{lf_{i,t}, rf_{i,t}, t\}$

Then the application sends fingerprints with signature to W_j. W_j signs the data with $IP_{j,t}$ for time t by its singing key sk_j, then send a host server them.

Step 4: $Sig_{j,t} = Sig_{sk_j}\{Sig_{i,t}, IP_{j,t}\}$

The host server verifies the information received with vk_i and vk_j and conduct **Test**.

Step 5: Test(f_L', f_R): Given f_L' = LFingerprint(lk, IP') which is the left-fingerprint of user's last IP routes from the blockchain and f_R which is right-fingerprint of user's current IP routes, host server tests whether they correspond to the same IP routes.

When host server finishes above equality testing, it sends the test result to smart contract for reward calculation. UUID, f_L, f_R, time stamp and signatures are also stored on blockchain via smart contract.

Calculate reward: At this phase, smart contract will calculate reward the user should receive using the calculation scheme described in Sect. 3.3.

Payout: The user exchanges their accumulated tokens for real world coupons/prizes from the reward organizations. The reward organization authenticates user for redeeming. If their identity is valid, the user will communicate to the organization which of their offered rewards they would like to take. In spending the reward, the amount will be adjusted at ledger on blockchain. To comply financial regulations, users cannot trade them with each other and are only able to redeem/spend the tokens in the ecosystem's preconfigured outlets.

5   Implementation

The priority of implementation is to develop key functionalities of the prototype system so we could evaluate security and efficiency of prototype system. These

Table 1. List of Java and Solidity files and their function

File	Function
FPScheme.java	Logic for fingerprinting scheme
Server.java	Logic for fingerprint generation of user IP information, equality test, updating duration of time at each location and store data to blockchain
CalculateReward.sol	Logic for reward calculation using duration of time at same location
CalculateReward.java	Same logic as CalculateReward.sol but a java wrapper of it

Table 2. Examples of user data on blockchain

UUID	IP_LFingerprint	IP_RFingerprint	Timestamp	Time duration	Rewards balance
1	JTB9BIcKcq	BaOwrtQKTH	06:00	0	0
1	rw1NGur2ME	WoK5d0sZ3C	07:00	1	0
1	xR7hpP2CIr	2yomU1icB8	08:00	2	0
1	HMJ3f1J97r	zpSMF6TDMK	09:00	0	0
2	j6LOQhHyos	NzhGph9omX	06:00	0	0
2	0w1Gu9wE+o	vnQ4f3NeCu	07:00	1	0
2	WfuM61rsVg	RFWpAjchj+	08:00	2	0
2	OvFO+75iAV	GmxhjyxLiq	09:00	3	5

key functionalities are equality test of user IP fingerprints and reward calculation. For equality test functionality, we first implemented fingerprint generation from user location info before it is stored on blockchain. Meanwhile, an equality test is offered to compare any two fingerprints stored on the blockchain. For reward calculation, we implemented two proposed calculation schemes.

Several Java classes which contain functions of fingerprint scheme and functions of reward calculation of Shannon entropy are developed. A smart contract is implemented in Solidity, which has functions for reward calculation as well as storing and retrieving data on blockchain. Table 1 lists the Java and Solidity files and their function. We also set up a private Ethereum blockchain to deploy the smart contract for use in our experiments. Table 2 shows examples of user data on blockchain. Rewards balance in this table is calculated based on an example protocol that user is rewarded for 5 tokens for staying at same place for 3 h. Note that each IP_LFingerprint and each IP_RFingerprint is 172 bytes but we only list 10 bytes for display in the table.

6   Evaluation

6.1   Privacy and Security

6.1.1   Privacy

The fingerprint is encrypted by using a public key encryption scheme with plaintext equality test. The only information obtainable from any set of encrypted fingerprints is if the plaintexts are the same or not. Even if the result of test algorithm of two different fingerprints is negative, the comparison does not reveal information about either plaintext. Thus, by comparing pairs of fingerprints, any party can compute users' behavior over time without access to individual points.

6.1.2 Security

Security against malicious user: For the first characteristic, the fingerprint is singed by signing key stored in TPM/TEE of the mobile device, which requires periodical authorization by the user

For the second characteristic, the source IP address of the user device is assigned by the WiFi router provided by ISP. For the case that, the user uses VPN to obtain the same IP address from different locations, the fingerprint contains the global IP address assigned to the WIFI router, then anyone can verify if the user connects via VPN.

For the third characteristic, the fingerprint is calculated by using randomness beacon and EUF-CMA digital signature scheme.

Security against malicious reward organization: The smart contract process and the result is public verifiable, thus, the reward organization cannot fake the time of staying at the same place and resulting amount of reward.

6.2 Efficiency

Let us consider practical efficiency of the system during widespread usage. Here we consider the scenario in which the application works from 12:00 h (noon) on Monday until to 12:00 h on Wednesday in order to generate an overlapping range of measurements (centered on Tuesday). Host servers permit the client to generate a location proof twice per hour. This time span accounts for 48 h of measurements or 96 individual proofs. While, in this configuration, each user generates 48 location proofs which are stored on blockchain each day, we intend to consider our derived scoring measurements as being centered in the 48 h interval covering half of the previous and subsequent days.

6.2.1 Space

Each location proof with attributes listed in Table 2 is 273 bytes. Without explicit consideration for the blockchain overhead, this is 13,104 bytes per user per day. While this is markedly more data than simply recording SHA256 or SHA512 hashes (32 bytes and 64 bytes respectively), we believe that the use of these fingerprints provides greater functionality in being user-decryptable when necessary and thus justifies retaining more information than either hash function would. In general, we consider this to be an acceptable growth rate (not particularly wasteful) that aligns with our interest in minimal data collection.

6.2.2 Time

The average running time for each plaintext equality check between ciphertexts off-chain is 0.08298 s.[3] Using location proofs from the blockchain were observed to

---

[3] The experiment was run on a mid-tier personal computer. This figure can likely be greatly reduced on higher end hardware.

take longer depending on network connectivity and server load on the blockchain testnet; however, by far, the bottleneck in this computation is the equality checking operation. The number of equality checking operations required to generate our scoring measures (such as the histogram required for the aforementioned entropy measure) will vary depending on the user behavior. This count is bounded above and below by the extremes of user behavior. If each fingerprint is identical (all equal) it will take p operations to fully sort them, where p is the number of proofs being considered. If each fingerprint is distinct (none equal) it will take $\sum_{i=1}^{p} i = 1 + 2 + ... + p = p * (p + 1)/2 \approx p^2$ operations. For the 96 fingerprints being considered, this equates to between 7.9661 s to 764.7437 s (12.75 min) of computation per user, per day. Clearly some heuristic is required to terminate computation for instances toward the latter case, however this can easily be done by running the much lighter computation of Eq. 1 intermittently and terminating early if S_{max} is already exceeded.

For the "streak" scoring measure, the calculation is much less variable and can simply be $R = t \times n$ where t is the time per operation and n is the number of proofs considered. This method is effectively constant time for very small n but then must be run much more frequently to completely score a user's behavior: run after every new proof instead of once a day. We note that in a practical setting with large number of users our protocol uses reasonable amounts of storage and has not quite ideal performance, but performance which may be considered acceptable given the low frequency of operations necessary per user per day.

6.3 Consideration of Regulations

The reward token should be structured so as not to be subject to financial regulation to avoid stringent compliance obligation. In the U.S., a token transfer can be deemed as money transmission and need to comply with anti-money laundering regulations if the issuance, acceptance and transmission of the token evidence the ownership of a certain amount of commodity, security or futures contract [5]. Our reward token will not fall under such regulations because the token does not represent any ownership and is not transferable to other users.

6.4 Discussion on Incentive Mechanism

Our method can contribute more than contact tracing because this system motivates people to stay home longer, which proactively prevents the spread of COVID-19. In contact tracing, all that can be done is follow up potential transmission with records given by interviews and likely encounters. As discussed, economic or public health incentives are put in place for each stakeholder to act otherwise. With our proposal, participants of the system can expect to earn the rewards. As for hosts, they will require economic compensations for providing the client application and hosting servers if private companies take the roles. While it is possible that reward organizations are to pay such fees to hosts, it is possible that public entities provide subsidies to the hosts as a public policy initiative. Private companies have realized that the pandemic impacts their economic well-being. They may join such a program to protect their business. A level of corporate social responsibility also motivates some to participate in this scheme. It is also expected that public entities such as governments will be motivated to join such a program to maintain public health and safety. Because essential workers are force to go outside and take risks to earn necessary income, we need tailored rewarding calculation to maximize the social benefit. Hence, further work is needed to determine how this system works quantitatively.

7   Conclusion

In this paper, we proposed an application of smart contracts to provide incentive to stay at the same location with maintaining the location privacy of each user. The reward calculation function should be tuned by using real situation of pandemic and its locality. This tuning needs actual data of operating this scheme. Conducting experiments in our real system and tuning the reward calculation function is future work to refine the incentive mechanism.

References

1. TraceTogether. https://www.tracetogether.gov.sg/
2. Anciaux, N., et al.: Anonymous tracing, dangerous oxymoron (2020). https://risques-tracage.fr/docs/risques-tracage.pdf
3. Canard, S., Pointcheval, D., Santos, Q., Traoré, J.: Privacy-preserving plaintext-equality of low-entropy inputs. In: Preneel, B., Vercauteren, F. (eds.) ACNS 2018. LNCS, vol. 10892, pp. 262–279. Springer, Cham (2018). https://doi.org/10.1007/978-3-319-93387-0_14
4. Kaafar, D., et al.: Joint Statement on Contact Tracing (2020). https://t.co/y803WQ0nV6
5. The Financial Crimes Enforcement Network (FinCEN). Application of FinCEN's regulations to certain business models involving convertible virtual currencies—fincen.gov, May 2019. https://www.fincen.gov/resources/statutes-regulations/guidance/application-fincens-regulations-certain-business-models
6. Centres for Disease Control and Prevention. Case investigation and contact tracing: part of a multipronged approach to fight the COVID-19 pandemic—CDC. https://www.cdc.gov/coronavirus/2019-ncov/php/principles-contact-tracing.html
7. Garay, J., Kiayias, A., Leonardos, N.: The bitcoin backbone protocol: analysis and applications. In: Oswald, E., Fischlin, M. (eds.) EUROCRYPT 2015. LNCS, vol. 9057, pp. 281–310. Springer, Heidelberg (2015). https://doi.org/10.1007/978-3-662-46803-6_10
8. Hinch, R., et al.: Effective configurations of a digital contact tracing app: a report to NHSX. https://www.research.ox.ac.uk/Article/2020-04-16-digital-contact-tracing-can-slow-or-even-stop-coronavirus-transmission-and-ease-us-out-of-lockdown
9. Apple Inc. and Google Inc.: Privacy-preserving contact tracing - apple and Google. https://www.apple.com/covid19/contacttracing
10. Kelly, L.: Top Researchers Condemn Centralized COVID-19 Tracking Approach (2020). https://cryptobriefing.com/top-researchers-condemn-centralized-covid-19-tracking-approach/

11. Sabt, M., Achemlal, M., Bouabdallah, A.: Trusted execution environment: what it is, and what it is not. In: 2015 IEEE Trustcom/BigDataSE/ISPA, vol. 1, pp. 57–64 (2015)
12. Su, J., Bartholic, M., Stange, A., Ushida, R., Matsuo, S.I.: How to dynamically incentivize sufficient level of IoT security. In: 4th Workshop on Trusted Smart Contracts, pp. 57–64 (2020)

CBT Workshop: Short Papers

Fundamental Properties of the Layer Below a Payment Channel Network

Matthias Grundmann$^{(\boxtimes)}$ and Hannes Hartenstein

Institute of Telematics, Karlsruhe Institute of Technology, Karlsruhe, Germany
{matthias.grundmann,hannes.hartenstein}@kit.edu

Abstract. Payment channel networks are a highly discussed approach for improving scalability of cryptocurrencies such as Bitcoin. As they allow processing transactions off-chain, payment channel networks are referred to as second layer technology, while the blockchain is the first layer. We uncouple payment channel networks from blockchains and look at them as first-class citizens. This brings up the question what model payment channel networks require as first layer. In response, we formalize a model (called RFL model) for a first layer below a payment channel network. While transactions are globally made available by a blockchain, the RFL model only provides the reduced property that a transaction is delivered to the users being affected by a transaction. We show that the reduced model's properties still suffice to implement payment channels. By showing that the RFL model can not only be instantiated by the Bitcoin blockchain but also by trusted third parties like banks, we show that the reduction widens the design space for the first layer. Further, we show that the stronger property provided by blockchains allows for optimizations that can be used to reduce the time for locking collateral during payments over multiple hops in a payment channel network.

1 Introduction

Payment channel networks (PCNs) became popular as an approach for improving the scalability of blockchain based cryptocurrencies such as Bitcoin [12]. While Bitcoin scales well in the amount of coins that can be transferred by a transaction, it can only process a limited number of transactions per second. PCNs, e.g., the Lightning Network [14] for Bitcoin, perform transactions off-chain in a second layer and they do not require global consensus for every transaction as long as all participants are honest.

PCNs have mostly been looked at as second layer on top of a blockchain. While the idea to use banks as a first layer has already been mentioned in 2015 by Tremback and Hess [17], to the best of our knowledge it has not been analyzed which properties PCNs require for the layer below. We look at PCNs as first-class citizen independent from the specific first layer and analyze whether PCNs can be used on top of models that are different from a blockchain (with the term blockchain, we refer to a public permissionless blockchain such as Bitcoin). As an affirmative answer, we present a reduced **model for the first layer** which

© Springer Nature Switzerland AG 2020
J. Garcia-Alfaro et al. (Eds.): DPM 2020/CBT 2020, LNCS 12484, pp. 409–420, 2020.
https://doi.org/10.1007/978-3-030-66172-4_26

we call **RFL model (Reduced First Layer)** whose properties give reduced guarantees compared to a blockchain but yet suffice to implement a protocol for a PCN on top. The reduced property of the RFL model in comparison to a blockchain is that a blockchain delivers each transaction to all peers participating in the network while in the RFL model a transaction is only guaranteed to be visible for a transaction's affected users. A transaction's affected users are the users who receive the transferred coins and the users who were able to spend the same coins that the transaction transfers. To show that a PCN can still securely be implemented using the RFL model as underlying first layer, we show the following property: A payment channel between two users can be closed within a given time so that each user u receives at least their correct balance if u is honest and checks the first layer regularly for new transactions. We will refer to this property as the security property and formally define it. We **prove this security property** for a PCN protocol that is executed on a first layer that implements the properties defined by the RFL model: liveness, affected user synchrony, persistence, and transaction validity.

Our analysis of the relationship between the RFL model and a blockchain shows that a blockchain instantiates the RFL model under typical assumptions for blockchains such as Bitcoin. Having shown that a PCN can be implemented on a reduced model compared to a blockchain, we show that the RFL model can not only be instantiated by blockchains but there is a wider design space for the first layer, e.g., using trusted third parties like banks. Implementation of PCNs on different first layers allows for a range of design opportunities, e.g., with respect to trust, privacy, liquidity, online requirements, and currencies. Having seen the advantages of a model for the first layer that is reduced compared to a blockchain, we also look at the advantages of using a blockchain that guarantees more than the RFL model: A blockchain's property to deliver a transaction to everyone can be used to **optimize payments in PCNs** so that collateral is locked for a shorter amount of time [11]. We show that this requires stronger assumptions than the basic construction of PCNs.

For readers, being not familiar with payment channels and PCNs, we provide a section on fundamentals in the extended version of this paper [6]. In the following section, we put our work in the context of related work. In Sect. 3, we present the RFL model. We show in Sect. 4 that a simplified version of the Lightning Network's protocol fulfills the security property if it is used on a first layer that instantiates the RFL model. Section 5 presents and compares instances of the RFL model using a blockchain and trusted banks. In Sect. 6, we show how the stronger properties fulfilled by a blockchain can be used to optimize payments in a PCN. Finally, we conclude in Sect. 7.

2   Related Work

Kiayias and Litos provide in [10] a formalization and security analysis of the Lightning Network using a global ledger functionality modeled in [2]. The global ledger fulfills a global synchrony property: An honest user that is connected to the required resources is being synchronized (receives the latest state) within a bounded time. Their work is orthogonal to our work because it appears that their proof would still work with the assumptions of the RFL model. We leave it for future work to provide a security proof for the Lightning Network that uses the RFL model instead of the global ledger functionality provided by Bitcoin.

Credit networks as proposed in [3] are a concept that is related to that of PCNs. A credit network, however, does not have an underlying layer. In a credit network, users are connected through credit links (IOUs) which represent the amount one user owes another user. This construction requires users to trust each other to an extent that is quantified by the size of the credit link. In a PCN, users are instead required to trust the first layer and not each other.

Recently, Avarikioti et al. proposed Cerberus channels, [1] a protocol for payment channels that includes watchtowers watching for outdated commitment transactions on the first layer. They also define a security property and show that Cerberus channels fulfill this property. The security property we define is inspired by the security property used in [1]; however, our definition does explicitly consider the timeouts and includes HTLCs which are required for payments over intermediaries.

3   RFL Model of First Layer

In this section, we present the RFL model, a model for the first layer that guarantees a reduced set of properties compared to a blockchain. The main difference of the RFL model to a blockchain is that, when using a blockchain, a transaction is delivered to all users. In this section, we define the *affected user synchrony* property which only requires the first layer to deliver a transaction to the users being affected by a transaction.

In the RFL model, we have a set of users U who can create transactions. Each user $u \in U$ has an asymmetric key pair with private key s_u and the public key p_u. A transaction t consists of an amount of coins and is associated with a set of *receivers* $\Omega_t^R \subseteq U$ that the coins are transferred to. The set of users who were able to spend the coins that are spent by t is referred to as the *potential senders* $\Omega_t^S \subseteq U$. We denote as *affected users* of the transaction t the set $\Omega_t = \Omega_t^S \cup \Omega_t^R$. For a transaction to be valid, it needs to fulfill conditions depending on the coins that are spent (e.g., a signature using a specified key or some timeout having passed). In general, it is possible that not all potential senders need to sign a transaction and thus some potential senders and receivers might not have seen the transaction before it has been published on the first layer.

We model the first layer as a (logically) single party $\mathcal{L}$ that is connected to all other parties via secure and reliable channels. Users can send transactions t to the first layer $\mathcal{L}$. We refer to this action as *publishing* t. $\mathcal{L}$ can send a confirmation that the transaction t has been executed, i.e. the coins have been transferred, and users can query $\mathcal{L}$ whether a transaction has been confirmed. The time a user has to wait for the confirmation is determined by the liveness property parametrized below by the waiting time Δl_{conf}. The first layer $\mathcal{L}$ can send transactions from other users and confirmations to users. Users can check the first layer $\mathcal{L}$ for the confirmation of a transaction. Whether the first layer's response about the confirmation is consistent among different users, is determined by the affected user synchrony property below parametrized by the time Δl_{sync}.

The first layer $\mathcal{L}$ has to have these essential properties:

- *Liveness:* If a user sends a valid transaction t to the first layer $\mathcal{L}$, then $\mathcal{L}$ will confirm the transaction after at most Δl_{conf}.
- *Affected User Synchrony:* If a user has received a confirmation from $\mathcal{L}$ for a transaction t with affected users Ω_t, then $\mathcal{L}$ makes t and the confirmation visible to all affected users $u \in \Omega_t$ within at most Δl_{sync}.
- *Persistence:* If a user has received a confirmation for transaction t from $\mathcal{L}$, then $\mathcal{L}$ will always report t as confirmed.
- *Transaction Validity:* A transaction t will only be confirmed by $\mathcal{L}$ if t is valid.

Note that instead of the affected user synchrony, a blockchain implements an unrestricted synchrony property: If a transaction is confirmed by the blockchain, the transaction will be seen as confirmed by all users within a given time. We will look deeper into the relationship between the RFL model and blockchains in Sect. 5.

For the RFL model, we use a UTXO (unspent transaction output) model for transactions which is also used by Bitcoin. In the UTXO model, a transaction consists of multiple inputs and multiple outputs. Each input spends an output of a previous transaction. An output specifies a condition that an input needs to meet to spend the output. An example for a condition is the signature of a public key that is specified in the output and the signature needs to be provided in the input. If a transaction is processed by the first layer, the first layer checks whether the transaction is *valid*. For a transaction to be valid, all inputs have to spend transaction outputs that are unspent and the conditions of the UTXOs need to be met. For a PCN as defined later, we require the following types of conditions: signature corresponding to a given public key, preimage for a given image of a hash function, time since confirmation of UTXO spent, and combinations thereof using logical operators OR and AND. The set of receivers Ω_t^{R} contains all users whose signature is required by at least one condition to spend an output of t. Analogously, the set of potential senders Ω_t^{S} of a transaction t is comprised of all users whose signature is required by at least one condition to spend an output that is spent by t.

4   Security Property for a Payment Channel Network Protocol Based on the RFL Model

In this section, we show that the RFL model suffices as a first layer to securely implement a PCN. To this end, we make use of a slightly simplified version of the Lightning Network's protocol, define a security property, and then show that the protocol fulfills this security property when it uses the RFL model as first layer. A more detailed description of the protocol can be found in the extended version of our paper [6]. Here, we only introduce the notation and explain some differences that we assume in comparison to the Lightning Network's protocol specification on Github[1] as a basis for the proof.

The current specification of the Lightning Network's protocol is only for single-funded channels, i.e. a channel is created by putting funds of only one participant in the channel. Payments are executed using HTLCs even if they are direct payments over just one channel. We use Alice and Bob as names for two users participating in the protocol. Alice has a secret key s_A associated with the public key p_A that she uses for commitment transactions and HTLCs. This is a simplification; the Lightning Network specification uses different keys to sign HTLCs and commitment transactions to allow for separating keys in cold and hot storage[2]. We count the states of a channel using $n \geq 1$ and denote the commitment transaction held by Alice for state n as t_{CnA} (t_{CnB} for Bob). For revocation, Alice creates a new revocation key s_{RnA} for each commitment transaction t_{CnA}. Each output of Alice's commitment transaction t_{CnA} is spendable using the revocation key s_{RnA} and Bob's public key, i.e. Bob can spend all outputs of t_{CnA} if Alice publishes t_{CnA} after she has revoked t_{CnA} by sending s_{RnA} to Bob. This is another simplification. The Lightning Network uses a construction that generates a revocation key for t_{CnA} from a long term secret created by Bob and the per-commitment secrets created by Alice and, to revoke a transaction, Alice shares the corresponding per-commitment secret with Bob.

Each commitment transaction t_{CnA} held by Alice for state n of the channel between Alice and Bob is built in the following way (t_{CnB} held by Bob is constructed analogously): The commitment transaction's input spends the channel's funding transaction's output which requires Alice's and Bob's signatures. We use the term *stable balance* for a user's balance that is not part of an HTLC. The HTLC outputs of t_{CnA} cannot directly be spent by Alice but only using the HTLC timeout transaction t_{TnyA} and the HTLC success transaction t_{SnyA} which will be explained below. Outputs spendable by Alice are locked for Δt_{comm} time to give Bob time to spend the output in case Alice publishes t_{CnA} after it has been outdated. Alice's commitment transaction t_{CnA} has the following outputs:

- An output for Alice's stable balance that is spendable
  - by Bob using Alice's revocation key s_{RnA} for state n or
  - by Alice after delay Δt_{comm}; aka 'to self delay'.
- An output for Bob's stable balance that is spendable by Bob.
- For each outgoing HTLC an output for the HTLC's balance that is spendable
  - by Bob if he provides a preimage for a given y, or
  - by Bob using Alice's revocation key for state n, or
  - by the HTLC-timeout transaction t_{TnyA} after point in time T_y^{HTLC}.
- For each incoming HTLC an output for the HTLC's balance that is spendable
  - by Bob after point in time T_y^{HTLC}, or

---

[1] https://github.com/lightningnetwork/lightning-rfc/blob/master/00-introduction.md.

[2] https://github.com/lightningnetwork/lightning-rfc/blob/master/02-peer-protocol.md#rationale.

- by Bob using Alice's revocation key for state n, or
- by the HTLC-success transaction t_{SnyA} using preimage for a given y.

There are two HTLC transactions per HTLC with preimage y that depend on t_{CnA}: An HTLC timeout transaction t_{TnyA} and an HTLC success transaction t_{SnyA}. The inputs for the HTLC transactions are the outputs indicated above for the commitment transaction t_{CnA} and need to be signed by Alice and Bob. Both HTLC transactions held by Alice have one output that is spendable

- by Alice after delay Δt_{comm}, or
- by Bob using Alice's revocation key for state n.

We define the forwarding timeout delta Δ_{forw} as a global value. This simplifies the Lightning Network's specification which uses values that are chosen by the users of each channel. Lastly, the closing of channels can be cooperative in the Lightning Network specification to allow both parties to access their funds immediately. However, we assume that users simply send their latest commitment transaction to the first layer.

Security Property for the Payment Channel Network Protocol Based on the RFL Model. We now show that the protocol described above fulfills the security property as defined in Lemma 1 when used with a first layer that implements the RFL model. We start by defining the term *correct balance*:

Definition 1. *The **correct balance** of a user Alice is the sum of Alice's stable balance and the amounts of outgoing HTLCs that she has not received the secret for and the amounts of incoming HTLCs that she has received the secret for.*

To facilitate understanding of the following lemma we give a brief review of the most important relative and absolute timings that are used: The first layer $\mathcal{L}$ confirms a valid transaction within Δl_{conf}, other users will see a confirmed transaction within Δl_{sync}, a user can spend their own commitment transaction's outputs after Δt_{comm}, and an HTLC with condition y times out at time T_y^{HTLC}.

Lemma 1. *The protocol as defined above fulfills the property **security**: At each point in time T_{now}, Alice can close the payment channel between Alice and Bob so that she has received at least her correct balance at time $T = \max(T_{max}^{HTLC}, T_{now}) + 2 \cdot \Delta l_{conf} + \Delta t_{comm}$ if she is honest and checks the first layer $\mathcal{L}$ for transactions at least once every Δ_{user} and $0 < \Delta_{user} < \Delta t_{comm} - \Delta l_{sync} - \Delta l_{conf}$, where T_{max}^{HTLC} denotes the maximal timeout of all HTLCs in the channel.*

Lemma 1 follows from the following arguments. We first look at the case that Alice initiates the closing of the channel and then at the case that Bob closes the channel and Alice did not want to close the channel. Let n be the number of the latest state. To close the channel, Alice sends her latest commitment transaction t_{CnA} and the associated HTLC transactions to $\mathcal{L}$ at T_{now}. Alice has Bob's signature for t_{CnA} because she receives Bob's signature for the initial commitment transaction t_{C1A} during the opening of the channel ($n = 1$) and during each update of the channel $(n > 1)$, Alice receives Bob's signature for the latest commitment transaction t_{CnA} and the associated HTLC transactions. If there are no conflicting transactions, t_{CnA} will be confirmed within Δl_{conf} according to the liveness property of $\mathcal{L}$. The funding transaction can only be spent by Alice and Bob and thus a transaction conflicting with t_{CnA} can only be sent to $\mathcal{L}$ by Bob until t_{CnA} is confirmed by $\mathcal{L}$. At time $T_{now} + \Delta l_{conf}$ one commitment transaction will be confirmed – either Alice's transaction or a transaction sent by Bob. Thus, we need to distinguish three scenarios:

Bob Does Not Publish a Commitment Transaction: The first layer $\mathcal{L}$ will confirm Alice's commitment transaction t_{CnA} within Δl_{conf} according to the liveness property. Alice can spend her stable balance after an additional Δt_{comm}. The associated output cannot be spent by Bob because Bob does not have the revocation key s_{RnA} for the latest commitment transaction. For the incoming HTLCs in t_{CnA} that Alice has the secret for, she publishes the success transactions t_{SnyA} together with t_{CnA} and the success transactions' outputs can be spent by Alice after Δt_{comm}. Bob cannot spend the HTLC output because the associated time T_y^{HTLC} has not come (else, Alice would have removed the HTLC or timely gone on-chain) and Bob does not have the revocation keys. Thus, Alice can spend her stable balance and her balance of incoming HTLCs at $T_{now} + \Delta l_{conf} + \Delta t_{comm}$. Her transaction to spend these outputs will be confirmed within Δl_{conf}. For the outgoing HTLCs in t_{CnA} that Alice does not have the secret for, she can spend the output using the timeout transaction t_{TnyA} after T_y^{HTLC}. The timeout transaction is confirmed by $\mathcal{L}$ and its output is spendable after $T_y^{HTLC} + \Delta l_{conf} + \Delta t_{comm}$. If Bob spends the HTLC using the preimage, Alice receives the preimage because of the affected user synchrony property of $\mathcal{L}$ because Alice is a potential sender of the HTLC output, so the HTLC's amount is not taken into account for this channel's correct balance. Thus, Alice has received her correct balance after at most $\max(T_{now}, T_{max}^{HTLC}) + 2 \cdot \Delta l_{conf} + \Delta t_{comm} = T$.

Bob has Published his Latest Commitment Transaction t_{CnB}: In this case, the affected user synchrony property of the first layer asserts that Alice can see Bob's commitment transaction t_{CnB} because she is a potential sender. Alice can instantly spend her stable balance in the channel once she sees the transaction t_{CnB} at time $T_{now} + \Delta l_{conf} + \Delta l_{sync}$. Alice's transaction spending her stable balance will be confirmed within Δl_{conf}. For each outgoing HTLC, Alice can spend the HTLC output after T_y^{HTLC}. If Bob spends the HTLC output using t_{SnyB} by providing a preimage for the given y, Alice receives the preimage because of the affected user synchrony property of $\mathcal{L}$. For each incoming HTLC, Alice must publish a transaction to redeem the HTLC if she has the preimage for the given y which takes Δl_{conf} to be confirmed. Thus, Alice has received her correct balance within $\max(T_{now} + \Delta l_{conf} + \Delta l_{sync}, T_{max}^{HTLC}) + \Delta l_{conf} \leq T$.

Bob has Published an Outdated Commitment Transaction: For each update to state number $i + 1$, Alice receives Bob's revocation key s_{RiB}. Say, Bob has published an outdated commitment transaction t_{CoB} with $o < n$. Alice can see the transaction after $T_{now} + \Delta l_{conf} + \Delta l_{sync}$. Bob can only spend his stable output of t_{CoB} after an additional Δt_{comm}. In case Bob publishes an HTLC success or timeout transaction, Alice also sees Bob's HTLC transaction because of the affected user synchrony property of $\mathcal{L}$ and Bob can only spend its output after Δt_{comm}. Thus, Alice must use her key s_A and Bob's revocation key s_{RoB} to create a revocation transaction that spends the whole balance in the channel (output for Alice, output for Bob, and all HTLC outputs). After Δl_{conf} this revocation transaction has been confirmed. Because $\Delta l_{conf} < \Delta t_{comm}$ (see Lemma 1), Bob cannot have spent his outputs before Alice. Thus, Alice has received her correct balance within $T_{now} + 2 \cdot \Delta l_{conf} + \Delta l_{sync} \leq T$.

In case Bob closes the channel by sending $t_{CiB}, i \leq n$ to $\mathcal{L}$ at T_{now} and Alice did not want to close the channel, too, Alice receives t_{CiB} from $\mathcal{L}$ within $T_{recvA} = T_{now} + \Delta l_{conf} + \Delta l_{sync} + \Delta_{user}$ because Alice is an affected user of the transaction and the affected user synchrony property of $\mathcal{L}$ asserts that she can see the transaction within Δl_{sync} and Alice checks the first layer $\mathcal{L}$ at least every Δ_{user} for new transactions. Bob's stable output and HTLC transaction outputs cannot be spent by him until $T_{spendB} = T_{now} + \Delta l_{conf} + \Delta t_{comm}$. If $i < n$, Alice must use her key s_A and Bob's revocation key s_{RiB} to spend the whole balance in the channel using a revocation transaction when she sees Bob's transaction at time T_{recvA}. This revocation transaction will be confirmed by the first layer after $T_{recvA} + \Delta l_{conf}$. Bob cannot have spent his outputs at this time because $T_{recvA} + \Delta l_{conf} = T_{now} + \Delta l_{conf} + \Delta l_{sync} + \Delta_{user} + \Delta l_{conf} < T_{now} + \Delta l_{conf} + \Delta t_{comm} = T_{spendB}$ because $\Delta_{user} < \Delta t_{comm} - \Delta l_{sync} - \Delta l_{conf} \implies \Delta l_{conf} + \Delta l_{sync} + \Delta_{user} < \Delta t_{comm}$. Thus, Alice has received her correct balance after $T_{now} + \Delta l_{conf} + \Delta l_{sync} + \Delta_{user} + \Delta l_{conf} < T_{now} + \Delta l_{conf} + \Delta t_{comm} \leq T$. If $i = n$, Alice reacts analogously to the case above that Bob has published his latest commitment transaction but the times are postponed by Δ_{user} (see [6]).

5   Instances and Options of the RFL model

The RFL model describes an ideal first layer that guarantees the properties required by a PCN. In this section, we show that, under certain assumptions, a blockchain instantiates such a first layer. We also sketch the idea of an instance of a first layer using a bank or a network of banks and provide a comparative exploration of design options.

Using a Blockchain. Garay et al. show in various works (e.g., [4,5]) that the Bitcoin protocol satisfies *consistency* and *liveness* with high probability under the assumption of a bounded-delay network model and an honest majority of computing power [5]. In comparison to our definition in Sect. 3, their definition of liveness assumes that a transaction is provided to all honest parties. This is implemented in Bitcoin by flooding transactions in the peer-to-peer network. The definition of consistency used in [5] implies our definition of persistence and affected user synchrony. It is even stronger and implies *synchrony* for all honest peers, i.e. the first layer $\mathcal{L}$ makes a transaction t and the confirmation visible to all honest peers. Assuming an honest majority of computing power and using a bounded-delay network model, the results of Garay et al. show that a blockchain similar to Bitcoin instantiates the RFL model with high probability.

Note that for a blockchain, liveness is not guaranteed because the blocksize is limited and there can be times during which the blockchain is congested so that users have to compete for publishing their transactions on the blockchain. Recent work [7,9,18] has shown attacks against payment channels that attack the liveness of a blockchain, e.g. by bribing miners to censor transactions. These works show the importance of considering the properties of the first layer when building second layer architectures.

Using a Single or Multiple Banks. Having an abstract model of the first layer allows for developing architectures that instantiate a first layer without a blockchain. For example, a network of banks can be used to instantiate a first layer under the assumption of trust in the banks. We assume the common features of banks as described in the following but the bank does not necessarily need to be a classical bank and can also be a payment service provider. A contemporary bank offers to their consumers an interface that implements liveness, transaction validity, and persistence. The usual visibility for a transaction matches the visibility required by affected user synchrony: A bank makes a transaction visible (only) to the potential senders and receivers of transferred funds. A transaction has multiple potential senders if it is sent from a joint account. Using banks as first layer, their customers could perform transactions using a PCN. While this requires trust into the bank to implement the RFL model, the transactions are hidden from the bank which improves privacy because the bank gains less information. So the PCN could be used for decentralized digital cash.

Comparative Exploration of Design Options. We now discuss differences between using a blockchain and trusted banks as different ways to instantiate the RFL model.

Trust. While banks have to be fully trusted, trust into a blockchain is more distributed (e.g., honest miners have the largest share of computation power).

Privacy. While PCNs do not categorically improve privacy [8,15,16], the privacy properties of the first layer are crucial for privacy in the PCN. While users are identified by pseudonyms on a blockchain, a bank is required to implement methods for customer identification. This reduces privacy for the users because the bank learns about their transactions. However, it allows the bank to implement access control on the transactions and to make a transaction only visible to the affected users of the transaction which, in turn, improves privacy. By facilitating tracing of money laundering, customer identification can be a way to increase chances of mainstream adoption of a digital payment system.

Liquidity. Payment channels require users to deposit funds by locking them on the first layer while the channel is open. On a blockchain, users can only use coins in their channel that they own on the blockchain. Using banks to implement a first layer allows for letting users open channels using credit they receive from their bank. This can improve the liquidity within the network because more users are able to forward payments if they have channels with higher capacity.

Online Requirement. While the first layer needs to provide affected user synchrony to make transactions visible, the corresponding part for the user is to check the first layer regularly for new transactions to react to outdated commitment transactions. With a blockchain as a first layer, this task requires a user to stay connected and analyze new blocks or to outsource this task to a watchtower. With a centralized system of banks as first layer, the bank needs to be trusted to run a system that provides affected user synchrony. Because the bank knows their customers, they could even contact them to inform about relevant transactions and, thus, include watchtower functionality in the first layer.

Currencies. The two different ways for instantiating the RFL model also differ in the type of currencies they can support. While a blockchain can provide a decentralized currency, a system of banks can make traditional currencies managed by central banks available for use in PCNs.

6   Optimization of HTLCs Using a Blockchain

The basic construction of PCNs leaves room for optimizations. One issue is that the amount of collateral that needs to be locked for one transaction allows for balance availability attacks [13] which lock the balance so that it cannot be used by honest parties. Recent research [11] has found ways to reduce the required collateral during one transaction over multiple hops assuming a blockchain as first layer that offers (global) synchrony instead of the reduced affected user synchrony. The Sprites protocol [11] uses a (logically) central "preimage manager" that can be read and written to by any party of the PCN. All channel updates on the route of a payment depend on the condition that the secret x has been published before a specific timeout that is the same across all channels. By using it as a "global synchronization gadget", the preimage manager is used to synchronize the timeouts so that all parts of the route timeout at the same time in contrast to increasing timeouts from the receiver's end in the Lightning Network. As all participants have the same view on the blockchain, either all updates that depend on the publication of the secret before a given timeout fail or all are valid. For a first layer instantiated by banks, a bank or another trusted party could implement such a preimage manager. However, this would add a central entity as dependency for the payments and thus, payments would not be decentralized anymore. This shows that, while the RFL model allows for a PCN to be implemented as second layer, the stronger properties fulfilled by a blockchain enable optimizations for HTLCs. The solution of Sprites can improve the PCN protocol because it makes use of the gap between the properties of the RFL model and a blockchain's properties.

7   Conclusion

For a PCN, a first layer can be used that delivers only a reduced set of properties compared to a blockchain. We defined these properties in the RFL model and showed that this model suffices to implement a secure protocol for PCNs. Furthermore, the RFL model can be instantiated by blockchains. We examined how the difference between the properties that blockchains have in comparison to the RFL model can be used to improve payments over HTLCs and we have shown that this difference has already been used by improvements that have been proposed in previous works. We also showed that banks can instantiate the RFL model. Implementing a first layer might be a role banks play in the future.

References

1. Avarikioti, Z., Thyfronitis Litos, O.S., Wattenhofer, R.: CERBERUS channels: incentivizing watchtowers for bitcoin. In: Bonneau, J., Heninger, N. (eds.) FC 2020. LNCS, vol. 12059, pp. 346–366. Springer, Cham (2020). https://doi.org/10.1007/978-3-030-51280-4_19
2. Badertscher, C., Maurer, U., Tschudi, D., Zikas, V.: Bitcoin as a transaction ledger: a composable treatment. In: Katz, J., Shacham, H. (eds.) CRYPTO 2017. LNCS, vol. 10401, pp. 324–356. Springer, Cham (2017). https://doi.org/10.1007/978-3-319-63688-7_11
3. Fugger, R.: Money as IOUs in a social trust network and a proposal for a secure, private, decentralized digital currency protocol. Technical report (2004)
4. Garay, J., Kiayias, A., Leonardos, N.: The bitcoin backbone protocol: analysis and applications. In: Oswald, E., Fischlin, M. (eds.) EUROCRYPT 2015. LNCS, vol. 9057, pp. 281–310. Springer, Heidelberg (2015). https://doi.org/10.1007/978-3-662-46803-6_10
5. Garay, J., Kiayias, A., Leonardos, N.: Full analysis of Nakamoto consensus in bounded-delay networks, p. 277. Technical report (2020). https://eprint.iacr.org/2020/277
6. Grundmann, M., Hartenstein, H.: Fundamental Properties of the Layer Below a Payment Channel Network (Extended Version). arXiv:2010.08316 [cs], October 2020. http://arxiv.org/abs/2010.08316
7. Harris, J., Zohar, A.: Flood & Loot: A Systemic Attack On The Lightning Network. arXiv:2006.08513 [cs], June 2020. http://arxiv.org/abs/2010.08316
8. Kappos, G., et al.: An Empirical Analysis of Privacy in the Lightning Network. arXiv:2003.12470 [cs], March 2020. http://arxiv.org/abs/2003.12470
9. Khabbazian, M., Nadahalli, T., Wattenhofer, R.: Timelocked bribes, p. 774. Technical report (2020). https://eprint.iacr.org/2020/774
10. Kiayias, A., Litos, O.S.T.: A composable security treatment of the lightning network. In: 2020 IEEE 33rd Computer Security Foundations Symposium (CSF), pp. 334–349, June 2020. https://doi.org/10.1109/CSF49147.2020.00031. ISSN 2374-8303
11. Miller, A., Bentov, I., Kumaresan, R., Cordi, C., McCorry, P.: Sprites and State Channels: Payment Networks that Go Faster than Lightning. arXiv:1702.05812 [cs], February 2017. http://arxiv.org/abs/1702.05812
12. Nakamoto, S.: Bitcoin: a peer-to-peer electronic cash system. Technical report (2008)
13. Pérez-Solá, C., Ranchal-Pedrosa, A., Herrera-Joancomartí, J., Navarro-Arribas, G., Garcia-Alfaro, J.: LockDown: balance availability attack against lightning network channels. In: Bonneau, J., Heninger, N. (eds.) FC 2020. LNCS, vol. 12059, pp. 245–263. Springer, Cham (2020). https://doi.org/10.1007/978-3-030-51280-4_14

14. Poon, J., Dryja, T.: The Bitcoin lightning network: scalable off-chain instant payments. Technical report (2016)
15. Rohrer, E., Tschorsch, F.: Counting Down Thunder: Timing Attacks on Privacy in Payment Channel Networks. arXiv:2006.12143 [cs], June 2020. http://arxiv.org/abs/2006.12143
16. Romiti, M., Victor, F., Moreno-Sanchez, P., Haslhofer, B., Maffei, M.: Cross-Layer Deanonymization Methods in the Lightning Protocol. arXiv:2007.00764 [cs], July 2020. http://arxiv.org/abs/2007.00764
17. Tremback, J., Hess, Z.: Universal Payment Channels, November 2015
18. Tsabary, I., Yechieli, M., Eyal, I.: MAD-HTLC: Because HTLC is Crazy-Cheap to Attack. arXiv:2006.12031 [cs], June 2020. http://arxiv.org/abs/2006.12031

Zerojoin: Combining Zerocoin and CoinJoin

Alexander Chepurnoy[1,2] and Amitabh Saxena[1(✉)]

[1] Ergo Platform, Saint Petersburg, Russia
kushti@protonmail.ch, alex.chepurnoy@iohk.io, amitabh123@gmail.com
[2] IOHK Research, Saint Petersburg, Russia

Abstract. We present Zerojoin, a privacy-enhancing protocol for UTXO blockchains. Like Zerocoin, our protocol uses zero-knowledge proofs and a pool of participants. However, unlike Zerocoin, our pool size is not monotonically increasing. Thus, our protocol overcomes the major drawback of Zerocoin. Our approach can also be considered a non-interactive variant of CoinJoin, where the interaction is replaced by a public transaction on the blockchain. The security of Zerojoin relies on the decisional-Diffie-Hellman (DDH) assumption. We also present ErgoMix, a practical implementation of Zerojoin on top of Ergo, a smart contract platform based on Sigma protocols. While Zerojoin contains the key ideas, it leaves open the practical issue of handling fees. The key contribution of ErgoMix is a novel approach to handle fee in Zerojoin.

1 Introduction

Privacy enhancing techniques in blockchains generally fall into two categories. The first is hiding the amounts being transferred, such as in Confidential Transactions [1]. The second is obscuring the input-output relationships such as in Zerocoin [2] and CoinJoin [3]. Some solutions such as Zcash [4,5] combine both.

In this work, we describe Zerojoin, yet another privacy enhancing protocol based on the latter approach of obscuring input-output relationships. This allows us to avoid expensive range proofs necessary for the first approach. Our protocol is motivated from Zerocoin and CoinJoin to overcome some of their limitations.

In particular, the protocol is designed to address two key problems with Zerocoin [2] and CoinJoin [3], namely the need for a monotonically increasing pool in Zerocoin and the need for off-chain interaction in CoinJoin. A monotonically increasing pool makes the protocol unusable in the long term because this pool has to be kept in memory to verify transactions. Many privacy oriented protocols including Zerocoin and Monero [6] suffer from this problem. On the other hand, CoinJoin, which does not have this weakness, has the problem of off-chain interaction, which again reduces its usability. Zerojoin aims to address this by creating a combined protocol that solves both these problems. Quisquis [7] is another protocol similar to Zerojoin. However, its proofs use generic NIZKs that are much larger than Zerojoin's proofs. The following table summarizes the various protocols. Note that unlike the other protocols, CoinJoin supports a covert mode,

© Springer Nature Switzerland AG 2020
J. Garcia-Alfaro et al. (Eds.): DPM 2020/CBT 2020, LNCS 12484, pp. 421–436, 2020.
https://doi.org/10.1007/978-3-030-66172-4_27

where it is not possible to identify if the protocol is in use. Some approaches, such as MW, CoinJoin and CS are vulnerable to eavesdropping attacks where an attacker has connectivity to a large part of the network. Hence they need additional off-chain mechanisms (such as "joiners" [8]) to counter such attacks before broadcasting transactions to the network.

	Monotonic pool	Generic NIZKs	Interaction needed	Eavesdropping attacks	Example implementation
CoinJoin [3]	No	No	Yes	Yes	JoinMarket [9]
Zerocoin [2]	Yes	Yes	No	No	Zcoin [10]
Monero	Yes	Yes	No	No	Monero [6]
Quisquis [7]	No	Yes	No	No	–
Zerojoin	No	No	No	No	ErgoMixer [11]

An interesting problem in CoinJoin-type protocols such as uis and Zerojoin is that of fee. Since the protocol requires multiple rounds where a box's value is preserved across rounds. If the fee is paid from an external source then privacy is broken. Thus, any fee must come from the boxes being mixed. However, then the value cannot be preserved. Our solution to the fee problem is ErgoMix, an implementation of Zerojoin on the Ergo blockchain. ErgoMix uses *mixing tokens*, a Ergo-specific approach to handle fee.

2   Background

Blockchain platforms such as Bitcoin [12], Zerocoin [2], Zcash [4] and Ergo [13] use short-lived immutable data structures called "coins" or UTXOs (short for unspent transaction outputs). In such blockchains, every node maintains an in-memory database of all current UTXOs, called the *UTXO-set*. A transaction consumes (destroys) some UTXOs and creates new ones. When a node receives a block, it updates its UTXO-set based on the transactions in that block. A UTXO is a single-use object, and its simplest form contains a public key (in which case, the UTXO can be "spent" using the corresponding private key). Spending a UTXO essentially involves executing any embedded code inside it and removing it from the UTXO-set. The alternative to UTXOs is the *account-based* model of Ethereum [14] or NXT [15]. Unlike UTXOs, accounts are mutable. While a UTXO must be completely spent (i.e., its balance cannot be changed), an account at the bare minimum allows changing the balance. Most privacy techniques including CoinJoin and Zerocoin are designed for UTXOs and cannot be easily adapted for accounts. Our protocol also works in the UTXO model only.

2.1   CoinJoin

CoinJoin [3] is a privacy enhancing protocol where multiple parties provide inputs and create outputs in a single transaction computed interactively such

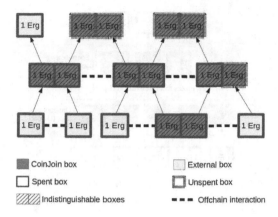

Fig. 1. Canonical multi-stage CoinJoin

that the original inputs and outputs are unlinked. The optimal use of CoinJoin is when two inputs of equal value are joined to generate two outputs of equal value, and the process is repeated, as depicted in Fig. 1.

In this model, each CoinJoin transaction has exactly two inputs (the boxes at the tail of the arrows) and two outputs (the boxes at the head of the arrows). Creating such a transaction requires a private off-chain interaction between the two parties supplying the inputs, which is denoted by the dashed line. We will ignore fee for now and revisit this issue in Sect. 4. The key idea of CoinJoin is that the two output boxes are *indistinguishable* in the following sense.

1. The owner of each input box controls exactly one output box.
2. An outsider has no idea which output corresponds to which input.

Thus, each CoinJoin transaction provides 50% unlinkability. The output box can be used as input to further CoinJoin transactions and the process repeated to increase the unlinkability to any desired level. We will use the same concept in Zerojoin. CoinJoin requires off-chain interaction and this interactive nature is the primary drawback of CoinJoin, which Zerojoin aims to overcome.

2.2 Zerocoin

Zerocoin is a privacy enhancing protocol depicted in Fig. 2. The protocol uses a pool of coins called the *unspent pool* (U-pool). A coin is added to the U-pool as a public commitment $c = \text{Comm}(s, r)$ of secrets s, r and later removed in a way that does not reveal c of the coin being removed. Instead, the removing transaction only reveals secret s, the "serial number", along with a zero-knowledge proof that one of the c's in the U-pool is of the form $\text{Comm}(s, r)$ for some r that is never revealed. Note that c is stored in the U-pool permanently. Additionally, to prevent double spending, the value s is also stored permanently in another pool

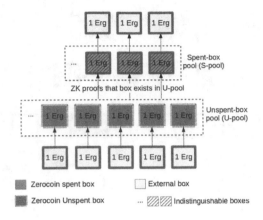

Fig. 2. Zerocoin protocol

called the *spent pool* (S-pool). A coin can be spent from the U-pool only if the corresponding serial number does not exist in the S-pool.

One consequence of this is that both the U-pool (the set of commitments) and the S-pool (the set of spent serial numbers) must be maintained in memory for verifying every transaction. Another consequence is that the sizes of the these two sets increase monotonically. This is the main drawback of Zerocoin (also Zcash [4]), which Zerojoin tries to address. In Zerojoin, once a box is spent, no information about it is kept in memory, and in particular no data sets of monotonically increasing sizes are maintained.

Considering the addition of a coin to the mix as a deposit and removal as a withdraw, the in-memory storage in Zerojoin is proportional to the number of deposits minus the number of withdraws, while that in ZeroCash is proportional to the number of deposits plus the number of withdraws.

2.3 Quisquis

One of the protocols closest in design to Zerojoin is Quisquis [7], since they both aim to prevent monotonic UTXO sets. At a conceptual level, both have the same fundamental CoinJoin-type primitive: a mix transaction consumes two 1-Erg boxes and creates two indistinguishable 1-Erg boxes. Similar to Zerojoin, Quisquis does this in a non-interactive manner, thereby overcoming the main drawback of CoinJoin. Both Zerojoin and Quisquis have the following structure:

1. Alice adds a box A to the pool and waits for someone (say Bob) to use it.
2. Bob selects a secret bit b and spends A along with some of his own boxes to create two identical looking boxes O_0, O_1 such that O_b is spendable by Alice and O_{1-b} by Bob. The boxes are indistinguishable to outsiders.
3. The protocol enforces Bob to create two identical looking boxes. However, it cannot be publicly verified if the boxes are created correctly. Thus, while the

protocol works if Bob is honest, a cheating Bob may create identical looking boxes containing invalid values, thereby rendering both unspendable.

4. The remaining part of the protocol enforces Bob's correct behavior using zero-knowledge proofs that the boxes were indeed created correctly. The difference is that Quisquis uses generic NIZKs, while Zerojoin uses sigma protocols: it only takes 8 exponentiations to verify a Zerojoin mix transaction and the proof size is around 200 bytes compared to several kilobytes.

2.4   Sigma Protocols

Let G be a cyclic multiplicative group where decisional Diffie-Hellman (DDH) problem is hard. Zerojoin uses two interactive proofs in this setting.

The first, a variation of Schnorr signatures [16], is a *proof of knowledge of discrete logarithm* of some u to base g, where the prover proves knowledge of x such that $u = g^x$. This is called `proveDlog(g, u)` and implemented as follows:

1. The prover, $\mathcal{P}$, picks $r \xleftarrow{R} \mathbb{Z}_q$ and sends $t = g^r$ to the verifier, $\mathcal{V}$.
2. $\mathcal{V}$ picks $c \xleftarrow{R} \mathbb{Z}_q$ and sends c to $\mathcal{P}$.
3. $\mathcal{P}$ sends $z = r + cx$ to $\mathcal{V}$, who accepts iff $g^z = t \cdot u^c$.

A protocol with this structure ($\mathcal{P} \xrightarrow{t} \mathcal{V}, \mathcal{P} \xleftarrow{c} \mathcal{V}, \mathcal{P} \xrightarrow{z} \mathcal{V}$) is called a sigma protocol if it satisfies *special soundness* and *honest-verifier zero-knowledge* [17].

The statement to be proved (example "I know the discrete logarithm of u to base g") is denoted by τ. Any sigma protocol can be made non-interactive via the Fiat-Shamir transform [18] by setting $c = H(t)$ where H is a hash function.

As shown in [19], any two sigma protocols for arbitrary statements τ_0, τ_1 can be efficiently composed to a single sigma protocol that proves knowledge of one of the witnesses without revealing which. Let $b \in \{0,1\}$ be such that $\mathcal{P}$ knows the witness of τ_b but not τ_{1-b}. $\mathcal{P}$ simulates the proof of τ_{1-b} to get an accepting transcript $(t_{1-b}, c_{1-b}, z_{1-b})$ and generates t_b properly. $\mathcal{P}$ sends (t_0, t_1) to $\mathcal{V}$. On receiving c, $\mathcal{P}$ computes $c_b = c \oplus c_{1-b}$ and then uses t_b, c_b to compute the response z_b properly. Finally $\mathcal{P}$ sends (z_0, z_1, c_0, c_1) to $\mathcal{V}$, who accepts iff both (t_0, c_0, z_0) and (t_1, c_1, z_1) are accepting transcripts and $c = c_0 \oplus c_1$. We call such a construction the OR operator.

The second primitive we need is a *proof of knowledge of a Diffie-Hellman tuple*, where the prover proves knowledge of x such that $u = g^x$ *and* $v = h^x$ for generators g, h. This is called `proveDHTuple(g, h, u, v)` and implemented using two parallel runs of the first protocol:

1. $\mathcal{P}$ picks $r \xleftarrow{R} \mathbb{Z}_q$ and sends $t = (g^r, h^r)$ to $\mathcal{V}$.
2. $\mathcal{V}$ picks $c \xleftarrow{R} \mathbb{Z}_q$ and sends c to $\mathcal{P}$.
3. $\mathcal{P}$ sends $z = r + cx$ to $\mathcal{V}$ who accepts iff $g^z = t_0 \cdot u^c$ and $h^z = t_1 \cdot v^c$.

Swapping h and u, we obtain `proveDHTuple(g, u, h, v)`, where $\mathcal{P}$ proves knowledge of y such that $h = g^y$ and $v = u^y$. This is the *dual* of the original protocol.

3   Zerojoin Protocol

Zerojoin uses a pool of *Half-Mix* boxes. The set of all unspent Half-Mix boxes is called the *H-pool*. To mix an arbitrary box B, one of the following is done:

1. **Pool:** Add B to the H-pool and wait for someone to mix it.
2. **Mix:** Pick any box A from the H-pool and a secret bit b. Spend A, B to output two boxes O_b and O_{1-b} spendable by A's and B's owners respectively.

Privacy comes from the fact that boxes O_b and O_{1-b} are indistinguishable so any outsider can only guess b with probability $\frac{1}{2}$. Thus, the probability of guessing the original box after n mixes is $\frac{1}{2^n}$. The protocol is depicted in Fig. 3.

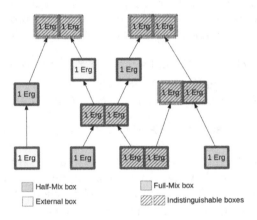

Fig. 3. Multi-round Zerojoin

3.1   One Zerojoin Round

Each individual Zerojoin round consists of two stages, the *pool* followed by the *mix* stage. Let g be some generator of G that is fixed beforehand. Each box has optional registers α, β that can store elements of G. Without loss of generality, Alice will pool and Bob will mix.

1. **Pool:** To add a coin to the H-pool, Alice picks a secret $x \in \mathbb{Z}$ and creates a box A containing $u = g^x$. The box is now considered added to the pool.
2. **Mix:** Bob picks secrets $(b, y) \in \mathbb{Z}_2 \times \mathbb{Z}$ and a box, say A, uniformly from the pool ensuring that $u \notin \{g, g^{-1}, g^0\}$. He spends A with some of his own boxes to create two output boxes O_0, O_1 having the same value as A such that:
   (a) Registers (α, β) of O_b and O_{1-b} store (g^y, u^y) and (u^y, g^y) respectively.
   (b) O_b, O_{1-b} are protected by the sigma statement given below:

$$\texttt{proveDHTuple}(g, \alpha, u, \beta) \text{ OR } \texttt{proveDlog}(g, \beta) \qquad (1)$$

O_b and O_{b-1} can be spent by Alice and Bob respectively using their secrets. Alice can identify her box as the one with $\beta = \alpha^x$. Assuming that the DDH problem is hard, no outsider can guess b with probability better than $\frac{1}{2}$.

The above protocol works assuming Bob behaves correctly. The protocol can enforce Bob to create two outputs with the same value as A and registers α, β swapped. However, since the DDH problem is hard, we cannot test whether the values in the registers are of the correct form (i.e., one is g^y and other is u^y). This is where the dual of `proveDHTuple` for secret y will come to our rescue. Concretely, Bob must adhere to the below rules when spending A:

1. Bob must create two outputs O_0, O_1 with the same value as A.
2. Both O_0, O_1 must be protected by the sigma statement of Eq. 1.
3. Let i_j be register i of O_j. Then the following must hold:

$$(\alpha_0, \beta_0) = (\beta_1, \alpha_1) \tag{2}$$

4. Bob must prove (via the dual) that one of $\{(g, u, \alpha_0, \beta_0), (g, u, \beta_0, \alpha_0)\}$ is of the form (g, g^x, g^y, g^{xy}). In other words, Bob must prove the sigma statement:

$$\texttt{proveDHTuple}(g, u, \alpha_0, \beta_0) \text{ OR } \texttt{proveDHTuple}(g, u, \beta_0, \alpha_0) \tag{3}$$

3.2   Analysis

For correctness, Alice requires that no one should be able to spend A in a manner that makes the resulting output(s) unspendable by her.

First note that due to Eqs. 2 and 3, Bob has no choice but to create two outputs O_0, O_1 such that the registers (α, β) of O_b and O_{1-b} contain (g^y, g^{xy}) and (g^{xy}, g^y) respectively for some integer y and bit b. Then the spending condition of Alice's Full-Mix box, O_b, reduces via Eq. 1 to:

$$\texttt{proveDHTuple}(g, g^y, g^x, g^{xy}) \text{ OR } \texttt{proveDlog}(g, g^{xy}).$$

The above statement can be proven by anyone who knows at least one of x or xy. Thus, Alice can spend this because she knows x.

For Alice's soundness, no one else apart from her should have the ability to spend O_b. Assume that there exists such a spender. Since only Alice knows x and the only other way to spend the box is via `proveDlog`(g, g^{xy}), that other spender must know xy. Such a spender cannot know y and so cannot spend O_{1-b}. We can model this spender as a black-box taking as input (g, g^x) and outputting (g^y, xy) for some $y \neq 0$. Since such a black-box can be used to solve the Computational Diffie-Hellman (CDH) problem in G, we can rule this out.

From Bob's point of view, the spending condition of O_{1-b} reduces to

$$\texttt{proveDHTuple}(g, g^{xy}, g^x, g^y) \text{ OR } \texttt{proveDlog}(g, g^y).$$

Since Bob knows y, he can spend the box using the right part of the statement. Finally, if someone apart from Bob spends O_{1-b} then they must have used the left part of the statement because using the right part would require knowledge of y. However, using the left part is not possible because (g, g^{xy}, g^x, g^y) is not a valid Diffie-Hellman tuple. Hence, no one else apart from Bob can spend O_{1-b}. Note that despite the left being an invalid tuple, the simulator must generate a valid proof for it, otherwise we could use the simulator to solve DDH.

For privacy, the only difference between O_b and O_{1-b} is that registers (α, β) are of the form (g^y, g^{xy}) and (g^{xy}, g^y) respectively. Assuming that the Decision Diffie-Hellman (DDH) problem in G is hard, no outsider has the ability to distinguish the boxes before they are spent. Since each box is spent using a sigma OR proof that is zero-knowledge [17], this applies even after they are spent.

Comparing with CoinJoin and Zerocoin: Both CoinJoin and Zerojoin use two indistinguishable outputs that provide the privacy (see Sect. 2.1). However, each CoinJoin transaction requires an off-chain interaction over a private channel. In Zerojoin, this interaction is replaced by a public transaction on the blockchain.

Both Zerocoin and Zerojoin add boxes to a pool and later spend them via zero-knowledge proofs (see Sect. 2.2). The difference is that the privacy in Zerocoin depends on the size of the pool, while that in Zerojoin depends on the number of rounds. Thirdly, Zerocoin's pool increases monotonically in size, while that of Zerojoin does not. Finally, the NIZK proofs in Zerocoin are much larger compared to the non-interactive sigma proofs of Zerojoin.

3.3   Implementing Zerojoin in ErgoScript

One way to implement Zerojoin would be to create a specialized privacy oriented blockchain with the protocol hardwired (such as Zcash [4]). A more pragmatic approach is to encode the protocol at the smart contract layer using a language that allows us to specify predicates on the entire transaction (i.e., one operating at context level C2 or higher using the terminology of [20]). We can then use the approach of [21] to encode the protocol into the smart contract of A, that is, by encoding Zerojoin as a two-stage protocol with the 'fingerprint' of the second stage embedded within a the first stage. One platform that supports such features is Ergo [13] and the following sections describe how to implement Zerojoin in ErgoScript, the programming language of Ergo. Note that ErgoScript is a strict subset of the Scala programming language [22,23].

For brevity, assume that `alpha`, `beta`, `gamma` are aliases for the registers α, β, γ of a box that contain elements of G. We already saw the first two used earlier. The third is to store u. We give some more notation below.

1. `script` refers to the guard script (in binary format) of the box.
2. `value` refers to the quantity of Ergo's primary token stored in the box.
3. `id` refers to the globally unique identifier of the box.
4. `SELF` is omitted, so `id` on its own, for example, must be read as `SELF.id`.

Let x be Alice's secret and let $u = g^x$. To create the Half-Mix box with u, first compile the following script of the second stage to get `fullMixScript`:

```
1 proveDHTuple(g, alpha, gamma, beta) || proveDlog(g, beta)
```

Contract 1. Full mix script

Next create a script, `halfMixScript`, with the following code:

```
1  val alpha0  = OUTPUTS(0).alpha
2  val alpha1  = OUTPUTS(1).alpha
3  val beta0   = OUTPUTS(0).beta
4  val beta1   = OUTPUTS(1).beta
5  val gamma0  = OUTPUTS(0).gamma
6  val gamma1  = OUTPUTS(1).gamma
7  val value0  = OUTPUTS(0).value
8  val value1  = OUTPUTS(1).value
9  val script0 = OUTPUTS(0).script
10 val script1 = OUTPUTS(1).script
11
12 INPUTS(0).id == id && // ensure this is the first box in transaction
13 alpha0 == beta1 && beta0 == alpha1 && gamma0 = gamma && gamma1 == gamma &&
14 value0 == value && value1 == value &&
15 script0 == fullMixScript && script1 == fullMixScript &&
16 alpha0 != beta0 && // to prevent Bob from setting y = 0
17 (proveDHTuple(g, gamma, alpha0, beta0) ||
18 proveDHTuple(g, gamma, beta0, alpha0))
```

Contract 2. Half mix script

Note that `OUTPUTS(0)` is the first output of the transaction, `OUTPUTS(1)` is the second output, and so on. Alice's box A is protected by `halfMixScript`. Alice must store u in register `gamma` of that box.

4 ErgoMix: Zerojoin with Fee

Similar to Zerocoin and CoinJoin (Fig. 1), each Half-Mix and Full-Mix box in Zerojoin must hold the same fixed value, which is carried over to the next stage. This implies zero-fee transactions because any fee must either be paid from the Full/Half-mix boxes (which breaks the fixed value requirement) or from a non-Zerojoin box (which breaks privacy). Zero-fee transactions are not practical.

Here we describe how to handle fee on the Ergo blockchain. To differentiate the generic protocol (Zerojoin) from the underlying implementation using Ergo, we give the name *ErgoMix* to any of the various extensions in this section that are largely specific to Ergo. We classify Zerojoin transactions into the following:

1. **Alice entry:** When someone plays the role of Alice to create a Half-Mix box and add to the H-pool. The inputs to the transaction are one or more non-ErgoMix boxes (*external* boxes) and the output is one Half-Mix box.
2. **Bob entry:** When someone plays the role of Bob to spend a Half-Mix box and remove from the H-pool. The other inputs of the transaction are one or more non-ErgoMix boxes and the outputs are two Full-Mix boxes.
3. **Alice or Bob exit:** When someone plays the role of Alice or Bob to spend a Full-Mix box and send the funds to a non-ErgoMix box.
4. **Alice or Bob reentry as Alice:** When someone plays the role of Alice or Bob to spend a Full-Mix box and create a Half-Mix box (i.e., send the coin back to the H-pool). The input is a Full-Mix box and the output is a Half-Mix box of the same amount.

5. **Alice or Bob reentry as Bob:** When someone plays the role of Alice or Bob to spend a Full-Mix box along with another Half-Mix box and create two new Full-Mix boxes. The input is a Half-Mix box and a Full-Mix box and the outputs are two new Full-Mix boxes.

Clearly, for both Alice and Bob entries, fee is not an issue because both parties can fund the fee component of the transaction from a known source. Similarly for case 3, when exiting the system, part of the amount in the Full-Mix box can be used to pay fee. The only time we need to hide the source of fee is when we spend a Full-Mix box and want to reenter as either Alice or Bob.

4.1 An Altruistic Approach

In this approach, fee is paid by a *sponsor* when spending a Full-Mix box for reentry. We use a variation of *Fee-Emission boxes* presented in [24].

Fee-Emission Box: A sponsor creates several Fee-Emission boxes to pay reentry fee. Such a box can be spent under the following conditions:

1. There is exactly one Fee-Emission box as input.
2. There is exactly one Full-Mix box as input.
3. Either exactly one input or exactly one output is a Half-Mix box.
4. The updated balance is stored in a new Fee-Emission box.

This is encoded in ErgoScript as follows:

```
1  def isFull(b:Box) = hash(b.script) == fullMixScriptHash
2  def isHalf(b:Box) = hash(b.script) == halfMixScriptHash
3  def isFee(b:Box) = hash(b.script) == feeScriptHash
4  def isCopy(b:Box) = b.script == script &&
5                      b.value == value - fee
6  val asAlice = INPUTS.size == 2 && OUTPUTS.size == 3 &&
7                isFull(INPUTS(0)) && isHalf(OUTPUTS(0)) &&
8                isCopy(OUTPUTS(1)) && isFee(OUTPUTS(2)
9  val asBob = INPUTS.size == 3 && OUTPUTS.size == 4 &&
10               isHalf(INPUTS(0)) && isFull(INPUTS(1)) &&
11               isCopy(OUTPUTS(2)) && isFee(OUTPUTS(3))
12 asAlice || asBob
```

Contract 3. Fee emission script

The condition `asAlice` encodes the rules of spending a Full-Mix box to emulate Alice for the next mix and create a Half-Mix box. Similarly, the condition `asBob` has the rules for spending a Full-Mix box as Bob's contribution in a mix.

The sponsor pays the fee whenever a Full-Mix box is remixed. However, there is no guarantee that some given Full-Mix box was actually created in a mix transaction. The only way to determine this is to examine the transaction that created the box. However, this is not yet possible in ErgoScript. Thus, the above approach is susceptible to freeloaders who store their funds in a Full-Mix box. However, such freeloaders must either create a Half-Mix box or spend another Half-Mix box, thereby forcing them participate in the protocol. This gives no advantage to freeloaders who still need to pay fee to create a fake full-mix box.

4.2 Mixing Tokens

Ergo's primary token is known as *Erg*, which is necessary to pay for transaction fees and storage rent [25]. An Ergo transaction conserves primary tokens (they can neither be created nor destroyed) and any box must have a positive quantity of primary tokens. Each box can optionally have *secondary tokens* which are uniquely identified by an id. Unlike primary tokens, an Ergo transaction can destroy secondary tokens. Additionally, each transaction can also create (i.e., *issue*) at most one new token in arbitrary quantity, whose id is the globally unique id of the first input box of that transaction.

In this approach, we will still use a Fee-Emission box (as in Sect. 4.1) to pay the fee in Ergs. However, we will also use secondary tokens issued by the creator of the Fee-Emission box, which we call *mixing tokens* (identified by `tokenId`). The Fee-Emission box can only be used by destroying a mixing token.

Approximate Fairness: We use the approximate fairness strategy described in [26]. At a high level the idea is as follows. Each mix transaction consumes one mixing token, which must be supplied by the inputs. Thus, there must be at least one mixing token among the inputs. Additionally, to keep the outputs indistinguishable, each must have the same number of tokens.

The approximate fairness strategy says that Bob must supply half the token, and is allowed to supply less tokens than Alice as long as both started with the same amount and Bob lost them in sequential mixes. The approximate-fairness strategy works only if two conditions are satisfied. The first is that mixing tokens are confined within the system by restricting their transfer to only those boxes that participate in a remix. The second is to ensure that tokens always enter the system in a fixed quantity, and that too in one of the two ErgoMix boxes.

4.3 Token Confinement

In this section we enforce the first requirement of approximate fairness, that of confining the tokens within the system. Recall that the Half-Mix box's script refers to the Full-Mix box's script via the constant `fullMixScriptHash`. Our approach additionally requires the Full-Mix box's script to refer back to the Half-Mix box's script. We do this by storing the hash of the Half-Mix script in one of the registers of the Full-Mix box. Let `delta` be an alias for this register that stores an array of bytes. The scripts are also modified.

Fee-Emission Box: We modify `isFull` method of the Fee-Emission box contract:

```
1  def isFull(b:Box) = hash(b.script) == fullMixScriptHash &&
2                       b.delta == halfMixScriptHash
3  (... remaining code same as Contract #3)
```

Contract 4. Fee emission script with confinement

Recall that the rule for spending the Fee-Emission box is to destroy one mixing token. While the above contract does not directly enforce this requirement, it does so indirectly via the Full-Mix and Half-Mix scripts discussed below.

Full-Mix Box: Modify `fullMixScript`, the contract of a Full-Mix box as well:

```
1  def isHalf(b:Box) = hash(b.script) == delta &&
2                       b.value == value
3  def isFull(b:Box) = b.script == script &&
4                       b.delta == delta && b.value == value
5  def noToken(b:Box) = b.tokens(tokenId) == 0
6  val nextAlice = isHalf(OUTPUTS(0)) && INPUTS(0).id == id
7  val nextBob = isHalf(INPUTS(0)) && INPUTS(1).id == id
8  val destroyToken = OUTPUTS.forall(noToken)
9  val nextAliceLogic = OUTPUTS(0).tokens(tokenId) ==
10                       INPUTS(0).tokens(tokenId) - 1 &&
11                       OUTPUTS(0).tokens(tokenId) > 0
12
13 ((nextAlice && nextAliceLogic) || nextBob || destroyToken)
14 && (... earlier condition from Contract #1)
```

Contract 5. Full mix script with confinement

The script enforces the transfer of mixing tokens when spending the Full-Mix box to create a Half-Mix box. In particular, the tokens can only be transferred if the transaction either outputs a Half-Mix box (i.e., the spender takes the role of Alice in the next mix step, in which case one mixing token is destroyed) or participates in a mix transaction as Bob and spends a Half-Mix box along with this Full-Mix box (in which case, the transfer of mixing tokens is governed by the contract in the Half-Mix box).

Half-Mix Box: Next, the Half-Mix contract (`halfMixScript`) is also modified:

```
1  val alice = INPUTS(0).tokens(tokenId)
2  val bob = INPUTS(1).tokens(tokenId)
3  val out0 = OUTPUTS(0).tokens(tokenId)
4  val out1 = OUTPUTS(1).tokens(tokenId)
5  val tLogic = alice + bob == out0 + out1 + 1 && bob > 0 && alice > 0
6
7  OUTPUTS(0).delta == hash(script) &&
8  OUTPUTS(1).delta == hash(script) && out0 == out1 && tLogic &&
9  && (... earlier condition from Contract #2)
```

Contract 6. Half mix script with confinement

The above contract assumes that the boxes already have some quantity of mixing tokens and enforces how these must be used. Each mix transaction is assumed to consume one such token, and to maintain privacy, the token balance must be equally distributed between the two outputs. The contract follows the *approximate-fairness* strategy where Alice requires Bob to contribute at least one mixing token [26]. For *perfect fairness* add the condition `alice == bob`.

4.4 Token Entry

Token-Emission Box: A Token-Emission box is used to get mixing tokens for entry into the system as either Alice or Bob. It contains the following contract.

```
1  def isCopy(b:Box) = b.script == script && b.value == value &&
2                       b.tokens(tokenId) == tokens(tokenId) - amt
3  def isFull(b:Box) = hash(b.script) == fullMixScriptHash &&
4                       b.delta == halfMixScriptHash
5  def isHalf(b:Box) = hash(b.script) == halfMixScriptHash
6  def isFee(b:Box) = hash(b.script) == feeScriptHash &&
```

```
 7                          b.value == fee
 8 def isEntry(b:Box) = (isFull(b) || isHalf(b)) &&
 9                          b.tokens(tokenId) == amt
10 def isZero(b:Box) = b.tokens(tokenId) == 0
11
12 INPUTS(0).id == id && isZero(INPUTS(1)) && INPUTS.size == 2 &&
13 isEntry(OUTPUTS(0)) && isCopy(OUTPUTS(1)) && isFee(OUTPUTS(2))
```

Contract 7. Token emission script

Anyone can spend the Token-Emission box to send a fixed amount **amt** of mixing tokens to either a Half-Mix box or a (fake) Full-Mix box, which should be the first output of the transaction. The other outputs are a copy of the token-emission box with the balance tokens and the fee paying output. The transaction must have exactly two inputs, with the token-emission box being the first and the second containing zero mixing tokens.

We can use mixing tokens to verify that a given Full-Mix box was indeed created in a mix transaction, and a given Half-Mix box was indeed created by spending a Full-Mix box. In particular, this is true if and only if the box contains less than **amt** and more than 0 mixing tokens.

While the above Token-Emission box gives the mixing tokens for free, it is trivial to modify the contract to sell the tokens at some given rate. The only change required is in the `isCopy` method:

```
1 def isCopy(b:Box) = b.script == script &&
2                       b.value == value + amt * rate &&
3                       b.tokens(tokenId) == tokens(tokenId) - amt
4 (... remaining code same as Contract #7)
```

Contract 8. Token emission script with sell capability

We also want the token issuer to be able to withdraw any Ergs deposited by token buyers. To achieve this, the token-emission box is again modified:

```
1 (... earlier condition from Contract #8) ||
2 (issuerPubKey && INPUTS.size == 1 &&
3   OUTPUTS(0).script == script && OUTPUTS(0).value > minErgs &&
4   OUTPUTS(0).tokens(tokenId) == tokens(tokenId))
```

Contract 9. Token emission script with withdraw capability

It is necessary to keep a certain amount of Ergs, `minErgs` inside each Token-Emission box, otherwise the box may be destroyed when miners collect storage rent. This value should be large enough to ensure sustenance for several years. In order to allow several people to buy tokens in the same block and to avoid collisions when multiple people try to spend the same token-emission box, there must be several token-emission boxes.

Analysis: Because of the condition **bob > 0** in `tLogic` of the Half-Mix box, a mix transaction requires Bob to supply at least one token, and since these tokens can only be stored in either Full or Half-Mix boxes, the second input of a mix transaction must be a Full-Mix box (as opposed to any box). That Full-Mix box can either be the output of a mix transaction (a real Full-Mix box) or the output of a token purchase transaction (a fake Full-Mix box).

Another consequence of `bob > 0` is that at least one token must exist in order to spend Alice's box. In the case that mixing tokens become unavailable, Alice's box is rendered unspendable. In order to handle this, we need to ensure that mixing tokens are always available. One way would be to have each token-emission box store a large number of tokens, much more than what can be purchased with all the available Ergs. Before storing any funds in a Half-Mix box, it must be ascertained that there are a large number of mixing tokens stored in at least one token-emission box.

An alternate way to ensure that Alice's Half-Mix box does not get stuck due to non-availability of tokens would be to allow Alice to spend the box using her secret. This requires modifying the Half-Mix box as follows:

```
1 def noToken(b:Box) = b.tokens(tokenId) == 0
2
3 (proveDlog(g, alpha) && INPUTS.size == 1 && OUTPUTS.forall(noToken)) ||
4 (... earlier condition from Contract #6)
```

Contract 10. Half script with withdraw capability

The above modification allows Alice to spend the Half-Mix box using her secret but she must destroy all mixing tokens in doing so.

Figure 4 gives an example flow with the above contracts in place. To avoid clutter, we skipped the fee output in the above flow. However, each transaction is implicitly assumed to have an additional box for paying fee.

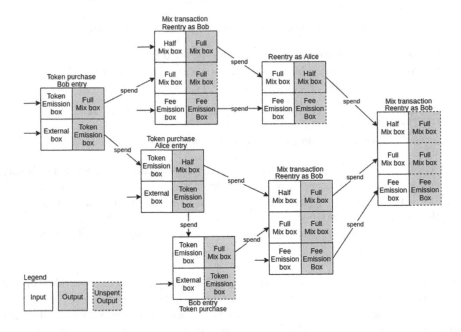

Fig. 4. Multi-round ErgoMix with Mixing Tokens to handle fee

A mix transaction is always a reentry as Bob and both Alice and Bob's entry is through a token purchase transaction.

The predicate `alice > 0` also requires that the Half-Mix box have at least one token, implying that the only way to create the Half-Mix box would be in a token purchase transaction or transaction for reentry as Alice. In particular, it is impossible to create a Half-Mix box in an other manner.

References

1. Maxwell, G.: Confidential transactions (2015). https://people.xiph.org/~greg/confidential_values.txt
2. Miers, I., Garman, C., Green, M., Rubin, A.D.: Zerocoin: anonymous distributed E-cash from bitcoin. In: Proceedings of the IEEE Symposium on Security and Privacy, pp. 397–411, May 2013
3. Coinjoin: Bitcoin privacy for the real world, August 2013. https://bitcointalk.org/?topic=279249
4. Sasson, E.B., et al.: Zerocash: decentralized anonymous payments from bitcoin. In: Proceedings of the 2014 IEEE Symposium on Security and Privacy, SP 2014, Washington, DC, USA, pp. 459–474. IEEE Computer Society (2014)
5. Zcash (2016). https://z.cash
6. Mastering Monero: The Future of Private Transactions. Independently Published (2018)
7. Fauzi, P., Meiklejohn, S., Mercer, R., Orlandi, C.: Quisquis: a new design for anonymous cryptocurrencies. In: Galbraith, S.D., Moriai, S. (eds.) ASIACRYPT 2019. LNCS, vol. 11921, pp. 649–678. Springer, Cham (2019). https://doi.org/10.1007/978-3-030-34578-5_23
8. Saxena, A., Misra, J., Dhar, A.: Increasing anonymity in bitcoin. In: Böhme, R., Brenner, M., Moore, T., Smith, M. (eds.) FC 2014. LNCS, vol. 8438, pp. 122–139. Springer, Heidelberg (2014). https://doi.org/10.1007/978-3-662-44774-1_9
9. Coinjoin implementation with incentive structure to convince people to take part, March 2016. https://github.com/JoinMarket-Org/joinmarket
10. Zcoin, August 2016. https://github.com/zcoinofficial/zcoin
11. Ergo mixer, June 2020. https://github.com/ergoMixer/ergoMixBack
12. Nakamoto, S.: Bitcoin: a peer-to-peer electronic cash system (2008). https://bitcoin.org/bitcoin.pdf
13. Ergo Developers: Ergo: a resilient platform for contractual money (2019). https://ergoplatform.org/docs/whitepaper.pdf
14. Wood, G.: Ethereum: A secure decentralised generalised transaction ledger. Ethereum project yellow paper **151**, 1–32 (2014)
15. The Nxt cryptocurrency. https://nxt.org/
16. Schnorr, C.-P.: Efficient signature generation by smart cards. J. Cryptol. **4**(3), 161–174 (1991). https://doi.org/10.1007/BF00196725
17. Damgård, I.: On Σ-protocols (2010). http://www.cs.au.dk/~ivan/Sigma.pdf
18. Fiat, A., Shamir, A.: How to prove yourself: practical solutions to identification and signature problems. In: Odlyzko, A.M. (ed.) CRYPTO 1986. LNCS, vol. 263, pp. 186–194. Springer, Heidelberg (1987). https://doi.org/10.1007/3-540-47721-7_12
19. Cramer, R., Damgård, I., Schoenmakers, B.: Proofs of partial knowledge and simplified design of witness hiding protocols. In: Desmedt, Y.G. (ed.) CRYPTO 1994. LNCS, vol. 839, pp. 174–187. Springer, Heidelberg (1994). https://doi.org/10.1007/3-540-48658-5_19. http://www.win.tue.nl/ berry/papers/crypto94.pdf

20. Chepurnoy, A., Saxena, A.: Bypassing non-outsourceable proof-of-work schemes using collateralized smart contracts. In: Bernhard, M., et al. (eds.) FC 2020. LNCS, vol. 12063, pp. 423–435. Springer, Cham (2020). https://doi.org/10.1007/978-3-030-54455-3_30

21. Chepurnoy, A., Saxena, A.: Multi-stage contracts in the UTXO model. In: Pérez-Solà, C., Navarro-Arribas, G., Biryukov, A., Garcia-Alfaro, J. (eds.) DPM/CBT -2019. LNCS, vol. 11737, pp. 244–254. Springer, Cham (2019). https://doi.org/10.1007/978-3-030-31500-9_16

22. Odersky, M., et al.: The scala language specification (2004)

23. Odersky, M., Spoon, L., Venners, B.: Programming in Scala: Updated for Scala 2.12, 3rd edn. Artima Incorporation, Sunnyvale (2016)

24. Paying fee in ergomix in primary tokens, August 2019. https://www.ergoforum.org/t/paying-fee-in-ergomix-in-primary-tokens/73

25. Chepurnoy, A., Kharin, V., Meshkov, D.: A systematic approach to cryptocurrency fees. In: Zohar, A., et al. (eds.) FC 2018. LNCS, vol. 10958, pp. 19–30. Springer, Heidelberg (2019). https://doi.org/10.1007/978-3-662-58820-8_2

26. Advanced ergoscript tutorial, March 2019. https://docs.ergoplatform.com/sigmastate_protocols.pdf

Who Let the $\mathcal{DOGS}$ Out: Anonymous but Auditable Communications Using Group Signature Schemes with Distributed Opening

Marina Dehez-Clementi[1,2(✉)], Jean-Christophe Deneuville[3], Jérôme Lacan[1],
Hassan Asghar[2,4], and Dali Kaafar[2,4]

[1] ISAE-SUPAERO, Toulouse, France
marina.dehez-clementi@isae-supaero.fr
[2] Macquarie University, Sydney, Australia
[3] ENAC, Toulouse, France
[4] Data61/CSIRO, Sydney, Australia

Abstract. Over the past two decades, group signature schemes have been developed and used to enable authenticated and anonymous peer-to-peer communications. Initial protocols rely on two main authorities, Issuer and Opener, which are given substantial capabilities compared to (regular) participants, such as the ability to arbitrarily identify users. Building efficient, fast, and short group signature schemes has been the focus of a large number of research contributions. However, only a few dealt with the major privacy-preservation challenge of group signatures; this consists in providing user anonymity and action traceability while not necessarily relying on a central and fully trusted authority. In this paper, we present $\mathcal{DOGS}$, a privacy-preserving Blockchain-supported group signature scheme with a distributed Opening functionality. In $\mathcal{DOGS}$, participants no longer depend on the Opener entity to identify the signer of a potentially fraudulent message; they instead collaborate and perform this auditing process themselves. We provide a high-level description of the $\mathcal{DOGS}$ scheme and show that it provides both user anonymity and action traceability. Additionally, we prove how $\mathcal{DOGS}$ is secure against message forgery and anonymity attacks.

1 Introduction

Developed in the 70's, digital signatures are one of the most important primitives in public key cryptography and provide *authentication*, *integrity* and *non-repudiation* to various applications. However, they do not provide privacy of the signer [12]. Our focus is on signature schemes that provide both **user anonymity** and **action traceability**, which fall in the realm of *group signature schemes*.

Introduced by Chaum and van Heyst [5], group signature schemes enable members of a group to sign messages on behalf of the group without revealing their identity. The signature can be verified by the recipient as a valid signature

© Springer Nature Switzerland AG 2020
J. Garcia-Alfaro et al. (Eds.): DPM 2020/CBT 2020, LNCS 12484, pp. 437–446, 2020.
https://doi.org/10.1007/978-3-030-66172-4_28

from the group, but cannot identify the member who generated the signature. However, signing members remain accountable for their messages as the *group manager*, a third-party managing the group, can open their signatures and hence identify them.

In [2], Bellare *et al.* presented some fundamental security notions for dynamic group signatures. A key feature of their scheme is that the group manager is split into two distinct entities: the *Issuer* which interacts with users to authenticate their credentials, and the *Opener* which is called when a signature needs to be opened.

Role of the Opener. The opener acts as the *tracing authority* in charge of linking a signed message to its origin, namely the signer. By definition, the role of the Opener entails no privacy preservation. Existing literature [9,10] usually considers a unique entity to be playing the role of the Opener, inducing strong assumptions of the level of trust in such an entity as well as its resilience. In Vehicular Ad-hoc Networks (VANETs) for instance, vehicles use group signatures to sign the (location and time-dependent) road-safety messages they broadcast. A vehicle's identity is protected by the scheme unless the Opener is compromised, in which case signatures may be opened which then breaches user privacy. An alternative way to relax these strong assumptions in the Opener is to implement a ***distributed tracing authority*** instead.

Related Work on Distributed Traceability. Studies that propose a distributed traceability functionality for group signature schemes (e.g., [3,6]) often leverage Shamir's Secret Sharing (SSS) scheme to generate shares of the Opener secret key and then distribute one share per user. This approach however presents a clear limitation: the computation of these shares is again centralized which still represents a single point of failure from an adversary perspective.

Our Contribution. In this paper, we propose the Distributed Opening Group Signature $\mathcal{DOGS}$ scheme, a BSZ group signature scheme [2] enhanced with the Distributed Key Generation (DKG) protocol from [11] (later denoted ETHDKG) for the distribution of the Opener secret key. The advantage of our DKG-enhanced group signature over SSS-based approaches is that the key generation is not entrusted to a third party. Instead, it is the result of the collaboration of a group of users. Hence, none of them knows all the shares, making the scheme strong against a more powerful adversary.

Structure of the Paper. Section 2 provides a description of the system model, desirable security features and the primitives used. Section 3 gives a generic presentation of the $\mathcal{DOGS}$ construction. Section 4 presents the security analysis of $\mathcal{DOGS}$. Section 5 concludes the paper.

2   Preliminaries

In this section, we present the adversary model and corresponding security features of $DOGS$. We describe the system, giving a real-world use case, and introduce our solution for the distribution of the Opener.

2.1   Adversary Model and Desirable Features

In $DOGS$, we consider an adversary that wants to break the underlying group signature scheme. Therefore it can perform de-anonymization attacks (i.e. intercept a message and identify the signer), key recovery attacks or forgery attacks (i.e. create a signature that would defeat the opening procedure or frame a legitimate user). All these scenarios are captured in Bellare *et al.* [2].

Desirable Features. Our main objectives are for our $DOGS$ scheme to be correct and to provide anonymity, traceability and non-frameability. Let λ denotes the security parameter.

Correctness. The correctness property guarantees that signatures issued by honest users:

  i) should pass the verification,
 ii) should trace to the correct issuer if opened with the Opening key, and
iii) the proof output by the *Open* process should verify the *Judge* algorithm. $\square$

Anonymity. Let U_0 and U_1 be two honest registered users, and σ a valid signature issued by U_b for some $b \in \{0, 1\}$. The anonymity property requires that no probabilistic polynomial-time (PPT) adversary $\mathcal{A}$ can guess b with non negligible (in λ) advantage. $\square$

Traceability. An adversary breaks the traceability property if she succeeds in creating a valid signature σ such that either:

  i) no registered (or revoked) user can be identified when σ is legitimately opened, or
 ii) the proof, produced by a honest opening, revealing that σ belongs to user U, does not convince the *Judge* algorithm. $\square$

Non-frameability. Finally, the non-frameability property requires that no PPT adversary $\mathcal{A}$ can create a valid signature that would trace to an honest user if opened, unless this user has effectively issued it. $\square$

We prove that $DOGS$ is compliant with these security goals in Sect. 4.

2.2   System Model

Involved in our $DOGS$ scheme are: an authority called the Issuer Iss for the generation of initial cryptographic information, and a body of users, each with a unique identity i (e.g. $i \in \mathbb{N}$). We assume over half of the participants are honest. Iss is public and has its own secret key. It interacts with users to issue them an authenticated signing key. We consider a Region of Interest (RoI), which users can join and leave and in which they can communicate. One Issuer is responsible for one RoI.

Use Case. In VANETs, we can assimilate the RoI to a neighbourhood. Vehicles are the users. They can enter, leave and move in the area, communicate with each other and broadcast road information. The Roadside unit acts as the Issuer.

2.3   Distributed Key Generation for $\mathcal{DOGS}$

Distributed Key Generation (DKG) protocols are fundamental building blocks for a variety of cryptographic schemes [8]. They enable a group of users to collaborate in order to obtain a common public key. The strength of DKG lies in that the public key can be computed by any honest participant, while the corresponding secret key cannot. Instead, it requires a threshold number of collaborating honest parties to derive it.

In this paper, we draw from Schindler *et al.*'s DKG implementation [11] (ETHDKG). The authors present a fully functioning DKG protocol for threshold signature generation, based on Ethereum smart contracts. In the following section, we explain how we combine this DKG proposition with BSZ group signature to produce a new Group Signature scheme with Distributed Opener called $\mathcal{DOGS}$.

3   Protocol Description

There are three phases in $\mathcal{DOGS}$:

  phase 1 *"Distributed Generation of an Opening Keys"*,
  phase 2 *"Inter Communications and App-related event logging"* and
  phase 3 *"Auditing and Identification"*.

We transpose them into five distinct modules (Fig. 1) namely **Bootstrapping**, **Registration** and **Opening Keys (OK) Generation** (phase 1), **Application** (phase 2) and **Audit** (phase 3).

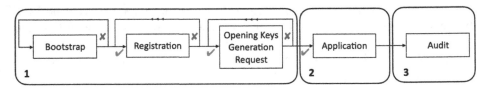

Fig. 1. $\mathcal{DOGS}$ Workflow diagram

Table 1. Description of the transaction (Tx) types and corresponding published data.

Module	Algorithm	Type	Comments
Bootstrap	GKg	BOOTSTRAP	Publication of the group public key gpk, and the Issuer public key ipk
Registration	UKg	None	U_i generates local identity **upk**$[i]$, **usk**$[i]$
	Join	JOINING REQUEST	By U_i, sends personal data to Issuer
	Iss	ISSUING REPLY	2 issues: accept/reject. If accept, the Issuer records the link between **upk**$[i]$, **usk**$[i]$ and (i, pk_i, sig_i)
Opening Keys Generation	sharing	OPENING KEYS (OK) GENERATION REQUEST	U_i generates and distributes commitments (C_{ij}), encrypted shares $\overline{s_{ij}}$ and value h^{s_i}, for $k = 0..t$, $j = 1..n$
	share_verification	CLAIM	A user U issues a claim $=< status, data, key, proof >$
	claim_verification	CLAIM VERIFICATION	All U check the validity of the claim; 2 issues: accept/reject
	key_derivation	KEY PUBLICATION	The Issuer determines and publishes the resulting Opening public key opk
Application	GSig	SIGNATURE	User U produces a group signature σ under opk
	GVf	VERIFICATION	User U verifies a group signature σ under opk. 2 issues: accept/reject
Audit	Request	OPEN REQUEST	User U requests the opening of a group signature σ under opk
	Collaborate	SECRET KEY PUBLICATION	One of the authorized users publishes the re-constructed Opening secret key osk
	Open	OPEN	The signature σ is opened and the result is published by the requester
	Judge	JUDGE	A user - not the requester - asserts and publishes the validity of the requester's opening

Algorithms and their Usage. Users can become group members by joining the Region of Interest and interacting with the Issuer. They become sub-opener authorities and participate to the opening process if they own a share of an Opening secret key. The group of sub-openers therefore replaces the Opener. The scheme is specified as a tuple $\mathcal{DOGS}$ =(GKg, dOKg, UKg, Join, Iss, GSig, GVf, Request, Collaborate, Open, Judge) of PPT algorithms, whose intended usage and functionalities are presented in this section. This protocol heavily relies on previous works [2, 11] and we advice the readers to briefly review them before they proceed. Indeed, (GKg, UKg, Join, Iss, GSig, GVf, Open, Judge) are inherited from [2], and dOKg invokes (sharing, share_verification, claim_verification, key_derivation) formalized from [11].

Usage of the Public Ledger. Throughout these phases, we assume the existence of a trusted message delivery service. To do so, we make use of a public ledger to record relevant information, i.e. any public data that can be used to assert the validity and integrity of the shared cryptographic parameters.

We leverage a classic blockchain implementation with the usual functionalities related to block addition, linkage and forking issues. In $\mathcal{DOGS}$ protocol, the transaction types and corresponding published data are summarized in Table 1, which includes the definition of: seven transaction types for Phase 1 (e.g. the *bootstrap transaction* corresponds to the publication of bootstrapping information); two transaction types for Phase 2, which illustrate the signing action of a user and verifying process of other members of the group; and finally, four transaction types for Phase 3.

Since the information published does not hold private or sensitive information, the public ledger is readable by anyone. However, we restrict the writing permissions to authenticated users only.

3.1   Phase 1: Distributed Generation of the Opening Keys

In the following paragraphs, we will explain each step of Phase 1.

Bootstrap. The scheme starts with the bootstrapping of the system. It consists in the Issuer executing the GKg algorithm and results in the publication of both the group public key *gpk* and the the Issuer's public key *ipk* (BOOTSTRAP transaction).

Registration. User U_i enters the RoI. First, U_i executes the UKg algorithm to obtain a personal public/private key pair, referring to its local identity (usk[i], **upk**[i]). Then, U_i starts the Join,Iss interactive protocols. It executes the Join function and triggers the JOIN REQUEST transaction. The generation and publication of related information (Table 1) is compliant with Bellare *et al.*'s $\mathcal{GS}$ Join algorithm, but enhanced with logging functionalities for traceability purposes. The Issuer receives encrypted data from U_i, including identifying information such as the public key pk_i used to verify U_i's signed messages. It compares it to the public record for data integrity checks; then executes the Iss function, triggering the publication of resulting data and the ISSUING REPLY transaction. The **Registration** step has two issues: the first ends up in U_i's request being rejected due to faulty data; the second grants U_i with a certificate $cert_i$ and allows it to perform subsequent actions such as OPENING KEYS (OK) GENERATION REQUEST, make a CLAIM, or a CLAIM VERIFICATION. If so, the Issuer records, in its local database, the relationship between the user's local identity given by UKg, and the authenticated identity (i, pk_i, sig_i) used in the RoI.

Opening Keys (OK) Generation. Since the Opener is no longer a single entity, from now on, we will use the wording "Opening" to designate the functionality it was in charge of. We now consider an authenticated user U_i and explain how it can request the generation of Opening keys to protect its future communications (see GSig [2]).

U_i executes the **sharing** function inherited from [11]. This function triggers the OPENING KEYS (OK) GENERATION REQUEST transaction. Subsequently, U_i generates and publishes the required information (commitments (C_{ik}), shares (s_{ij}) and value h^{s_i} according to [11]) for the computation of an Opening public key.

The broadcasting of this new transaction triggers an update of the local ledgers of the users. They individually execute the **share_verification** function to check the correctness of the share that has been sent to them by U_i (note: each share s_{ij} is encrypted with a symmetric encryption scheme of key $k_{ij} = g^{sk_i sk_j} = pk_i^{sk_j} = pk_j^{sk_i}$). The execution of this function triggers a CLAIM transaction and publishes the result as $< status, data, key, proof >$. Depending on *status*, there are two different results: if *status* contains the value "*no_claim*" or U_j does not reveal k_{ij} or its proof $\pi(k_{ij})$, then the share is accepted and U_j in turn has to broadcast its own shares (see **Case** 1). Else if, *status* value is equal to "*claim*", then the protocol holds as others check the claim (see **Case** 2).

Case 1. Therefore, U_j in turn executes the **sharing** function, distributes the resulting shares and publishes related data. Again, **share_verification** function is used to check the validity of the shares but this time either the peers $\{U_k\}_{k \neq j \in N}$ accepts U_j's share and it ends there, or it rejects it.

Case 2. In this case, a share has been rejected and a claim has been broadcast. Hence, users execute **claim_verification** function to check its validity. Doing so, they trigger a CLAIM VERIFICATION transaction which results in either the claim being denied or accepted.

Once all the shares and claim have been verified, the Issuer can execute **key_derivation** function. It browses the public records and determines which shares are usable to compute the final Opening public key. It finally publishes this key *opk* and $\mathcal{R}$ the list of authenticated local identities which participated to the establishment of this Opening key.

In the following sub-section, we explain how anyone in the RoI can use *opk* in GSig to encrypt its signature, ensuring its anonymity in communications while still providing action traceability.

3.2 Phase 2: Inter Communications and Application-Related Event Logging

Application. Our *DOGS* scheme has been initially thought to be applied in the context of local logging of events, especially for VANETs. Let us consider U_i has a road-safety information to share with vehicles in the neighbourhood, for instance an alert about a car accident. However, U_i does not want to reveal its identity nor its position at this particular time (to prevent location-based identity inference [7]). If U_i applies GSig function on the alert message, it is able to produce a signature that refers to the group but protects its identity. It additionally triggers the SIGNATURE transaction. The use of [2]'s GSig along with the DKG-computed Opening public key ensures that no single sub-opener can open this signature, hence identify U_i. However, users in the neighbourood can still individually execute GVf [2] to assert the correctness of the received signature and trust U_i's alert. The result gets published along with VERIFICATION transaction.

That is how user anonymity is provided in $\mathcal{DOGS}$. In the following subsection, we consequently explain how $\mathcal{DOGS}$ also provides action traceability.

3.3   Phase 3: Auditing and De-anonymization

Audit. This module regroups the required functionalities implemented in $\mathcal{DOGS}$ for providing action traceability.

With Request, the requester U_i triggers the OPEN REQUEST transaction, hence summoning users in the RoI to collaborate in order to reconstruct an Opening secret key. U_i therefore communicates the signature σ it wants to open, the message m it signs and the corresponding Opening public key opk. For traceability guarantees, this request gets published on to the public ledger.

Then, the Collaborate function is executed. All U_j in the set $\mathcal{R}$ related to opk will collaborate to reconstruct the Opening secret key osk (by consecutively summing their shares to previous partial results). The last peer to add its own secret s_{t+1} also publishes the result while triggering the SECRET KEY PUBLICATION transaction. It includes the initial data $<m, opk, \sigma>$, the set $\mathcal{R}$, and the result of their work osk.

Finally, by retrieving osk, the requester U_i can identify the origin of σ and publishes the result via the Open function (OPEN transaction). Other peers in the RoI can consequently check this identification by executing the Judge function (JUDGE transaction).

4   Security Analysis

In this section, we show that the use of ETHDKG functionalities is compatible with the security environment related to group signature schemes as presented in [2], hence that $\mathcal{DOGS}$ presents all the security properties we aimed for. Due to space restrictions, the security proofs are only sketc.hed, but most of them are directly inherited from the BSZ construction and the ETHDKG protocol. Only the anonymity property requires a careful treatment. We refer the reader to BSZ [2] for a complete description of the experiments for each security feature.

Let λ be $\lambda = 100$ bits of security provided by the instantiation of the ETHDKG with the elliptic curve BN254 [1].

Correctness. Properties i) and iii) are directly satisfied using BSZ. Assuming the Opening key is correctly reconstructed, which is the case with overwhelming probability (in λ) thanks to ETHDKG, then ii) is also satisfied.   □

Anonymity. In the original experiment [2], A does *not* have access to the opening oracle. In $DOGS$, we weaken this assumption to "A has access to at most t shares of the Opening secret key (including her own, if she is a registered user)". Then A has negligible advantage in λ in recovering osk [11] and our anonymity feature boils down to the original one, which is fulfilled by using BSZ.   □

Traceability. Similarly, in [2], A is granted access to the Opening secret key osk. Therefore, A learns nothing more by corrupting users and $DOGS$ traceability is inherited from BSZ.   □

Non-frameability. Here again, since A has already access to osk in the original experiment, she obtains no additional advantage by exploiting the shares of the Opening secret key, and $DOGS$ satisfies non-frameability as BSZ.   □

Discussion. Most of the security features are directly inherited from the BSZ and ETHDKG constructions. However, the anonymity experiment as described in [2] needs to be slightly modified. Indeed, an adversary A against the original property could create and corrupt sufficiently many (more than t) users to obtain their respective shares of the Opening secret key osk, and hence reconstruct it. Using osk, A could trivially break the original anonymity property. Therefore, an upper bound has to be integrated to compensate for the extra knowledge A gets by corrupting users.

5   Conclusion

In this work, we present $DOGS$, a Blockchain-supported group signature scheme which implements a distributed Opening functionality.

It would be meaningful, in future works, to include additional materials notably regarding the algorithms and their explicit definitions, ways to contact users from the group of sub-openers that are no longer in the Region of Interest or potential solutions to redistribute their shares to newcomers, an implementation of the scheme with performance analysis to compare to real-world scenarios (e.g. VANETs), and the establishment of more formal security proofs. Also, it would be interesting to complete the current scheme with the addition of a distributed Issuing functionality hence proposing a fully distributed Blockchain-supported group signature scheme. Camenisch *et al.* [4] recently came up with their own proposition and it might be interesting to analyse and compare both to some extent.

Nonetheless, being the combination of a BSZ group signature scheme and the ETHDKG protocol, we already succeed in formulating DOGS and show that, only by distributing the Opener among a group of users, we preserve the traceability feature of group signatures while enhancing their anonymity feature. Indeed, our scheme is proven stronger than BSZ's in terms of anonymity due to the use of DKG. Furthermore, the scheme brings an additional novelty as it enables the dynamic definition of the set of sub-opener authorities which makes it more practical to applications with variable topologies such as VANETs.

Acknowledgements. We would like to express our great appreciation to E. Lochin for his valuable and constructive suggestions during the planning and development of this research work.

This work was partly supported by the French government through the Toulouse graduate School of Aerospace Engineering (TSAE). Contract ANR-17-EURE-0005. This work has also been supported by the Optus Macquarie University Cyber Securiy Hub.

References

1. Barreto, P.S.L.M., Naehrig, M.: Pairing-friendly elliptic curves of prime order. In: Preneel, B., Tavares, S. (eds.) SAC 2005. LNCS, vol. 3897, pp. 319–331. Springer, Heidelberg (2006). https://doi.org/10.1007/11693383_22
2. Bellare, M., Shi, H., Zhang, C.: Foundations of group signatures: the case of dynamic groups. In: Menezes, A. (ed.) CT-RSA 2005. LNCS, vol. 3376, pp. 136–153. Springer, Heidelberg (2005). https://doi.org/10.1007/978-3-540-30574-3_11
3. Blömer, J., Juhnke, J., Löken, N.: Short group signatures with distributed traceability. In: Kotsireas, I.S., Rump, S.M., Yap, C.K. (eds.) MACIS 2015. LNCS, vol. 9582, pp. 166–180. Springer, Cham (2016). https://doi.org/10.1007/978-3-319-32859-1_14
4. Camenisch, J., Drijvers, M., Lehmann, A., Neven, G., Towa, P.: Short threshold dynamic group signatures. IACR Cryptol. ePrint Arch. **2020**, 16 (2020)
5. Chaum, D., van Heyst, E.: Group signatures. In: Davies, D.W. (ed.) EUROCRYPT 1991. LNCS, vol. 547, pp. 257–265. Springer, Heidelberg (1991). https://doi.org/10.1007/3-540-46416-6_22
6. Ghadafi, E.: Efficient distributed tag-based encryption and its application to group signatures with efficient distributed traceability. In: Aranha, D., Menezes, A. (eds.) International Conference on Cryptology and Information Security in Latin America, pp. 327–347. Springer, Cham (2014)
7. Kalnis, P., Ghinita, G., Mouratidis, K., Papadias, D.: Preventing location-based identity inference in anonymous spatial queries. IEEE Trans. Knowl. Data Eng. **19**(12), 1719–1733 (2007)
8. Neji, W., Blibech, K., Rajeb, N.B.: A survey on e-voting protocols based on secret sharing techniques. Proc. CARI **2018**, 142 (2018)
9. Perera, M.N.S., Koshiba, T.: Fully dynamic group signature scheme with member registration and verifier-local revocation. In: Ghosh, D., Giri, D., Mohapatra, R.N., Sakurai, K., Savas, E., Som, T. (eds.) ICMC 2018. SPMS, vol. 253, pp. 399–415. Springer, Singapore (2018). https://doi.org/10.1007/978-981-13-2095-8_31
10. Sakai, Y., Schuldt, J.C.N., Emura, K., Hanaoka, G., Ohta, K.: On the security of dynamic group signatures: preventing signature hijacking. In: Fischlin, M., Buchmann, J., Manulis, M. (eds.) PKC 2012. LNCS, vol. 7293, pp. 715–732. Springer, Heidelberg (2012). https://doi.org/10.1007/978-3-642-30057-8_42
11. Schindler, P., Judmayer, A., Stifter, N., Weippl, E.: Ethdkg: Distributed key generation with ethereum smart contracts. Technical Report, Cryptology ePrint Archive, Report 2019/985, 2019. https://eprint.iacr.org (2019)
12. Yang, G., Wong, D.S., Deng, X., Wang, H.: Anonymous signature schemes. In: Yung, M., Dodis, Y., Kiayias, A., Malkin, T. (eds.) PKC 2006. LNCS, vol. 3958, pp. 347–363. Springer, Heidelberg (2006). https://doi.org/10.1007/11745853_23

Tracking Mixed Bitcoins

Tin Tironsakkul$^{(\boxtimes)}$ (ID), Manuel Maarek (ID), Andrea Eross (ID), and Mike Just (ID)

Heriot-Watt University, Edinburgh, UK
`tt28@hw.ac.uk`

Abstract. Mixer services purportedly remove all connections between the input (deposited) Bitcoins and the output (withdrawn) mixed Bitcoins, seemingly rendering taint analysis tracking ineffectual. In this paper, we introduce and explore a novel tracking strategy, called *Address Taint Analysis*, that adapts from existing transaction-based taint analysis techniques for tracking Bitcoins that have passed through a mixer service. We also investigate the potential of combining address taint analysis with address clustering and backward tainting. We further introduce a set of filtering criteria that reduce the number of false-positive results based on the characteristics of withdrawn transactions and evaluate our solution with verifiable mixing transactions of nine mixer services from previous reverse-engineering studies. Our findings show that it is possible to track the mixed Bitcoins from the deposited Bitcoins using address taint analysis and the number of potential transaction outputs can be significantly reduced with the filtering criteria.

1 Introduction

A Bitcoin *mixer service* (also commonly known as *tumbler* or *laundering service*) is a cryptocurrency service that allows users to "anonymise" their Bitcoins by eliminating any possible connection between their original deposited Bitcoins and the *mixed* Bitcoins that they withdraw later from the service [12]. This mixing process can make the tracking of Bitcoin movements between addresses challenging, such as when using techniques like *taint analysis* [7]. Mixer services are also frequently used as one of the core components in transaction obscuring for illicit activities, such as theft, ransomware, and dark market trade [11,13].

In a normal Bitcoin transaction, address A would send Bitcoins directly to address B. However, this interaction establishes a connection between the two addresses in the blockchain, allowing anyone to observe the movement of Bitcoins [9]. Mixer services attempt to prevent this traceability by serving as an intermediary between the two addresses where address A deposits Bitcoins to a mixer service address (named the receiver address) for mixing purposes. Next, the mixer service uses another address(es) (named the delivery address) to deliver completely unrelated Bitcoins to address B in withdrawn transactions.

For the full version of the paper please visit: https://arxiv.org/abs/2009.14007.

© Springer Nature Switzerland AG 2020
J. Garcia-Alfaro et al. (Eds.): DPM 2020/CBT 2020, LNCS 12484, pp. 447–457, 2020.
https://doi.org/10.1007/978-3-030-66172-4_29

As a result, the interaction between address A and B is obscured in the blockchain, as there is no direct connection or transaction between the two endpoint addresses. Furthermore, simple transaction tracking methods are incapable of tracking the actual exchange of Bitcoins between the two addresses. One method used to track the mixed Bitcoins is to calculate every possible combination on every transaction within the mixing time for the potential withdrawn transaction outputs [15], which requires significant computational resources.

Few studies have investigated reverse-engineered mixer services to discover their mixing pattern [2,7,14]. We are aware of only one study that proposed a tracking method for mixed Bitcoins, which adapted from the aforementioned approach, and evaluated their method on a single mixer service [15]. In particular, we are not aware of any proposed tracking method to overcome the transaction obscuring feature of mixer services.

Hence, in this paper we introduce a novel tracking method called *address taint analysis* that focuses on tainting at the address level, whereas previous taint analysis approaches have focused on tainting at the transaction level. We investigate this method, both on its own and in combination with other tracking methods such as *address clustering* and *backward tainting*. We also introduce a set of filtering criteria in an attempt to reduce the number of false-positive results, and we evaluate our solutions with verifiable mixing transactions of nine mixer services used in previous reverse-engineering studies.

2   Related Work

2.1   Taint Analysis

Taint analysis is a transaction tracking method that determines the relationship or connection of addresses based on exchanges of specific Bitcoins in transactions [7]. It is often adapted to track the movement of specific Bitcoins (e.g., stolen Bitcoins) by classifying the tracked Bitcoins as tainted or clean and calculating the distribution of tainted Bitcoins used in subsequent transactions.

One taint analysis method, the *Poison method*, considers all of the resulting transaction outputs as fully tainted [8]. There are other tainting strategies that utilise different approaches of tracking and distributing Bitcoins, such as the *Haircut method* [8] and *FIFO method* (First In, First Out) [1]. Taint analysis can also be performed backwards, where instead of tainting forward to the next transaction, the algorithm taints backwards following previous transactions [1].

Aside from transaction tracking, taint analysis is utilized to measure the effectiveness of transaction obscuring methods where results with tainted connections indicate that the obscuring method is ineffective and can still be tracked [5,10]. We hereafter refer to the original transaction-based taint analysis as *transaction taint analysis* to distinguish it from the address-based taint analysis we define in this paper (see Sect. 3.1).

2.2   Address Clustering

Address clustering is a method that operates by grouping addresses into a cluster based on specific transaction behaviours. Address clustering methods are utilised in de-anonymisation which attempts to classify Bitcoin addresses likely to belong to the same user for tackling illegal activities [6].

One address clustering method, called *input-sharing clustering* or *multi-input heuristic*, is based on the assumption that all the addresses that share inputs in the same transaction belong to the same entity because every input address must sign a digital signature with its private key for the transaction to be valid. As such, if there are two or more input addresses in the same transaction, these addresses are being controlled by the same user [3].

Another clustering approach, *change address clustering*, operates by clustering the input addresses with the output addresses that are likely to be the change addresses – this is an address that is owned by the transaction's sender and which receives the remaining change Bitcoins in the transaction [6].

3   Methodology

In this section, we describe the address taint analysis method and its combination with other tracking methods (address clustering and backward tainting). Subsequently, we discuss the filtering criteria we developed and the rationale behind them.

3.1   Address Taint Analysis

The majority of mixer services usually utilise either a group of central addresses in order to combine and mix deposited Bitcoins from their users [2,7,14]. We assume that the receiver and delivery addresses within the mixer services are both likely to interact with the central addresses at some point in time. Our taint analysis method, *address taint analysis*, shown in Fig. 1, operates at the address connection level, where any address that receives Bitcoins from tainted addresses will be considered as a tainted address including every Bitcoin it possesses at any point in time. Existing taint analysis methods operate at the transaction level, where the tainted Bitcoins of a received address do not affect other Bitcoins belonging to that address, unless they are used together in the same transactions.

The assumption for address taint analysis is that any transaction and address that can be connected to the receiver addresses at any point in time, whether directly or indirectly, may be related to the mixer service in some way. Therefore the objective of address taint analysis is not only to track the mixed Bitcoins, but also to map the network of address clusters and their transactions that may involve the mixer service operation, as in Bitcoin network analysis [4].

The tainting methods used in our experiment are shown in Table 1. The **Baseline method** considers all outputs of every transaction recorded in the blockchain within the tainting time frame for a given sample case to be potentially the targeted withdrawn outputs; therefore these are considered tainted [15].

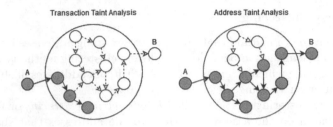

Fig. 1. Transaction taint analysis and address taint analysis. The figure depicts the difference between the transaction taint analysis and address taint analysis methods on an example mixing case that shows the deposited transaction from address A and the withdrawn transaction to address B. A darker arrow and circle indicate a transaction and address that involves tainted Bitcoins, while a lighter one indicate it being clean.

Table 1. Tainting methods implemented in this investigation.

Method 0	(or Baseline method) All outputs of every transaction recorded in the blockchain within the tainting time frame of a given sample case
Method 1	Address taint analysis
Method 2	Address taint analysis with input-sharing clustering
Method 3	Address taint analysis with input-sharing and output-sharing clustering
Method 4	Perform Method 3 on the results of backward address taint analysis on the known pre-existing withdrawn transactions from the same mixer service

Method 1 employs only address taint analysis. For Method 2 and Method 3, we investigate the potential of incorporating address clustering methods into the address taint analysis in order to improve the address cluster tracking results.

Due to the fact that the address taint analysis method operates with the assumption that the deposited and withdrawn mixer addresses may have a connection with each other via the central addresses, the analysis will not connect deposited inputs to the withdrawn outputs if there is no connection between the addresses involved, as shown in Fig. 2. We therefore introduce Method 4 by combining backward tainting with address taint analysis to create another tracking method called *backward address taint analysis*. This method operates by tainting any address that sends Bitcoins to a tainted address. The idea is that these addresses could subsequently be used to find the targeted withdrawn transaction outputs. Thus, this method operates in two steps, as presented next.

Using the example from Fig. 2, Method 4 starts by performing the backward address taint analysis variation from the withdrawn transactions of a case from the same mixer service (B_K) for three days to trace the mixed Bitcoins back to the central address clusters. Next, we use the results of the backward address taint analysis to perform address taint analysis at the time of the deposited transactions of the targeted sample case (A).

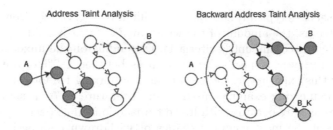

Fig. 2. Address taint analysis and backward address taint analysis. The figure depicts a mixer service with two separate central groups tainted without and with backward address taint analysis. Notice the lack of any interaction between the address A and B groups. B_K represents the withdrawn output(s) from a known case used for backward address tainting in Method 4. The lighter grey colour circles represent tainting results of backward address taint analysis and the darker grey colour circles represent tainting results of address taint analysis performed after backward address taint analysis.

3.2   Filtering Criteria

To further reduce the number of false-positive results, we define five filtering criteria based on the information of the withdrawn transactions obtained from reverse-engineering experiments used in previous studies [2, 7, 14].

Table 2. Filtering criteria.

Criteria 1	(Value of withdrawn bitcoins) The transaction output value of the targeted withdrawn transaction outputs cannot be higher than the deposited input value minus the mixing fee
Criteria 2	(Withdrawn transaction's shape) The number of transaction inputs and outputs of the targeted withdrawn transactions must be in the same pattern as the other withdrawn transactions used by the same mixer service
Criteria 3	(Withdrawn transaction chain's shape) If the mixing algorithm follows a continuous withdrawn transaction chain pattern, either the transaction prior or after the targeted withdrawn transactions must have the same number of transaction inputs and outputs as the common pattern
Criteria 4	(Reused input address) The input address in the targeted withdrawn transactions is not used as transaction input more than once in its lifetime
Criteria 5	(Withdrawn transaction fee) The transaction fee value of the targeted withdrawn transactions must be the same as in other withdrawn transactions in the same time period

As mixer services typically subtract a specific mixer service fee from the initial deposited Bitcoins, the amount of the withdrawn Bitcoins would be lower than the original deposited amount (Criteria 1). Depending on the mixer service, the mixing fee can vary in a specific range, such as between 1–2% of the deposited Bitcoins. For this experiment, we use a minimum mixing fee for this criterion.

Reverse-engineering examples used in the literature [2,7,14] show that the mixer services usually perform withdrawn transactions in a specific pattern. For example, one of the most common shapes of withdrawn transaction is in the form of a one-to-two addresses transaction where a single transaction output is sent to two addresses, one belonging to the user and the other to the mixer service. The number of transaction inputs and outputs of the targeted withdrawn transactions must be in the same pattern as the other withdrawn transactions by the same mixer service (Criteria 2).

Reverse-engineering results of the mixing sample cases indicate that multiple mixer services usually perform the withdrawn transactions in a continuous peeling chain, where a single transaction input with a large amount of Bitcoins is continuously peeled into two transaction outputs with one typically much smaller than the other [2]. As such, either the previous or next transaction of the targeted withdrawn transactions must also follow a similar pattern, accounting for the possibility that the targeted withdrawn transactions can be at the start or at the end of the withdrawn transaction chain (Criteria 3).

Our analysis of the verifiable mixing transactions from previous studies shows that the majority of the mixer services never reuse their delivery addresses before and after the withdrawn transaction. We therefore exclude any transaction with reused input addresses (Criteria 4).

In our analysis, we also detect a specific pattern in the transaction fee values of the withdrawn transactions. In particular, the transaction fee values are of the same specific amount even with a different transaction fee per byte ratio, while also considering a different time and day. This suggests that mixer services generally do not automatically adjust the transaction fee setting in real-time but after a specific amount of time has passed. As such, if the transaction fee always remains constant for the withdrawn transactions over a similar time period. We can exclude those transactions that do not conform to our transaction fee criteria (Criteria 5).

The criteria can be applied for mixed Bitcoins in general, with appropriate calibration to the service's mixing algorithm – the specific calibration parameters for our evaluation are shown in Table 3. The criteria parameters can also be specified to be stricter in order to reduce the false-positive results even further but this can increase the risk of missing the targeted withdrawn outputs.

3.3   Sample Cases

We use 15 mixing transaction samples from previous studies [2,7,14] which have shown that transaction taint analysis could not taint the withdrawn Bitcoins from the deposited Bitcoins. These studies perform reverse engineering on prominent mixer services shown in Table 3. As one study [14] chose to not publicly

Table 3. Sample mixer services and calibration of the filtering criteria.

Service	Criteria 1	Criteria 2	Criteria 3	Criteria 4	Criteria 5
Blockchain.info	0.5%	one-to-one	one-to-two	Y	10,000 Sat
Bitcoin Fog	1%	one-to-two	one-to-two	Y	50,000 Sat
BitLaundry	2.49%	one-to-two	one-to-two	Y	50,000 Sat
Unnamed 1	1.5%	one-to-two	one-to-two	Y	10,000 Sat
Unnamed 2	1%	one-to-two	one-to-two	Y	10,000 Sat
Bitlaunder	2%	N	N	Y	N
Darklaunder	2%	N	N	Y	N
Alphabay	10,000 Sat	one-to-two	N	N	N
Helix Light	2%	one-to-many	N	Y	50,000 Sat

The letter Y/N indicates that the criteria can/cannot be applied to the mixer services.

name their tested mixer services, we exclude any identifiable information of the services and transactions, and refer to the mixer services from that study as "Unnamed".

4   Results and Discussion

4.1   Address Taint Analysis

As mixer services typically perform the mixing operation continuously, it is possible for the service to deliver Bitcoins that are already mixed prior to the time of the deposited transactions. We set the time limit for the address taint analysis operation to begin tainting from five days before the deposited transactions until the maximum amount of mixing time allowed by the mixer service (e.g., BitLaundry allows up to maximum 10 days mixing time). If the mixer service did not have a mixing time setting, we set the time limit to three days.

As shown in Table 4, the results of our experiment demonstrate that even mixed Bitcoins are not always perfectly immune to tracking as the new tracking methods were able to connect the deposited and withdrawn Bitcoins together. The majority of the sample cases show successful results overall except for the Blockchain.info and Bitcoin Fog cases. For the majority of sample cases, Method 1 yields the lowest number of transaction outputs compared to the other three methods and the Baseline method, followed by Method 2 and lastly Method 3. The number of transaction outputs for Method 1 is considerably lower than those of the Baseline method at roughly 20%. For example, Method 1 has 21% fewer transactions than the Baseline method results for Case 9, and 17% fewer transactions for Case 4.

Table 4. Address tainting results with and without filtering criteria.

Case & service	Baseline	Method (%)				Baseline criteria	Method criteria (%)			
		1	2	3	4		1	2	3	4
1 Blockchain.info	485,155	—	—	93	n/a	87	—	—	96	—
2 Bitcoin Fog	713,899	—	—	—	95	9,804	—	—	—	96
3 Bitcoin Fog	1,525,276	—	—	—	98	12,945	—	—	—	99
4 BitLaundry	1,013,374	83	83	96	97	24,885	95	95	99	99
5 BitLaundry	1,016,043	82	83	96	45	22,712	96	96	98	45
6 Unnamed 1	1,337,727	83	84	92	n/a	51,099	73	74	75	—
7 Unnamed 2	1,264,966	84	85	92	n/a	48,626	78	79	80	—
8 Bitlaunder	1,867,536	80	81	93	89	385,811	87	87	96	90
9 Bitlaunder	2,156,487	79	80	93	89	428,042	86	86	96	89
10 Darklaunder	1,712,521	82	83	94	95	333,400	84	86	96	96
11 Darklaunder	1,845,130	81	83	93	94	367,516	81	85	96	96
12 Alphabay	1,949,670	81	83	93	96	181,512	85	86	96	96
13 Alphabay	2,175,263	81	83	94	94	227,718	78	79	94	94
14 Helix Light	1,858,540	75	77	93	94	6,329	91	91	97	97
15 Helix Light	1,777,542	74	76	94	94	6,160	93	94	97	97

We indicate with — that the method's experiment for the sample case was unsuccessful and with n/a the absence of an experiment. The percentage result represents the method's transaction output number compared to the baseline before and after applying the filtering criteria. The lower percentage, the less false positive results.

The results of Method 2 are generally similar to those of Method 1. For example, Method 2 has only 1% more transactions than Method 1 for Case 7, and 2% more for Case 12. Meanwhile, Method 3 produces a greater number of transaction outputs compared to the first two methods and is much closer to the results of the Baseline method. For example, Method 3 has 12% more transaction output than Method 1 for Case 10, and 6% fewer than the results of the Baseline method. As such, our results suggest that the incorporation of address clustering and backward tainting methods is not always necessary for the tracking of mixer services though a few cases, Bitcoin.info's Shared Send and Bitcoin Fog are notable exceptions.

Method 1, 2 and 3 for the Bitcoin Fog cases (2 and 3) produce unsuccessful results. This is because the mixer service keeps the deposited Bitcoins idle for as long as 6 months, which is outside the time period verification for our experiments. This is similar to the situation for Case 3. This type of scenario indicates that the central address clusters used for deposited and withdrawn transactions are separate and cannot be connected.

Method 4 shows successful results for all sample cases as shown in Table 4. Although, aside from the Bitcoin Fog cases, the Method 4 tainting results (and the results after applying filtering criteria – see Sect. 4.2) generally do not provide improved results compared to the other three methods. In particular, the number of transaction outputs resulting from Method 4 is higher than those of Method 3 for most cases. However, there are some exceptions where Method 4 performs better than Method 3 such as in Cases 5 and 9, where the number of transaction outputs are 53% and 5% lower than those of Method 3, respectively.

Nevertheless, the results of the backward address tainting of Method 4 show that it is possible to defeat the mixer service operation with separate central address clusters. If one can initiate the mixing transactions at the same time as the targeted mixing transactions so as to perform backward address tainting, one also can discover the central address clusters that are being used for the withdrawal of targeted mixed Bitcoins.

4.2   Filtering Criteria

After performing address taint analysis on each sample case, we applied the filtering criteria listed in Sect. 3.2 on each method's results for every case, as shown in Table 3. The address tainting results show significant improvement in terms of the number of transaction outputs for all of the methods including the Baseline method after applying the filtering criteria, as can be seen in the extensive reduction in the transaction outputs number shown in Table 4.

For the sample cases for which we can apply more filtering criteria, namely Cases 1 to 7, 14 and 15, the number of false-positive transaction outputs is reduced by 90% to as high as 99%. However, the transaction output number after applying filtering criteria for the first three methods is closer to the Baseline method outputs at around 10% lower. While the sample cases that have less applicable filtering criteria, which are Cases 8 to 13, generally have lower reduction number of transaction outputs at around 80%. When compared to the results of the Baseline method, the number of transaction outputs show an increased reduction than for the other cases at around 20% lower.

However, there are cases where the results yield different patterns. For example, for Cases 7 and 8, the number of transaction outputs is much lower for the three methods compared to those of the baseline method. Interestingly, the Helix light cases (Case 14 and 15) show the largest reductions in the number of transaction outputs. We hypothesise this is due to the constant 50,000 Satoshis transaction fee used in the one-to-many transaction type that makes the withdrawn transactions extremely unusual compared to other transactions.

The differences in the results may be because the exploitable transaction patterns of mixer services have exceedingly unique patterns that make their transactions have characteristics that are considerably different from other transactions. Thus, this makes them less difficult to distinguish. Nevertheless, the significant reduction in transaction outputs suggests that the filtering criteria can be adopted for other tracking methods of mixer services in general.

5   Conclusion

The address taint analysis methods we propose in this paper have the potential for reconnecting the original deposited Bitcoins to the mixed Bitcoins – this has not been possible with earlier taint analysis methods. We also illustrate that address taint analysis can be incorporated into other tracking methods such as address clustering and backward tainting methods for mixer services that utilise an irregular mixing algorithm. Although the number of false-positive results is still not substantially different between the Baseline and the other methods, by exploiting the transaction pattern of the withdrawn transactions to create filtering criteria, the number of false-positive results can be reduced further.

With further improvement, our approach could possibly be used to assist cryptocurrency crime forensics in clearing the mystery of past illegal activities, such as exchange service thefts. Nevertheless, more mixing samples from other mixer services are still required for evaluating and improving the tracking method further, considering that mixer services are constantly evolving as new transaction obscuring techniques are introduced.

Acknowledgment. We thank the authors of previous studies [2,7,14] for providing Bitcoin mixing transactions information. Thanks also to Sasa Radomirovic who provided some feedback on earlier drafts of this paper.

References

1. Anderson, R., Shumailov, I., Ahmed, M.: Making bitcoin legal. In: Cambridge International Workshop on Security Protocols (2018)
2. de Balthasar, T., Hernandez-Castro, J.: An analysis of bitcoin laundry services. In: Nordic Conference on Secure IT Systems (NordSec) (2017)
3. Harrigan, M., Fretter, C.: The unreasonable effectiveness of address clustering. In: IEEE Advanced and Trusted Computing (ATC) (2016)
4. Lischke, M., Fabian, B.: Analyzing the bitcoin network: the first four years. Future Internet, **8** (2016)
5. Meiklejohn, S., Orlandi, C.: Privacy-enhancing overlays in bitcoin. In: Financial Cryptography and Data Security (2015)
6. Meiklejohn, S., et al.: A fistful of bitcoins: characterizing payments among men with no names. In: ACM Internet Measurement Conference (IMC) (2013)
7. Möser, M., Böhme, R., Breuker, D.: An inquiry into money laundering tools in the bitcoin ecosystem. In: APWG eCrime Researchers Summit (2013)
8. Möser, M., Böhme, R., Breuker, D.: Towards risk scoring of bitcoin transactions. In: Financial Cryptography and Data Security (2014)
9. Nakamoto, S.: Bitcoin: A Peer-to-Peer Electronic Cash System White Paper (2009). https://bitcoin.org/bitcoin.pdf
10. Ruffing, T., Moreno-Sanchez, P.: ValueShuffle: mixing confidential transactions for comprehensive transaction privacy in bitcoin. In: Financial Cryptography and Data Security (2017)
11. Samsudeen, Z., Perera, D., Fernando, M.: Behavioral analysis of bitcoin users on illegal transactions. Adv. Sci. Technol. Eng. Syst. J. **4**(2) (2019)

12. Simon, B., Xavier, B., Elaine, S., Ersin, U.: Bitter to better–how to make bitcoin a better currency. In: Financial Cryptography and Data Security (2012)
13. Turner, A., Irwin, A.S.M.: Bitcoin transactions: a digital discovery of illicit activity on the blockchain. J. Financ. Crime, **25**(1) (2017)
14. van Wegberg, R., Oerlemans, J.J., van Deventer, O.: Bitcoin money laundering: mixed results? an explorative study on money laundering of cybercrime proceeds using bitcoin. J. Financ. Crime, **25** (2018)
15. Younggee, H., Hyunsoo, K., Jihwan, L., Junbeom, H.: A practical de-mixing algorithm for bitcoin mixing services. In: ACM Blockchains, Cryptocurrencies, and Contracts (BCC) (2018)

Author Index

Printed in the United States
By Bookmasters